Military Neuropsychology

Carrie H. Kennedy, PhD, is a Lieutenant Commander in the Medical Service Corps of the U.S. Navy. She received her doctoral degree from Drexel University and completed her postdoctoral fellowship in clinical neuropsychology at the University of Virginia. She currently serves as an aerospace neuropsychologist at the Naval Aerospace Medical Institute and is the Navy's only dual designated clinical and aerospace experimental psychologist. Dr. Kennedy recently constructed the Navy's training program for battlefield concussion management, and she serves as the chair of the Conflict of Interest Committee for the National Academy of Neuropsychology, is the past chair of the American Psychological Association's Division 19 (Military Psychology) Ethics Consultation Committee, and serves as Member-at-Large of Division 19. She was selected as the Navy's Junior Psychologist of the Year in 2007 and is the coeditor of *Military Psychology: Clinical and Operational Applications*. She serves on the editorial boards of *Military Psychology* and *Psychological Services*.

Jeffrey L. Moore, PhD, received his doctoral degree from Auburn University and completed his postdoctoral fellowship in clinical neuropsychology at the University of Texas Medical Branch, Galveston, Texas. He retired from active duty U. S. Naval service in 1997. While a naval officer, he established neuropsychological laboratories at Naval Medical Center Portsmouth and the Naval Aerospace Medical Institute. Since his active duty retirement, Dr. Moore has served as clinical neuropsychologist for the Robert E. Mitchell Center for Prisoner of War Studies. Dr. Moore is a fellow in both the National Academy of Neuropsychology and the Aerospace Medical Association and is a recipient of the Raymond F. Longacre Award for his contributions regarding the psychological aspects of aerospace medicine.

Military Neuropsychology

CARRIE H. KENNEDY, PhD
JEFFREY L. MOORE, PhD
EDITORS

SPRINGER PUBLISHING COMPANY
NEW YORK

The views expressed in this book are those of the authors and do not reflect the official policy or position of the Department of the Air Force, Department of the Army, Department of the Navy, Department of the Defense, the United States Government or any other organization with which the authors are affiliated.

Springer Publishing Company, LLC
11 West 42nd Street
New York, NY 10036
www.springerpub.com

Acquisitions Editor: Philip Laughlin
Project Manager: Molly Morrison
Cover design: Mimi Flow
Composition: Newgen

Ebook ISBN: 978-0-8261-0449-6

10 11 12 13/ 5 4 3 2 1

The author and the publisher of this Work have made every effort to use sources believed to be reliable to provide information that is accurate and compatible with the standards generally accepted at the time of publication. The author and publisher shall not be liable for any special, consequential, or exemplary damages resulting, in whole or in part, from the readers' use of, or reliance on, the information contained in this book. The publisher has no responsibility for the persistence or accuracy of URLs for external or third-party Internet Web sites referred to in this publication and does not guarantee that any content on such Web sites is, or will remain, accurate or appropriate.

Library of Congress Cataloging-in-Publication Data

Military neuropsychology / edited by Carrie H. Kennedy, Jeffrey L. Moore.
  p. ; cm.
Includes bibliographical references.
ISBN 978-0-8261-0448-9
1. Military psychiatry—United States. 2. Psychology, Military. 3. Clinical neuropsychology.
I. Kennedy, Carrie H. II. Moore, Jeffrey L.
[DNLM: 1. Trauma, Nervous System. 2. Military Personnel—psychology. 3. Nervous System Diseases—psychology. 4. Neuropsychology—methods. 5. Psychology, Military—methods. WL 140 M644 2009]
  UH629.3.M55 2009
  616.80024'355—dc22   2009043105

Printed in the United States of America by Hamilton Printing

To our heroes: the sailors, marines, soldiers, and airmen who are fighting this war.

—Carrie H. Kennedy and Jeffrey L. Moore

Contents

Contributors

Thomas J. Balkin, PhD
Chief
Department of Behavioral Biology
Walter Reed Army Institute of
    Research
Silver Spring, Maryland

Jeffrey T. Barth, PhD, ABPP (CN)
John Edward Fowler Professor and
    Director
Department of Psychiatry and
    Neurobehavioral Sciences
Brain Injury and Sports Concussion
    Institute
University of Virginia School of
    Medicine
Charlottesville, Virginia

Mark C. Bender, PhD
Neuropsychologist
Polytrauma Transitional Rehabilitation
    Program
Mental Health Service, McGuire VA
    Medical Center
Richmond, Virginia

Corwin Boake, PhD, ABPP (CN)
Associate Professor of Physical
    Medicine and Rehabilitation
University of Texas-Houston Medical
    School
Neuropsychologist
The Institute for Rehabilitation and
    Research
Houston, Texas

Shane S. Bush, PhD, ABPP (CN, RP), ABN
United States Marine Corps Active
    Reserves 1984–1987, United States
    Navy Active Reserves 1997–2001
VA New York Harbor Healthcare System
Queens, New York
Long Island Neuropsychology, P.C.
Lake Ronkonkoma, New York

George M. Cuesta, PhD
United States Military Academy
    1973–1978, United States Army
    1978–1985, United States Army
    Reserves 1999–2004
Clinical Assistant Professor of
    Neuropsychology in Neurology and
    Neuroscience
Department of Neurology and
    Neuroscience
Weill Medical College of Cornell
    University at the Burke
    Rehabilitation Hospital
White Plains, New York

Louis M. French, PsyD
Director
Traumatic Brain Injury Program
Department of Orthopaedics and
    Rehabilitation
Walter Reed Army Medical Center
Site Director
Defense and Veterans Brain Injury Center
Walter Reed Army Medical Center
Assistant Professor of Neurology
Department of Neurology
Uniformed Services University of the
    Health Sciences
Washington, DC

Eugene Gourley, PhD
Neuropsychologist
Polytrauma Network Site
Mental Health Service
McGuire VA Medical Center
Richmond, Virginia

Manfred F. Greiffenstein, PhD, ABPP (CN)
Certified Neuropsychologist
Fellow of the American Psychological
   Association
Psychological Systems
Royal Oak, Michigan

Rebecca A. Hardin, MS
Argosy University
Washington, DC

Robert K. Heaton, PhD, ABPP (CN)
United States Air Force 1961–1969
Professor of Psychiatry
HIV Neurobehavioral Research
   Center
University of California at
   San Diego
La Jolla, California

Katherine M. Helmick, MS, CRNP
Interim Senior Executive, Traumatic
   Brain Injury, and Director
TBI Clinical Standard of Care
Defense Centers of Excellence for
   Psychological Health and Traumatic
   Brain Injury
Silver Spring, Maryland
Deputy Director
Clinical and Educational Affairs
Defense and Veterans Brain Injury
   Center
Washington, DC

David W. Hess, PhD, ABPP (RP)
Neuropsychologist
Neuropsychology Clinic
Naval Medical Center Portsmouth
Portsmouth, Virginia

Lieutenant Colonel William C. Isler III, PhD
United States Air Force
Psychologist
Air Force Medical Operations Agency
   Lackland/Kelly
San Antonio, Texas

Colonel Michael S. Jaffee, MD
United States Air Force
National Director
Defense and Veterans Brain Injury
   Center
Defense Centers of Excellence for
   Psychological Health and Traumatic
   Brain Injury
Silver Spring, Maryland

Robert L. Kane, PhD, ABPP (CN)
Neuropsychologist and NCAT Program
   Director
Defense and Veterans Brain Injury
   Center
Washington, DC
Adjunct Associate Professor
   (Neurology)
University of Maryland
   Medical School
Baltimore, Maryland

Mark P. Kelly, PhD, ABPP (CN)
Chief
Neuropsychology Service
Walter Reed Army Medical Center
Director
Neuropsychology Postdoctoral
   Fellowship
Walter Reed Army Medical Center
Washington, DC

Carrie H. Kennedy, PhD, ABPP (CL)
Assistant Professor of Psychiatry and
   Neurobehavioral Sciences
University of Virginia School of Medicine
Charlottesville, Virginia

Thomas Kupke, PhD
Psychology Training Director and Head
Neuropsychology Clinic
Naval Medical Center Portsmouth
Portsmouth, Virginia

Helen Z. MacDonald, PhD
VA Boston Healthcare System
Boston University School of Medicine
Boston, Massachusetts

J. Allen McCutchan, MD, MSc
Professor of Medicine, Emeritus
University of California
San Diego, California
Codirector
HIV Neurobehavioral Research
Center (HRNC)
Director
International Core
HRNC
San Diego, California

Major Jeffrey A. McNeil, PhD
United States Army
Operational Psychologist
Fort Bragg, North Carolina

Commander Mark C. Monahan, PhD
United States Navy
Neuropsychologist
Comprehensive Combat and Complex
   Casualty Care
Naval Medical Center
San Diego, California

Jeffrey L. Moore, PhD
United States Army 1972–1975
United States Navy 1980–1997

C. A. Morgan III, MD, MA
Associate Clinical Professor of Psychiatry
Yale University School of Medicine
New Haven, Connecticut
Research Affiliate
National Center for PTSD
Washington, DC

Kevin P. Mulligan, PsyD, ABPP (CN)
United States Air Force (Ret)
Professor and Chair
Clinical Psychology Program
Florida Institute of Technology
Melbourne, Florida

Treven C. Pickett, PsyD, ABPP (RP)
Neuropsychologist and Rehabilitation
   Psychologist
Mental Health Service
McGuire VA Medical Center
Neuropsychologist and Coinvestigator
Defense and Veterans Brain Injury
   Center
Richmond, Virginia

Nicole Rodier, BA
VA Boston Healthcare System
Boston, Massachusetts

Robert A. Seegmiller, PhD, ABPP (CN)
United States Air Force (Ret)
Neuropsychologist
Brooke Army Medical Center
Fort Sam Houston, Texas

Jack Spector, PhD, ABPP (CN)
United States Army 1983–1988
Independent Practice
Baltimore, Maryland, and Greensboro,
North Carolina

William Stiers, PhD, ABPP (RP)
Department of Physical Medicine and
   Rehabilitation
The Johns Hopkins University School of
   Medicine
Baltimore, Maryland

Erin W. Ulloa, PhD
VA Boston Healthcare System
Assistant Professor
Boston University School of Medicine
Boston, Massachusetts

Jennifer J. Vasterling, PhD
Chief of Psychology
VA Boston Healthcare System
Professor of Psychiatry
Boston University School of Medicine
Boston, Massachusetts

Erica Weber, BA
Graduate Student Researcher
Joint Doctoral Program
San Diego State University and
University of California at San Diego
San Diego, California

Nancy J. Wesensten, PhD
Supervisory Psychologist
Walter Reed Army Institute of
  Research
Silver Spring, Maryland

Major Ilaina M. Wingler, PsyD
United States Air Force
Psychologist and Neuropsychology
  Fellow
University of Virginia School of
  Medicine
Charlottesville, Virginia

Steven Paul Woods, PsyD
Associate Professor of Psychiatry
HIV Neurobehavioral Research Center
University of California at San Diego
La Jolla, California

Preface

As interest in clinical neuropsychology has grown and become a recognized subspecialty, so too have the unique contributions of clinicians and researchers practicing within the Departments of Defense and Veterans Affairs. Today's war has propelled the field of neuropsychology in general and military neuropsychology in particular given what are being called the signature injuries, namely mild traumatic brain injury and posttraumatic stress disorder. The demand for neuropsychological expertise has never been so great, in traditional hospital and clinic settings as well as on the battlefield.

Within the military, neuropsychologists contribute to such important components of military medicine as fitness and suitability determinations, acute evaluations, postdeployment evaluations, rehabilitation, disability determinations, and consultation to commands, to name but a few. These evaluations and the knowledge to provide consultation to commands require significant expertise and informed decision making, though no single resource had yet been produced in which to find this information. As is so often the case, it was our own need for such a volume that resulted in this work. It is our intention that *Military Neuropsychology* will provide a necessary resource for those who are treating and making life-changing career and medical decisions for our warriors. Whether the neuropsychologist or psychologist is consulting because of an acute concussion after an IED blast, writing a medical board report that will help determine long-term medical and financial benefits, or assessing the cognitive decrements of a given unit in the field due to recent sleep patterns, our service personnel demand and deserve the best professional expertise we have to offer.

Such a text required an edited volume due to the scope of the project and in recognition of the vast expertise of the authors who participated. Each author was selected in recognition of their clinical expertise, their documented record of research in the specific topic area, and/or their recognized status as subject matter experts. Thus, each author has an appreciation of how best to integrate lessons learned from the nonmilitary setting with the practical problems of applying that knowledge to military clinical and operational settings. It is our hope that you will be able to use this information in your daily work to provide the very best services to our service members.

Carrie H. Kennedy
Jeffrey L. Moore
Pensacola, Florida
September 2009

Acknowledgments

We would like to express our gratitude to everyone who has contributed to making *Military Neuropsychology* a reality. First and foremost we are indebted to the outstanding group of professionals who contributed the chapters for this book. Not only did the quality of their work meet or exceed our expectations, but their adherence to the time schedule and their willingness to accept editorial guidance made the process flow smoothly. Next we would like to thank our very supportive editorial staff: our original editor Phil Laughlin, and Kerry Vegliando, Jennifer Perillo, and Nancy Hale who saw it through. Not only would we have been unable to complete this effort without their assistance but the process would not have been as gratifying.

Each of us would also like to acknowledge the patient mentoring, training, and supervision we received early in our careers. These valued relationships helped mold our professional identities as military officers, clinicians, researchers, and especially as neuropsychologists:

CAPT Frank Mullins, USN/RET
CAPT J. R. "Buck" Aitken, USN/RET
CAPT Bruce Becker, USNR/RET
Ralph M. Reitan, PhD
H. Julia Hannay, PhD
Harvey S. Levin, PhD
CAPT Ralph Bally, USN/RET
Dr. Leo Kormann, PhD
Dr. Jeffrey Barth, PhD
Dr. Donna Broshek, PhD
Dr. Jason Freeman, PhD
Dr. Scott Bender, PhD
Dr. Eric Zillmer, PsyD

Finally, and perhaps most important, we would like to thank our spouses for their love, support, and encouragement to broaden our professional horizons. We acknowledge that one of the hardest jobs anywhere is that of a military spouse and giving up that spouse to work on a book during cherished liberty is difficult.

Military Neuropsychology

1

A History and Introduction to Military Neuropsychology

CARRIE H. KENNEDY, CORWIN BOAKE, AND
JEFFREY L. MOORE

THE INTRODUCTION OF PSYCHOLOGISTS INTO THE ARMED FORCES

"When the United States declared war on Germany on April 6, 1917, the psychologists undertook at once to promote the useful application of psychology within the armed forces" (Boring, 1945, p. 12). The United States was at a significant disadvantage to Germany, which already had a pool of well-trained and well-assigned warfighters, due to Germany's policy of compulsory service (Terman, 1918). Terman described the problem presented to the United States:

> Contrast this situation with that in an American cantonment receiving each month perhaps twenty thousand men, from all walks of life, with every kind of training and experience, of all degrees of ability, and alike only in their universal ignorance of the science and art of modern warfare. Such a body of men is not an army; it is only the raw material for an army. It will only become an efficient army in proportion as each man is assigned to the kind of duty for which he is best fitted, and is trained in the performance of that duty. As long as it remains but an assembled horde, it could easily be vanquished by a trained army of a twentieth its size. (Terman, 1918, p. 177)

The president of the American Psychological Association (APA), Robert Yerkes, set aside all other tasks in order to prepare for the war

1

(Kevles, 1968), and in an environment of some disagreement amongst the testing movement pioneers, the war provided a singular purpose and united the efforts of Yerkes and fellow psychologists Lewis M. Terman, Edward L. Thorndike, and Walter Dill Scott (von Mayrhauser, 1992; see also Kevles, 1968). The resulting creation of the intelligence tests, the Army alpha and beta, used to screen 1.75 million men (Zeidner & Drucker, 1988), and the validation of their statistical properties have been described as "the profession's most influential contribution to American society" (von Mayrhauser, 1992, p. 252).

The creation of the alpha and beta would have significant consequences for the psychology profession. With regard to psychological testing, the Army tests were transformed into the individual intelligence tests of today by David Wechsler, who worked at an Army camp scoring alpha administrations, initially under the supervision of Edwin G. Boring (Boake, 2002). While verbal instructions no longer begin with "Attention!" subtests and even individual test items continue to be used from the Army alpha in current versions of the Wechsler Adult Intelligence Scale and the Wechsler Memory Scale (Bronner, Healy, Lowe, & Shimberg, 1929; Wechsler, 1997a; Wechsler, 1997b; Wechsler, 2008; Yoakum & Yerkes, 1920). The beta examination continues to serve as a nonverbal ability measure for persons with limited English and literacy skills (Kellogg & Morton, 1999).

Along with the successful creation of the Army alpha and beta, and the subsequent development of the Army Performance Scale for individual testing (Bronner et al., 1929; Yoakum & Yerkes, 1920), came the commission of Yerkes as a major in the Army, setting the precedent for active duty psychologists (Kennedy & McNeil, 2006). During World War I, 132 psychologists were commissioned (Zeidner & Drucker, 1988) at a time when there were 336 members of the fledgling APA (Driskell & Olmstead, 1989). As officers, the skills of psychologists in the military were applied not only to the psychological examination of the intelligence of recruits, the selection of men for special assignments, and occupational placement based on specific aptitudes (e.g., Personnel Research Section, 1943), but also to the reeducation of men incapacitated for further military service (Baldwin, 1919).

Another development of World War I had a considerable impact on modern clinical psychology. Robert S. Woodworth created the first personality test geared toward assessing neurotic tendencies in order to screen draftees. His adjustment inventory consisted of 100 questions. "Normals" (i.e., college students) reported 10 symptoms on average, shell-shock cases, 30, and hysterics, 40 (Woodworth, 1919). This inventory and like tests have evolved over time and now constitute integral parts of both traditional psychological and neuropsychological assessment batteries.

Unfortunately, at the end of the war "the psychologists went back to their universities, the research stopped and the accepted procedures remained about where they were" (Boring, 1945, p. 14). Yerkes in particular was frustrated with the decision to end the involvement of psychologists as soon as the war was over and felt that if the work had been allowed to continue, the country would have been better prepared to meet the demands of World War II (Kevles, 1968). Despite the temporary hiatus of psychologists working within the military, there was significant impact. Recruiters continued to administer tests to some enlistees, schools implemented widespread intellectual testing; aptitude tests started being used for entrance into college; businesses became interested in personnel testing; and the practical value of psychological science was made evident to the military (Driskell & Olmstead, 1989; Kevles, 1968).

THE BIRTH OF CLINICAL MILITARY PSYCHOLOGY AND MODERN NEUROPSYCHOLOGICAL ASSESSMENT

Psychologists in World War II picked up where those in World War I had to stop. At one point in the war, the military was able to use "seven classification tests, eleven aptitude tests, thirteen educational achievement examinations and five trade knowledge tests" (Boring, 1945, p. 17) that were developed by psychologists. The Army General Classification Test, which replaced the Army alpha and beta tests (Driskell & Olmstead, 1989), was taken by 12 million men (Harrell, 1992), and brief intellectual screening instruments were developed at a rapid pace (Hunt & Stevenson, 1946). The Minnesota Multiphasic Personality Inventory (MMPI) made its debut during World War II and was used experimentally for selection based on personality factors by the Army (Page, 1996).

Other tests made their way into the mainstream where they remain as valuable neuropsychological instruments today. The Trail Making Test, for example, currently found in the Halstead-Reitan Neuropsychological Battery, comprised part of the Army Individual Test Battery used during World War II (Armitage, 1946; Lezak, Howieson, & Loring, 2004). The Army Individual Test was created largely in response to clinicians' needs for tests that would provide a wider variety of information regarding behaviors and abilities and to assist with diagnostic clarification (Staff, Personnel Research Section, Classification and Replacement Branch, 1944). A compendium of individually administered tests was created as a resource for military clinical psychologists (Wells & Ruesch, 1942). Other cognitive testing was performed to choose men and women (for a discussion of women in the military, see Kennedy & Malone, 2009) for specific jobs, such as aviation (Driskell & Olmstead, 1989; Staff, Psychological Research Unit No. 2, Department of Psychology Research Section, 1944), recognizing that assessment of intelligence was not sufficient in and of itself.

In addition to testing, occupational placement, and performance evaluations, new technology (e.g., aircraft, weaponry) and other demands required an expansion of roles, and World War II saw psychologists making further advances in the areas of human factors and the effects of stress on performance (Driskell & Olmstead, 1989). As in World War I, psychologists rose to meet the call of the defense of the country. World War II saw the active duty service of 986 commissioned psychologists, and 276 additional psychologists were employed by government agencies supporting the war effort. In other words, 1,262 of the 4,500 psychologists (28%) in the United States at that time served either in the U.S. military or worked in direct support of the war effort (Boring, 1945).

As work of research psychologists grew exponentially, psychologists as military clinicians entered the scene. The formal initiation of Army clinical psychology may be dated to 1942 when six psychologists were assigned to neuropsychiatric centers of Army hospitals (Seidenfeld, 1966). The major expansion occurred during 1944 when the shortage of psychiatrists was recognized and the psychiatrist William Menninger, head of the Army mental health program, requested that psychologists be assigned to assist psychiatrists in hospitals and other facilities (Capshew, 1999). The need for appropriately trained psychologists was partly met by a clinical training program at the Adjutant General's School, Fort Sam Houston, Texas, which graduated 281 students by the end of the war. In a move that symbolized the role of Army psychologists as health service providers, as well as physician supervisees, administrative authority over Army clinical psychologists was transferred from the Classification and Replacement Branch of the Adjutant General's Office to the Neuropsychiatry Consultants Division of the Surgeon General's Office.

Toward the end of the war many psychologists' duties were shifted from classification, assessment, and selection to clinical duties due to a shortfall of psychiatrists to meet the mental health needs of the 40,000 psychiatrically hospitalized veterans and the hundreds of thousands of veterans who were seen as outpatients (Cranston, 1986; see also Baganz & Strotz, 1941). Psychologists' assessment abilities transferred readily from occupational categorization and selection to clinical assessment and "retraining of disabled soldiers and sailors" (Boring, 1945, p. 18). To ensure quality personnel, the Veterans Administration (VA) pushed the APA to define both the field and the basic education and training requirements for psychologists, adopting the scientist-practitioner model. The adoption of this model of training was influenced by the significant work done by research psychologists through the world wars and to the new need for clinicians. The VA created the first psychology internships in 1946 (Cranston, 1986; Phares & Trull, 1997). Following World War II, psychologists were again demobilized as after World War I. However, in 1947 psychologists achieved permanent active duty status, which has been maintained consistently since that time (Kennedy & McNeil, 2006; McGuire, 1990).

Military neuropsychologists hold a wide array of current positions and require as many clinical and consultative skills. The remainder of this chapter briefly addresses those issues deemed most pertinent to military neuropsychologists and neuropsychologists serving military personnel in today's wartime environment. Historical issues are addressed when indicated, and the chapters comprising this volume are introduced.

ETHICS OF MILITARY NEUROPSYCHOLOGY

Clinical military psychologists have faced unique ethical challenges since they first became involved with the military. Dual agency, multiple relationships, confidentiality, and issues related to competence (Grinker & Spiegel, 1945; Johnson, 2008; Kennedy & Johnson, 2009; McCauley, Hughes, & Liebling-Kalifani, 2008; Reger, Etherage, Reger, & Gahm, 2008) are perhaps the most challenging ethical dilemmas confronted, problems that began to evolve when military psychologists began to assume clinical duties during World War II (Kennedy & Moore, 2008; Page, 1996). This occurred during a time when there was no ethics code, psychology licensure, as we know it, was decades away, and the duties performed by psychologists were unprecedented. While the Ethics Code began to be developed following World War II (APA

Committee on Ethical Standards for Psychology, 1949), the first code was not established until 1953 (Canter, Bennett, Jones, & Nagy, 1996). Military psychologists were not mandated to maintain licensure until 1988 (Jeffrey, 1989).

Since that time, with the continued expansion of roles of military psychologists, ethical analysis has become more complex. Clinical psychologists and neuropsychologists now serve in every venue offered by the military, including combat zones (e.g., Campise, Geller, & Campise, 2006), with Special Forces (e.g., Picano, Williams, & Roland, 2006), and wartime detention facilities (Kennedy, Malone, & Franks, 2009). Issues related to dual agency and dual roles in these expeditionary and operational environments become magnified (Kennedy & Johnson, 2009; Kennedy & Williams, in press), and civilian psychologists serving the military are being thrust into new roles as they fill gaps created by deployed active duty providers.

Each service has begun to hire civilian psychologists and neuropsychologists at a rapid rate, creating a situation in which providers, who may be very well trained clinically, have not had any opportunity to develop the competencies required to work in the military environment. These providers are bound by military-imposed limits of confidentiality and are impacted by the inevitable dual agency conflicts that arise when working with service members. This has become especially difficult for VA clinicians, who are being asked to make fitness-for-duty recommendations, in a population that previously would not have returned to war (Stone, 2008). Fitness for military duty is a complex issue that requires understanding of specific military jobs, operational requirements, and military laws and regulations (Budd & Harvey, 2006; Budd & Kennedy, 2006). Cultural competency is further complicated since the military is an incredibly diverse organization from racial and ethnic perspectives (Kennedy, Jones, & Arita, 2007), and has its own behavioral norms, belief systems, and language (Reger et al., 2008). Providers who lack experience and training with the military in general and with service members in particular may be ineffective, resulting in ill-informed recommendations about such matters as flight status, security clearances, weapons handling, and a host of other serious matters. Bush and Cuesta (chapter 2, this volume) will address the most pertinent ethical dilemmas encountered by neuropsychologists working within the military and provide an illustrative case example demonstrating the ethical analysis recommended for use with the military population.

NEUROPSYCHOLOGICAL FITNESS-FOR-DUTY EVALUATIONS

Fitness-for-duty evaluations became a core requirement for military psychologists toward the end of World War II as psychologists began to take on clinical roles. This capacity has rapidly become the most frequently performed duty of military psychologists and neuropsychologists. Each time any mental health provider sees an active duty patient for any reason, determinations of fitness, suitability (i.e., primarily issues related to maladaptive personality traits), and deployability must be made.

The neuropsychological fitness-for-duty evaluation is essentially a comprehensive assessment of an individual's current cognitive and psychological functioning as compared to prior levels, as well as a prognosis for the future. This information is used to make significant life decisions for the individual, so it is imperative that the neuropsychological evaluation be thorough and tailored appropriately for that individual. These evaluations include not only standard portions of traditional neuropsychological evaluations but also unique components related to the military and an individual's military service. Among these are sources and interpretation of military cognitive baselines (e.g., Armed Services Vocational Aptitude Battery, Aviation Selection Test Battery, etc.), collateral information from a variety of sources to include the chain of command and service record, and unique factors related to the variety of deployment locations and missions. In addition, the military neuropsychologist must possess an excellent working knowledge of combat trauma/posttraumatic stress disorder, preexisting learning disorders (LD) and attention deficit hyperactivity disorder (ADHD), and traumatic brain injury (TBI). Kelly, Mulligan, and Monahan (chapter 3) dissect the fitness-for-duty evaluation and describe in detail the required components of these assessments. These are demonstrated by a series of illustrative cases.

MALINGERING OF COGNITIVE DEFICITS

"During the war, 1914 to 1918, an authoritative recommendation was made that malingerers should be treated by a very strong faradic current, the forcible application of which was said to be almost infallible. It was held that the malingerer might stand one or two applications, but quickly recovered under the prospect of a daily repetition" (Doherty & Runes, 1943, p. 133; see also Shephard, 2000). This extreme "treatment" reflects the frustration that exists with regard to those suspected of malingering, an issue that has been formally addressed by the U S. military since the Civil War (Lande, 1997; see also Greiffenstein, chapter 4). Sick-call riders, sick-call rangers, sick-call ninjas, sickbay commandos, malingering racketeers, masters of malingering, goldbrickers, frequent flyers, profile rangers, shirkers, gripers, those riding the sick book, or just plain malingerers and fakers provide a challenge to all medical professionals, and this is no more true than in the military (Altus & Bell, 1945; Budd & Harvey, 2006; Campbell, 1943; Hulett, 1941; Kennedy & McNeil, 2006; Waud, 1942). While there is a rather vast literature on malingering in the military, it is notable that other early researchers and clinicians also described malingering among criminals (Hopwood & Snell, 1933; Karpman, 1926; Myerson, 1931), work-related compensation seekers (Edgar, 1931; Garner, 1939), and amnestic husbands seeking to avoid negative consequences of contraindicated marital behavior (Kanzer, 1939).

Early military malingerers adopted such strategies as placing sugar in urine samples to mimic diabetes; placing blood in urine samples; using a variety of drugs, alcohol, and fasting; and claiming nonexistent sensory defects (largely visual and auditory; e.g., Bruner, 1934; Jackson, 1897), paralysis, pain conditions, tuberculosis, brain injury, speech disorders, encephalitis, meningitis, epilepsy, psychosis, feeblemindedness, illiteracy, and amnesia (Brussel, Grassi, & Malniker, 1942; Dillon, 1939; Gill, 1941; Good, 1942; Kahn, 1943; Myers, 1916; Seltzer, 1936; No author noted, 1943). While there are no data that elucidate good estimates of malingerers through the various conflicts, Seltzer (1936) states of World War I that there were 300,000 veterans with service-connected disabilities but 1,060,000 applications to the VA for disability compensation.

Military malingerers have been depicted in numerous ways. A U.S. Army psychiatrist following World War I described malingerers as "marked psychopaths, emotionally unstable, or decidedly inadequate" (Meagher, 1919, p. 969). Lumsden (1916) noted that malingering during times of both peace and war was "a disease of the highest conscious cerebral centres in the frontal lobes" (p. 862). In the Royal Air Force during World War II, military malingerers were noted to present "a clinical picture of symptoms without signs, ruthless egocentricity with little sense of social responsibility" (Ballard & Miller, 1944, p. 40). Others noted that they were "never seen as an isolated phenomenon but most frequently as a manifestation of psychopathic personality" (Rosenberg & Feldberg, 1944, p. 141; see also Good, 1942). Still others noted of military malingerers, "there has been an unmistakable, severe neurosis or infantilism"

(Saul, 1943, p. 77). During World War II the issue of shell shock was questioned by some to be an issue of malingering (No author noted, 1943). The concept of shell shock is covered in more detail below.

During World War II, psychologists at the U.S. Naval Training Station in Rhode Island were tasked with determining whether or not an individual might be malingering "feeblemindness or illiteracy" to avoid military service. The initial screening method consisted of a brief intelligence test, a passing score resulting in a return to duty, a borderline score resulting in a trial-duty period, and a failing score resulting in further testing. These psychologists employed a flexible battery; "the specific tests given vary with the demands of each case" (Hunt, 1943, p. 598). Tests and methods employed at the training center within the neuropsychiatry department included the Wechsler-Bellevue, the General Classification Test, Rorschach Ink Blots (see also Rosenberg & Feldberg, 1944), "the importance of test scatter as a diagnostic aid" (p. 599; see also Hunt & Older, 1944), and the electroencephalogram (see Jasper, Kershman, & Elvidge, 1940; Serota, 1940). The Rorschach Method in particular enjoyed widespread use and was used in the Army to delineate postconcussion syndrome from neurotics and malingerers by differentiating between organic and neurotic indicators upon testing (Brussel, Grassi, & Melniker, 1942). In other locations barbiturate narcosis or narcoanalysis was utilized (Ludwig, 1944; Wilde, 1942), as were the hand dynamometer and the tuning fork pressure test (Fetterman, 1943).

Hunt and Older (1943), again working at the Newport Naval Training Station, employed psychometric testing to parse out the malingerers from the truly feebleminded, noting that "it is not as easy to appear feebleminded as the layman might believe....A malingerer attempting to appear feebleminded does act dumb and makes mistakes, but the dumbness is not the dumbness nor are the mistakes the mistakes which are typical of true feeblemindedness" (p. 1318). They instructed a group of normal individuals to simulate feeblemindedness on Arithmetical Reasoning, the Easy Directions Test, and the Kent Emergency Test, and they compared their scores to an adult group of individuals with an average mental age of 9.7 years. They found that the simulated malingerers demonstrated significant inconsistency of performance throughout the tests, a phenomenon the authors dubbed internal scatter.

It is notable that while most think of the production or exaggeration of symptoms of disorders as malingering, the military frequently sees those who attempt to reverse malinger (Hulett, 1941) to be accepted into the military (Kahn, 1943; Saul, 1943), to obtain special jobs within the military (e.g., aviation, special forces), or to avoid a mental health diagnosis (Budd & Harvey, 2006). Hunt and Older (1943) surmised that this phenomenon was much more common than that seen in individuals who attempted to feign illness to get out of military duty.

In the military, the label of malingering has historically brought legal consequences. This has presented a challenge to military physicians/ psychiatrists and later to psychologists throughout the history of the American military. Bowers cautioned in 1943 that "extreme care must be exercised in recommending court-martial on the grounds of malingering because a grave injustice may be done the patient" (p. 509). While today's military mental health providers have no role in the recommendation of legal action, the malingering label may result in such action. In the same light the outcome of disability determinations is profoundly impacted by a finding or suspicion of malingering. These issues become even more complicated in the context of current blast injuries and concussion, posttraumatic stress disorder, and other mental health sequelae of combat, and the rapidly increasing need for mental health and neuropsychological services for active duty, reserve and guard personnel, and veterans. Greiffenstein (chapter 4) will address military regulations as they pertain to malingering, the current state of the art of neuropsychological assessment of malingering, and the unique challenges presented by today's service personnel.

BLAST INJURIES

Blast injuries have been described since the Civil War, though not on a grand scale until World War I when hundreds of thousands of men were exposed to blast waves of exploding shells, while also being somewhat protected from shell fragments and peripheral injury due to being sheltered in trenches. Cases of those who experienced unconsciousness following an explosion but with no external injuries "complained of headache, dizziness, lethargy and inability to concentrate—in short, they exhibited all the major signs and symptoms of the postconcussion syndrome of peacetime" (Fulton, 1942, p. 228). These cases came to be differentiated from shell shock cases described below. World War II then saw an even greater use of high explosive bombs and shells, both on civilian and military populations during the war, though little research was conducted on the effects this had on humans (Fulton, 1942).

The issue of blast injuries has arisen again in today's war, where the enemy utilizes improvised explosive devices heavily and modern protective equipment serves to protect service members from many forms of physical injury. Unfortunately, the question of whether or not primary blast effects directly cause TBI and if so, to what extent is still unanswered. French, Spector, Stiers, and Kane (chapter 5) discuss what is known about blast injury in today's conflict. The authors will address the pathophysiology of mild TBI (mTBI), the gamut of blast effects, and the influence of other comorbid injuries and disorders.

BATTLEFIELD NEUROPSYCHOLOGICAL EVALUATIONS

Today's conflict marks the first time where neuropsychologists are needed on the ground in the war zone, due to the large numbers of suspected concussion/mTBI. To address the issue of mTBI, in October 2008, Congress mandated predeployment cognitive testing for all service members due to the large numbers of TBIs and the pressing need to make better assessments of possible impairment without unnecessarily removing service members from the war zone.

A history of this kind of assessment does not exist in the military. The most appropriate parallel comes from the arena of sideline sports concussion assessment. From the assessment and recovery literature on athletes involved in sports with a high risk of head injury (e.g., football, ice hockey, etc.), the military has modeled its current predeployment assessment and clinical practice guidelines for in-theater assessment and decision making. Barth, Isler, Helmick, Wingler, and Jaffee (chapter 6) discuss the evolution of sports concussion assessment to battlefield assessment, the various instruments used in assessment (e.g., Military Acute Concussion Evaluation, Neurocognitive Assessment Tool), confounds to assessment (e.g., effort, sleep issues, mental health symptoms), and the various guidelines used for making return-to-duty decisions in the war zone.

TBI ASSESSMENT AND REHABILITATION

Prior to World War I most significant brain trauma resulted in death; subsequently assessment and rehabilitation was not often required.

However, this changed in World War I due to advances in neurosurgery and consequent high numbers of head injury survivors from war wounds (Boake, 1989). This was not just an issue in the United States. Other countries faced the need for head injury assessment and rehabilitation as well. Germany, for example, employed a highly progressive model that included care from the initial injury through community reentry and vocational rehabilitation to long-term follow-up (Poser, Kohler, & Schönle, 1996).

The United States was apparently not as organized as Germany in its implementation of specialized head injury services. One of these reasons was due to a professional argument between orthopedic surgeons, who felt that all rehabilitation services should fall under medical control, and vocational educators, who disagreed. Consequently, rehabilitation services formed in military general hospitals, as opposed to specialty clinics or hospitals, and services were not generally felt to be optimal (Boake, 1989).

There were some organized efforts to implement brain injury rehabilitation within these U.S. hospitals to address the needs of the military's wounded. Franz (1923), of the Government Hospital for the Insane, published an unprecedented work on nervous and mental reeducation, in essence an early primer for rehabilitation. He addressed such issues as paralysis, ataxia, speech problems, and psychosis (a catch-all category for mental health, cognitive and behavioral problems), using the techniques of electrotherapy, hydrotherapy, physiotherapy, rudimentary cognitive strategies and involving the family in the treatment program. His goals for those with personality and behavioral disturbance were to reconstruct the activities of the individual so that "he becomes capable of behaving like the normal people in his environment" (p. 203). He noted four conditions that made for poor outcomes: lack of insight into the need for behavior change, lack of motivation, lack of self-confidence "in his ability to overcome the condition or abnormality" (p. 205), and lack of proper goal setting on the part of the reeducation program.

The two World Wars served as significant research opportunities for TBI (Figure 1.1). Egas Moniz, Nobel Prize winner for his controversial work with lobotomy, furthered the understanding of neurological injuries following World War I (El-Hai, 2005). In Germany during World War I, Kurt Goldstein (1942) and Walther Poppelreuter (1917/1990) produced seminal works on aphasia rehabilitation and visual attention disorders. Teuber, working at the Naval Hospital in San Diego, researched the behavioral effects of penetrating brain injuries in both World War II and

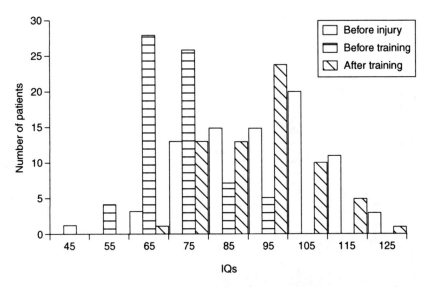

Figure 1.1 Distribution of IQs obtained by psychological tests before injury and before and after training. Wepman (1951) used estimates of general cognitive ability to demonstrate the benefit of intensive aphasia therapy in a sample of 68 World War II veterans with traumatic aphasia. The veterans' preinjury score was estimated from the Army General Classification Test administered at induction. The "before training" score represents the Wechsler-Bellevue performance scale and the "after training" score the full Wechsler-Bellevue scale. Wepman concluded that "while there is a measurable loss of IQ after injury, this loss is frequently not permanent and may be reversed through training" (p. 75). The work by Wepman and others at specialized brain-injury rehabilitation centers contributed to the design of civilian stroke rehabilitation. (Reproduced by permission from Wepman, J. M. [1951]. *Recovery from aphasia*. New York: Ronald Press. Reprinted with permission of John Wiley & Sons.)

Korea veterans (Meier, 1992), and Weinstein and Teuber (1957) examined the effects of preinjury education and intelligence on head-injured soldiers after World War II. Reitan and Benton (Figures 1.2 and 1.3) also began their long career of neuropsychological research and test construction with brain-injured service members in the 1940s (Aita, Armitage, Reitan, & Rabinovitz, 1947; Benton, 2003; Meier, 1992; Reitan, 1989). Zangwill (1945) conducted evaluations of British military personnel in the Brain Injuries Unit at Edinburgh to determine fitness-for-duty status, using intelligence, memory, comprehension, motor, sensory perception, and emotional assessment. His work during the war established a role for psychologists as valued members of the interdisciplinary team in neurological units in Britain (Collins, 2006).

Figure 1.2 Captain Ralph Reitan, U.S. Army, circa 1945. After completing his military service, Reitan studied with Ward Halstead and went on to assemble the best known neuropsychological test battery used to date. (Photo courtesy of Ralph Reitan.)

Treatment of brain-wounded World War II veterans created the basic model for multidisciplinary physical rehabilitation programs. In Russia, Luria directed a rehabilitation hospital where he applied his theories of cortical functioning to the benefit of many wounded veterans (Glozman, 2007), and he worked to promote and define relationships between psychologists and neurologists to optimize services for patients (Teuber, 1950). In the United States, military clinical psychologists helped to pioneer rehabilitation of aphasia. For example, Wepman (1951) reported on outcomes of a specialized aphasia rehabilitation program at Dewitt General Hospital and Letterman General Hospital, both in California, where veterans received intensive treatment for up to 18 months.

In the United States, neuropsychological research on soldiers with penetrating brain wounds resumed during the Vietnam conflict (Black, 1973) and continues through the Vietnam Head Injury Study (VHIS;

Figure 1.3 Lieutenant Arthur Benton (1909–2006), U.S. Navy, circa 1945. Benton pioneered modern objective assessment of brain-injured service members, stimulated by the neurologist Morris Bender, a coworker during their service at the Naval Hospital in San Diego in World War II. (Photo courtesy of Abigail Sivan.)

Salazar, Schwab, & Grafman, 1995). The VHIS was initially designed as a registry to obtain outcome data for the survivors of combat-related brain injuries. Approximately 2000 veterans were registered, and data from the first two phases of the long-term medical follow-up program have provided valuable data regarding how the brain compensates for injury, how frontotemporal areas of the brain function, and how specific injury characteristics are related to posttraumatic epilepsy (Grafman & Salazar, 1999). In 1993 the VHIS was integrated into the Defense and Veterans Head Injury Program.

Currently, active duty military members and veterans, within both military treatment facilities and the Veterans Health Administration, are afforded the gamut of care required by today's brain injuries. Pickett, Bender, and Gourley (chapter 7) present the current state of brain injury rehabilitative services available to service members, with an emphasis on services provided by the Department of Veterans Affairs (VA).

ATTENTION DEFICIT HYPERACTIVITY DISORDER AND LEARNING DISORDERS

ADHD has had a significant impact on the military. Recognized as a disorder for the first time in 1980 (American Psychiatric Association), it has created a situation in the last decade, as those first diagnosed grew to adulthood, for significant military resources to be devoted to the issue. This has been observed largely in making determinations as to whether the disorder renders a particular individual suitable or unsuitable for duty. While the assessment of LD has evolved over the years into a fairly well-understood and structured process, ADHD assessment continues to be varied among a diverse array of providers (e.g., psychologists/neuropsychologists, pediatricians, family practice physicians, psychiatrists, etc.). To maintain the safety of individual military members and fellow troops, the military has begun to lean heavily on neuropsychological assessment in this determination. Most often this is not done to establish the diagnosis of ADHD, but rather to objectively assess the continued presence of cognitive impairment into adulthood or to establish likely resolution of ADHD symptoms.

Hess, Hardin, and Kupke (chapter 8) discuss military regulations as they pertain to ADHD and LD and provide case examples of fitness-for-duty evaluations. In addition, evolving guidelines for aviation personnel seeking waivers for histories of ADHD and LD are described as is the experience of an active duty ADHD clinic.

HUMAN IMMUNODEFICIENCY VIRUS

As much more has been discovered about HIV, its progression and treatment, military regulations and practice have adapted. Early in the years of the epidemic, HIV was considered medically disqualifying for military service, and service members testing positive were automatically medically retired. However, these policies have changed significantly over the years as research into the disease has improved the medical management and outcomes of these individuals. The Department of Defense has excellent medical treatment facilities and resources for HIV-positive service members, beginning with early detection, given military policies about routine HIV testing of all service members.

Once diagnosed, HIV positive service members undergo mandatory routine medical evaluations to monitor the progression of the disease so that optimal treatment decisions can be made in a timely manner. A part of these routine visits includes psychological evaluation and, increasingly, neuropsychological assessment. HIV-Associated Neurocognitive Disorders impact a large percentage of HIV-positive individuals. In the military the more subtle Mild Neurocognitive Disorder and Asymptomatic Neurocognitive Impairment (i.e., impairment on neurocognitive testing that is not evident in daily functioning) are the more difficult to disposition from a fitness-for-duty perspective. Woods, Weber, McCutchan, and Heaton (chapter 9) provide an overview of HIV, discuss the range of cognitive disorders associated with HIV, and provide recommendations regarding neuropsychological assessment of HIV-positive military members.

REPATRIATED PRISONERS OF WAR

Of all military members, repatriated prisoners of war (RPW) are perhaps the best studied psychologically and neuropsychologically. The prisoner-of-war (POW) experience through the various conflicts is diverse, and while all World War I RPWs are now deceased, those from World War II and all other conflicts since continue to receive specialized care. To understand an RPW, one must take into consideration his or her unique POW experience with a focus on where and by whom they were held, duration of captivity, availability of medical care, nutritional factors, torture experience, and pertinent individual characteristics.

Following the repatriation of the Vietnam POWs in the 1970s, the Army, Air Force, and Navy medical departments undertook structured

POW studies. The Army and Air Force discontinued their programs in 1978 but the Navy's continued under the leadership of Captain Robert E. Mitchell, a Navy flight surgeon. The Robert E. Mitchell Prisoner of War Studies Center now falls under the command of the Naval Operational Medicine Institute in Pensacola, Florida, where RPWs from all services from the Vietnam era forward are seen routinely for medical care and routine reevaluation. This has included serial neuropsychological testing. Moore (chapter 10) discusses the literature as it relates to RPWs, the current operations of the Robert E. Mitchell Center, and the longitudinal neuropsychological data acquired from the Vietnam RPWs.

NEUROPSYCHOLOGY AND SUSTAINED OPERATIONS

Military personnel face significant challenges in the routine course of their work. By virtue of frequent service in a combat zone in today's conflict, work hours are long and the need for vigilance and self-protection is high. In these dangerous and fast-paced environments, sleep is often sacrificed. Fatigue is a service member's enemy, and decisions regarding rest and sleep significantly impact cognition (Boring, 1945). Sleep deprivation and fatigue have historically been major topics of study for the military, particularly in high-risk populations such as aviation (McFarland, 1942).

The military has searched for solutions to the problem of fatigue and sleep deprivation since World War II. In some populations, such as aviation, special forces, and medical personnel, stimulants have been studied and are used as one solution (Ryan, Zazeckis, French, & Harvey, 2006). Researchers have dedicated significant time to the issue, with particular emphasis on the negative impact upon higher order or executive cognitive abilities, namely performing novel and/or complex tasks or having to find a novel solution to a problem (Wesensten, Belenky, & Balkin, 2006). In the high-risk combat environment, in particular, a declination of these cognitive abilities creates significant risk and is known to result in poor decision making and problem solving leading to unnecessary loss of life.

Wesensten and Balkin (chapter 11) review the cognitive effects of sleep deprivation on service members and the operational implications of lack of sleep. To effectively relate the impact of sleep deprivation on individuals in operational environments, they review both aviation and ground catastrophes, linked directly to the sleep deprivation of personnel. They provide cogent recommendations for the optimization of sleep in operational environments, which military psychologists can use to provide valuable consultation to commands. Of particular benefit to neuropsychologists, using these guidelines regarding sleep needs and time needed to restore normal cognitive functioning following a variety of sleep deprivation scenarios can inform in-theater neuropsychological assessment and return-to-duty decisions. In particular, and with the large numbers of concussed individuals requiring assessment, better determinations regarding return to duty and appropriate waiting periods with which concussed individuals must wait prior to engaging meaningfully in neuropsychological screening can be made.

POSTTRAUMATIC STRESS DISORDER

Historically, the concept of a psychological reaction to the trauma of war has been described in many ways. While the labels change with each new war, the struggle does not. In World War I a comparable term was "shell shock," though other labels of mental health sequelae were "effort syndrome, war neurosis, gas hysteria, Da Costa's syndrome, irritable heart syndrome, and not yet diagnosed nervous" (Campise, Geller, & Campise, 2006, p. 215). Early in World War I, shell shock was described as a "mysterious kind of nervous disorganization (which) occurred in those who were submitted to close shelling, and it was natural that this clinical syndrome should be thought to be due to the physical effects of explosion" (Denny-Brown, 1943, p. 509), and the term "shell shock" was synonymous with "shell concussion" (Fulton, 1942). However, these symptoms of sensory and motor disturbance, "loss of memory, insomnia, terrifying dreams, pains, emotional instability, attacks of unconsciousness or of changed consciousness, epileptic fits, obsessive thoughts, usually of the gloomiest and most painful kind, even in some cases hallucinations and incipient delusions" (Smith & Pear, 1917, pp. 12–13) became largely reconceptualized as an emotional response to trauma as opposed to the neurological consequence of shelling injury. Shell shock became an umbrella term for a variety of conditions, to include concussion, malingering, cowardice, hysteria (Lumsden, 1916), psychopathy, exhaustion delirium, psychosis, and even schizophrenia when wartime experiences were felt to have propagated the illness (Baganz & Strotz, 1941). Shell shock was considered to be the most difficult war-related diagnosis to treat (Jones & Wessely, 2005).

By World War II the term had been dropped in favor of such diagnoses as "psychoneurosis, effort syndrome, combat exhaustion, battle fatigue and operational fatigue" (Campise, Geller, & Campise, 2006, p. 215). Korea saw battle fatigue and combat exhaustion. During Vietnam the current diagnostic and descriptive labels of combat stress and posttraumatic stress disorder (PTSD) first arose to be further described as "combat stress reaction" during the first Gulf War, an umbrella term used today. Service members currently experience high rates of PTSD and brain injury, with some researchers concluding that mTBI cases are strongly associated with PTSD (Hoge et al., 2008), akin to that of World War I's shell shock. Early military providers struggled with differentiating psychogenic war neurosis (i.e., shell shock) from concussion resulting from a blast (i.e., shell concussion, Fulton, 1942), a direct parallel to today.

Vasterling, MacDonald, Ulloa, and Rodier (chapter 12) present the current status of PTSD in the context of military service and trauma. The neuroanatomical findings, neuropsychological correlates, difficulties related to comorbidities, functional impact, and clinical implications of PTSD are addressed. The chapter concludes with a description of emerging empirically based treatments for PTSD.

COGNITION IN EXTREME SITUATIONS AND ENVIRONMENTS

While much of neuropsychology is concerned about changes in cognitive and emotional functioning as a result of injury, disease, or psychological trauma, cognition in military environments can be impaired in healthy, high-functioning service members. The combat theater and other environments in which military members operate are frequently life threatening (search and rescue, special operations, humanitarian missions, etc.). Making decisions and being able to implement learned skills in these environments can be inordinately challenging, and it is known that there can be an observed cognitive decline in these situations. This concept of Operational Demand Related Cognitive Decline (ODRCD) is intimately linked to known physiological aspects of functioning. McNeil and Morgan (chapter 13) will address the literature as it pertains to military cognitive demands and the interrelationships between extreme stress and norepinephrine, epinephrine, cortisol, neuropeptide-Y, and dehydroepiandrosterone.

THE TRAINING OF NEUROPSYCHOLOGISTS IN THE MILITARY

The history of neuropsychologists in the military is a relatively short one. The Air Force began training neuropsychologists in the early 1980s. By the mid-1980s, neuropsychologists were assigned to Wilford Hall (Texas), Wright-Patterson (Ohio), David Grant (California), and Malcolm Grow (Maryland) Medical Centers, and the Air Force personnel system began to recognize neuropsychology as a subspecialty of clinical psychology. This designation, called a shred-out, required completion of a fellowship. During the early 1990s, Air Force neuropsychologists went to civilian institutions for 1 year of training; from 1992 on, the training period was extended to 2 years. Training sites include the University of Texas at Galveston, the University of California at San Diego, the University of Florida, the University of Oklahoma, Brown University, the University of Virginia, Ohio State University, and the Oregon Health Sciences University. One Air Force neuropsychologist was trained at Walter Reed Army Medical Center. More than 20 active duty Air Force psychologists have now been trained as neuropsychologists.

The Army provides 2-year in-service postdoctoral fellowships in clinical neuropsychology for Army psychologists at Walter Reed Army Medical Center in Washington, DC, and Tripler Army Medical Center in Honolulu, Hawaii. The program at Walter Reed Army Medical Center began in 1991 and has graduated a total of 14 fellows, 6 of whom remain on active duty. The program was accredited by the APA in 2002 and was the first postdoctoral program in the country with a specialization in clinical neuropsychology to obtain accreditation. The program at the Tripler Army Medical Center began in 1994 and was recognized by the Association of Psychology Postdoctoral and Internship Centers in 1995. The program has graduated a total of nine fellows consisting of five active duty and four civilian neuropsychologists. All of the five active duty fellows remain on active duty. Operational needs and individual preferences determine the nature of assignments following completion of the fellowships. While it is not typical for Army neuropsychologists to remain in assignments with a major focus on clinical neuropsychology following a utilization tour, most will apply skills gained during fellowship to a broad variety of other activities involving leadership, telemedicine, deployment health, and special operations.

The Navy has been providing the 2-year postdoctoral fellowship since the mid-1980s in a duty under instruction model. In essence this means that the Navy (like the Air Force) sends commissioned psychologists to a civilian site for 2 years of training. Navy psychologists have trained at the University of Texas Medical Branch at Galveston (1), University of Alabama (1), University of Oregon (2), University of Florida (2), Georgetown University (2), University of Virginia (4), and University of California, Los Angeles (1). To date, the Navy has trained 13 neuropsychologists, 4 of whom currently serve on active duty. While the three branches of service adopt slightly varying methods of delivery of the fellowship, they are united in their commitment to the Houston Conference training model (Hannay et al., 1998).

THE FUTURE OF MILITARY NEUROPSYCHOLOGY

The future of military neuropsychology cannot ignore its past. Major current challenges include the assessment and treatment of blast injuries and the psychological trauma of war, the most profound psychology-oriented problems encountered in all of the prior wars. New to this war is the need for active duty neuropsychologists to serve in the combat zone to address these challenges. Seegmiller and Kane (chapter 14) summarize the most pertinent directions for military neuropsychology in both the near and distant future. Included in these challenges are improving battlefield concussion assessment, denoting the appropriate use of predeployment cognitive assessment, better delineating strategies to differentiate the complex interplay of war-related cognitive and psychiatric diagnoses, improving training and manning needs, using teleneuropsychology, and remaining relevant. In many ways, the challenges faced by military neuropsychologists are not new; however, there is perhaps more at our disposal at this time to more successfully meet the needs of service members and the military. This volume is intended to delineate the current state of military neuropsychology and provide a primary resource to any neuropsychologist serving our active, reserve, guard, and veteran populations.

REFERENCES

Aita, J. A., Armitage, S. G., Reitan, R. M., & Rabinovitz, A. (1947). The use of certain psychological tests in the evaluation of brain injury. *Journal of General Psychology*, 37, 24–44.
Altus, W. D., & Bell, H. M. (1945). The validity of certain measures of maladjustment in an army special training center. *Psychological Bulletin*, 42, 98–103.

American Psychiatric Association. (1980). *Diagnostic and statistical manual of mental disorders* (3rd ed.). Washington, DC: Author.

American Psychological Association Committee on Ethical Standards for Psychology. (1949). Developing a code of ethics for psychologists: A first report of progress. *American Psychologist, 4,* 17.

Armitage, S. G. (1946). An analysis of certain psychological tests used for the evaluation of brain injury. *Psychological Monographs, 60* (Whole No. 277).

Baganz, C. N., & Strotz, C. M. (1941). So-called "shell shock": Types, etiological factors and means for its prevention. *The Military Surgeon, 88,* 282–286.

Baldwin, B. T. (1919). The function of psychology in the rehabilitation of disabled soldiers. *Psychological Bulletin, 16,* 267–290.

Ballard, S. I., & Miller, H. G. (1944). Neuropsychiatry at a Royal Air Force centre. *British Medical Journal, 2,* 40–43.

Benton, A. (2003). Recollections of a part-time amateur neurohistorian. *Journal of the History of the Neurosciences, 12,* 25–33.

Black, F. W. (1973). Cognitive and memory performance in subjects with brain damage secondary to penetrating missile wounds and closed head injury. *Journal of Clinical Psychology, 29,* 441–442.

Boake, C. (1989). A history of cognitive rehabilitation of head-injured patients, 1915–1980. *Journal of Head Trauma Rehabilitation, 4,* 1–8.

Boake, C. (2002). From the Binet-Simon to the Wechsler-Bellevue: Tracing the history of intelligence testing. *Journal of Clinical and Experimental Psychology, 24,* 383–405.

Boring, E. G. (1945). *Psychology for the armed forces.* Washington, DC: The Infantry Journal.

Bowers, W. F. (1943). Hysteria and malingering on the surgical service. *The Military Surgeon, 92,* 506–511.

Bronner, A. F., Healy, W., Lowe, G. M., & Shimberg, M. E. (1929). *A manual of individual mental tests and testing.* Boston: Little, Brown, and Company.

Bruner, A. B. (1934). Malingering tests. *American Journal of Ophthalmology, 17,* 490–496.

Brussel, J. A., Grassi, J. R., & Melniker, A. A. (1942). The Rorschach method and postconcussion syndrome. *The Psychiatric Quarterly, 16,* 707–743.

Budd, F. C., & Harvey, S. (2006). Military fitness-for-duty evaluations. In C. H. Kennedy & E. A. Zillmer (Eds.), *Military psychology: Clinical and operational applications* (pp. 35–60). New York: Guilford.

Budd, F., & Kennedy, C. H. (2006). Introduction to clinical military psychology. In C. H. Kennedy & E. A. Zillmer (Eds.), *Military psychology: Clinical and operational applications* (pp. 21–34). New York: Guilford.

Campbell, M. M. (1943). Malingery in relation to psychopathy in military psychiatry. *Northwest Medicine, 42,* 349–354.

Campise, R. L., Geller, S. K., & Campise, M. E. (2006). Combat stress. In C. H. Kennedy & E. A. Zillmer (Eds.), *Military psychology: Clinical and operational applications* (pp. 215–240). New York: Guilford.

Canter, M. B., Bennett, B. E., Jones, S. E., & Nagy, T. F. (1996). *Ethics for psychologists: A commentary on the APA ethics code.* Washington, DC: American Psychological Association.

Capshew, J. H. (1999). *Psychologists on the march: Science, practice, and professional identity in America, 1929–1969.* New York: Cambridge University Press.

Collins, A. F. (2006). An intimate connection: Oliver Zangwill and the emergence of neuropsychology in Britain. *History of Psychology, 9,* 89–112.

Cranston, A. (1986). Psychology in the Veterans Administration. *American Psychologist, 41,* 990–995.

Denny-Brown, D. (1943). "Shell shock" and effects of high explosives. *Journal of Laboratory and Clinical Medicine, 28,* 509–514.

Dillon, F. (1939). Simulated mental disorders among soldiers in the late war. *The Lancet, 237,* 706–709.

Doherty, W. B., & Runes, D. D. (1943). *Rehabilitation of the war injured: A symposium.* New York: Philosophical Library.

Driskell, J. E., & Olmstead, B. (1989). Psychology and the military: Research applications and trends. *American Psychologist, 44,* 43–54.

Edgar, T. W. (1931). Industrial disability versus pain intensity. *Medical Journal and Record, 133,* 157–160.

El-Hai, J. (2005). *The lobotomist.* Hoboken, NJ: John Wiley & Sons.

Fetterman, J. L. (1943). Two clinical tests valuable in war medicine and in medicolegal practice. *War Medicine, 3,* 155–159.

Franz, S. I. (1923). *Nervous and mental re-education.* New York: The Macmillan Company.

Fulton, J. F. (1942). Blast and concussion in the present war. In W. S. Pugh (Ed.), *War medicine: A symposium* (pp. 226–240). New York: Philosophical Library.

Garner, J. R. (1939). Malingering. *American Journal of Medical Jurisprudence, 2,* 173–177.

Gill, M. M. (1941). Malingering. *Bulletin of the Menninger Clinic, 5,* 157–160.

Glozman, J. M. (2007). A. R. Luria and the history of Russian neuropsychology. *Journal of the History of the Neurosciences, 16,* 168–180.

Goldstein, K. (1942). *Aftereffects of brain injuries in war: Their evaluation and treatment. The application of psychologic methods in the clinic.* New York: Grune & Stratton.

Good, R. (1942). Malingering. *British Medical Journal, 2,* 359–362.

Grafman, J., & Salazar, A. M. (1999). Defense and Veterans Head Injury Program (DVHIP): The William Fields Caveness Vietnam Head Injury Study—Past and future. *Brain Injury Source, 3,* 10–17.

Grinker, R. R., & Spiegel, J. P. (1945). *War neuroses.* Philadelphia: The Blakeston Company.

Hannay, H. J., Bieliauskas, L., Crosson, B. A., Hammeke, T. A., Hamsher, K. de S., & Koffler, S. (1998). Proceedings of the Houston conference on specialty education and training in clinical neuropsychology. *Archives of Clinical Neuropsychology, 13,* 203–249.

Harrell, T. W. (1992). Some history of the Army General Classification Test. *Journal of Applied Psychology, 77,* 875–878.

Hoge, C. W., McGurk, D., Thomas, J. L., Cox, A. L., Engel, C. C., & Castro, C. A. (2008). Mild traumatic brain injury in U.S. soldiers returning from Iraq. *The New England Journal of Medicine, 358,* 453–463.

Hopwood, J. S., & Snell, H. K. (1933). Amnesia in relation to crime. *Journal of Mental Science, 79,* 27–41.

Hulett, A. G. (1941). Malingering: A study. *The Military Surgeon, 89,* 129–139.

Hunt, W. A. (1943). Psychology in the selection of recruits at the U.S. Naval Training Station, Newport, Rhode Island. *Psychological Bulletin, 40,* 598–600.

Hunt, W. A., & Older, H. J. (1943). Detection of malingering through psychometric tests. *Naval Medical Bulletin, 41,* 1318–1323.

Hunt, W. A., & Older, H. J. (1944). Psychometric scatter pattern as a diagnostic aid. *Journal of Abnormal and Social Psychology, 39,* 118–123.

Hunt, W. A., & Stevenson, I. (1946). Psychological testing in military clinical psychology: Intelligence testing. *Psychological Review, 53,* 25–35.

Jackson, E. (1897). Tests for visual malingering and hysterical blindness. *Medicine and Surgery Reports, 76,* 109–114.

Jasper, H. H., Kersman, J., & Elvidge, A. (1940). Electroencephalographic studies of injury to the head. *Archives of Neurology and Psychiatry, 44,* 328–350.

Jeffrey, T. B. (1989). Issues regarding confidentiality for military psychologists. *Military Psychology, 1,* 49–56.

Johnson, W. B. (2008). Top ethical challenges for military clinical psychologists. *Military Psychology, 20,* 49–62.

Jones, E., & Wessely, S. (2005). *Shell shock to PTSD: Military psychiatry from 1900 to the Gulf War.* New York: Psychology Press.

Kahn, S. (1943). Malingering in the army. *Medical Record, 156,* 416–418.

Kanzer, M. (1939). Amnesia: A statistical study. *The American Journal of Psychiatry, 96,* 711–716.

Karpman, B. (1926). Psychoses in criminals: Clinical studies in the psychopathology of crime. *The Journal of Nervous and Mental Disease, 64,* 482–502.

Kellogg, C. E., & Morton, N. W. (1999). *Beta-III.* Bloomington, MN: Pearson Assessments.

Kennedy, C. H., & Johnson, W. B. (2009). Mixed agency in military psychology: Applying the American Psychological Association's Ethics Code. *Psychological Services, 6,* 22–31.

Kennedy, C. H., Jones, D. E., & Arita, A. A. (2007). Multicultural experiences of U.S. military psychologists: Current trends and training target areas. *Psychological Services, 4,* 158–167.

Kennedy, C. H., & Malone, R. C. (2009). Integration of women into the modern military. In S. M. Freeman, B. A. Moore, & A. Freeman (Eds.), *Living and surviving in harm's way: A psychological treatment handbook for pre- and post-deployment of military personnel* (pp. 67–81). New York: Routledge.

Kennedy, C. H., Malone, R. C., & Franks, M. J. (2009). Provision of mental health services at the detention hospital in Guantanamo Bay. *Psychological Services, 6,* 1–10.

Kennedy, C. H., & McNeil, J. A. (2006). A history of military psychology. In C. H. Kennedy & E. A. Zillmer (Eds.), *Military psychology: Clinical and operational applications* (pp. 1–17). New York: Guilford.

Kennedy, C. H., & Moore, B. A. (2008). Evolution of clinical military psychology ethics. *Military Psychology, 20,* 1–6.

Kennedy, C. H., & Williams, T. J. (in press). *Ethical practice in operational psychology: Examining dilemmas in military and intelligence arenas.* Washington, DC: American Psychological Association .

Kevles, D. (1968). Testing the army's intelligence: Psychologists and the military in World War I. *The Journal of American History, 55,* 565–581.

Lande, R. G. (1997). The history of forensic psychiatry in the U.S. military. In R. G. Lande & D. T. Armitage (Eds.), *Principles and practice of military forensic psychiatry* (pp. 3–27). Springfield, IL: Charles Thomas.

Lezak, M., Howieson, D. B., & Loring, D. (2004). *Neuropsychological assessment* (4th ed.). New York: Oxford University Press.

Ludwig, A. O. (1944). Clinical features and diagnosis of malingering in military personnel. *War Medicine, 5,* 378–382.

Lumsden, T. (1916). The psychology of malingering and functional neurosis in peace and war. *The Lancet, 191,* 860–862.

McCauley, M., Hughes, J. H., & Liebling-Kalifani, H. (2008). Ethical considerations for military clinical psychologists: A review of selected literature. *Military Psychology, 20,* 7–20.

McFarland, R. A. (1942). Fatigue in aircraft pilots. In W. S. Pugh (Ed.), *War medicine: A symposium* (pp. 430–448). New York: Philosophical Library.

McGuire, F. L. (1990). *Psychology Aweigh: A History of Clinical Psychology in the United States Navy, 1900-1988.* Washington, DC: American Psychological Association.

Meagher, J. F. W. (1919). Malingering in relation to war neuropsychiatric conditions, especially hysteria: A criticism. *Medical Record, 96,* 963–972.

Meier, M. J. (1992). Modern clinical neuropsychology in historical perspective. *American Psychologist, 47,* 550–558.

Myers, C. S. (1916). Contributions to the study of shell shock. Being an account of certain disorders of speech, with special reference to their causation and their relation to malingering. *The Lancet, 191,* 461–467.

Myerson, A. (1931). Three cases of malingering in persons accused of crime. *The Journal of Nervous and Mental Disease, 73,* 646–648.

No Author Noted. (1943). The refusal to remember. *The Lancet, 245,* 231–232.

Page, G. D. (1996). Clinical psychology in the military: Developments and issues. *Clinical Psychology Review, 16,* 383–396.

Personnel Research Section. (1943). Personnel research in the Army VI: The selection of truck drivers. *Psychological Bulletin, 40,* 499–508.

Phares, E. J., & Trull, T. J. (1997). *Clinical psychology: Concepts, methods, and profession* (5th ed.). Pacific Grove, CA: Brooks/Cole.

Picano, J. J., Williams, R. J., & Roland, R. R. (2006). Assessment and selection of high risk operational personnel. In C. H. Kennedy & E. A. Zillmer (Eds.), *Military psychology: Clinical and operational applications* (pp. 353–370). New York: Guilford.

Poppelreuter, W. (1990). *Disturbances of lower and higher visual capacities caused by occipital damage: With special reference to the psychopathological, pedagogical, industrial, and social implications* (J. Zihl, Trans.). New York: Oxford University Press. (Original work published 1917)

Poser, U., Kohler, J. A., & Schönle, P. W. (1996). A historical review of neuropsychological rehabilitation in Germany. *Neuropsychological Rehabilitation, 6,* 257–278.

Rosenberg, S. J., & Feldberg, T. M. (1944). Rorschach characteristics of a group of malingerers. *Rorschach Research Exchange, 8,* 141–158.

Reger, M. A., Etherage, J. R., Reger, G. M., & Gahm, G. A. (2008). Civilian psychologists in an army culture: The ethical challenge of cultural competence. *Military Psychology, 20,* 21–36.

Reitan, R. M. (1989). A note regarding some aspects of the history of clinical neuropsychology. *Archives of Clinical Neuropsychology, 4*, 385–391.

Ryan, L. M., Zazeckis, T. M., French, L. M., & Harvey, S. (2006). Neuropsychological practice in the military. In C. H. Kennedy & E. A. Zillmer (Eds.), *Military psychology: Clinical and operational applications* (pp. 105–129). New York: Guilford.

Salazar, A. M., Schwab, K., & Grafman, J. H. (1995). Penetrating injuries in the Vietnam war. Traumatic unconsciousness, epilepsy, and psychosocial outcome. *Neurosurgery Clinics of North America, 6*(4), 715–726.

Saul, L. J. (1943). Some aspects of psychiatry in the training station. *The American Journal of Psychiatry, 100*, 74–79.

Seidenfeld, M. A. (1966). Clinical psychology. In A. J. Glass & R. J. Bennucci (Eds.), *Neuropsychiatry in World War II (vol. 1, Zone of Interior)* (pp. 567–603). Washington, DC: Office of the Surgeon General.

Seltzer, A. P. (1936). Malingering. *Medical Record, 143*, 228–231.

Serota, H. M. (1940). Applicability of the electroencephalogram (EEG) to military medical problems. *The Military Surgeon, 87*, 537–539.

Shephard, B. (2000). *A war of nerves: Soldiers and psychiatrists in the twentieth century*. Cambridge, MA: Harvard University Press.

Smith, G. E., & Pear, T. H. (1917). *Shell shock and its lessons*. Manchester, England: Manchester University Press.

Staff, Personnel Research Section, Classification and Replacement Branch. (1944). The new Army individual test of general mental ability. *Psychological Bulletin, 41*, 532–538.

Staff, Psychological Research Unit No. 2, Department of Psychology Research Section. (1944). Research program on psychomotor tests in the Army Air Forces. *Psychological Bulletin, 41*, 307–321.

Stone. (2008). Dual agency for VA clinicians: Defining and evolving ethical question. *Military Psychology, 20*, 37–48.

Terman, L. M. (1918). The use of intelligence tests in the army. *The Psychological Bulletin, 15*, 177–187.

Teuber, H. (1950). Neuropsychology. In R. E. Harris, J. G. Miller, G. A. Muench, L. J. Stone, H. Teuber, & J. Zubin (Eds.), *Recent advances in diagnostic psychological testing* (pp. 30–52). Springfield, IL: Charles C. Thomas.

von Mayrhauser, R. T. (1992). The mental testing community and validity: A prehistory. *American Psychologist, 47*, 244–253.

Waud, S. P. (1942). Malingering. *The Military Surgeon, 91*, 535–538.

Wells, F. L., & Ruesch, J. (1942). *Mental examiner's handbook*. New York: Psychological Corporation.

Wechsler, D. (1997a). *Wechsler adult intelligence scale-III*. San Antonio: The Psychological Corporation.

Wechsler, D. (1997b). *Wechsler memory scale*. San Antonio: The Psychological Corporation.

Wechsler, D. (2008). *Wechsler adult intelligence scale-IV*. San Antonio: The Psychological Corporation.

Weinstein, S., & Teuber, H. (1957). The role of preinjury education and intelligence level in intellectual loss after brain injury. *Journal of Comparative and Physiological Psychology, 50*, 535–539.

Wepman, J. M. (1951). *Recovery from aphasia*. New York: Ronald Press.

Wesensten, N. J., Belenky, G., & Balkin, T. J. (2006). Sleep loss: Implications for operational effectiveness and current solutions. In T. W. Britt, C. A. Castro, & A. B. Adler (Eds.), *Military life: The psychology of serving in peace and combat* (Vol. 1, pp. 81–107). Westport, CT: Praeger Security International.

Wilde, J. F. (1942). Narco-analysis in the treatment of war neuroses. *British Medical Journal, 2*, 4–7.

Woodworth, R. S. (1919). The first adjustment inventory. *Psychological Bulletin, 16*, 59. Reprinted in W. Dennis (Ed.), *Readings in general psychology* (1949, p. 451). New York: Prentice-Hall.

Yoakum, C. S., & Yerkes, R. M. (1920). *Army mental tests.* New York: Henry Holt and Company.

Zangwill, O. L. (1945). A review of psychological work at the Brain Injuries Unit, Edinburgh, 1941–1945. *British Medical Journal, 2*, 248–250.

Zeidner, J., & Drucker, A. J. (1988). *Behavioral science in the army: A corporate history of the Army Research Institute.* Alexandria, VA: United States Army Research Institute for the Behavioral and Social Sciences.

Ethical Issues in Military Neuropsychology

2

SHANE S. BUSH AND GEORGE M. CUESTA

Psychologists enter the military for a variety of personal and professional reasons. For those psychologists who take pride in donning the uniform of the military psychologist, few activities are as personally and professionally rewarding as serving U.S. military personnel and their families. Military psychologists, in general, and neuropsychologists, more specifically, typically hold multiple roles within the military, which provide them numerous avenues through which to apply their knowledge and skills. However, those same roles and activities tend to expand ethical considerations and amplify the potential for ethical challenges and conflicts.

With traumatic brain injury emerging as "the signature injury" of combat operations in Iraq and Afghanistan (Committee on Gulf War and Health: Brain Injury in Veterans and Long-Term Health Outcomes, 2008), neuropsychologists have begun assuming a greater role in the military mission. Neuropsychologists currently have a greater presence in combat theaters than ever before, serving multiple roles as military officers, psychologists, and neuropsychologists. Each role has its own obligations and responsibilities, which in turn have the potential to conflict with each other and with the values held by the profession of psychology and the individual neuropsychologist.

As the roles, methods, and knowledge of military neuropsychology evolve, so too will areas of ethical uncertainty be confronted and addressed. Clinicians must consider the unique ethical issues, and unique variations on traditional ethical issues, that are encountered in military neuropsychology. Servicemen and women are not only encountered by neuropsychologists within active duty units but are also evaluated and treated in Veterans Administration (VA) facilities and in a variety of civilian contexts. The various clinical contexts, whether representing one step in a continuum of care or a distinct phase of clinical service, are associated with overlapping and unique ethical considerations of which neuropsychologists must be aware. The goals of this chapter are to clarify the relevant ethical considerations in military neuropsychology and provide clinicians with an approach to addressing ethical challenges.

PRIMARY ETHICAL CONCERNS IN PSYCHOLOGY AND NEUROPSYCHOLOGY

For psychologists in general, results of a survey of American Psychological Association (APA) members published in 1992 revealed that the three major ethical dilemmas encountered in daily work were confidentiality; blurred, dual, or conflictual relationships; and payment issues (Pope & Vetter, 1992). Forensic issues were fifth, assessment issues were ninth, and competence was eleventh. With regard to military clinical psychologists, a survey of ethical concerns of U.S. Air Force clinicians (Orme & Doerman, 2001) identified the five most common areas of ethical concerns as (a) conflicts between ethics and organizational demands, (b) maintaining confidentiality, (c) multiple relationships, (d) disclosures, and (e) avoiding harm.

In contrast, board-certified neuropsychologists considered boundaries of competence, appropriate use of assessments, and interpretation of assessment results to be of primary importance (Brittain, Frances, & Barth, 1995). More recently, a panel of neuropsychologists with considerable experience addressing ethical issues considered the primary ethical challenges to involve professional competence, the increasing involvement of neuropsychologists in forensic activities, and the apparent misconduct of colleagues (Bush, Grote, Johnson-Greene, & Macartney-Filgate, 2008).

In addition, Bush (2007), noting that considerable differences exist as a function of practice context, described the top 12 sources of ethical conflict for neuropsychologists. We have compared those sources of ethical conflict for neuropsychologists in general to a list of sources of ethical conflict for military neuropsychologists that we have proposed, based on our experience and familiarity with the literature on this topic (Table 2.1).

Our list of primary ethical considerations for military neuropsychologists closely resembles the list relevant for military clinical psychologists in a more general way (Johnson, 2008; Kennedy & Moore, 2008; McCauley, Hughes, & Liebling-Kalifani, 2008). Military neuropsychologists must understand and learn to address the ethical issues that are common to the military clinical psychologist's experience as their foundation of ethical competence before focusing on sources of ethical concern that are more specific to neuropsychological practice.

Table 2.1

COMMON SOURCES OF ETHICAL CONCERN IN NEUROPSYCHOLOGY AND MILITARY NEUROPSYCHOLOGY

NEUROPSYCHOLOGY[a]	MILITARY NEUROPSYCHOLOGY[b]
Professional competence	Professional competence
Roles/relationships (dual/multiple)	Third-party requests for services/informed consent
Test security/release of raw test data	Privacy and confidentiality
Third-party observers	Roles/relationships (dual/multiple)
Confidentiality	Avoiding harm
Assessment	Assessment (methods, norms)
Conflicts between ethics and law	Conflicts between civilian and military ethical and legal requirements
False or deceptive statements	Record keeping
Objectivity	Test security/release of raw test data
Cooperation with other professionals	Objectivity
Informed consent/third party	Third-party observers' requests for services
Record keeping and fees	Psychological services delivered to or through organizations

[a]From Bush (2007). This list is based on the combination of interviews of ethically knowledgeable neuropsychologists (Bush, Grote, Johnson-Greene, & Macartney-Filgate, 2008), review of the literature, and the author's clinical experiences.
[b]This list is proposed based on our experiences and our familiarity with the literature on this topic. It is recognized that the order of importance of these ethical issues will vary considerably depending on the practice context.

PRIMARY ETHICAL ISSUES IN MILITARY NEUROPSYCHOLOGY

Because extensive coverage of all areas of ethical concern in military neuropsychology is beyond the scope of a single chapter, in this section we present some ethical issues that are considered to be particularly challenging, and we provide a detailed case vignette to illustrate some of the challenges encountered.

Competence

Military clinical psychologists, including neuropsychologists, are often required to provide a diverse array of psychological services. When confronted with novel tasks or responsibilities for which professional competence is lacking, clinicians have an ethical obligation to "take reasonable steps" to obtain the necessary knowledge and skills (APA Ethical Standard 2.01, Boundaries of Competence). However, "in emergencies, when psychologists provide services to individuals for whom other mental health services are not available and for which psychologists have not obtained the necessary training, psychologists may provide such services in order to ensure that services are not denied" (Ethical Standard 2.02, Providing Services in Emergencies). Nevertheless, once the emergency has ended, clinicians should discontinue the services, transfer care to a qualified provider, and/or obtain the necessary knowledge and skills to continue to serve the population. Advances in, and availability of, information technology and telecommunications facilitate the education, training, and supervision of military neuropsychologists.

Military neuropsychologists may be asked or directed to provide services by superiors who have inadequate understanding or unrealistic expectations of neuropsychology. Consider the case of a Navy neuropsychologist who is assigned to a busy fleet hospital in a forward area. Upon arrival, she is given the names of eight Marine riflemen who sustained concussions of different types and severities over the past few days and have been awaiting "neuropsych testing" before being returned to their units. She is informed by the physician officer-in-charge, "Let's go. Let's get these guys back to their units." She has access to a computerized neuropsychological screening test but does not have the more comprehensive measures that she thinks will be needed. She is not assigned private space to perform her examinations and ultimately depends on the radiology technician to sacrifice his space for brief periods. The sounds of helicopters, loud voices, and heavy machinery fill the environment.

The neuropsychologist wonders how she will make meaningful determinations about the neuropsychological functioning of these eight Marines and the others that are sure to follow.

As with other military occupations, military neuropsychologists must be able to improvise, adapt, and overcome obstacles. For creative and determined clinicians there may be a number of reasonable solutions to nontraditional requests for services or there may be no acceptable solutions. Neuropsychologists who strive to *educate* all relevant parties, particularly the primary decision makers, and *advocate* for their professional needs and the needs of their patients often find their efforts rewarded. With such efforts, persistence maximizes chances for success.

Military and VA Cultural Competence

The U.S. military represents a discrete cultural group with unique features of language, dress, manners, behavioral norms, and belief systems. In addition to general professional competence in the practice of psychology and neuropsychology, clinicians serving military populations must have or develop an understanding of military and veteran cultures. Neuropsychologists may evaluate and/or treat military personnel or veterans while on active duty, in a reserve status, in a VA setting, or in a variety of other civilian contexts. When deployed overseas, neuropsychologists may be embedded with mobile medical units or base hospitals. Although each context is associated with unique priorities and concerns, the cultural commonalities include an overarching set of values, beliefs, and experiences, and a manner of communication that civilians will not immediately understand. In addition, to the extent that cultural differences include subtle or obvious variations in language, behaviors, belief and value systems, dress, and rituals, each branch of the military represents a unique cultural group.

Currently, the significant majority of psychologists serving in the Army medical treatment facilities are civilian employees of the federal government. For example, Reger, Etherage, Reger, and Gahm (2008) reported that at Madigan Army Medical Center in Fort Lewis, Washington, over 90% of the licensed psychologists in the psychology department were civilians. The demand for civilian psychologists and neuropsychologists is likely to remain high as military operations in Afghanistan (Operation Enduring Freedom) and Iraq (Operation Iraqi Freedom) have resulted in large numbers of service members sustaining traumatic brain injury, postconcussion syndrome, and posttraumatic stress disorder (Fischer,

2008; Vasterling et al., 2006). To help meet the growing demand for neuropsychological evaluation and rehabilitation services, civilian neuropsychologists will increasingly be called upon to meet the neuropsychological needs of service members and veterans.

Because an understanding of military culture is required for the provision of competent neuropsychological services to military personnel and veterans, civilian neuropsychologists working in such contexts have an ethical obligation to strive to understand those aspects of military life that bear upon the evaluation and treatment services provided (Ethical Standard, 2.01, Boundaries of Competence). Training procedures, military cultural exposure experiences, education about relevant regulations, observation of experienced military neuropsychologists, and mentoring have been recommended to assist civilian neuropsychologists in obtaining the knowledge, skills, and abilities necessary for ethical practice in military and veteran contexts (Reger et al., 2008). Although neuropsychologist veterans possess the military cultural foundation to provide clinical services to military personnel and veterans, they nevertheless must familiarize themselves with the traditions and culture of the branches of service with which they are less familiar, in order to be culturally competent when working with individuals from other branches of service.

Military language and acronyms, rank, and behavioral norms are some aspects of military culture that unprepared clinicians will encounter and may misunderstand immediately. Acronyms and abbreviations are commonly used within all branches of military service to facilitate communication about a wide variety of topics. It is essential for newly commissioned clinicians and nonveteran civilian clinicians to become familiar with the acronyms most commonly used in their setting (General Principle E, Respect for People's Rights and Dignity). Such familiarization will facilitate communication between the neuropsychologist and the service member and will provide the clinician with important information about the service member.

As with language, rank plays a fundamental role within all branches of the military. In all branches of the military there are enlisted personnel, noncommissioned officers, warrant officers, and commissioned officers. These discrete groups within the military have their own corresponding affiliations, roles, and influence. Even within enlisted, warrant, noncommissioned, and commissioned ranks there are distinctions in rank that have corresponding expectations of behavior and decorum, the understanding of which facilitates the provision of clinical services.

Related to rank, a defining feature of a culture is a group's expectations for behavior (Reger et al., 2008). Within the military, numerous behavioral norms are well defined. In addition to basic training and indoctrination, there are books written for officers and noncommissioned officers of each of the service branches on how to conduct oneself in conformity with the culture (Benton, 2002; Bonn, 2002; Field Manual 7–22.7, 2002; Mack, Seymour, & McComas, 1998). Many of the cultural norms for behavior have implications for clinicians (Reger et al., 2008) and can be important for avoiding errors in diagnosis and patient management. Neuropsychologists should understand that they are viewed by enlisted personnel as the equivalent of an officer in uniform. Accordingly, they may address civilian neuropsychologists as "sir" or "ma'am," wait to sit until the neuropsychologist is seated, and apologize after using inappropriate language. Service members may present themselves in a polite, deferential, and guarded manner, especially in the initial sessions, which can sometimes hinder open and clear communication.

Multiple Roles, Relationships, and Obligations

Military neuropsychologists are first and foremost military officers and "therefore carefully and diligently discharge the duties of the office to which appointed by doing and performing all manner of things thereunto belonging."[1] As such, the neuropsychologist's primary responsibility is to the military command and the military mission. However, as clinicians, military neuropsychologists are also diagnosticians and healers, with an obligation to patients as human beings as well as essential members of the fighting force. Whether patients are self-referred or command-referred, neuropsychologists must, at the outset, clarify for all parties who the client is, what determinations will be made or services provided, and what information will be shared (Ethical Standard 3.10, Informed Consent). When identifying the client, clinicians must take care to remember that "the client" is not the only one with whom the clinician has relationships and ethical obligations. Neuropsychologists have ethical obligations to all involved parties. Clinicians should ask not only "Who is the client?" but also "What are my ethical responsibilities to each of the parties involved?" (Fisher, 2009).

   Neuropsychologists must be prepared to be pressured by patients or the command to make certain determinations, often regarding fitness for duty, and are best served by determining in advance how such pressures will be handled. In addition, military neuropsychologists might be required to switch from a clinical to a forensic or administrative role with their patient (Johnson, Ralph, & Johnson, 2005). Therefore, all parties are well served when careful informed consent is provided and documented as early as possible during the initial clinical contact and thereafter as needed.

Because neuropsychologists may be deployed to installations where there are no other mental health professionals, let alone neuropsychologists, they may be asked to provide clinical services to senior officers, persons over whom they have command authority, or persons with whom they have personal relationships such as colleagues and friends. Although the APA Ethics Code (Standard 3.05, Multiple Relationships) requires psychologists to refrain "from entering into a multiple relationship if the multiple relationship could reasonably be expected to impair the psychologist's objectivity, competence, or effectiveness in performing his or her functions as a psychologist or otherwise risks exploitation or harm to the person with whom the professional relationship exists," military service may require neuropsychologists to enter such relationships, thus placing neuropsychologists in a bind. In such instances, clinicians should clarify role expectations and process, to the extent necessary, the potential impact of the clinical interaction on the previous relationship between clinician and patient.

Although dual loyalty situations can occur, military medicine is similar to civilian medicine in most aspects (Institute of Medicine of the National Academies, 2009). Occupational medicine, sports medicine, and prison medicine offer models for addressing ethical issues that can be applied to military medicine. "Ethical considerations relevant to military medicine include parity, elasticity, and *primum non nocere*...In this context, *parity* refers to equality in treating patients, *elasticity* refers to flexibility in implementing policies, and *primum non nocere* is the historic principle of 'first, do no harm'" (Institute of Medicine of the National Academies, 2009, p. 4).

Confidentiality

The right of patients to have their thoughts, feelings, and personal information remain private has long been a cornerstone of medicine and mental health. As Hippocrates[2] stated, "What I may see or hear in the course of the treatment or even outside of the treatment in regard to the life of men, which on no account one must spread abroad, I will keep to myself, holding such things shameful to be spoken about." Trust that the doctor will maintain the privacy of sensitive information is central to the promotion of sincere communication between patient and doctor. In addition, diagnostic accuracy and the usefulness of recommendations depend upon the accuracy and completeness of relevant patient information. The obligation of neuropsychologists to safeguard sensitive patient information is reflected in the APA (2002) Ethics Code (Ethical Standard 4, Privacy and Confidentiality).

Neuropsychologists and their patients in civilian clinical contexts face multiple threats to confidentiality (Bush & Martin, 2008). In addition, the military has long held little regard for the privacy or confidentiality of individual service members (Johnson, 2008). Although the Department of Defense (DoD; 2003, 2007) has reported a commitment to the privacy of DoD personnel, its privacy directives include exceptions that allow dissemination of private information without the service member's authorization when necessary for the completion of the military mission (e.g., fitness for duty, illegal activities). In addition, military neuropsychologists do not maintain control over their patients' records. When clinicians transfer to new duty stations, the neuropsychological records remain with the clinic in which the records were generated.

Neuropsychologists may help to reduce unwanted dissemination of sensitive patient information by thoroughly informing patients of the potential limits to confidentiality during the informed consent process so that the patients can determine whether to share the sensitive information. However, neuropsychologists should be aware that the willingness of individuals to disclose personal information, which is often essential for making accurate diagnostic determinations and recommendations, is reduced when patients are informed that there are limits to confidentiality (Haut & Muehleman, 1986; Nowell & Spruill, 1993; Woods & McNamara, 1980).

"The freedom of competent adults to allow or restrict access to their bodies, thoughts, and feelings has long been a fundamental value of medicine and the cornerstone of clinical psychology, and neuropsychologists are obligated to defend that value" (Bush & Martin, 2008, pp. 527–528). However, neurologically compromised patients and the obligation of clinicians to support the military mission provide challenges for neuropsychologists. Patients with neurological injuries often do not have the cognitive capacity to fully understand privacy and confidentiality issues and exceptions, requiring the military neuropsychologist to bear the additional responsibility of weighing the best interests of both the patient and the military mission.

Assessment Methods and Bases for Professional Judgments

The APA (2002) requires psychologists to base their work upon established scientific and professional knowledge of the discipline (Ethical Standard 2.04, Bases for Scientific and Professional Judgments). In addition, "psychologists base the opinions contained in their recommendations, reports, and diagnostic or evaluative statements, including forensic testimony, on information and techniques sufficient to substantiate their findings" (Ethical Standard 9.01, Bases for Assessments). Unfortunately, perhaps out of necessity and/or expediency, neuropsychological practices seem to have outpaced research in recent clinical activities.

With the relatively high incidence of blast injuries in the wars in Iraq and Afghanistan, neuropsychologists have been struggling to understand the nature of blast injuries on neuropsychological functioning and recovery *while* needing to assist persons who have sustained such injuries. Published research only began to emerge years after the problem of blast injuries was identified. In addition, the comorbidities, including posttraumatic stress and symptom validity issues, that complicate the emerging understanding of the neurocognitive effects of blast injuries are currently being studied.

Furthermore, the neuropsychological measures that are currently selected and the manner in which they are used to assess persons prior to deployment and/or after injury may be questioned, based on limited empirical evidence to support their use in these contexts. Policy makers and clinicians are likely doing the best that they can given the novel circumstances, but "the best that they can do" may not meet APA's requirement that "psychologists administer, adapt, score, interpret, or use assessment techniques, interviews, tests, or instruments in a manner and for purposes that are appropriate in light of the research on or evidence of the usefulness and proper application of the techniques" (Ethical Standard 9.02 Use of Assessments). In general, the provision of innovative services is consistent with ethical practice in those instances in which the potential costs and risks are minimal (nonmaleficence), the potential for benefit exists (beneficence), conclusions are conservative, and expectations can be carefully managed (Bush & Martin, 2005). Nevertheless, evidence-based services are preferred, and military neuropsychologists will increasingly be provided and/or will conduct the research needed to help direct their services.

Sexual Orientation Considerations and Effective Treatment

When the National Defense and Authorization Act of 1994 (1993), otherwise known as the "don't ask, don't tell" policy, came into effect, it codified into law a policy that prohibits gay, lesbian, and bisexual men and women from openly serving in the armed forces of the United States. This policy creates personal and occupational stress for gay, lesbian, and bisexual Airmen, Marines, Sailors, and Soldiers.

Despite positive changes in attitudes of the American public (Johnson & Buhrke, 2006) and military personnel (Belkin & Embser-Herbert, 2002; Jones & Koshes, 1995; Varnell, 2003) in recent years, gay, lesbian, and bisexual men and women in the military continue to face sources of occupational stress and exclusion (Biaggio, Orchard, Larson, Petrino, & Mihara, 2003; Blue Ribbon Commission report, 2006; Johnson & Buhrke, 2006; Meyer, 1995; Smith & Ingram, 2004; United States Government Accountability Office, 2005). Clinicians encounter ethical dilemmas when determining whether issues related to sexual orientation are clinically relevant and should be included in reports or are not essential to the clinical issues and should be omitted. In such situations, clinicians are vulnerable to having their personal values affect decisions about omitting clinically relevant information or including clinically irrelevant information about sexual orientation.

Conflicting requirements involving the APA Ethics Code and "don't ask, don't tell" policy further complicate the clinician's decision making. Johnson and Buhrke (2006) reported that although most military psychologists attempt to follow what has been termed a *best-interest model* (Johnson & Wilson, 1993) that involves working to balance ethical and federal obligations while attempting to promote the best interests of their clients, there are times when dilemmas related to sexual orientation are not easily resolved.

The clinical and confidentiality parameters pertaining to this issue are clarified during the informed consent process when clinicians inform or remind patients about confidentiality limitations in the military. Neuropsychologists have control over what client information is documented; however, confidentiality considerations must be balanced with federal regulations that grant commanders access to information that is relevant to the service member's deployability.

Detention and Interrogation Support

The widely publicized and highly politicized abuses at Guantánamo Bay and Abu Ghraib brought issues of detention and interrogation support by psychologists to the forefront of the APA's agenda in recent years. A primary concern is that involvement in detainee interrogations contradicts psychology's mission to help and that psychologists' presence at interrogations at military and Central Intelligence Agency detention sites presents an ethical conflict. Others believe that psychologists improve the accuracy of information gathering and work to make interrogations safer by emphasizing rapport-building techniques (see Galvin, 2008, for a complete review of the debate).

According to the Institute of Medicine of the National Academies (2009), when working with detainees, clinicians "should strive to gain the detainee's trust, rather than act as an agent of security forces" (p. 17). Furthermore, "under DoD policy, military health professionals are obligated to report suspected or observed abuse to the operational chain of command or, if they do not believe appropriate investigations or actions are occurring, to go through the medical chain of command, the DoD or Service Inspectors General, or the Criminal Investigative Services" (Institute of Medicine of the National Academies, 2009, p. 19).

On September 17, 2008, the APA Office of Public Affairs published an announcement that the APA membership approved a petition resolution on detainee settings. The resolution stated that psychologists may not work in settings where "persons are held outside of, or in violation of, either International Law (e.g., the United Nations Convention Against Torture and the Geneva Conventions) or the U.S. Constitution (where appropriate), unless they are working directly for the persons being detained or for an independent third party working to protect human rights." The approval of the petition resolution limited the role of psychologists in settings where persons are detained to working directly for detainees or for an independent third party to protect human rights or to providing treatment to other military personnel. It is important to note that this resolution did not change the Ethics Code and it is consequently not an ethical violation for a psychologist to serve in these locations. Although this issue is not specific to neuropsychology, all military psychologists should be aware of the relevant issues surrounding this debate because of the potential to find oneself confronting such issues (for further reading, see Kennedy & Johnson, 2009; Kennedy, Malone, & Franks, 2009).

Evolving VA Roles and Dual Agency

Prior to Operations Iraqi Freedom and Enduring Freedom, all patients evaluated and treated at VA clinics and medical centers were veterans who had completed their service to the nation. However, the situation has changed. Currently, veterans may return from the war only to return again to the war. Policy changes now allow for recipients of services at VA health care facilities to be eligible to return to active duty. For example, an active member of the Marine Corps Reserve might receive services at the local VA medical center for a complicated concussion and post-traumatic stress disorder. She (and her commander) might wish to have her declared by the neuropsychologist to be healthy enough to return to duty and fit to be deployed. Stone (2008) explored how potential deployments of patients seen at VA health care facilities raise questions and ethical challenges for VA mental health practitioners. The potential for deployment of brain injured military personnel and service members with a history of concussion, for example, raises similar questions and ethical challenges for VA neuropsychologists.

A primary conflict for neuropsychologists arises between assisting in the patient's rehabilitation and serving the mission of the institution to which the patient belongs. The mission of the U.S. military medical services is clearly delineated as conserving the fighting strength. By extension, the military neuropsychologist's primary mission is to ensure the health and fitness of military personnel to return to the field of battle. Neuropsychologists in the active military are commissioned officers. As such, they pledge fidelity to the nation, the U.S. Constitution, and this mission. Implementing this mission can create ethical dilemmas for the neuropsychologist by pitting fidelity to the organization versus the needs of the individual service member. In contrast, the VA (civilian) neuropsychologist is focused more on the evaluation and care of the individual veteran.

Carr (2005) defined dual agency, also called mixed agency, as a situation in which one person performs or acts for two entities. Military physicians, mental health providers, and neuropsychologists have historically had to struggle with allegiance to the medical missions of the military and their ethical oaths to do no harm to their patients. In the current military climate, neuropsychologists who work for the VA are faced with similar conflicts. Howe (2003) described three areas in which the goal of conserving the fighting strength was central to medical decision making: (a) return to duty, (b) setting priorities for triage, and, (c) when necessary, removing soldiers from combat. While civilian neuropsychologists working for the VA will not be faced with making decisions about setting priorities for triage or removing soldiers from combat, they are now faced with making clinical decisions about recommendations for return to duty, which might include deployment.

The primary ethical challenge in the context of dual agency is the need to balance the interests of the patient with the interests of the organization (Jeffrey, Rankin, & Jeffrey, 1992). APA (2002) General Principles A (Beneficence and Nonmaleficence) and B (Fidelity and Responsibility) are primary. According to General Principle A, "Psychologists strive to benefit those with whom they work and take care to do no harm," and "When conflicts occur among psychologists' obligations or concerns, they attempt to resolve these conflicts in a responsible fashion that avoids or minimizes harm. Because psychologists' scientific and professional judgments and actions may affect the lives of others, they are alert to and guard against personal, financial, social, organizational, or political factors that might lead to misuse of their influence."

In addition to these aspirational general principles, a number of enforceable ethical standards are also relevant, including Standards 1.02 (Conflicts Between Ethics and Law, Regulations, or Other Governing Legal Authority), 1.03 (Conflicts Between Ethics and Organizational Demands), 3.11 (Psychological Services Delivered to or Through Organizations), 4.02 (Discussing the Limits of Confidentiality), 6.01 (Documentation of Professional and Scientific Work and Maintenance of Records), and 9.03 (Informed Consent in Assessments). In addition, because many, if not most, VA neuropsychologists have little or no expertise or knowledge of the specific occupational demands of combat roles, questions of competence to make fitness-for-duty recommendations may be quite relevant (Ethical Standard 2.01, Boundaries of Competence).

The Neuropsychologist's Psychological Fitness

A combat theater of operations such as in Iraq or Afghanistan presents unique physical, cognitive, mental, and spiritual stressors on all military personnel, and neuropsychologists are no exception (Hoge, Auchterlonie, & Milliken, 2006; Hoge et al., 2004). Some examples of physical stressors include extreme heat or cold, long and irregular work hours, sleep deprivation, decreased nutrition, and the need to carry heavy equipment on one's person including body armor and weapons. Examples of cognitive stresses include needing to think clearly under conditions of sleep deprivation and hunger. Examples of mental stressors include fear of being killed or injured, fear or actual experience of seeing comrades or civilians killed or injured, missing loved ones at home, and pressure exerted from members higher in the chain of command. Examples of spiritual stressors include discouragement about one's faith in religious beliefs or about one's faith in humanity.

APA (2002) General Principle A (Beneficence and Nonmaleficence) states, "Psychologists strive to be aware of the possible effect of their own physical and mental health on their ability to help those with whom they work." Further, Ethical Standard 2.06 (Personal Problems and Conflicts) states, "(a) Psychologists refrain from initiating an activity when they know or should know that there is a substantial likelihood that their personal problems will prevent them from performing their work-related activities in a competent manner. (b) When psychologists become aware of personal problems that may interfere with their performing work-related duties adequately, they take appropriate measures, such as obtaining professional consultation or assistance, and determine whether they should limit, suspend, or terminate their work-related duties." Although neuropsychologists are sensitive to the potential adverse effects of military and combat service on mental health, they are not immune to them. Failure of neuropsychologists to address their own mental health needs can lead to an erosion of the trust and confidence placed in them by others and can cause them to become a liability to the safety of others and the military mission.

When neuropsychologists realize that they have reached a breaking point in their ability to cope and adjust to the demands of the combat environment, to the extent possible they should take steps to, at least temporarily, remove themselves from service. Neuropsychologists then have the opportunity and responsibility to strive to revive their resilience and readiness to resume their duties.

ETHICAL DECISION-MAKING PROCESS

Ethical decision making, like clinical decision making, should follow a structured, logical process and should be evidence based (Bush, 2007). Many ethical and legal resources exist to inform neuropsychologists about appropriate conduct (Figure 2.1). The professional activities of military neuropsychologists may be informed and governed by both civilian and military codes, regulations, and laws. In addition to such resources,

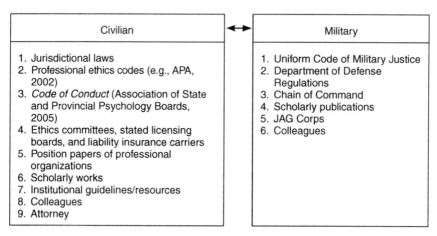

Civilian	←→	Military
1. Jurisdictional laws 2. Professional ethics codes (e.g., APA, 2002) 3. *Code of Conduct* (Association of State and Provincial Psychology Boards, 2005) 4. Ethics committees, stated licensing boards, and liability insurance carriers 5. Position papers of professional organizations 6. Scholarly works 7. Institutional guidelines/resources 8. Colleagues 9. Attorney		1. Uniform Code of Military Justice 2. Department of Defense Regulations 3. Chain of Command 4. Scholarly publications 5. JAG Corps 6. Colleagues

Figure 2.1 Resources for ethical decision making in military neuropsychology.

scholarly publications and experienced and knowledgeable colleagues are important resources for facilitating sound ethical decision making.

With the availability of such resources, there is no reason for clinicians to rely on their own subjective impressions and "I think" solutions. Neuropsychologists typically make diagnostic decisions after gathering needed information and considering appropriate resources; it is typically advisable to follow a similar process for ethical decision making. In addition, to make good ethical decisions and determine appropriate courses of professional behavior, it can be beneficial to employ a decision-making model (Figure 2.2).

It is recognized that in some contexts, such as remote locations without ready access to telecommunications or in combat or other situations in which decisions must be made urgently, the opportunities for gathering and reviewing multiple resources and following a comprehensive decision-making model will not be practical. As Johnson (2008) stated, "the exigencies of war may thwart elegant solutions" (p. 53). In isolated or combat situations, clinicians must rely on previous familiarity with ethical and legal requirements, guidelines and their own internalized decision-making process. Because of the potential for military neuropsychologists to find themselves in such situations, advanced preparation and anticipation of ethical conflicts and resolutions are vital. Military neuropsychologists should engage in ethical decision-making exercises as part of their commitment to maintaining ethical competence (APA

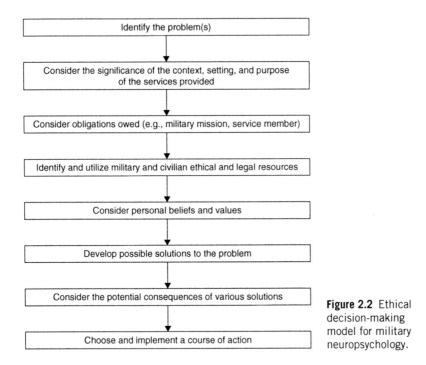

Identify the problem(s)

Consider the significance of the context, setting, and purpose of the services provided

Consider obligations owed (e.g., military mission, service member)

Identify and utilize military and civilian ethical and legal resources

Consider personal beliefs and values

Develop possible solutions to the problem

Consider the potential consequences of various solutions

Choose and implement a course of action

Figure 2.2 Ethical decision-making model for military neuropsychology.

Ethical Standard 2.03, Maintaining Competence). Advanced preparation for ethical challenges is consistent with positive ethics.

Case Illustration

Lance Corporal (LCPL) Boonkue, a native of Palau serving in the U.S. Marine Corps in his third deployment to Operation Iraqi Freedom, was on patrol when a large improvised explosive device exploded less than a half klick away. When asked later, he recalled having felt a wave of pressure and heat but did not think he was struck by flying debris and did not fall. However, he recalled feeling stunned and confused about what had happened and acknowledged that there may have been a couple of minutes after the event that he could not recall. The events that followed were chaotic and stressful. The following day he experienced a severe headache, which recurred daily for 6 days, and ringing in the ears. He was informed by the corpsman that he had sustained a concussion. He was taken to a Navy fleet hospital where he was diagnosed with a concussion, based on Department of Veterans Brain Injury Center (DVBIC) criteria (DVBIC,

2006; Schwab et al., 2006), and postconcussion headaches. It was not long before LCPL Boonkue's command requested his return to his unit.

Commander Jones, a physician and the officer in charge of the fleet hospital, reviewed the case and told Lieutenant Greenberg, a neuropsychologist, to "see this kid so we can get him back to his unit ASAP." LT Greenberg performed a clinical interview, completed the Military Acute Concussion Evaluation, and administered the Automated Neuropsychological Assessment Metrics (ANAM). The Military Acute Concussion Evaluation revealed no Level 2 or Level 3 red flags. LCPL Boonkue's ANAM score was one standard deviation below the mean; however, because of "technical problems," his predeployment ANAM score was not immediately available for comparison. LT Greenberg believed that LCPL Boonkue should remain at the fleet hospital for a few days for monitoring and further assessment, and so that the predeployment ANAM score could be obtained. CDR Jones, however, was of the opinion that the headaches were the result of a very mild concussion and would resolve quickly, that the ANAM score likely reflected predeployment cultural issues, and that LCPL Boonkue should be returned to his unit, with light duty for 3 days. LT Greenberg felt pressure, although nothing specific had been said, to concur with CDR Jones. However, he questioned whether concurring with CDR Jones, which might be the prudent course of action, would be "the ethical thing to do."

Identify the problem(s). LT Greenberg is invested in both the health care interests of LCPL Boonkue and in supporting the military mission. He suspects that the headaches may be more the result of psychological distress than a concussion and believes that following a psychological treatment protocol may be the most appropriate course of action. However, he is struggling with meeting the needs of all parties, and he is concerned about disagreeing with CDR Jones. He would like to have more time to perform a more comprehensive psychological evaluation and to obtain LCPL Boonkue's predeployment ANAM scores. In addition, he would like more time to investigate cultural issues that may impact symptom presentation and testing implications for a service member from Palau. Finally, he questions CDR Jones' professional competence to make clinical decisions of a neuropsychological nature.

Consider the significance of the context, setting, and purpose of the services provided. The fleet hospital is in a forward area, serving troops immediately removed from theaters of operation. Medical personnel triage casualties, treating those that can be treated in that setting and sending others on to other medical facilities. For troops treated at the fleet hospital, there is a need to return them to their units as quickly as possible. Neuropsychologists in such settings may not have their full complement of assessment measures and are likely to experience numerous environmental (e.g., noises from helicopters and heavy machinery, intrusions from other medical personnel) threats to the validity of neuropsychological test results obtained in such settings. In addition, in this context the physician with whom LT Greenberg must agree or disagree is also the officer-in-charge and, as such, holds some influence over LT Greenberg's experiences in the fleet hospital and will write his fitness report, which will significantly impact his career.

Consider obligations owed. LT Greenberg has an obligation to LCPL Boonkue to make appropriate diagnostic determinations and recommendations. He also has an obligation to support the military mission by recommending that service members be returned to duty as soon as they are ready and by helping to insure that service members not be returned to an operational environment prematurely. In addition, he has an obligation to CDR Jones to be open and forthright with him regarding their differences of opinion about LCPL Boonkue's clinical condition and the appropriate course of action. LT Greenberg also considers whether he has an obligation to himself and his career to not "ruffle any feathers" in such an ambiguous situation as this one.

Identify and utilize military and civilian ethical and legal resources. LT Greenberg refers to the 2002 APA Ethics Code. He is reminded of his primary obligation to avoid harming his patients (General Principle A, Beneficence and Nonmaleficence; Ethical Standard 3.04, Avoiding Harm). He reaffirms that his clinical decisions must be based on sufficient evidence and knowledge (Ethical Standard 2.04, Bases for Scientific and Professional Judgments), but he believes that such evidence is currently lacking.

LT Greenberg also has psychological and neuropsychological colleagues, both military and civilian, available via the Internet. He reaches out to a more senior military neuropsychologist who has experience in the Middle East, and he identifies a civilian psychologist in Hawaii who has evaluated and treated many people from South Pacific islands, including Palau. He also reviews the DVBIC (2006) clinical practice guidelines, including the algorithm for evaluating and managing persons with possible traumatic brain injury and posttraumatic stress disorder.

Consider personal beliefs and values. LT Greenberg appreciates the importance of balancing patient care and mission goals. However, he is particularly interested in LCPL Boonkue not returning to his unit prematurely and possibly increasing the risk of harm to himself or others. He believes that service members should be returned to their units as soon as possible but also believes that a conservative approach to return to duty decisions is in the best interest of all parties. He firmly believes that it is his responsibility to advocate for the neuropsychological needs of patients and to promote a conservative approach to return to duty decision making. However, he is also respectful of rank and is hesitant to contradict the opinions or decisions of more senior officers, including CDR Jones.

Develop possible solutions to the problem. LT Greenberg considers the following options: (a) agree with CDR Jones that LCPL Boonkue's headaches are the result of a very mild concussion and will resolve soon, and he should be returned to his unit; (b) disagree with CDR Jones by noting that LCPL Boonkue's symptoms are more likely the result of a complex stress reaction and that it will be in everyone's best interest if LCPL Boonkue can be evacuated for appropriate mental health treatment; and (c) discuss his concerns with CDR Jones and request additional time to conduct a more thorough evaluation, obtain the predeployment ANAM scores, and consult with identified colleagues.

Consider the potential consequences of various solutions. LT Greenberg considers the following possible consequences: (a) LCPL Boonkue may be (1) appropriately returned to duty where he can continue to assist his unit in a manner consistent with the military mission or (2) prematurely returned to duty, placing him and others at increased risk of harm. (b) LCPL Boonkue will receive additional services and recovery time, which may or may not be necessary. The military mission may suffer from, or be better served by, his absence. Disagreement with CDR Jones may have implications, positive or negative, for LT Greenberg. (c) Open discussion with CDR Jones may help him to appreciate the potential benefits of more time and assessment for LCPL Boonkue. The military mission may be better served by having LCPL Boonkue return to duty at the appropriate time. CDR Jones may develop increased respect for LT Greenberg as a clinician and officer because of LT Greenberg's direct but deferential approach to the situation.

Choose and implement a course of action. LT Greenberg chose the third option and found CDR Jones to appear irritated initially, but ultimately CDR Jones became more understanding and agreeable. LCPL Boonkue received further neuropsychological evaluation before being evacuated for longer term mental health services.

Discussion. This case, like most ethical challenges, involved a variety of clinical, ethical, and professional issues, some of which conflicted with each other. LT Greenberg considered the issues in a thoughtful manner and selected a good solution. However, when the chosen solutions do not work out as intended or the outcome is not what was expected, clinicians have an additional obligation to modify their choices or behaviors or strive to address unanticipated consequences.

POSITIVE ETHICS

The ability to avoid and resolve ethical conflicts requires both a proactive approach and a personal commitment to ethical practice. In contrast to the traditional remedial approach to ethics whereby "disciplinary codes represent only the ethical 'floor' or minimum standards to which psychologists should adhere" (Knapp & VandeCreek, 2006, p. 9), *positive ethics* represents a shift toward a voluntary commitment to pursuing ethical ideals. Thus, rather than simply doing the minimum necessary to avoid ethical misconduct, a positive ethics approach is proactive, requiring clinicians to promote exemplary behavior in all their professional activities, not only when confronting ethical dilemmas.

At a minimum, military neuropsychologists have unique identities as military officers, psychologists, and neuropsychologists, although a variety of additional roles are also typically held. The adoption of multiple identities and roles brings diverse responsibilities. The ability to understand ethical issues and address ethical challenges across multiple roles cannot be established by chance; such skill must be developed. In their development and maintenance of ethical competence, military neuropsychologists should adhere to the four As of ethical practice and decision making: *Anticipate, Avoid, Address*, and *Aspire* (Bush, 2009). That is, they should (a) *anticipate* and prepare for ethical issues and challenges commonly encountered in their specific practice contexts, (b) strive to *avoid* ethical misconduct, (c) *address* ethical challenges when they are anticipated or encountered, and (d) *aspire* to the highest standards of ethical practice. A personal commitment to the four As of ethical practice and decision making promotes sound ethical practice and is consistent with positive ethics.

APPLYING ETHICAL PRINCIPLES TO MILITARY NEUROPSYCHOLOGY

Bioethical Principles

Four core principles have been described as being particularly important to biomedical ethics (Beauchamp & Childress, 2001). Those principles are (a) respect for autonomy, (b) beneficence, (c) nonmaleficence, and (d) justice. Respect for autonomy refers to the right of competent adults to make the decisions that govern their lives, as long as such decisions do not adversely impact the rights of others. Nonmaleficence refers to a moral obligation for clinicians to do no harm. Beneficence refers to the promotion of the rights and welfare of others, defense of the rights of others, and the prevention of harm. Justice, which includes both distributive justice and formal justice, refers to "fair, equitable, and appropriate treatment in light of what is due or owed to persons" (Beauchamp & Childress, 2001, p. 226). Fidelity and general beneficence are two additional principles that are also relevant to neuropsychology. Fidelity (Bersoff & Koeppl, 1993; Kitchener, 1984) refers to the obligation to be truthful and faithful, keep promises, and maintain loyalty. General beneficence (Knapp & VandeCreek, 2006) refers to the clinician's responsibility to the public at large (i.e., society).

Although the value of these ethical principles and the neuropsychologist's moral obligation to practice in a manner consistent with the principles is self-evident to most clinicians in most clinical contexts, considerable challenges arise in contexts in which (a) principles conflict with each other or (b) there are inherent contradictions between a principle and the neuropsychologist's role. In military contexts, determinations regarding which actions or inactions constitute harm, or which individual, organization, or system is primary with regard to obligations owed can be extremely difficult to make. It is generally accepted that obligations owed to society via the military mission outweigh the obligations owed to individual military personnel, a perspective that can be difficult for some clinicians to adopt.

It can be argued that general bioethical principles do not apply to neuropsychological services provided to military personnel in the same manner that they do with civilians. Consider the case of an army infantryman who reports postconcussive symptoms after falling off a wall during a combat mission. A neuropsychological evaluation reveals no neurocognitive deficits. The neuropsychologist informs the soldier of the "good news," including the fact that he will be returned to his unit. The soldier confesses that he does not want to return to combat. The neuropsychologist believes that it will be in the best interests of both the mission and the soldier for the soldier to return to his unit and makes recommendations accordingly.

In this situation, the neuropsychologist made a decision that conflicts with the patient's wishes and places the soldier back into harm's way. Thus, the neuropsychologist, consistent with loyalty (fidelity) to the military mission rather than the individual patient, determined that the principle of general beneficence would be afforded greater weight than respect for the patient's autonomy, beneficence, or nonmaleficence. Although developing an appreciation of the relative emphases placed on bioethical principles should occur as early as possible in the training of military neuropsychologists, the military stance can be extremely trying for clinicians when faced with individual servicemen and women whose lives are being adversely affected in significant ways by military service, deployment, and/or combat.

APA Ethics Code

The Ethics Code of the APA (2002) provides guidance for ethical practice. The code has as its goal "the welfare and protection of the individuals and groups with whom psychologists work and the education of members, students, and the public regarding ethical standards of the discipline" (Preamble). However, in military contexts, the welfare and protection of the individual patients to whom neuropsychologists provide services are not always the neuropsychologist's primary obligation. Thus, from the beginning of the APA Ethics Code, an inherent conflict exists for military neuropsychologists. Specific conflicts are also encountered in specific sections throughout the code, but particularly with Ethical Standards 3 (Human Relations) and 4 (Privacy and Confidentiality).

Laws and Regulations

Consideration of jurisdictional laws, both civilian and military, that govern professional behavior can assist clinicians with making appropriate decisions. However, neuropsychologists have simultaneous allegiances to professional (e.g., ethical standards and guidelines) and military (e.g., federal statutes; DoD regulations) requirements. Competing and conflicting requirements between military and civilian laws and regulations in multiple aspects of practice, including privacy/confidentiality and informed consent, can continue to confuse and frustrate clinicians.

Military neuropsychologists, faced with competing ethical and professional obligations, must first accept that such contradictions exist and then strive to reconcile the specific competing demands in each case. Senior colleagues can help prepare less experienced clinicians to anticipate and address competing ethical and legal requirements that are commonly encountered in specific military practice contexts.

CONCLUSIONS

Uniformed neuropsychologists have very exciting and rewarding opportunities to evaluate and treat the men and women who sacrifice a tremendous amount to defend our country. However, to provide such services competently requires awareness of the ethical issues and challenges that are commonly encountered in clinical psychology and neuropsychology in general and in military contexts specifically. In this chapter we provided an overview of ethical issues that military neuropsychologists are likely to confront. We also described an approach to addressing ethical challenges. This information is intended to promote ethical competence and facilitate ethical decision making. However, a personal commitment to meeting the needs of both the individual service member and the military mission is the foundation of ethical practice, despite the apparent incongruity of these efforts at times. Nevertheless, we are confident that military neuropsychologists are up to the task.

NOTES

1. This statement was taken from the first author's commission certificate.
2. From the Hippocratic Oath; translated from Greek by Ludwig Edelstein. Retrieved June 23, 2009, from www.pbs.org/wgbh/nova/doctors/oath_classical.html.

REFERENCES

American Psychological Association. (2002). Ethical principles of psychologists and code of conduct. *American Psychologist, 57*(12), 1060–1073.
Association of State and Provincial Psychology Boards. (2005). *ASPPB code of conduct.* Retrieved January 28, 2005, from www.asppb.org
Beauchamp, T. L., & Childress, J. F. (2001). *Principles of biomedical ethics* (5th ed.). New York: Oxford University Press.

Belkin, A., & Embser-Herbert, M. S. (2002). A modest proposal: Privacy as a flawed rationale for the exclusion of gays and lesbians from the U.S. military. *International Security, 27*, 178–197.

Benton, J. C. (2002). *Air Force officer's guide* (33rd ed.). Mechanicsburg, PA: Stackpole Books.

Bersoff, D. N., & Koeppl, P. M. (1993). The relation between ethical codes and moral principles. *Ethics & Behavior, 3*(3/4), 345–357.

Biaggio, M., Orchard, S., Larson, J., Petrino, K., & Mihara, R. (2003). Guidelines for gay/lesbian/bisexual-affirmative educational practices in graduate psychology programs. *Professional Psychology: Research and Practice, 34*, 548–554.

Blue Ribbon Commission Report. (2006). *Financial analysis of "Don't Ask, Don't Tell": How much does the gay ban cost?* Retrieved December 8, 2008, from www.palmcenter.org/files/active/0/2006

Bonn, K. (2002). *Army Officer guide* (49th ed.). Mechanicsburg, PA: Stackpole Books.

Brittain, J. L., Frances, J. P., & Barth, J. T. (1995). Ethical issues and dilemmas in neuropsychological practice reported by ABCN diplomates. *Advances in Medical Psychotherapy, 8*, 1–22.

Bush, S. S. (2007). *Ethical decision making in clinical neuropsychology*. New York: Oxford University Press.

Bush, S. S. (2009). *Geriatric mental health ethics: A casebook*. New York: Springer.

Bush, S. S., Grote, C., Johnson-Greene, D., & Macartney-Filgate, M. (2008). A panel interview on the ethical practice of neuropsychology. *The Clinical Neuropsychologist, 22*, 321–344.

Bush, S. S., & Martin, T. A. (2005). Ethical issues in geriatric neuropsychology. In S. S. Bush & T. A. Martin (Eds.), *Geriatric neuropsychology: Practice essentials* (pp. 507–536). New York: Psychology Press.

Bush, S. S., & Martin, T. A. (2008). Confidentiality in neuropsychological practice. In A. M. Horton, Jr., & D. Wedding (Eds.), *The neuropsychology handbook* (3rd ed., pp. 517–532). New York: Springer.

Carr, V. F. (2005). Dual agency and fiduciary responsibilities in modern medicine. *Physician Executive, 31*, 56–58.

Committee on Gulf War and Health: Brain Injury in Veterans and Long-Term Health Outcomes. (2008). *Gulf War and health: Volume 7: Long-term consequences of traumatic brain injury*. Retrieved December 7, 2008, from www.nap.edu/catalog/12436.html

Defense and Veterans Brain Injury Center (DVBIC) Working Group on the Acute Management of Mild Traumatic Brain Injury in Military Operational Settings. (2006). *Clinical practice guidelines and recommendations*. Retrieved February 9, 2009, from www.pdhealth.mil/downloads/clinical_practice_guideline_recommendations.pdf

Department of Defense (DoD). (2003). *Department of Defense Health Information Privacy Regulation* (DoD Directive 6025.18-R). Retrieved November 28, 2008, from www.dtic.mil/whs/directives/corres/pdf/602518r.pdf

DoD. (2007). *Department of Defense Privacy Program* (DoD Directive 5400.11-R). Retrieved November 28, 2008, from www.dtic.mil/whs/directives/corres/pdf/540011r.pdf

Field Manual 7–22.7. (2002, December). *The Army Noncommissioned Officers Guide*. Headquarters, Department of the Army.

Fischer, H. (2008). United States Military Casualty Statistics: Operation Iraqi Freedom and Operation Enduring Freedom. *Congressional Research Service (CRS) Report for Congress*, September 9, 2008.

Fisher, M. A. (2009). Replacing "Who is the client?" with a different ethical question. *Professional Psychology: Research and Practice, 40*, 1–7.

Galvin, M. (Producer/Director). (2008). *Interrogate this: Psychologists take on terror* [Motion picture]. (Available from MG Productions, 1112 Boylston St. #163, Boston, MA 02215)

Haut, M. W., & Muehleman, T. (1986). Informed consent: The effects of clarity and specificity on disclosure in a clinical interview. *Psychotherapy, 23*, 93–101.

Hoge, C. W., Auchterlonie, J. L., & Milliken, C. S. (2006). Mental health problems, use of mental health services, and attrition from military service after returning from deployment to Iraq or Afghanistan. *Journal of the American Medical Association, 295*, 1023–1032.

Hoge, C. W., Castro, C. A., Messer, S. C., McGurk, D., Cotting, D. I., & Koffman, R. L. (2004). Combat duty in Iraq and Afghanistan, mental health problems, and barriers to care. *The New England Journal of Medicine, 351*, 13–22.

Howe, E. G. (2003). Mixed agency in military medicine: Ethical roles in conflict. In E. Pellegrino (Ed.), *Textbook of military medicine: Military medical ethics* (pp. 331–365). Washington, DC: Office of the Surgeon General, U.S. Department of the Army.

Institute of Medicine of the National Academies. (2009). *Military medical ethics: Issues regarding dual loyalties: Workshop summary*. Washington, DC: The National Academies Press. Retrieved February 2, 2009, from www.nap.edu/catalog. php?record_id=12478#toc

Jeffrey, T. B., Rankin, R. J., & Jeffrey, L. K. (1992). In service of two masters: The ethical-legal dilemma faced by military psychologists. *Professional Psychology: Research and Practice, 23*, 91–95.

Johnson, W. B. (2008). Top ethical challenges for military clinical psychologists. *Military Psychology, 20*, 49–62.

Johnson, W. B., & Buhrke, R. A. (2006). Service delivery in a "Don't Ask, Don't Tell" world: Ethical care of gay, lesbian, and bisexual military personnel. *Professional Psychology: Research and Practice, 37*, 91–98.

Johnson, W. B., & Wilson, K. (1993). The military internship: A retrospective analysis. *Professional Psychology: Research and Practice, 24*, 312–318.

Johnson, W. B., Ralph, J., & Johnson, S. J. (2005). Managing multiple roles in embedded environments: The case of aircraft carrier psychology. *Professional Psychology: Research and Practice, 36*, 73–81.

Jones, F. D., & Koshes, R. J. (1995). Homosexuality and the military. *American Journal of Psychiatry, 152*, 16–21.

Kennedy, C. H., & Johnson, W. B. (2009). Mixed agency in military psychology: Applying the American Psychological Association's Ethics Code. *Psychological Services, 6*, 22–31.

Kennedy, C. H., Malone, R. C., & Franks, M. J. (2009). Provision of mental health services at the detention hospital in Guantanamo Bay. *Psychological Services, 6*, 1–10.

Kennedy, C. H., & Moore, B. A. (2008). Evolution of clinical military psychology ethics. *Military Psychology, 20*, 1–6.

Kitchener, K. S. (1984). Intuition, critical evaluation and ethical principles: The foundation for ethical decisions in counseling psychology. *Counseling Psychologist, 12,* 43–55.

Knapp, S., & VandeCreek, L. (2006). *Practical ethics for psychologists: A positive approach.* Washington, DC: American Psychological Association.

Mack, W. P., Seymour, H. A., & McComas, L. A. (1998). *The Naval officer's guide* (11th ed.). Annapolis, MD: U.S. Naval Institute Press.

McCauley, M., Hughes, J. H., & Liebling-Kalifani, H. (2008). Ethical considerations for military clinical psychologists: A review of selected literature. *Military Psychology, 20,* 7–20.

Meyer, I. H. (1995). Minority stress and mental health in gay men. *Journal of Health Sciences and Social Behavior, 36,* 38–56.

National Defense Authorization Act for Fiscal Year 1994, Pub. L. 103–160, 107 Stat. 1547. (1993).

Nowell, D., & Spruill, J. (1993). If it's not absolutely confidential, will information be disclosed? *Professional Psychology: Research and Practice, 24,* 367–369.

Orme, D. R., & Doerman, A. L. (2001). Ethical dilemmas and U.S. Air Force clinical psychologists: A survey. *Professional Psychology: Research and Practice, 32,* 305–311.

Pope, K. S., & Vetter, V. A. (1992). Ethical dilemmas encountered by members of the American Psychological Association: A national survey. *American Psychologist, 47,* 397–411.

Reger, M. A., Etherage, J. R., Reger, G. M., & Gahm, G. A. (2008). Civilian psychologists in an Army culture: The ethical challenge of cultural competence. *Military Psychology, 20,* 21–35.

Schwab, K. A., Baker, G., Ivins, B., Sluss-Tiller, M., Lux, W., & Warden, D. (2006). The Brief Traumatic Brain Injury Screen (BTBIS): Investigating the validity of a self-report instrument for detecting traumatic brain injury (TBI) in troops returning from deployment in Afghanistan and Iraq. *Neurology, 66*(5), (Suppl. 2), A235. Retrieved February 9, 2009, from www.dvbic.org/pdfs/3-Question-Screening-Tool.pdf

Smith, N. G., & Ingram, K. M. (2004). Workplace heterosexism and adjustment among lesbian, gay, and bisexual individuals: The role of unsupportive social interactions. *Journal of Counseling Psychology, 51,* 57–67.

Stone, A. M. (2008). Dual agency for VA clinicians: Defining an evolving ethical question. *Military Psychology, 20,* 37–48.

United States Government Accountability Office. (2005). *Military personnel: Financial cost and loss of critical skills due to DOD's homosexual conduct policy cannot be completely estimated.* Report to Congressional Requesters (GAO-05–299). Retrieved October 1, 2007, from www.gao.gov/new.items/d05299.pdf

Varnell, P. (2003). *Don't ask don't mind.* Retrieved December 8, 2008, from www.indegayforum.org/authors/varnell/varnell21.html

Vasterling, J. J., Proctor, S. P., Amoroso, P., Kane, R., Heeren, T., & White, R. F. (2006). Neuropsychological outcomes of army personnel following deployment to the Iraq war. *Journal of the American Medical Association, 296*(5), 519–529.

Woods, K. M., & McNamara, J. R. (1980). Confidentiality: Its effect on interviewee behavior. *Professional Psychology, 11,* 714–721.

3

Fitness for Duty

MARK P. KELLY, KEVIN P. MULLIGAN, AND
MARK C. MONAHAN

The military health care system has a systematic, well-defined process for the determination of medical fitness for duty. In service members with known or suspected brain disorders, neuropsychological assessment plays a key role in fitness-for-duty decisions. Neuropsychologists evaluating service members with conditions that potentially render them unfit must be thoroughly familiar with the military fitness-for-duty process to ensure examinations are properly conducted and results effectively communicated.

OVERVIEW OF MEDICAL FITNESS FOR DUTY IN THE MILITARY

The Department of Defense (DoD) has mandated that standards for determining medical fitness for duty be uniform among the services (DoD, 1996): the same general standards apply to determination of fitness for Soldiers, Sailors, Airmen, and Marines. Each service, however, has developed individual procedures for implementation (Secretary of the Air Force, 2006a, 2006b, 2006c, 2006d; Secretary of the Army, 2006, 2007; Secretary of the Navy, 2002, 2005).

DoD policy stipulates that a service member will be found unfit for duty if he or she has a disease or injury that prevents performance of the duties of his or her office, grade, rank, or rating (DoD, 1996). Stated succinctly, to be found fit, a service member must be able to physically, cognitively, and emotionally perform the essential functions of his or her job safely in any locale around the world. Active duty service members are assigned to an occupational field, and there are many available, ranging from boatswain's mate to air traffic controller to finance specialist. In addition, all service members hold rank, and with progression there are higher levels of responsibility and greater expectations for leadership. As determination of fitness depends upon the ability to perform the functions of one's job, service members with identical diseases of similar severity may have discrepant fitness-for-duty decisions. For example, a right-shoulder injury accompanied by range-of-motion limitations may prevent a cavalry scout from performing the duties of his or her military occupational specialty (MOS), yet have little impact on duty performance for a finance specialist. Likewise, while a mild impairment in spatial skills may have little impact on duties of a chaplain assistant, the consequences for an aircraft structural repairer would be significant.

Determination of fitness for duty is a multistep process. When a service member's health, safety, or ability to perform his or her job effectively are at risk due to a medical (including psychiatric) condition, providers are required to inform the member's command. In the Air Force and Army this occurs via a physical profile serial report. The physical profile system is based upon the function of six major body systems factors (physical capacity, upper extremity, lower extremity, hearing and ears, eyes, and psychiatric). Each system is rated on a numerical scale ranging from 1 (high level of medical fitness) to 4 (performance of military duty drastically limited), and specific duty limitations are recommended. These recommended limitations outlined in a profile may be temporary or permanent. The U.S. Navy and Marine Corps do not use the profile system but have an equivalent system designated as a limited duty board.

The second step in the medical fitness-for-duty process is the medical evaluation board (MEB). Service members can be referred to the MEB by either their treating provider or their command. Each service has established explicit medical fitness standards (Secretary of the Air Force, 2006b; Secretary of the Army, 2007; Secretary of the Navy, 2002), outlining conditions that *may* render a service member unfit. The MEB determines whether or not a service member has an injury or illness and documents severity. The MEB then decides if the injury or illness is severe enough to call into question the member's ability to continue on active duty, according to the established retention standards.

A critical component of the military medical fitness system is the narrative summary prepared by the provider leading the MEB. The narrative summary describes in detail the history of the illness, objective examination findings, results of laboratory and radiology results, consultation reports, diagnosis, treatment and response, and subjective conclusion with rationale. Depending on the service, the neuropsychological report may serve as the narrative summary or be included as an addendum to the narrative summary, along with other consultant reports. The MEB does not determine fitness for duty nor do contributing providers.

Also included in MEB documentation is a memorandum from the service member's commanding officer describing the member's ability to perform duties in the currently assigned position. Additional information is also solicited including annual evaluation letters from the chain of command, credential reports, or personal testimony from third parties. Such information may be particularly helpful in cases where the illness is chronic or where objective findings are sparse.

If the MEB determines that the service member does not meet retention standards, the case is referred to the physical evaluation board (PEB). The PEB constitutes the final step in the fitness-for-duty determination process. The PEB is the sole body authorized to determine if a service member is unfit for duty. The PEB is typically composed of experienced officers (including a medical officer) trained in adjudication standards and procedures. In the Army, for example, the PEB is composed of a presiding officer, a personnel management officer, and a medical member. Medical expertise and vocational expertise are represented: the medical member can interpret complex medical data, while the other two senior officers serve as "vocational experts."

Each case is reviewed first by an informal PEB. The informal PEB evaluates documents including the MEB narrative summary with addenda (including the neuropsychological evaluation), the commander's memorandum, the physical serial profile or limited duty board findings, and other related information. There is no live testimony, and the service member is not permitted to attend. The informal PEB determines by majority vote, based on the preponderance of the evidence, whether the service member is fit for duty in his or her current MOS based on specific performance standards. If the service member is found unfit, the PEB assigns a disability rating percentage for each disorder found to be unfitting. Service members found unfit may request a formal hearing with or without a personal appearance. The formal PEB provides the service member an opportunity, with assistance of counsel, to present additional evidence.

Fitness-for-duty determination is a medicolegal process. Neuro-psychologists involved in military medical fitness-for-duty determinations should keep the following points in mind. First, the neuropsychological evaluation report will be the sole source of neuropsychological evidence in the majority of cases. As live testimony is not permitted at the informal PEB and is rarely sought at the level of a formal PEB, the burden to communicate findings completely and clearly falls to the report preparation skills of the examining neuropsychologist. Second, though virtually all service members seen for neuropsychological evaluation for PEB purposes will have known or suspected neurological or psychiatric illness or injury, the physician member of the PEB may not have a great deal of familiarity with neuropsychological assessment. The responsibility rests with the examining neuropsychologist to write the report in language that is clear and understandable to a layperson. Third, the PEB is the sole body for determination of fitness for duty and does not mandate a fitness-for-duty opinion from examining providers. Fourth, third-party observations are a vital component of the PEB process.

When conducting neuropsychological evaluations of service members, there are instances where developmental disorders such as attention deficit hyperactivity disorder or learning disorder are discovered. By definition these conditions existed prior to military service and cannot be a cause for medical unfitness. However, if these disorders are present and are causing impaired duty performance, there may be grounds for administrative separation from the military (e.g., Secretary of the Air Force, 2006b; see Budd & Harvey, 2006; Ryan, Zazeckis, French, & Harvey, 2006; chapter 8).

REQUIREMENTS FOR CONDUCTING NEUROPSYCHOLOGICAL EVALUATIONS TO ASSIST FITNESS-FOR-DUTY DETERMINATIONS

When consulted to provide a neuropsychological evaluation for fitness-for-duty purposes, it is incumbent upon the neuropsychologist to provide a diagnosis and prognosis, answer a number of medicolegal questions, and recommend possible treatment alternatives. The main aim of the evaluation is to establish the presence or absence of a cognitive disorder and then to determine whether cognitive deficits affect the service member's ability to perform his or her job not just at the home station but also in the deployed environment.

All neuropsychological evaluations conducted for fitness-for-duty reasons should be comprehensive. Screening evaluations and those that do not include a thorough history will normally be rejected by the PEB. The evaluation should include a detailed history, comprehensive record review (with imaging and laboratory studies), reports of other consultants, summaries of interviews with pertinent collateral sources, review of Armed Service Vocational Aptitude Battery (ASVAB) (DoD, 1984) scores or other baseline measures where applicable, and findings of prior neuropsychological evaluations. Background evidence for a comprehensive fitness-for-duty evaluation also includes service records, officer or enlisted evaluation reports, and collateral data from sources such as family, senior noncommissioned officers, and commanders. Gathering this information may or may not fall to the neuropsychologist, depending on the service, the referral question, and the composition/organization of the MEB team.

A thorough clinical interview is critical. In traumatic brain injury (TBI) cases, determination of duration of loss of consciousness, alteration of consciousness, and posttraumatic amnesia is necessary.

A determination of premorbid ability is recommended in most cases. As Strauss, Sherman, and Spreen (2006) point out, such data can provide evidence of abnormality and have clinical value. Even if the comparison of expected versus obtained performance fails to exceed the established cutoff, the patient may still show evidence of significant decline via other methods. The authors also note that although these methods have limited sensitivity, they mention that clinicians' informal estimates are usually even less accurate. Orme, Brehm, and Ree (2001) suggest a method using the Armed Forces Qualification Test score, which is derived from the ASVAB. All enlisted personnel take the ASVAB as part of the enlistment process. In the case of career officers, who in most instances do not take the ASVAB, and when ASVAB scores cannot be located, a measure such as the North American Adult Reading Test (Blair & Spreen, 1989) or the Wechsler Test of Adult Reading (The Psychological Corporation, 2001) is recommended. Consideration should also be given to demographic methods of estimating premorbid ability (Barona, Reynolds, & Chastain, 1984) or the use of methods that combine demographic and psychometric variables (Oklahoma Premorbid Intelligence Estimate). The latter technique was developed by Krull, Scott, and Sherer (1995). The neuropsychologist should choose tests with demographically corrected normative samples when available (Heaton, Miller, Taylor, & Grant, 2004). The DoD has recently mandated that all service members take a baseline brief computerized cognitive assessment known as Automated Neuropsychological Assessment Metrics (ANAM) prior to deployment, and as these baseline studies accumulate and become available, they may also prove useful to military neuropsychologists in establishing premorbid level of ability.

The test battery should include tests from all of the neurocognitive domains typically included in comprehensive evaluations. Intellectual ability, verbal and nonverbal memory, language, perceptual abilities, attention, executive functioning, academic abilities, sensorimotor skills, and measures of personality and psychopathology should be included. Lezak, Howieson, and Loring (2004) provide further information on the domains typically included in comprehensive evaluations. In most instances regulations do not stipulate a specific battery of tests, but there are exceptions. In each service, for example, where the question relates to a return to flying or air traffic control duties, a specific battery is required or at least preferred. The reasoning here relates to the existence of specific military aircrew norms for existing neuropsychological tests and differing assumptions regarding levels of functioning required by personnel. The Neuropsychiatry Branch of the Aeromedical Consultation Service at the Air Force School of Aerospace Medicine, the Naval Aerospace Medical Institute (for both Naval and Marine Corps aviation personnel), or the U.S. Army Aeromedical Activity should be consulted prior to conducting a neuropsychological assessment on military aviation personnel. This will assist in the provision of a requisite battery, use of appropriate norms, and enabling the neuropsychologist to conduct an assessment geared to determine whether there are any contraindications to return to duties involving flying, operation of unmanned aerial vehicles, or air traffic control duties. It is also important to note that each Air Force pilot has baseline cognitive data available. In each service, being declared physically qualified (PQ) for flight duties is separate from being declared fit for duty. General military fitness is a prerequisite, but special duties, such as for those on flight status, submarine duty, special operations, and special forces must meet higher standards.

Effort and motivation measures should always be included in neuropsychological evaluations conducted for fitness-for-duty reasons. Boone (2007) provides a comprehensive approach to assessing effort and motivation in neuropsychological evaluations. Greiffenstein (chapter 4) provides specific guidance in the military population with discussions of symptom validity measures and the issue of malingering.

FITNESS FOR DUTY: THE NEUROPSYCHOLOGICAL REPORT

Just as there are no regulations dictating that a specific neuropsychological battery should be used in military fitness-for-duty assessments except as noted above, there are also no regulations outlining specific requirements for the neuropsychological report. The guidelines that follow are based on the authors' collective experience in preparing neuropsychological reports as a component of the MEB process and incorporate feedback they have received from the PEB as well as knowledge of the pertinent regulations governing the overall fitness-for-duty process for each service branch. The following segment of this chapter is organized by sections of the report commonly used by neuropsychologists.

Chief Complaint and Reason for Referral

A review of the referral question and the patient's chief complaint is included by the majority of neuropsychologists in their reports (Donders, 2001). Detailing the specific referral question and chief complaint is particularly important in planning and ultimately writing the report for MEB purposes. When completed for fitness-for-duty purposes, the neuropsychological report should be written to address the service member's potential impairment. Likewise, the report should reflect that the evaluation (including, for example, composition of the neuropsychological test battery) addresses a specific referral question, and should address the applicability of the Boxer amendment (i.e., whether the evaluation is the result of a command directed referral). In our experience the most frequent questions are related to diagnosis, fitness for duty, or treatment planning.

History of Present Illness

The portion of the report on history of the present illness should include information pertaining to baseline level of functioning, onset of deficits, progression and severity of symptoms, and current level of functioning. This will reflect a summary of information obtained from the clinical interview and review of medical records at a minimum. This may include evaluations by other services, an accounting of the incident that caused the head injury (if applicable), reports of assessments provided in theater when combat related, and an understanding of all hospital services involved in the patient's care. If collateral information regarding problems with day-to-day functioning has been obtained from the service member's command or family, it should be integrated into this section of the report. It is important to know not only how the patient views the problems, but also how the command and/or close family member sees the problems affecting the service member's performance, particularly if the service member has limited insight.

Past Medical History

The focus of the review is to provide background information regarding the context in which the current illness or injury occurred. This data may be important for differential diagnosis, treatment planning, and prognosis.

In some cases neuropsychological screening data conducted in theater may be available for mild head injury cases. In Figure 3.1, Commander Mark Monahan, one of only four active duty Navy neuropsychologists, performs an evaluation on a soldier following an improvised explosive device (IED) blast in Iraq.

Past Psychiatric History

Clinical experience suggests that patients frequently minimize histories of mental health problems. Since mental health issues can affect test results, it is important to incorporate this history. Combat veterans returning from deployment often have symptoms of posttraumatic stress disorder (PTSD; chapter 12) overlapping the symptoms for mild TBI (TBI; e.g., Hoge et al., 2008). Likewise, depression and anxiety can mimic neuropsychological symptoms of mild TBI.

Social History

There are key questions to address when taking and reporting a social history. It is important to determine and report the service member's birthplace and native language. Cultural and linguistic factors will affect interpretation of neuropsychological test results and at times affect the choice of tests, certainty of conclusions, or even the possibility of conducting the examination. In our experience many consumers of neuropsychological reports, including MEB and PEB members, have limited understanding of these issues, and the examining neuropsychologist must detail them explicitly in the report.

Figure 3.1 Commander Mark Monahan, the first Navy neuropsychologist to serve in the current combat theater, performs an evaluation in Iraq.

All reports should contain a detailed educational and occupational history. The service member's level of education, his or her approach to academics, and success in school will offer insight into premorbid functioning. Patients often exaggerate their grades (Greiffenstein, Baker, & Johnson-Greene, 2002) and in some circumstances (e.g., discrepancy between reported grades and other indicators of premorbid ability such as word reading recognition scores) copies of transcripts will clarify premorbid status and should be requested. The ASVAB can be used as an objective estimate of premorbid intellectual functioning (Orme et al., 2001) and should be reported if available. As in the general population, in the military it is not uncommon for a patient referred for neuropsychological assessment to have a history of special education, attention deficits, or lack of academic success (Centers for Disease Control and Prevention, 2005a, 2005b). These factors may significantly impact interpretation of test results and should always be described in the report. Preenlistment jobs, with information about the number, types, and success, can give an indication of interpersonal skills, work ethic, and previous occupational accomplishment. These data can also help in estimating baseline cognitive functioning. Informants from the command should be able to provide a clear picture of current functioning. Evaluations, fitness reports, personal awards, and decorations provide useful and unique data for the military neuropsychological evaluation.

Information regarding the patient's family and upbringing offers insight into childhood influences, relationship skills, and personality features. This information can often be summarized more succinctly in a neuropsychological report than in a more generic psychological report. Marital problems are a common reason for emotional distress, and conversely, if the patient is in a strong marriage, then this can be a tremendous support in aiding an individual coping with cognitive problems. As such this information may require more in-depth description.

Substance abuse can impair cognition (Morrow, RoBards, Saxton, & Metheney, 2008), and this can be compounded in service members who are coping with mild TBI and/or PTSD or depression. A comprehensive alcohol and drug use history is an essential part of the neuropsychological report.

The report should also contain information about legal history, as it provides valuable data on previous behavior and patterns of misbehavior. A pattern of counseling and nonjudicial punishment in the military raises questions about effort and secondary gain (American Psychiatric Association, 2000).

Family Medical History

Family risk factors should be reviewed, with emphasis on mental health problems, serious or chronic illness, and hereditary conditions (e.g., Huntington's disease).

Laboratory and Imaging Results

While a neuropsychologist is not expected to interpret lab results or neuroimaging studies, he or she should understand how to interpret the reports generated from these studies and be familiar with the neuropsychological correlates of abnormal results (De Zubicaray, 2006; McConnell, 2006). Results of these studies are readily available for service members in the electronic medical record (Armed Forces Longitudinal Technology Application, also known as AHLTA) and can easily be incorporated into the report.

Current Medications

Many medications may confound neuropsychological evaluations, particularly those causing drowsiness (Stein & Strickland, 1998). Even over-the-counter medication and nutritional supplements may alter cognitive functioning (Bower et al., 2003), and use should be reviewed and described in the report. While it is best if such medications are not taken prior to a neuropsychological evaluation, sometimes this is not possible; therefore, test results must be interpreted cautiously and medication effects must be discussed.

Mental Status Examination and Behavioral Observations

Reporting how the patient looks and behaves is essential in the neuropsychological fitness-for-duty report. Behavioral observations and mental status findings may reveal impairment in comportment and emotional regulation characteristic of frontal lobe involvement that is difficult to detect with formal testing (Kelly & Kirshner, 1986). Behavioral observations are also important in detecting characteristics that may affect interpretation of test results (such as drowsiness). Do behavioral observations match the presenting complaint and results of formal testing? A discrepancy serves as a potential indication of malingering (Slick, Sherman, & Iverson, 1999; chapter 4), an important consideration in fitness-for-duty assessments.

Tests Administered and Normative System Employed

A summary of tests and procedures used should be in the report for other neuropsychologists who may need to review the findings. This is most important when a different neuropsychologist must compare and contrast the current results with previous assessments. Neuropsychologists employ different approaches to selecting normative data. Therefore, it is best to identify the normative source in the report. Including this information also makes the basis for the conclusions rendered in the report clearer for the adjudicating body.

Test Results

It is imperative that the neuropsychologist communicate test results clearly and in sufficient detail so that results can be understood by a layperson, keeping in mind that the PEB, who ultimately makes the determination of fitness for duty, is often composed of two officers with no medical background and a physician who may have only basic training in neurology and psychiatry. Jargon and unnecessary verbiage should be avoided. A recent survey (Donders, 2001) indicated that most neuropsychologists organize their reports according to cognitive domains, and the authors endorse this approach as one way to achieve clarity for PEB readers. This survey also indicated that most neuropsychologists include test scores (e.g., percentiles, t scores) and utilize descriptive terms (e.g., "mildly impaired") in their reports.

Conclusions

Informal contact with physician colleagues suggests that this is the section that most readers of neuropsychological reports turn to first. As such it should summarize the neuropsychological findings and integrate them with all other pertinent data that have been reviewed in the report: all pieces of the puzzle are examined, organized, and explained to the reader. Performance across cognitive domains is described, compared, and interpreted. If present or suspected, confounding factors should be described and discussed: pain, medication effects, emotional disturbance, ethno-cultural factors, learning disabilities, physical limitations, attention deficit hyperactivity disorder, fatigue, and effort can all significantly influence test results. The conclusion section must tie together all pertinent data contained in the report. Educational history and past military performance can be used to contrast current deficits and decline in functioning. Confounding factors are discussed and weighted in terms of their effects on test findings. Reviewing implications of test results for functioning on a day-to-day basis will be helpful to adjudicators, who look to the neuropsychologist first and foremost to provide information about objective evidence of cognitive and functional impairment.

Diagnosis

A well-written report should methodically lead the reader to the diagnostic conclusion. If the neuropsychological findings result in a diagnosis, it should be reported in multiaxial terms and conform to the latest edition of the *Diagnostic and Statistical Manual of Mental Disorders* (American Psychiatric Association, 2000). In some instances there may be multiple diagnoses or a need to make a complex differential diagnosis. The contemporary practice of clinical neuropsychology in the military environment finds many service members returning from lengthy and multiple combat deployments. Frequently they have suffered mild TBI (single or multiple) due to IEDs and other causes as well as comorbid depression, PTSD, and adjustment disorders (Hoge, Auchterlonie, & Milliken, 2006; Hoge et al., 2008; Hotopf et al., 2006). Multiple diagnoses should be coded in the report as appropriate. Explaining the rationale for differential diagnosis in terms that can be understood by a layperson will facilitate PEB adjudication. Neuropsychologists evaluating service members should be aware that there are special considerations when making a diagnosis of malingering. In the military, malingering can result in Uniformed Code of Military Justice charges and significant punitive action, per Article 115 (Ritchie, 1997; see also chapter 4). A thorough assessment and systematic review of the neuropsychological data and additional background information (Slick et al., 1999) should occur prior to considering a diagnosis of malingering in the report.

Recommendations

Recommendations must be written with care and precision. As with most other neuropsychological reports, there may be recommendations involving additional evaluation or consultation, follow-up neuropsychological assessment, treatment and rehabilitation, strategies for adapting to deficits, and suggestions involving compensation for limitations or assistance with daily activities. Military neuropsychologists go beyond these typical recommendations in every neuropsychological evaluation they conduct with a service member; however, in a sense every evaluation poses fitness-for-duty questions.

Should the evaluation result in a diagnosis of an acquired disorder, the neuropsychologist must determine whether the signs and symptoms noted are severe enough to impact fitness for duty. The determination must be made as to whether the service member's case should be adjudicated through the disability evaluation system or whether the noted deficits are mild, enabling the service member to remain on active duty or as a member of the reserve component. Milder deficits might allow the service member to remain on active duty but may necessitate cross training into another career field. It should be noted that the decision to change jobs (i.e., ratings, MOS, or Air Force Specialty Code) in the military is entirely up to the command. The neuropsychologist can only recommend this course of action.

In cases where the deficits are judged to be severe enough to warrant processing through the disability evaluation system, the evaluation report should state this fact along with additional information that will assist the PEB in determining impairment percentage ratings to be assigned to each diagnosis. This information, in turn, will affect the disability retirement pay of the service member. At the time of this writing, the DoD and the Department of Veterans Affairs have agreed to explore ways to merge the disability evaluation systems of the two departments with the desired goal being a streamlined method to quickly and correctly process the service member's case (DoD, 2007). Currently, the Department of Veterans Affairs conducts a separate disability determination following a similar (but not identical) determination by the Army, Navy, or Air Force.

THE NEUROPSYCHOLOGICAL REPORT: POSSIBLE ADDITIONAL COMPONENTS

As indicated earlier, there are uniform DoD standards governing fitness-for-duty determinations, but each service has developed somewhat different procedures and informal practices for implementation. While all service branches ultimately require that the same information be gathered and integrated for MEB and PEB purposes, the role of the neuropsychologist in gathering and presenting information varies from service to service and at times from occasion to occasion within a single service.

In this section, we present information that is essential for processing a service member through the fitness-for-duty system but that may or may not, depending on circumstances, be included as an element of the neuropsychological report. Neuropsychologists need to work in collaboration with their command, physician colleagues, and PEB to determine which of the elements below are expected as a component of their neuropsychological report and to avoid duplication of effort. Information in this section of the chapter currently applies to neuropsychological evaluations conducted for the Air Force, and at times to evaluations conducted for the Army, Marine Corps, and Navy.

Additional Issues in Diagnosis

When performing a fitness-for-duty evaluation on airmen, the following information should be included to assist the Air Force MEB and PEB in their deliberations (these terms are explained in Air Force Regulation 168–4 which has been superseded by Air Force Instruction 48–123).

When it is determined that the severity of the disorder is such that the service member can no longer remain on active duty, additional information must be included in the diagnostic statement of neuropsychological reports. For Axis I disorders, a statement concerning severity must be included along with the specific manifestations of the disorder, its date of onset and duration, the external precipitating stress and its severity, the premorbid disposition and its severity, the degree of impairment for military service, and the degree of impairment for civilian industrial adaptability.

The severity and the disorder-specific manifestations are relatively simple. For example, if making the diagnosis of dementia secondary to head trauma, one should also note the severity and how the dementia is manifested. Additives such as "mild," "moderate," or "severe" should be used and followed by a description of the major symptoms, such as "…manifested by global intellectual decline, verbal and nonverbal memory impairment, and executive dysfunction." If the diagnosis rendered relates to a traumatic event, such as a motor vehicle accident or IED, the date of the injury must be noted. Following the date, a description of the duration is needed and is usually best described as "…and continuous since that time." The external precipitating stress is usually noted as "mild, routine military duty" unless the injury occurred when under hostile fire. In such cases a statement such as "intense prolonged combat" should be used instead. With most neuropsychological disorders the premorbid predisposition should be listed as "none."

When the service member's case is presented to an MEB, the degree of impairment for military service must be noted. The service member's current and projected future capacity to perform military duties should be used as a baseline in these cases. The neuropsychologist must note one of four degrees of impairment: no impairment, minimal impairment, moderate impairment, or marked impairment. Those service members deemed to be moderately or markedly impaired are usually not returned to duty.

Finally, the evaluating neuropsychologist must list in the diagnostic statement the degree of impairment for civilian social and industrial adaptability. This is essentially an assessment of the service member's civilian earning capacity. Listing the degree of impairment for social and industrial adaptability also assists the Department of Veterans Affairs in determining a disability rating for the service member. In this area the neuropsychologist must list one of six possibilities; total impairment, severe impairment, considerable impairment, definite impairment, mild impairment, or full remission. Service members deemed to have total or severe impairment for civilian industrial adaptability are usually those who are completely unable to work or at best able to work only in a sheltered setting. Those with considerable and definite impairment may be able to perform duties similar to their military job in a civilian environment but most often are unable to work at the same level of independence as prior to the injury or onset of the illness. An example of this is a service member who is an aircraft mechanic exposed to an IED while performing convoy duty and suffers a TBI severe enough to make it difficult for him complete checklist items without supervisory oversight. Guidelines for rating social and industrial adaptability can be found in section B-107 of the Army Regulation 635–40 (Secretary of the Army, 2006) and Air Force Regulation 168–4 (Secretary of the Air Force, 1990).

Additional Issues in Making Recommendations

In circumstances where the neuropsychologist concludes that the service member's condition warrants presentation of the case to an MEB, a number of additional requirements must appear in the body of some reports. A statement concerning the service member's competency for pay and records may be needed. A service member who is not competent for pay and records is usually one who exhibits fundamental problems with language and numerical concepts. The neuropsychologist's opinion should be based on the relevant test data. The competency statement is essentially a recommendation to the PEB, which makes the final determination on competency for pay and records.

It also needs to be mentioned that a line of duty determination was made in some reports. DoD regulations prohibit payment of disability retirement pay when the injury or illness is due to the service member's intentional misconduct or willful negligence. The line of duty determination made by Medical Service officers is strictly administrative in nature. When the neuropsychologist has concerns about stating "Line of Duty: No," consultation with a medical law consultant is warranted. A senior commander in the service member's chain of command makes a more formal line of duty determination. This formal determination supersedes that made by the Medical Service officer.

CASE VIGNETTES

Case 1: Army Corporal

Case 1 is a 25-year-old ambidextrous Army Corporal with an MOS 88M (truck driver). During a physical training test he developed a severe headache and lost consciousness. Cranial computed tomography revealed a large left parietal juvenile pilocytic astrocytoma. He underwent left parietal craniotomy. Following surgery he developed right hemiparesis, right homonymous hemianopsia, almost daily headaches, and mild anxiety. He also suffered one generalized seizure. He received postoperative rehabilitation therapy, and psychiatry treated him for anxiety. He underwent neuropsychological testing approximately 4 months after surgery with a battery that included the Portland Digit Recognition Test, Wechsler Adult Intelligence Scale-III (WAIS-III), Wechsler Memory Scale-III (WMS-III), Wide Range Achievement Test-4, Halstead-Reitan Neuropsychological Battery with Allied Procedures, Boston Naming Test, Thurstone Verbal Fluency Test, California Verbal Learning Test-II (CVLT-II), and MMPI-2. Medications at the time of testing included melatonin, levetiracetam, and sertraline. During testing the patient was cooperative, and Portland Digit Recognition Test results contained no indications of malingering or suboptimal effort. Intellectual functioning was in the average range (Full Scale IQ 97), whereas scores on measures of academic achievement were low average to borderline, consistent with educational history (lacked interest in school and dropped out, later obtained GED) and his ASVAB score at the time of enlistment (ASVAB General Technical Score of 98). Performance on measures of language, visuoconstructive ability, most measures of learning and memory, executive function, and left-sided motor function was normal. He did, however, show mild impairment on selected measures of visual and verbal memory. There were also indications of mild impairment of working memory and processing speed, though it was possible that the information processing speed deficit was secondary to the impact of his visual field deficit on the ability to perform these tasks (e.g., WAIS-III Digit Symbol, Trail Making Test). He had a severe impairment of grip strength on the right side. His MMPI-2 profile was normal. Diagnosis was Cognitive Disorder Not Otherwise Specified (NOS). The MEB found the patient's neurological condition (pilocytic astrocytoma with residual right homonymous hemianopsia, right-sided hemiparesis, persistent frequent headaches, and cognitive impairment) warranted referral to the PEB. The PEB in turn found the patient was unfit for further military service in his rank and MOS and rated his overall disability at 50%. The patient accepted the PEB determination.

Case 2: Air Force Major

In most fitness-for-duty cases involving a psychiatric or neurological condition, the prognosis is difficult to determine at the time the patient first presents for evaluation. As a result the PEB often temporarily retires service members from active duty, and they are placed on the temporary disability retirement list (TDRL). Regulations require that service members on TDRL be reevaluated at 18-month intervals for up to a 5-year period by all specialties involved in the original evaluation. Following reevaluation, the service member can be returned to active duty, continued on the TDRL, or permanently retired. Case 2 is a TDRL reevaluation of a service member who had undergone a PEB review approximately 2 years earlier.

Case 2 is a 46-year-old right-handed male Air Force Major who had been employed as an electrical engineer and was status post-cerebrovascular accident secondary to a ruptured left middle cerebral artery aneurysm. The PEB retired him with a disability rating of 100%. Following his temporary retirement he underwent both inpatient and outpatient rehabilitation. At the time of the neuropsychological evaluation he worked part time in a job arranged through his state department of vocational rehabilitation. When interviewed, both the patient and his wife noted functional improvements (relative to 2 years prior) in a variety of areas but also noted that significant problems including aphasia, memory difficulties, right-sided weakness and numbness remained. They also noted that he was now quick to anger, which was often exacerbated by his inability to express himself verbally. His wife further noted problems with impulse control.

Given his aphasia, no formal symptom validity testing was attempted. On a short form of the WAIS-III, the patient obtained an estimated verbal IQ of 74, an estimated performance IQ of 68, and an estimated full scale IQ of 69, which placed him in the extremely low range of overall intellect. Due to his language disability and hemiparesis, results were not felt to represent an adequate estimate of his current intellectual functioning and the Test of Nonverbal Intelligence–Second Edition (TONI-2) was also administered. He obtained a TONI-2 quotient of 97, which placed him in the average range of overall intellectual functioning. This result was felt to reflect more accurately the patient's current level of functioning; however, this level was still felt to represent a decline from premorbid levels (as this patient was an officer, no ASVAB scores were available).

Despite his aphasia, the patient's performance on the WMS-III logical memory subtest was average. On the CVLT-II his performance was markedly impaired for both short-delay and long-delay recall.

Due to the patient's right hemiparesis, nonverbal memory tests requiring motor output were not administered. The patient's performance on both the Continuous Visual Memory Test and the Warrington Recognition Memory Test–Faces subtest was average suggesting intact nonverbal/visual memory.

During the clinical interview the patient's spontaneous speech was noted to be dysfluent. Specifically his speech was noted to be telegraphic in nature with numerous phonemic paraphasic errors and stiff prosody. Confrontation naming ability was significantly impaired as was verbal fluency. In contrast the patient's auditory comprehension was relatively spared as per tests of body-part identification, response to auditory commands, comprehension of complex ideational material, and comprehension of sentences and paragraphs (Boston Diagnostic Aphasia Exam). The patient's ability to read aloud was impaired, again with numerous phonemic paraphasic errors.

Visuospatial and visuoconstructive abilities were high average as assessed by the Benton Judgment of Line Orientation and WAIS-III

Block Design subtest. Abstract concept formation ability and cognitive set shifting ability were also intact (Booklet Category Test and Wisconsin Card Sorting Test). The patient's motor speed as assessed by the Finger Tapping Test was borderline with the nonpreferred left hand and was not attempted with the preferred right hand due to the right hemiparesis.

As noted the patient and his wife described problems with anger and impulse control. However, the patient denied significant depression or anxiety during the clinical interview; the patient's wife also stated that she did not note signs or symptoms suggestive of a depressive or anxiety disorder. This finding was replicated on brief self-report measures that were administered (Beck Depression Inventory–Second Edition, Beck Anxiety Inventory).

As a result of the TDRL evaluation, case 2 received a diagnosis of vascular dementia manifested by global intellectual decline, Broca's aphasia, verbal memory impairment, and personality change. Because case 2 was already on the TDRL, it was recommended to the PEB, due to the severity of his impairments, that he be either maintained on the TDRL or more preferably permanently retired.

Case 3: Marine Lance Corporal

Case 3 is a 22-year-old, right-handed, male Marine Lance Corporal with 4 years of continuous active duty. Six months prior to his neuropsychological assessment he was the gunner in a Humvee when it was struck by an IED near the driver's side door. He was wearing a Kevlar helmet but struck his head violently against the metal forming the gun turret. He lost consciousness for 2–3 minutes, with 15 minutes of retrograde amnesia and 2 hours of anterograde amnesia. During the days after the incident he appeared slow to process information, speech was slow, and he complained of ear and head pain, dizziness, and poor balance. He was evacuated to Germany and then to the United States. A brain MRI raised the question of an axonal injury in the frontal and temporal lobes but was not definitive. He received care in the vestibular clinic and continued to experience problems with headaches, hearing loss, balance, and dizziness. The patient is married with two children. He is a high school graduate who described himself as an average student. ASVAB scores were not available. Neuropsychological assessment revealed normal performance on embedded validity measures and formal symptom validity measures including the Test of Memory Malingering and the Victoria Symptom Validity Test. Based on WAIS-III performance, the patient's intellectual abilities were within the average range, with a full scale IQ of 104. His performance demonstrated variability across cognitive domains, with a general tendency to perform below expectation on tests associated with frontal and left hemisphere functions. Visuospatial abilities were a relative strength. Vocabulary, confrontation naming, immediate recall on measures of visual memory, and left-handed fine motor skills were within the average range, consistent with his intellectual level. On measures of delayed visual memory, category fluency, mental flexibility, and right-hand fine motor functions, he performed within the below-average range. A number of abilities were within the impaired range. Working memory, processing speed, phonemic fluency, verbal learning and memory, and attention and concentration abilities were all impaired. Personality Assessment Inventory results were valid and revealed elevated levels of anxiety and depression. Based on this neuropsychological assessment, the patient was found cognitively unfit for duty and diagnosed with Cognitive Disorder NOS. Vestibular clinic wrote the MEB report, and the neurology service wrote an addendum for chronic headaches.

SUMMARY AND CONCLUSIONS

Clinical neuropsychologists working with military populations can expect to continue to play a significant role in medical fitness-for-duty determinations, in keeping with increasing roles of clinical neuropsychology in the medicolegal arena and the high incidence of traumatic survivable TBI in contemporary military conflicts (Hoge et al., 2008). To provide effective consultation, military clinical neuropsychologists must be thoroughly familiar with the service-specific regulations governing determination of fitness for duty as well as the steps in the fitness-for-duty process. In addition, they must understand in detail the military-relevant requirements for conducting an effective and useful neuropsychological evaluation, including gathering of history and background information, appropriate test selection, and selection of the most suitable normative system. Finally, military clinical neuropsychologists must prepare reports that provide the reader with a clear review and integration of background information and neuropsychological test results and the implications for adequate duty performance.

Military neuropsychologists assume responsibility that is unique and of great consequence. A neuropsychologically healthy fighting force is critical to mission success and national security. Service members who fall ill with a disease involving the brain or incur a TBI in the line of duty require a thorough neuropsychological assessment for treatment planning purposes, determination of fitness for duty, and decision making regarding the presence and extent of disability.

REFERENCES

American Psychiatric Association. (2000). *Diagnostic and statistical manual of mental disorders* (text revision) (4th ed.). Arlington, VA: Author.

Barona, A., Reynolds, C. R., & Chastain, R. (1984). A demographically based index of premorbid intelligence for the WAIS-R. *Journal of Consulting and Clinical Psychology, 52*, 885–887.

Blair, J. R., & Spreen, O. (1989). Predicting premorbid IQ: A revision of the National Adult Reading Test. *The Clinical Neuropsychologist, 3*, 129–136.

Boone, K. B. (2007). *Assessment of feigned cognitive impairment: A neuropsychological perspective.* New York: The Guilford Press.

Bower, A., Moore, J., Moss, M., Selby, K., Austin, M., & Meeves, S. (2003). The effects of single dose fexofenadine, diphenhydramine, and placebo on cognitive performance in flight personnel. *Aviation, Space, and Environmental Medicine, 74*(2), 145–152.

Budd, F. C., & Harvey, S. (2006). Military fitness-for-duty evaluations. In C. H. Kennedy & E. A. Zillmer (Eds.), *Military psychology: Clinical and operational applications* (pp. 35–60). New York: Guilford.

Centers for Disease Control and Prevention. (2005a). Prevalence of diagnosis and medication treatment for attention-deficit/hyperactivity disorder—United States, 2003. *Morbidity and Mortality Weekly Report, 54*(34), 842–847.

Centers for Disease Control and Prevention. (2005b). Percentage of children aged 5–17 years ever having diagnoses of attention deficit/hyperactivity disorder (ADHD) or learning disability (LD) by sex and diagnosis—United States, 2003. *Morbidity and Mortality Weekly, 54*(43), 1107.

De Zubicary, G. (2006). Neuroimaging and clinical neuropsychological practice. In P. Snyder, P. Nussbaum, & D. Robins (Eds.), *Clinical neuropsychology: A pocket handbook for assessment* (pp. 56–74). Washington, DC: American Psychological Association.

Department of Defense (DoD). (1984). *Test manual for the armed services vocational aptitude battery.* North Chicago: United States Military Entrance Processing Command.

DoD. (1996). *Separation or retirement for physical disability* (DoD Directive 1332.18). Washington, DC: Author.

DoD. (2007, November 30). *Pilot program cuts disability evaluation time, speeds veterans' benefits.* Retrieved October 6, 2008, from http://www.defenselink.mil/news/newsarticle.aspx?id=48289

Donders, J. (2001). A survey of report writing by neuropsychologists, I: General characteristics and content. *The Clinical Neuropsychologist, 15*, 137–149.

Greiffenstein, M., Baker, W., & Johnson-Greene, D. (2002). Actual versus self-reported scholastic achievement of litigating postconcussion and severe closed head injury claimants. *Psychological Assessment, 14*(2), 202–208.

Heaton, R., Miller, S., Taylor, M., & Grant, I. (2004). *Revised comprehensive norms for an expanded Halstead Reitan battery: Demographically adjusted neuropsychological norms for African American and Caucasian adults.* Lutz, FL: Psychological Assessment Resources.

Hoge, C., Auchterlonie, J., & Milliken, C. (2006). Mental health problems, use of mental health services, and attrition from military service after return from deployment to Iraq or Afghanistan. *Journal of the American Medical Association, 295*(9), 1023–1032.

Hoge, C., McGurk, D., Thomas, J., Cox, A., Engel, C., & Castro, C. (2008). Mild traumatic brain injury in U.S. soldiers returning from Iraq. *New England Journal of Medicine, 358*(5), 453–463.

Hotopf, M., Hull, L., Fear, N., Browne, T., Horn, O. Iverson, A., et al. (2006). The health of UK military personnel who deployed to the 2003 Iraq war: A cohort study. *Lancet, 367*, 1731–1741.

Kelly, M. & Kirshner, H. (1986). Syndromes of the frontal lobes. In H. Kirshner (Ed.), *Behavioral neurology: A practical clinical approach.* New York: Churchill Livingstone.

Krull, K. R., Scott, J. G., & Sherer, S. K. (1995). Evaluation of two methods for estimating premorbid intelligence from combined performance and demographic variables. *The Clinical Neuropsychologist, 9*, 83–88.

Lezak, M. D., Howieson, D. B., & Loring, D. W. (2004). *Neuropsychological assessment* (4th ed.). New York: Oxford University Press.

McConnell, H. (2006). Laboratory testing in neuropsychology. In P. Snyder, P. Nussbaum, & D. Robins (Eds.), *Clinical neuropsychology: A pocket handbook for assessment* (pp. 34–55). Washington, DC: American Psychological Association.

Morrow, L., RoBards, M., Saxton, J., & Metheny, K. (2008). Toxins in the CNS: Alcohol, illicit drugs, heavy metals, solvents, and related exposure. In J. Morgan & J. Ricker (Eds.), *Textbook of clinical neuropsychology* (pp. 588–598). New York: Taylor and Francis.

Orme, D., Brehm, W., & Ree, M. (2001). Armed Forces Qualification Test as a general measure of premorbid intelligence. *Military Psychology, 13*, 187–197.

The Psychological Corporation. (2001). *Wechsler test of adult reading.* San Antonio, TX: Author.

Ritchie, E. (1997). Malingering and the United States Military. In R. Lande & D. Armitage (Eds.), *Principles and practice of military forensic psychiatry.* Springfield, IL: Charles C. Thomas.

Ryan, L. M., Zazeckis, T. M., French, L. M., & Harvey, S. (2006). Neuropsychological practice in the military. In C. H. Kennedy & E. A. Zillmer (Eds.), *Military psychology: Clinical and operational applications* (pp. 105–129). New York: Guilford.

Secretary of the Air Force. (1990). *Air Force administration of medical activities (Air Force Regulation 168–4).* Washington, DC: Author.

Secretary of the Air Force. (2006a). *Medical examinations and standards. Volume 1—General provisions (Air Force Instruction 48–123, Vol. 1).* Washington, DC: Author.

Secretary of the Air Force. (2006b). *Medical examinations and standards. Volume 2—Accession, retention, and administration (Air Force Instruction 48–123, Vol. 2).* Washington, DC: Author.

Secretary of the Air Force. (2006c). *Medical examinations and standards. Volume 3—Flying and special operational duty (Air Force Instruction 48-123, Vol. 3).* Washington, DC: Author.

Secretary of the Air Force. (2006d). *Medical examinations and standards. Volume 4—Special standards and requirements (Air Force Instruction 48-123, Vol. 4).* Washington, DC: Author.

Secretary of the Army. (2006). *Physical evaluation for retention, retirement, and separation (Army Regulation 635–40).* Washington, DC: Author.

Secretary of the Army. (2007). Standards *of medical fitness (Army Regulation 40–501).* Washington, DC: Author.

Secretary of the Navy. (2002). *Department of the Navy disability determination manual (Secretary of the Navy Instruction 1850.4E).* Washington, DC: Author.

Secretary of the Navy. (2005). *Manual of the medical department U.S. Navy (NAVMED P-117).* Washington, DC: Author.

Slick, D., Sherman, E., & Iverson, G. (1999). Diagnostic criteria for malingered neurocognitive dysfunction: Proposed standards for clinical practice and research. *The Clinical Neuropsychologist, 13,* 545–561.

Strauss, E., Sherman, E. M. S., & Spreen, O. (2006). A *compendium of neuropsychological tests: Administration, norms, and commentary.* New York: Oxford University Press.

Stein, R. A. & Strickland, T. (1998). A review of the neuropsychological effects of prescription medications. *Archives of Clinical Neuropsychology, 13,* 259–284.

4

Noncredible Neuropsychological Presentation in Service Members and Veterans

MANFRED F. GREIFFENSTEIN

INTRODUCTION

It is important to note at the outset of this chapter that neuropsychological evaluations of active duty service members may be regulated by the Boxer law. The Boxer law was passed to protect service members from receiving a command-directed mental health evaluation as a form of retaliation (i.e., whistle blowing). Essentially, this Department of Defense Directive (Department of Defense, 1997) regulates involuntary mental health referrals, which are differentiated from self-referrals and those referrals that are initiated by other clinicians. This process requires a formal request by the individual's commanding officer/commander and adequate rationale such that the provider feels the request is a valid one. The service member is provided the option of legal consultation prior to being seen by the provider, as mental health evaluations in the military can have serious repercussions, such as loss of career (e.g., being deemed unfit or unsuitable for duty), hospitalization or legal charges, as is the case with malingering.

With that said, this chapter concerns the measurement and evaluation of noncredible neuropsychological presentations. A noncredible cognitive deficit is defined as a poor performance that is unrelated to brain dysfunction and is accompanied by compelling evidence that effort is a major influence. Noncredible presentation can take two forms: Poor effort (not trying hard enough) or directed effort (working hard to leave an impression of impairment).

The term "noncredible deficits" is preferred in a military setting because the diagnosis of malingering is a crime under the Uniform Code of Military Justice (Article 115). Article 115 reads, "any person subject to this chapter who for the purpose of avoiding work, duty, or service (1) feigns illness, physical disablement, mental lapse or derangement; or (2) intentionally inflicts self-injury; shall be punished as a court-martial may direct." Maximum penalties for malingering of neurocognitive deficits include a dishonorable discharge, forfeiture of all pay and allowances, and confinement for a year, unless this is done in a hostile fire pay zone or in a time of war. Then, maximum penalties include the same as above except that confinement can be extended to 3 years (Joint Service Committee on Military Justice, 2008).

There will be cases where a malingering diagnosis is appropriate, such as capital crimes with questionable insanity pleas, or avoiding deployment or other duty for mental health reasons. But in general, the consequences of this diagnosis are much greater in active military circles than in civilian ones. I will use the term malingering only when accuracy in quoting research literature and accepted diagnostic treatises is required. More often, I use terms like *noncredible* and similar terms to define instances where deviant or abnormal neurocognitive scores are unrelated to brain disease. The terms include pseudoabnormalities, invalid scores, improbable deficits, illogical history, impression management, and so on. Such language removes the onus, while taking the neutral stance that noncredible presentation can represent adaptation to difficult life problems. Hence I am taking the respectful attitude of the French neurologist Jean-Martin Charcot, but more about him later.

My final word on the mental framework for reading this chapter is: emphasis is on the invalidity of data during a specific evaluation, *not the general credibility of the service member*. The existence of noncredible findings does not automatically rule out coexisting problems, nor does it make the service member a liar or psychopath. A good example is pseudoseizures: Persons with documented seizures may still produce noncredible fits to cope with stress (Goldstein, Drew, Mellers, Mitchell-O'Malley, & Oakley, 2000).

This chapter begins with a brief history of the clinical and scientific measurement of feigned impairments (see chapter 1 for additional history of malingering in the military). Next, I describe the three behavioral domains in which implausible impairments are expressed: cognitive, sensory-motor, and symptom expression. Each form of noncredible impairment helps the examinee solve an important problem in living. Such problems may include avoidance of severe legal penalty (death, imprisonment), avoidance of military service or combat exposure, avoidance of work, access to drugs, and/or need for money. There is also a review of the various quantitative and qualitative methods for assessing noncredible status. Finally, I summarize the most defensible practices with regard to assessment and clinical reasoning.

A BRIEF HISTORY OF EXAMINATION FOR SIMULATION

The objective study of deception in neurological presentation has a long history dating back to the early days of modern neurology. Charcot, the founder of modern neurology, invented a device for detecting feigned movement disorders (Goetz, 2007). Charcot respected the artistry of noncredible presentations, but his American contemporary Weir Mitchell did not. Mitchell, a Civil War neurologist enmeshed in wartime pressures to produce able-bodied men, developed behavioral techniques for quickly resolving feigned presentations. This included setting fires in the tents of soldiers with unexplained paraplegia. Mitchell wrote with contempt and made no distinction between hysteria and malingering (Goetz, 1997).

The advent of self-administered personality inventories offered new threats to validity, but also opportunity to measure it objectively. Face-valid items made it easier for even naïve respondents to discriminate abnormal from normal answers. But the ease of scoring made statistical discrimination of plausible versus implausible findings easier as well. The most commonly used personality test is the Minnesota Multiphasic Personality Inventory (MMPI); it was updated in 1989 to the MMPI-2 (Butcher, Dahlstrom, Tellegen, & Kaemmer, 1989). The MMPI-2 was replaced in the fall of 2008 by the MMPI-RF (MMPI Restructured Form), although the MMPI-2 is still available. The MMPI/MMPI-2 have validity scales made up of items infrequently reported in either the standardization group or genuine psychiatric patients; hence, deviant scores represent frequent endorsement of atypical symptoms. If such overreporting of problems is marked, the MMPI-2 profile is invalid, and misrepresentation of psychological disturbance becomes a diagnostic hypothesis.

The *Diagnostic and Statistical Manual* (*DSM*), now in its fourth edition (*DSM-IV*; American Psychiatric Association, 1994), provided qualitative criteria for malingering. The *DSM-IV* defines malingering as the intentional production of false or exaggerated psychological symptoms motivated by external incentives; the avoidance of military duty is prominently named as one motivation. The diagnosis requires clinical judgments to determine whether at least two of four indicia are present: medicolegal setting of assessment (e.g., something to be gained from misleading impairment), marked discrepancy between the claimed disability and objective findings, lack of cooperation during evaluation and/or compliance with treatment, and the presence of antisocial personality disorder. The specific assessment methods are left to the examiner ("objective findings" not specified), and the final judgments are qualitative, not quantitative.

Slick, Sherman, and Iversen (1999) published multifaceted criteria for refining the diagnosis. The Slick paper offered rules for assigning a confidence level to the diagnosis of malingered neurocognitive deficits: definite, probable, or possible. Slick et al. (1999) defined malingered neurocognitive deficits as "the volitional exaggeration or fabrication of cognitive dysfunction for the purpose of obtaining substantial material gain, or avoiding or escaping formal duty or responsibility. Material gain includes money, goods, or services" (p. 552).

The Slick criteria were strongly influenced by a number of considerations. First, the operational definitions and methodology of Greiffenstein, Baker, and Gola (1994) and Nies and Sweet (1994) were relied upon by employing a multidimensional, multi-method approach to validate the detection of malingering. Second, the Slick system was formatted to parallel the *DSM-IV* template of a general definition, followed by various criteria to consider. The Slick criteria for malingered neurocognitive deficits thus allowed for a standardized creation of "known groups" or "at-risk for exaggeration" samples necessary for the validation of malingering measures. Third, Slick criteria are easily translated into other settings where secondary gain is prominent. For example, the Slick guidelines were adapted to malingered pain-related disability (Bianchini, Etherton, & Greve, 2004; Bianchini, Greve, & Glynn, 2005). Fourth, the criteria merged quantitative and qualitative methods, which required the integration of biographical, case history, mental status, and test scores. In summary, the Slick criteria were a clear departure from past attempts to define malingering, which frequently placed the clinician in the position of intuiting intention from a single event, single test score, or unproven heuristic. Prior to Slick et al., it was generally accepted that clinicians were poor at rendering clinical judgments of noncredibility based on observation alone (Faust & Ziskin, 1988).

DOMAINS OF NONCREDIBLE PRESENTATION

The work of Richard Lanyon (Lanyon, 2001; Lanyon & Almer, 2001) is persuasive regarding diversity of noncredible presentations. Lanyon argues that assessment of misrepresentation should rely on tests addressing the nature of the misrepresentation. Put differently, there are multiple forms of noncredible presentation one can expect in a military setting, each form solves a different problem or achieves a different goal, and the methods used to capture this must be content valid. No single test can capture any form of misrepresentation (there is no universal sensitivity) or rule it out (there is no universal specificity). Because mild head injury is associated with cognitive issues and not psychotic symptoms, the Infrequency scale should not be effective, and in fact it is not. For example, Greiffenstein, Gola, and Baker (1995) showed that in persons reporting prolonged disability after minor head injury, the Infrequency scale of the MMPI/MMPI-2 did not detect noncredible status, but cognitive effort tests did. This finding was later replicated through factor analysis by Nelson, Sweet, Berry, Bryant, and Granacher (2007).

There are three content domains in which service members can give misleading portrayals of deficit: noncredible cognitive, perceptual-motor, and symptom presentations. Anecdotal examples of each noncredible presentation are provided. Military psychologists, who are tasked with evaluating credibility versus noncredibility of mental health presentation, must be familiar with the three variations (Department of Veteran Affairs, 2008).

Domain: Noncredible Cognitive Scores

Noncredible cognitive impairments refer to the production of invalid results on tests or informal assessments of mental function. Noncredible cognitive impairments can serve to solve a number of dilemmas. If charged with a serious crime under the UCMJ, abnormal neurocognitive findings can reduce culpability (not guilty by reason of insanity), evade the death penalty (by reason of mitigation or mental retardation; see U.S. Supreme Court case Adkins v Virginia 2002), or excuse noncompliance with military police (amnesia for crime elements). Such "impairments" may also be a gateway of disability benefits in perpetuity.

A good military example is provided by Kennedy (2008). She reports evaluating a petty officer who sustained benign head trauma (no altered mentation or neurological sequelae). She gave an ad hoc test of general knowledge, which draws on semantic memory, a mental function impervious to all but the most debilitating brain disease (Schachter, 2001). The sailor gave wrong answers such as "carbon monoxide" (as opposed to commanding officer) to basic questions such as "What does CO stand for?" She further determined the sailor was enmeshed in difficult psychosocial circumstances, being unable to solve mounting family problems while at sea. The petty officer's answers are noncredible because they violate a fundamental law of neuropsychology: semantic memory (facts, definitions, socially shared ideas) is resistant to head injury, but episodic memory (personal recall of specific events) is very vulnerable. Interestingly, the wrong answers also betrayed the sailor's underlying intelligence: CO actually is the chemical shorthand for carbon monoxide. Kennedy (2008) concluded the sailor was trying to solve personal problems with unusual means.

Noncredible cognitive deficits are not easily detected by examining score patterns on commonly used cognitive measures, and such noncredible patterns can look legitimate on the surface (Greiffenstein et al., 1994). The literature documents the widely used cognitive measures that are vulnerable to expression of response bias. This list includes episodic memory (Bernard, Houston, & Natoli, 1993; Hilsabeck et al., 2003; Langeluddecke & Lucas, 2003; Sinnett & Holen, 2001), intelligence (Chafetz, Abrahams, & Kohlmaier, 2007; Graue et al., 2007), executive function (DenBoer & Hall, 2007; Greve, Bianchini, & Roberson, 2007), and concentration (Harrison, Edwards, & Parker, 2007; Iverson, Lange, Green, & Franzen, 2002; Iverson & Tulsky, 2003; Mathias, Greve, Bianchini, Houston, & Crouch, 2002). Depending on stringency of criteria for invalid scores, base rates for noncredible performance in compensation-seeking samples cluster tightly around 40% (Gervais, Green, Allen, & Iverson, 2001; Greiffenstein & Baker, 2006; Greiffenstein et al., 1994; Larrabee, 2003a; Mittenberg, Patton, Canyock, & Condit, 2002). More importantly, specificity of invalidity signs (chances of falsely diagnosing malingering) is good in genuinely injured persons not seeking compensation (for a Wechsler Memory Scale example, only 6% false positives were reported by Iverson & Slick, 2001).

Domain: Noncredible Sensory-Motor Scores

Measurement of motor skills and sensory function are a fundamental component of the neuropsychological examination (Spreen & Strauss, 2006). The requirement of being "able bodied" implies that simple sensory and motor functions may be face valid (from the standpoint of the claimant) evidence relevant to duty fitness. The inference follows, those poor scores on sensorimotor tests may not always represent the effects of focal damage to the sensorimotor cortex; instead, there is strong evidence that sensory-motor measures are vulnerable to response bias (Greiffenstein, 2007). Measures found to distinguish between persons with genuine brain injury and atypical head injury include finger tapping (Arnold et al., 2005; Greiffenstein, Baker, & Gola, 1996b; Mittenberg, Rotholc, Russell, & Heilbronner, 1996), grip strength (Chengalur, Smith, Nelson, & Sadoff, 1990; Gilbert & Knowlton, 1983; Sweeney, 1999), and tactile perception (Binder, 1992; Greve, Bianchini, & Ameduri, 2003; Greve et al., 2005; Mittenberg et al., 1996). Interestingly, fine-motor coordination, which is most susceptible to brain injury, is performed better by compensation seekers with questionable brain injury (Greiffenstein et al., 1996b). This finding informs inquiries into qualitative analysis for atypical patterns, which is discussed later.

A civilian case from my files can easily be imagined as possible in a military setting. A 40-year-old laborer was struck in the head by the side mirror of a slow-moving work truck. He was "stunned" but was able to report the accident in detail to the occupational physician he saw an hour later. Reporting only low-grade headache initially, he left work early the following 2 days, retained an attorney, received referrals to neurological specialists including a neuropsychologist, and received a diagnosis of "delayed TBI." When seen for an independent neuropsychological evaluation, his many concerns included weakness, greater in his preferred left hand. Tested with the Smedley Dynamometer, he pressed 3 kg on the left and 5 kg on the right, peak grip scores one would expect in a hemiparetic patient. But manual speed (finger tapping) and fine-motor dexterity (Lafayette Grooved Pegboard) were in the low-normal to normal range. Arranging these scores into a gradient from simple motor to complex sensorimotor integration, the examinee's gradient implied impairment of simple motor function, but sparing of complex function. This gradient contradicts the nomothetic law that impaired function begins with the most complex because complex functions contain many elements, the loss of any one affecting the whole. It is neurologically impossible to lose strength but retain motor speed and accuracy. Greiffenstein, Baker, and Gola (1996b) demonstrate how to distinguish between genuine and atypical motor skills patterns.

Domain: Noncredible Symptom History

Psychological and psychiatric assessment relies heavily on self-report. Self-report is the verbal communication of symptoms and problems. Our diagnostic classification systems, in particular the *DSM-IV*, heavily weight the patient's verbal report of psychological distress with an assumption of accuracy. Self-reported symptoms are classified by their nature, frequency, and association. Further, we also rate functional impact of symptoms based on the intensity of self-report. With the exception of organic brain syndromes and developmental disorders, the *DSM-IV* criteria rarely mention objective behavioral or laboratory findings as a basis of diagnosis.

The perils of self-report are evident in settings associated with incentives for disability (or disincentives for return to premorbid service duties). One drawback is difficulty of symptom validation, as the self-report describes a private experience that is not independently verifiable through observation. Try proving someone *does not* have headaches. Second, self-report is particularly prone to recall bias. Korgeski and Leon (1983) reported a strong correlation between self-reported Agent Orange exposure and abnormal personality test findings, but low correlations when relying on military deployment records showing actual chemical exposure. Third, self-report is influenced by suggestion and secondary gain. Maugh (1982) reported an eruption of somatic symptoms in residents of a Memphis neighborhood that was newly designated as a toxic dump site. But the health alert was cancelled when a new investigation showed an error: the real dump site was not only located far away but blocked off by barriers preventing chemical seepage.

The best approaches to assessing symptom validity include endorsement of rare symptoms, overall symptom severity, and erroneous stereotypes held by the examinee. These approaches combine quantitative and qualitative considerations. A recent case involving an interpreter embedded with a Marine unit in Iraq exemplifies all three approaches. The interpreter experienced a brief mortar attack at the base where he was assigned; one shell landed nearby. His earliest account to medics was that a shock wave threw him back on his buttocks; he was uncertain if he bumped his head, but he denied memory loss and did not witness any horrific effects (no Marine killed or hurt). After completing his contract and returning stateside a year later he applied for worker's compensation, claiming delayed onset of dual posttraumatic stress disorder (PTSD) and mild brain injury. His MMPI-2 profile was invalid. Evidence for erroneous stereotype held by the examinee was a symptom validity scale of 90-T, implying great suffering. Promotion of rare symptoms was shown by an Infrequency scale of 85-T. These scores increase certainty that he was most similar to persons known to be overreporting symptoms (Greiffenstein, Fox, & Lees-Haley, 2007; Pope, Butcher, & Seelen, 2005). Implausibly severe symptoms were shown by the extreme elevations on most MMPI-2 clinical scales, and the qualitative consideration of multiple physical complaints during the interview, in a man only 39 years old. The final consideration was nomothetic: There is no injury mechanism that would cause both brain injury with associated amnesia, and hypergraphic recall of the trauma.

MEASUREMENT TECHNIQUES

Forced Choice

The most effective effort tests are simple verbal or visual two-choice recognition memory tests. All but the most profoundly impaired neurological patients pass these tests with ease (Green, Rohling, Lees-Haley, & Allen, 2001; Tombaugh, White, Cyrus, Krengel, & Rose, 1997). Examples of two-choice verbal memory tests include the Computerized Assessment of Response Bias (Allen, Iversen, & Green, 2002), the Word Memory Test (Green, Lees-Haley, & Allen, 2002), and the Warrington Recognition Memory Test verbal subtest (Millis, 2002). Examples of two-choice visual memory tests include the Test of Memory Malingering (TOMM; Rees, Tombaugh, Gansler, & Moczynski, 1998; Tombaugh, 1995; Tombaugh, 2003) and the Warrington Recognition Memory Test "faces" subtest (Millis, 2002).

The main advantage of forced-choice testing is the mathematical precision. The binomial formula can be applied to state the chances a score could be explained by mere guessing. The logic is that persons with substantial memory defect have to guess; any scores below chance are widely considered definitive evidence for feigned defect (Larrabee, 2005b; Slick et al., 1999). A disadvantage is length; it takes many trials to achieve a sample large enough to create reliable probability. For example, the TOMM requires 100 to 150 trials to complete (the last 50 trials are optional) and requires 20 to 30 minutes to administer (Tombaugh, 1995).

Level of Performance

Another validity determination method is a floor effects strategy. This means validity concerns are justified when observing performances at or below the lower performance limit of clinical groups with known brain disease (Taylor, Kreutzer, & West, 2003; van Gorp et al., 1999). The logic is that brain injury should obey nomothetic laws such as a dose–response relation; the more severe the brain disease, the greater the impairment. Persons with minor concussion or neck strain are expected to outperform such patients, so they must be using insufficient effort if they perform below the severe brain injury floor. Examples of tests keyed to empirically established floors (or cut scores) include the Rey Fifteen Item Memory Test (Greiffenstein, Baker, & Gola, 1996a; Lezak, Howieson, Loring, Hannay, & Fischer, 2004; Taylor et al., 2003), Dot Counting Test (Boone et al., 2002; Nelson et al., 2003), and the b-Test (Boone et al., 2000; Nitch, Glassmire, & Boone, 2007). Persons with moderate to severe closed head injury obtain a group mean of 12 items (4 rows) with a lower limit of 10 items; they rarely produce intrusion errors. For example, persons with remote mild trauma (mean of 2.2 years postinjury) often score <9, while patients with moderate to severe brain injury typically score >9 out of 15 (Greiffenstein et al., 1994, 1996b). These tests take advantage of laymen's poor understanding of how brain damage influences cognition. For example, the b-Test requires only automatic recognition of well-learned material, typically unaffected by brain injury (see Kennedy's case example on page 88).

The advantage of level of performance measures is brevity; the Rey Fifteen Item Memory Test, b-Test, and Dot Counting Test can be administered quickly. The disadvantages are transparency and vulnerability to coaching. Examinees can quickly intuit the Rey Fifteen Item Memory Test as "easy," and the basic concept is easy to communicate in advance of the testing ("Soldier, watch for that sheet with 15 symbols on it!"). In contrast, the TOMM is subjectively perceived as hard, even though it is objectively easy (Tombaugh, 1995).

Symptom Inventories

Prospects for over- or underreporting psychological disturbance through personality tests have been recognized as a threat to validity for many decades (Greiffenstein et al., 2007). Most modern personality inventories contain validity scales that measure various forms of response bias. The MMPI-2 contains scales measuring fixed response bias (True Response Inconsistency), exaggerated virtue or "faking good" (Lie scale or L), grossly exaggerated psychopathology (Infrequency or MMPI-F; Frequency [psychopathology] or MMPI-Fp), and overreporting of suffering and disability (Symptom Validity Scale, or MMPI-FBS).[1]

The MMPI-FBS is of particular value in civil settings, where persons may magnify pain or functional disability, in excess of objective physical (typically soft tissue) injury (Larrabee, 1998; Nelson, Sweet, & Demakis, 2006). The clinical validity of the FBS is supported by its proven association with atypical head injury history (Greiffenstein, Baker, Gola, Donders, & Miller, 2002), exaggerated pain (Larrabee, 2003b), forensic evaluation context (Wygant et al., 2007), multichemical sensitivity claims (Binder, Storzbach, & Salinsky, 2006; Staudenmayer & Phillips, 2007), and failures on cognitive effort tests (Greiffenstein et al., 2007; Ross, Millis, Krukowski, Putnam, & Adams, 2004).

To date, the MMPI-FBS has not been researched in active duty settings. However, the scale is relevant for a current development: dual claims of brain injury and PTSD associated with blast exposure in Iraq and Afghanistan. Claims of psychogenic and neurogenic injury sharing the same trauma have logical problems, such as opposing injury mechanism: acute amnesia for versus acute remembering of trauma. Greiffenstein and Baker (2008) showed higher validity test failure, particularly on the MMPI-FBS and TOMM, in persons claiming both reexperiencing symptoms and amnesia for head trauma. Persons with less numerous or conflicting symptoms were less likely to fail validity tests. Conflicting symptom reports in returning veterans will most certainly require validity testing, in light of Hoge et al.'s (2008) findings that injured soldiers reporting loss of consciousness were much more likely also to meet PTSD criteria than injured soldiers with partially or fully retained consciousness. Because it is reasonable to expect amnesia to be protective against threat encoding, greater PTSD claims in those losing consciousness justifies closer scrutiny of symptom validity.

Other personality and symptom inventories containing validity scales include the Personality Assessment Inventory (Demakis et al., 2007; Haggerty, Frazier, Busch, & Naugle, 2007), Miller Forensic Assessment of Symptoms Test (Alwes, Clark, Berry, & Granacher, 2008; Vagnini et al., 2006), and the Structured Inventory of Reported Symptoms (Hanlon, Mayfield, & Heilbronner, 2005; Wynkoop, Frederick, & Hoy, 2006). Too few studies of these validity scales have been published to make recommendations about clinical use, although they should stimulate research. In comparison, there have been many high-quality studies of the MMPI-FBS in neuropsychological and forensic settings.

Qualitative Indicators

Qualitative analysis means the *nature* of score patterns or errors are examined for commonness versus atypicality, when placed against expectations of genuine brain injury. Atypical findings mean uncommon expressions of brain damage and refer to pairs or groups of test scores that are inconsistent with neuropsychological first principles. Atypical patterns may include (a) violations of test difficulty hierarchy, (b) extreme variability on tests measuring the same underlying cognitive processes, (c) incompatibility of test pairs, or (d) disease-deficit incompatibility (Larrabee, 2005a). Examples include failing easy but passing more difficult items in the same domain (e.g., poorer yes/no recognition than free recall), large discrepancies between test scores measuring the same underlying construct (poor and good episodic memory scores), and violation of dependent cognitive processes (poor attention scores but good memory scores), when memory depends on quality of attention (Mittenberg, Azrin, Millsaps, & Heilbronner, 1993). Disease-deficit incompatibility means an abnormal score is not consistent with the claimed disease. For example, brief working memory tasks are not affected by nondementing brain disorders with the exception of conduction aphasia. Persons feigning brain injury are not aware of this and perform poorly on digit span tasks (Greiffenstein et al., 1994; Greve, Bianchini, Mathias, Houston, & Crouch, 2003; Mittenberg et al., 2001). Another example is implausible motor dysfunction. Damage to motor control centers of the brain results in a gradient of increasing impairment as a function of task complexity (Haaland, Harrington, & Yeo, 1987; Haaland, Temkin, Randahl, & Dikmen, 1994), but Greiffenstein et al. (1996b) showed that compensation seekers with minor traumas show the inverse pattern: grip strength performed worst, finger tapping intermediate, and small parts dexterity best.

Lack of ecological validity is the neuropsychologist's judgment that a respondent's scores are not consistent with injury history or observable behavior (Larrabee, 1990; Sweet, 1999). This is a subjective judgment that requires a comparison of cognitive behavior during the interview (or other settings) and the cognitive impairments implied by poor test scores. Persons with extremely low episodic memory scores should display obvious problems during an interview. For example, a person with genuine organic amnesia will exhibit considerable difficulty recalling postaccident information. Ecological validity takes advantage of the pressure created by misrepresentation: Persons must prove their claims through two clashing tactics: (a) relying on intact cognitive processes to communicate disability during the interview but (b) proving cognitive defects by underperforming on neurocognitive measures.

A good example of poor ecological validity is the person who performs <3 *SD* below expectations on memory and language tests but who spontaneously and fluently verbalizes many symptoms during face-to-face interview. More sophisticated simulators may anticipate this dilemma and bring typewritten lists of symptoms to the interview, carefully explaining that they prepared the list because of "poor memory." But such behavior still implies good executive-cognitive skills, that is anticipating and planning for future events. Greiffenstein et al. (1994) and Slick et al. (1999) offer behavioral criteria for rating unusual interview behaviors and improbable reports. It has been empirically demonstrated that persons with genuine memory disorders report fewer complaints than normal controls (Feher, Larrabee, Sudilovsky, & Crook, 1994; Prigatano, Altman, & O'Brien, 1990).

BEST PRACTICES AND CONCLUSIONS

The main teaching point of this chapter is that effort and symptom validity testing are an integral part of the neuropsychological evaluation. The reasons include the goal of accurate diagnosis. Misdiagnosis of noncredible presentations as genuine diseases of the mind or personality will incur many costs both human and financial. It is inadvisable to ignore the problem based on the belief that malingering or noncredible presentation represents a small minority of service members ("the overall probability is low so we shouldn't bother"); one must also weigh the costs associated with missing dubious symptoms. Costs and risks include undeserved disability payments in perpetuity, other benefits, access to pleasure-inducing drugs, injurious side effects of unneeded medications, permanent labeling of the service member as "brain damaged," and loss of military contributions in an era of manpower constraints. The main reason that military members see a neuropsychologist is in the context of disability rating and benefits, so the costs of missing noncredibility can be huge, even if simulators represent a minority of applicants.

There are several other teaching points. First, it is critical to recognize at the outset that *assessment of effort and symptom validity is an entire process*, of which formal test instruments are only one component. The entire process requires a multimethod, convergent evidence model, no different than the assessment of genuine clinical syndromes. With the exception of a below chance score on a two choice test, there is no single test of "faking." Scores do not come with flag pins that state the cause. Scores have to be combined with other *qualitative* indicia, such as history from the examinee compared to expectations of disease course, collateral interviews with reliable observers of the examinee's conduct when not being tested, and behavioral presentation during testing compared to the impairments implied by test scores. The data analysis must always be context sensitive. A chance level score on a simple memory test, combined with observation of a coherent and talkative service member who acts as his/her own historian, is evidence for noncredible presentation, while those same chance level scores seen in an apathetic and tearful service member are insufficient evidence for noncredible status.

Second, the Slick et al. (1999) criteria best capture the multimethod considerations necessary for sifting and weighing evidence. Their diagnostic reasoning can be applied without using the term "malingering." The Slick criteria require combining quantitative and qualitative, multimethod indicia. Quantitatively, the clinical implication is to use at least one sensitive test for each domain of noncredible performance; for example, TOMM or Word Memory Test (to address implausible memory deficits), MMPI-2 or MMPI-RF validity scales (misrepresentation of symptoms through verbal report), and evaluation of gross- and fine-motor skills (perceptual-motor pseudoabnormalities relevant to physical fitness for duty). Qualitatively, the Slick criteria suggest standardized coding of injury severity (to determine correlation between test scores and initial trauma), biographical data (preservice difficulties and academic achievement), and service record (personality traits conflicting with regimentation). Finally, there is the purely subjective, but defensible, task of weighing incentives for chronic illness behavior against incentives for duty return. Subjective methods include collateral interview and data sources such as service record, fitness reports, and counseling statements. Peers and members of the chain of command are also invaluable sources of information, particularly if they were present for the injury and have direct knowledge of it.

Third, military psychologists should always keep the disease-illness distinction in mind (Albers & Schiffer, 2007). This is the medical doctrine that discrepancy always exists between structural neuropathology (the diseased brain tissue) and the functional impairment it produces (the illness, or lived experience of the patient). In the terminology of neuropsychology, traumatic brain injuries of the same magnitude can cause different functional impairments in many, within broad limits imposed by the dose–response relationship. Brain injury severity and neurocognitive outcome are significantly correlated, but the association is imperfect ($r < 1$). Hence, there is room for postinjury variation in symptoms if one holds injury severity constant. This gap between disease and illness behavior is exploited by some patients, but it also pressures the clinician to determine how much illness behavior (e.g., poor test scores) is noncredible overlay, and how much represents valid impairment. In general, the task becomes easier the more minor or ambiguous the neurological injury, and it does appear that persons with minor injury are more likely to exaggerate (Greiffenstein & Baker, 2008). The work of differentiation is also made easier by the breadth and quality of neuropsychology training. Assessment experience with bona fide patients with well-documented brain disease also makes disease-illness distinctions easier. As stated by Charcot (1879) more than 100 years ago (as cited in Goetz, 2007, p. 108),

> But to learn how to unveil simulation in such cases, at the very least, one must have completely studied the real condition in the greatest and most serious detail...and to know it in all its most serious forms.

NOTE

1. Symptom Validity Scale does not match the acronym FBS for historical reasons. The FBS was renamed the Symptom Validity Scale to avoid literal interpretation of "faking bad" with deviant FBS scores. But the acronym FBS was retained over SVS, to preserve continuity with the extensive research literature on the FBS. For unclear reasons, the Lie (L) scale retains its original name, despite the even greater potential for misuse and harm.

REFERENCES

Albers, J., & Schiffer, R. (2007). Features of the neurological evaluation that suggest noncredible performance. In G. Larrabee (Ed.), *Assessment of malingered neuropsychological deficits* (pp. 312–333). New York: Oxford University Press.

Allen, L., Iverson, G. L., & Green, P. (2002). Computerized assessment of response bias in forensic neuropsychology. *Journal of Forensic Neuropsychology, 3,* 205-225.

Alwes, Y. R., Clark, J. A., Berry, D. T. R., & Granacher, R. P. (2008). Screening for feigning in a civil forensic setting. *Journal of Clinical and Experimental Neuropsychology, 30,* 1–15.

American Psychiatric Association. (1994). *Diagnostic and statistical manual of mental disorders* (4th ed.). Washington, DC: Author.

Arnold, G., Boone, K. B., Lu, P., Dean, A., Wen, J., Nitch, S., et al. (2005). Sensitivity and specificity of finger tapping test scores for the detection of suspect effort. *Clinical Neuropsychologist, 19,* 105–115.

Bernard, L. C., Houston, W., & Natoli, L. (1993). Malingering on neuropsychological memory tests: Potential objective indicators. *Journal of Clinical Psychology, 49*, 45–53.

Bianchini, K. J., Etherton, J. L., & Greve, K. W. (2004). Diagnosing cognitive malingering in patients with work-related pain: Four cases. *Journal of Forensic Neuropsychology, 4*, 65–85.

Bianchini, K., Greve, K., & Glynn, G. (2005). On the diagnosis of malingered pain-related disability: Lessons from cognitive malingering research. *The Spine Journal, 5*, 414–417.

Binder, L. M. (1992). Malingering detected by forced-choice testing of memory and tactile sensation: A case report. *Archives of Clinical Neuropsychology, 7*, 155–163.

Binder, L. M., Storzbach, D., & Salinsky, M. C. (2006). MMPI-2 profiles of persons with multiple chemical sensitivity. *Clinical Neuropsychologist, 20*, 848–857.

Boone, K. B., Lu, P., Back, C., King, C., Lee, A., Philpott, L., et al. (2002). Sensitivity and specificity of the Rey Dot Counting Test in patients with suspect effort and various clinical samples. *Archives of Clinical Neuropsychology, 17*, 625–642.

Boone, K. B., Lu, P., Sherman, D., Palmer, B., Back, C., Shamieh, E., et al. (2000). Validation of a new technique to detect malingering of cognitive symptoms: The b-Test. *Archives of Clinical Neuropsychology, 15*, 227–241.

Butcher, J., Dahlstrom, W., Graham, J., Tellegen, A., & Kaemmer, B. (1989). *MMPI-2: Manual for administration and scoring.* Minneapolis: University of Minnesota Press.

Chafetz, M. D., Abrahams, J. P., & Kohlmaier, J. (2007). Malingering on the social security disability consultative exam: A new rating scale. *Archives of Clinical Neuropsychology, 22*, 1–14.

Chengalur, S. N., Smith, G. A., Nelson, R. C., & Sadoff, A. M. (1990). Assessing sincerity of effort in maximal grip strength tests. *American Journal of Physical Medicine Rehabilitation, 69*, 148–153.

Demakis, G. J., Hammond, F., Knotts, A., Cooper, D. B., Clement, P., Kennedy, J., et al. (2007). The personality assessment inventory in individuals with traumatic brain injury. *Archives of Clinical Neuropsychology, 22*, 123–136.

DenBoer, J. W., & Hall, S. (2007). Neuropsychological test performance of successful brain injury simulators. *Clinical Neuropsychologist, 21*, 943–955.

Department of Defense (DoD). (1997). *Mental health evaluations of members of the armed forces* (DoD Directive 6490.1). Washington, DC: Author.

Department of Veteran Affairs. (2008). *Schedule for rating disabilities; Evaluation of residuals of Traumatic Brain Injury (TBI).* 38 CFR Part 4RIN 2900-AM75.

Faust, D., & Ziskin, J. (1988). The expert witness in psychology and psychiatry. *Science, 241*, 31–35.

Feher, E. P., Larrabee, G. J., Sudilovsky, A., & Crook, T. H. (1994). Memory self-report in Alzheimer's disease and in age-associated memory impairment. *Journal of Geriatric Psychiatry and Neurology, 7*, 58–65.

Gervais, R. O., Green, P., Allen, L. M., III, & Iverson, G. L. (2001). Effects of coaching on symptom validity testing in chronic pain patients presenting for disability assessments. *Journal of Forensic Neuropsychology, 2*, 1–19.

Gilbert, J. C., & Knowlton, R. G. (1983). Simple method to determine sincerity of effort during a maximal isometric test of grip strength. *American Journal of Physical Medicine, 62*, 135–144.

Goetz, C. G. (1997). Jean-Martin Charcot and Silas Weir Mitchell. *Neurology, 48*, 1128–1132.

Goetz, C. G. (2007). J.-M. Charcot and simulated neurologic disease: Attitudes and diagnostic strategies. *Neurology, 69*, 103–109.

Goldstein, L. H., Drew, C. M., Mellers, J., Mitchell-O'Malley, S., & Oakley, D. A. (2000). Dissociation, hypnotizability, coping styles and health locus of control: Characteristics of pseudoseizure patients. *Seizure, 9*, 314–322.

Graue, L. O., Berry, D. T. R., Clark, J. A., Sollman, M. J., Cardi, M., Hopkins, J., et al. (2007). Identification of feigned mental retardation using the new generation of malingering detection instruments: Preliminary findings. *The Clinical Neuropsychologist, 21*, 929–942.

Green, P., Lees-Haley, P. R., & Allen, L. M., III. (2002). The word memory test and the validity of neuropsychological test scores. *Journal of Forensic Neuropsychology, 2*, 97–124.

Green, P., Rohling, M. L., Lees-Haley, P. R., & Allen, L. M., III. (2001). Effort has a greater effect on test scores than severe brain injury in compensation claimants. *Brain Injury, 15*, 1045–1060.

Greiffenstein, M., Baker, W. J., Gola, T., Donders, J., & Miller, L. (2002). The fake-bad scale in atypical and severe closed head injury litigants. *Journal of Clinical Psychology, 58*, 1591–1600.

Greiffenstein, M. F. (2007). Motor, sensory, and perceptual-motor pseudoabnormalities. In G. Larrabee (Ed.), *Assessment of malingered neuropsychological deficits* (pp. 100–130). New York: Oxford University Press.

Greiffenstein, M. F., & Baker, W. J. (2006). Miller was (mostly) right: Head injury severity inversely related to simulation. *Legal and Criminological Psychology, 11*, 131–143.

Greiffenstein, M. F., & Baker, W. J. (2008). Validity testing in dually diagnosed PTSD and mild closed head injury. *The Clinical Neuropsychologist, 22*, 565–582.

Greiffenstein, M. F., Baker, W. J., & Gola, T. (1994). Validation of malingered amnesia measures with a large clinical sample. *Psychological Assessment, 6*(3), 218–224.

Greiffenstein, M. F., Baker, W., & Gola, T. (1996a). Comparison of multiple scoring methods for Rey's malingered amnesia measures. *Archives of Clinical Neuropsychology, 4*, 283–293.

Greiffenstein, M. F., Baker, W. J., & Gola, T. (1996b). Motor dysfunction profiles in traumatic brain injury and postconcussion syndrome. *Journal of the International Neuropsychology Society, 2*, 477–485.

Greiffenstein, M. F., Fox, D., & Lees-Haley, P. R., (2007). The MMPI-2 fake-bad scale in detection of noncredible brain injury claims. In K. B. Boone (Ed.), *Assessment of feigned cognitive impairment: A neuropsychological perspective* (pp. 210–235). New York: Guilford Press.

Greiffenstein, M. F., Gola, T., & Baker, W. J. (1995). MMPI-2 validity scales versus domain specific measures in detection of factitious traumatic brain injury. *Clinical Neuropsychologist, 9*, 230–240.

Greve, K. W., Bianchini, K. J., & Ameduri, C. J. (2003). Use of a forced-choice test of tactile discrimination in the evaluation of functional sensory loss: A report of 3 cases. *Archives of Physical Medicine and Rehabilitation, 84*, 1233–1236.

Greve, K., Bianchini, K., Mathias, C. W., Houston, R. J., & Crouch, J. A. (2003). Detecting malingered performance on the Wechsler Adult Intelligence Scale: Validation of Mittenberg's approach in traumatic brain injury. *Archives of Clinical Neuropsychology, 18*, 245–260.

Greve, K. W., Bianchini, K. J., & Roberson, T. (2007). The booklet category test and malingering in traumatic brain injury: Classification accuracy in known groups. *The Clinical Neuropsychologist, 21*, 318–337.

Greve, K. W., Love, J. M., Heinly, M. T., Doane, B. M., Uribe, E., Joffe, C. L., et al. (2005). Detection of feigned tactile sensory loss using a forced-choice test of tactile discrimination and other measures of tactile sensation. *Journal of Occupational and Environmental Medicine, 47*, 718–727.

Haaland, K. Y., Harrington, D. L., & Yeo, R. (1987). The effects of task complexity on motor performance in left and right CVA patients. *Neuropsychologia, 25*, 783–794.

Haaland, K. Y., Temkin, N., Randall, G., & Dikmen, S. (1994). *Recovery of simple motor skills after head injury. Journal of Clinical and Experimental Neuropsychology, 16*, 448–456.

Haggerty, K. A., Frazier, T. W., Busch, R. M., & Naugle, R. I. (2007). Relationships among Victoria Symptom Validity Test indices and personality assessment inventory validity scales in a large clinical sample. *Clinical Neuropsychologist, 21*, 917–928.

Hanlon, R. E., Mayfield, M. W., & Heilbronner, R. L. (2005). Murder in Chicago: Insanity and tragedy. In R. L. Heilbronner (Ed.), *Forensic neuropsychology casebook* (pp. 268). New York: Guilford Press.

Harrison, A. G., Edwards, M. J., & Parker, K. C. H. (2007). Identifying students faking ADHD: Preliminary findings and strategies for detection. *Archives of Clinical Neuropsychology, 22*, 577–590.

Hilsabeck, R. C., Thompson, M. D., Irby, J. W., Adams, R. L., Scott, J. G., & Gouvier, W. D. (2003). Partial cross-validation of the Wechsler memory scale-revised (WMS-R) general memory–attention/concentration malingering index in a nonlitigating sample. *Archives of Clinical Neuropsychology, 18*, 71–79.

Hoge, C. W., McGurk, D., Thomas, J. L., Cox, A. L., Engel, C. C., & Castro, C. A. (2008). Mild traumatic brain injury in US soldiers returning from Iraq. *New England Journal of Medicine, 358*, 453–463.

Iverson, G. L., Lange, R. T., Green, P., & Franzen, M. D. (2002). Detecting exaggeration and malingering with the trail making test. *Clinical Neuropsychologist, 16*, 398–406.

Iverson, G. L., & Slick, D. J. (2001). Base rates of the WMS-R malingering index following traumatic brain injury. *American Journal of Forensic Psychology, 19*, 5–14.

Iverson, G. L., & Tulsky, D. S. (2003). Detecting malingering on the WAIS-III: Unusual digit span performance patterns in the normal population and in clinical groups. *Archives of Clinical Neuropsychology, 18*, 1–9.

Joint Service Committee on Military Justice. (2008). *Manual for courts-martial United States (2008 Edition)*. Author.

Kennedy, C. (2008). Spotlight on ethics. The case of the amnestic petty officer. *The Navy Psychologist, 1*, 10.

Korgeski, G. P., & Leon, G. R. (1983). Correlates of self reported and objectively determined exposure to Agent Orange. *American Journal of Psychiatry, 140*, 1443–1449.

Langeluddecke, P. M., & Lucas, S. K. (2003). Quantitative measures of memory malingering on the Wechsler Memory Scale–Third edition in mild head injury litigants. *Archives of Clinical Neuropsychology, 18*, 181–194.

Lanyon, R. I. (2001). Dimensions of self-serving misrepresentation in forensic assessment. *Journal of Personality Assessment, 76*, 169–179.

Lanyon, R. I., & Almer, E. R. (2001). Multimodal assessment of self-serving misrepresentation during personal injury evaluation. *American Journal of Forensic Psychology, 19*, 5–12.

Larrabee, G. J. (1998). Somatic malingering on the MMPI and MMPI-2 in personal injury litigants. *The Clinical Neuropsychologist, 12,* 179–188.

Larrabee, G. J. (1990). Cautions in the use of neuropsychological evaluation in legal settings. *Neuropsychology, 4,* 239–247.

Larrabee, G. J. (2003a). Detection of malingering using atypical performance patterns on standard neuropsychological tests. *The Clinical Neuropsychologist, 17,* 410–425.

Larrabee, G. J. (2003b). Exaggerated pain report in litigants with malingered neurocognitive dysfunction. *Clinical Neuropsychologist, 17,* 395–401.

Larrabee, G. J. (2005a). A scientific approach to forensic psychology. In G. Larrabee (Ed.), *Forensic neuropsychology. A scientific approach* (pp. 3–28). New York: Oxford University Press.

Larrabee, G. J. (Ed.). (2005b). *Assessment of malingering.* New York: Oxford University Press.

Lezak, M. D., Howieson, D. B., Loring, D. W., Hannay, H. J., & Fischer, J. S. (2004). *Neuropsychological assessment* (4th ed.). New York: Oxford University Press.

Mathias, C. W., Greve, K. W., Bianchini, K. J., Houston, R. J., & Crouch, J. A. (2002). Detecting malingered neurocognitive dysfunction using the reliable digit span in traumatic brain injury. *Assessment, 9,* 301–308.

Maugh, T. H. (1982). The dump that wasn't there. *Science, 215*(4533), 645–646.

Millis, S. R. (2002). Warrington's Recognition Memory Test in the detection of response bias. *Journal of Forensic Neuropsychology, 2,* 147–166.

Mittenberg, W., Azrin, R., Milsaps, C., & Heilbronner, R. (1993). Identification of malingered head injury on the Wechsler Memory Scale–Revised. *Psychological Assessment, 5,* 34–40.

Mittenberg, W., Patton, C., Canyock, E. M., & Condit, D. C. (2002). Base rates of malingering and symptom exaggeration. *Journal of Clinical & Experimental Neuropsychology, 24,* 1094–1102.

Mittenberg, W., Rotholc, A., Russell, E., & Heilbronner, R. (1996). Identification of malingered head injury on the Halstead-Reitan battery. *Archives of Clinical Neuropsychology, 11*(4), 271–281.

Mittenberg, W., Theroux, S., Aguila-Puentes, G., Bianchini, K., Greve, K., & Rayls, K. (2001). Identification of malingered head injury on the Wechsler Adult Intelligence Scale—3rd edition. *The Clinical Neuropsychologist, 15,* 440-445.

Nelson, N. W., Boone, K., Dueck, A., Wagener, L., Lu, P., & Grills, C. (2003). Relationships between eight measures of suspect effort. *Clinical Neuropsychologist, 17*(2), 263–272.

Nelson, N. W., Sweet, J. J., Berry, D. T. R., Bryant, F. B., & Granacher, R. P. (2007). Response validity in forensic neuropsychology: Exploratory factor analytic evidence of distinct cognitive and psychological constructs. *Journal of the International Neuropsychological Society, 13,* 440–449.

Nelson, N. W., Sweet, J. J., & Demakis, G. J. (2006). Meta-analysis of the MMPI-2 fake-bad scale: Utility in forensic practice. *Clinical Neuropsychologist, 20,* 39–58.

Nies, K., & Sweet, J. (1994). Neuropsychological assessment and malingering: A critical review of past and present strategies. *Archives of Clinical Neuropsychology, 9,* 501–552.

Nitch, S. R., Glassmire, D. M., & Boone, K. B. (2007). Non-forced-choice measures to detect noncredible cognitive performance. In K. B. Boone (Ed.), *Assessment of feigned cognitive impairment: A neuropsychological perspective* (pp. 78–102). New York: Guilford Press.

Pope, K. S., Butcher, J. N., & Seelen, J. (2006). *The MMPI, MMPI-2 and MMPI-A in court.* Washington, DC: American Psychological Association.

Prigatano, G. P., Altman, I. M., & O'Brien, K. P. (1990). Behavioral limitations that brain-injured patients tend to underestimate. *The Clinical Neuropsychologist, 4*, 163–176.

Rees, L. M., Tombaugh, T. N., & Gansler, D. A. (1998). Five validation experiments of the Test of Memory Malingering (TOMM). *Psychological Assessment, 10*, 10–20.

Ross, S. R., Millis, S. R., Krukowski, R. A., Putnam, S. H., & Adams, K. M. (2004). Detecting incomplete effort on the MMPI-2: An examination of the fake-bad scale in mild head injury. *Journal of Clinical and Experimental Neuropsychology, 26*, 115–125.

Schachter, D. (2001). The seven sins of memory. In D. Schacter (Ed.), *The seven sins of memory. How the mind remembers and forgets*. New York: Houghton Mifflin.

Sinnett, E. R., & Holen, M. C. (2001). Possible artifacts in memory assessment with the Wechsler Memory Scale-III. *Psychological Reports, 88*, 869–870.

Slick, D. J., Sherman, E. M. S., & Iverson, G. L. (1999). Diagnostic criteria for malingered neurocognitive dysfunction: Proposed standards for clinical practice and research. *Clinical Neuropsychologist, 13*, 545–561.

Spreen, O., & Strauss, E. (2006). *A compendium of neuropsychological tests. Administration, norms, and commentary* (3rd ed.). New York: Oxford University Press.

Staudenmayer, H., & Phillips, S. (2007). MMPI-2 validity, clinical and content scales, and the fake bad scale for personal injury litigants claiming idiopathic environmental intolerance. *Journal of Psychosomatic Research, 62*, 61–72.

Sweeney, J. E. (1999). Raw, demographically altered, and composite Halstead-Reitan battery data in the evaluation of adult victims of nonimpact acceleration forces in motor vehicle accidents. *Applied Neuropsychology, 6*, 79–85.

Sweet, J. (1999). *Forensic neuropsychology*. Lisse, NL: Swets & Zeitlinger.

Taylor, L. A., Kreutzer, J. S., & West, D. D. (2003). Evaluation of malingering cut-off scores for the Rey 15-item test: A brain injury case study series. *Brain Injury, 17*, 295–308.

Tombaugh, T. N. (1995). *Tests of memory malingering (TOMM)*. Toronto, ON: Multi-Health Systems.

Tombaugh, T. N. (2003). Test of Memory Malingering (TOMM) in forensic psychology. *Journal of Forensic Neuropsychology, 2*, 69–96.

Tombaugh, T. N., White, R. F., Cyrus, P., Krengel, M., & Rose, F. (1997). Validation of the Test for Memory Malingering (TOMM) with cognitively intact and neurologically impaired subjects. *Archives of Clinical Neuropsychology, 12*, 418–430.

Vagnini, V. L., Sollman, M. J., Berry, D. T. R., Granacher, R. P., Clark, J. A., Burton, R., et al. (2006). Known-groups cross-validation of the letter memory test in a compensation-seeking mixed neurologic sample. *The Clinical Neuropsychologist, 20*, 289.

van Gorp, W. G., Humphrey, L. A., Kalechstein, A. L., Brumm, V. L., McMullen, W. J., Stoddard, M. A., et al. (1999). How well do standard clinical neuropsychological tests identify malingering? A preliminary analysis. *Journal of Clinical and Experimental Neuropsychology, 21*, 245–250.

Wygant, D. B., Sellbom, M., Ben-Porath, Y. S., Stafford, K. P., Freeman, D. B., & Heilbronner, R. L. (2007). The relation between symptom validity testing and MMPI-2 scores as a function of forensic evaluation context. *Archives of Clinical Neuropsychology, 22*, 489–500.

Wynkoop, T. F., Frederick, R. I., & Hoy, M. (2006). Improving the clinical utility of the SIRS cognitive items: Preliminary reliability, validity, and normative data in pretrial and clinical samples. *Archives of Clinical Neuropsychology, 21*, 651–656.

Blast Injury and Traumatic Brain Injury

5

LOUIS M. FRENCH, JACK SPECTOR,
WILLIAM STIERS, AND ROBERT L. KANE

INTRODUCTION

Due to the current conflicts in Iraq and Afghanistan, Defense and Veterans Brain Injury Center sites have seen 9,286 service members with traumatic brain injury (TBI) (January 1, 2003–January 31, 2009), with the largest number of those seen at Landstuhl Regional Medical Center and transferred to Walter Reed Army Medical Center (WRAMC). Overall, of those medically evacuated from Iraq or Afghanistan, 25% have suffered injuries to the head or neck (Xydakis, Fravell, Nasser, & Casler, 2005).

In addition to those numbers, military efforts at screening the larger group (nonmedically evacuated) of deployed service members for mild TBI (mTBI) during deployment suggest that as many as 10–20% may have suffered a concussion during their deployment (Traumatic Brain Injury Task Force, 2008). Terrio et al. (2009) reported a 22.9% positive rate of mTBI in a brigade combat team evaluated as they returned to the United States. Further, those with TBI were significantly more likely to report postinjury and postdeployment somatic and/or neuropsychiatric symptoms than those without this injury history. These relatively high numbers are related to a number of factors, including better reporting, a strong effort by the military to increase awareness, and efforts to increase overall survival in the field through advanced protective equipment and a sophisticated system of emergency medical care.

Historically much of the focus in military-related brain injuries has been on penetrating brain injury (e.g., Carey, Sacco, & Merkler, 1982), usually through a bullet (often high velocity) or shrapnel (often low velocity). However, TBI due to closed head injury is a greater concern at present, especially through explosions or blasts. Much of this focus is due to the enemy's choice of weapons in the current conflict. Murray et al. (2005) found that 78% of injuries seen in one combat field setting were due to explosions. This number is consistent with other reports on mechanism of injury in U.S. troops in Iraq in which 80% of the casualties (wounded and killed) were due to blast ("Iraq Index," 2008). The mechanism of injury for 87.9% of the service members with traumatic limb amputation was some form of explosive device (Stansbury et al., 2008). One recent study (Hoge et al., 2008) reported that in those sustaining TBI with loss of consciousness, blast was involved in 79%. These numbers for blast-induced TBI are also consistent with internal data from the Defense and Veterans Brain Injury Center.

TBI DEFINITION AND SEVERITY

TBI is described as penetrating or closed. A penetrating brain injury occurs when a foreign object or bone penetrates the dural lining surrounding the brain. In a military setting, this is most commonly a metallic fragment or a bullet. It can, however, involve bone from the skull or the penetration of other foreign bodies. In closed TBI, there is no such penetration, but forces acting on the head cause some damage to the brain. While there is some variability in the definitions of TBI, most accepted definitions possess common elements. The current definition (Department of Defense Memo from S. Ward Casscells, October 1, 2007) in the Department of Defense (DoD) (and accepted by the U.S. Department of Veterans Affairs) defines TBI as a traumatically induced structural injury and/or physiological disruption of brain function as a result of an external force that is indicated by new onset or worsening of at least one of the following clinical signs, immediately following the event:

1. Any period of loss of or a decreased level of consciousness
2. Any loss of memory for events immediately before or after the injury
3. Any alteration in mental state at the time of the injury (e.g., confusion, disorientation, slowed thinking)

4. Neurological deficits (e.g., weakness, balance disturbance, praxis, paresis/plegia, change in vision, other sensory alterations, aphasia) that may or may not be transient
5. Intracranial abnormalities (e.g., contusions, diffuse axonal injury, hemorrhages, aneurysms)

These external forces include the head being struck by an object, the head striking an object, the brain undergoing an acceleration/deceleration movement without direct external trauma to the head, a foreign body penetrating the brain, forces generated from events such as a blast or explosion, or other forces yet to be defined.

In TBI, injuries can be categorized as mild, moderate, or severe based on associations between early indicators of injury severity and long-term (greater than 6 months) outcomes. Injuries are usually categorized by the Glasgow Coma Scale (Teasdale & Jennett, 1974), length of post-traumatic amnesia (PTA), and/or length of unconsciousness (Table 5.1). The World Health Organization Collaborating Centre Task Force and the Centers for Disease Control each define mTBIs in similar terms, as marked by brief loss of consciousness and/or by transient alterations in consciousness following central nervous system insult.

Leaving for the moment the question as to whether blast injuries should be treated as a unique entity, or are better grouped with brain injuries of similar severities regardless of mechanism, the majority of blast-related head injuries sustained in combat meet the diagnostic criteria set forth by the American College of Rehabilitation Medicine with respect

Table 5.1

U.S. DEPARTMENT OF DEFENSE TRAUMATIC BRAIN INJURY SEVERITY CLASSIFICATION SYSTEM

CLASSIFICATION	DURATION OF UNCONSCIOUSNESS	ALTERATION OF CONSCIOUSNESS (AOC)	POSTTRAUMATIC AMNESIA
Mild	<30 minutes	≤24 hours	<24 hours
Moderate	30 min–24 hours	If AOC >24 hours then severity based on other criteria	1–7 days
Severe	>24 hours		>7 days

Source: Assistant Secretary of Defense for Health Affairs Memorandum, March 23, 2007.

to mTBI. As summarized in McCrea (2008), the American College of Rehabilitation Medicine criteria (and consistent with DoD criteria) note that "a patient with mild traumatic brain injury is a person who has had a traumatically induced physiological disruption of brain function, as manifested by at least one of the following: any period of loss of consciousness, and loss of memory for events immediately before or after the accident, any alteration of mental state at the time of the accident, and/or focal neurological deficits that may or may not be transient, so long as the severity of the injury does not exceed (1) loss of consciousness for more than 30 minutes, (2) after 30 minutes, a Glasgow Coma Scale score of 13–15, and (3) a period of post-traumatic amnesia not to exceed 24 hours."

Overall, however, even in the well-studied area of TBI, there is some inconsistency in these severity categories. For example, some authors have categorized persons as having "mild" injuries based on PTA less than 24 hours (Tucker & Hanlon, 1998), while other studies categorized "mild" injuries as having PTA less than 10 minutes (Sunderland, Harris, & Gleave, 1984). Some studies categorized persons as having "severe" (McDonald & Saunders, 2005) or "very severe" (Sunderland et al., 1984) injuries based on PTA of greater than 24 hours, while other studies categorized persons as having "severe" injuries based on PTA greater than 28 days (Bond & Godfrey, 1997). Thus, in some studies, persons with "moderate" injuries had significantly greater indications of injury (more similar to other categorizations of "severe" injuries), while in other studies persons with "moderate" injuries had significantly less indications of injury (more similar to other categorizations of "mild" injuries). This lack of consensus about what constitutes a "moderate" injury complicates understanding of the effects of such injuries.

PATHOPHYSIOLOGY AND OUTCOME IN TBI

In brain injury, it is important to consider both microscopic and macroscopic elements. With regard to microscopic elements, the recent Institute of Medicine (2009) report on TBI describes brain damage following TBI as resulting from both the initial physical trauma as well as the subsequent pathophysiology that occurs in response. The pathophysiology of TBI can be considered in four phases:

1. Phase 1 involves the rupture of cellular and vascular membranes, release of intracellular contents, and impaired cerebral blood flow.

2. Phase 2 involves necrotic and apoptotic cell death. Necrotic cell death is rapid and involves membrane failure, loss of homeostasis, and breakdown of the cytoskeleton. Apoptotic cell death is less rapid and involves DNA breakage, chromosome compaction, and cytoplasmic disintegration. Cell death occurs because of the release of excitatory neurotransmitters such as glutamate, the increase in intracellular calcium, the generation of free radicals, and inflammation. Increase in glutamate results in overstimulation of ion channels, with prolonged depolarization and increases in intracellular calcium, which leads to cytoskeletal damage, free-radical generation, and cell injury and death. Inflammatory responses in the brain, although partially neuroprotective, also include significant neurotoxic properties. In addition, neurons depend on astrocytes for their survival, and the loss of astrocytes contributes to neuronal death.

3. Phase 3 involves hypoxia, hypotension, increased intracranial pressure, and metabolic imbalance that contribute to cell injury. Hypoxia and hypotension occur in one third of patients with TBI, despite aggressive medical management including endotracheal intubation, and are independently predictive of death. These are related to damage to blood vessels as well as autoregulatory failure. Increased intracranial pressure is a consequence of brain swelling following disruption of the blood–brain barrier and has a significant effect on the brain because of the restrictions imposed by the skull. Metabolic imbalance occurs when neuronal overexcitation is not adequately compensated for by increased cerebral blood flow.

4. Phase 4 involves recovery, including wound-healing processes such as phagocytic removal of cellular debris, glial scar formation, and adaptive changes in neural networks (cell repair, modification of existing pathways, and formation of new pathways).

Earlier work regarding the mechanism of injury associated with mTBI invoked the concept of axonal shearing, that is that biomechanical forces affecting the differentially dense brain in an acceleration–deceleration injury stretched axons beyond the point of survival, in more severe cases producing an observable pattern of diffuse white matter changes resembling shear-strain. However, this model of axonal injury in mTBI was based upon observations in much more severely injured adults, or in laboratory models involving a much more contrived set of injury parameters. Work by Povlishock and others, summarized in Iverson, Lange, Gaetz, and Zasler (2006), suggests that instead of biomechanical strain the more appropriate model is one of biochemical stress. This model describes a complex interaction between cellular and vascular factors in response to injury, characterized by time-limited changes in ionic balance, energy metabolism, axonal transport, cerebral blood flow, and neurotransmission, which temporarily impair the efficiency of neuronal function. These changes permanently injure very few brain cells, perhaps no more than would be accounted for by natural processes alone. That is, that axons are unexpectedly resistant to permanent injury following stretch, shear, or strain and that necrosis of brain cells following mTBI likely does not significantly exceed expected cell deaths due to normal attrition or pruning (apoptosis) in the absence of mild head injury.

In any case, this more measured approach to the pathophysiology of mTBI appears to better account for the consistent finding that the vast majority of individuals who suffer mTBIs recover in full, usually within weeks of their injuries. Significant changes in neuropsychological functioning are typically not observed in athletes 1–2 weeks following their head injuries (Bleiberg et al., 2004), or in mixed trauma samples 1–3 months following injury (Belanger, Curtiss, Demery, Lebowitz, & Vanderploeg, 2005). Prospective studies of such at-risk populations such as professional, collegiate, and high school football players, professional and amateur hockey players, Army paratroopers, and military academy intramural boxers suggest that what memory and attention-related inefficiencies are observed immediately after injury quickly dissipate, such that subjects have returned to their physical, cognitive, and emotional baseline within 5–10 days after injury (Belanger & Vanderploeg, 2005). While there is evidence of slowed recovery in those who have suffered multiple concussions, and special vulnerability when a second concussion occurs in the 7- to 10-day period following one concussion (Guskiewicz et al., 2003), there is no evidence of cumulative effects of two concussions (Iverson, Brooks, Lovell, & Collins, 2006).

The results of the meta-analysis published by the World Health Organization Collaborating Centre Task Force on mTBI suggest that the vast majority of adults have good outcome following uncomplicated mTBI, typically recovering in full within months. A more recent meta-analytic study by Schretlen and Shapiro (2003) also revealed that what decrements in neuropsychological functioning are apparent after mTBI resolve in 1–3 months.

For the purposes of discussion of mTBI sustained in military operations, it would seem that the literature on mTBI in athletes would be particularly germane. The similarity between mTBI in athletes and soldiers are readily apparent: most of the subjects are young, male, well-conditioned, helmeted, and not naive or unprepared as to the possibility of being injured in the course of their normal activities. In professional and collegiate football players, hockey players, and similar samples, what subtle neurocognitive aftereffects that are seen in the hours to days after mild head injuries largely resolve within the week (McCrea, 2008). In such samples, symptoms may persist for as long as a month, but even these symptoms are likely to resolve, with less than 3% of subjects suffering an uncomplicated mild head injury still symptomatic at 30 days (McCrea, 2008). In general, however, there is value in using both self-reported symptoms and some more formal measure of cognition in determining return to ready status (McCrea et al., 2005).

However, one of the potential differences between athlete and military samples is the potential contingencies affecting return to the full range of activities. There is evidence from the sports concussion literature that athletes will underreport the frequency and severity of their injuries and minimize or deny the presence of aftereffects so that they might return to play sooner rather than later. While this dynamic is also frequently observed in military settings, there are obvious benefits with respect to personal safety and secondary gain for service members to report more severe or persisting symptoms than may be the case. It is reasonable to expect that such contingencies for overreporting symptoms or disability might increase in concert with the dangers associated with the combat environment and be mediated by a number of other factors to include the expectations of the service member that additional injuries might occur; the previous duration of exposure to the combat environment; the degree of commitment to fellow soldiers, command, and mission; and other factors affecting compensation or gain. There may be other important differences between these two groups. It is uncommon for an mTBI on the playing field to be accompanied by significant physical trauma, and the emotional context in which these injuries may occur differ dramatically (for a comprehensive discussion of combat posttraumatic stress, see chapter 12).

If military head injuries associated with blast mirror their civilian mTBI counterparts in most other meaningful ways, then it follows that the issues related to motivation and malingering that affect the rate and course of civilian mTBI would also have bearing on the frequency and course of military blast-related trauma (for a comprehensive discussion of the detection of poor effort and malingering in the military population, see chapter 4). In fact, it could be argued that the contingencies associated with military blast injury (relief from combat and escape from dangerous conditions) might even contribute to an increased rate of poor effort or malingering relative to civilian head injury.

Available data suggest a 30% or higher rate of insufficient test-taking effort or malingering invalidating test performance in civilians with persistent mTBI complaints (Bianchini, Mathias, & Greve, 2001). However, for any of a number of practical and political reasons, there is scant information with regard to the rates of insufficient effort or malingering in global war on terror veterans claiming cognitive deficits due to mTBI/concussion. Belanger and associates (2009) report having to exclude 31 of 137 (22%) consecutively examined subjects at the Tampa Veterans Affairs Medical Center and other Department of Veterans Affairs (VA) Medical Centers belonging to the Mid-Atlantic Mental Illness Research, Education, and Clinical Center because of evidence of poor effort or malingering on standardized symptom validity tests or on other embedded measures sensitive to test-taking effort. In this study there were no differences in test performance between those with blast and nonblast mechanisms of injury. In another recent study (Vasterling et al., 2006), a small number of deployed subjects were excluded due to insufficient test-taking effort, but it is uncertain what percentage of subjects claiming combat-related head injuries this actually represented. One sample at Walter Reed undergoing neuropsychological evaluation showed a 26% failure rate on symptom validity measures (Conrad et al., 2008).

Despite compelling evidence from prospective and meta-analytic studies confirming that mild head injuries resolve rapidly and completely, absent other psychological or incentive-related factors, there persists a clinical lore that as many as 15% of patients exhibit persistent or severe sequelae of their mild head injuries. This group has been identified as the "miserable minority" by Ruff, Camenzuli, and Mueller (1996), and, more recently, the Centers for Disease Control's Web site (http://www.cdc.gov/ncipc/factsheets/tbi.htm) notes that "an estimated 15% of persons who sustain a mild brain injury continue to experience negative consequences 1 year after injury" (Guerrero, Thurman, & Sniezek, 2000). However, when the original studies are reviewed, objective data are employed, and factors related to psychopathology and incentive accounted for, uncomplicated mild head injuries recover quickly and completely, and rarely result in prolonged (or delayed) neurobehavioral consequences requiring prolonged neurobehavioral intervention.

In short, it is well accepted that severe TBI results in significant cognitive and functional impairments. The 2009 Institute of Medicine study found no association between mTBI and objectively measured neurocognitive deficits or between mTBI and long-term adverse social functioning (unemployment, diminished social relationships, and decrease in the ability to live independently; Institute of Medicine, 2009). However, there was an association between moderate to severe TBI and neurocognitive deficits and between moderate to severe TBI and long-term adverse social-function outcomes (particularly unemployment and diminished social relationships).

BLAST EFFECTS

Blast injuries may be defined as primary, secondary, tertiary, or quaternary (DePalma, Burris, Champion, & Hodgson, 2005). Primary blast effects refer to injuries caused by the blast wave itself, wherein a highly pressurized force may cause injury as a result of barotraumas, or via the displacement of organs or tissues accelerating at different rates. Secondary trauma refers to the displacement of a person (e.g., being thrown through the air as a result of a blast wave) and tertiary, to the effects of an object striking a person as a result of blast. Further (quaternary) effects can be caused by toxic gases or burns. Nelson et al. (2006) reported on a series of consecutive close proximity blast injury patients presenting to a forward deployed surgical unit in Iraq. They concluded that blast injury of this type caused severe anatomic and physiological damage. They found that sustained hypotension or the presence of two or more other injury factors (e.g., multiple long bone fractures, penetrating head injury, etc.) were significantly associated with increased mortality.

The mechanisms and effects of blunt-force TBI have been extensively studied. However, blast-induced neurotrauma (BINT) is a newer area of research. BINT can develop without the usual acceleration–deceleration forces that are seen with blunt-force trauma to the head. In fact, animal models have shown that BINT can occur when the head is protected from a blast wave but the body is exposed. This appears to occur when the blast wave compresses the abdomen and chest, transferring the kinetic energy of the blast wave through the large blood vessels in the abdomen and chest to the brain (Cernak et al., 1999a, 2001b; Bhattacharjee, 2008). However, these hypothesized hydraulic effects of blast waves on the brain are complicated by the fact that blast injuries usually involve polytrauma, which may include bradycardia, hypotension, apnea, blood loss, and pulmonary impairment, all of which can result in cerebral hypoxia (Cernak et al., 1996a, 1996b; Ohnishi et al., 2001). These additional complications may be the cause of findings that patients with brain injuries acquired in explosions can develop sudden, unexpected brain edema and cerebral vasospasm despite continuous monitoring (Armonda et al., 2006), as well as changes in blood chemistry and electrolyte imbalance, and neuroendocrine alterations (Cernak et al., 1999a, 1999b, 1999c, 2000).

In animal models, BINT has been also associated with cerebral edema, metabolic imbalance, ion imbalance, cytoskeletal damage, and breakdown of cell membranes. There are no data indicating that the microscopic-level processes are different for TBI versus BINT. However, in TBI the most common locations for microscopic damage are in the gray matter–white matter junctions (particularly in the frontal and temporal areas), internal capsule, deep gray matter, upper brainstem, and corpus callosum (Taber, Warden, & Hurley, 2006), while in BINT (in animal models) the most common locations for microscopic damage are in the hippocampus (Cernak et al., 2001b) and the temporal cortex, cingulate gyrus, pirifom cortex, and dentate gyrus (Saljo, Bao, Haglid, & Hansson, 2000).

It is also not clear that the macroscopic effects are the same. The most common macroscopic effects of TBI are contusions of the gray matter of the inferior, lateral, and anterior aspects of the frontal and temporal lobes, and subdural hemorrhage of the frontal and parietal convexities (Taber et al., 2006). Contusion and subdural hemorrhage are not common in BINT. However, regardless of these differences, there is no evidence that the neuropsychological effects of TBI versus BINT are different (Belanger, Kretzmer, Yoash-Gantz, Pickett, & Tupler, 2009). In addition, Sayer et al. (2008) describe the characteristics and rehabilitation outcomes of those injured through blast and treated in the VA polytrauma system. In their sample, in which 56% of those injured had blast-related injuries, the pattern of injuries was unique among those with injuries due to blasts. Soft tissue, eye, oral and maxillofacial, otologic, penetrating brain injuries, symptoms of posttraumatic stress disorder, and auditory impairments were more common in blast-injured patients than in those with war injuries of other etiologies. Despite the differences, the mechanism of the injury did not predict functional outcomes.

Despite suggestive animal evidence, the evidence supporting brain injury due to a primary blast effect is very limited in humans (Taber et al., 2006; Warden et al., 2009). However, as noted above, it may be that physical injuries (extracranial) or emotional effects are greater in those injured in blast. In a group of terror attack victims, those injured in blast had more body regions injured than did gunshot wound patients and had greater numbers of injuries overall (Peleg, Aharonson-Daniel, Michael, & Shapira, 2003). In a sample at WRAMC, those with TBI related to blast were significantly more likely to have had a skull fracture, seizure, and lower limb amputation than those not injured in a blast. They also were more likely to have symptoms of acute stress than their counterparts who had TBI through other mechanisms (Warden, 2006).

POLYTRAUMA AND COMORBID CONDITIONS

The high rates of injuries in those hurt by blast have important rehabilitation and outcome implications for those with blast-related TBI. Further, TBI may affect recovery from other injuries, or the other injuries and their associated factors may retard the natural recovery of even mTBI. Minimal extracranial injuries and low pain predict better outcomes for return to work after mTBI (Stulemeijer et al., 2006). Polytrauma patients, even without brain injury, have high rates of neurobehavioral symptoms (Frenisy et al., 2006), including memory difficulties, irritability, mood swings, suspiciousness, amotivation, and guilt. In a group of individuals who sustained mTBI and who also suffered extracranial injuries, at 6 months after injury, 44% of the patients with additional injuries were still in treatment, compared to just 14% of the patients with isolated mTBI. They also had resumed work less frequently and reported more limitations in physical functioning. Those individuals that required continued treatment also reported significantly more severe postconcussive symptoms (Stulemeijer et al., 2006).

Sensory difficulties in this population are one area of concern. In a group of polytrauma patients injured by blast (Goodrich, Kirby, Cockerham, Ingalla, & Lew, 2007) the rates of visual impairment were more than double compared to other causes of polytrauma (i.e., motor vehicle accidents, gunshot and/or shrapnel, assault, falls, or anoxia). Overall, the rate of visual impairment in blast-related injury was 52% compared with 20% for all other sources of injury. The authors concluded that comprehensive eye examinations should be routinely administered in polytrauma, particularly when the mechanism of injury involves a blast. In a group of patients at WRAMC (Weichel, Colyer, Bautista, Bower, & French, 2009) with TBI and combat ocular trauma (COT), explosive fragmentary munitions accounted for 79% of TBI-associated COT. Severe TBI was more frequently associated with COT than milder

TBI. Overall, TBI occurred in two-thirds of all COT and ocular trauma was a common finding in all TBI cases. Lew, Jerger, Guillory, and Henry (2007a) examined a group in a VA polytrauma center. In those injured by blast since the beginning of the war in Iraq, 62% complained of hearing loss and 38% reported tinnitus, sensorineural loss being the most prevalent type of hearing loss. This compares to rates of 44% with hearing loss and 18% with tinnitus in those injured through some mechanism other than blast.

Other conditions that sometimes follow TBI may have implications for overall recovery. In the trauma population, these conditions may also occur independently of the brain injury. In general, it is important to assess and treat these conditions regardless of etiology, as longer-term prognosis may be improved. Such conditions may include sleep disturbance (for a comprehensive discussion of sleep issues in operational environments, see chapter 11), pain including headache (Nampiaparampil, 2008), vestibular dysfunction (Hoffer, Balough, & Gottshall, 2007), sexual dysfunction (Kreuter, Dahllof, Gudjonsson, Sullivan, & Siosteen, 1998), or cognitive dysfunction. It is our clinical experience in the general trauma population at WRAMC that it is not uncommon for patients with mTBI or no history of TBI to be agitated and require restraint and/or psychotropic medication in the first 24 hours following extubation. This delirium may be a response to pain, medication, or other factors. Cognitive performance may remain impaired secondary to narcotics and other factors for weeks after the injury. Further, polytrauma patients, especially those with traumatic amputations, often due to blast, may have a history of extensive blood loss and hypovolemic shock, which may have additional negative effects on their cognitive or behavioral functioning.

Psychological conditions are also of concern. In the injured, psychological health affects recovery from physical trauma (Holbrook, Anderson, Sieber, Browner, & Hoyt, 1999; Michaels et al., 2000). In those acutely hospitalized for physical trauma, general recovery is enhanced through the identification and treatment of comorbid psychological conditions including posttraumatic stress disorder (PTSD), a condition of significant concern in the combat-exposed population overall (chapter 12). Hoge et al. (2004) reported that in their survey of combat troops returning from Iraq or Afghanistan that the rates of PTSD ranged from 12.2–12.9%, with higher rates of PTSD associated with greater combat exposure and wounds of any type. In those service members seriously enough injured to be medically evacuated and hospitalized at WRAMC, slightly over 4% had PTSD and/or depression at 1 month. These rates increased to 12.2% for PTSD and 8.9% for depression at 4 months. At 7 months these rates were 12% and 9.3%, respectively. High levels of self-reported physical problems at 1 month postinjury were significantly predictive of PTSD and depression at 7 months post-injury. Significant to the initial identification and management of these individuals, the majority of soldiers with PTSD or depression at 7 months postinjury did not have those conditions at 1 month (Grieger et al., 2006). Koren, Norman, Cohen, Berman, and Klein (2005), in a study looking at rates of PTSD in injured Israeli war veterans, found that bodily injury is a risk factor for PTSD, with odds of developing PTSD following traumatic injury about eight times higher than a group that suffered significant emotional trauma without associated physical trauma.

The relationship between PTSD and TBI is a complex one. In one study of active duty service members who sustained moderate TBI with associated neurogenic amnesia for the event, none of them developed full criteria for PTSD (Warden & Labbate, 2005). In a similar civilian study (Gil, Caspi, Ben-Ari, Koren, & Klein, 2005) of 120 individuals who sustained TBIs, those who reported amnesia for the event were unlikely to develop PTSD. Glaesser, Neuner, Lutgehetmann, Schmidt, and Elbert (2004) examined 46 patients who had experienced a TBI due to an accident. In that study, 27% of patients with TBI, with associated briefer loss of consciousness (LOC), developed PTSD, whereas only 3% who were unconscious for more than 12 hours developed the disorder. Furthermore, intrusive memories were more common in participants who had not been unconscious. They were also more likely to reexperience symptoms, experience marked psychological distress, and evidence physiological reactivity to antecedent stimuli associated with the traumatic event. These studies suggest that more severe TBI, with associated extended loss of consciousness, is protective against the development of PTSD, presumably through an individual's inability to "reexperience" the traumatic experience. Further, more recent data from the Vietnam Head Injury Study, composed predominantly of penetrating head injuries, demonstrated that those veterans with damage to the amygdala and ventromedial prefrontal cortex had reduced likelihood of developing PTSD (Koenigs et al., 2008). However, other studies (e.g., Bryant & Harvey, 1995, 1998; Harvey & Bryant, 2001) suggest that TBI and PTSD can co-occur, even in more severe TBI, through a range of possible mechanisms.

Gaylord et al. (2008) examined the relationship between PTSD and TBI in a group of 76 burned military service members. In that study the incidence rate of PTSD was 32% and mTBI was 41%. Eighteen percent screened positive for both conditions. The incidence of PTSD among burned service members diagnosed with mTBI was significant when compared with those not diagnosed with mTBI. Hoge et al. (2008) examined mTBI and psychiatric symptoms in U.S. Soldiers following a year-long Iraq deployment. In a survey administered about 3 months after their return, service members answered questions about their deployment including whether they sustained mTBI while deployed or suffered other injuries. Mild TBI was strongly associated with PTSD. Forty-four percent of the soldiers who had injuries with loss of consciousness met criteria for PTSD, while only about 16% who endorsed sustaining other types of injuries and about 9% who reported having no other injuries met criteria for PTSD. The soldiers who reported mTBI were more likely to report poor general health, more days of missed work, increased medical visits, and a higher number of somatic and post-concussive symptoms than did Soldiers with other injuries. Depression was also more frequent in those with loss of consciousness than in those with other injuries. However, after adjustment for PTSD and depression, the occurrence of mTBI was no longer significantly associated with these physical concerns (except for headache in the loss of consciousness group). While the study showed some limitations, including a failure to account for the effect of retrospective self-report bias, where individuals with health problems may more often recall negative past events than persons without health problems, the study reinforced the well-known association between the physical and psychological and how they interact to affect functioning.

Besides PTSD, other psychological conditions related to TBI can have an effect on outcome. These include substance abuse. Direct injuries to the frontal and temporal lobes may predispose one to substance abuse through diminished self-control and increased impulsivity. The relation of TBI to substance abuse may also be more indirect. Corrigan and Cole (2008) suggest that one of the key features of PTSD, hyperarousal, may lead to substance abuse problems. In this model, hyperarousal leads to hypervigilance, which in turn leads to avoidance of things and feelings associated with high levels of distress. This in turn leads to emotional numbing and social detachments. All of these factors can lead to substance abuse through attempts to self-medicate anxiety, avoid traumatic memories, or increase emotional numbing and detachment. The substance abuse in turn may contribute to poor TBI outcomes through increased involvement with the criminal justice system, increased social friction or unemployment, increased possibility of another injury while intoxicated, or diminished health conditions.

PREDEPLOYMENT COGNITIVE TESTING AND BATTLEFIELD ASSESSMENT

Freidl et al. (2007) point out that "the complexity, speed, and lethality of modern warfare means that even small mental lapses may have catastrophic consequences." These "mental lapses," whether related to TBI, fatigue, or conditions related to the battlefield environment, have operational significance. Identification and characterization of these difficulties, especially as related to TBI, have taken on increased importance.

Clinical practice guidelines for managing concussion/mTBI have been developed for settings both in-theater and outside the theater of operations (chapter 6). The guidelines are not dependent on the mechanism of injury, although the specifics of the injury may necessitate the need for particular medical interventions. From the standpoint of the neuropsychologist, the essential questions following conditions producing alterations or loss of consciousness have to do with assessing whether there has been a change in cognition, assessing the severity of cognitive change, and monitoring recovery. The nature of war-related injury also requires the neuropsychologist be aware of other physical and emotional factors that might impact cognitive functioning. While the mechanisms associated with war-related injuries producing concussion/mTBI may be varied, the clinical model for management is essentially consistent with that found in sports medicine.

To enhance the initial postinjury assessment of service members, the Defense and Veterans Brain Injury Center developed the Military Acute Concussion Evaluation (French, McCrea, & Baggett, 2008) with items based on those from the Standardized Assessment of Concussion (McCrea, Kelly, Kluge, Ackley, & Randolph, 1997). The Military Acute Concussion Evaluation supplements the Standardized Assessment of Concussion by adding questions related to type of injury and symptoms. Like the Standardized Assessment of Concussion it can be given by various trained medical personnel and is designed as an initial assessment; it is not intended to be a detailed neurocognitive examination. It offers a number of alternate forms to decrease the chance of practice effect.

A recent effort by the DoD to enhance the assessment of concussion/mTBI is the introduction of the Neurocognitive Assessment Tool (NCAT) program. This DoD program officially launched in May 2008 following a directive from Dr. S. Ward Casscells, the Assistant Secretary of Defense for Health Affairs. The directive was based on health concerns related to tactics used by enemies in Iraq and Afghanistan resulting in service members sustaining concussion and TBI and was spurred by congressional legislation. The directive specified that all deploying service members should receive a neurocognitive baseline. The memorandum also dictated that the automated neuropsychological assessment (ANAM) test system would serve as the NCAT while efforts continued to evaluate potential NCAT candidate measures. Because of the magnitude of the endeavor, the focus from Health Affairs has been on obtaining baseline evaluations. As of this writing, DoD has exceeded the 200,000 mark with respect to the number of service members tested prior to deployment. One proposed use of the NCAT is for routine postdeployment screening to capture undetected cognitive residuals following concussion. This use is not being advocated. A study is under way to evaluate using the NCAT for routine postdeployment screening. Results from other studies where ANAM tests have been used for postdeployment assessments have not supported this use of the test instrument (Ivins, Kane, & Schwab, 2009; Vasterling et al., 2006) especially in the absence of specific indications.

Information on the military and VA medical care system is described elsewhere (e.g., Butler, Holcomb, Giebner, McSwain, & Bagian, 2007; Lew et al., 2007b). In those individuals seriously injured enough to require evacuation from the theater of operations, some may require eventual transfer to hospitals in the United States. At WRAMC, where the largest number of seriously injured casualties has been treated, we have had a program of TBI screening since the beginning of the war. In general, mTBI is not a reason for evacuation to this level of care, but such an injury may co-occur in the context of significant systemic trauma or limb loss. Many of these individuals may require ongoing care for their injuries followed by a period of lengthy rehabilitation. Outpatient evaluation and ongoing management of ambulatory service members with a history of mTBI is coordinated through a specialty clinic. All patients are discussed before their appointments by a multidisciplinary TBI working group that includes staff providers from PM&R, neurology, neuropsychology, and psychiatry, as well as speech and language pathology, physical and occupational therapies, and case management. Service members are seen in the clinic by residents and staff from the various disciplines to address medical and psychiatric issues specifically related to their TBI, including management of typical issues such as headache, sleep disturbance, and irritability. This model provides for integration of the care of individuals with complex clinical presentations. It is our experience that it is important to address all symptoms, regardless of their particular etiology, to have successful outcomes.

CASE STUDIES

Note: The following case studies are intended to illustrate some common clinical conditions and concerns for individuals with blast-related TBI. While these illustrations are loosely based on cases seen at WRAMC, they represent composites of several cases and details have been altered to preserve anonymity.

Case Study 1: Staff Sergeant A

Staff Sergeant A is a married Hispanic active duty soldier who was serving in Afghanistan when he sustained a moderate TBI due to a blast and subsequent motor vehicle accident. SSG A has no memory of the incident and was told by the members of his unit that he was the restrained driver of a Humvee wearing his Kevlar and full body armor when the vehicle was hit by a rocket propelled grenade. The vehicle was thrown by the blast and hit a concrete barrier in the center of the road. He was told he was conscious at the scene and was observed to try to drive the incapacitated Humvee out of the kill zone per protocol. SSG A's last memory before the blast was checking his gear before going out on the mission. He reports this retrograde amnesia to be a period of about 2 hours. He reports PTA for a period of 3 weeks, much of which was likely medication induced. His first memory after the injury was of being at WRAMC. He recalls being informed that he was not going to be able to keep his badly damaged right leg and that they would have to amputate it.

SSG A's injuries include an above-the-knee amputation of the right lower extremity; diffuse shrapnel wounds to his face, arms, and right torso; a vertebral burst fracture; right clavicle fracture; and a TBI. A computed tomography (CT) scan of the brain revealed a right frontal contusion. SSG A completed 2 months of cognitive rehabilitation at an inpatient VA facility.

At 12 months postinjury, SSG A was endorsing difficulty with rote memorization and recall such as remembering phone numbers and birthdays he would previously have remembered without difficulty.

He reported increased irritability and some mild depression with rumination about losing his leg and poor self-esteem related to his appearance. He denied any behavioral changes and denied any difficulty controlling his temper or acting out his irritability.

SSG A reported having a strong, supportive relationship with his wife. He reported being grateful that they had not had children yet as he would not want to have been an additional burden on them during his period of rehabilitation. He expressed a sense of hope for the future and expressed an interest in starting a family as soon as they were able to leave WRAMC. SSG A was planning on getting out of the military and leading a more settled life with his wife close to extended family members. He expressed understanding that his deficits might make having additional support for them beneficial.

Neuropsychological testing was valid, as indicated by appropriate scores on symptom validity testing, and revealed mild to moderate impairment in areas of sustained attention, executive functioning involving problem solving and mental flexibility, and verbal memory. Self-report measures of emotional functioning revealed some mild mood and self-esteem difficulties that seemed consistent with his self-reported symptoms. SSG A demonstrated good awareness during the interview and testing process. Findings from the testing were deemed consistent with residual impairments related to SSG A's TBI.

SSG A was referred for group counseling routinely offered to service members who are transitioning out of the military. He was also referred for a vocational rehabilitation evaluation to determine needed services. He continued with physical therapy to maximize his mobility and use of his lower extremity prosthetic. Speech pathology worked with him on compensatory memory and organization strategies, including the use of a PDA. SSG A was also offered supportive psychotherapy to address his mild depression and his feelings about his amputation and other injuries. He declined the referral stating that he felt the support of his wife, his buddies, and his family was sufficient for him at that time.

Case Study 2: Sergeant J

Sergeant J is a divorced White male infantry NCO who was on his third deployment to Iraq. He reported being on a dismounted patrol when a firefight ensued. He was injured during the fight when an explosive device detonated. A metallic fragment entered SGT J's left orbit and fractured his mandible as it exited. SGT J reported having comprehensive memory of the events leading up to and including being injured. Because of the nature of the firefight, SGT J's men were unable to remove him from the area immediately, and he recalled being stuck in the house where they had taken cover, wondering if he was going to die there as his face bled profusely and his shattered jaw made him unable to communicate with his team. He reported patchy memory for the 10 or 15 minutes after the injury followed by 48 hours of medically induced loss of consciousness. He reported one hazy memory of his time in Landstuhl and then regaining full and continuous memory upon arrival at WRAMC 3 days after being hurt. A CT scan of his brain noted no abnormalities. Magnetic resonance imaging was not possible due to retained metallic fragments.

At 6 months postinjury, SGT J reported difficulty with memory, concentration, and maintaining focus when he was not interested in the task or subject at hand. SGT J also reported social isolation, difficulty engaging with others, and a preference for spending time alone in his room watching movies. He denied headaches, dizziness, or fatigue. SGT J had regained some very limited vision in his left eye, including the ability to differentiate light and dark and detect gross movement when he is looking directly at an object.

SGT J reported that during his two prior tours he had seen a lot of action and had lost several buddies. However, he had been married during those deployments and had the support of his wife. SGT J had been divorced shortly before deploying for his final tour and reported having thoughts of courting harm or injury in combat due to his disappointment and pain over losing his wife. He reported that during the first months at WRAMC after having been injured, when his jaw was wired shut and he was still in danger of losing his left eye, he wished he had been killed outright and had not survived to be "a freak." SGT J also reported increased irritability and having difficulty controlling impulses such as making inappropriate remarks to women about their appearance.

SGT J's neuropsychological testing showed mild to moderate deficits in areas of memory, attention, and visuospatial construction. He also showed intact abilities in areas of verbal and nonverbal reasoning, deliberate memorization, and visuospatial analysis and construction. Symptom validity testing indicated good effort, and his findings were considered to be consistent with cognitive residua of his recent injury. SGT J also endorsed symptoms associated with depression, social isolation, and passive suicidal ideation on self-report measures administered during testing.

SGT J was referred for individual psychotherapy on a weekly basis to address mood and psychological symptoms. He was also encouraged to address issues of impulsivity and disinhibition with his therapist to hone his social skills and regain a sense of confidence in his ability to interact appropriately with women.

CONCLUSION

TBI is an important concern in the military, both in peacetime and wartime. Given the demographics of the military, mostly populated by young men, there is an inherent risk for TBI. Complicating this is the additional risk associated with combat operations. In the current conflicts the explosive device has been a major cause of injury overall, and TBI in particular. Explosions can cause injury through a variety of mechanisms. It is clear that TBI can be caused by secondary, tertiary, and potentially quaternary effects of blast. Further, there are animal data and some limited human data to suggest that primary blast effect may cause brain injury. It is important to note, however, that there is no evidence to suggest that blast exposure in itself (without associated alteration of consciousness) can cause damage to the brain. That is, we have no evidence to suggest that subclinical exposure even if that occurs over an extended period of time is damaging in itself. That is, however, an area of active scientific investigation.

In assessing or treating an individual injured by blast, it is important to think in a comprehensive fashion taking into account the full range of possible consequences of that injury to include TBI, sensory impairment, pain issues, vestibular dysfunction, effort and motivation, and the emotional context in which the injury occurred. PTSD, mood changes, substance abuse, family dynamics, the disability process, and individual personality characteristics of the injured individual will all have an impact on symptom presentation, rehabilitation, and recovery. Information obtained in our clinical care of those injured through blast and in our research studies may have implications for the civilian population in the future (Rutland-Brown et al., 2007; Schwartz et al., 2008).

REFERENCES

Armonda, R. A., Bell, R. S., Vo, A. H., Ling, G., DeGraba, T. J., Crandall, B., et al. (2006). Wartime traumatic cerebral vasospasm: Recent review of combat casualties. *Neurosurgery, 59*(6), 1215–1225.

Barr, W. B. (2006). Assessing mild traumatic brain injury on the sideline. In R. Echemendia (Ed.), *Sports neuropsychology* (pp. 87–109). New York: The Guilford Press.

Barth, J. T., Alves, W. M., Ryan, T. V., Maciocchi, S. N., Rimel, R. W., Jane, J. A., et al. (1998). Mild head injury in sports: Neuropsychological sequelae and recovery of function. In H. L. Levin, H. M. Eisenberg, & A. L. Benton (Eds.), *Mild head injury* (pp. 257–275). New York: Oxford University Press.

Barth, J. T., Freeman, J. R., Broshek, D. K., & Varney, R. N. (2001). Acceleration-deceleration sport-related concussion: The gravity of it all. *Journal of Athletic Training, 36*(3), 253–256.

Belanger, H. G., Curtiss, G., Demery, J. A., Lebowitz, B. K., & Vanderploeg, R. D. (2005). Factors moderating neuropsychological outcomes following mild traumatic brain injury: A meta-analysis. *Journal of the International Neuropsychological Society, 11*(3), 215–227.

Belanger, H. G., Kretzmer, T., Yoash-Gantz, R., Pickett, T., & Tupler, L. A. (2009) Cognitive sequelae of blast-related versus other mechanisms of brain trauma. *Journal of the International Neuropsychological Society, 15*(1), 1–8.

Belanger, H. G., & Vanderploeg, R. D. (2005). The neuropsychological impact of sports-related concussion: A meta-analysis. *Journal of the International Neuropsychological Society, 11*(4), 345–357.

Bhattacharjee, Y. (2008). Neuroscience. Shell shock revisited: Solving the puzzle of blast trauma. *Science, 319*(5862), 406–408.

Bianchini, K. J., Mathias, C. W., & Greve, K. W. (2001). Symptom validity testing: A critical review. *The Clinical Neuropsychologist, 15*(1), 19–45.

Bleiberg, J., Cernich, A. N., Cameron, K., Sun, W., Peck, K., Ecklund, P. J., et al. (2004). Duration of cognitive impairment after sports concussion. *Neurosurgery, 54*(5), 1073–1078; discussion 1078–1080.

Bond F., & Godfrey, H. (1997). Conversation with traumatically brain-injured individuals: A controlled study of behavioural changes and their impact. *Brain Injury, 11*(5), 319–329.

Bryant, R. A., & Harvey, A. G. (1995). Psychological impairment following motor vehicle accidents. *Australian Journal of Public Health, 19*(2), 185–188.

Bryant, R. A., & Harvey, A. G. (1998). Traumatic memories and pseudomemories in posttraumatic stress disorder. *Applied Cognitive Psychology, 12*(1), 81–88.

Butler, F. K., Jr., Holcomb, J. B., Giebner, S. D., McSwain, N. E., & Bagian, J. (2007). Tactical combat casualty care 2007: Evolving concepts and battlefield experience. *Military Medicine, 172*(11 Suppl.), 1–19.

Carey, M. E., Sacco, W., & Merkler, J. (1982). An analysis of fatal and nonfatal head wounds incurred during combat in Vietnam by U.S. forces. *Acta Chirurgica Scandinavica Supplement, 508*, 351–356.

Cernak, I., Savic, J., Ignjatovic, D., & Jevtic, M. (1999a). Blast injury from explosive munitions. *Journal of Trauma-Injury Infection and Critical Care, 47*(1), 96–103.

Cernak, I., Savic, V., Kotur, J., Prokic, V., Veljovic, M., & Grbovic, D. (2000). Characterization of plasma magnesium concentration and oxidative stress following graded traumatic brain injury in humans. *Journal of Neurotrauma, 17*(1), 53–68.

Cernak, I., Savic, V., Lazarov, A., Joksimovic, M., & Markovic, S. (1999c). Neuroendocrine responses following graded traumatic brain injury in male adults. *Brain Injury, 13*(12), 1005–1015.

Cernak, I., Savic, J., Malicevic, Z., Zunic, G., Radosevic, P., & Ivanovic, I. (1996a). Leukotrienes in the pathogenesis of pulmonary blast injury. *Journal of Trauma-Injury Infection and Critical Care, 40*(3 Suppl.), S148–S151.

Cernak, I., Savic, J., Malicevic, Z., Zunic, G., Radosevic, P., Ivanovic, I., et al. (1996b). Involvement of the central nervous system in the general response to pulmonary blast injury. *Journal of Trauma-Injury Infection and Critical Care, 40*(3 Suppl.), S100–S104.

Cernak, I., Savic, J., Zunic, G., Pejnovic, N., Jovanikic, O., & Stepic, V. (1999b). Recognizing, scoring, and predicting blast injuries. *World Journal of Surgery, 23*(1), 44–53.

Cernak, I., Wang, Z., Jiang, J., Bian, X., & Savic, J. (2001b). Ultrastructural and functional characteristics of blast injury-induced neurotrauma. *Journal of Trauma-Injury Infection and Critical Care, 50*(4), 695–706.

Conrad, A. K., Pancholi, S. K., Bhagwat, A. A., & French, L. M. (2008). Improvement of effort in military patients undergoing neuropsychological assessment for traumatic brain injury [Abstract]. *Archives of Clinical Neuropsychology, 23*, 710.

Corrigan, J. D., & Cole, T. B. (2008). Substance use disorders and clinical management of traumatic brain injury and posttraumatic stress disorder. *Journal of the American Medical Association, 300*(6), 720–721.

DePalma, R. G., Burris, D. G., Champion, H. R., & Hodgson, M. J. (2005). Blast injuries. *New England Journal of Medicine, 352*(13), 1335–1342.

French, L. M., McCrea, M., & Baggett, M. R. (2008). The Military Acute Concussion Evaluation (MACE). *Journal of Special Operations Medicine, 8*(1), 68–77.

Frenisy, M. C., Benony, H., Chahraoui, K., Minot, D., d'Arthis, P., Pinoit, J. M., et al. (2006). Brain injured patients versus multiple trauma patients: Some neurobehavioral and psychopathological aspects. *The Journal of Trauma Injury, Infection, and Critical Care, 60*, 1018–1026.

Friedl, K. E., Grate, S. J., Proctor, S. P., Ness, J. W., Lukey, B., J., & Kane, R. L. (2007). Army research needs for automated neuropsychological tests: Monitoring soldier health and performance status. *Archives of Clinical Neuropsychology, 22*(1), S7–14.

Garvey Wilson, A. L., Lange, J. L., Brundage, J. F., & Frommelt, R. A. (2003). Behavioral, demographic and prior morbidity risk factors for accidental death among men: A case–control study of soldiers. *Preventive Medicine, 36*(1), 124–130.

Gaylord, K. M., Cooper, D. B., Mercado, J. M., Kennedy, J. E., Yoder, L. H., & Holcomb, J. B. (2008). Incidence of posttraumatic stress disorder and mild traumatic brain injury in burned service members: Preliminary report. *Journal of Trauma, 64*(2 Suppl.), S200–205; discussion S205–206.

Gil, S., Caspi, Y., Ben-Ari, I. Z., Koren, D., & Klein, E. (2005). Does memory of a traumatic event increase the risk for posttraumatic stress disorder in patients with traumatic brain injury? A prospective study. *American Journal of Psychiatry, 162*(5), 963–969.

Glaesser, J., Neuner, F., Lutgehetmann, R., Schmidt, R., & Elbert, T. (2004). Posttraumatic stress disorder in patients with traumatic brain injury. *BMC Psychiatry, 4*, 5.

Goodrich, G. L., Kirby, J., Cockerham, G., Ingalla, S. P., & Lew, H. L. (2007). Visual function in patients of a polytrauma rehabilitation center: A descriptive study. *Journal of Rehabilitation Research and Development, 44*(7), 929–936.

Grieger, T. A., Cozza, S. J., Ursano, R. J., Hoge, C., Martinez, P. E., Engel, C. C., et al. (2006). Posttraumatic stress disorder and depression in battle-injured soldiers. *American Journal of Psychiatry, 163*(10), 1777–1783; quiz 1860.

Guerrero, J. L., Thurman, D. J., & Sniezek, J. E. (2000). Emergency department visits associated with traumatic brain injury: United States, 1995–1996. *Brain Injury, 14,* 181–186.

Guskiewicz, K. M., McCrea, M., Marshall, S. W., Cantu, R. C., Randolph, C., Barr, W., et al. (2003). Cumulative effects associated with recurrent concussion in collegiate football players: The NCAA Concussion Study. *Journal of the American Medical Association, 290*(19), 2549–2555.

Harvey, A. G., & Bryant, R. A. (2001). Reconstructing trauma memories: A prospective study of "amnesic" trauma survivors. *Journal of Traumatic Stress, 14*(2), 277–282.

Hoffer, M. E., Balough, B. J., & Gottshall, K. R. (2007). Posttraumatic balance disorders. *International Tinnitus Journal, 13*(1), 69–72.

Hoge, C. W., Castro, C. A., Messer, S. C., McGurk, D., Cotting, D. I., & Koffman, R. L. (2004). Combat duty in Iraq and Afghanistan, mental health problems, and barriers to care. *New England Journal of Medicine, 351*(1), 13–22.

Hoge, C. W., McGurk, D., Thomas, J. L., Cox, A. L., Engel, C. C., & Castro, C. A. (2008). Mild traumatic brain injury in U.S. soldiers returning from Iraq. *New England Journal of Medicine, 358*(5), 525–527.

Holbrook, T. L., Anderson, J. P., Sieber, W. J., Browner, D., & Hoyt, D. B. (1999). Outcome after major trauma: 12-month and 18-month follow-up results from the Trauma Recovery Project. *Journal of Trauma, 46*(5), 765–771; discussion 771–783.

Institute of Medicine. (2009). *Gulf war and health, volume 7: Long-term consequences of traumatic brain injury.* Washington, DC: The National Academies Press.

Iverson, G. L., Brooks, B. L., Lovell, M. R., & Collins, M. W. (2006). No cumulative effects for one or two previous concussion. *British Journal of Sports Medicine, 40*(1), 72–75.

Iverson, G. L., Lange, R. T., Gaetz, M., & Zasler, N. D. (2006). Mild TBI. In N. D. Zasler, D. I. Katz, & R. D. Zafonte (Eds.), *Brain injury medicine: Principles and practice* (pp. 333–371). New York: Demos Medical.

Ivins, B. J., Kane, R., & Schwab, K. A. (2009). Performance on the automated neuropsychological assessment metrics in a nonclinical sample of soldiers screened from mild TBI after returning from Iraq and Afghanistan: A descriptive analysis. *Journal of Head Trauma Rehabilitation, 24*(1), 24–31.

Koenigs, M., Huey, E. D., Raymont, V., Cheon, B., Solomon, J., Wassermann, E. M., et al. (2008). Focal brain damage protects against posttraumatic stress disorder in combat veterans. *Nature Neuroscience, 11*(2), 232–237.

Koren, D., Norman, D., Cohen, A., Berman, J., & Klein, E. M. (2005). Increased PTSD risk with combat-related injury: A matched comparison study of injured and uninjured soldiers experiencing the same combat events. *American Journal of Psychiatry, 162*(2), 276–282.

Kreuter, M., Dahllof, A. G., Gudjonsson, G., Sullivan, M., & Siosteen, A. (1998). Sexual adjustment and its predictors after traumatic brain injury. *Brain Injury, 12*(5), 349–368.

Lew, H. L., Jerger, J. F., Guillory, S. B., & Henry, J. A. (2007a). Auditory dysfunction in traumatic brain injury. *Journal of Rehabilitation Research and Development, 44*(7), 921–928.

Lew, H. L., Poole, J. H., Vanderploeg, R. D., Goodrich, G. L., Dekelboum, S., Guillory, S. B., et al. (2007b). Program development and defining characteristics of returning military in a VA Polytrauma Network Site. *Journal of Rehabilitation Research and Development, 44*(7), 1027–1034.

Lovell, M. R., & Collins, M. W. (1998). Neuropsychological assessment of the college football player. *Journal of Head Trauma Rehabilitation, 13*(2), 9–26.

McCrea, M. (2008). *Mild traumatic brain injury and postconcussion syndrome. The new evidence base for diagnosis and treatment.* New York: Oxford University Press.

McCrea, M., Barr, W. B., Guskiewicz, K., Randolph, C., Marshall, S. W., Cantu, R., et al. (2005). Standard regression-based methods for measuring recovery after sport-related concussion. *Journal of the International Neuropsychological Society, 11*(1), 58–69.

McCrea, M., Kelly, J. P., Kluge, J., Ackley, B., & Randolph, C. (1997). Standardized assessment of concussion in football players. *Neurology, 48*(3), 586–588.

McDonald, S., & Saunders, J. (2005). Differential impairment in recognition of emotion across different media in people with severe traumatic brain injury. *Journal of the International Neuropsychological Society, 11*, 392–399.

Michaels, A. J., Michaels, C. E., Smith, J. S., Moon, C. H., Peterson, C., & Long, W. B. (2000). Outcome from injury: General health, work status, and satisfaction 12 months after trauma. *Journal of Trauma, 48*(5), 841–848; discussion 848–850.

Murray, C. K., Reynolds, J. C., Schroeder, J. M., Harrison, M. B., Evans, O. M., & Hospenthal, D. R. (2005). Spectrum of care provided at an echelon II Medical Unit during Operation Iraqi Freedom. *Military Medicine, 170*(6), 516–520.

Nampiaparampil, D. E. (2008). Prevalence of chronic pain after traumatic brain injury: A systematic review. *Journal of the American Medical Association, 300*(6), 711–719.

Nelson, T. J., Wall, D. B., Stedje-Larsen, E. T., Clark, R. T., Chambers, L. W., & Bohman, H. R. (2006). Predictors of mortality in close proximity blast injuries during Operation Iraqi Freedom. *Journal of the American College of Surgeons, 202*(3), 418–422.

Ohnishi, M., Kirkman, E., Guy, R. J., & Watkins, P. E. (2001). Reflex nature of the cardiorespiratory response to primary thoracic blast injury in the anaesthetised rat. *Experimental Physiology, 86*(3), 357–364.

Peleg, K., Aharonson-Daniel, L., Michael, M., & Shapira, S. C. (2003). Patterns of injury in hospitalized terrorist victims. *American Journal of Emergency Medicine, 21*(4), 258–262.

Ruff, R. M., Camenzuli, L., & Mueller, J. (1996). Miserable minority: Emotional risk factors that influence the outcome of a mild traumatic brain injury. *Brain Injury, 10*(8), 551–565.

Rutland-Brown, W., Langlois, J. A., Nicaj, L., Thomas, R. G., Jr., Wilt, S. A., & Bazarian, J. J. (2007). Traumatic brain injuries after mass-casualty incidents: Lessons from the 11 September 2001 World Trade Center attacks. *Prehospital and Disaster Medicine, 22*(3), 157–164.

Saljo, A., Bao, F., Haglid, K. G., & Hansson, H. A. (2000). Blast exposure causes redistribution of phosphorylated neurofilament subunits in neurons of the adult rat brain. *Journal of Neurotrauma, 17*(8), 719–726.

Sayer, N. A., Chiros, C. E., Sigford, B., Scott, S., Clothier, B., Pickett, T., et al. (2008). Characteristics and rehabilitation outcomes among patients with blast and other injuries sustained during the Global War on Terror. *Archives of Physical Medicine and Rehabilitation, 89*(1), 163–170.

Schretlen, D. J., & Shapiro, A. M. (2003). A quantitative review of the effects of traumatic brain injury on cognitive functioning. *International Review of Psychiatry, 15*(4), 341–349.

Schwartz, I., Tuchner, M., Tsenter, J., Shochina, M., Shoshan, Y., Katz-Leurer, M., et al. (2008). Cognitive and functional outcomes of terror victims who suffered from traumatic brain injury. *Brain Injury*, *22*(3), 255–263.

Scott, B. A., Fletcher, J. R., Pulliam, M. W., & Harris, R. D. (1986). The Beirut terrorist bombing. *Neurosurgery*, *18*(1), 107–110.

Stansbury, L. G., Lalliss, S. J., Branstetter, J. G., Bagg, M. R., & Holcomb, J. B. (2008). Amputations in U.S. military personnel in the current conflicts in Afghanistan and Iraq. *Journal of Orthopaedic Trauma*, *22*(1), 43–46.

Stulemeijer, M., van der Werf, S. P., Jacobs, B., Biert, J., van Vugt, A. B., Brauer, J. M., et al. (2006). Impact of additional extracranial injuries on outcome after mild traumatic brain injury. *Journal of Neurotrauma*, *23*(10), 1561–1569.

Sunderland, A., Harris, J., & Gleave, J. (1984). Memory failures in everyday life following severe head injury. *Journal of Clinical Neuropsychology*, *6*(2), 127–142.

Taber, K., Warden, D., & Hurley, R. (2006) Blast-related traumatic brain injury: What is known? *Journal of Neuropsychiatry and Clinical Neuroscience*, *18*, 2.

Teasdale, G., & Jennett, B. (1974). Assessment of coma and impaired consciousness. A practical scale. *Lancet*, *2*(7872), 81–84.

Terrio, H., Brenner, L. A., Ivins, B. J., Cho, J. M., Helmick, K., Schwab, K., et al. (2009). Traumatic brain injury screening: Preliminary findings in a US Army Brigade Combat Team. *Journal of Head Trauma and Rehabilitation*, *24*(1), 14–23.

Traumatic Brain Injury Task Force. (2008). *Army TBI Taskforce Report*. Retrieved February 28, 2008, from http://www.armymedicine.army.mil/prr/tbitfr.html

Tucker, F. M., & Hanlon, R. E. (1998). Effects of mild traumatic brain injury on narrative discourse production. *Brain Injury*, *12*(9), 783–792.

Vasterling, J. J., Proctor, S. P., Amoroso, P., Kane, R., Heeren, T., & White, R. F. (2006). Neuropsychological outcomes of army personnel following deployment to the Iraq War. *Journal of the American Medical Association*, *296*(5), 519–529.

Warden, D. (2006). Military TBI during Iraq and Afghanistan wars. *Journal of Head Trauma and Rehabilitation*, *21*, 398–402.

Warden, D., & Labbate, L. A. (2005). Posttraumatic stress disorder and other anxiety disorders. In J. Silver, T. McAllister, & S. Yudofsky (Eds.), *Textbook of traumatic brain injury* (pp. 231–244). Arlington, VA: American Psychiatric Publishing.

Warden, D., French, L. M., Shupenko, L., Fargus, J., Riedy, G., Erickson, M. E., et al. (2009). Case report of a soldier with primary blast brain injury. *Neuroimage*, *47*, 152–153.

Weichel, E. D., Colyer, M. H., Bautista, C., Bower, K. S., & French, L. M. (2009). Traumatic brain injury associated with combat ocular trauma. *Journal of Head Trauma and Rehabilitation*, *24*(1), 41–50.

Xydakis, M. S., Fravell, M. D., Nasser, K. E., & Casler, J. D.(2005). Analysis of battlefield head and neck injuries in Iraq and Afghanistan. *Otolaryngological Head and Neck Surgery*, *133*, 497–504.

6

Acute Battlefield Assessment of Concussion/Mild TBI and Return-to-Duty Evaluations

JEFFREY T. BARTH, WILLIAM C. ISLER,
KATHERINE M. HELMICK, ILAINA M. WINGLER,
AND MICHAEL S. JAFFEE

INTRODUCTION

The War on Terror has brought to the forefront a new era in conflict and an urgent need for innovative ways to manage war-related injuries. The "invisible wounds of war," including sequelae from concussion or mild traumatic brain injury (mTBI), as well as acute stress disorder (ASD) and other mental health conditions, have challenged clinicians in the areas of detection, assessment, and treatment paradigms while remaining mission-focused in the care of our wounded warriors. The RAND report (Tanielian et al., 2008) suggested that as many as 320,000 veterans from Operation Iraqi Freedom (OIF) and Operation Enduring Freedom (OEF) may have experienced a TBI. It is difficult to gauge incidence and prevalence of concussion/mTBI in previous conflicts based on the lack of system-wide efforts to promote early detection of concussion sustained in an austere environment. For the current conflict, the Defense and Veterans Brain Injury Center (DVBIC) serves as the office of responsibility for TBI surveillance. The DVBIC estimates that 10–20% of those returning home after combat exposure may have sustained a concussion/mTBI, which is now considered the signature injury in the OEF/OIF conflict (Department of Defense Task Force on Mental Health, 2007; Independent Review Group, 2007). Moderate and severe

TBI resulting from penetrating and closed head injuries are identified quickly due to obvious symptomology and cared for immediately, while concussion/mTBI can go unrecognized. This is particularly likely when a service member also receives other more obvious injuries that require immediate life-saving interventions (e.g., burns or amputations). Due to enemy tactics and the frequency of operational missions, many service members are at risk for sustaining more than one concussion during a deployment. In addition, since many service members will experience several deployments, the opportunity for exposures to multiple blasts has greatly increased.

The purpose of this chapter is to focus on concussion/mTBI rates in the military, present the history and mechanisms of mTBI as described in the clinical and sports medicine literature, discuss how blast injury may or may not be different from concussion, and make recommendations for conducting in-theater assessments (as per the DVBIC Guidelines for the Acute Management of Concussion/mTBI in the Deployed Setting), short-term interventions, and return-to-duty evaluations. The terms *concussion* and *mTBI* will be used interchangeably in this chapter, because both terms are defined by trauma or acceleration of the head and brain causing a brief alteration or loss of consciousness, with possible retrograde and/or posttraumatic amnesia, and in most cases, rapid recovery. The Department of Defense (DoD) has defined TBI as a traumatically induced structural injury or physiological disruption of brain function as a result of external force to the head and new or worsening of at least one of the following clinical signs:

1. Loss of consciousness or decreased consciousness
2. Loss of memory immediately before or after injury
3. Alteration in mental status (confused, disoriented, slow thinking)
4. Neurological deficits
5. Intracranial lesion

The DoD definition is consistent with other nationally and internationally recognized definitions of TBI offered by the Centers for Disease Control and Prevention, the World Health Organization, the American Academy of Neurology, and the American Congress of Rehabilitation Medicine.

Although a small minority of concussed patients have longer and perhaps less complete recoveries, it is important to provide education and convey positive expectations to the patient (while not overlooking or minimizing important symptoms) to maximize recovery. For this reason, it is suggested that the term "concussion" be utilized when working with military personnel who have sustained such an injury, to minimize the social bias or perception of permanent disability often associated with the terms *TBI* or *brain damage.*

DEPARTMENT OF DEFENSE TBI SURVEILLANCE

The DoD initiated a TBI surveillance system in October 2007 after the DVBIC conducted system-wide TBI surveillance throughout their network. Beginning in 2003, the DVBIC started to collect surveillance data on wounded OIF/OEF service members receiving treatment at the Walter Reed Army Medical Center. In 2005, the DVBIC expanded their surveillance efforts for the remaining affiliated sites that included military treatment facilities, polytrauma Veterans Administration centers, and civilian sites. There are 25 variables collected in this surveillance system to include patient demographics, mechanism of injury, severity of brain injury, where wounded and others. The cases that are in this database represent clinician-confirmed diagnosis of TBI as reported by International Classification of Diseases (ICD-9) codes. Recently there was collaborative work between numerous federal agencies to standardize the ICD-9 codes used to identify TBI patients.

There are various TBI-related statistics that have been recently released to include rates of those who have come back after deployment and been screened using a brief questionnaire and those who are thought to have sustained a concussion and continue to report symptoms that require clinical evaluation. Rates of continued symptoms after concussion from a combat-exposed army brigade team were 7.5% (Terrio, 2009). Screening also occurs during the postdeployment health reassessment phase. As of September 2008, 15,808 Air Force personnel had taken the new version of the postdeployment health reassessment and 1.8% had reported an event along with symptoms that would indicate a possible concussion. These data indicate that the problem of TBI symptoms, although very real in Air Force deployers, is reported much less frequently than in the Army, where there is potentially much greater exposure to improvised explosive device blast injuries.

The Army conducted the Mental Health Advisory Team V (MHAT-V, 2008) well-being survey of 2,279 soldiers serving in OIF and OEF during October and November of 2007. Of the OIF soldiers surveyed, 19.7%

reported having an injury that involved "being dazed, confused or seeing stars" but only about one third reported actually being medically evaluated for a concussion. Whereas 11.2% of the Soldiers who met the criteria for a positive mTBI screen (an injury to the head coupled with being dazed and confused, not remembering the injury, or losing consciousness), only 5.1% (less than half) reported being evaluated for concussion. This estimate is likely less than the actual number, because those identified with a potentially more serious TBI or those with other injuries are typically evacuated and would not have been available for the survey.

The true incidence and prevalence of TBI is unknown, which is similar in context to the civilian sector's inability to capture all mTBI cases. There are multiple reasons for this including some who do not seek care, resolution of symptoms within a short time period, medical providers attending to other needs, and lack of proper assessment tools. The DoD is continuing to use the best science to guide the process of improving efforts to identify, document, and treat service members who experience TBI.

HISTORY AND MECHANISMS OF MILD TBI

TBI assessment, care, and research began to gain momentum in the mid-1970s with the development of the Glasgow Coma Scale (Teasdale & Jennett, 1974), which aided clinicians with the gross assessment of severity in head injury. The 1990s were deemed the "Decade of the Brain" by the U.S. Congress, and more money went into research and development for tools to help clinicians care for this very complex and clinically challenging population. In 1995, the first evidence-based guidelines for the care of severe TBI were released by the Brain Trauma Foundation, paving the way for standardized care across the United States. The guidelines for severe TBI are continually revised to incorporate more current research findings (Brain Trauma Foundation, 2007).

Moderate and severe TBI were the focus of most research in these early years because mild head injury and concussion were not thought to result in identifiable neurologic trauma or poor outcomes. A series of papers by Gronwall and Wrightson from 1974 to 1980 began to suggest that concussions could result in some neurocognitive compromise, slow recovery, and delayed return to work (Gronwall & Wrightson, 1974; Gronwall & Wrightson, 1980; Wrightson & Gronwall, 1980). In 1981, researchers at the University of Virginia Department of Neurological Surgery published results from their large epidemiological study, which demonstrated that the majority of TBIs in their sample were mild in severity, most related to motor vehicle crashes (MVCs), and that more than 30% had not returned to work 3 months postinjury (Rimel, Giordani, Barth, Boll, & Jane, 1981). Barth et al. (1983) discovered neurocognitive deficits in a substantial number of these patients. Subsequent research on different populations using matched controls found rapid (from hours to 3 months) recovery curves for the vast majority of mTBI patients, with a small percentage of outliers demonstrating lengthier recoveries (Dikmen, McLean, & Temkin, 1986; Levin, Mattis, Ruff, & Eisenberg, 1987; McLean, Temkin, Dikmen, & Wyler, 1983).

At about the same time, animal research initiated at the University of Pennsylvania, utilizing an acceleration–deceleration model in primates, found that mild head injury could cause twisting, stretching, or tearing of axonal fibers in the brain, called shear-strain or axonal injury (Gennarelli, Adams, & Graham, 1981). These findings supported the notion that mild head injury or concussion could result in identifiable neuropathology, at a histological level, which would not necessarily be evident on neuroimaging. Later histological, glucose utilization work by Hovda and colleagues, employing brain fluid percussion models with rodents (Hovda et al., 1990), identified a physiological cascade of potassium expulsion and calcium influx, which is associated with all levels of TBI severity.

CONCUSSION IN SPORTS

Even with the growing clinical and animal research evidence of significant consequences in a small minority of mild head injury patients, most human studies were limited by their inability to fully control for variables such as preexisting conditions (i.e., previous head injuries, substance abuse, etc.) and premorbid neurocognitive functioning. To address this issue, University of Virginia researchers initiated studies to assess neurocognitive functions pre- and postconcussion in young healthy athletes (Barth et al., 1989). They chose football players because their concussions were often of the acceleration–deceleration variety, the mechanism of which is similar to MVCs, which are a main focus of clinical mTBI research (Barth, Freeman, Broshek, & Varney, 2001). By getting brief, baseline measures of neurocognitive functioning and testing again at intervals on the sidelines and several days post concussion, the football player served as his own control and any decrement or decline in functioning from baseline could presumably be attributed to the effects of the head trauma. This 1985–1989 study of 2,350 football players from 10 universities captured almost 200 mild concussions and revealed mild neurocognitive deficits (attention and rapid problem solving) within 24 hours of injury, with a 5- to 10-day recovery curve.

The Sports as a Laboratory Assessment Model, using a baseline evaluation methodology to study concussion, has offered further evidence for neurocognitive consequences even in a controlled laboratory setting using young, bright, healthy, motivated athletes with very mild injuries (Barth, Broshek, & Freeman, 2006). This study, as well as many follow-up investigations by other sports concussion researchers, has informed our clinical research and sensitized clinicians to the potential for even greater neurocognitive impairment in situations where the injuries (acceleration and impact) are more severe and the populations have more risk factors (e.g., older, poor health, substance abuse, depression, anxiety/stress, sleep disturbance, pain, previous head injury, etc.) leading to slower and less complete recovery.

An unanticipated benefit of these sports concussion studies was the application of recovery curve data to the return-to-play decision making on the athletics fields. Until baseline and sideline neurocognitive evaluations were available, such return-to-play decisions were based solely upon self-report of neurological symptoms if the player was identified as having a concussion, and even then, some players returned to play. As Collins et al. (2002) point out in their study of high school athletes, the cumulative effects of multiple concussions can result in more severe trauma and a weakening of the threshold for incurring another concussion. In addition, Cantu describes the potential catastrophic consequences of returning to play before full recovery from even a mild concussion in his papers on second impact syndrome (SIS) (Cantu, 1998; Cantu & Mueller, 2000; Cantu & Voy, 1995). In rare cases, some young (<24 years of age) athletes who suffer two mild concussions within 4 or 5 days of each other can suffer severe brain damage or death based upon increase in intracranial pressure and related dysfunction of vascular autoregulation. This is not a common phenomenon, as Maroon and colleagues suggest that there were 26 SIS-related deaths from 1984 to 2000 (Maroon et al., 2000). It is, however, avoidable with careful and conservative evaluation of potential concussions and waiting for all symptoms to resolve prior to return to play. Consensus opinion and most return-to-play guidelines, such as those developed by Cantu (1986) and the American Academy of Neurology (1997), support waiting to return to play and practice until there has been a complete resolution of all symptoms (neurologic, neurocognitive, and emotional), even upon physical exertion testing and when there has been sufficient rest (several days to several weeks, depending on the severity and length of symptom experience).

CONCUSSION IN THE MILITARY ENVIRONMENT

Blast Injury: A Unique TBI?

Improvised explosive device blast injuries are the most common cause of war trauma in Iraq and Afghanistan (Okie, 2005; DVBIC, 2009). Forty percent of all blast injuries in the Iraq and Afghanistan conflict involve TBI (DVBIC, 2009). TBIs are more common in the OIF/OEF conflicts than in past wars because more service members survive blasts due to advanced body armor and better medical treatment. Unfortunately many mild and moderate head injuries may be overlooked in the presence of blast-related polytrauma such as amputations and burns (Martin, Lu, Helmick, French, & Warden, 2008).

The mechanism of these blast injuries is multifaceted and includes the following:

1. *Primary blast dynamics:* Wave-induced changes in atmospheric pressure (overpressure wave followed by underpressure or vacuum)
2. *Secondary blast dynamics:* Objects placed in motion by the blast hitting the service member (blunt and penetrating injuries)
3. *Tertiary blast dynamics:* Service members being put in motion by the blast, and hitting other objects
4. *Quaternary blast dynamics:* Other injuries from blast-related burns, toxic fumes, crush trauma, hypertension, etc.

The similarities between blast injury, sports concussion, and MVC mechanisms lie in the blunt trauma and acceleration–deceleration actions noted in the secondary and tertiary dynamics. In addition, blast injury may take place while the service member is in a motor vehicle, adding to the similarities to MVCs. Blast injury, however, is considerably more complex based upon the primary and quaternary blast dynamics. The atmospheric overpressure and underpressure have their most serious effects on hollow organs such as the lungs (pulmonary barotrauma), but may also affect the vascular system and other tissues by possibly creating microbubbles or acute gas emboli (AGE) that can occlude blood vessels of the brain (DePalma, Burris, Champion, & Hodgson, 2005; Taber, Warden, & Hurley, 2006). Other consequences of blast injury can include neuropathology associated with more-severe head trauma such as edema, hemorrhage, diffuse axonal injury, electroencephalogram abnormalities, the release of oxygen-free radicals, and overstimulation of the immune system and toxic levels of nitric oxide (Taber et al., 2006). For more information on blast injuries, see chapter 5.

DEFENSE AND VETERANS BRAIN-INJURY CENTER CLINICAL PRACTICE GUIDELINES

Responding to an identified need to provide clinical guidance to both theaters of war, the DVBIC convened 32 military and civilian subject matter experts in November 2006 to build a literature-based concussion/mTBI clinical practice guideline (CPG). Because of the dearth of literature on blast concussions, this CPG is considered to be evidence informed, but not evidence based. Nevertheless, this CPG was quickly adopted for use in theater, emphasizing four main topic areas: (a) an operational definition of concussion/mTBI, (b) assessment of concussion/mTBI, (c) management of concussion/mTBI, and (d) operational issues that could impact the ability to conduct evaluations and provide treatment in theater.

In August 2008, the DVBIC was asked to reconvene 33 military and civilian subject matter experts who gleaned information from published literature and from the Joint Theater Trauma System, Special Forces/Ranger, and Multi-National Corps-I algorithms to update the theater guidelines. Taking operational conditions into consideration, they updated the original guidelines to produce a medic/corpsman and provider-specific concussion CPG for use in deployed settings, focusing on three areas: (a) diagnosis and evaluation, (b) treatment, and (c) follow-up and return to duty.

In-Theater Assessment Issues

Operational Considerations

Acute assessment of TBI symptoms is very important on the battlefield. All services have recognized for decades that assessing and treating people near the action, and closer to the time of injury, is helpful because it leads to better outcomes and increased rates of return to duty. Unit cohesion is an important component of military life, lengthy separations can reduce expectations of return to duty, and service members may become less likely to recover and return to full duty. Keeping people out of action or evacuating them so they can recover must be balanced with the negative expectations about not returning to duty that may arise when they are removed from their units.

Providing medical care in a combat environment poses a unique set of challenges for the clinician. Patient care must often be balanced within the context of mission goals and safety for the patient and others. There are times when a service member should be evacuated to a higher level of care, and this decision should be determined in collaboration between the medical staff and the commander/commanding officer. In addition, potential psychological costs should be considered before removing a service member from duty. The services have long recognized this, but in the case of mTBI there may be some time frames to examine. For example, most studies of sports-related concussions find rapid recovery curves that average less than 7 days. Most symptoms of mTBI resolve without any formal treatment, and most service members should remain in place for several days of rest to allow this brief time of healing to occur. Yet too quickly returning a neurocognitively impaired service member back to full unrestricted duty could potentially put the individual, his unit, and the operational mission in jeopardy. In this situation, an ounce of prevention is truly worth a pound of cure.

Screening/Initial Assessment

The 2008 DVBIC Consensus Conference on the Acute Management of Concussion/Mild Traumatic Brain Injury in the Deployed Setting developed three separate algorithms for in-theater assessment and treatment. The algorithms include Combat Medic/Corpsman Concussion Triage, Initial Management of Concussion in Deployed Setting, and the Comprehensive Concussion Evaluation.

Level I: Combat Medic/Corpsman Concussion Triage Algorithm

The Combat Medic/Corpsman Concussion Triage Algorithm (Figure 6.1) is used before the patient reaches a hospital setting or when no medical officer is in the immediate area. It includes the administration of the

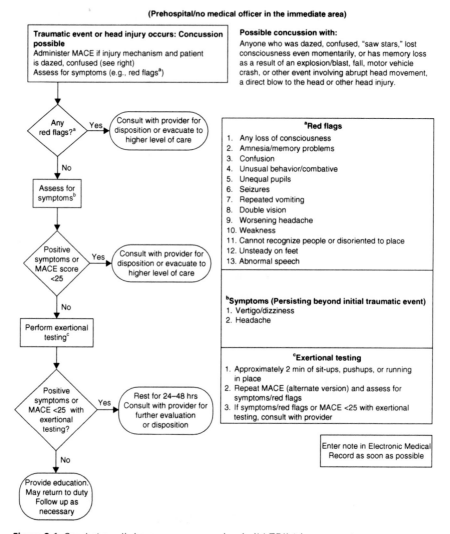

Figure 6.1 Combat medic/corpsman concussion (mild TBI) triage.

Military Acute Concussion Evaluation (MACE; described later; DVBIC, 2006) and the assessment of high-risk symptoms called red flags. Red flag symptoms require immediate attention and include seizures, repeated vomiting, and worsening headache. When the patient is evaluated and red flags are present and/or the cognitive score on the MACE is less than 25, then an immediate consult with a medical provider for disposition or evacuation to a higher level of care should take place. Careful consideration for return-to-duty determinations should be made for any service member with symptoms reported on the MACE or a cognitive score on the MACE less than 25. If no symptoms are present and the MACE score is 25 or greater, then exertional testing (described later) should be conducted. If symptoms are detected following the exertional testing, then observation for 24–48 hours and a consult with a medical provider is warranted. If no symptoms are evident, then clinical judgment should be used in the decision to conduct education and provide return-to-duty instructions along with the possibility for follow-up.

Level II: Initial Management of Concussion in the Deployed Setting

The second algorithm (Figure 6.2) was developed for the initial management of concussion and specifically designed for locations that would likely have physicians available to provide detailed assessment and management of the concussed patient. This algorithm has many of the same initial assessment recommendations as the Combat Medic algorithm, including the assessment of red flags, the MACE cut off of less than 25, and exertional testing to elicit dormant symptoms. This algorithm includes an additional evaluation by a primary care asset along with the suggestion for a reevaluation every 3 days if symptoms persist. If the symptoms have not resolved at the end of 7 days, then the patient should be screened for depression and ASD symptoms, with a referral to a combat stress provider (mental/behavioral health) if needed. This last step addresses the significant impact of psychological symptoms in the management of postconcussive symptoms. If combat stress symptom management is indicated, then the patient should be followed for at least 14 days or even longer if symptoms are improving. If symptoms are not improving or the patient appears to be getting worse, then evacuation to the next level of care should be considered.

Level III: Comprehensive Concussion Algorithm

The third algorithm (Figure 6.3) was developed for the highest level of care found in a battlefield environment where additional resources are available that are not typically present at other treatment facilities. These additional resources allow for a much more comprehensive assessment than might be possible at other locations. This assessment might include

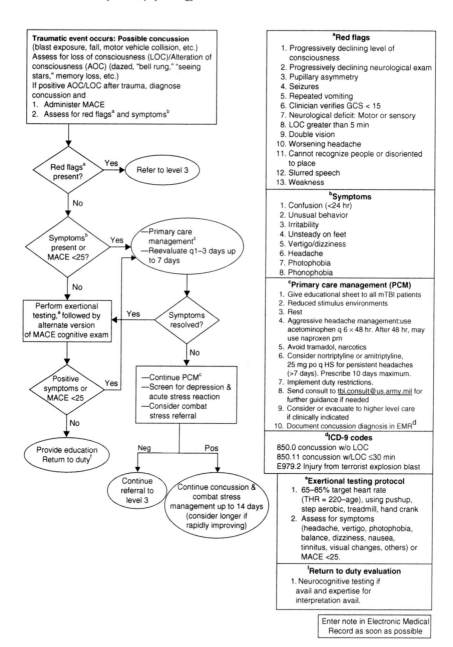

Figure 6.2 Initial management of concussion in a deployed setting.

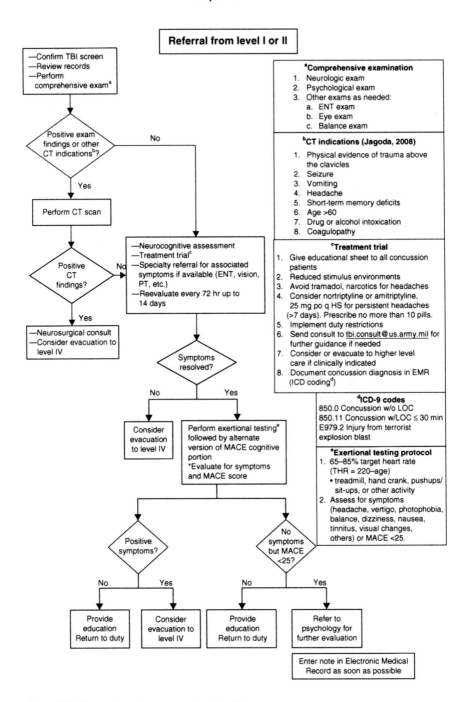

Figure 6.3 Comprehensive concussion algorithm.

more advanced technology such as computed tomography scan or other brain imaging and laboratory facilities, as well as more traditional medical specialty evaluations such as neurology, neurosurgery, ophthalmology, optometry, psychology, physical therapy, and occupational therapy. After confirming the TBI diagnosis, reviewing the records, and conducting a comprehensive neurological exam, the patient might receive brain imaging if positive indicators (confusion, unusual behavior, irritability, balance difficulties, vertigo/dizziness, headache, diplopia, and/or photosensitivity) are present. Positive brain-imaging results likely indicate the need for neurosurgical consultation with possible evacuation to a higher level of treatment.

Continuing symptoms with negative neuroimaging suggest the need for a neurocognitive assessment. This neurocognitive assessment is not fully described within the algorithm but will initially comprise the Automated Neuropsychological Assessment Metric (ANAM; Reeves, Kane, Elsmore, Winter, & Bleiberg, 2002; see below). DoD has required all the services to begin using this instrument, and over 200,000 service members have already had predeployment testing conducted with this measure. When individuals manifest cognitive problems on the ANAM, more traditional pen and paper neuropsychological screening is needed because the ANAM has not yet been validated for use in the military concussion population.

One significant improvement in this algorithm over the last iteration is the addition of the section entitled Treatment Trial. This section has eight suggestions:

1. Give an educational sheet to all concussion patients. A two-page concussion information sheet (see Appendix A at the end of this chapter) has been provided by the DVBIC, which is brief yet comprehensive enough to provide good quality information to both the concussed patient and their command on the diagnosis, symptoms, management, and recovery.
2. Reduce stimulus environments.
3. Avoid certain headache medications, such as tramadol and narcotics, which could increase the risk of rebound headaches.
4. Consider nortriptyline or amitriptyline for persistent headaches greater than 7 days.
5. Implement duty restrictions.
6. Send consult to tbi.consult@us.army.mil.
7. Consider evacuation to higher level care if clinically indicated.

8. Document concussion diagnosis in electronic medical record including the appropriate ICD coding (potential ICD-9 codes are listed in the algorithm).

The algorithm suggests that reevaluations take place every 72 hours for up to 14 days. Although other theater guidelines dictate how long patients can remain in theater when symptoms persist despite ongoing treatment, we recommend that these additional guidelines be consulted in the management of unresolved postconcussive symptoms and that evacuation to a higher level of care be strongly considered. If the symptoms have resolved and the clinician is considering a return to full duty, then exertional testing, along with a follow-up MACE (alternate version), is recommended. If dormant symptoms are recognized or a score of less than 25 is recorded, then evacuation to a higher level of care should be conducted. If no symptoms are present, a full return to duty should take place. Overall, we recommend that the clinician consider the progression of symptoms over time. For example, if the symptoms seem to be resolving, then more time might be allowed between follow-ups. If symptoms remain stable or are increasing in severity, then steps need to be taken to appropriately care for the patient, perhaps even evacuating the patient to a higher level of care.

Concussion Screening Measures for the Battlefield

The Military Acute Concussion Evaluation

The DVBIC has recommended that anyone involved in or exposed to a blast, fall, vehicle crash, or with direct impact or acceleration to the head and becomes dazed, confused, or loses consciousness, even momentarily, should be screened for a concussion. The MACE (DVBIC, 2006; McCrea et al., 2003; McCrea, Kelly, Randolph, Cisler, & Berger, 2002; Appendix B), as a result of its simplicity and ease of administration, is the measure of choice in the deployed setting. It combines the documentation of acute injury characteristics and symptoms with a brief cognitive screening tool previously validated for evaluation of concussion/mTBI. The MACE was developed in collaboration with the DVBIC and includes eight questions designed to assess the event history in an attempt to establish the diagnosis of concussion/mTBI. The first eight topics of assessment on the MACE include asking the patient for a description of the incident; cause of the injury; helmet worn; amnesia before or after the incident; self-report and others' report of loss of consciousness; and a list of nine possible symptoms including headache, dizziness, memory problems, balance problems, nausea/vomiting, difficulty concentrating, irritability, visual disturbances, or ringing in the ears.

The second half of the MACE includes brief questions from the Standardized Assessment of Concussion (SAC; McCrea, Kelly, & Randolph, 2000) that assess the level of neurocognitive deficits. The SAC has been validated for use in a sports concussion model. Validation of the use of the MACE in an austere environment is ongoing. The MACE was introduced to the services for use in the military assessment of concussion in 2006. It typically takes less than 10 minutes to administer, comes in three different forms, and can be conducted in an interview format by medics or corpsmen to confirm a suspected diagnosis of concussion. The MACE measures four cognitive domains including orientation, immediate memory, concentration, and delayed recall. Although the MACE is available in three different forms, it was not originally developed for serial testing and is likely most accurate at establishing the presence or absence of a concussion if used within the first 24 hours. In a battlefield assessment, it may be the best instrument available. The MACE is intended to be given by a medic/corpsman, which is the most available medical asset on the battlefield, as opposed to specialty services such as neuropsychology or neurology.

NEUROCOGNITIVE ASSESSMENT TOOLS

To assess the immediate and future needs of injured service members across the continuum of care, and to facilitate rapid data access and transfer, computerized neurocognitive assessment is emerging in the evaluation of battlefield concussion/mTBI. Recognizing the need to employ a baseline assessment model similar to that used in sports concussion (Sports Laboratory Assessment Model), the DoD initiated a requirement in 2008 that all deployers receive a baseline predeployment neurocognitive assessment. The current mandated military NCAT (neurocognitive assessment tool) is the ANAM (Reeves et al., 2002). The ANAM has been developed over the course of three decades as a joint DoD effort and is a library of computer-based measures developed for assessing cognition and human performance.

The ANAM4 TBI Battery was developed in cooperation with the University of Oklahoma specifically for assessing a military population

(Center for the Study of Human Operator Performance, 2007). This battery of selected ANAM4 tests can be completed in approximately 20–30 minutes and measures six domains considered to be impacted by concussion: simple and complex reaction time, code substitution, delayed code substitution, matching to sample, procedural reaction time, and mathematical processing. Embedded within this program are demographic questions, a sleepiness scale, and a measure of mood. As with all psychological testing, the clinician interpreting the ANAM4 test should consider, in addition to the ANAM4 scores, a broad range of assessment information such as the patient's premorbid status, previous injuries, past clinical notes, and current symptoms as well as environmental and psychometric factors that can influence testing.

Following the administration of the ANAM4, the results are automatically saved and can be viewed on the computer or printed. The patient's pretest ANAM4 data, when available, can be used for comparison. The ANAM4 Performance Report (APR) gives a summary comparing patient scores to those of a reference group based on patient gender and age. The clinician might choose to select additional comparison options and observe the changes this makes in relationship to the selected reference group. This is accomplished by clicking on the "Comparison Group" button on the report to open up the dialog box.

In the predeployment scenario, the APR displays an alert box on the top right for three types of alerts that may trigger a referral for further evaluation: (a) a response that in the past 4 years the service member has experienced an injury that resulted in an alteration of consciousness and postconcussive symptoms that continue either at rest or following exertion; (b) a score of >85% on the anger or depression sections of the mood scale; and (c) responses that are at approximately chance levels on at least one of the neurocognitive tests. Chance levels are defined as accuracy scores of <56%. We recommend that some type of follow-up evaluation be conducted for all positive alerts on ANAM4 testing.

In the postinjury scenario, the APR alert box is replaced by a summary performance indicator, which provides information at a glance on the patient's aggregate performance across all tests. According to the *ANAM4 User Manual* (Center for the Study of Human Operator Performance, 2008), having two or more tests that deviate significantly from the baseline evaluation should be a "serious cause for concern" (p. 36). Patient characteristics such as sleep and hydration, which can influence cognition, should be considered when interpreting the results of the APR. The sleep and mood scales, as well as a brief interview, may be particularly useful. The provider observation section, available only for the postinjury assessments, allows the clinician to include MACE scores, previous injuries or concussions, and any other important evaluation information. The clinician will then want to review the performance-at-a-glance section of the APR, which lists the sequence of ANAM4 tests. Each test is displayed with a set of boxes checked on the right-hand side of the report as either average or above, below average, or clearly below average to indicate the performance pattern. When using a baseline test for comparison, the APR will contain a column of boxes on the left side of the report, which will indicate any tests that significantly vary, according to a Reliable Change Index. The values inside these boxes are the index of reliable change, and when this value exceeds –1.96, the box will be highlighted in red. These highlighted test boxes will be of particular interest to the clinician because they indicate a significant change from the patient's baseline scores.

There is also a section of the APR entitled Performance Detail, which provides additional summary in graphical form for each test. The test name, correct, incorrect, lapse, mean reaction time, percent correction, throughput, score, and percentile will be displayed. Lapses are defined as the number of trials for which the patient did not respond in the allowable time. The number of correct/incorrect and number of lapses become important when reviewing the results and may lead to questions about whether the patient was attending well enough to answer in the allotted time or may have avoided responding at all to the questions. The mean reaction time for the correct responses is measured in milliseconds and the percentage correct is the number of correct responses divided by the sum of correct, incorrect, and lapse responses. The throughput is the number of correct responses per minute of available response time. Any clinician conducting ANAM4 test interpretation should have the most recent user manual available as a reference.

The main criticism of the ANAM4 is the limited research-based evidence of its effectiveness for identifying combat mTBI injuries. Additional criticisms of the ANAM4 include (a) its lack of a web-based option for immediate comparison of baseline assessment to postconcussion testing and (b) its challenges with data storage and retrieval because it must be used on stand-alone, nonnetworked computers. Future studies are required to investigate the sensitivity and specificity of this measure, its effectiveness for identifying those with mTBI, and its ability to assist with combat injury return-to-duty decisions.

Military psychologists are currently being trained to administer a more traditional battery of neurocognitive screening measures. These include a personality measure, such as the Minnesota Multiphasic Personality Inventory-2 or the Personality Assessment Inventory, Trail Making Test A and B, and the Repeatable Battery for the Assessment of Neuropsychological Status (RBANS; Gold, Queern, Iannone, & Buchanan, 1999). The RBANS was initially selected for use in battlefield neuropsychological assessment for its ease of use, portability, short administration time, the cognitive domains assessed, and most importantly its equivalent alternate forms (repeatability). The RBANS is individually administered and includes both easy-to-use flip charts and response booklets to cue the examiner and record answers. It takes approximately 30 minutes to administer and includes 12 subtests. The cognitive domains assessed include immediate memory, visuospatial/constructional memory, language, attention, and delayed memory.

One of the RBANS memory tasks involves a word list. It should be noted that half of word list A on the RBANS is identical to the word list in form A of the MACE, and the other half of the word list from the RBANS A appears as the word list in form B of the MACE. This must be taken into account when interpreting the RBANS word list memory if the MACE has been taken previously by the service member. Recovery from concussion is best seen in ability to take advantage of the practice effect, which may be reflected in a good word memory score on the RBANS. Conversely, if the service member has previously taken the MACE and subsequently does poorly on the RBANS word memory, it is likely that they have not recovered sufficiently to take advantage of the practice effect. It should be noted that corpsmen/medics in the field are currently being encouraged to use MACE form C and avoid using A and B when possible. DVBIC is currently working on creating more alternative forms of the MACE to address this problem, as well as the fact that it has been reported that service members have obtained copies of the existing MACE stimulus cards.

With any of the neuropsychological measures described above, the clinician should acquire training in standardized test administration and appropriate use of measurement statistics. The clinician should also be thoroughly familiar with the test manual and be comfortable with his or her level of competence in administering and interpreting the psychological measure appropriately. This is not always fully achievable prior to a battlefield assessment, but the ethics of psychological testing should be attended to in order to ultimately protect both the patient being evaluated and the clinician (for a discussion of military neuropsychology ethics, see chapter 2).

ASSESSMENT OF EFFORT

While the majority of service members in theater will put forth their greatest effort on the above measures, as they tend to be highly motivated to return to their units, there are some cases in which an individual may be giving suboptimal effort. Fears and anxiety, a strong desire to return to family, potential secondary gains, and outright malingering are some possible reasons for this. Regardless of the reason, suboptimal effort could result in significant overestimation of impairment. As important decisions are being made based upon these evaluations, with significant mission impact as well as substantial cost, it would be wise to formally screen for effort. Formal effort screening measures, along with good clinical judgment and addressing the issue directly if suboptimal effort is suggested, can be quite beneficial in the battlefield management of concussion.

Military psychologists are currently being encouraged to utilize the RBANS embedded effort measure to assess suboptimal effort (Silverberg, Wertheimer, & Fichtenberg, 2007) to avoid overexposure to commonly used symptom validity tests. However, when this is insufficient or more than one measure is indicated, one widely accepted measure of effort is the Test of Memory Malingering (Tombaugh, 1996), which employs a forced choice recognition task for visually presented stimuli. It gives the impression of being a difficult measure of memory, but is actually quite easy. Subjects are given two learning trials during which they are shown 50 pictures of common objects. They are then presented with one of the previously presented pictures and a new picture and must select the previously shown target picture. Research on this measure indicates that it is sensitive to deception and insensitive to genuine memory impairment (Rees, Tombaugh, Gansler, & Moczynski, 1998; Tombaugh, 1996, 1997). Another widely accepted measure of effort is the Victoria Symptom Validity Test (Slick, Hopp, Strauss, & Thompson, 1997), which employs a forced choice recognition task for visually presented numbers. As with the Test of Memory Malingering, the task appears to be a difficult measure of memory, but in actuality, scores around 50% suggest random responding, whereas scores below this suggest deliberate choice of incorrect answers. Although this is a computer-based test, a flip card version can be made if a computer is not available. If suboptimal effort is suggested on screening measures, a frank discussion with the individual would be indicated. Providing feedback to the service member and assessing potential contributing factors for the suboptimal effort can be helpful in increasing effort, and thus getting a more accurate reflection of current functioning. For more information on issues of effort and neuropsychological assessment in the military, see chapter 4.

IMPACT OF SLEEP DEPRIVATION

Many service members who will be presenting for concussion evaluations will have been exposed to chronic sleep deprivation due to the current operational tempo and demands in the field. Chronic sleep deprivation has been shown to have a number of deleterious effects on cognitive functioning and may result in the service member looking impaired upon neuropsychological testing. This impairment may be temporary and related to the chronic sleep deprivation, versus a concussion. Therefore, chronic sleep deprivation will be an important differential diagnosis for service members presenting for concussion evaluations.

There are three general types of sleep deprivation: long-term total sleep deprivation (>45 hours), short-term total sleep deprivation (≤45 hours), and partial sleep deprivation (<7 hours in a 24-hour period). Total sleep deprivation has been well studied, and in a review of the literature, Durmer and Dinges (2005) note that following wakefulness in excess of 16 hours, deficits in attention and executive function tasks are demonstrable through well-validated testing protocols. Thus, it would be very important in the initial assessment to determine whether or not the service member has been awake beyond 16 hours, and to consider the acute sleep deprivation as a differential. If the service member demonstrates deficits but has also been awake for over 16 hours, it may be prudent to allow the member to sleep and then reevaluate.

However, even if acute sleep deprivation is not an issue, the operational tempo is such that most service members have been exposed to partial sleep deprivation for a significant period of time. Studies find that four or more days of partial sleep restriction results in cumulative adverse effects on neurobehavioral functions (Drake et al., 2001; Van Dongen, Maislin, Mullington, & Dinges, 2003; Dinges et al., 1997; Belenky et al., 2003). Furthermore, repeated days of sleep restriction to between 3 and 6 hours in bed has been shown to decrease cognitive speed/accuracy as reflected in working memory tasks (Drake et al., 2001; Van Dongen et al., 2003) and increase lapses of attention on psychomotor vigilance tasks (Drake et al., 2001; Van Dongen et al., 2003; Dinges et al., 1997; Belenky et al., 2003). A comprehensive study on chronic sleep restriction found that, after 2 weeks of sleep restriction to 4 hours in bed per night, deficits in attention, working memory, and cognitive throughput were equivalent to those seen after two nights of total sleep deprivation (Van Dongen et al., 2003). In addition, 2 weeks of restriction to 6 hours in bed per night resulted in cognitive deficits equivalent to those found after one night of total sleep deprivation.

In addition to chronic partial sleep deprivation, sleep fragmentation has also been shown to have a deleterious effect on cognitive functioning. Sleep fragmentation refers to arousals during sleep with abrupt increases in the electroencephalogram frequency for a minimum of 3 seconds during non-REM sleep and in association with increases in the electromyographic frequency during REM sleep (American Sleep Disorders Association Atlas Task Force, 1992). These arousals do not result in awakenings but have been associated with cognitive performance deficits (Bonnet, 1986a; Bonnet, 1986b, 1987, 1989a; 1989b; Bonnet, Berry, & Arand, 1991; Martin, Engleman, Deary, & Douglas, 1996) and mood alterations (Martin et al., 1996; Bonnet, 1987; Bonnet et al., 1991, Kingshott, Cosway, Deary, & Douglas, 2000). In effect, sleep fragmentation appears to have the same effect as sleep deprivation on waking behavior. In deployed military populations, it is highly likely that individuals may also be experiencing chronic sleep fragmentation, particularly if they are in high-threat areas. Obviously sleeping conditions are not ideal, with noise, threat, and associated hypervigilance potentially leading to chronic sleep fragmentation.

Based on the forgoing information, as part of the assessment, it will be important to assess the service member's sleep history. However, the service member's reported level of sleepiness and fatigue is not a good indicator of the impact of chronic sleep deprivation, as there appears to be an escalating dissociation between subjective perceptions of sleepiness and actual cognitive performance capability (Van Dongen et al., 2003). Thus it will be important to gather a good history regarding the service member's sleep schedule and quality prior to the concussion assessment. If sleep deprivation is suspected to be playing a role in the service member's deficits, it is recommended to allow the member time to sleep and then reevaluate. Studies in young adults indicate that 8–9 hours of extended nocturnal sleep are needed to resolve sleepiness caused by decreased sleep time (Roehrs, Merlotti, Petrucelli, Stepanski, & Roth, 1994; Roehrs, Timms, Zwyghuizen-Doorenbos, & Roth, 1989). Although this may not be feasible in the deployed area due to the environment and its impact on sleep fragmentation, at least allowing the member 8–9 hours time in bed may help to address the confounding effects of sleep deprivation. In addition, following the sleep hygiene guidelines discussed later in this chapter can be helpful as well. Evacuation to a level III facility would make it more likely that this recommendation would be able to be implemented. At least one level III facility has implemented a TBI tent where members arriving for TBI assessments are housed in a relatively comfortable setting, allowing them a better opportunity to receive restful sleep while still remaining in theater. In addition, the importance of managing sleep deprivation in the field due to its impact on functioning becomes clear. For more information on the contribution of sleep loss to operational effectiveness, see chapter 11.

PHYSICAL EXERTIONAL TESTING

When the concussed patient reports no symptoms, then physical exertional testing is recommended. This type of evaluation is used in sports medicine to uncover dormant symptoms (Guskiewicz et al., 2004). If physical or cognitive symptoms return with brief physical exertion, then continued rest and observation must be considered. Retesting with the MACE or the neuropsychological assessment procedures described above can be performed periodically until the patient is asymptomatic and able to return to full duty. Exertional testing is typically conducted by requesting that the service member engage in some type of aerobic activity such as push-ups, step aerobics, or run in place to raise their heart rate to 65–85% of their target heart rate (THR = 220 – age). This is thought to increase intracranial pressure, which in turn may then activate the dormant symptoms. Immediately following the exertion the clinician should query/assess for symptoms such as headache, vertigo, photophobia, balance, dizziness, nausea, tinnitus, or visual changes. The clinician should also keep in mind there may be contraindications for conducting exertional testing such as a suspected spinal injury or shrapnel to an extremity. Remember, exertional testing is reserved for those who are asymptomatic and as a last screener for a return to unrestricted duty. It is advisable not to perform exertional testing prior to 24 hours post concussion, even in cases where the service member is denying physical symptoms, has exhibited no red flags, and has a MACE score above the cut-off.

DIFFERENTIAL DIAGNOSIS: MILD TBI VERSUS ASD/PTSD

The one notable difference between many stateside concussions and those that occur on the battlefield is the ongoing threat to one's life. Most stateside concussions occur in MVCs or sports-related events where the intent is not to kill. Battlefield concussions, however, are usually blast related and potentially life threatening. In addition, these injuries take place in an environment of constant stress. The quick return to play experienced post sports concussion is likely to be a much different experience than the return-to-duty expectations that most service members face (e.g., high-threat situations).

Concussion/mTBI is the signature injury of the OIF/OEF conflicts, and as such, there has been considerable discussion regarding the comorbidity of concussion/mTBI (and related postconcussion syndrome or disorder), acute stress disorder, and posttraumatic stress disorder (PTSD). Mild TBI in soldiers deployed to Iraq is strongly associated with PTSD (Hoge et al., 2008). It is recognized in the civilian literature that the rates of ASD and PTSD are high in those with concussion/mTBI because many of these patients have experienced a traumatic event that caused the injury (Glaesser, Neuner, Lutgehetmann, Schmidt, & Elbert, 2004). Research with service members indicates that sustaining a physical injury of any kind in-theater increases the risk for PTSD (Hoge et al., 2004, 2008). When beginning any thorough evaluation, the clinician should gather a good clinical history from the service member regarding the course of events before, during, and after a traumatic event. Posttraumatic amnesia is very common in TBI, yet is less common in ASD/PTSD. There is some overlap in the *DSM-IV-TR* (American Psychiatric Association, 2000) symptom lists for PTSD and postconcussion disorder, which includes decrease in attention and memory, irritability, and sleep disturbance. Some distinguishing symptoms in the acute assessment period include the presence of headache, dizziness, diplopia, photosensitivity, balance problems, and nausea or vomiting in the TBI patient. This list of symptoms could potentially help the clinician make a judgment call on how to proceed with the evaluation.

Although much attention has been paid to attempting to differentiate these two disorders, regardless of the presence or absence of ASD/PTSD or combat operational stress reactions, the acute management and treatment of either or both remain similar. Overall, the importance of trying to make the distinction in the acute management stage may not contribute much to the overall treatment plan for the patient because with either disorder one treats the symptoms. However, if a concussion is identified, clinicians can evaluate for subclinical symptoms that may affect recovery if they remain undetected and untreated.

The symptoms of concussion and ASD/PTSD will often overlap and include the following:

1. Memory/learning impairment
2. Impaired attention
3. Slowed mental processing
4. Problems in abstract reasoning
5. Mental confusion
6. Lowered frustration tolerance/irritability
7. Mental and physical fatigability
8. Apathy/poor motivation
9. Depression and stress
10. Sleep disturbance

It is worth noting that many subjective complaints can be very nonspecific; therefore, a thorough evaluation with a comprehensive history of the injury event, including how symptoms may be temporally related, is crucial. For further discussion of combat-related PTSD, see chapter 12.

TREATMENT ISSUES AND SYMPTOM MANAGEMENT

The treatment of mTBI can be organized into three separate areas including symptom management, return to duty, and interventions. Headaches, sleep difficulties, and depression/anxiety are among the most commonly reported postconcussive symptoms (McCrea, 2008; Ryan & Warden, 2003).

Headaches and Associated Pain

Because headache pain can be associated with cognitive deficits, a brief headache assessment can be very important in the treatment of patients who have been concussed, and consultation with a physician should be initiated where possible. The patient should be asked to describe their headache frequency, intensity, and duration both before and after their injury. This will provide the clinician with information about baseline headache activity and changes postinjury. We suggest the clinician ask the service member to rate his/her headache on a 0–10 scale with 0 being no pain and 10 being the worst headache imaginable. The clinician should be listening for responses that indicate the service member's experience of the headache pain, getting diagnostic and clarifying information on topics such as location of headache, throbbing versus band-like pain, sensitivity to light and noise, and increasing levels of pain on exertion. Headache pain is among the most enduring symptoms of mTBI and postconcussion disorder, and we recommend that it be aggressively assessed, monitored, and treated.

It is recommended that opiates be avoided in the case of concussion because of their potential to exacerbate confusional states and contribution to rebound headaches (Mathew, Kurman, & Perez, 1990). Rebound headaches occur when some medications, which are typically taken for pain control, begin to actually contribute to the onset and maintenance of headache. The mechanism of rebound headaches is thought to be from the body's desire to maintain a homeostatic level of the medication that contributes to the initiation of a new headache (Rapoport, 1988).

If service members have a prior history of migraine, then intervention for posttraumatic migraines can include previously successful treatment procedures and medications. If daily headaches continue, then it is highly recommended that a full neurological exam be conducted. Other possible referrals to be considered for continued headache pain include physical therapy, during which time a range of motion assessment may be conducted. It is not uncommon postinjury for patients to experience increased muscle tension or neck and shoulder injuries that can contribute to the initiation and maintenance of headache. Additional referrals to ophthalmology or optometry should be considered if headaches persist, given the possibility of photosensitivity and other visual disturbances. Finally, stress reduction and deep muscle relaxation can contribute to improved outcomes.

Sleep Difficulties

Sleep and fatigue problems are also frequently reported in those who have experienced a concussion (Beetar, Guilmette, & Sparadeo, 1996). If the service member is reporting insomnia-type symptoms such as difficulty falling asleep or staying asleep, a behavioral assessment should be initiated to define the parameters of the sleep disturbance and to inform the behavioral intervention. The most common assessment measure is the Insomnia Severity Index (ISI), which is a self-report questionnaire that has the patient rate their difficulty falling asleep, staying asleep, waking up too early, interference with life activities, and concern over sleep problems (Bastien, Vallieres, & Morin, 2001). The Epworth Sleepiness Scale (Johns, 1991) may also prove useful in evaluating fatigue.

Morin (1993) suggests that the basics of treatment are best initiated through cognitive behavioral therapy (CBT) and that once you have identified the parameters of the insomnia, helping the patient to adhere to six basic rules should positively affect sleep architecture (Morin, 1993, p. 111):

1. Restrict time in bed to actual time you sleep.
2. Only go to bed when you are sleepy.
3. Do not stay in bed if you cannot fall asleep in 15 minutes.
4. Be consistent regarding the time you rise in the morning.
5. Only use the bed for sleep; do not read, listen to the radio, or eat in bed.
6. Do not nap during the day.

Under normal circumstances, these rules would be difficult to enforce in the deployed setting. Yet they should be adhered to in the rest and observation/assessment or treatment stages following a concussion.

Mood (Irritability, Stress, and Depression)

The authors have found that many times the service member does not complain of mood problems, although others around them may be picking up on this symptom. Collateral information is always helpful and is usually available from members of the service member's chain of command. The clinician should also consider using the Physical Health Questionnaire (PHQ-9; Spitzer, Kroenke, & Williams, 1999), the Beck Depression Inventory (Beck, Steer, & Brown, 1996), or the Beck Anxiety Inventory (Beck & Steer, 1990) if there are concerns about possible depression/anxiety, and PTSD may be assessed in theater with the PTSD Checklist-Military Version (PCL-M; Blanchard, Jones-Alexander, Buckley, & Forneris, 1996; Weathers, Litz, Herman, Huska, & Keane, 1993). Since substance use can be a major complicating factor in identified mood disorders, it should also be investigated, and a brief, ten-item alcohol use inventory, the Alcohol Use Disorders Identification Test (Babor, Higgins-Biddle, Saunders, & Monteiro, 2001) is recommended. This is recommended even in combat theaters of operation where alcohol is restricted, as alcohol-dependent service members have been known to be very creative in obtaining alcohol while deployed (e.g., receiving via mail from home, buying from locals, abusing over-the-counter cold medicine, etc.). It should also be noted that huffing and prescription pain medications have been reported by clinicians to be a current problem in theater, and these should also be evaluated.

RETURN-TO-DUTY DECISION MAKING

An important question becomes apparent to the clinician conducting acute assessment and management of TBI on the battlefield, "Can you return someone to duty when he/she is still symptomatic?" The key issues here are whether this injury will place the service member in danger of further injury to themselves, place their fellow service members at risk, and/or jeopardize the mission. If we consider other medical conditions such as shrapnel wounds or broken limbs, we would see that many service members return to some form of duty following injuries. Even though they return to duty, they may continue to experience symptoms such as pain and limited range of movement but are placed on profiles where they are able to manage their continued symptoms while performing some duties. The belief is that the symptoms will continue to improve and that the person will follow up for care as needed.

To make the determination of a return to duty in the case of a concussion, the clinician should reexamine the patient and look for evidence of an improving pattern of physical symptoms, cognitive performance, and emotional functioning. When this pattern is established, it may indicate that a return to duty with some limitations is in order. Headaches may be one of the most enduring symptoms, and it is recommended that these be aggressively addressed. It is likely that many service members with concussion/ mTBI symptoms could return to light or full duty with self-care instructions. These instructions should describe the symptoms of concussion, ways to manage their symptoms, what to expect in their recovery period and appropriate positive expectations, warning signs or signals to return for care, and how to access services if symptoms do not resolve. If significant symptoms persist past the rest and observation stage, the service member should not return to duty and should be referred to the next level of care, as outlined in the clinical practice guidelines discussed earlier.

Duty Restrictions

There may be both positive and negative consequences associated with return-to-duty decisions. A quick return to duty may enhance the therapeutic outcome through unit cohesion. If the unit welcomes the person back and quickly reintegrates them, this may actually improve the expectation for recovery and subsequent outcomes. There can also be potential negative outcomes associated with a quick return to duty, which could ultimately put both the individual and the unit at greater risk. Since the battlefield is inherently dangerous, the clinician should take the person's physical, cognitive, functional, and emotional symptoms into consideration, recognizing that these symptoms may not be evident on any psychological or neuropsychological tests. Although the operational mission should always consider the service member's safety first, unit effectiveness and safety, and mission requirements should also be thoroughly considered.

Often, restricting duties will not be possible in the deployed environment given the dangerous nature of the missions inherent to these settings. Consequently, if an individual is not symptom free, they are not able to return to their units. However, if the command can support a service member with duty restrictions, the clinician should consider the tactical setting when describing functional limitations. Some safety-related considerations should include quarters for 24 hours, with the requirement that the service member should not leave the immediate area for the duration of the light duty without medical permission, limit airborne operations, and name a battle buddy or wingman who could periodically check on the individual. The functional limitations that should be considered when writing the profile/recommending duty restrictions include those typically found on a battlefield such as not moving with a fighting load, not constructing an individual fighting position, no high-impact activities, no standing greater than 20 minutes, and setting a maximum weight of 35 pounds for lifting and/or carrying things.

When discussing current concussion symptoms with a service member in theater, the clinician should take into consideration that the patient may not recognize cognitive problems while in the deployed environment. It is most probable that he/she will be more cognizant of physical symptoms such as headaches and dizziness. Some patients have reported that they did not recognize their true limitations until returning stateside and being confronted with multiple demands, an unstructured or different environment, and/or new and unfamiliar tasks. This is understandable if one is aware of the sometimes-limited number of tasks and the repetition of daily life that takes place within deployed settings. There are several additional reasons why service members might not report concussion symptoms including (a) limited understanding of the signs and symptoms of the injury, (b) high unit cohesion and desire to return to their buddies, (c) limited duration of time since injury (cognitive or emotional symptoms may not have had time to surface), and (d) fear of being returned stateside and guilt regarding leaving their unit.

Clinicians should also take into consideration the potential for harm when conducting a concussion evaluation on the battlefield. There may be a risk to service members identifying themselves as having a TBI because they may perceive that this injury is permanent or something from which they may not recover. In addition, delays to return to duty could also impact the service member's expectations. Unit cohesion is known to impact resilience in service members (Bartone, 2006), and a lengthy evaluation process with limitations on full return to duty could contribute to the unit identifying the individual as "broken" and no longer able to reach operational usefulness despite a full recovery. It is therefore incumbent on the clinician to emphasize the natural recovery process and the expectation that symptoms will resolve to both the injured service member and his/her command.

Clinicians should also consider that their goal in the evaluation might not always be the goal of the service member being evaluated. By this we mean that most service members in theater have a very strong desire to return to their unit. The strong cohesion that fighting units build over the course of time is evident during the interview portion of many evaluations. This cohesion may contribute to both a conscious and/or subconscious tendency to limit self-reported symptoms. The clinician, however, typically wishes to fully evaluate all symptoms and estimate the level of functional impact. Being aware of these issues is critical when trying to get a clear understanding of the service member's functioning.

It is recommended that the clinician evaluating the service member postinjury consider using the Neurobehavioral Symptom Checklist (Cicerone & Kalmar, 1995). This list of symptoms may help the clinician identify those problems that need to be addressed in the immediate situation and those that might be labeled for future follow-up. In addition, this simple measure can be used to track the outcome of symptom management.

Documentation is important in any patient care activities, but it may be especially important in concussion assessment and management. For example, when considering return-to-duty decisions, other clinicians may need to better understand the outcome of the assessment and decision making regarding why he/she should or should not return the person to full or partial duty. Another reason to provide complete documentation of the assessment could be the potential long-term sequelae of concussion. In 2008, the Veterans Administration announced that the benefits to those who have experienced a TBI will increase, and without documentation of the event and resulting symptoms, the service member may not be able to receive a full review for benefits. Last, documentation may be important to service members who may have the opportunity to receive a Purple Heart.

TREATMENT OF CONCUSSION IN THE DEPLOYED SETTING

In any clinical population, the most significant symptoms of concussion usually occur immediately or soon after the injury, followed by a gradual abatement of symptoms to a complete recovery within days to weeks in the majority of single injury cases (Iverson, 2005). The strongest evidence for successful treatment for concussion/mTBI involves education regarding symptoms and possible expectations for rapid recovery (Hinkle, Alves, Rimel, & Jane, 1986; Ponsford et al., 2002). Providing educational intervention has resulted in a faster recovery and reduction of symptoms in a civilian population (Ponsford et al., 2002; Von Holst & Cassidy, 2004). It is therefore recommended that an educational handout (Concussion Information Sheet—Appendix A at the end of the chapter) with specific information be provided to all concussed patients, with the strong expectation of complete and rapid recovery. Any handout should contain information on how the diagnosis of concussion is reached, typical symptoms, symptoms that may be warning signs, how to seek further care if needed, when to expect recovery and to return to duty, and a list of self-care instructions such as getting rest/sleep, avoiding exertional activities such as recreational sports, and a gradual return to normal physical activities.

In addition to the patient informational sheet describing symptoms and recovery process, there should be communication with the service member's command about these same topics, which could take the form of a very similar information sheet. In addition, these information sheets should provide a very clear outline of the specific duty recommendations and duty restrictions that are expected for the individual service member. These communications should clearly reinforce not only the expectation of rapid recovery but also the safety of the individual and his/her unit. The recent RAND study (Tanielian et al., 2008) recognized the need for appropriate risk communication strategies in the concussion population: "Another area for improvement is the development of appropriate strategies and materials to educate the military community, service providers, and families about mild TBI. Materials developed for more-severe brain injury can misguide or unnecessarily alarm those suffering from only mild TBI. Military leadership, medical providers, service members, and families need to understand signs and symptoms of mild TBI and the importance of documentation, general guidelines in the management of mild TBI, and the expected course of TBI-related impairments and recovery. The Defense and Veterans Brain Injury Center has been increasing its outreach and training to meet this need" (p. 324).

CONCLUSIONS

Identification of concussion/mTBI at the earliest possible time in theater is critical to safety for the service member and his/her unit, good outcome/recovery, and rapid return to duty to service the mission goals. In most cases, following the CPG algorithm, beginning with brief history of injury and assessment, rest, education with appropriate attention and concern to the presenting symptoms, and instilling positive expectations for full and rapid concussion recovery will result in good outcomes. For the minority of service members who demonstrate continued concussion symptoms over days or weeks (perhaps due to a more severe concussion, multiple concussions, or exacerbating factors such as PTSD), specialized health care services may be required at higher level medical facilities in theater, and occasionally in the continental United States.

REFERENCES

American Academy of Neurology. (1997). Practice parameters: The management of concussion in sports. *Neurology, 48*, 581–585.

American Psychiatric Association. (2000). *Diagnostic and statistical manual of mental disorders* (4th ed.). Washington, DC: American Psychological Association.

American Sleep Disorders Association Atlas Task Force. (1992). EEG arousals: Scoring rules and examples. *Sleep, 15*, 173–184.

Babor, T. F., Higgins-Biddle, J. C., Saunders, J. B., & Monteiro, M. G. (2001) *Alcohol Use Disorders Identification Test (AUDIT): Guide for use in primary care*. Geneva, Switzerland: Department of Mental Health and Substance Dependence, World Health Organization.

Barth, J. T., Alves, W. M., Ryan, T. V., Macciocchi, S. N., Rimel, R. W., Jane, J. A. et al. (1989). Mild head injury in sports: Neuropsychological sequelae and recovery of function. In H. S. Levin, H. M. Eisenberg, & A. L. Benton (Eds.), *Mild head injury* (pp. 257–276). New York: Oxford University Press.

Barth, J. T., Broshek, D. K., & Freeman, J. R. (2006). Sports: A new frontier for neuropsychology. In R. Echemendia (Ed.), *Sports neuropsychology: Assessment and management of traumatic brain injury* (pp. 3–16). New York: Guilford.

Barth, J. T., Freeman, J. R., Broshek, D. K., & Varney, R. N., (2001). Acceleration-deceleration sports-related concussion: The gravity of it all. *Journal of Athletic Training, 36*(3), 253–256.

Barth, J. T., Macciocchi, S. N., Giordani, B., Rimel, R., Jane, J. A., & Boll, J. T. (1983). Neuropsychological sequelae of minor head injury. *Neurosurgery, 13,* 529–533.

Bartone, P. T. (2006). Resilience under military operational stress: Can leaders influence hardiness? *Military Psychology, 18*(Suppl.), S131–S148.

Bastien, C. H., Vallieres, A., & Morin, C. M. (2001). Validation of the insomnia severity index as an outcome measure for insomnia research. *Sleep Medicine, 2*(4), 297–307.

Beck, A. T., & Steer, R. A. (1990). *Manual for the Beck anxiety inventory.* San Antonio, TX: Psychological Corporation.

Beck, A. T., Steer, R. A., & Brown, G. K. (1996). *Manual for the Beck depression inventory-II.* San Antonio, TX: Psychological Corporation.

Beetar, J. T., Guilmette, T. J., & Sparadeo, F. R. (1996). Sleep and pain complaints in symptomatic traumatic brain injury and neurologic populations. *Archives of Physical Medicine & Rehabilitation, 77,* 1298–1302.

Belenky, G., Wesensten, N. J., Thorne, D. R., Thomas, M. L., Sing, H. C., Redmond, D. P., et al. (2003). Patterns of performance degradation and restoration during sleep restriction and subsequent recovery: A sleep dose–response study. *Journal of Sleep Research, 12,* 1–12.

Blanchard, E. B., Jones-Alexander, J., Buckley, T. C., & Forneris, C. A. (1996). Psychometric properties of the PTSD Checklist (PCL). *Behavior Research and Therapy, 34*(8), 669–673.

Bonnet, M. H. (1986a). Performance and sleepiness as a function of frequency and placement of sleep disruption. *Psychophysiology, 23,* 263–271.

Bonnet, M. H. (1986b). Performance and sleepiness following moderate sleep disruption and slow wave sleep deprivation. *Physiology and Behavior, 37,* 915–918.

Bonnet, M. H. (1987). Sleep restoration as a function of periodic awakening, movement, or electroencephalographic change. *Sleep, 10,* 364–373.

Bonnet, M. H. (1989a). Infrequent periodic sleep disruption: Effects on sleep, performance and mood. *Physiology and Behavior, 45,* 1049–1055.

Bonnet, M. H. (1989b). The effect of sleep fragmentation on sleep and performance in younger and older subjects. *Neurobiology and Behavior, 10,* 21–25.

Bonnet, M. H., Berry, R. B., & Arand, D.L. (1991). Metabolism during normal, fragmented, and recovery sleep. *Journal of Applied Physiology, 71,* 1112–1118.

Brain Trauma Foundation; American Association of Neurological Surgeons; Congress of Neurological Surgeons. (2007) Guidelines for the management of severe traumatic brain injury. *Journal of Neurotrauma, 24*(Suppl. 1), S1–S106.

Cantu, R. C. (1986). Guidelines for return to contact sports after cerebral concussion. *Physicians in Sports Medicine, 14*(10), 75–83.

Cantu, R. C. (1998). Second impact syndrome. *Clinical Sports Medicine, 17,* 37–44.

Cantu, R. C., & Mueller, F. O. (2000). Catastrophic football injuries. *Neurosurgery, 47*(3), 673–675.

Cantu, R. C., & Voy, R. (1995). Second impact syndrome: A risk in contact sport. *The Physician in Sports Medicine, 23*(6), 114.

Center for the Study of Human Operator Performance. (2007). *Automated neuropsychological assessment metrics* (Version 4) [Computer software]. University of Oklahoma, Norman, OK: Author.

Center for the Study of Human Operator Performance. (2008). *ANAM4 user manual.* Norman, OK: Author.

Cicerone, K. D., & Kalmar, K. (1995). Persistent postconcussive syndrome: Structure of subjective complaints after mild traumatic brain injury. *Journal of Head Trauma Rehabilitation, 10*(3), 1–17.

Collins, M. W., Lovell, M., Iverson, G., Cantu, R. C., Maroon, J. C., & Field, M. (2002). Cumulative effects of concussion in high school athletes. *Neurosurgery, 51*(5), 1175–1181.

Defense and Veterans Brain Injury Center. (2006). Retrieved April 15, 2009, from www.dvbic.org

Defense and Veterans Brain Injury Center. (2009). Retrieved April 15, 2009, from www.dvbic.org

DePalma, R. G., Burris, D. G., Champion, H. R., & Hodgson, M. J. (2005). Blast injuries. *New England Journal of Medicine, 352*(13), 1335–1342.

Department of Defense Task Force on Mental Health. (2007, June). *An achievable vision.* Retrieved April 17, 2009, from //www.ha.osd.mil/dhb/mhtf/MHTF-Report-Final.pdf

Dikmen, S., McLean, A., & Temkin, N. (1986). Neuropsychological and psychological consequences of minor head injury. *Journal of Neurology, Neurosurgery, and Psychiatry, 48*, 1227–1232.

Dinges, D. F., Pack, F., Williams, K., Gillen, K. A., Powell, J. W., Ott, G. E., et al. (1997). Cumulative sleepiness, mood disturbance, and psychomotor vigilance performance decrements during a week of sleep restricted to 4–5 hours per night. *Sleep, 20*, 267–277.

Drake, C. L., Roehrs, T. A., Burduvali, E., Bonahoom, A., Rosekind, M., & Roth, T. (2001). Effects of rapid versus slow accumulation of eight hours of sleep loss. *Psychophysiology, 38*, 979–987.

Durmer, J. S., & Dinges, D. F. (2005). Neurocognitive consequences of sleep deprivation. *Seminars in Neurology, 25*, 117–129.

Gennarelli, T. A., Adams, G. H., & Graham, D. I. (1981). Acceleration induced head injury in the monkey: The model, its mechanisms, and physiological correlates. *Acta Neuropathologica, 7*(Suppl.), 23–25.

Glaesser, J., Neuner, F., Lutgehetmann, R., Schmidt, R., & Elbert, T. (2004). Posttraumatic stress disorder in patients with traumatic brain injury. *British Journal of Medical Psychiatry, 9*(4), 5.

Gold, J. M., Queern, C., Iannone, V. N., & Buchanan, R. W. (1999). Repeatable battery for the assessment of neuropsychological status as a screening test in schizophrenia, I: Sensitivity, reliability, and validity. *American Journal of Psychiatry, 156*, 1944–1950.

Gronwall, D., & Wrightson, P. (1974). Delayed recovery of intellectual function after minor head injury. *Lancet, 2*, 604–609.

Gronwall, D., & Wrightson, P. (1980). Duration of posttraumatic amnesia after mild head injury. *Journal of Clinical Neuropsychology, 1*, 51–60.

Guskiewicz, K. M., Bruce, S. L., Cantu, R. C., Ferrara, M. S., Kelly, J. P., McCrea, M., et al. (2004). Recommendations on management of sport-related concussion:

Summary of the National Athletic Trainers' Association position statement. *Neurosurgery, 55*(4), 891–895; discussion 896.

Hinkle, J. L., Alves, W. M., Rimel, R. W., & Jane, J. A. (1986) Restoring social competence in minor head-injury patients. *Journal of Neuroscience and Nursing, 18*(5), 268–271.

Hoge, C. W., Castro, C. A., Messer, S. C., McGurk, D., Cotting, D. I., & Koffman, R. L. (2004). Combat duty in Iraq and Afghanistan, mental health problems and barriers to care. *New England Journal of Medicine, 35*(1), 13–22.

Hoge, C. W., McGurk, D., Thomas, J. L., Cox, A. L., Engel, C. C., & Castro, C. A. (2008). Mild traumatic injury in U.S. Soldiers returning from Iraq. *New England Journal of Medicine, 358,* 455–463.

Hovda, D. A., Yoshino, A., Kawamata, T., Katayama, Y., Fineman, I., & Becker, D. P. (1990). The increase in local cerebral glucose utilization following fluid percussion brain injury is prevented with kynurenic acid and is associated with an increase in calcium. *Acta Neurochirurgica Suppl (Wien), 51,* 331–333.

Independent Review Group. (2007, April). *Rebuilding the trust: Report on rehabilitative care and administrative processes at Walter Reed Army Medical Center and National Naval Medical Center.* Alexandria, VA: Retrieved January 26, 2009, from http://www.ha.osd.mil/dhb/recommendations/2007/IRG-Report-Final.pdf

Iverson, G. L. (2005) Outcome from mild traumatic brain injury. *Current Opinions in Psychiatry, 18*(3), 301–317.

Johns, M. W. (1991). A new method for measuring daytime sleepiness: The Epworth sleepiness scale. *Sleep, 14*(6), 540–545.

Kingshott, R. N., Cosway, R. J., Deary, I. J., & Douglas, N. J. (2000). The effect of sleep fragmentation on cognitive processing using computerized topographic brain mapping. *Journal of Sleep Research, 9,* 353–357.

Levin, H. S., Mattis, S., Ruff, R. M., & Eisenberg, H. M. (1987). Neurobehavioral outcome following minor head injury: A three center study. *Journal of Neurosurgery, 66,* 234–243.

Maroon, J. C., Lovell, M., Norwig, J., Podell, K., Powell, J. W., & Hartl, R. (2000). Cerebral concussion in athletes: Evaluation and neuropsychological testing. *Neurosurgery, 47*(3), 659–669.

Martin, S. E., Engleman, H. M., Deary, I. J., & Douglas, N. J. (1996). The effect of sleep fragmentation on daytime function. *American Journal of Respiratory Critical Care Medicine, 153,* 1328–1332.

Martin, E. M., Lu, W. C., Helmick, K., French, L., & Warden, D. L. (2008) Traumatic brain injuries sustained in the Afghanistan and Iraq wars. *American Journal of Nursing, 108*(4), 40–47.

Mathew, N. T., Kurman, R., & Perez, F. (1990). Drug induced refractory headache—clinical features and management. *Headache, 30*(10), 634–638.

McCrea, M. A. (2008). *Mild traumatic brain injury and postconcussion syndrome: The new evidence base for diagnosis and treatment* (pp. 153–158). New York: Oxford University Press.

McCrea, M., Guskiewicz, K. M., Marshall, S. W., Barr, W., Randoph, C., & Cantu, R. C. (2003). Acute effects and recovery time following concussion in collegiate football players: The NCAA concussion study. *Journal of the American Medical Association, 290*(19), 2556–2563.

McCrea, M., Kelly, J., & Randolph, C. (2000). *Standardized Assessment of Concussion (SAC): Manual for administration, scoring, and interpretation* (2nd ed.). Waukesa, WI: Oxford University Press.

McCrea, M., Kelly, J.P., Randolph, C., Cisler, R., & Berger, L. (2002). Immediate neurocognitive effects of concussion. *Neurosurgery, 50*(5), 1032–1040.

McLean, A., Temkin, N. R., Dikmen, S., & Wyler, A. R. (1983). The behavioral sequelae of head injury. *Journal of Clinical Neuropsychology, 5*, 361–376.

Mental Health Advisory Team (MHAT-V) Operation Iraqi Freedom 06–08, chartered by the Office of the Surgeon General Multi-National Forces-Iraqi and Office of the Surgeon General United States Army Medical Command. (2008, February 14). Retrieved April 3, 2009, from http://www.armymedicine.army.mil

Morin, C. M. (1993). *Insomnia: Psychological assessment and management.* New York: Guilford Press.

Okie, S. (2005). Traumatic brain injury in the war zone. *New England Journal of Medicine, 352*(2), 2043–2047.

Ponsford, J., Willmott, C., Rothwell, A., Cameron, P., Kelly, A. M., Nelms, R., et al. (2002). Impact of early intervention on outcome following mild head injury in adults. *Journal of Neurology, Neurosurgery, and Psychiatry, 73*(3), 330–332.

Rapoport, A. M. (1988). Analgesic rebound headache. *Headache, 28*(10), 662–665.

Rees, L. M., Tombaugh, T. N., Gansler, D. A., & Moczynski, N. P. (1998). Five validation experiments of the Test of Memory Malingering (TOMM). *Psychological Assessment, 10*, 10–20.

Reeves, D., Kane, R., Elsmore, T., Winter, K., & Bleiberg, J. (2002). *ANAM 2001 user's manual: Clinical and research modules.* San Diego, CA: National Cognitive Recovery Foundation, Publication SNRF-SF-2002-1.

Rimel, R. W., Giordani, B., Barth, J. T., Boll, T. J., & Jane, J. A. (1981). Disability caused by minor head injury. *Neurosurgery, 9*, 221–228.

Roehrs, T., Merlotti, L., Petrucelli, N., Stepanski, E., & Roth, T. (1994). Experimental sleep fragmentation. *Sleep, 17*, 438–443.

Roehrs, T. A., Timms, V., Zwyghuizen-Doorenbos, A., & Roth, T. (1989). Sleep extension in sleepy and alert normals. *Sleep, 12*, 449–457.

Ryan, L. M., & Warden, D. L. (2003). Post concussion syndrome. *International Review of Psychiatry, 15*(4), 310–316.

Silverberg, N. D., Wertheimer, J. C., & Fichtenberg, N. L. (2007). An effort index for the Repeatable Battery for the Assessment of Neuropsychological Status (RBANS). *The Clinical Neuropsychologist, 21*, 841–854.

Slick, D., Hopp, G., Strauss, E., & Thompson, G. B. (1997). *Victoria Symptom Validity Test.* Odessa, FL: Psychological Assessment Resources.

Spitzer, R. L., Kroenke, K., & Williams, J. B. (1999). Validation and utility of a self-report version of the PRIME-MD: The PHQ primary care study. *Journal of the American Medical Association, 282*, 1737–1744.

Taber, K. H., Warden, D. L., & Hurley, R. A. (2006). Blast-related traumatic brain injury: What is known? *Journal of Neuropsychiatry and Clinical Neuroscience, 18*(2), 141–145.

Tanielian, T., Jaycox, L. H., Schell, T. L., Marshall, G. N., Burnam, M. A., Eibner, C., et al. (2008). *Invisible wounds of war: Summary and recommendations for addressing psychological and cognitive injuries.* Santa Monica, CA: RAND Corporation, MG-720/1-CCF, 64. Retrieved April 3, 2009, from http://veterans.rand.org

Teasdale, G., & Jennett, B. (1974). Assessment of coma and impaired consciousness. A practical scale. *Lancet, 13*(2), 81–84.

Terrio, H., Brenner, L. A., Ivins, B. J., Cho, J. M., Helmick, K., Schwab, K., et al. (2009). Traumatic brain injury screening: Preliminary findings in a U.S. Army brigade combat team. *The Journal of Head Trauma Rehabilitation, 24*, 14–23.

Tombaugh, T. N. (1996). *Test of Memory Malingering (TOMM)*. North Tonawanda, NY: Multi Health Systems.

Tombaugh, T. N. (1997). The Test of Memory Malingering (TOMM): Normative data from cognitively intact and cognitively impaired individuals. *Psychological Assessment, 9*, 260–268.

Van Dongen, H. P. A., Maislin, G., Mullington, J. M., & Dinges, D. F. (2003). The cumulative cost of additional wakefulness: Dose-response effects on neurobehavioral functions and sleep physiology from chronic sleep restriction and total sleep deprivation. *Sleep, 26*, 117–126.

Von Holst, H., & Cassidy, J. D. (2004). Mandate of the WHO Collaborating Centre Task Force on mild traumatic brain injury. *Journal of Rehabilitation Medicine* (43, Suppl.), 8–10.

Weathers, F., Litz, B., Herman, D., Huska, J., & Keane, T. (1993, October). *The PTSD Checklist (PCL): Reliability, validity, and diagnostic utility.* Paper presented at the Annual Convention of the International Society for Traumatic Stress Studies, San Antonio, TX.

Wrightson, P., & Gronwall, D. (1980). Time off work and symptoms after mild head injury. *Injury, 12*, 445–454.

Appendix A

Concussion Information Sheet

What is a concussion?

A concussion is a blow or jolt to the head that briefly knocks you out (loss of consciousness) or makes you confused or "see stars" (change in consciousness, getting your "bell rung"). In combat, concussions are usually caused by a blast, fall, direct impact, or motor vehicle crash. Some, but not all, persons with a concussion lose consciousness. A concussion is also called "mild traumatic brain injury."

Why is this important?

Often after a concussion service members think they are OK, yet they have actually suffered a brain injury that needs immediate attention. You should seek medical treatment from the nearest aid station as soon as possible after any head injury where there may be a chance of a concussion. Your doctor will determine if your head injury is serious and will decide when it is safe for you to return to duty. It is important that your doctor decides this; because if you get another concussion before healing from the first one, you are likely to be at greater risk for a more serious injury.

What are the symptoms of a concussion?

Confusion
Difficulty concentrating
Difficulty remembering
Dizziness
Drowsiness
Excessive tiredness
Fatigue
Headache
Insomnia/sleep disturbances
Irritability
Loss of balance
Nausea/vomiting
Ringing ears
Sensitivity to noise and light
Vision changes/blurred vision

Symptoms of concussion usually recover quickly, often within a few minutes to hours. However, if symptoms persist and do not improve, seek medical treatment.

How is concussion diagnosed?
A concussion diagnosis is based on the history of the event, your physical symptoms, and a physical examination. Your provider may use the Military Acute Concussion Evaluation (MACE) to guide your assessment. The MACE also includes measures of memory and concentration to see if there are any effects from your concussion. Physical exertion may also be included in your evaluation. You will heal rapidly from the concussion.

Does medicine help?
The treatment for concussion is limited duty and rest. If you have a headache, you can usually take acetaminophen (brand name: Tylenol). Taking stronger pain medications (like Percocet or hydrocodone) may actually make your headache worse, and medicines like aspirin or ibuprofen (Advil, Motrin) should be used only with advice from your provider. Always ask your provider before you take any medicines.

What are the warning signs of concussion?
Certain signs and symptoms of a concussion require immediate care. If you experience any of the following go *immediately* to the nearest aid station or emergency room, at any time of day or night.

Double vision
Progressively declining level of consciousness
Repeated vomiting
Seizures
Slurred speech
Unable to recognize people and places
Unequal pupils
Unsteadiness on feet
Weakness or numbness in arms or legs
Worsening headache

When can I return to duty?
After your medical evaluation, you may be given a short period of light duty restrictions to give your brain time to heal. If your concussion was very mild, you may be allowed to return to duty quickly. You should not return to full duty until the symptoms of concussion, like headache or dizziness, are gone. It's important to let your provider decide when it's time to return to duty.

Are there any lasting effects from a concussion?
Almost all people recover completely following a concussion. If you have had multiple concussions, you may have a longer recovery time. Even if you've had more than one concussion during deployment, full recovery is expected.

What else should I know about my recovery?
Get plenty of sleep; do not overexert yourself.
Return to normal activities gradually, not all at once.
Until you are better, avoid activities such as contact or recreational sports that could lead to a second brain injury. Remember to wear helmets and safety belts to decrease your risk of having a second brain injury.
Do not drink alcohol; it may slow your brain recovery and put you at further risk of injury.
Sleep, rest, and gradual return of normal physical activities will help.

Appendix B

Patient Name: _____
SS#: _____-_____-_____Unit: _____
Date of Injury: _____/_____/_____ Time of Injury: _____
Examiner: _____
Date of Evaluation: _____/_____/_____ Time of Evaluation: _____

History: (I–VIII)

I. Description of Incident
Ask:
a) What happened?
b) Tell me what you remember.
c) Were you dazed, confused, "saw stars"? ❏ Yes ❏ No
d) Did you hit your head? ❏ Yes ❏ No

II. Cause of Injury (Circle all that apply):
1) Explosion/Blast   4) Fragment
2) Blunt object   5) Fall
3) Motor Vehicle Crash 6) Gunshot wound
7) Other _____

III. Was a helmet worn? ❏ Yes ❏ No Type _____

IV. Amnesia Before: Are there any events just BEFORE the injury that are not remembered? (Assess for continuous memory prior to injury)
❏ Yes ❏ No If yes, how long _____

V. Amnesia After: Are there any events just AFTER the injury that are not remembered? (Assess time until continuous memory after the injury)
❏ Yes ❏ No If yes, how long _____

VI. Does the individual report loss of consciousness or "blacking out"?
❏ Yes ❏ No If yes, how long _____

VII. Did anyone observe a period of loss of consciousness or unresponsiveness? ☐ Yes ☐ No If yes, how long _____

VIII. Symptoms (Circle all that apply)

1) Headache   2) Dizziness
3) Memory Problems   4) Balance problems
5) Nausea/Vomiting   6) Difficulty Concentrating
7) Irritability   8) Visual Disturbances
9) Ringing in the ears   10) Other _____

Evaluate each domain. Total possible score is 30.

Examination: (IX–XIII)

IX. Orientation: (1 point each)

Month:	0	1
Date:	0	1
Day of Week:	0	1
Year:	0	1
Time:	0	1

Orientation Total Score _____/5

X. Immediate Memory:

Read all 5 words and ask the patient to recall them in any order. Repeat two more times for a total of three trials. (1 point for each correct, total over 3 trials)

List	Trial 1	Trial 2	Trial 3
Elbow	0 1	0 1	0 1
Apple	0 1	0 1	0 1
Carpet	0 1	0 1	0 1
Saddle	0 1	0 1	0 1
Bubble	0 1	0 1	0 1
Trial Score			

Immediate Memory Total Score _____/15

XI. Neurological Screening

As the clinical condition permits, check
Eyes: pupillary response and tracking

Verbal: speech fluency and word finding
Motor: pronator drift, gait/coordination
Record any abnormalities. **No points are given for this**.

XII. Concentration

Reverse Digits: (go to next string length if correct on first trial. Stop if incorrect on both trials.) 1 pt. for each string length.

4-9-3	6-2-9	0	1
3-8-1-4	3-2-7-9	0	1
6-2-9-7-1	1-5-2-8-5	0	1
7-1-8-4-6-2	5-3-9-1-4-8	0	1

Months in reverse order: (1 pt. for entire sequence correct)
Dec-Nov-Oct-Sep-Aug-Jul-Jun-May-Apr-Mar-Feb-Jan
0   1
Concentration Total Score _____ **/5**

XIII. Delayed Recall (1 pt. each)

Ask the patient to recall the 5 words from the earlier memory test (Do NOT reread the word list.)

Elbow	0	1
Apple	0	1
Carpet	0	1
Saddle	0	1
Bubble	0	1

Delayed Recall Total Score _____ **/5**
TOTAL SCORE _____ **/30**

Notes: _____

_____

Diagnosis: (circle one or write in diagnoses)

No concussion
850.0 Concussion without Loss of Consciousness (LOC)
850.1 Concussion with Loss of Consciousness (LOC)

Other diagnoses _____

_____

Instruction Sheet

Purpose and Use of the MACE

A concussion is a mild traumatic brain injury (TBI). The purpose of the MACE is to evaluate a person in whom a concussion is suspected. The MACE is used to confirm the diagnosis and assess the current clinical status.

Tool Development

The MACE has been extensively reviewed by leading civilian and military experts in the field of concussion assessment and management. While the MACE is not, yet, a validated tool, the examination section is derived from the Standardized Assessment of Concussion (SAC) (McCrea, M., Kelly, J., & Randolph, C. (2000). *Standardized Assessment of Concussion (SAC): Manual for Administration, Scoring, and Interpretation* (2nd ed.), Waukesa, WI: Authors.), which is a validated, widely used tool in sports medicine. Abnormalities on the SAC correlate with formal comprehensive neuropsychological testing during the first 48 hours following a concussion.

Who to Evaluate

Anyone who was dazed, confused, "saw stars" or lost consciousness, even momentarily, as a result of an explosion/blast, fall, motor vehicle crash, or other event involving abrupt head movement, a direct blow to the head, or other head injury is an appropriate person for evaluation using the MACE.

Evaluation of Concussion

History: (I–VIII)

I. Ask for a description of the incident that resulted in the injury; how the injury occurred, type of force. Ask questions A–D.

II. Indicate the cause of injury.

III. Assess for helmet use. Military: Kevlar or ACH (Advanced Combat Helmet), sports helmet, motorcycle helmet, etc.

IV–V. Determine whether and length of time that the person wasn't registering continuous memory both prior to injury and after the injury. Approximate the amount of time in seconds, minutes or hours, whichever time increment is most appropriate. For example, if the assessment of the patient yields a possible time of 20 minutes, then 20 minutes should be documented in the "how long?" section.

VI–VII. Determine whether and length of time of self-reported loss of consciousness (LOC) or witnessed/observed LOC. Again, approximate the amount of time in seconds, minutes or hours, whichever time increment is most appropriate.

VIII. Ask the person to report their experience of each specific symptom since injury.

Examination: (IX–XIII)

Standardized Assessment of Concussion (SAC):
Total possible score = 30
Orientation = 5
Immediate Memory = 15
Concentration = 5
Memory Recall = 5

IX. Orientation: Assess patient's awareness of the accurate time.
Ask: WHAT MONTH IS THIS?
WHAT IS THE DATE OR DAY OF THE MONTH?
WHAT DAY OF THE WEEK IS IT?
WHAT YEAR IS IT?
WHAT TIME DO YOU THINK IT IS?
One point for each correct response for a total of 5 possible points.
It should be noted that a correct response on time of day must be
within 1 hour of the actual time.

X. Immediate memory is assessed using a brief repeated list learning
test. Read the patient the list of 5 words once and then ask them to
repeat it back to you, as many as they can recall in any order. Repeat
this procedure 2 more times for a total of 3 trials, even if the patient
scores perfectly on the first trial. Trial 1: I'M GOING TO TEST
YOUR MEMORY, I WILL READ YOU A LIST OF WORDS AND
WHEN I AM DONE, REPEAT BACK AS MANY WORDS AS
YOU CAN REMEMBER, IN ANY ORDER.
Trial 2 & 3: I AM GOING TO REPEAT THAT LIST AGAIN.
AGAIN, REPEAT BACK AS MANY AS YOU CAN REMEMBER
IN ANY ORDER, EVEN IF YOU SAID THEM BEFORE.
One point is given for each correct answer for a total of 15 possible
points.

XI. Neurological screening
Eyes; check pupil size and reactivity.
Verbal: notice speech fluency and word finding.
Motor: pronator drift—ask patient to lift arms with palms up, ask
patient to then close their eyes, assess for either arm to "drift" down.
Assess gait and coordination if possible. Document any abnormalities.
No points are given for this section.

XII. Concentration: Inform the patient:
I'M GOING TO READ YOU A STRING OF NUMBERS AND
WHEN I AM FINISHED, REPEAT THEM BACK TO ME

BACKWARDS, THAT IS, IN REVERSE ORDER OF HOW I READ THEM TO YOU. FOR EXAMPLE, IF I SAY 7-1-9, YOU WOULD SAY 9-1-7.

If the patient is correct on the first trial of each string length, proceed to the next string length. If incorrect, administer the 2nd trial of the same string length. Proceed to the next string length if correct on the second trial. Discontinue after failure on both trials of the same string length. Total of 4 different string lengths; 1 point for each string length for a total of 4 points.

NOW TELL ME THE MONTHS IN REVERSE ORDER, THAT IS, START WITH DECEMBER AND END IN JANUARY. 1 point if able to recite ALL months in reverse order. 0 points if not able to recite ALL of them in reverse order. Total possible score for concentration portion: 5.

XIII. Delayed recall

Assess the patient's ability to retain previously learned information by asking him/her to recall as many words as possible from the initial word list, without having the word list read again for this trial. DO YOU REMEMBER THAT LIST OF WORDS I READ A FEW MINUTES EARLIER? I WANT YOU TO TELL ME AS MANY WORDS FROM THE LIST AS YOU CAN REMEMBER IN ANY ORDER.

One point for each word remembered for a total of 5 possible points.

Total score = Add up from the 4 assessed domains: immediate memory, orientation, concentration and memory recall.

Significance of Scoring

In studies of non-concussed patients, the mean total score was 28. Therefore, a score less than 30 does not imply that a concussion has occurred. Definitive normative data for a "cut-off" score are not available. However, scores below 25 may represent clinically relevant neurocognitive impairment and require further evaluation for the possibility of a more serious brain injury. The scoring system also takes on particular clinical significance during serial assessment where it can be used to document either a decline or an improvement in cognitive functioning.

Diagnosis

Circle the ICD-9 code that corresponds to the evaluation. If loss of consciousness was present, then circle 850.1. If no LOC, then document 850.0. If another diagnosis is made, write it in.

MACE Form B

Due to test-retest issues (e.g. service members memorizing words and numbers) validated, alternative versions B or C should be used.

Immediate Memory

Read all 5 words and ask the patient to recall them in any order. Repeat two more times for a total of three trials. (1 point for each correct, total over 3 trials.)

List	Trial 1	Trial 2	Trial 3
Candle	0 1	0 1	0 1
Paper	0 1	0 1	0 1
Sugar	0 1	0 1	0 1
Sandwich	0 1	0 1	0 1
Wagon	0 1	0 1	0 1
Total			

Concentration

Reverse Digits: (go to next string length if correct on first trial. Stop if incorrect on both trials.) 1 pt. for each string length.

5-2-6	4-1-5	0	1
1-7-9-5	4-9-6-8	0	1
4-8-5-2-7	6-1-8-4-3	0	1
8-3-1-9-6-4	7-2-4-8-5-6	0	1

Delayed Recall (1 pt each)

Ask the patient to recall the 5 words from the earlier memory test (DO NOT reread the word list.)

Candle	0	1
Paper	0	1
Sugar	0	1
Sandwich	0	1
Wagon	0	1

MACE Form C

Due to test-retest issues (e.g. service members memorizing words and numbers) validated, alternative versions B or C should be used.

Immediate Memory

Read all 5 words and ask the patient to recall them in any order. Repeat two more times for a total of three trials. (1 point for each correct, total over 3 trials.)

List	Trial 1	Trial 2	Trial 3
Baby	0 1	0 1	0 1
Monkey	0 1	0 1	0 1
Perfume	0 1	0 1	0 1
Sunset	0 1	0 1	0 1
Iron	0 1	0 1	0 1
Total			

Concentration

Reverse Digits: (go to next string length if correct on first trial. Stop if incorrect on both trials.) 1 pt. for each string length.

1-4-2	6-5-8	0	1
6-8-3-1	3-4-8-1	0	1
4-9-1-5-3	6-8-2-5-1	0	1
3-7-6-5-1-9	9-2-6-5-1-4	0	1

Delayed Recall (1 pt each)

Ask the patient to recall the 5 words from the earlier memory test (DO NOT reread the word list.)

Baby	0	1
Monkey	0	1
Perfume	0	1
Sunset	0	1
Iron	0	1

7

Head Injury Rehabilitation of Military Members

TREVEN C. PICKETT, MARK C. BENDER, AND
EUGENE GOURLEY

INTRODUCTION

America's armed forces have sustained complex patterns of injuries since the onset of military operations of 9/11 (DePalma, Burris, Champion, & Hodgson, 2005; Gawande, 2004). Available data indicate that, as of July 24, 2009, 34,750 service members have suffered nonmortal injuries in association with Operation Enduring Freedom (OEF) and Operation Iraqi Freedom (OIF) and, according to this data source, 15,957 of these individuals did not return to duty within 72 hours, presumably because of the severity of sustained injuries (U. S. Department of Defense, 2009). Data indicate that the majority of OEF–OIF combat injuries are blast related and include those resulting from artillery, rocket and mortar shells, mines, booby traps, aerial bombs, improvised explosive devices, and rocket-propelled grenades (Coupland & Meddings, 1999; Gondusky & Reiter, 2005; Murray et al., 2005). Traumatic brain injury (TBI) is often referred to as the "signature injury" in the wars in Iraq and Afghanistan with estimates that over 60% of blast injuries result in TBI (Okie, 2006; Warden et al., 2005). Soldiers survive injuries at higher rates after suffering blast injuries due to improvements in body armor and acute trauma care (for more on blast injury, see chapter 5) and, consequently, the military and Department of Veterans Affairs (VA) health care systems have adjusted to accommodate the medical and rehabilitation needs of these veterans who survive TBI. The Veterans Health Administration (VHA) officially implemented the (VA) Polytrauma System of Care (PSC) in 2005 in recognition of the need to provide long-term and specialized rehabilitation to these injured active duty military and veterans.

In this chapter, we endeavor to chronicle the varying levels of rehabilitation care that are available for TBI rehabilitation including acute, subacute, and transitional rehabilitation. The PSC is highlighted at the conclusion of the chapter. We acknowledge that across all levels of the PSC, comorbid psychiatric symptoms common in postdeployed soldiers complicate traditional TBI assessment and rehabilitation approaches. For the purposes of this chapter, however, relative emphasis is placed on TBI rehabilitation. Later chapters will cover posttraumatic stress and related conditions in greater detail (chapter 12). The PSC is highlighted as the VHA system addresses the complex medical and psychosocial needs of polytrauma patients and their families.

TBI SEVERITY AND LEVELS OF REHABILITATION

Classification of TBI severity plays an important role in the patient's treatment, rehabilitation potential, and prognosis. The most common classification system for TBI severity is based on the Glasgow Coma Scale (GCS) score determined at the time of injury. Considered a gold standard of measuring TBI severity, the GCS is a 3- to 15-point scale used to assess a patient's level of consciousness and level of neurologic functioning (McDonald et al., 1994; Teasdale & Jennett, 1974). The GCS consists of three sections: best motor response, best verbal response, and eye opening. A total score of 3–8 for the three sections suggests severe TBI, a score of 9–12 indicates moderate TBI, and a score of 13–15 indicates mild TBI (mTBI) (for the purposes of this chapter, mTBI and concussion are used interchangeably). Duration of loss of consciousness (LOC) and duration of posttraumatic amnesia (PTA), both challenging indicators to approximate in clinical interviews with patients, are other indicators of TBI severity. PTA is defined as the time elapsed from injury to the moment when patients can demonstrate continuous memory for what is happening around them (Russell, 1932). PTA shows evidence of being the strongest predictor of functional outcome following TBI and may best reflect the overall severity of injury (Levin, O'Donnell, & Grossman, 1979; Zafonte et al., 1997). PTA is challenging to measure in that medical records are often inadequate to estimate PTA duration.

In acute rehabilitation settings, prospective monitoring of PTA is recommended using instruments such as the Galveston Orientation and Amnesia Test (Levin et al., 1979) or Orientation Log (Novack, 2000).

Using all three severity indices, ranges of TBI severity have been outlined by the American Academy of Physical Medicine and Rehabilitation. According to these guidelines, when considering the injury event, severe TBI is defined as LOC greater than 6 hours, PTA more than 7 days, and GCS less than 9. Moderate TBI is defined as LOC less than 6 hours, PTA less than 7 days, and GCS between 9 and 12. Mild TBI is defined as LOC less than 30 minutes, with normal CT and/or MRI findings, PTA less than 24 hours, and initial GCS between 13 and 15. Complicated mTBI captures those situations where there are similar LOC, PTA, and GCS parameters as in mTBI, but with positive neuroimaging findings (Veterans Administration Health Initiative, 2003).

In most cases, only patients with TBI classified as severe, moderate, or complicated-mild are hospitalized for initial medical stabilization. For these cases, when acute medical or surgical care is no longer required, a definitive recommendation for a rehabilitation program is typically made with appropriate consideration for factors such as medical acuity, functional need, and general cognitive functioning. Options for discharge rehabilitation settings range from intensive inpatient programs to community-based settings where patients are assigned a case manager to coordinate needed clinical services. An uninterrupted, seamless transfer between treatment settings is a key element in successful patient management (McNamee, Pickett, Benedict, & Cifu, 2009).

COGNITIVE, BEHAVIORAL, AND EMOTIONAL REHABILITATION CONSIDERATIONS IN ACUTE REHABILITATION

TBI is a heterogeneous construct that can produce an array of medical, physical, cognitive, and emotional symptoms. Because of its multidimensional impacts, a dynamic interdisciplinary team rehabilitation process is vital to assist patients' recovery of function, or compensation for lost functional abilities. Importantly, this process ideally includes the family system, as TBI affects multiple aspects of a patient's psychosocial functioning. Whereas immediately postinjury the most pressing concern is medical stabilization, a more holistic treatment approach is embraced later in the TBI recovery process. Rehabilitation approaches vary according to the severity and type of injury and individual patient characteristics, necessitating dynamic rehabilitation treatment plans to meet patients' changing needs over time. At every level of care, TBI rehabilitation aims to restore maximum independence within the framework of individual limitations (Cifu, Kreutzer, Kolakowsky-Hayner, Marwitz, & Englander, 2003).

Cognitive Problems and Rehabilitation Issues

Cognitive problems are expected in patients with TBI classified as moderate or severe and may consist of (but are not limited to) difficulties with attention and concentration, new learning and memory, executive control, reasoning, judgment, and self-awareness. Learning compensatory strategies is paramount, beginning at the acute inpatient rehabilitation level (Cicerone et al., 2000). Cognitive rehabilitation strategies are generally developed within the context of the interdisciplinary team and reinforced throughout the inpatient rehabilitation stay by the interdisciplinary team and family.

Cognitive problems may occur in areas of orientation (especially in the early phases of recovery), processing speed, language, visual-perceptual skills, and motor dexterity and/or speed. Other changes may include a patient's ability to appreciate subtle social and interpersonal nuances. Nonverbal aspects of communication such as voice volume, rate, tone, gestures and body posture, and interpersonal/relational style reflect areas of postinjury deficit that are not easily captured by scores on standardized neuropsychological measures, but nonetheless may impede resumption of adaptive social-relational and/or vocational functioning. Problems in "executive functioning," often associated with damage to the frontal lobe (or neural circuits in association with the frontal lobe), include problems with abstraction, reasoning, problem solving, planning, organization, flexibility, initiation, behavioral inhibition, persistence, and self-awareness. Individuals with executive problems may lack spontaneity or, alternatively, they may be impulsive, unable to shift flexibly between tasks, or perseverate. Impaired awareness of deficits or anosognosia is a common and particularly challenging problem in rehabilitation. This may manifest as the individual asserting unrealistic goals, and seeing no purpose for the use of overall compensatory strategies or rehabilitation. A variety of methods for assessment and treatment of impaired awareness have been proposed (Cheng & Man, 2006; Goverover, Johnston, Toglia, & DeLuca, 2007; Vanderploeg, Belanger, Duchnick, & Curtiss, 2007).

There are two schools of thought with regard to cognitive rehabilitation techniques. Approaches either involve rehabilitation "directed to achieve functional changes by reinforcing, strengthening, or reestablishing previously learned patterns of behavior, or establishing new patterns of cognitive activity or compensatory mechanisms for impaired neurological systems" (Harley et al., 1992, p. 63). Empirical evidence exists for some cognitive rehabilitation techniques, but more research is needed to substantiate effectiveness of rehabilitation techniques for specific cognitive domains. Attention process training is a technique with some evidence for improving attention and aspects of memory (Sohlberg & Mateer, 1987). Other cognitive rehabilitation interventions teach time-pressure management strategies to compensate for slowed information processing, and handling multiple information sources (e.g., Sohlberg, McLaughlin, Pavese, Heidrich, & Posner, 2000).

New learning and memory problems are common following TBI and, consequently, patients may experience difficulty encoding new material, retaining it, and retrieving it after a delay. A variety of cognitive rehabilitation techniques have been developed and proposed to teach patients how to use visualization, repetition, and reduction of distracters to increase encoding of information, and categorical, multiple choice, or phonemic cues to assist in the retrieval of previously encoded information. Some evidence supports the use of such compensatory strategies for mild memory impairment after TBI (Berg, Konning-Haanstra, & Deelman, 1991; Kaschel et al., 2002; Schmitter-Edgecombe, Fahy, Whelan, & Long, 1995). External cognitive compensatory devices have been long employed to address memory deficits. One of the earliest and most common methods, memory notebooks, is used by patients and rehabilitation facilities as an efficacious compensatory strategy that leads to fewer everyday memory problems (Schmitter-Edgecombe et al., 1995). With advances in technology, cognitive assistive devices are proving to be of benefit for patients with sufficient residual cognitive abilities to integrate these devices into their daily lives (e.g., Galvin & Scherer, 1996). The reader is referred to two review articles that provide cognitive rehabilitation practice guidelines following TBI (Cicerone et al., 2000, 2005).

Another means of providing cognitive rehabilitation is through computer-based programs. A wide variety of such programs are available via the Internet or for purchase to be loaded on one's personal computer. Such intervention strategies are appealing for a number of reasons, including their availability, relative ease of use, self-directed nature following initial instruction and guidance, and serial nature of training and feedback often provided. While they are often utilized as part of a comprehensive cognitive rehabilitation program, evidence about their ability to generalize and improve performance on functional tasks remains scarce (Lynch, 2002).

Comprehensive-holistic cognitive rehabilitation, defined as treatment targeting multiple areas of functional deficit (e.g., cognitive, behavioral, emotional), is recommended during postacute rehabilitation with individuals who have sustained a moderate to severe TBI. Furthermore, due to evidence that psychosocial interventions facilitate the effectiveness of treatment for cognitive impairments following TBI, individual cognitive and interpersonal treatment tailored for each patient is recommended as a practice option (Cicerone et al., 2005).

Executive functioning deficits may be present but not readily apparent through analysis of neuropsychological test scores, which is why assessment of patients' functioning in real-world environments is critical in a rehabilitation context. TBI patients with executive functioning deficits may not show problems in familiar or highly structured tasks. Rehabilitation teams should consider involving patients with suspected executive deficits in novel and complex real-world situations as part of the assessment and treatment plan to assess for the presence of executive functioning problems (and intervene accordingly). Treatment of executive dysfunction may take a variety of forms often involving feedback about performance from the rehabilitation team. A recent meta-analysis concluded that meta-cognitive strategy instruction approaches (involving step-by-step task instruction, a priori performance predictions, solution generation, self-monitoring, and strategy reassessment resulting from self-assessment) are effective and recommended for young to middle-aged adults with TBI experiencing problems with problem solving, planning, and organization (Kennedy et al., 2008).

Behavioral and Emotional Problems and Rehabilitation Issues

Agitation, hypoarousal, and depression are common in the early stages following moderate or severe TBI (Morton & Wehman, 1995; Sohlberg & Mateer, 2001). Though expected, these symptoms can be both difficult to manage and present a significant barrier to optimal functional recovery. In the acute rehabilitation setting, agitation is perhaps the most commonly reported behavioral problem. Sandel and Mysiw (1996) define agitation as a special subtype of delirium specific to TBI that includes PTA and behaviors such as disinhibition, emotional lability, aggression, and akasthesia. Behaviors such as extreme psychomotor restlessness, yelling, cursing, angry outbursts, striking out, and inappropriate sexual gestures can occur.

Agitation can be distressing to family members and clinicians who are unfamiliar with TBI sequelae. For those more familiar with TBI rehabilitation, the emergence of such behaviors may signal neurologic recovery, though importantly other medical etiologies may be contributing to agitation including hydrocephalus, intracranial bleeding, seizure, pulmonary embolism, electrolyte disturbance, infection, medications, undertreated pain, and disturbed sleep, and these potential contributors should be fully explored (McNamee, Pickett, Benedict, & Cifu, 2009).

Appropriate characterization of agitation is helpful to inform rehabilitation interventions. The Agitated Behavior Scale (Corrigan, 1989) and the Overt Agitation Severity Scale (Yudofsky, Silver, & Jackson, 1986) are two useful measures constructed to assess agitation.

Typically, behavioral and environmental approaches should be explored as a first-line intervention method when agitation behaviors are not severe or dangerous. Behavioral management plans, typically devised by the staff psychologist on an interdisciplinary team, can be implemented by individuals involved in the patient's care (including the patient's family). Environmental manipulations are common and effective interventions helpful for managing agitation, but must be consistently and sufficiently implemented by interdisciplinary teams to hope to effect meaningful behavior change. Such interventions may include regulating sleep/wake cycles, controlling noise levels and minimizing environmental stimulation, treating pain, and/or frequently reorientating the patient to reduce confusion to person, place, time, and situation. All of the aforementioned may have a behavioral calming effect. However, staff responding on an interpersonal level by using a calm tone of voice, presenting requests for nonagitated behavior, underreacting, and not taking agitated behavior personally has been quite helpful. Physical restraints are discouraged save for those instances when agitation may lead to self-harm or harm of others. Pharmacologic approaches are generally utilized when environmental and/or behavioral management strategies fail (Gordon et al., 2006).

Hypoarousal is problematic during acute rehabilitation in that a patient's ability to remain awake and alert during treatment may be compromised. Motor restlessness, involuntary yawning, drowsiness, and waning attention over a therapy session all indicate inadequate arousal. Patients with hypoarousal may be able to tolerate only short periods of active therapy. Behaviorally, many patients may begin to opt out of therapeutic activities that require cognitive exertion, as they may associate these cognitive or physical tasks with fatigue (Matthies, Kreutzer, & West, 2004). Frequent breaks, early discrimination of fatigue, and promotion of sleep hygiene are all effective strategies to improve arousal. The art of scaffolding therapeutic intensity to meet a TBI patient's energy levels is demonstrated by sophisticated interdisciplinary teams. For patients with hypoarousal, cognitive or physical rehabilitation should ideally occur when they are at peak alertness. To gradually increase endurance, within sessions, therapists may consider alternating between challenging and less-intense tasks. Likewise, patients may be taught how to discriminate between tasks that require intense focus and tasks that do not, the latter offering a period of rest and recuperation before the next task when they would need to adaptively focus (e.g., when important medical information is being communicated). Staff should be vigilant to patient arousal levels within treatment sessions and, importantly, reduce task demands well in advance of fatigue onset. This practice will reduce the extent to which patients may begin to associate cognitive or physical rehabilitation activities with a fatigue state. Pharmacologic interventions such as the use of psychostimulants (e.g., methylphenidate) may complement environmental and behavioral strategies (McElligott, Greenwald, & Watanabe, 2003).

Estimates of the incidence of depressive disorders after TBI range from 6% to 77% in the literature (Levin & Grossman, 1978; Rutherford, Merrett, & McDonald, 1997; Varney, Martzke, & Roberts, 1987), and the proper evaluation and treatment of depression are vital across rehabilitation stages. Depressive symptoms can significantly contribute to long-term disability and TBI rehabilitation outcomes are adversely affected by depression (Jorge et al., 2004), perhaps because depressive symptoms interfere with optimal participation in (and benefit from) available therapies (Matthies et al., 2004). Following TBI, depressive symptoms may either present as a component of TBI symptoms or as a discrete major depressive episode. For this reason, the assessment of post-TBI depression often requires an appreciation for the natural course of emotional recovery after a TBI and determining whether there is presence of a mood disorder beyond that which would be expected secondary to TBI.

For some patients, cognitive symptoms may affect the accuracy of symptom reporting. Also, the injury itself, or the hospitalization process, may bring about "depressive" symptoms such as low energy, fatigue, reduced motivation, or anhedonia. Depressive symptoms include sadness, irritability, hopelessness, tearfulness, anhedonia, suicidal ideation, and sleep/appetite disturbances. Given the overlap between somatic and cognitive symptoms of depression and consequences of TBI, the assessment of depressed affect or lack of positive affect is helpful in determining depression from more transient TBI-related symptoms (Dikmen, Bombardier, Machamer, Fann, & Temkin, 2004).

Many depression screening questionnaires have been developed such as the Beck Depression Inventory (Beck, Steer, & Brown, 1996) and Zung Depression Inventory (Zung, 1965), which are patient-administered instruments, and the Hamilton Depression Inventory (Hamilton, 1967), which is a rating form completed by the provider. Referral to a psychologist, neuropsychologist, or psychiatrist familiar with TBI sequelae is indicated when there are uncertainties regarding differential diagnosis or treatment approach.

Effective treatment strategies for post-TBI depressive symptoms are multimodal. Normalization of post-TBI problems, shaping positive expectations regarding recovery, focusing on improvements, and psychotherapy may all be useful strategies. A positive, upbeat, rehabilitation program is also important because this context is incompatible with depressed mood. Staff behavior and interpersonal reactions to the post-TBI patient also play a vital role in managing patients' mood states. Interdisciplinary teams should be forward thinking, encouraging, and improvement-focused. The appropriate use of humor and normalization of reactions to disability may be helpful interventions. Across rehabilitation contexts, TBI patients should be encouraged to maintain a positive outlook about the treatment benefits and, importantly, to focus on accomplishments relative to recent status (as opposed to engaging in comparisons to premorbid functioning).

Group, individual, and family counseling may be recommended during inpatient hospitalization. Group therapy provides an avenue for peer-to-peer normalization of problems and social support and can facilitate return of self-awareness. An adapted form of cognitive behavioral therapy provided in a group or telephone format has been found effective in improving the emotional well-being of TBI survivors (Bradbury et al., 2008). Educational interventions empower patients and families in the short term, shape positive expectations for recovery, and may provide a buffer against negative emotional experiences in the long term, in that patients will have sufficient knowledge about deficits (and compensatory strategies) in advance. Antidepressant medication may also serve as a useful adjunct to psychotherapy, but careful consideration of side effects is encouraged, and side effect profiles should be reviewed regularly with the patient and family. Finally, TBI patients may experience exacerbation of depressive symptoms once confronted with cognitive or neurobehavioral deficits postdischarge. For this reason, education should focus on identifying warning signs for depression, coping strategies, and when/how to pursue treatment if needed (Matthies et al., 2004; McNamee et al., 2009).

REHABILITATION LEVELS OF CARE

Intensive Care Units and Neurologic Step-Down Units

Following a TBI, an interdisciplinary team composed of rehabilitation specialists should be involved in patient care as soon as clinically indicated. Initial assessments by physiatry or neuropsychiatry, neuropsychology, physical therapy, occupational therapy, and speech and language pathology are typical. Ideally, detailed neurologic and medical examinations should be performed as soon as medical stability is achieved, followed by general medical management in the ICU via serial evaluations to inform disposition planning. Particular attention should be paid to seizure prophylaxis, deep vein thrombosis (DVT) prevention, pain management, bowel and bladder functioning, management of pathologic tone, nutritional status, behavioral issues, and sleep cycles. Initial physical therapy and occupational therapy assessments should address body positioning to prevent contractures, pressure sores, and peripheral nerve compression injuries. Ranges of motion exercises may be recommended to maximize functional range in all major joints and to ensure proper positioning. Specific activity training such as toileting and ambulation may be delayed until later in the rehabilitation process. The speech and language pathology assessment provides information about communication abilities and swallowing safety. The initial rehabilitation plan implemented in the ICU should be continued and expanded in the neurologic step-down unit. Often, sedating medications that are utilized in the ICU setting are weaned in favor of medications that optimize cognitive arousal. Comprehensive assessment of cognitive and behavioral capabilities should be conducted once sedating agents have been removed. A broader array of rehabilitation therapies are introduced in this setting, as strict bed rest is no longer necessary or beneficial (McNamee et al., 2009).

Acute Inpatient Rehabilitation

Acute inpatient rehabilitation programs have become the mainstay of care following moderate to severe TBI. These programs are characterized by an interdisciplinary treatment milieu that strives to promote optimal medical status, assess cognitive and functional strengths and weaknesses, and develop individually tailored treatment plans to maximize functional independence. The principal goals of acute interdisciplinary rehabilitation are to set the stage for optimal community reintegration post discharge and to restore functional independence. This model of treatment is also thought to bring about self-awareness in the moderate to severely injured (Goranson, Craves, Allison, & La Freniere, 2003; Klonoff, Lamb, Henderson, & Shepherd, 1998; Malec, 2001; Salazar et al., 2000; Seale, Caroselli, & High, 2002).

For admission to an acute inpatient rehabilitation program, it is vital to determine whether a patient will be able to tolerate and benefit from the intensity of a daily therapy regimen. Therapy services at the acute care level include, on average, 3 hours of structured therapy per day. After admission, interdisciplinary teams often must decide about appropriate therapeutic intensity keeping in mind the patient's capacity and functional level. The conversation around discharge planning occurs early in the inpatient's rehabilitative stay, which sets the tone for rehabilitation as a goal-oriented endeavor, with the focus to restore functional independence to the extent possible. Key points that are emphasized to patients and families include expectations of a positive recovery course and a primary focus on community reintegration.

One frequent dilemma for interdisciplinary teams is that the pace and extent of recovery following TBI can vary considerably between patients, even between those with similar injuries based on established injury severity indices. Prediction models about the extent of recovery expected are sometimes perceived by patients and family members as ambiguous. Most professionals in the TBI field are familiar with at least one case where a severe TBI recovers much better than injury severity indices might otherwise predict and, conversely, also a case where a patient with mTBI does not recover as well as might be expected. This presents a perplexing state of affairs for rehabilitation professionals, patients, and families alike, who continuously attempt to predict short- and long-term rehabilitation outcome for pragmatic considerations (i.e., postdischarge living arrangement, vocational involvement) and emotional considerations, such as worrying that their loved one's personality is forever altered (that they have lost their loved one psychologically, while physically they are still present).

A vital element in acute rehabilitation is the patient's support system. The presence of an interested, committed, and resilient family system can facilitate progress toward rehabilitation goals in the acute setting. Ideally, families become active collaborators with interdisciplinary teams to establish and reinforce treatment strategies to shape patients toward greater functional independence.

Acute inpatient rehabilitation programs support cognitive and functional recovery—while maximizing safety. These types of programs are typically separate, with the option of being locked, as a way to ensure environmental control. Treatment decisions and care plans are made with appreciation that optimal rehabilitative care occurs in the least restrictive environmental setting. Nursing and medical services, typically provided by physiatry, are available 24 hours a day. Interdisciplinary teams are most commonly led by a physician (physiatrist) with other team members including specialists from rehabilitation nursing, physical therapy, occupational therapy, speech-language pathology, psychology and/or neuropsychology, social work/case management, and recreation therapy.

Other consultative services may be needed for such targeted problems as orthopedics, neurosurgery, wound care, and neuroophthalmology. Interdisciplinary team meetings occur on a regular basis and provide a forum to apprise staff of medical status, allow for revisions in rehabilitation goals, address psychosocial issues, and plan for discharge (McNamee et al., 2009).

Subacute Rehabilitation

Not all individuals suffering a moderate to severe TBI are appropriate for acute rehabilitation programs. For instance, those who have yet to return to consciousness cannot actively participate in acute inpatient rehabilitation. Patients need to have achieved a return of consciousness that would indicate placement in an acute intensive inpatient rehabilitation program. To progress, at a minimum, a patient must be able to follow simple commands. Some hospital programs have been developed to provide supportive services to accelerate return to consciousness and typically employ environmental control of stimuli as a way of bringing about increased cortical arousal. Numerous titles are given to this approach, including "coma stimulation" and "cortical stimulation." To date, the literature provides little support for acceleration to return to consciousness using this approach (Lombardi, Taricco, De Tanti, Telaro, & Liberati, 2002).

Second, those too frail to tolerate at least 3 hours of therapy per day, elderly patients with numerous comorbid medical problems, severely debilitated patients, minimally conscious patients, or those with medical restrictions (i.e., numerous fractures with weight-bearing restrictions) may be more appropriate for subacute rehabilitation units. Such programs provide supportive nursing and therapy, albeit at a reduced intensity relative to acute inpatient rehabilitation units. Physical and occupational therapy services are typically available, whereas speech and intensive cognitive therapies are less commonly available. The goal for subacute rehabilitation programs is to build functional capability for eventual discharge to a community setting or for participation in an acute rehabilitation facility.

Transitional Rehabilitation

While many TBI survivors make recoveries in the acute rehabilitation setting that permit return to approximately normal premorbid social, occupational, and familial roles, others may be challenged by residual cognitive, emotional, and/or neurobehavioral symptoms that interfere with optimal community reentry. The overarching goal of transitional TBI rehabilitation is community reintegration, or to put it another way, a return to the least restrictive environment. This goal would include return to active duty military service, work, school, or independent living in the community with meaningful daily activities. Transitional brain injury rehabilitation models vary widely and range from residential programs, facility- or community-based day treatment, or a home-based (possibly hybrid) model (Ben-Yishay, 2000; Glenn, Rotman, Goldstein, & Selleck, 2005; Malec & Basford, 1996).

A transitional rehabilitation level of care for TBI is vital for a variety of reasons. Some injuries, while limiting full independence, do not require the intensive medical or nursing services of the acute rehabilitation environment. An additional advantage of transitional programs is that, relative to clinic-based settings, transitional brain injury rehabilitation often takes place in environments more closely resembling the "real world." Transitional rehabilitation programs emphasize ecological validity, meaning that assessment and intervention services are carried out in environmental contexts that aspire to closely resemble real-world settings.

For some patients, transitional rehabilitation offers an accessible, progressive return to independent living through a structured program focused on restoring home, community, leisure, and psychosocial and vocational skills in a controlled, therapeutic setting. Transitional rehabilitation programs attempt to shape adaptive functional outcomes through graduated therapeutic exercises, and active participation in community and work settings. Treatments target cognitive, social, and neurobehavioral functioning in an ecologically valid treatment setting to enhance the likelihood of transfer of training to the community setting. The scope of transitional rehabilitation services includes medical, psychiatric, health and wellness, cognitive rehabilitation, independent living skills, psychosocial adjustment, community reintegration, and vocational rehabilitation services. Treatment, whether conducted in the clinic or community setting, is often provided by rehabilitation specialists spanning multiple disciplines (e.g., neuropsychology, recreation therapy, and vocational rehabilitation).

POLYTRAUMA SYSTEM OF CARE

The polytrauma system of care (PSC) is a national, multi-tiered system of rehabilitation care in the VA designed to address the specialized rehabilitation needs of patients who have sustained TBI, along with other life-threatening injuries, while addressing the broad geographic distribution of patients (and their families) and their potential lifelong treatment needs (Sigford, 2008). The four common elements across all levels of the PSC are (a) proactive case management, (b) lifelong specialized follow-up care, (c) telehealth, and (d) care for patients who are unable to return to their homes or require extensive in-home services because of the severity of their injuries (www.va.polytrauma.gov). The PSC has five levels of care. Each is detailed below.

Level I: Polytrauma Rehabilitation Center

Level 1 consists of four regional polytrauma rehabilitation centers (PRCs), which are located in Minneapolis, Minnesota; Palo Alto, California; Richmond, Virginia; and Tampa, Florida. Regional PRCs serve as hubs for acute medical and rehabilitation care, research, and education related to polytrauma and TBI. Clinical care is provided by a dedicated staff of rehabilitation specialists and medical consultants with expertise in the treatment of the physical, cognitive, emotional, and neurobehavioral problems that accompany TBI. PRCs maintain accreditation by the Commission on Accreditation of Rehabilitation Facilities for both TBI and comprehensive rehabilitation. Inpatient rehabilitation in the PSC occurs at the level of the four PRCs.

PRC programs are characterized by a collaborative, patient- and family-centered process involving an interdisciplinary team of rehabilitation professionals. Interdisciplinary team members include physiatry, nursing, neuropsychology, rehabilitation psychology, vocational counseling, social work, occupational therapy, physical therapy, speech therapy, recreation therapy, and low-vision specialists. All aforementioned team members coordinate individualized assessment and treatment planning in close collaboration with the injured veteran and their family. Individualized treatments are aimed at using strengths and compensatory strategies to decrease barriers and maximize functioning (Collins & Kennedy, 2008).

The clinical complexity of PRC patients was demonstrated in a study describing the characteristics and rehabilitation outcomes of veterans with TBI and other combat injuries in the four PRCs between October 2001 and January 2006 (Sayer et al., 2008). These authors found that, in a sample of 188 PRC patients, the modal patient was a white male Army service member deployed to Iraq from active duty status, admitted to a PRC from a military treatment facility, and who had undergone surgeries prior to PRC admission. The vast majority in the sample had sustained injuries to more than one body structure or system, and 56% had sustained blast-related combat injuries that were associated with injuries to more body systems and/or organs than other injury mechanisms. The presence of brain lesion was confirmed for 156 of the 175 patients with structural imaging available. Pain was the second most common impairment. Of the psychiatric impairments, posttraumatic stress disorder (PTSD) was the most common among all, and more common among those with blast injuries.

Level 2: Polytrauma Network Site

Level 2 consists of 21 polytrauma network sites (PNS) located in each of the Veterans Integrated Service Networks. These sites provide specialized, postacute rehabilitation in a setting appropriate to the needs of the injured veterans and their family. These network sites provide proactive case management for existing and emerging conditions and identify local resources for VA and non-VA care.

Level 3: Polytrauma Support Clinical Team

Level 3 consists of polytrauma support clinical teams (PSCT). PSCTs assume a proactive case management role and take responsibility for managing and coordinating care for relatively stable TBI sequelae. PSCTs are generally located in nearer proximity to veterans' homes. PSCTs monitor for acute physical, cognitive, or emotional changes that would signal potential need for more intensive clinical services at a PNS (level 2), polytrauma transitional program (level 5), or PRC (level 1).

Level 4: Polytrauma Points of Contact

At level 4, polytrauma points of contact are designated staff at all other VHA facilities who are responsible for assisting identified patients in their local area with accessing necessary and appropriate services from the PSC.

Level 5: Polytrauma Transitional Program

At level 5, recently created polytrauma transitional programs, which are colocated with PRC programs, are residential programs that are designed to be time limited and goal oriented and emphasize improving the person's physical, cognitive, communicative, behavioral, psychological, and social functioning (in real-world settings). All polytrauma transitional programs are applying for Commission on Accreditation of Rehabilitation Facilities accreditation under residential/brain injury medical rehabilitation. The overall treatment approach recognizes and appreciates the role of biological, psychological, and social factors in the treatment of TBI/polytrauma injuries. Treatment is designed to be time limited and goal oriented to improve the person's physical, cognitive, communicative, behavioral, psychological, and social functioning in an environment that provides the necessary support and supervision.

REHABILITATION OF THE VETERAN FOLLOWING MILD TBI

In civilian literature, most individuals sustaining a TBI are classified as mTBI (Alexander, 1995). Patients with mTBI are expected to make a rapid recovery with few postinjury complications. It is for these reasons that mTBI patients often bypass acute medical attention or hospitalization. Nevertheless, some mTBI patients develop chronic symptoms (Alexander, 1995; Binder, 1997; Vanderploeg, Curtiss, & Luis, 2001). For such individuals, treatments targeting cognitive remediation and psychotherapy have demonstrated improvements in emotional and cognitive functioning (Tiersky et al., 2005).

Postconcussive syndrome (PCS) refers to an array of physical, emotional, and cognitive symptoms that can occur following mTBI. While these same symptoms occur in the general population, there is a greater incidence of these symptoms in PCS among mTBI patients (Mittenberg, 2002). PCS symptoms include headaches, postural imbalance, insomnia, memory problems, fatigue, and irritable or depressed mood. Treatment for PCS symptoms often includes "normalization" of symptoms through education about the expected symptoms following mild head injury, expected recovery course, and transient nature of postconcussive symptoms; recommendations for improved rest; stress management; and headache management (McCrea, 2008; Mittenberg, Canyock, Condit, & Patton, 2001). More intensive interdisciplinary treatment shortly following mTBI has not been shown to produce better outcomes relative to controls, though there is some evidence suggesting improved cost-effectiveness targeting those with premorbid psychiatric difficulties (Ghaffar, McCullagh, Ouchterlony, & Feinstein, 2006). There is some literature supporting the use of medications such as nonsteroidal anti-inflammatory drugs, tricyclic antidepressants, and selective serotonin reuptake inhibitor antidepressant medications (Mittenberg et al., 2001). Therapeutically, a stance emphasizing "validation" of PCS symptoms paired with setting reasonable expectations for recovery is recommended (Salazar & Warden, 1999). Morbid psychiatric problems increase the risk for TBI, and these same problems may be amplified following mTBI (Bennett & Raymond, 1997; Hanks, Tempkin, Machamer, & Dikmen, 1999; McCauley, Boake, Levin, Contant, & Song, 2001; Sarapata, Herrman, Johnson, & Aycock, 1998).

Some findings show that a percentage of individuals with mTBI change or lose their jobs within 6 months of the injury (Gasquoine, 1997) and some may be at risk for not understanding why they are now having problems in their life (Prigatano & Schacter, 1991). Finally, it can also be the case that, for individuals with mTBI, emotional symptoms may go unreported until the symptoms have produced a significant negative impact on the person's life. Unless history of TBI is queried in a clinical interview, it may be that patients come to the attention of a mental health provider with distressing psychiatric symptoms or psychosocial adjustment difficulties, and these are never etiologically related to the TBI event.

It is recommended that TBI history be incorporated into the regular clinical intake process, as mTBI patients may enter the health-care system through a variety of channels including primary care, mental health, or other specialty clinics. There are times when emotional symptoms are the direct result of neurological damage rather than psychological reactions secondary to having a brain injury, despite similar clinical appearance (e.g., Judd & Wilson, 1999). In either case emotional dysfunction in the postacute period can contribute to problems.

DISCUSSION

Military activities in the post-9/11 era have resulted in a new cohort of active duty service members and veterans who are seeking rehabilitation care through the VA. Injuries sustained in OEF/OIF combat arenas are most often to multiple bodily systems (polytrauma) and, as such, a unique rehabilitation-service-delivery model is required.

It is important to note that these injuries may be unhidden, as in the case of fractures or burns, and also hidden, as in the case of combat stress reactions, PTSD, and depression. The presence of comorbid TBI and combat stress symptoms has resulted in a necessary adaptation of traditional TBI rehabilitation methods to more strongly incorporate mental health programming.

The needs of veterans who have experienced mTBI (or potentially a series of mild concussive events) have become a major focus of assessment and treatment for PNS and PCST levels of care. In a large percentage of these cases, veterans who screen positive for history of concussion injury may also screen positive for PTSD or other mental health conditions. In one cross-sectional study of military personnel who had left combat theatres by September 30, 2004, 11% were classified as having PTSD and 12% reported a history consistent with mTBI (Schneiderman, Braver, & Kang, 2008). Persistent symptoms were associated with more severe mTBI, multiple injury mechanisms, and PTSD. PTSD was also associated with persisting postconcussive symptoms suggesting that veterans presenting themselves to the VA system of care with a history of mTBI are likely to present with a complex profile of neuropsychiatric symptoms and show symptoms consistent with postconcussion syndrome, PTSD, and other psychiatric disorders such as depression. In one study, approximately 15% of OIF combat veterans had experienced concussions marked by either lost or altered consciousness (Hoge et al., 2008). These authors asserted a strong association between history of combat-related concussion and the later development of PTSD symptoms. Statistical analysis confirmed that experiencing mTBI was significantly associated with psychiatric symptoms.

A marked challenge facing health care diagnosticians has been the differential diagnosis of persisting symptoms attributable to TBI, in particular mTBI presenting with postconcussive symptoms, from other comorbid (or stand alone) psychiatric diagnoses including PTSD, depression, sleep disturbance, pain, and substance abuse. Difficulty with differential diagnosis occurs in part because the mTBI and PTSD diagnoses share many symptoms (Bryant & Harvey, 1999) including attention and concentration problems, slowed processing speed and efficiency, and short-term memory difficulties. Regardless of etiology, cognitive and behavioral symptoms of TBI and/or PTSD can present veterans with significant impairments in functioning that interfere with community adjustment.

Taking an etiological approach requires clinicians to make judgments about the most likely cause of presenting symptoms and provide a pathway of care. For example, if a patient's symptoms were determined to likely have mTBI as an etiological factor, traditional rehabilitation therapy services (e.g., cognitive rehabilitation, occupational therapy, vocational rehabilitation, along with psychological services) would likely be provided through physical medicine and rehabilitation. However, if the veteran's symptoms were judged to be primarily attributable to PTSD, then the patient would be referred to the VA's mental health providers who are specially trained to treat PTSD. In the etiology-driven model, veterans presenting with nearly identical symptoms may have access to different service pathways, not based on presenting symptoms or severity of problems, but because of a clinician's judgment of likely etiology of symptoms.

An alternative model, as has been proposed by Ruff (2005), is to attempt to treat presenting symptoms as functional deficits rather than focusing on etiology. In this case, patients presenting with a history of mTBI and having symptoms of postconcussion syndrome and/or a mental health disorder will be provided services, not based on judgments of etiology, but based on presenting symptoms, functional impairment, and a more phenomenologically based (patient centered) understanding of how the individual's life has changed. Despite the need for increased understanding of etiology in polytrauma patient care, there is broad recognition that the goal of polytrauma rehabilitation is to assist combat veterans' efforts to reintegrate into their community, achieve educational and vocational success, and be positive, loving members of their families. As a result, polytrauma programs in the VA have continued to develop and change as understanding of the OEF/OIF war veteran has evolved. While some clinicians coming from traditional rehabilitation programs have emphasized only treating patients with clearly established brain injuries within multidisciplinary models, polytrauma rehabilitation teams have evolved to coordinate more effectively with mental health treatment providers in their facilities and the community.

REFERENCES

Alexander, M. P. (1995). Mild traumatic brain injury: Pathophysiology, natural history, and clinical management. *Neurology, 45*, 1253–1260.

Beck, A. T., Steer, R. A., & Brown, G. K. (Eds.). (1996). *Manual for the Beck depression inventory* (2nd ed.). San Antonio, TX: The Psychological Corporation.

Bennett, T. L., & Raymond, M. J. (1997). Emotional consequences and psychotherapy for individuals with mild brain injury. *Applied Neuropsychology, 4*, 51–61.

Ben-Yishay, Y. (2000). Postacute neurobehavioral rehabilitation: A holistic approach. In A. L. Christensen & B. P. Uzell (Eds.), *International handbook of neuropsychological rehabilitation* (pp. 127–136). New York: Kluwer Academic/Plenum Publishers.

Berg, I., Konning-Haanstra, M., & Deelman, B. (1991). Long-term effects of memory rehabilitation. A controlled study. *Neuropsychological Rehabilitation, 1*, 97–111.

Binder, L. M. (1997). A review of mild head trauma. Part II: Clinical implications. *Journal of Clinical and Experimental Neuropsychology, 19*, 432–457.

Bradbury, C. L., Christensen, B. K., Lau, M. A., Ruttan, L. A., Arundine, A. L., & Green, R. E. (2008). The efficacy of cognitive behavior therapy in the treatment of emotional distress after acquired brain injury. *Archives of Physical Medicine and Rehabilitation, 89*(2), 61–68.

Bryant, R. A., & Harvey, A. G. (1999). Postconcussive symptoms and posttraumatic stress disorder after mild traumatic brain injury. *Journal of Nervous and Mental Disease, 187*, 302–305.

Cheng, S. K. W., & Man, D. W. K. (2006). Management of impaired self-awareness in persons with traumatic brain injury. *Brain Injury, 20*, 621–628.

Cicerone, K. D., Dahlberg, C., Kalmar, K., Langenbahn, D. M., Malec, J. F., Bergquist, T. F., et al. (2000). Evidence-based cognitive rehabilitation: Recommendations for clinical practice. *Archives of Physical Medicine and Rehabilitation, 81*, 1596–1615.

Cicerone, K. D., Dahlberg, C., Malec, J. F., Langenbahn, D. M., Felicetti, T., Kneipp, S., et al. (2005). Evidence-based cognitive rehabilitation: Updated review of the literature from 1998 through 2002. *Archives of Physical Medicine and Rehabilitation, 86*, 1681–1692.

Cifu, D. X., Kreutzer, J. S., Kolakowsky-Hayner, M. A., Marwitz, J. H., & Englander, J. (2003). The relationship between therapy intensity and rehabilitative outcomes after traumatic brain injury: A multicenter analysis. *Archives of Physical Medicine and Rehabilitation, 84*, 1441–1448.

Collins, R. C., & Kennedy, M. C. (2008). Serving families who have served: Providing family therapy and support in interdisciplinary polytrauma rehabilitation. *Journal of Clinical Psychology, 64*(8), 993–1003.

Corrigan, J. D. (1989). Development of a scale for assessment of agitation following traumatic brain injury. *Journal of Clinical and Experimental Neuropsychology, 11*, 261–277.

Coupland, C. R. M., & Meddings, D. R. (1999). Mortality associated with use of weapons in armed conflicts, wartime atrocities, and civilian mass shootings: Literature review. *British Medical Journal, 319*, 410–412.

DePalma, R. G., Burris, D. G., Champion, H. R., & Hodgson, M. J. (2005). Blast injuries. *New England Journal of Medicine, 352*, 1335–1342.

Department of Veterans Affairs. (2003). Veterans Administration Health Initiative. Employee Education System. *Traumatic Brain Injury* (p. 24).

Dikmen, S. S., Bombardier, C. H., Machamer, J. E., Fann, J. R., & Temkin, N. R. (2004). Natural history of depression in traumatic brain injury. *Archives of Physical Medicine and Rehabilitation, 85*, 1457–1464.

Galvin, J. C., & Scherer, M. J. (Eds.). (1996). *Evaluating, selecting an appropriate assistive technology.* Gaithersburg: Aspen.

Gasquoine, P. G. (1997). Postconcussion symptoms. *Neuropsychology Review, 7*, 77–85.

Gawande, A. (2004). Casualties of war—military care for the wounded from Iraq and Afghanistan. *New England Journal of Medicine, 351*, 2471–2475.

Ghaffar, O., McCullagh, S., Ouchterlony, D., & Feinstein, D. (2006). Randomized treatment trial in mild traumatic brain injury. *Journal of Psychosomatic Research, 61*, 153–160.

Glenn, M. B., Rotman, M., Goldstein, R., & Selleck, E. A. (2005). Characteristics of residential community integration programs for adults with brain injury. *Journal of Head Trauma Rehabilitation, 20*, 393–401.

Gondusky, J. S., & Reiter, M. P. (2005). Protecting military convoys in Iraq: An examination of battle injuries sustained by a mechanized battalion during Operation Iraqi Freedom II. *Military Medicine, 170*, 546–549.

Goranson, T. E., Craves, R. E., Allison, D., & La Freniere, R. (2003). Community integration following multidisciplinary rehabilitation for traumatic brain injury. *Brain Injury, 17*, 759–774.

Gordon, W. A., Zafonte, R., Cicerone, K., Cantor, J., Brown, M., Lombard, L., et al. (2006). Traumatic brain injury rehabilitation: State of the science. *American Journal of Physical Medicine and Rehabilitation, 85*, 343–382.

Goverover, Y., Johnston, M. V., Toglia, J., & DeLuca, J. (2007). Treatment to improve self-awareness in persons with acquired brain injury. *Brain Injury, 21*, 913–923.

Hamilton, M. (1967). Development of a rating scale for primary depressive illness. *British Journal of Social and Clinical Psychology, 6*, 278–296.

Hanks, R. A., Tempkin, N., Machamer, J., & Dikmen, S. S. (1999). Emotional and behavioral adjustment after traumatic brain injury. *Archives of Physical Medicine and Rehabilitation, 80*, 991–997.

Harley, J. P., Allen, C., Braciszewski, T. L., Cicerone, K. D., Dahlberg, C., Evans, S., et al. (1992). Guidelines for cognitive rehabilitation. *NeuroRehabilitation, 2*, 62–67.

Hoge, C. W., McGurk, D., Thomas, J. L., Cox, A. L., Engel, C. C., & Castro, C. A. (2008). Mild traumatic brain injury in U.S. soldiers returning from Iraq. *New England Journal of Medicine, 358*, 453–463.

Jorge, R. E., Robinson, R. G., Moser, D., Tateno, A., Crespo-Facorro, B., & Arndt, S. (2004). Major depression following traumatic brain injury. *Archives of General Psychiatry, 61*, 42–50.

Judd, D. P., & Wilson, S. L. (1999). Brain injury and identity: The role of counseling psychologists. *Counseling Psychology Review, 14*, 4–16.

Kaschel, R., Della Sala, S., Cantagallo, A., Fahlbock, A., Laaksonen, R., Kazan, M., et al. (2002). Imagery mnemonics for the rehabilitation of memory: A randomized group controlled trial. *Neuropsychological Rehabilitation, 12*, 127–153.

Kennedy, M. R. T., Coelho, C., Turkstra, L., Ylvisaker, M., Sohlberg, M. M., Yorkston, K., et al. (2008). Intervention for executive functions after traumatic brain injury: A systematic review, meta analysis and clinical recommendations. *Neuropsychological Rehabilitation, 1*, 1–43.

Klonoff, P. S., Lamb, D. C., Henderson, S. W., & Shepherd, J. (1998). Outcome assessment after milieu-oriented rehabilitation: New considerations. *Archives of Physical Medicine and Rehabilitation, 79*, 684–690.

Levin, H. S., & Grossman, R. G. (1978). Behavioral sequelae of closed head injury: A quantitative study. *Archives of Neurology, 35*, 720–727.

Levin, H. S., O'Donnell, V. M., & Grossman, R. G. (1979). The Galveston orientation and amnesia test: A practical scale to assess cognition after head injury. *Journal of Nervous and Mental Disease, 167*, 675–684.

Lombardi, F., Taricco, M., De Tanti, A., Telaro, E., & Liberati, A. (2002). Sensory stimulation for brain injured individuals in coma or vegetative state. *Cochrane Database of Systematic Reviews*, (2), CD001427.

Lynch, B. (2002). Historical review of computer-assisted cognitive retraining. *Journal of Head Trauma Rehabilitation, 17*, 446–457.

Malec, J. F. (2001). Impact of comprehensive day treatment on societal participation for persons with acquired brain injury. *Archives of Physical Medicine and Rehabilitation, 82*, 885–895.

Malec, J. F., & Basford, J. S. (1996). Postacute brain injury rehabilitation. *Archives of Physical Medicine and Rehabilitation, 77*, 198–207.

Matthies, B. K., Kreutzer, J. S., & West, D. D. (2004). *The behavior management handbook: A practical approach to patients with neurological disorders.* Richmond, VA: National Resource Center for Traumatic Brain Injury.

McCauley, S. R., Boake, C., Levin, H. S., Contant, C. F., & Song, J. X. (2001). Postconcussional disorder following mild to moderate traumatic brain injury: Anxiety, depression, and social support as risk factors and comorbidities. *Journal of Clinical and Experimental Neuropsychology, 23*, 792–808.

McCrea, M. A. (2008). *Mild traumatic brain injury and postconcussion syndrome.* New York: Oxford University Press.

McDonald, C. M., Jaffe, K. M., Fay, G. C., Polissar, N. L., Martin, K. M., Liao, S., et al. (1994). Comparison of indices of traumatic brain injury severity as predictors of neurobehavioral outcome in children. *Archives of Physical Medicine and Rehabilitation, 75*, 328–337.

McElligott, J. M., Greenwald, B. D., & Watanabe, T. K. (2003). Congenital and acquired brain injury. 4. New frontiers: Neuroprotective agents, cognitive enhancing agents, new technology, and complementary medicine. *Archives of Physical Medicine and Rehabilitation, 84*(Suppl.), S18–S22.

McNamee, S., Pickett, T., Benedict, S., & Cifu, D. X. (2009). TBI rehabilitation. In J. Jallo (Ed.), *Neurotrauma and clinical care of the brain* (1st ed., pp. 385–403). New York: Thieme.

Mittenberg, W. (2002). Base rates of malingering and symptom exaggeration. *Journal of Clinical and Experimental Neuropsychology, 24*(8), 1094–1102.

Mittenberg, W., Canyock, E. M., Condit, D., & Patton, C. (2001). Treatment of postconcussion syndrome following mild head injury. *Journal of Clinical and Experimental Neuropsychology, 23*, 829–836.

Morton, M. V., & Wehman, P. (1995). Psychosocial and emotional sequelae of individuals with traumatic brain injury: A literature review and recommendations. *Brain Injury, 9*(1), 81–92.

Murray, C. K., Reynolds, J. C., Schroeder, J. M., Harrison, M. B., Evans, O. M., & Hospenthal, D. R. (2005). Spectrum of care provided at an echelon II medical unit during Operation Iraqi Freedom (OIF). *Military Medicine, 170*, 516–520.

Novack, T. (2000). *The orientation log.* Retrieved July 13, 2009, from, http://www.tbims.org/combi/olog

Okie, S. (2006). Reconstructing lives—A tale of two soldiers. *New England Journal of Medicine, 355*, 2609–2615.

Prigatano, G. P., & Schacter, D. L. (Eds.). (1991). *Awareness of deficit after brain injury: Clinical and theoretical issues.* New York: Oxford University Press.

Ruff, R. (2005). Two decades of advances in understanding mild traumatic brain injury. *Journal of Head Trauma Rehabilitation, 20*, 5–18.

Russell, W. R. (1932). Cerebral involvement in head injury. *Brain, 55*, 549–603.

Rutherford, W. H., Merrett, J. D., & McDonald, J. R. (1997). Sequelae of concussion caused by minor head injuries. *Lancet, 1*, 1–4.

Salazar, A., & Warden, D. (1999). Traumatic brain injury. *Scientific American Medicine, 11*, 1–8.

Salazar, A. M., Warden, D. L., Schwab, K., Spector, J., Braverman, S., Walter, J., et al. (2000). Cognitive rehabilitation for traumatic brain injury: A randomized trial. Defense and veterans head injury program (DVHIP) study group. *Journal of the American Medical Association, 283*, 3075–3081.

Sandel, M. E., & Mysiw, M. J. (1996). The agitated brain injured patient. Part 1: Definitions, differential diagnosis, and assessment. *Archives of Physical Medicine and Rehabilitation, 77*, 617–623.

Sarapata, M., Herrman, D., Johnson, T., & Aycock, R. (1998). The role of head injury in cognitive functioning, emotional adjustment, and criminal behavior. *Brain Injury, 12*, 821–842.

Sayer, N. A., Chiros, C., Sigford, B., Scott, C., Pickett, T. C., Lew, H., et al. (2008). Characteristics and rehabilitation outcomes among patients with blast and other combat injuries. *Archives of Physical Medicine and Rehabilitation, 89*(1), 163–170.

Schmitter-Edgecombe, M., Fahy, J., Whelan, J., & Long, C. (1995). Memory remediation after severe closed head injury. Notebook training versus supportive therapy. *Journal of Consulting and Clinical Psychology, 63*, 484–489.

Schneiderman, A. I., Braver, E. R., & Kang, H. K. (2008). Understanding sequelae of injury mechanisms and mild traumatic brain injury incurred during the conflicts in Iraq and Afghanistan: Persistent postconcussive symptoms and posttraumatic stress disorder. *American Journal of Epidemiology, 167*(12), 1446–1452.

Seale, C. S., Caroselli, J. S., & High, W. M. (2002). Use of community integration questionnaire (CIQ) to characterize changes in functioning for individuals with traumatic brain injury who participated in a post-acute rehabilitation programme. *Brain Injury, 16*, 955–967.

Sigford, B. J. (2008). To care for him who shall have borne the battle and for his widow and his orphan (Abraham Lincoln): The Department of Veterans Affairs Polytrauma System of Care. *Archives of Physical Medicine and Rehabilitation, 89*(12), 2227–2238.

Sohlberg, M. M., & Mateer, C. A. (1987). Effectiveness of an attentional training program. *Journal of Clinical and Experimental Neuropsychology, 9*, 117–130.

Sohlberg, M. M., & Mateer, C. A. (2001). *Cognitive rehabilitation: An integrative neuropsychological approach.* New York: Guilford Press.

Sohlberg, M. M., McLaughlin, K. A., Pavese, A., Heidrich, A., & Posner, M. (2000). Evaluation of attention process training and brain injury education in persons with acquired brain injury. *Journal of Clinical and Experimental Neuropsychology, 22*, 656–676.

Teasdale, G., & Jennett, B. (1974). Assessment of coma and impaired consciousness. A practical scale. *Lancet, 2*, 81–84.

Tiersky, L. A., Anselmi, V., Johnston, M. V., Kurtyka, J., Roosen, E., Schwartz, T., et al. (2005). A trial of neuropsychological rehabilitation in mild-spectrum traumatic brain injury. *Archives of Physical Medicine and Rehabilitation, 86*(8), 1565–1575.

United States Department of Defense. (2009). *Operation Iraqi Freedom (OIF) U.S. casualty status.* Retrieved March 30, 2009, from, http://www.defenselink.mil/news/casualty.pdf

Vanderploeg, R. D., Belanger, H. G., Duchnik, J. D., & Curtiss, G. (2007). Awareness problems following moderate to severe traumatic brain injury: Prevalence, assessment methods, and injury correlates. *Journal of Rehabilitation Research and Development, 44*(7), 937–950.

Vanderploeg, R. D., Curtiss, G., & Luis, C. A. (2001). *Resolving controversies in mild TBI: Neuropsychological, psychosocial, and psychiatric outcomes.* Paper presented at the Annual Convention of the American Psychological Association, San Francisco.

Varney, N. R., Martzke, J. S., & Roberts, R. J. (1987). Major depression in patients with closed head injury. *Neuropsychology, 1*, 7–9.

Warden, D. L., Ryan, L. M., Helmick, K. M., Schwab, K., French, L. M., Lu, W., et al. (2005). War neurotrauma: The Defense and Veterans Brain Injury Center (DVBIC) experience at Walter Reed Army Medical Center (WRAMC). *Journal of Neurotrauma, 22*, 1178.

Yudofsky, S. C., Silver, J. M., & Jackson, W. (1986). The overt aggression scale for the objective rating of verbal and physical aggression. *The American Journal of Psychiatry, 143*, 35–39.

Zafonte, R. D., Mann, N. R., Millis, S. R., Black, K. L., Wood, D. L., & Hammond, F. (1997). Posttraumatic amnesia: Its relation to functional outcome. *Archives of Physical Medicine and Rehabilitation, 78*, 1103–1106.

Zung, W. W. K. (1965). A self-rating depression scale. *Archives of General Psychiatry, 12*, 63–70.

8

Attention Deficit/Hyperactivity Disorder and Learning Disorders

DAVID W. HESS, CARRIE H. KENNEDY,
REBECCA A. HARDIN, AND THOMAS KUPKE

Attention deficit/hyperactivity disorder (ADHD) and learning disabilities (LD) are two developmental disorders characterized by cognitive deficiencies that are likely to be encountered in a military population. This chapter provides a brief overview of these disorders and then addresses them from the perspectives of military regulations and the practice of neuropsychology within military settings. It is not our intent to provide exhaustive reviews of the neuropsychological or neuroanatomical research available for these disorders, and the reader is directed elsewhere for comprehensive treatment of these literatures (e.g., Barkley, Murphy, & Fischer, 2008; Bridgett & Walker, 2006; Collins & Rourke, 2003; Hervey, Epstein, & Curry, 2004; Krain & Castellanos, 2006; Mapou, 2009; Makris et al., 2007; Schneider, Retz, Coogan, Thome, & Rösler, 2006; Seidman, Biederman, Weber, Hatch, & Farone, 1998; Wender, Wolf, & Wasserstein, 2001).

ATTENTION DEFICIT/HYPERACTIVITY DISORDER

ADHD is a developmental disorder characterized by problematic functioning in the areas of attention, hyperactivity, and impulse control. Current diagnostic criteria, as per the *Diagnostic and Statistical Manual, 4th edition* (*DSM-IV-TR*; American Psychiatric Association,

2000), require the presence of six of nine specified features of inattention (e.g., difficulties sustaining attention, not listening when spoken to directly) and/or six of nine characteristics of hyperactivity/impulsivity (e.g., fidgeting with hands or feet, interrupting, or intruding on others). Diagnostically, qualifying symptoms must be present for a period of at least 6 months and exist to a degree that is maladaptive and inconsistent with the individual's developmental level. Further, at least some of these symptoms must have developed by the age of seven, exist within two or more settings (e.g., school and home), cause clinically significant impairment in some aspect of everyday functioning, not occur exclusively during the course of another major developmental or Axis I psychiatric disorder (e.g., pervasive developmental disorder, schizophrenia), and not be better accounted for by another diagnostic entity (e.g., mood disorder, anxiety disorder, personality disorder). Based on the presenting constellation of symptoms, this diagnostic classification is subdivided into combined type, predominantly inattentive type, or hyperactive-impulsive type.

The above criteria were developed for children and may not be completely applicable to adults. Indeed, Barkley et al. (2008) provide data that challenge the age at onset criterion established by *DSM-IV-TR*, this data suggest that four versus six symptoms of either inattention or hyperactivity accurately diagnose the condition in adults relative to a community sample, and support the use of just six symptoms for separating ADHD from other mental health disorders. These authors conclude with a recommendation that the upcoming revision of the DSM provide separate ADHD diagnostic criteria for adults and children.

ADHD has been historically viewed as a childhood disorder that one would "outgrow." However, data have accumulated since the 1960s that attest to the persistence of this disorder into adulthood. Currently available estimates indicate that from 20–70% of children with this disorder have problems that persist into adulthood and lead to an estimated adult prevalence of 3.3–5.3% (Barkley et al., 2008). Accordingly, ADHD is a relatively common disorder among adults and affects nearly 11 million in the United States alone.

The adult expression of this disorder carries with it significant risk of comorbidities. Adults with ADHD, relative to the general public, are four times as likely to contract sexually transmitted disease and three times as likely to be unemployed (Barkley, Fischer, Smallish, & Fletcher, 2002). In a population survey, 500 adults with ADHD were twice as likely to be divorced and twice as likely to have been arrested (Biederman et al., 2006). In another epidemiological study, the National Comorbidity

Survey Replication, it was determined that the lifetime prevalence rates were 45% for mood disorders, 59% for anxiety, 36% for substance abuse, 70% for impulse disorders (antisocial personality, oppositional defiant conduct, intermittent explosive disorder), and 89% for any psychiatric disorder (Kessler et al., 2006). In the National Comorbidity Survey Replication study, individuals with ADHD also experienced high rates of occupational failure, low social functioning, and low cognitive functioning. Recent data presented by Barkley et al. (2008) summarize findings from two large comprehensive studies of adult ADHD in which functional limitations experienced by patients with ADHD exceeded those found among adults presenting to outpatient mental health clinics with other disorders.

Multiple neuropsychological correlates of ADHD have been identified. Though the bulk of this literature addresses the childhood expression of this disorder, a sizable adult literature has developed over the past two decades. Specifically, multiple studies and several meta-analyses have demonstrated that adults with ADHD perform more poorly in aspects of attention, processing speed, executive functioning, and learning and memory than control samples do (e.g., Barkley, 1997b; Barkley et al., 2008; Boonstra, Oosterlaan, Sergeant, & Buitelaar, 2005; Doyle, 2006; Frazier & Demaree, 2004; Johnson et al., 2001; Schoechlin & Engle, 2005; Simon, Czobor, Balint, Meszaros, & Bitter, 2009).

LEARNING DISABILITIES

Learning disabilities (LD) are a collection of disorders that have at their core a discrepancy between one or more discrete components of academic achievement with global intellectual status. The *DSM-IV-TR* defines LD as academic discrepancies that are substantially below that expected given the person's chronological age, measured intelligence, and age-appropriate education in reading, mathematics, or written expression. In addition, the specific disturbance significantly interferes with areas of achievement or activities of daily living and, if a sensory deficit is present, the difficulties posed by the specific learning disorder are in excess to what is typically expected given the nature of the sensory abnormality. *DSM-IV-TR* further notes that the term "substantially below" is usually defined by a discrepancy of more than 2 *SD* between academic achievement and intellectual capacity, though a smaller discrepancy (e.g. 1–2 *SD*) may be appropriate in instances where IQ test data have been compromised by an associated disorder in cognitive processing, a comorbid mental disorder or general medical condition, or the individual's ethnic or cultural background.

Substantial research has documented the presence of at least two learning disability types that go beyond the three primary *DSM-IV-TR* learning disabilities. First, a nonverbal learning disability subtype characterized by deficits in visuospatial and nonverbal organizational skills has been studied by Rourke and others (e.g., Tsatsanis & Rourke, 2008; Wasserstein, Vadhan, Barboza, & Stefanatos, 2008). In addition, a learning disorder subtype characterized by attention and executive functioning deficits, which do not meet diagnostic criteria for ADHD, has also been identified (Cutting & Denckla, 2003; Wasserstein & Denckla, 2009).

The adequacy of *DSM-IV-TR* conceptualizations of LD has recently been challenged for more than just its limited delineation of subtypes. The basic discrepancy model that serves as the underpinning of the DSM conceptualization of LD has been scrutinized by several investigators (Fletcher, Lyon, Fuchs, & Barnes, 2007; Siegel, 2003). A recommended alternative, described by Mapou (2009) as the clinical model, is characterized as a comprehensive assessment that includes a broad range of academic and neuropsychological skills as well as historical information from the client and other sources of information. In addition, consideration of social, economic, emotional, and behavioral contributions to observed academic and cognitive difficulties is added to the assessment process.

Katz, Goldstein, and Beers (2001) estimated that 3–20% of adults in the general population have a learning disorder. Approximately 80% of diagnosed learning disorders among children affect reading (Katz et al., 2001), and Mapou (2009) considers it reasonable to assume that similar rates persist into adulthood. Comorbidities associated with LD among adults are less well studied than those for ADHD. There are indications, however, that risk for psychosocial difficulties and psychiatric disorders is elevated among adults with LD (e.g., Gregg, Hoy, King, Moreland, & Jagota, 1992; Hooper & Olley, 1996, Hoy & Manglitz, 1996; Katz et al., 2001). Furthermore, there are indications that individuals with nonverbal learning disabilities may be particularly vulnerable to emotional distress due to the impact of their disabilities on everyday functioning and interpersonal skills (Tsatsanis & Rourke, 2008). Also there are data among adult prison inmates in Sweden indicating high proportions of reading disorders that are associated with higher frequencies of emotional distress, personality disorders, and lower degrees of socialization than is seen in inmates who do not have reading disorders (Jensen, Lindgren, Meurling, Ingvar, & Levander, 1999).

Neuropsychological features of LD vary as a function of the specific disorder. The core deficit associated with reading disorders is linguistic in nature and characterized by a primary deficit in auditory phonological processing (Birch & Chase, 2004; de Gelder & Vrooman, 1996; Elbro, 1998; Katz et al., 2001; Shaywitz, Lyon, & Shaywitz, 2006; Shaywitz & Shaywitz, 2005), though processing speed, especially naming speed, is also believed to play a role (Wolf & Bowers, 1999). There is less agreement regarding the cognitive underpinnings of mathematic disorders. Greiffenstein and Baker (2002) report problems with nonverbal reasoning and constructional skills of adults with mathematics disabilities. Osman, Schwartz, Braun, and Plambeck (2006) found evidence of subtypes of mathematics-disabled college students characterized by impaired executive functioning, impaired spatial skills, or both. Research regarding disorders of written language is quite limited. Peverly (2006) suggested that handwriting speed, spelling, working memory, and higher-level cognitive capacities form the basis for effective writing. Last, nonverbal learning disabilities have been linked to deficits in visuospatial skills, motor skills, complex problem solving, and arithmetic (Rourke, Young, Strang, & Russell, 1986; Rourke, 2000, Tsatsanis & Rourke, 2008). Considering the above as a whole, a wide array of neuropsychological domains would appear to play a role in LD.

ADHD/LD AND THE MILITARY

The exact prevalence of ADHD and LD in the military is unknown, though there is no doubt that these disorders are represented among the men and women who serve in the armed forces. As testament to this fact, Cigrang, Carbone, Todd, and Fiedler (1998) in a study of new Air Force recruits found that 5% of mental health attrition was linked to ADHD. Standards for enlistment in the armed forces relevant to persons with ADHD and LD are addressed in two Department of Defense (DoD) instructions. DoD Instruction 6130.4 (2005) stipulates that the presence of ADHD or perceptual/learning disorder(s) are disqualifying unless the applicant can demonstrate passing academic performance and there has been no use of medications in the previous 12 months. It further stipulates that applicants with current or histories of academic skills or perceptual defects secondary to organic or functional mental disorders, including but not limited to dyslexia, that interfere with school or employment are disqualifying. Yet applicants who demonstrate passing academic and employment performance without utilization or recommendation of academic and/or work accommodations at any time in the previous 12 months may be qualified.

The second DoD instruction pertinent in the present context (DoDI 1304.26, 2007) addresses aptitude requirements for enlistment based on scores on the Armed Forces Qualification Test (AFQT) as derived from the Armed Services Vocational Aptitude Battery (ASVAB). Individuals who score below the 10th percentile on composite measures, composed of subtests assessing word knowledge, paragraph comprehension, arithmetic reasoning, and mathematics knowledge, are ineligible to enlist. Currently, depending on the branch of service, individuals wanting to enlist must score anywhere between 31 (Army standard) and 40 (Coast Guard standard). (However, a limited number of applicants with scores falling between the 10th and 30th percentiles may be given waivers for entry into the military.) This preenlistment cognitive screening effort is believed to screen out many persons with LD.

Service members with histories of ADHD who gain access into the military may receive ADHD medications subsequent to their completion of basic training, though this is handled on a case-by-case basis. The Coast Guard, which now falls under the Department of Homeland Security, but receives medical services through DoD facilities, is an exception to this rule. Members of the Coast Guard are not allowed to remain on active duty if they must take medication to control symptoms of ADHD (Department of Homeland Security, 2008). In addition, it is notable that any active duty service member with ADHD or LD who is unable to perform his/her duties adequately with, or without medication, may be administratively separated from any branch of service. Furthermore, histories of ADHD/LD or current use of ADHD medications may restrict service members from some career paths. For example, Navy personnel working in nuclear fields may not take psychotropic medications. In addition, use of stimulant medication to control ADHD symptoms is incompatible with being granted flight status and even a history of ADHD/LD will warrant submission of an exception to policy or waiver request prior to being permitted to perform any role within military aviation communities.

In brief, some persons with ADHD/LD will be barred from entering the military as a result of the above directives, but many persons with these disorders will also be granted entry into the armed services. Affected active duty members will have access to treatment, in many instances, and quite likely function at an acceptable level within the structured military setting. Some active duty members will either be restricted from specific career paths or will need to submit waiver requests and demonstrate the ability to function without psychotropic medications or workplace accommodations before being allowed to function in some positions.

ADHD/LD AND MILITARY NEUROPSYCHOLOGY

When considering appropriate uses of neuropsychological testing procedures within military settings, it is clear that LD must be addressed within the context of a comprehensive neuropsychological evaluation that includes a thorough examination of basic academic capacities. The situation is less clear regarding the use of neuropsychological instruments within the context of ADHD evaluations. If one is solely concerned with making an accurate diagnosis of this condition, one may elect not to include neuropsychological testing in the assessment package. As voiced by Barkley (Barkley, 1997a, 1997b; Barkley et al., 2008), neuropsychological tests may not substantially improve the accuracy of this diagnosis. He notes the presence of excessive false negatives in studies differentiating adults with ADHD from community samples and excessive false positives when discriminating adults with ADHD from persons with other psychiatric disorders. Rather the diagnosis can be adequately established with a thorough review of the history of the patient and school records, plus a detailed interview of the patient, and ideally, a parent, possibly supplemented with use of one of a number of symptom rating scales or checklists.

However, if the military neuropsychologist is charged with determining fitness or suitability for duty, be it for general military duty or for a special duty assignment (e.g., flight status or high-risk training instructor), neuropsychological instruments are the standard of care. Indeed, such testing is required under specific circumstances by regulations. Persons with ADHD/LD who wish to be on flight status within any service's aviation community must submit a waiver request that includes neuropsychological/psychological test data. The inherent assumption linked to this requirement is that evidence of cognitive impairment is more predictive of a person's capacity to function safely within a restricted career field than the diagnosis of ADHD or LD, per se.

Unfortunately, there is no evidence that cognitive status, objectively assessed with neuropsychological tests, is more predictive of occupational competency than the presence of an accurate diagnosis of ADHD/LD. Yet this notion may not run counter to similar assumptions operating within the civilian community. In particular, educational institutions and companies that offer standardized testing services must adhere to the Americans with Disabilities Act (ADA). The ADA mandates the granting of accommodations (e.g., extra time for tests, a quiet room for testing, use of a tape recorder during lectures) for persons who have qualifying disabilities. ADHD and LD fall under the rubric of the ADA, yet, the diagnosis in and of itself is usually insufficient evidence to support the granting of accommodations. For example, the policy of the Educational Testing Service (ETS) with regard to ADHD and LD stipulates that "relevant testing" must be provided as part of the application for accommodations (ETS, 2008). Some universities defer to the standards established by ETS whereas others have developed their own. For example, with regard to ADHD accommodations at Harvard University, "neuropsychological or psycho-educational assessment can be helpful in identifying the individual's pattern of strengths and weaknesses and therefore whether there are patterns supportive of attention problems" (2008). In addition, policies of the University of Texas at Austin stipulate that "comprehensive psychoeducational or neuropsychological evaluations may be required to support specific accommodation requests" for ADHD/LD (2008). Our intent is neither to provide an exhaustive review of the requirements established by educational facilities regarding ADHD/LD nor to address specific test data as they relate to the granting of educational accommodations, but rather to illustrate that neuropsychological testing is viewed as appropriate when decisions regarding the functional capacities of individuals with ADHD/LD must be made.

In light of this discussion, it is important to point out that the military does not operate under the dictates of the Americans with Disabilities Act. Consequently, the mission is not to determine what modifications of the educational/work environment can be offered to suit the particular needs of the individual. Rather, it must be determined if the individual possesses the requisite skills to meet the challenges of a particular military career field. In a sense, the Americans with Disabilities Act is designed to assist the individual in meeting his or her needs, while military policies are designed to use testing to meet the necessary safety requirements of the service member and the military. Within both contexts, the underlying assumption remains that neuropsychological/

psychological test data offer pertinent information above and beyond that garnered simply from the diagnosis of ADHD/LD.

In everyday practice, this is expressed through two basic functions of the military neuropsychologist: (a) in the recommendation of waivers that permit individuals with ADHD/LD to work within specific service areas and (b) in clinical settings where the emphasis is on the care of the patient within the context of ensuring suitability for continued military duty. The remaining pages of this chapter illustrate two examples of the application of military neuropsychology to ADHD/LD-related issues. The first offers a review of procedures followed across the services in granting waivers for persons with histories of ADHD/LD to work within aviation communities. The second describes the operation of a Navy neuropsychology clinic that handles among its various referrals requests for ADHD and LD assessments.

AEROMEDICAL WAIVER PROCEDURES

Determination of flight status in individuals with histories of ADHD and/or LD is complicated. First, this is a unique population that must maintain a higher standard of functioning than that required by those on general military duty. Military pilots, for example, exhibit an average full scale IQ of 120 (Ryan, Zazeckis, French, & Harvey, 2006) and must have comparable cognitive abilities as they relate to the aviation environment (e.g., visual scanning, psychomotor speed, ability to dual task, etc.). Enlisted aircrew and air traffic controllers also exhibit high levels of aptitude, as they must meet certain criterion levels on the ASVAB/AFQT and line scores to be selected for an aviation career field. Second, while all jobs in the military are dangerous and can result in death or serious harm to individuals, the flight environment is particularly hazardous and unforgiving to mistakes. Consequently, waivers for any disorder must be considered very carefully.

Persons with any history of ADHD/LD are not permitted flight status in the Navy, Air Force, Army, Marines, or Coast Guard unless they submit a request for a waiver or exception to policy and it is approved. Aviation guidelines in all services apply to aviators/pilots, flight officers/navigators, aircrew (to include aerospace psychologists, flight surgeons, aerospace optometrists, and aerospace physiologists), air traffic controllers, and operators of unmanned aerial vehicles. Aeromedical risks associated with ADHD/LD include slowed information processing; error proneness secondary to lapses of judgment, impulsivity, and poor problem-solving skills; limited capacity to multitask or perform when divided attention is required; difficulties with set shifting; problems with attention to detail; and difficulties with task organization. Symptomatic LDs also offer significant risks specific to the particular disorder, such as inability to work rapidly through complex written emergency procedures or to calculate necessary formulas in air (adjusting for winds, fuel requirements, course, etc.). In addition, ADHD/LD symptoms may result in requirements for excessive supervision and monitoring to ensure completion of tasks and may also interfere with crew resource management. Waiver requests must provide convincing evidence that there are no cognitive deficits, no comorbidities frequently associated with ADHD/LD, and that the individual has an established history of high behavioral function without medication or recent academic accommodation.

Packages submitted for aviation waivers in all branches of service require extensive documentation regarding the service members' condition. In the Navy and Marine Corps, records must encompass all periods during which medication used to treat the disorder occurred. A narrative summary (i.e., Aeromedical Summary) from the individual's flight surgeon must be prepared documenting all prior symptoms: the absence of persistent features, when medication was discontinued (if used), and evidence of current academic performance proficiency. A current neuropsychological evaluation, obtained after discontinuation of ADHD medications, may also be required (see Naval Aerospace Medical Institute, 2008).

For the Air Force, the waiver package must document that the individual is symptom free, has not manifested a degradation of their performance of aircrew duties, and has not taken medication for the disorder for the past 12 months. In addition, there must be a mental health evaluation summary specifically including psychological and neuropsychological evaluation reports (with raw data) and any pertinent past medical or mental health records. This must be accompanied by any pertinent neurological or other medical consultation report and an Aeromedical Summary detailing any social, occupational, administrative, or legal problems. It should also include an individualized analysis of the aeromedical implications of the particular case history of the service member seeking a waiver. For aircrew applicants there must be a detailed history of academic achievement and the use of any educational accommodations.

The Army regulations require a detailed clinical interview by a psychologist or psychiatrist. There must be a review of all treatment records and if positive findings for ADHD/LD are present, a detailed neuropsychological assessment to include cognitive domains, IQ, and achievement testing is required. The Army is the only branch of service that considers waiving any kind of medication for ADHD: Wellbutrin and Strattera, both of which are nonstimulants. However, if an individual is taking either medication, an assessment must be conducted both on and off the medication. An in-flight evaluation is recommended concurrently with each of the neuropsychological assessments.

As a comparison standard, the Federal Aviation Administration requires administration of a neuropsychological battery based on a history of ADHD/LD and mandates specific tests. Depending on the history, a period of 3–90 days without medication is required prior to the evaluation (Virtual Flight Surgeons, 2009). Similar to most branches of the military, the Federal Aviation Administration waives no medications.

In the presence of the above waiver requirements, the Navy and Marine Corps have granted waivers to 57% of 204 ADHD waiver requests submitted since 2001 and 54.5% of 11 LD waiver requests between 1999 and 2008. Since 2001, the Air Force has considered 57 ADHD waiver applications. All of the 14 applications for Flight Class I (i.e., student pilot or navigator) status were granted while 87.5% of eight requests were granted for Flight Class II (i.e., designated pilot, navigator, or flight surgeon). Waiver packages submitted in support of waivers for Flight Class III (i.e., aircrew and air traffic control) resulted in 42% of 36 packages being granted. Since 1999, the Army has entertained 30 ADHD waiver requests for flight status. Of these, nine were granted an exception to policy and seven were granted waivers, three of which involved the use of Strattera (two aeromedical physician's assistants and one designated aviator).

Recently, changes have been recommended to the ADHD/LD waiver requirements for the Navy and Marine Corps. Changes were proposed following a review of 38 waiver packages for which comprehensive neuropsychological evaluations had been performed over a period of 18 months. Of the 15 waiver submissions offered by college graduates (14 aviator and flight officer candidates and one aircrew candidate), none were determined to have active or impairing symptoms as per the results of the neuropsychological evaluation. Consequently, all were granted waivers. Of the 22 noncollege graduates, 27% were found to be not physically qualified for duties involving flight due to their neuropsychological evaluation. Four of these individuals were disqualified for ADHD or LD symptoms observed upon testing whereas two had other significant mental health disorders that had been misdiagnosed (i.e., major depressive disorder and posttraumatic stress disorder). One designated aviator was found to be not physically qualified for continued flight status due to a history of previously undisclosed ADHD and active symptomatology that threatened the safety of others in the aviation environment. Stemming from this case review, modifications to the necessary information required in waiver packages were proposed that differentiate between those with college degrees and those without and provide specific guidance regarding documentation, mental health evaluation, and neuropsychological evaluation.

For individuals with college degrees from campus-based educational systems, transcripts are required along with a memorandum from the institution's learning needs/assistance center noting that the individual has never been evaluated or accommodated academically. In addition, a statement from the service member stating they do not now use and did not use medications or require special assistance for their condition throughout college is required. Assuming successful completion of the entire college degree with no psychopharmacologic or academic assistance, no mental health or neuropsychological evaluation is required for waiver application.

College graduates from nontraditional programs (e.g., Internet-based institutions) are required to obtain a mental health evaluation, and must submit transcripts. Individuals without a college degree must undergo a mental health evaluation. The guidelines stipulate the requirements of the mental health evaluation, which must be performed by a clinical psychologist or psychiatrist. This evaluation must include an interview with a parent or primary caregiver, a review of report cards and high school transcripts, a review of individual education plans (if applicable), a review of childhood medical records, and inclusion of standard elements of a mental health evaluation (i.e., substance use history, social history, mental health and medical history, family mental health and medical history, legal history, and mental status examination). In addition, upon review of the mental health evaluation the service member or civilian applicant may be required to undergo a neuropsychological evaluation. Any college graduate requiring medication or academic assistance during their studies will automatically be required to undergo neuropsychological evaluation (see requirements below), though someone with documented impairment as an adult is likely not to be waived.

For waiver packages coming from midshipmen/graduates of the U.S. Naval Academy, given the unavailability of academic accommodations, no documentation of academic success or a memorandum regarding academic assistance is considered necessary. Accordingly, U.S. Naval Academy midshipmen do not require documentation regarding childhood functioning, though the member must provide a statement indicating that he or she neither took medication for ADHD or received private, professional assistance with academic course work at any time during his or her 4 years of college.

Under the proposed changes to navy policy, neuropsychological testing will be required when an individual: (a) does not have a college degree and ADHD/LD cannot be ruled out from a mental health evaluation, (b) has a college degree but took medication and/or received academic accommodations at any time during their college studies, or (c) has a nontraditional college degree (e.g., Internet degree) and the mental health evaluation cannot rule out ADHD/LD. It is hypothesized that individuals who have obtained a college degree do not demonstrate neurocognitive deficits linked to ADHD/LD due to their older age than the traditional enlisted aircrew applicants (e.g., 22 vs. 18 years), and that the college experience in conjunction with adequate scoring on the Aviation Selection Test Battery, a requirement for pilot or flight officer program entry, operate as a suitable selection process.

In addition to the aforementioned components of the mental health evaluation, specifications for the neurocognitive and personality testing components of the neuropsychological evaluation, which must be performed by a credentialed neuropsychologist, are also provided. In particular, general intellectual functioning must be documented using the full current edition of the Wechsler Adult Intelligence Scale (Wechsler, 2008) to include all indices. Memory assessment, including verbal and visual memory capacities (e.g., current Wechsler Memory Scale Logical Memory subtests; Wechsler, 1997, California Verbal Learning Test; Delis, Kaplan, Kramer, & Ober, 2000, Rey Complex Figure Test; Meyers & Meyers, 1995), must be documented. In addition an assessment of executive functioning must be contained in the evaluation with at least four of the following (or comparable tasks) included: Trail Making Test Parts A and B (Reitan, 1958), Stroop Color and Word Test (Golden & Freshwater, 2002), Paced Auditory Serial Addition Task (Gronwall, 1977), Tower of London-Drexel (Brickencamp & Zillmer, 1998), Iowa Gambling Task (Bechara, 2007), and/or Booklet Category Test (DeFilippis & McCampbell, 1997). Documentation of results of vigilance testing must also be included and may be based on such tests as the Conner's Continuous Performance Test-II (Conners, 2000) or the Aviation Vigilance Test (Kay & Moore, 2002). Personality assessment should include an ADHD self-report measure, an alcohol screen, depression screen, and formal personality testing (e.g., Minnesota Multiphasic Personality Inventory-2; MMPI-2; University of Minnesota, 2001). In the case of LD assessment, pertinent academic achievement tests must also be administered (e.g., Woodcock-Johnson Tests of Achievement and Cognitive Abilities; Woodcock, McGrew & Mather, 2001a, 2001b).

At their core, these policy changes are intended to reduce the need for unnecessary neuropsychological evaluation and improve the quality of evaluations that are deemed necessary for making an aeromedical disposition. Other efforts are also under way to improve the assessment process further. Normative data for aviation personnel is necessary given that they all function at a high level. There are some tests normed solely on pilots, such as the CogScreen–Aeromedical Edition (Kay, 1995) and the Aviation Vigilance Test. Military aviator norms were recently collected for the d2 Test of Attention (Brickenkamp & Zillmer, 1998), a test that measures processing speed and visual tracking accuracy (Table 8.1) (Kennedy, Walker, & Moore, 2008). On average, these individuals performed three standard deviations above the general population norm on this test. It is also notable that there are consistent findings on personality testing in this population as well. For example, military aviator norms exist for the NEO Personality Inventory–Revised (Costa & McCrae, 2000) and poor outcomes in military aviation are associated with elevated neuroticism and depressed extraversion on this test (Campbell, Moore, Poythress, & Kennedy, 2009). It is important when conducting evaluations of aviation personnel that the assessment is tailored and the interpretation is based on aviation norms as opposed to the general population whenever possible.

The need to gather outcome data on individuals with ADHD or LD who have received waivers is necessary. In preliminary data from the Naval Aerospace Medical Institute, student aviators and flight officers in preflight training (i.e., Introductory Flight Screening and Aviation Preflight Indoctrination) with waivers for ADHD/LD show no decrement in performance in comparison to their peers. Academic grades in aerodynamics, air navigation, aviation weather, engines and systems, and flight rules and regulations are comparable between those waived and those with no diagnosis. Of interest is that Aviation Selection Test Battery scores (Flight Aptitude Ratings and Officer Aptitude Ratings) are higher

Table 8.1

NAVAL AND MARINE CORPS AVIATORS AND FLIGHT OFFICERS NORMATIVE DATA FOR THE D2 TEST OF ATTENTION

	MEAN	SD	PERCENTILES				
			5th	15th	50th	85th	95th
Male Age 21–23 (*n* = 77)							
TN	583	(±53)	482	535	587	643	656
E1	18	(±20)	2	4	13	30	62
E2	2	(±5)	0	0	1	3	10
E	21	(±21)	2	5	15	33	69
TNE	562	(±54)	467	504	563	616	650
E percent	4	(±3)	0	1	3	6	12
CP	240	(±33)	185	201	244	275	290
FR	12	(±6)	2	6	13	18	23
Age 24–31 (*n* = 91)							
TN	583	(±62)	452	507	593	644	655
E1	12	(±10)	1	3	10	22	34
E2	1	(±4)	0	0	0	3	5
E	14	(±11)	1	3	11	24	36
TNE	569	(±63)	441	490	573	633	647
E percent	2	(±2)	0	1	2	4	7
CP	245	(±37)	172	202	251	283	293
FR	11	(±6)	1	6	10	16	22
Female Age 21–27 (*n* = 13)							
TN	583	(±38)	511	546	578	639	646
E1	12	(±12)	3	4	8	25	46
E2	2	(±2)	0	0	1	4	7
E	14	(±13)	4	4	10	32	46
TNE	572	(±39)	506	532	559	631	636
E percent	2	(±2)	1	1	2	5	8
CP	244	(±22)	215	220	236	279	282
FR	12	(±4)	6	7	13	18	18

TN = total number of items processed; E1 = omission errors; E2 = commission errors; E = total errors; TNE = overall performance; E percent = percentage of errors; CP = concentration performance; FR = fluctuation rate.

in the ADHD/LD group, lending some evidence to the theory that there is a self-selection bias for this group of individuals.

CLINICAL EVALUATIONS OF ADHD/LD IN A MILITARY NEUROPSYCHOLOGY CLINIC

Neuropsychological evaluations conducted in support of aeromedical waiver packages are performed for the needs of the military, for example, to ensure that service members are capable of executing duties to which they are assigned. In contrast, within the clinical arena, services are primarily provided to meet the needs of the individual, though this is performed in a manner that simultaneously insures that the service member is fit and suitable for meeting the demands of military service. At the Naval Medical Center in Portsmouth, Virginia (NMCP), referrals for ADHD/LD workups are seen within the neuropsychology clinic. Individuals referred for LD workups are given appointments within the regular neuropsychology clinic while ADHD referrals are seen within a specialized adult ADHD clinic staffed by neuropsychology personnel. Most referrals for ADHD/LD evaluations come from primary care physicians and mental health clinicians, though some patients are seen on a self-referral basis.

Evaluations of LD

The NMCP standard LD workup consists of a detailed clinical interview addressing the history and current characteristics of the learning difficulty plus a thorough review of current emotional/psychiatric symptomatology and the developmental history. The typical test battery includes the Woodcock-Johnson III Tests of Cognitive Abilities (Woodcock et al., 2001b), the Woodcock-Johnson III Tests of Achievement (Woodcock et al., 2001a), and administration of various sensory/motor tasks from the expanded Halstead-Reitan as delineated by Heaton et al. (1991). A case illustrating LD and the question of suitability for duty follows.

Case Example

This individual was a 24-year-old, right-handed, Caucasian male, Seaman/E-3, active duty Navy service member who presented with complaints of difficulties comprehending and retaining information he read.

He dated the onset of his reading problems to about the eighth grade, when he was specially tutored in reading but was not formally diagnosed with an LD. He was placed within lower-tiered reading classes in high school but, again, was not technically diagnosed with an LD. When seen for this assessment he stated that his reading problems were interfering with his ability to advance in his Navy career and he felt they interfered with his ability to perform well in college course work. He denied feeling depressed or anxious, and did not have vegetative signs associated with depression. He did not report a history of significant birth complications or problems with early physical/social development. He had recurrent ear infections as a child and frequent episodes of strep throat but was otherwise healthy. There was no history of childhood abuse or juvenile legal/criminal problems. There was no significant history of disciplinary problems across his 3 years of active duty service in the Navy. His preenlistment ASVAB/AFQT score was documented as falling at the 39th percentile. In addition to the educational history offered above, it is notable that he repeated the second grade because "my parents didn't think I was ready to continue." He was able to earn a high school diploma and had completed less than one semester of college at the time of the evaluation. He did not give a history of significant psychiatric problems, alcohol/substance abuse, or neurological abnormalities.

Test findings were notable for essentially average intellectual development (Woodcock-Johnson General Intellectual Ability Scale Score = 93), though cognitive efficiency (scale score = 83) and working memory (scale score = 75) represented relative cognitive weaknesses. Verbal ability, thinking ability, and phonemic awareness were all essentially average with scale scores ranging from 91 to 103. Performances on achievement subtests of the Woodcock-Johnson indicated that oral language skills were average to above average (scale score =110) and broad math was average (scale score = 93), but broad reading and broad written language were borderline to low average (scale scores = 78 and 79, respectively). Among specific achievement subtests, letter-word identification (scale score = 77), reading fluency (scale score = 74), and spelling (scale score = 75) were most notably deficient. Discrepancy analyses indicated that broad reading and broad written language were significantly worse than expected relative to GIA. In addition, predicted versus actual achievement discrepancies were significant for broad reading and broad written language. Examination of sensory-motor "soft signs" revealed essentially normal grip strength, bilaterally, though fine-motor dexterity was slightly worse than expected in both hands. Sensory perceptual functioning was intact.

The above findings were felt to be consistent with the presence of a mild LD impacting reading and writing/spelling skills. Within the context of essentially average general intellectual capacity, he was also noted to exhibit weaknesses in the areas of processing speed and working memory. It is notable in this case that auditory phonological processing was not compromised and thus this individual would not appear to be typical of adults with reading disorders. It would appear that elements of processing speed and mild limitations in working memory played a role in the development of his academic difficulties. When provided feedback regarding the results of the examination, the patient was informed that the military did not grant occupational accommodations due to LD but he was advised to seek academic accommodations for his college class work. In addition, given the mild nature of his disorder, he was informed that he was judged to be suitable for continued military service.

Evaluations of ADHD

Within the adult ADHD component of the neuropsychology clinic, patients receive a full diagnostic workup during which a structured interview specifically based on the *DSM-IV-TR* criteria for ADHD is completed. Features of childhood and adult functioning are assessed during this interview, as well as age at symptom onset, settings in which symptoms occurred, duration of symptoms, and functional compromise linked to these symptoms. A telephone interview with a parent is performed, and the same structured interview format is used. A full review of current psychiatric symptoms is also pursued, along with the individual's developmental, educational, social, occupational, medical, and substance use/misuse history. A set of standardized assessment instruments is administered to address core ADHD features and probe for possible comorbid disorders.

The assessment battery for ADHD includes administration of a brief neuropsychological test battery tapping inattention/impulsivity, planning deficits, processing speed, and working memory via listening skills. Specifically, we use the Connor's Continuous Performance Test-2 (CPT-2) and three Woodcock-Johnson subtests—Understanding Directions from the Woodcock-Johnson III Tests of Achievement, and the Planning and Cancellation subtests from the Woodcock-Johnson III Tests of Cognitive Abilities. The rationale for inclusion of this cluster of measures is one of efficiency—most of the neuropsychology clinic's resources are dedicated to adult onset disorders (e.g., traumatic brain injury)—and these tasks appear to adequately sample core deficits as reflected in the ADHD neuropsychological literature. While Barkley's (Barkley et al., 2008) position is acknowledged that neuropsychological tests are not needed to diagnosis ADHD, the use of these measures establishes a basis for making objective decisions regarding fitness/suitability for duty; for example, the underlying rationale inherent in both the aeromedical waiver process and the granting of academic accommodations is that test data contribute to decision making above and beyond diagnosis alone. Last, these measures were chosen because they have minimal overlap with standard neuropsychological test batteries and consequently patients are not exposed to any test that is not specifically indicated in the assessment of their known or suspected disorder. In addition to this brief neuropsychological battery, patients are administered the MMPI-2 (University of Minnesota, 2001), Beck Anxiety Inventory (Beck & Steer, 1993), Beck Depression Inventory-2 (Beck, Steer, & Brown, 1996), and the Mood Disorder Questionnaire (Hirschfeld et al., 2000).

Case Example

This service member is a right-handed, Caucasian male who presented with complaints of problems focusing and sustaining his attention for long periods of time as well as decreased memory. He reported that his parents noticed these problems from the time he was 5 years old, though he denies a diagnosis of ADHD or being prescribed medications. In addition, he noted that problems have been more remarkable since being in the Navy for the past 2 years and 10 months. He does not report a depressed mood but identifies vegetative symptoms that include poor appetite, sleep, decreased interest in routine activities, and irritability. These symptoms have persisted for the last 3 months.

There is no history of birth complications or developmental problems. He was the second of three children born within a divorced family structure when he was 8 years old. He endorsed both emotional and verbal abuse as a child. He denied problems with juvenile authority figures or unusual health problems as a youth. He describes himself as an average student. He has completed 2 years of college but has not earned an AA degree. There is no history of psychiatric illness. There is no family history of psychiatric disease or ADHD. There is a history of significant alcohol/substance abuse, specifically he reported a DUI (driving under the influence) with a BAC of 0.16 six months ago, but he reports compliance with military abstinence rules regarding his subsequent diagnosis of Alcohol Abuse. The family history is also positive for alcohol/substance abuse/dependence with four of his six maternal and paternal uncles. He has a positive family history of suicide related to substance abuse.

Specific *DSM-IV* diagnostic criteria were assessed with a structured interview addressing both childhood and adult symptomatology. His responses to this structured interview resulted in positive endorsements of eight out of nine features of inattention and four of nine symptoms of hyperactivity/impulsivity as characteristic of his childhood behavior. Regarding adult functioning, nine of nine features of inattention and six of nine dimensions of hyperactivity/impulsivity were reported. His parents were not available via telephone for interview.

The service member's profile on the CPT-2, a measure of sustained attention, had an 84.76% probability of matching an ADHD profile. Most notable were the higher than expected omissions and impulsivity. Although his performance on the Woodcock-Johnson III Planning subtest was in the average range, the Pair Cancellation subtest (Visual Attention/Processing Speed) and Understanding Directions subtest (Auditory Attention/Processing) were deficient. Assessment of depression, anxiety, mood disorder, and serious psychopathology were within expected limits.

In this case, both data collected from the structured interview and psychometric assessment provide adequate justification for the diagnosis of ADHD. Treatment recommendations included a trial of an anti-ADHD pharmacological agent and behaviorally-based therapy to address interpersonal problems and work-related problems that have resulted from his ADHD. While this service member is considered fit for full duty in the sense that there is no medical/psychological disorder eligible for coverage under the medical board process, if he is unable to perform his duties adequately, he may be considered for an administrative separation in the future.

THE EXPERIENCE OF AN ACTIVE DUTY ADHD CLINIC

Within the Naval Medical Center Portsmouth, a process improvement review of 25 cases was recently completed for service members presenting to the adult ADHD clinic, the results of which appear to be worthy of mention in this chapter, as no other descriptions of clinical services offered to military service members presenting for ADHD evaluations are available. In the following discussion of findings from this review, we make no claims of generalizability; that is, this is a process improvement effort and not research. Basic characteristics of these 25 clinic referrals are presented in Table 8.2.

Table 8.2

CHARACTERISTICS OF ACTIVE DUTY ADULT ADHD CASES REVIEWED

CHARACTERISTIC	
Gender	76% male
Age	Mean = 29.8 years; *SD* = 7.0
Education	56% High school/GED
	28% Some college
	16% Bachelor's degree or higher
Service	72% Navy
	16% Army
	8% Marines
Rank	64% E-5 or below
	24% E-6 to E-8
	12% Officers

In all, 60% of these individuals had a concurrent psychiatric diagnosis, and 64% had a family history of ADHD. A parent interview was secured in only 28% of the cases—often parents were not available at all or were not able to be reached after a reasonable number of attempts to do so.

In 64% of the cases referred, the patients' self-reported symptoms did not meet *DSM-IV-TR* diagnostic criteria for ADHD. Of the nine cases reporting diagnosable levels of ADHD symptoms, clinicians judged three to have possible ADHD (i.e., clinicians were less than fully convinced that they met full diagnostic criteria for the disorder) and the remaining six were deemed by clinicians to have met *DSM-IV* criteria.

Average scores, with standard deviation in parentheses, for various measures used in assessments are shown in Table 8.3. No data from the MMPI-2 are included due to the finding that 8 of 25 cases exhibited questionably reliable findings secondary to either over- or underreporting of symptoms.

Several statistical analyses were performed with these data, and selected findings are listed below:

1. Number of self-reported childhood features of inattention correlated significantly with performance on the Pair Cancellation task, a measure of processing speed ($r = -.45$, $p < .05$).

Table 8.3

AVERAGE TEST SCORES AND STANDARD DEVIATION

TEST	AVERAGE SCORE (*SD*)
CPT-2–ADHD Confidence Index	53.32 (23.40)
Woodcock-Johnson Planning Scale Score	101.67 (7.40)
Woodcock-Johnson Pair Cancellation Scale Score	88.79 (12.57)
Woodcock-Johnson Understanding Directions Scale Score	94.42 (7.12)
Beck Anxiety Inventory	10.76 (11.56)
Beck Depression Inventory	19.12 (14.73)

2. Number of self-reported adult features of hyperactivity/impulsivity correlated significantly with CPT-2–ADHD Confidence Index ($r = .45, p < .05$).

3. Number of self-reported adult features of inattention correlated significantly with total score on the Beck Depression Inventory-2 ($r = -.52, p < .01$).

Mean score comparisons of patients judged to not have ADHD versus those who had either possible or diagnosable ADHD were explored. CPT-2 performance and number of symptoms each for childhood inattention, childhood hyperactivity/impulsivity, and adult inattention were found to differ significantly ($p < .05$) across these groupings.

What was learned from this process improvement effort? First, it is clear that some active duty members who have complaints of ADHD-like symptoms do not meet *DSM-IV-TR* diagnostic criteria for the disorder (64% in this case). Considering that 60% of these service members had previously diagnosed psychiatric disorders, and that the average scores on the Beck Anxiety Inventory and Beck Depression Inventory-2 suggest mild problems with anxiety and depression, this perhaps is to be expected. However, it should be pointed out that Barkley et al. (2008) recommend less stringent criteria for assessing ADHD among adults (e.g., requiring four versus six features or either inattention or hyperactivity/impulsivity) and adoption of this more liberal diagnostic criteria would increase our diagnostic rate.

Second, success in securing telephone interviews with parents was significantly limited. It is possible that the diagnostic conclusions would have been altered in the presence of more parental input. Efforts to improve outreach to collateral information sources are needed.

Third, several of the objective measures of cognitive performance and affective status demonstrate reasonable associations with ADHD criteria. It is not contended that the presence of these data impacted diagnostic decisions substantially, yet, at a clinical level, the clinicians were more comfortable making the diagnosis of ADHD when there was a convergence of clinical and test data.

Fourth, the clinicians felt that the methods adequately protected the interests of the military. That is, inclusion of cognitive test instruments allowed for the screening of patients for functionally significant cognitive compromise. Major deficits were not found among the 25 patients examined, though it is apparent that mild problems with attentional capacities were present on the CPT-II for a number of patients and that the average score on the Pair Cancellation Subtest from the Woodcock-Johnson fell in the upper limits of the low-average range relative to same-aged peers. These levels of performance are not considered functionally problematic in the context of judging fitness/suitability for general, versus specialized, duty status. Overall, these data reflect minor cognitive compromise expected of this patient population and do not suggest that these patients are sufficiently impaired, cognitively, to render them unsuitable for their military responsibilities.

ADHD/LD FUTURE DIRECTIONS

Our understanding of the impact of ADHD and LD on individual service members and on the larger military mission is remarkably limited. Though policies are in place to evaluate service members with histories of ADHD or LD prior to assignment to specialized duties (e.g., flight status, Basic Underwater Demolition/SEAL) and the provision of clinical services to patients with known or suspected ADHD/LD is commonplace, we do not know the extent to which screening and diagnostic/treatment efforts are successful. Some data, presented above, indicate that persons with ADHD or LD who obtain aeromedical waivers for flight status perform as well as individuals never diagnosed with ADHD/LD, at least in the early stages of training. Yet there is no longitudinal data attesting to the long-term suitability of such persons for these missions. Likewise, it is unknown the extent to which service members with ADHD or LD diagnoses receive effective interventions or the extent to which their behavior contributes positively or negatively to the larger military mission. Considering the known array of emotional and functional problems exhibited by civilian adults with ADHD/LD, the increasing numbers of waiver requests for special duty and the difficulties in parsing out preexisting ADHD and LD from acquired neurological injuries in the war zone, research addressing these issues is needed.

REFERENCES

American Psychiatric Association. (2000). *Diagnostic and statistical manual of mental disorders* (4th ed., text rev.). Washington, DC: Author.

Barkley, R. A. (1997a). *ADHD and the nature of self-control*. New York: Guilford Press.

Barkley, R. A. (1997b). Behavioral inhibition, sustained attention, and executive functions: Constructing a unifying theory of ADHD. *Psychological Bulletin, 121*, 65–94.

Barkley, R. A., Fischer, M., Smallish, L., & Fletcher, K. (2002). The persistence of attention-deficit/hyperactivity disorder into young adulthood as a function of reporting source and definition of disorder. *Journal of Abnormal Psychology, 111*, 279–289.

Barkley, R. A., Murphy, K. R., & Fischer, M. (2008). *ADHD in adults: What the science says*. New York: Guilford Press.

Bechara, A. (2007). *Iowa gambling task*. Lutz, FL: Psychological Assessment Resources.

Beck, A. T. & Steer, R. A. (1993). *Beck anxiety inventory manual*. San Antonio, TX: The Psychological Corporation.

Beck, A. T., Steer, R. A., & Brown, G. K. (1996). *Beck depression inventory-2 manual*. San Antonio, TX: The Psychological Corporation.

Biederman, J., Faraone, S. V., Spencer, T. J., Mick, E., Monuteaux, M. C., & Aleardi, M. (2006). Functional impairments in adults with self-reports of diagnosed ADHD: A controlled study of 1001 adults in the community. *Journal Clinical Psychiatry, 67*(4), 524–540.

Birch, S., & Chase, C. (2004). Visual and language processing deficits in compensated and uncompensated college students with dyslexia. *Journal of Learning Disabilities, 37*, 389–410.

Boonstra, A. M., Oosterlaan, J., Sergeant, J. A., & Buitelaar, J. K. (2005). Executive functioning in adult ADHD: A meta-analytic review. *Psychology Medicine, 35*(8), 1097–1108.

Brickenkamp, R., & Zillmer, E. (1998). *d2 test of attention manual*. Seattle, WA: Hogrefe & Huber.

Bridgett, D. J., & Walker, M. E. (2006). Intellectual functioning in adults with ADHD: A meta-analytic examination of full scale IQ differences between adults with and without ADHD. *Psychological Assessment, 18*, 1–14.

Campbell, J. S., Moore, J. L., Poythress, N. G., & Kennedy, C. H. (2009). Personality traits in clinically referred aviators: Two clusters related to occupational suitability. *Aviation, Space and Environmental Medicine, 80*, 1049–1054.

Cigrang, J. A., Carbone, E. G., Todd, S., & Fiedler, E. (1998). Mental health attrition from Air Force basic military training, *Military Medicine, 163*(12), 834–838.

Collins, D. W., & Rourke, B. P. (2003). Learning-disabled brains: A review of the literature. *Journal of Clinical and Experimental Neuropsychology, 25*(7), 1011–1034.

Conners, C. K. (2002). *Continuous performance test II.* Toronto, Canada: MultiHealth Systems.

Costa, P., Jr., & McCrae, R. (2000). *Revised NEO personality inventory.* Lutz, FL: Psychological Assessment Resources.

Cutting, L. E., & Denckla, M. B. (2003). Attention: Relationships between attention-deficit hyperactivity disorder and learning disabilities. In H. L. Swanson, K. R. Harris, & S. Graham (Eds.), *Handbook of learning disabilities* (pp. 125–139). New York: Guilford Press.

De Filippis, N. A., & McCampell, E. (1997). *Booklet Category Test (BCT)* (2nd ed.). Odessa, FL: Psychological Assessment Resources.

De Gelder, B., & Vrooman, J. (1996). Auditory illusions as evidence for a role of the syllable in adult developmental dyslexics. *Brain and Language, 52*, 373–385.

Delis, D. C., Kaplan, E., Kramer, J. H., & Ober, B. A. (2000). *California Verbal Learning Test–Second Edition (CVLT-II).* San Antonio, TX: Psychological Corporation.

Department of Defense. (2005). *Department of Defense Instruction 6130.4: Medical standards for appointment, enlistment, or induction in the armed forces.* Washington, DC: Author.

Department of Defense. (2007). *Department of Defense Instruction 1304.26: Qualification standards for enlistment, appointment, and induction.* Washington, DC: Author.

Department of Homeland Security, United States Coast Guard. (2008). *COMDTINST M6000.1C: Medical Manual.* Washington, DC: Author.

Doyle, A. E. (2006). Executive functions in attention-deficit/hyperactivity disorder. *Journal of Clinical Psychiatry, 67*(Suppl. 8), 21–26.

Educational Testing Service. (2008). *Policy statement for documentation of attention-deficit/hyperactivity disorder in adolescents and adults* (2nd ed.). Princeton, NJ: Office of Disability Policy.

Elbro, C. (1998). When reading is "readn" or somethn: Distinctiveness of phonological representations of lexical items in normal and disabled readers. *Scandinavian Journal of Psychology, 39*, 149–153.

Faraone, S. V., Biederman, J., Spencer, T., Mick, E., Murray, K., Petty, C., et al. (2006). Diagnosing adult attention deficit hyperactivity disorder: Are late onset and subthreshold diagnoses valid? *American Journal of Psychiatry, 163*, 1720–1729.

Faraone, S. V., Biederman, J., Spencer, T., Wilens, T., Seidman, L. J., Mick, E., et al. (2000). Attention deficit/hyperactivity disorder in adults: An overview. *Biological Psychiatry, 48*, 9–20.

Fletcher, J. M., Lyon, G. R., Fuchs, L. S., & Barnes, M. A. (2007). *Learning disabilities: From identification to intervention.* New York: Guilford Press.

Frazier, T. W., Demaree, H. A., & Youngstrom, E. A. (2004). Meta-analysis of intellectual and neuropsychological test performance in attention-deficit/hyperactivity disorder. *Neuropsychology, 18*, 543–555.

Golden, C. J., & Freshwater, S. M. (2002). *The Stroop color and word test manual.* Wood Dale, IL: Stoelting.

Gregg, N., Hoy, C., King, W. M., Moreland, C. M., & Jagota, M. (1992). The MMPI-2 profile of adults with learning disabilities in university and rehabilitation settings. *Journal of Learning Disabilities, 25,* 386–395.

Greiffenstein, M. F., & Baker, W. J. (2002). Neuropsychological and psychosocial correlates of adult arithmetic deficiency. *Neuropsychology, 16,* 451–458.

Gronwall, D. M. A. (1977). Paced auditory serial addition task: A measure of recovery from concussion. *Perceptual and Motor Skills, 44,* 367–373.

Harvard University. (2008). *Information for students: Clinical documentation.* Retrieved April 1, 2009, from Harvard University Department of Accessible Education Office Web site: http://www.aeo.fas.harvard.edu/documentation.html

Heaton, R. K., Grant, I., & Matthews, C. G. (1991). *Comprehensive norms for an expanded Halstead-Reitan battery: Demographic corrections, research findings, and clinical applications.* Odessa, FL: Psychological Assessment Resources.

Hervey, A. S., Epstein, J. N., & Curry, J. F. (2004). Neuropsychology of adults with attention-deficit/hyperactivity disorder: A meta-analytic review. *Neuropsychology, 18,* 485–503.

Hirschfeld, R., Williams, J., Spitzer, R., Calabrese, J., Flynn, L., Keck, P., et al. (2000). Development and validation of a screening instrument for bipolar spectrum disorder: The mood disorder questionnaire. *The American Journal of Psychiatry, 157*(11), 1873–1875.

Hooper, S. R., & Olley, J. G. (1996). Psychological comorbidity in adults with learning disabilities. In N. Gregg, C. Hoy, & A. F. Gay (Eds.), *Adults with learning disabilities* (pp. 162–183). New York: Guilford Press.

Hoy, C., & Manglitz, E. (1996). Social and affective adjustment of adults with learning disabilities: A life-span perspective. In N. Gregg, C. Hoy, & A. F. Gay (Eds.), *Adults with learning disabilities* (pp. 208–231). New York: Guilford Press.

Jensen, J., Lindgren, M., Meurling, A. W., Ingvar, D. H., & Levander, S. (1999). Dyslexia among Swedish prison inmates in relation to neuropsychology and personality. *Journal of the International Neuropsychological Society, 5,* 452–461.

Johnson, D. E., Epstein, J. N., Waid, L. R., Latham, P. K., Konstantin, E. V., & Anton, R. F. (2001). Neuropsychological performance deficits in adults with attention deficit/hyperactivity disorder. *Archives of Clinical Neuropsychology, 16,* 587–604.

Katz, L. J., Goldstein, G., & Beers, S. S. (2001). *Learning disabilities in older adolescents and adults.* New York: Kluwer Academic/Plenum.

Kay, G. G. (1995). *CogScreen–Aeromedical edition: Professional manual.* Washington, DC: CogScreen, LLC.

Kay, G. G., & Moore, J. L. (2002). *Aviation vigilance test.* Washington, DC: CogScreen, LLC.

Kennedy, C. H., Walker, P. B., & Moore, J. S. (2008). Military aviator norms for the d2 test of attention. *Archives of Clinical Neuropsychology, 23,* 750.

Kessler, R. C., Adler, L., Barkley, R. A., Biederman, J., Conners, C. K., Demler, O., et al. (2006). The prevalence and correlates of adult ADHD in the United States: Results from the National Comorbidity Survey replication. *American Journal of Psychiatry, 163,* 716–723.

Krain, A. L., & Castellanos, F. X. (2006). Brain development and ADHD. *Clinical Psychology Review, 26*(4), 477–484.

Makris, N., Biederman, J., Valera, E. M., Bush, G., Kaiser, J., Kennedy, D. N., et al. (2007). Cortical thinning of the attention and executive function networks in adults with attention-deficit/hyperactivity disorder. *Cerebral Cortex, 17*(6), 1364–1375.

Mapou, R. L. (2009). *Adult learning disabilities and ADHD: Research-informed assessment.* New York: Oxford University Press.

Meyers, J. E., & Meyers, K. R. (1995). *Rey complex figure test and recognition trial: Professional manual.* Odessa, FL: Psychological Assessment Resources.

Naval Aerospace Medical Institute. (2008). *Aeromedical reference and waiver guide.* Pensacola, FL: Author. Retrieved April 11, 2009, from http://www.med.navy.mil/sites/navmedmpte/nomi/nami/arwg/Pages/default.aspx

Osmon, D. C., Smerz, J. M., Braun, M. M., & Plambeck, E. A. (2006). Processing abilities associated with math skills in adult learning disability: A simulation study. *The Clinical Neuropsychologist, 20,* 315–324.

Peverly, S. (2006). The importance of handwriting speed in adult writing. *Developmental Neuropsychology, 29,* 197–216.

Reitan, R. (1958). Validity of the Trail Making Test as an indicator of organic brain damage. *Perceptual and Motor Skills, 8,* 271–276.

Rourke, B. (2000). Characteristics and dynamics of the NLD syndrome in adults. *Journal of the International Neurological Society, 6,* 210.

Rourke, B. P., Young, G. C., Strang, J. D., & Russell, D. L. (1986). Adult outcomes of childhood central processing deficiencies. In I. Grant & K.M. Adams (Eds.), *Neuropsychological assessment of neuropsychiatric disorders* (pp. 244–267). New York: Oxford University Press.

Ryan, L. M., Zazeckis, T. M., French, L. M., & Harvey, S. (2006). Neuropsychological practice in the military. In C. H. Kennedy & E. A. Zillmer (Eds.), *Military psychology: Clinical and operational applications* (pp. 105–129). New York: Guilford.

Schneider, M., Retz, W., Coogan, A., Thome, J., & Rosler, M. (2006). Anatomical and functional brain imaging in adult attention-deficit/hyperactivity disorder (ADHD)—A neurological view. *European Archives of Psychiatry and Clinical Neuroscience, 256*(Suppl. 1), i32–i41.

Schoechlin, C., & Engle, R. R. (2005). Neuropsychological performance in adult attention-deficit hyperactivity disorder: Meta-analysis of empirical data. *Archives of Clinical Neuropsychology, 20,* 727–744.

Seidman, L. J., Biederman, J., Weber, W., Hatch, M., & Farone, S. (1998). Neuropsychological function in adults with attention-deficit hyperactivity disorder. *Biological Psychiatry, 44,* 260–268.

Shaywitz, B. A., Lyon, G. R., & Shaywitz, S. E. (2006). The role of functional magnetic resonance imaging in understanding reading and dyslexia. *Developmental Neuropsychology, 30,* 613–632.

Shaywitz, S. E., & Shaywitz, B. A. (2005). Dyslexia (specific reading disability). *Biological Psychiatry, 57,* 1301–1309.

Siegel, L. S. (2003). IQ-discrepancy definitions and the diagnosis of LD: Introduction to the special issue. *Journal of Learning Disabilities, 36,* 2–3.

Simon, V., Czobor, P., Balint, S., Meszaros, A., & Bitter, I. (2009). Prevalance and correlates of adult attention-deficit hyperactivity disorder: Meta-analysis. *British Journal of Psychiatry, 194*(3), 204–211.

The University of Minnesota. (2001). *Minnesota multiphasic personality inventory-2.* Minneapolis, MN: University of Minnesota.

The University of Texas at Austin. (2008). *Guidelines for documenting attention-deficit/hyperactivity disorder.* Retrieved April 1, 2009, from the University of Texas at Austin Division of Diversity and Community Engagement Website: http://www.utexas.edu/diversity/ddce/ssd/doc_adhd.php

Tsatsanis, K. D., & Rourke, B. P. (2008). Syndrome of nonverbal learning disabilities in adults. In L. E. Wolf, H. Schreiger, & J. Wasserstein (Eds.), *Adult learning disorders: Contemporary issues* (pp. 159–190). New York: Psychology Press.

Virtual Flight Surgeons, Inc. (2009). *FAA Medical Certification: Attention Deficit Disorder.* Retrieved May 1, 2009, from Virtual Flight Surgeons Website: http://aviationmedicine.com/medications/index.cfm

Wasserstein, J., & Denckla, M. B. (2009). ADHD and learning disabilities in adults: Overlap with executive dysfunction. In T. E. Brown (Ed.), *ADHD comorbities: Handbook for ADHD complications in children and adults* (pp. 267–285). Washington, DC: American Psychiatric Publishing.

Wasserstein, J., Vadhan, N. P., Barboza, K., & Stefanatos, G. A. (2008). Outcomes in proable nonverbal learning disabled (NLD) adults: A naturalistic study. In L. E. Wolf, H. Schreiger, & J. Wasserstein (Eds.), *Adult learning disorders: Contemporary issues* (pp. 462–491). New York: Psychology Press.

Wechsler, D. (2008). *Wechsler adult intelligence scale-IV.* San Antonio, TX: The Psychological Corporation.

Wechsler, D. (1997). *Wechsler memory scale* (3rd ed.). San Antonio, TX: The Psychological Corporation.

Wender, P. H., Wolf, L. E., & Wasserstein, J. (2001). Adults with ADHD: An overview. In J. Wasserstein, L. E. Wolf, & F. F. LeFever (Eds.), Adult attention-deficit disorder: Brain mechanisms and life outcomes. *Annals of the New York Academy of Sciences, 931,* 1–16.

Wolf, M., & Bowers, P. G. (1999). The double-deficit hypothesis for the developmental dyslexias. *Journal of Educational Psychology, 91,* 415–438.

Woodcock, R. W., McGrew, K. S., & Mather, N. (2001a). *Woodcock-Johnson III: Tests of achievement.* Itasca, IL: Riverside.

Woodcock, R. W., McGrew, K. S., & Mather, N. (2001b). *Woodcock-Johnson III: Tests of cognitive abilities.* Itasca, IL: Riverside.

HIV-Associated Neurocognitive Disorders in the Military

STEVEN PAUL WOODS, ERICA WEBER,
J. ALLEN McCUTCHAN, AND ROBERT K. HEATON

Neuropsychological assessment has become increasingly relevant to the medical care of HIV-infected active duty military personnel, reservists, and veterans of the armed forces. Prevalence estimates suggest that approximately 0.15–0.20 per 1,000 active duty military personnel are infected with HIV and annual seroconversion (i.e., incidence) rates are currently estimated at 0.10–0.15 per 1,000 (Army Medical Surveillance Activity, 2007). Although the incidence of HIV infection in the military has decreased over the past 15 years, new infections are still relatively common among certain subpopulations, including African American men, unmarried individuals, and health care professionals (Bautista et al., 2006). HIV is transmitted via exposure to infected blood, semen, or vaginal fluid, which in active duty military personnel is most often a consequence of unprotected sexual contact rather than injection drug use (e.g., Brodine et al., 1999).

In the early years of the epidemic (i.e., from the 1980s to the mid-1990s), HIV seropositivity was grounds for immediate retirement or separation from military service because disease progression was presumed to be invariably rapid and debilitating. The past decade has witnessed tremendous advancements in the management of systemic HIV infection, however, and the disease is increasingly viewed as a chronic, but manageable, medical illness. Although HIV infection is still exclusionary for entry into the armed forces (Department of Defense, 2006), the regulations governing incident HIV infection among active duty and reservists have been updated to reflect the changing face of the epidemic (Department of Homeland Security, 2008; Department of the Air Force, 2004; Department of the Army, 2005; Department of the Navy, 2006).

Specifically, the Department of Defense (2006) dictates biannual screening for all service members for HIV infection. However, individuals who test seropositive for HIV are no longer released from military service unless the medical condition is sufficiently severe to warrant such actions. Given the medical complications often seen with HIV infection, however, the military does restrict duty assignments based on HIV status, generally, so that service members are near major military treatment facilities designed to monitor and treat HIV. HIV-positive service members may not be deployed or stationed overseas in most areas, and restrictions may apply in such career fields as recruiting, health care, explosive ordnance, and aviation. All branches of service mandate that service members are routinely sent for a comprehensive medical evaluation to ensure that immunological, general medical, or neurological (e.g., neuropsychological) complications of infection do not render them unfit for duty. As such, a comprehensive neuropsychological evaluation provides a valuable contribution to the process of determining an HIV-infected service member's medical fitness for active duty. With these issues in mind, this chapter provides an overview of HIV-associated neurocognitive disorders, focusing on issues related to their epidemiology, neurobiology, diagnosis, impact on everyday functioning, comorbidities, and responsiveness to treatment.

NEUROPATHOGENESIS OF HIV

HIV is a lentivirus, which belongs to the class of enveloped viruses known as *Retroviridae* that replicate by integrating themselves into the DNA of the host cell. HIV preferentially infects T-helper cells (e.g., CD4+ lymphocytes), along with monocytes and macrophages. Accordingly, HIV infection can severely compromise the host's immune system, making them vulnerable to contracting various opportunistic infections (e.g., toxoplasmosis) and cancers (e.g., Kaposi's sarcoma). Although its primary adverse effects are immunological, HIV is also highly neurotropic, meaning that it is able to infiltrate the central nervous system (CNS). The virus uses an effective "Trojan horse" mechanism to invade the CNS by hiding inside of monocytes (and other white blood cells) that readily traffic across the blood–brain barrier (Haase, 1986). Although HIV is not known to productively infect neurons, the virus can nevertheless trigger neuronal apoptosis and/or synaptoden-dritic degeneration in about 50% of seropositive individuals, which can arise by both direct (i.e., viral) and indirect (i.e., host) mechanisms (Ellis, Langford, & Masliah, 2007). The direct CNS effects of HIV are characterized by its replication in microglia, astrocytes, and perivascu-lar macrophages, which can release neurotoxic viral proteins, such as gp120 and Tat (Ellis et al., 2007). The indirect (i.e., "bystander") CNS effects of HIV, on the other hand, may arise via several different neu-ropathogenic mechanisms, most notably neuroinflammatory processes (Gonzalez-Scarano & Martin-Garcia, 2005).

HIV RNA is detectable throughout brain parenchyma, and neu-roimaging studies show that a subset of HIV-infected individuals dem-onstrate generalized cerebral atrophy (e.g., Stout et al., 1998), as well as abnormalities in the macrostructure (e.g., nonspecific hyperinten-sities; Archibald et al., 2004) and microstructure (e.g., reduced aniso-tropy; Pomara, Crandall, Choi, Johnson, & Lim, 2001) of the cerebral white matter. When this is present, HIV-associated neurodegeneration is most readily observed in the structure and function of the fronto-striatal (e.g., caudate) and temporolimbic (e.g., hippocampus) networks. Although the neurotoxic effects of HIV may be evident in many neu-ral networks, including both primary and associational cortices (e.g., Thompson et al., 2005), a convergence of evidence suggests that the virus may preferentially disrupt the structure and function of the fronto-striato-thalamo-cortical circuits. For example, the frontal cortex and striatum of HIV-infected individuals appear to be especially sus-ceptible to structural abnormalities (e.g., Castelo, Courtney, Melrose, & Stern, 2007), neuroinflammation (e.g., elevated myoinositol and choline; Chang, Ernst, Speck, & Grob, 2005), neuronal injury (i.e., decreased N-acetyl asparate; Chang et al., 2005), and altered blood-oxygen-level dependent response during the performance of cognitive tasks (e.g., Melrose, Tinaz, Castelo, Courtney, & Stern, 2008). Whether the rela-tively disproportionate frontostriatal neuropathogenesis of HIV is attrib-utable to regional differences in permeability of the blood–brain barrier (e.g., Berger & Arendt, 2000), the differential prevalence of vulnerable neuronal populations (e.g., large spiny neurons), and/or the involvement of specific neurotransmitters (e.g., glutamate and dopamine) has yet to be determined (e.g., Langford, Hurford, Hashimoto, Digicaylioglu, & Masliah, 2005).

HIV-ASSOCIATED NEUROCOGNITIVE DISORDERS

HIV-associated neuropathologies can produce mild-to-moderate impairment in numerous lower-order (e.g., motor skills) and higher-order (e.g., executive functions and episodic memory) cognitive abilities upon which successful everyday functioning depend. Depending on stage of HIV disease, global neuropsychological impairment is evident in an estimated 30–50% of individuals with HIV (e.g., Heaton et al., 1995; Robertson et al., 2007), with yearly incidence rates of approximately 10–25% (e.g., Robertson et al., 2007). It is nevertheless important to note that, in the absence of significant comorbid conditions (e.g., developmental disabilities, hepatitis C co-infection), as many as 50–70% of HIV-infected adults therefore *do not* have significant brain involvement or resultant neurocognitive impairments. Currently, it is unclear why some individuals are spared CNS involvement, but it is likely that a variety of viral (e.g., genetics, compartmentalization), host (e.g., cognitive reserve, comorbidities), and treatment factors contribute to the expression of HIV-associated neurocognitive disorders (HAND).

In an effort to facilitate research on this important phenomenon, the AIDS Task Force of the American Academy of Neurology (1991) proposed specific guidelines for the diagnosis of HAND, which included HIV-associated dementia (HAD) and minor cognitive-motor disorder (MCMD). In 1995, Grant and Atkinson extended the HAND nosology to include "subsyndromic neuropsychological impairment" to capture patients who exhibit mild neurocognitive deficits that do not noticeably interfere with everyday functioning.

Most recently, a National Institutes of Health working group (Antinori et al., 2007) updated the research diagnostic criteria for HAND, taking into consideration the many clinical and scientific advancements in treatment (i.e., the introduction of highly active antiretroviral therapies [HAART]) and neuropsychological assessment (e.g., new tests and improved normative standards) of HIV infection, as well as emerging appreciation of important comorbidities (e.g., hepatitis C co-infection). As shown in Figure 9.1, these updated HAND criteria allow for three possible diagnoses: (a) HIV-associated asymptomatic neurocognitive impairment (ANI); (b) HIV-associated mild neurocognitive disorder (MND) and (c) HIV-associated dementia (HAD). For each of these diagnoses, an individual must demonstrate at least mild neuropsychological impairment (i.e., >1 *SD* below the appropriate normative mean) in at least two cognitive domains that is attributable, at least in part, to HIV infection.

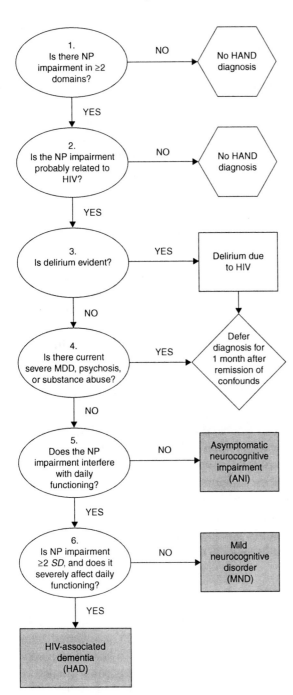

Figure 9.1 An algorithm for diagnosing HIV-associated neurocognitive disorders (HAND). (Adapted from Antinori et al., 2007.)

Since HIV infection is sometimes associated with comorbidities that may affect CNS functioning, the updated HAND criteria provide guidelines for secondary (e.g., an individual with remote alcohol abuse that is unlikely to have residual cognitive effects from their alcohol use), contributing (e.g., an individual with alcohol dependence within 6 months that may be affecting cognition, but who nevertheless shows clear evidence of HIV-related cognitive and functional difficulties), and confounding (e.g., an individual experiencing acute withdrawal from alcohol dependence in whom it is not possible to attribute cognitive problems to HIV infection) conditions (Antinori et al., 2007).

Asymptomatic Neurocognitive Impairment

The most notable addition to the updated HAND nosology is the diagnosis of ANI, which requires demonstrable evidence of impairment (i.e., >1 SD below the mean of demographically adjusted normative scores) in at least two areas of cognitive functioning in the absence of noticeable functional impairment. It has been argued that this diagnosis encompasses a sizeable and previously ignored portion of the HIV-infected population (Grant & Atkinson, 1995). It is estimated that ANI diagnoses make up over 50% of HAND diagnoses and approximately 15–30% of the HIV population overall (Grant, Sacktor, & McArthur, 2005). Nevertheless, critical questions remain regarding the diagnostic methods for distinguishing between ANI and the "syndromic" HAND conditions, which have historically relied upon self-report (e.g., questionnaires), rather than performance-based laboratory measures of daily functioning that may be more sensitive to functional declines (e.g., Mitchell & Miller, 2008). Nevertheless, early identification of ANI may be clinically important to predict future functional impairment, as well as to monitor health-related behaviors that are particularly sensitive to even the mildest impairment (e.g., medication adherence).

Mild Neurocognitive Disorder

Although ANI is the most prevalent form of HAND in the HAART era, approximately 30–50% of individuals with HIV-associated neuropsychological impairment experience problems with their basic and/ or instrumental activities of daily living (IADLs) as a consequence of their cognitive deficits (Antinori et al., 2007; Grant et al., 2005). The epidemiology of MND is not well understood, but it is estimated that approximately 20–40% of those with HAND and 5–20% of the HIV population overall may meet criteria for MND (Grant et al., 2005). Formerly referred to as MCMD, a diagnosis of MND requires acquired mild-to-moderate impairment (i.e., >1 *SD* below the normative mean) in at least two areas of cognitive functioning, which also interferes with ADLs and cannot be entirely explained by comorbidities or delirium.

The mild functional decline requirement for a diagnosis of MND may be met by evidence of two or more of the following that are not exclusively attributable to a comorbid condition: (a) self- or proxy-report of declines in ≥2 IADLs (e.g., financial management); (b) unemployment or a significant reduction in job responsibilities secondary to reduced cognitive abilities; (c) decline in vocational functioning (e.g., increased errors, decreased productivity, or greater effort is required to achieve prior levels of productivity); (d) self- or proxy-report of increased problems in ≥2 cognitive ability areas in day-to-day life (NB: this criterion cannot be used if based only on the self-report of an individual with current depression, since depression may bias self-report); or (e) scores >1 *SD* below mean on a performance-based laboratory measure of everyday functioning (e.g., medication management).

HIV-Associated Dementia

A diagnosis of HAD is defined by an acquired moderate-to-severe impairment (i.e., at least 2 *SD* below demographically adjusted normative means) in at least two cognitive domains along with marked ADL declines that are not fully attributable to comorbidities or delirium. Thus, HAD represents the most severe form of HAND, both in the magnitude and breadth of the observed neurocognitive impairment and its impact on daily functioning, which requires two or more of the following: (a) unemployment due to cognitive impairment; (b) self-or proxy-report of dependence in >2 IADLs related to cognitive problems; (c) self- or proxy report of declines in ≥4 cognitive ability areas in day-to-day life (*NB*: As with a diagnosis of MND, this criterion is not applicable if based exclusively on the self-report of an individual with current depression, which can be defined as having a BDI score > 17); (d) performance that is >2 *SD* below the mean on a performance-based laboratory measure of everyday functioning (e.g., or >1 *SD* below the mean on two functional tests).

The incidence of HAD has decreased dramatically since the introduction of HAART in 1996 (e.g., Sacktor et al., 2001), but prevalence rates remain fairly constant, and relative to the pre-HAART era, may be slightly higher among individuals who are not immunosuppressed (e.g., Grant et al., 2005). Unlike the classic neurodegenerative dementias (e.g., Alzheimer's disease), HAD is not invariably progressive; in fact, there is considerable variability in the long-term course of all of the HAND classifications, which may improve, deteriorate, or fluctuate over time (Antinori et al., 2007). This is influenced by a variety of factors, such as incident and remitting comorbidities (e.g., psychiatric disorders) and treatment effects (e.g., commencement of HAART). A diagnosis of "HAD in remission" may be given to individuals with a prior diagnosis of HAD who no longer meet the neurocognitive and/or functional criteria.

ASSESSMENT METHODOLOGIES FOR DIAGNOSING HAND

Although the updated HAND criteria (Antinori et al., 2007) allow for the use of mental status exams (e.g., the HIV Dementia Scale; Power, Selnes, Grim, & McArthur, 1995; Morgan et al., 2008) in resource-limited settings, they recommend that the diagnoses be based on a comprehensive neuropsychological evaluation. The neurocognitive test battery should (a) assess at least five of the ability areas known to be affected by HIV (e.g., executive functions, episodic memory, speed of information processing, motor skills, attention/working memory, language, and sensoriperception); (b) include at least two tests per cognitive domain assessed; and (c) utilize the best available demographically adjusted normative standards. There are several different summary methods used to classify domain-specific and global neurocognitive impairment in HIV, including the Global Deficit Score (see Carey et al., 2004a) and the clinical ratings methodology, which provides an algorithm for the neuropsychologist to assign scores of 1 (above average) to 9 (severely impaired) based on demographically adjusted T-scores, with scores of 5 and higher (i.e., T-score < 40) indicating cognitive impairment (Woods et al., 2004b). Table 9.1 displays select neuropsychological and functional measures that have demonstrated predictive validity in HIV infection and have adequate demographically adjusted normative standards for U.S. populations.

Despite the inclusion of everyday functioning capacity in the diagnostic criteria for HAND (and many other neurological and psychiatric disorders), there are no widely agreed-upon methods for determining the presence of functional impairment (for a review, see Morgan & Heaton, 2009). In a recent survey of assessment practices (Rabin,

Table 9.1

A SELECTION OF NEUROPSYCHOLOGICAL TESTS THAT HAVE DEMONSTRATED CONSTRUCT VALIDITY IN HIV DISEASE AND HAVE AVAILABLE NORMATIVE STANDARDS

DOMAIN	TEST
Neurocognitive functions	
Executive functions	Halstead category test
	Stroop color and word test
	Trailmaking test, Part B
	Wisconsin card sorting test
Episodic memory	Brief visuospatial memory test–revised
	California verbal learning test (2nd ed.)
	Hopkins verbal learning test-revised
	Rey auditory verbal learning test
	Rey complex figure test
	Wechsler memory scale (3rd ed.)
Language	Action (verb) fluency
	Animal fluency
	Boston naming test
	Controlled oral word association test
Information processing speed	Digit vigilance test
	Symbol digit modalities test
	Trailmaking test, Part A
	WAIS-III processing speed index
Attention and working memory	Paced serial addition test
	WAIS-III/WMS-III working memory index
Motor skills	Finger tapping
	Grooved pegboard
	Timed gait
Everyday functioning	
Questionnaires	Modified Lawton & Brody ADL
	Patients' assessment of own functioning inventory
Laboratory	Medication management task–revised
	Valpar standardized work samples
	ACTG adherence questionnaire

Barr, & Burton, 2005), fewer than 40% of neuropsychologists reported "frequently" using direct functional assessments, and no functional measure appeared among the top 40 tests used in clinical practice. Although there are innumerable research-based measures of daily functioning in HIV, there are few such tests that are adequately validated for clinical use in the diagnosis of HAND. Most commonly implemented are self- and proxy-report questionnaires, such as the modified Lawton & Brody's ADL Scale (Heaton et al., 2004) and Patients' Assessment of Own Functioning Inventory (Chelune, Heaton, & Lehman, 1986), which have the benefit of considerable research support. However, the clinical diagnostic value of these assessments is tempered by confounds such as cognitive impairment (e.g., underreporting due to poor insight or lack of awareness), psychiatric comorbidities (e.g., overreporting secondary to depression), and possible issues of personal gain (e.g., underreporting to minimize risk of discharge). Laboratory measures, such as the Medication Management Task-Revised (Heaton et al., 2004), Valpar standardized work sample (Heaton et al., 2004) and driving simulators (e.g., Marcotte et al., 2004), offer objective, performance-based assessments of functional abilities (e.g., see Heaton et al., 2004), but are limited in scope, are sometimes viewed as contrived, lack validated demographically adjusted normative standards, and are quite time-intensive, making them less practical for use in most clinical settings. Although these limitations must be considered in interpreting data derived from functional assessments, the inclusion of such instruments may nevertheless provide some additional value in the diagnostic evaluation of HAND (Table 9.1).

EFFORT AND SYMPTOM VALIDITY

Military personnel infected with HIV face a variety of serious career consequences that hinge on the outcome of their medical disability evaluations (e.g., duty restrictions, retirement, or discharge). As such, some individuals may minimize genuine neurocognitive, psychiatric, and neurological symptoms to reduce their risk of discharge. Moreover, some individuals may feign or exaggerate such symptoms in an attempt to secure a medical discharge with additional disability compensation. Thus, practitioners must carefully evaluate under- or overreporting of symptoms and/or suboptimal effort in interpreting neuropsychological data from individuals undergoing medical disability evaluations for HIV infection (see chapter 4 for a more comprehensive discussion of this issue). Practitioners are advised to include well-validated measures of symptom validity and effort in their neuropsychological test battery. Although research on the clinical utility of effort tests in HAND is limited, low false-positive rates have been shown using Mittenberg and colleagues' (1993) "embedded" WMS-R effort index (Slick, Hinkin, van Gorp, &

Satz, 2001) and the Hiscock Digit Memory Test (Hiscock & Hiscock, 1989), with the latter showing a 2% failure rate in a noncompensation-seeking population with HAND (Woods et al., 2003).

HAND AND SEVERITY OF HIV DISEASE

In 1993, the Centers for Disease Control and Prevention (CDC, 1992) proposed a set of criteria for staging HIV disease severity that remain the current standard of practice. The classification scheme is composed of nine exclusive categories based on a patient's nadir (i.e., lowest) CD4 lymphocyte count (i.e., stage $1 \geq 500$ c/ml; stage 2 = 499–200 c/ml; and stage 3 < 200 c/ml) and severity of clinical symptoms (i.e., category A = asymptomatic; category B = mild symptoms [e.g., peripheral neuropathy]; and category C = AIDS-defining illnesses [e.g., Kaposi's sarcoma, toxoplasmosis]). Individuals falling within stage 3 and/or category C are diagnosed with AIDS, which is an immutable classification, meaning that a patient will retain an AIDS diagnosis even if the defining opportunistic infection is successfully treated or they experience a significant improvement in CD4 count (i.e., immune reconstitution). A commonly used estimate of current HIV disease severity is HIV RNA, which can be detected and quantified in blood plasma and cerebrospinal fluid (CSF). Such measures of "viral load" reflect the frequency of HIV replication and provide a yardstick with which to gauge the success (i.e., viral suppression) of antiretroviral therapies (Hammer et al., 2008).

Current CD4 count and plasma viral load are not considered valuable indicators of neuro-AIDS in the era of HAART because they no longer accurately reflect the primary neuropathogenic mechanisms of HAND (e.g., neuroinflammatory processes). CSF viral load has been hypothesized to provide a more direct window on the CNS effects of HIV (e.g., Ellis et al., 1997b) and is predictive of incident HAND (e.g., Ellis et al., 2002), but more recent studies raise questions about the robustness of such associations in the HAART era (e.g., Sevigny et al., 2004). Lower nadir CD4 lymphocyte counts are also associated with an increased risk of current HAND, even after considering the possible confounding influence of demographics, current CD4 count, and estimated HIV disease duration (e.g., Valcour et al., 2006). Indeed, the prevalence and magnitude of HAND generally increase in step with advancing HIV disease, with approximately 50% of individuals with AIDS showing impairment across a range of cognitive ability areas (Heaton et al., 1995) that is broadly of moderate severity (Reger, Welsh, Razani, Martin, & Boone, 2002).

There is considerable controversy about the nature and extent of neurobehavioral sequelae in the acute (i.e., the period between transmission and seroconversion), early (i.e., <1 year posttransmission), and asymptomatic phases of HIV disease. It is known that HIV crosses the blood–brain barrier early after initial infection (Davis et al., 1992). Moreover, animal models of acute and early HIV infection demonstrate that rapid viral replication and neuroinflammatory changes occur during these stages of infection (e.g., Greco et al., 2004). Research on the neuropsychological effects of acute and early HIV infection is sparse, but elevated viral loads during the period of early infection may be a harbinger of incident HAND, particularly in individuals with lower CD4 counts (Marcotte et al., 2003).

In contrast, numerous studies have been published on HAND in persons with asymptomatic HIV disease, a topic that engendered much debate in the late 1980s and early 1990s. Findings from early studies were mixed, likely reflecting the subtle, "spotty" nature of the impairment (Grant et al., 1987), as well as across-study variability in cohort composition, statistical power, the breadth and depth of neuropsychological test batteries, and the operationalization of "impairment" (e.g., Newman, Lunn, & Harrison, 1995). Subsequent, large-scale studies have similarly revealed that approximately 30% of individuals with asymptomatic HIV disease demonstrate global impairment (Heaton et al., 1995). In fact, a recent multisite study ($N = 1,556$) found that over 30% of persons with CDC classifications of A1 or A2 who are without significant confounding conditions meet criteria for HAND (Heaton et al., 2009). The magnitude of impairment, however, is quite mild, as evidenced by generally small effect sizes at the group level (Reger et al., 2002).

The extent to which the asymptomatic HAND literature generalizes to military populations remains to be determined, as very few studies have been published on such cohorts (e.g., Goethe et al., 1989; Mapou et al., 1993; White et al., 1995). One early study reported that approximately 38% of asymptomatic HIV-infected active duty men in the U.S. Army demonstrated neurocognitive impairment, as defined by test scores at least 2 SD below the normative mean in two or more functional domains (Klusman et al., 1991). Findings from these limited investigations are inconsistent, making it difficult to draw any reliable inferences, particularly since no studies have been conducted in the era of HAART. The issue of CNS complications in individuals with asymptomatic disease is nevertheless highly pertinent to the neuropsychological assessment of active duty military personnel with HIV, who may be referred for evaluation in the early and asymptomatic stages of infection. The population of seropositive active duty personnel is also likely to include a subset of individuals that have remained asymptomatic for extended periods of time (i.e., "long-term nonprogressors"), who may demonstrate preserved cognitive functioning (Cole et al., 2007).

COGNITIVE PROFILE OF HAND

At the group level, the pattern of cognitive deficits observed in association with HIV infection is largely commensurate with the preferential disruption of frontostriatal systems. Impairment is most commonly observed in the areas of executive functions, working memory, information processing speed, episodic memory, and motor skills, with relative sparing of simple attentional, language, visuoperceptual, and somatosensory functions (e.g., Heaton et al., 1995). In fact, numerous studies demonstrate direct associations between biomarkers of frontostriatal neural injury and HIV-associated neuropsychological impairment; for example, Paul et al. (2008) found robust correlations between basal ganglia volumes and measures of executive dysfunction, bradykinesia, and bradyphrenia in HIV. Nevertheless, the specificity of these associations is tempered by studies that demonstrate the contributions of pathologies in the medial temporal (e.g., Moore et al., 2006) and posterior parietal (Thompson et al., 2005) cortices to the cognitive expression of HAND.

Also of note, among the particular cognitive ability areas that are most commonly affected by HIV, there appears to be no prototypical profile of impairment at the level of the individual (Dawes et al., 2008). Deficits tend to be in the mild-to-moderate range of severity and are classically referred to as "spotty" (Butters et al., 1990). In other words, there is considerable variability in which individuals demonstrate impairment in which cognitive abilities areas; for example, an individual with HAND may demonstrate impairment on measures of learning and psychomotor speed, but not on tests of working memory and executive functions (or vice versa). As a result, only relatively comprehensive assessments are likely to detect most cases of HIV-associated neuropsychological impairment. Below we review the cognitive domains that are most often affected in HAND and provide recommendations for clinical assessment and interpretation.

Motor and Psychomotor Processing

Although gross motor abnormalities (e.g., chorea and dystonia) are uncommon (e.g., Tse et al., 2004), bradykinesia (i.e., slowed movement) and bradyphrenia (i.e., slowed mentation) represent cardinal clinical features of HAND. Slowing is evident in myriad aspects of psychomotor functioning, including gait (e.g., Robertson et al., 2006), fine-motor coordination (e.g., Carey et al., 2004b), and complex information processing (e.g., Reger et al., 2002). In fact, it has been suggested that motor and cognitive slowing may even be the primary deficits of HIV disease and drive the impairments observed in other cognitive abilities, such as attentional, memory, and executive functions (e.g., Becker & Salthouse, 1999). Clinical tests of motor and psychomotor abilities with strong evidence of construct validity in HAND include Trailmaking Test-Part A, WAIS-III Processing Speed Index, Grooved Pegboard, Finger Tapping, and Timed Gait. HIV-associated distal sensory polyneuropathy is most often observed in the lower extremities but should nevertheless be considered in the interpretation of motor and psychomotor deficits.

Attention and Executive Functions

Although simple attention (e.g., forward digit span) is generally spared in nondemented persons with HIV infection, deficits on measures of complex attention, working memory, and executive functions are considerably more prevalent (e.g., Heaton et al., 1995; Reger et al., 2002). HIV disease can be associated with deficits in multiple components of complex attention (Levine et al., 2008), including selective (e.g., Martin et al., 1995), divided (e.g., Hinkin, Castellon, & Hardy, 2000), and sustained (e.g., Levine et al., 2006) attentional processes, as well as working memory, for which deficits are apparent across numerous information processing modalities (i.e., auditory, spatial, visual, and verbal; e.g., Martin et al., 2001). Similarly, executive dysfunction can be expressed in a wide variety of higher-order processes, the most studied of which are abstraction and novel problem solving (e.g., Heaton et al., 1995), cognitive flexibility (e.g., Reger et al., 2002), prepotent response inhibition (e.g., Martin et al., 2004a), and planning (e.g., Bartok et al., 1997). Emergent data also indicate that individuals infected with HIV may be prone to risky decision making (Hardy, Hinkin, Levine, Castellon, & Lam, 2006), perhaps as a function of cognitive impulsivity (Martin et al., 2004b). Tests of attention, working memory, and executive functions that have shown particularly strong clinical utility in HAND include WAIS-III/WMS-III (Working Memory Index), Paced Auditory Serial Addition Test, Stroop Color-Word Test, Trailmaking Test-Part B, Wisconsin Card Sorting Test, and Halstead Category Test.

Learning and Memory

The pattern of episodic memory impairment in HAND is most consistent with the prototypical mixed encoding and retrieval profile that is often observed in populations with compromised frontostriatal systems (e.g., Parkinson's disease). At the group level, HAND is associated with generally comparable impairment in immediate and delayed free recall, which improves but does not always normalize when the individual is provided with the structure of recognition trials (e.g., Delis et al., 1995). HAND is also marked by limited use of higher-order strategic organizational encoding strategies (e.g., Delis et al., 1995), including semantic clustering during list learning (e.g., Gongvatana et al., 2007). Individuals with HAND may also evidence impairment in prospective memory (i.e., the ability to execute a future intention or "remembering to remember"; Carey, Woods, Rippeth, Heaton, & Grant, 2006b), which is associated with an increased risk of dependence in everyday functioning (e.g., Woods et al., 2008a). Dysregulation of both prefrontal and medial temporal systems has been implicated in the profile of memory deficits observed in HAND (e.g., Castelo, Sherman, Courtney, Melrose, & Stern, 2006). Nevertheless, the hallmarks of memory impairment in disorders of the medial temporal lobes (e.g., Alzheimer's disease), including shallow encoding (e.g., recency effects), semantic intrusion errors, rapid forgetting (i.e., consolidation impairment), and remote memory deficits with a temporal gradient, are not typically observed in uncomplicated HAND. Clinical evaluations of learning and memory in HAND would benefit from the inclusion of empirically supported measures such as the California Verbal Learning Test (2nd ed.), Hopkins Verbal Learning Test–Revised, Brief Visuospatial Memory Test–Revised, Heaton Story and Figure Memory Tests, Rey Complex Figure Test, and WMS-R/III Logical Memory and Visual Reproduction tests.

Language Abilities

The elementary aspects of speech and language, including basic receptive and expressive abilities, are largely intact in patients with HIV (with the rare exception of individuals with focal perisylvian CNS opportunistic infections). Very mild word retrieval deficits may be observed during confrontation naming, but evidence of moderate-to-severe anomia, even in the setting of HAD (White et al., 1997), should raise strong suspicions about the presence of a comorbid neuropathogenic (e.g., neurodegenerative) process. Verbal fluency deficits, on the other hand, are a common feature of HAND, which is associated with comparably mild impairment on measures of letter and category fluency (Iudicello et al., 2007), thereby suggesting a common mechanism of deficient strategic search and retrieval from lexico-semantic memory stores (Woods et al., 2004a). The process of switching between lexico-semantic categories during verbal fluency appears to be particularly affected in HAND, especially during alternating fluency trials (Iudicello et al., 2008). Relative to traditional letter and category fluency tasks, the action (verb) fluency test (i.e., "things...that people do") developed by Piatt and colleagues (1999) may be particularly sensitive to HAND, perhaps as a function of this task's presumed demands on motor imagery and associated frontal systems (Woods, Carey, Tröster, & Grant, 2005, 2006). Empirically supported recommendations for the clinical assessment of language functions in HAND include the Controlled Oral Word Association Test, Category Fluency (animals or supermarket items), Action (Verb) Fluency, DKEFS Category Switching, and the Boston Naming Test.

Visuoperceptual Functioning

It has been widely reported that most aspects of visuoperceptual processing, including basic spatial perception, judgment of line orientation, and visuoconstructional abilities, are not commonly impaired in HAND (Cysique, Maruff, & Brew, 2006). However, deficits may be observed in higher-level aspects of spatial cognition, especially on tasks that place concurrent demands on complex attention and working memory processes. For example, HIV-associated deficits have been reported on experimental measures of egocentric spatial cognition (Martin, 1994), mental rotation (Olesen, Schendan, Amick, & Cronin-Golomb, 2007), and number line orientation (Bogdanova, Neargarder, & Cronin-Golomb, 2008). Indeed, thinning of the posterior parietal cortex, which is critical to numerous aspects of spatial cognition (e.g., Lawrence, Watkins, Sahakin, Hodges, & Robbins, 2000) and maintains reciprocal connections with the frontostriatal circuits, has been correlated with greater severity of cognitive impairment in HIV (Thompson et al., 2005). Given the relative insensitivity of more basic visuoperceptual tasks to HAND, clinical assessment of this ability may be kept brief, perhaps to include Judgment of Line Orientation and/or the Hooper Visual Organization Test. In interpreting evidence of visuoperceptual impairments in patients with HIV, clinicians may also wish to consider the possible influence of basic visual abnormalities sometimes observed in this population, including infectious (e.g., cytomegalovirus) and noninfectious (e.g., cotton wool spots secondary to microvascular disease) conditions.

IMPACT OF HAND ON EVERYDAY FUNCTIONING

Although HIV infection is no longer sufficient grounds for dismissal from the military, seroconversion nevertheless immediately raises questions regarding the individual's functional capacity, responsibilities, and disposition (Department of the Navy, 2006). The myriad medical, psychiatric, and neurocognitive complications that may accompany HIV infection can decrease one's efficiency in completing instrumental and even basic ADLs. Neurocognitive impairment is an important and independent contributor to ADL declines, which are the defining characteristic of symptomatic HAND (i.e., MND and HAD). Among those with a diagnosis of HAND (i.e., approximately 30–50% of persons infected with HIV), approximately 50% are estimated to experience significant interference with normal daily functioning. Since the majority of HIV-related cognitive deficits are in the mild-to-moderate range of severity, gross impairment of basic ADLs exclusively due to a cognitive etiology is relatively rare. However, even subtle HIV-associated neurocognitive deficits can contribute to problems in numerous aspects of everyday functioning, including dependence in instrumental ADLs (Heaton et al., 2004), poorer health-related quality of life (e.g., Trepanier et al., 2005), increased engagement in risk behaviors (e.g., Gonzalez et al., 2005), and even higher mortality rates (e.g., Ellis et al., 1997a).

For instance, Heaton et al. (2004) found that individuals with HAND performed significantly worse than unimpaired HIV-infected persons on a series of performance-based tasks that were designed to mimic real-world IADLs (e.g., medication management, cooking, and financial management). Research shows that individuals with deficits in psychomotor speed (van Gorp, Baerwald, Ferrando, McElhiney, & Rabkin, 1999), attention and executive functions (Marcotte et al., 2006), and episodic memory (e.g., prospective memory; Woods et al., 2008b, 2009) may be at greatest risk for declines in everyday functioning. Below we review the literature on the impact of HAND on three important functional outcomes that are of direct relevance to military settings: (a) vocational functioning; (b) automobile driving; and (c) medication adherence.

Vocational Functioning

As described above, determining whether an HIV-infected individual may experience difficulties performing core job functions is of central importance to neuropsychological disability evaluations in military settings. HAND has been associated with higher rates of unemployment and incident disability, as well as poorer performance on standardized work samples, even after controlling for effects of disease severity (Heaton et al., 2004). Specifically, those with deficits in executive functions and learning abilities may be at greater risk for reducing or terminating employment (van Gorp et al., 1999). Even more relevant in the age of HAART is the ability to return to work after one's health status improves. Although the policies of various branches of military (e.g., Navy) state that job duties may change after seroconversion (e.g., restriction from deployable units), HIV status may not be cause for denial of reenlistment (Department of the Navy, 2006). In the event that health status allows for an individual to reseek employment, cognitive status must also be a consideration. van Gorp et al. (2007) found that HIV-associated impairment in verbal learning (i.e., California Verbal Learning Test total trials 1–5) was the most robust predictor of difficulties successfully reattaining gainful employment. As such, these findings can provide useful information for HIV-related career reassignments and reenlistments, such as skill assessment and related cognitive rehabilitation (e.g., compensatory strategies). However, it is important to note that predictions in the relevant studies are far from perfect and that considerable clinical judgment may be required to decide whether a particular pattern of neurocognitive deficits is likely to be problematic in the vocational functioning of the individual patient. This having been said, more severe and widespread deficits, perhaps especially involving episodic memory, executive functions, and processing speed, within the context of a job that is cognitively demanding and/or involves significant safety risks, would be especially concerning and cause for a medical board (see chapter 3).

The military may also make vocational determinations based on a given, asymptomatic, individual's case, particularly if the military has a high demand for an individual's specific skills. Take the recent cases of a Navy air traffic controller and a Naval Flight Officer, both diagnosed with HIV approximately 1 year ago. As per the *Aviation Reference and Waiver Guide* (Naval Aerospace Medical Institute, 2008), HIV is a disqualifying condition. However, individuals in aviation fields with disqualifying conditions can seek a waiver through a rather intensive medical process culminating in a Special Board of Flight Surgeons, conducted at the Naval Aerospace Medical Institute in Pensacola, Florida. Prior to these two cases, no individual with flight status had ever been considered for a waiver for HIV to work in an aviation career field in the Navy. However, given negative medical findings (i.e., general immune and neurological health) and neurocognitive findings on an extensive battery of neuropsychological tests, both were granted waivers with requirements for annual neurocognitive assessment. As an aside, the Army has waived an HIV-positive helicopter pilot, suggesting that the military may be more open to allow asymptomatic HIV-positive service members greater access to some jobs.

Automobile Driving

Automobile driving is a complex psychomotor skill that is a key component of successful daily functioning. The safe operation of military vehicles (e.g., trucks, tanks, aircraft) and other heavy equipment is a central component of many military occupational specialties. Safe and effective automobile driving draws upon several cognitive processes, including visuoperception, selective and sustained attention, psychomotor processing speed, motor sequencing, judgment, and planning. Given the above-described potential for HIV infection to adversely impact many of these cognitive ability areas, persons with HAND are at risk for a variety of adverse automobile driving outcomes. For example, individuals with HAND often demonstrate impaired performance during driving simulations, are more likely to fail on-road driving evaluations, and tend to experience more on-road driving accidents than HIV-infected persons who are not cognitively impaired (e.g., Marcotte et al., 2004). Importantly, neurocognitive deficits are uniquely predictive of automobile driving impairments, independent of HIV disease severity and depression (Marcotte et al., 2004). Poor driving performance was most closely associated with deficits in executive functions, complex attention, speed of information processing, fine-motor dexterity, and sensoriperception (Marcotte et al., 1999, 2004). Of note, a comprehensive neuropsychological evaluation is just one component of the decision to limit or suspend driving privileges, which should also include formal medical (e.g., ophthalmological) and driving (i.e., knowledge-based and on-road) evaluations.

Medication Adherence

As with many chronic medical illnesses, adequate adherence to sometimes complex medication regimens is essential to favorable health outcomes in individuals infected with HIV. Antiretroviral (ARV) therapies often require very high (i.e., 90–95%) levels of adherence to optimize their efficacy by preventing viral replication and/or the development of treatment-resistant mutations (Harrigan et al., 2005). While comorbid psychiatric conditions (e.g., depression and substance use disorders) contribute to poor ARV adherence (Dilorio et al., 2009), deficits in executive functions, episodic memory, and psychomotor speed are independently predictive of nonadherence (Hinkin et al., 2004). For example, Hinkin et al. (2002) observed that HAND was associated with a two-fold risk of ARV nonadherence as measured by electronic monitoring devices, particularly for individuals on complex medication regimens (i.e., more than two doses per day). One cognitive ability that is particularly relevant to medication adherence and is frequently impaired in HIV infection (Carey et al., 2006b) is prospective memory (ProM; "remembering to remember"). Relative to other cognitive deficits (e.g., executive functions) and psychiatric risk factors (e.g., depression), subjective ProM complaints and performance-based ProM deficits demonstrate incremental validity as predictors of poorer medication management (Woods et al., 2008b). In fact, individuals with impaired time-based ProM are approximately six times more likely to be nonadherent to their ARVs (Woods et al., 2009). As such, clinicians are encouraged to formally assess medication adherence in their evaluations, taking into consideration neuropsychological, psychiatric, and psychosocial factors that may be predictive of nonadherence.

COMORBIDITIES OF HIV-ASSOCIATED NEUROCOGNITIVE DISORDERS

Persons living with HIV can present with a variety of comorbid conditions that might contribute to both neurocognitive impairment and functional disability. Risk factors for acquiring HIV infection such as intravenous drug abuse and high-risk sexual activity predispose to chronic infections such as hepatitis C, which can contribute to impairment (for discussion see below). In developing countries, tuberculosis, malaria, and a variety of tropical infections may increase rates of progression of HIV to AIDS. Mood disorders can accompany the diagnosis of HIV infection and increase high-risk behaviors thereby increasing risk of acquiring other infectious diseases (e.g., hepatitis C infection). Not only do such comorbid conditions greatly impact everyday functioning and quality of life, but they may also amplify HIV-associated neural injury and subsequently increase risk of cognitive impairment.

Mood Disorders

Mood disorders are among the most common neuropsychiatric comorbidities in HIV infection, with prevalence rates of lifetime major depressive disorder (MDD) being estimated as high as 50% (Ciesla & Roberts, 2001). The etiology of depression in HIV is multifactorial. In the United States, premorbid depression is more common in HIV-infected than in the general population (Atkinson & Grant, 1997) and may promote risk behaviors linked to HIV infection. Subsequent to HIV infection, neurobiological (e.g., frontostriatal dysfunction), immunological (e.g., general health status), and/or psychosocial factors (e.g., dependence, fear of death or disability, or loss of relationships or jobs) may all contribute to depression.

Depression in HIV infection is associated with poorer quality of life (Jia et al., 2004), medication nonadherence (Starace et al., 2002), worse functional outcomes (Heaton et al., 2004), and increased mortality (Mayeux et al., 1993). Frontal systems pathology (e.g., Cotter, Mackay, Landau, Kerwin, & Everall, 2001) and subsequent neurocognitive effects of depression can follow a deficit pattern resembling that of HIV (e.g., attentional deficits and executive dysfunction) even in remitted MDD (Weiland-Fiedler et al., 2004), yet depression does not appear to exacerbate HAND (e.g., Cysique et al., 2007). Subjectively, MDD is related to increased cognitive complaints in HIV (Rourke, Halman, & Bassel, 1999), and indeed, depressive symptoms weakly correlate with poor objective performance across a variety of domains (e.g., executive functions, motor skills; Castellon et al., 2006). However, there is no strong evidence that current or past MDD increases the risk or impact of HAND (e.g., Cysique et al., 2007), regardless of MDD etiology (e.g., primary). Of note, the current HAND diagnostic criteria preclude the diagnosis of impairment in the setting of very severe MDD that interferes with the validity of testing (e.g., suboptimal effort secondary to depression). Despite a lack of evidence for elevated risk of cognitive impairment, the negative health- and functional-related outcomes associated with comorbid depression in HIV necessitate increased clinical awareness and monitoring.

Given the prevalence of depression in this population, the military regularly screens all active duty members for mental health symptoms in the course of their mandated medical evaluations. Serial psychological evaluations/screenings are initiated during their first comprehensive medical evaluation/education period, which follows quickly after notification of a positive HIV test (approximately 14 days). Screening for depression should also account for the risk of false-positive errors on traditional self-report measures (e.g., Beck Depression Inventory), which may be mildly elevated due to the expected medical complications of HIV (e.g., fatigue).

Substance Use Disorders

Substance use is a major risk factor for HIV transmission (CDC, 2006), and approximately 20% of U.S. patients living with HIV infection meet criteria for a recent substance use disorder (e.g., Pence, Miller, Whetten, Eron, & Gaynes, 2006). In some individuals, chronic substance dependence can be associated with neural injury (e.g., Schweinsburg et al., 2003) and mild-to-moderate neurocognitive impairment (e.g., Scott et al., 2007), which may worsen HIV-associated neurotoxicity and HAND (e.g., Chana et al., 2006; Rippeth et al., 2004). Limited research exists on the potentially additive effects of cocaine (e.g., Durvasula et al., 2000), marijuana (e.g., Cristiani, Pukay-Martin, & Bornstein, 2004), and opiates (Selnes et al., 1997) on HAND. Accordingly, the present review focuses on the combined effects of HIV and alcohol and methamphetamine, which are the most-studied substances in HAND and are ostensibly relevant to military populations.

Alcohol

Alcohol-related substance disorders are highly prevalent in HIV infection, with reports estimating heavy drinking to be twice as likely as in the general population (Galvan et al., 2002). In the active duty military population, alcohol is usually the drug of choice as the zero tolerance policy makes abusing other substances a crime, which will result in discharge from the military with no financial or medical benefits. As with other comorbid conditions, alcohol abuse may predate seroconversion and, in fact, adds to the risk for contracting HIV due to increased risk behaviors (e.g., sexual disinhibition) for HIV transmission (Meyerhoff, 2001). Alcohol consumption could alter the progression of HIV infection through immunosuppression (e.g., upregulation of CCR5 receptor expression; Wang et al., 2002), interfering with HAART (Miguez, Shor-Posner, Morales, Rodriguez, & Burbano, 2003), and potentiating the neurotoxic effects of HIV-specific protein-induced apoptosis (Chen et al., 2005). Structural neural changes are also evident due to excessive alcohol consumption, namely exacerbated HIV-associated white matter damage (e.g., fractional anisotropy in the corpus callosum; Pfefferbaum, Rosenbloom, Adalsteinsson, & Sullivan, 2007).

While effects of alcohol on cognition are potentially confounded by the high prevalence of polysubstance use in HIV-infected persons, several well-controlled studies have noted additive effects of alcohol in HIV-associated cognitive deficits, particularly in the areas of selective attention (Schulte, Mueller-Oehring, Rosenbloom, Pfefferbaum, & Sullivan, 2005), verbal reasoning and auditory processing (Green, Saveanau, & Bornstein, 2004), and psychomotor speed (Durvasula, Myers, Mason, & Hinkin, 2006). Some research has alluded to poorer quality of life in alcohol-dependent individuals with HIV (e.g., Rosenbloom et al., 2007), but further work is needed to elucidate its impact on other functional outcomes, including IADL dependence and mortality.

Methamphetamine

Among substances of abuse in HIV infection, the cognitive effects of methamphetamine are the most extensively studied, likely because of its widespread use (Woody et al., 1999). Independently, methamphetamine use is associated with structural abnormalities in frontostriatal pathways (e.g., evidence of neuronal injury in basal ganglia and frontal white matter; Ernst, Chang, Leonido-Yee, & Speck, 2000) and cognitive deficits in the areas of episodic memory, executive functions, motor skills, information processing speed, and visuocontructional abilities (Scott et al., 2007). Although associated with similar neural pathway dysfunction, the resulting neuropathology of methamphetamine use on frontostriatal systems (e.g., increases in cortical and basal ganglia volume; Jernigan et al., 2005) may be distinct from that of HIV infection (e.g., frontal cortex and caudate atrophy). Despite evidence of distinguishable effects on brain structure (Jernigan et al., 2005), methamphetamine use in the presence of HIV may produce an additive neuronal injury (e.g., interneuron loss; Chana et al., 2006) and abnormal brain metabolism (Chang et al., 2005) in frontostriatal pathways. Not surprisingly, this combination is also associated with higher rates of neuropsychological impairment than either of the independent conditions, in addition to specific deficits in learning, memory, motor skills, and attention/working memory (Rippeth et al., 2004). Methamphetamine also interacts with HIV disease severity, such that immunosuppression among HIV-infected methamphetamine users is associated with greater neural abnormalities (e.g., increased myoinositol; Taylor et al., 2007) and cognitive impairment (Carey et al., 2006a), which may amplify the risk of poorer functional outcomes (e.g., Sadek, Vigil, Grant, Heaton, & The HNRC Group, 2007).

Hepatitis C

Hepatitis C virus (HCV) and HIV often (15–50%) coinfect the same patients due to common means of transmission (especially intravenous drug use; Mohsen, Murad, & Easterbrook, 2005). In addition to its well-known effects on liver functioning, HCV is neurotropic, which is evidenced by the presence of HCV RNA in neural tissue (Letendre et al., 2007; Radkowski et al., 2002) and elevated markers of neuronal injury and neuroinflammation in HCV-infected persons (e.g., Forton et al., 2005). Co-infection with HCV and HIV may exacerbate the neuroinflammatory processes associated with each of these conditions alone (Letendre et al., 2005), which may in turn heighten the risk of neurocognitive impairment in co-infected persons (e.g., Hinkin, Castellon, Levine, Barclay, & Singer, 2008). Consistent with its apparent effects on frontostriatal systems (Letendre et al., 2007), HCV infection is also associated with neurocognitive deficits, particularly in the areas of psychomotor speed, executive functions, and complex attention, even independent of related confounding factors, such as liver disease and substance use (e.g., Cherner et al., 2005). HCV-associated neurocognitive deficits, specifically motor impairment and slowed processing speed, predict poorer functional outcomes, including ADL declines (Vigil et al., 2008). Several studies have shown that co-infection is associated with greater impairment in areas of psychomotor speed (e.g., Clifford, Evans, Yang, & Gulick, 2005) and episodic memory (Hinkin et al., 2008), as well as increased emotional distress (von Giesen et al., 2004). However, not all studies support an effect of HCV on cognition (e.g., Ryan, Morgello, Isaacs, Nasser,

Naseer, & Gerits, 2004; von Giesen et al., 2004) that may be related to the confounding effects of demographic (e.g., ethnicity), medical (e.g., HIV disease severity), and psychiatric (e.g. overrepresentation of injection drug users in coinfected samples) factors.

Posttraumatic Stress Disorder and Traumatic Brain Injury

Although of relatively lower prevalence in HIV populations than the above-described comorbidities, posttraumatic stress disorder (PTSD) and traumatic brain injury (TBI) are highly prevalent in military populations and are therefore worth examining in the context of HIV infection. Both PTSD and TBI may be independently associated with deficits in learning and memory, executive functions, attention, and processing speed (e.g., Mathias, Beall, & Bigler, 2004; Samuelson et al., 2006). However, research into these effects in the context of HIV infection is minimal. Defined broadly, anxiety disorders are more prevalent in HIV samples than in the general population, with cumulative rates cited as high as 38% (Elliott, 1998). Although research has noted that heightened self-reported anxiety in HIV populations is predictive of poorer quality of life and medication nonadherence (Tucker, Burnam, Sherbourne, Kung, & Gifford, 2003), these symptoms are not related to actual cognitive deficits (Mapou et al., 1993). No studies have directly examined the combined effects of PTSD and HIV on brain structure or function. One study reported no effect of prior mild TBI on neurocognitive performance of persons with HIV infection (Bornstein et al., 1993), but these data may not generalize to populations with more severe TBI (e.g., lower Glasgow Coma Scale scores, longer durations of unconsciousness). (For further reference regarding these comorbidities, see chapter 12.)

TREATMENT OF HIV-ASSOCIATED
NEUROCOGNITIVE DISORDERS

The widespread use of highly active antiretroviral therapies (HAART) in the United States has greatly reduced the morbidity and mortality of HIV infection (CDC), including the incidence of the most severe form of HAND (i.e., HAD; Sacktor et al., 2006) and most CNS opportunistic infections. Moreover, the initiation of HAART has been associated with improvements in neurocognitive functioning (e.g., Ferrando et al., 1998), particularly for those individuals who are ART naïve (e.g.,

Letendre et al., 2004) and/or achieve viral suppression (e.g., McCutchan et al., 2007). Nevertheless, milder forms of HAND (e.g., ANI and MND) remain prevalent in the era of HAART (e.g., Robertson et al., 2007), thereby raising questions about the effectiveness of HAART in fully ameliorating the CNS complications of HIV infection. Several factors may play a role in the persistence of HAND in the HAART era, including treatment guidelines that defer ART until CD4 counts drop below 200 or 350 cells/µL (e.g., Panel on Antiretroviral Guidelines for Adults and Adolescents, 2008; Powderly, 2002), which could allow ongoing damage to the brain and heighten the risk of HAND (Munoz-Moreno et al., 2007).

Another possible contributor to the persistence of HAND is the considerable variability in the CNS penetrance of ARVs (Letendre et al., 2008). Prior research shows that more highly penetrating ARV regimens are associated with better cognitive outcomes, at least partly by way of reducing viral burden in the CNS (e.g., Letendre et al., 2004). A randomized clinical trial is currently examining the effect of ART regimens designed to either maximize or minimize CNS penetration in reversal of cognitive impairment. Results of this trial should lead to recommendations about whether selecting better penetrating regimens is helpful in that setting. If optimal CNS penetration is desirable, application will be hindered by the lack of a practical screening tool for detection of mild and moderate cognitive impairment by clinicians.

Although several promising preliminary studies have been published on the possible effectiveness of adjunctive, nonantiretroviral agents, including selegiline (e.g., Sacktor et al., 2000) and various psychotropics (e.g., lithium; Letendre et al., 2006) and cognitive-behavioral rehabilitation (e.g., Neundorfer et al., 2004) for the treatment of HAND, such interventions await systematic evaluation in larger patient cohorts (e.g., Schifitto et al., 2006).

CLINICAL RECOMMENDATIONS

The primary roles of clinical neuropsychologists in the management of HIV disease are to help identify patients who do (and do not) have HAND and to advise patients and caregivers regarding the possible impact (and treatment) of the observed neurocognitive deficits and psychiatric comorbidities on everyday functioning, including safety risks. Based on the neuroAIDS literature reviewed in this chapter, we offer the following recommendations to help guide clinicians through the difficult process of determining whether an individual infected with HIV may be unfit for duty as a consequence of HAND.

The first point of emphasis is that not all persons infected with HIV demonstrate cognitive impairment; in fact, the estimated prevalence rates of HAND are only 30–50%, which means that HIV seropositivity itself does not justify a recommendation for duty restrictions or reassignment, especially for individuals in the acute, early, and asymptomatic phases of the disease. However, if a comprehensive neuropsychological assessment supports a diagnosis of MND or HAD, which by definition indicate substantial cognitive and functional impairment, then release from active duty would likely be the most prudent course of action. Although there is potential for CNS-penetrating ARVs to remediate (and possibly even normalize) cognitive impairment in some individuals with MND or HAD (see Letendre et al., 2008), the most appropriate short-term course of action would be suspension (e.g., limited duty) from any active duty assignment or position in which errors, inefficiencies, or other performance difficulties could have serious adverse consequences.

The clinician is faced with a more complicated decision for individuals diagnosed with ANI, who represent a majority of HAND cases and evidence only mild-to-moderate NP impairment but no obvious functional declines. As noted above, current methods of ascertainment for syndromic HAND diagnoses rely heavily on self-report and therefore may be insensitive to a subset of individuals with HIV-associated neurocognitive impairment who are actually experiencing functional problems, or who may experience such problems when faced with novel and/or complex problems in their daily lives. Collateral information from commands will be highly informative as to the ability of the service member to continue in the military. Dispositional decision making in cases with ANI may also hinge on the presence of serious psychiatric (e.g., bipolar disorder) or neurological (e.g., TBI) comorbidities, as well as the profile of neurocognitive impairment in relation to the individual's current job responsibilities. For instance, an individual with mild deficits in complex attention and verbal fluency may perform adequately in a position that primarily involves manual labor or simple administrative work but may be at risk of experiencing job-related difficulties if working in a position that places considerable demands on higher-level cognitive abilities, such as a pilot, air traffic controller, or flight surgeon. Furthermore, repeated assessments may be useful to screen for incident neurocognitive and functional decline in at-risk individuals (e.g., especially those with ANI), as well as to document possible neurocognitive improvement in individuals who have experienced significant immune and virologic recovery.

CASE ILLUSTRATION

To illustrate, consider the case of an HIV-infected 29-year-old USMC Staff Sergeant with 14 years of education who is referred for neuropsychological evaluation in the context of his fitness for duty as an Arabic linguist. Aside from HIV infection, the service member's medical, neurological, and psychiatric histories are unremarkable. He has been living with HIV for 5 years and has undergone annual medical, neurological, and neuropsychological evaluations, which have revealed excellent immune health (e.g., CD4 counts > 500, undetectable viral load) and no evidence of neuroAIDS (e.g., T-scores > 40 on all cognitive tests using appropriate demographic adjustments). However, over the past year, his CD4 counts have dropped below 200 and his viral load is now detectable in both plasma and CSF, thus prompting initiation of ARV therapy. Neuropsychological evaluation prior to ARV therapy reveals moderate impairment (T-scores < 30) on multiple measures of information processing speed and episodic memory. Application of published reliable change indices confirms the clinical impression of a significant decline from prior levels of performance. Self-report measures of cognitive complaints, ADLs, and affective distress are all within normal limits, but proxy reports from superiors reveal evidence of cognitive slowing, forgetfulness, and reduced efficiency and productivity on the job.

In this case, a diagnosis of MND is likely warranted (i.e., impairment in two cognitive domains that is likely due to HIV disease and is interfering with daily functioning). Given the considerable cognitive demands of this gentleman's work as an Arabic linguist, and the potentially critical consequences of poor job performance due to neuroAIDS, the most prudent course of action is to recommend suspension of his active duty assignment. Since it is possible that recovery of cognitive function may occur with effective treatment (especially since the patient is ARV naïve), follow-up neuropsychological evaluation in 6–12 months may be recommended if his immune health recovers in response to cART, which may be bolstered by ARVs with higher levels of CNS penetration if medically indicated. In the event of a medical discharge, recommendations may be offered with respect to vocational rehabilitation.

ACKNOWLEDGMENTS

This chapter was supported by grants R01-MH073419 and P30-MH62512 from the National Institute of Mental Health. The authors thank Cynthia Hight for her assistance with the graphics.

REFERENCES

American Academy of Neurology AIDS Task Force. (1991). Nomenclature and research case definitions for neurologic manifestations of human immunodeficiency virus-type 1 (HIV-1) infection. *Neurology, 41*, 778–785.

Antinori, A., Arendt, G., Becker, J. T., Brew, B. J., Byrd, D. A., Cherner, M., et al. (2007). Updated research nosology for HIV-associated neurocognitive disorders. *Neurology, 69*, 1789–1799.

Archibald, S. L., Masliah, E., Fennema-Notestine, C., Marcotte, T. D., Ellis, R. J., McCutchan, J. A., et al. (2004). Correlation of in vivo neuroimaging abnormalities with postmortem human immunodeficiency virus encephalitis and dendritic loss. *Archives of Neurology, 61*, 369–376.

Army Medical Surveillance Activity. (2007). Routine screening for antibodies to HIV-1, U.S. Army, Navy, Marine Corps, and civilian applicants for U.S. military service, January 1990–June 2007. *Medical Surveillance Monthly Report, 14*, 10–18.

Atkinson, J. H., & Grant, I. (1997). Mood disorder due to human immunodeficiency virus: Yes, no, or maybe? *Seminars in Clinical Neuropsychiatry, 2*, 276–284.

Bartok, J. A., Martin, E. M., Pitrak, D. L., Novak, R. M., Pursell, K. J., Mullane, K. M., et al. (1997). Working memory deficits in HIV-seropositive drug users. *Journal of the International Neuropsychological Society, 3*, 451–456.

Bautista, C. T., Sanchez, J. L., Montano, S. M., Laguna-Torres, A., Suarez, L., Sanchez, J., et al. (2006). Seroprevalence of and risk factors for HIV-1 infection among female commercial sex workers in South America. *Sexually Transmitted Infections, 82*, 311–316.

Becker, J. T., & Salthouse, T. A. (1999). Neuropsychological test performance in the acquired immunodeficiency syndrome: Independent effects of diagnostic group on functioning. *Journal of the International Neuropsychological Society, 5*, 41–47.

Berger, J. R., & Arendt, G. (2000). HIV dementia: The role of the basal ganglia and dopaminergic systems. *Journal of Psychopharmacology, 14*, 214–221.

Bogdanova, Y., Neargarder S., & Cronin-Golomb, A. (2008). Mapping mental number line in physical space: Vertical and horizontal visual number line orientation in asymptomatic individuals with HIV. *Neuropsychologia, 46*, 2914–2923.

Bornstein, R. A., Podraza, A. M., Para, M. F., Whitacre, C. C., Fass, R. J., Rice, R. R., Jr., et al. (1993). Effect of minor head injury on neuropsychological performance in asymptomatic HIV-1 infection. *Neuropsychology, 7*, 228–234.

Brodine, S. K., Shaffer, R. A., Starkey, M. J., Tasker, S. A., Gilcrest, J. L., Louder, M. K., et al. (1999). Drug-resistance patterns, genetic subtypes, clinical features, and risk factors in military personnel with HIV-1 seroconversion. *Annals of Internal Medicine, 131*, 502–506.

Butters, N., Grant, I., Haxby, J., Judd, L. L., Martin, A., McClelland, J., et al. (1990). Assessment of AIDS-related cognitive changes: Recommendations of the NIMH Workshop on neuropsychological assessment. *Journal of Clinical and Experimental Neuropsychology, 12*, 963–978.

Carey, C. L., Woods, S. P., Gonzalez, R., Conover, E., Marcotte, T. D., Grant, I., et al. (2004a). Predictive validity of global deficit scores for detecting neuropsychological impairment in HIV infection. *Journal of Clinical and Experimental Neuropsychology, 26*, 307–319.

Carey, C. L., Woods, S. P., Rippeth, J. D., Gonzalez, R., Heaton, R. K., Grant, I., et al. (2006a). Additive deleterious effects of methamphetamine dependence and immunosuppression on neuropsychological functioning in HIV infection. *AIDS and Behavior, 10*, 185–190.

Carey, C. L., Woods, S. P., Rippeth, J. D., Gonzalez, R., Moore, D. J., Marcotte, T. D., et al. (2004b). Initial validation of a screening battery for the detection of HIV-associated cognitive impairment. *The Clinical Neuropsychologist, 18*, 234–248.

Carey, C. L., Woods, S. P., Rippeth, J. D., Heaton, R. K., & Grant, I. (2006b). Prospective memory in HIV-1 infection. *Journal of Clinical and Experimental Neuropsychology, 28*, 536–548.

Castellon, S. A., Hardy, D. J., Hinkin, C. H., Satz, P., Stenquist, P. K., van Gorp, W. G., et al. (2006). Components of depression in HIV-1 infection: Their differential relationship to neurocognitive performance. *Journal of Clinical and Experimental Neuropsychology, 28*, 420–437.

Castelo, J. M., Courtney, M. G., Melrose, R. J., & Stern, C. E. (2007). Putamen hypertrophy in nondemented patients with human immunodeficiency virus infection and cognitive compromise. *Archives of Neurology, 64*, 1275–1280.

Castelo, J. M., Sherman, S. J., Courtney, M. G., Melrose, R. J., & Stern, C. E. (2006). Altered hippocampal-prefrontal activation in HIV patients during episodic memory encoding. *Neurology, 66*, 1688–1695.

Centers for Disease Control. (1992). 1993 revised classification system for HIV infection and expanded surveillance case definition for AIDS among adolescents and adults. *Morbidity and Mortality Weekly Report, 41*, 1–19.

Centers for Disease Control. (2006). *Epidemiology of HIV/AIDS—United States, 1981–2005*.

Chana, G., Everall, I. P., Crews, L., Langford, D., Adame, A., Grant, I., et al. (2006). Cognitive deficits and degeneration of interneurons in HIV+ methamphetamine users. *Neurology, 67*, 1486–1489.

Chang, L., Ernst, T., Speck, O., & Grob, C. S. (2005). Additive effects of HIV and chronic methamphetamine use on brain metabolite abnormalities. *American Journal of Psychiatry, 162*, 361–369.

Chelune, G. J., Heaton, R. K., & Lehman, R. A. (1986). Neuropsychological and personality correlates of patients' complaints of disability. In R.E. Tarter (Ed.), *Advances in clinical neuropsychology* (3rd ed., pp. 95–126). New York: Plenum Press.

Chen, W., Tang, Z., Fortina, P., Patel, P., Addya, S., Surrey, S., et al. (2005). Ethanol potentiates HIV-1 gp120-induced apoptosis in human neurons via both the death receptor and NMDA receptor pathways. *Virology, 334*, 59–73.

Cherner, M., Letendre, S., Heaton, R. K., Durelle, J., Marquie-Beck, J., Gragg, B., et al. (2005). Hepatitis C augments cognitive deficits associated with HIV infection and methamphetamine. *Neurology, 64*, 1343–1347.

Ciesla, J. A., & Roberts, J. E. (2001). Meta-analysis of the relationship between HIV infection and risk for depressive disorders. *American Journal of Psychiatry, 158,* 725–730.

Clifford, D. B., Evans, S. R., Yang, Y., & Gulick, R. M. (2005). The neuropsychological and neurological impact of hepatitis C virus coinfection in HIV-infected subjects. *AIDS, 19*(Suppl. 3), S64–71.

Cole, M. A., Margolick, J. B., Cox, C., Li, X., Selnes, O. A., Martin E. M., et al. (2007). Longitudinally preserved psychomotor performance in long-term asymptomatic HIV-infected individuals. *Neurology, 69,* 2213–2220.

Cotter, D. R., Mackay, D., Landau, S., Kerwin, R., & Everall, I. (2001). Reduced glial cell density and neuronal size in the anterior cingulated cortex in major depressive disorder. *Archives of General Psychiatry, 58,* 545–553.

Cristiani, S. A., Pukay-Martin, N. D., & Bornstein, R. A. (2004). Marijuana use and cognitive function in HIV-infected people. *The Journal of Neuropsychiatry and Clinical Neurosciences, 16,* 330–335.

Cysique, L. A., Deutsch, R., Atkinson, J. H., Young, C., Marcotte, T. D., Dawson, L., et al. (2007). Incident major depression does not affect neuropsychological functioning in HIV-infected men. *Journal of the International Neuropsychological Society, 13,* 1–11.

Cysique, L. A., Maruff, P., & Brew, B. J. (2006). The neuropsychological profile of symptomatic AIDS and ADC patients in the pre-HAART era: A meta-analysis. *Journal of the International Neuropsychological Society, 12,* 368–382.

Davis, S. J., Schockmel, G. A., Somoza, C., Buck, D. W., Healey, D. G., Rieber, E. P., et al. (1992). Antibody and HIV-1 gp120 recognition of CD4 undermines the concept of mimicry between antibodies and receptors. *Nature, 358,* 76–79.

Dawes, S., Suarez, P., Casey, C. Y., Cherner, M., Marcotte, T. D., Letendre, S., et al. (2008). Variable patterns of neuropsychological performance in HIV-1 infection. *Journal of Clinical and Experimental Neuropsychology, 30,* 613–626.

Delis, D. C., Peavy, G., Heaton, R., Butters, N., Salmon, D. P., Taylor, M., et al. (1995). Do patients with HIV-associated minor cognitive/motor disorder exhibit a "subcortical" memory profile? Evidence using the California Verbal Learning Test. *Assessment, 2,* 151–165.

Department of the Air Force. (2004). *Air Force Instruction 48–135 human immunodeficiency virus program.* Washington, DC: Author.

Department of the Army. (2005). *Army Regulation 600–110 identification, surveillance, and administration of personnel infected with human immunodeficiency virus (HIV).* Washington, DC: Author.

Department of Defense. (2006). *Department of Defense Instruction 6485.01 human immunodeficiency virus.* Washington, DC: Author.

Department of Homeland Security. (2008). *Coast Guard Human Immunodeficiency Virus (HIV) Program.* Washington, DC: Author.

Department of the Navy. (2006). *Management of human immunodeficiency virus (HIV) infection in the Navy and Marine Corps* (SECNAVIST publication No. 5300.30D). Washington, DC: Author.

Dilorio, C., McCarty, F., Depadilla, L., Resnicow, K., Holstad, M. M., Yeager, K., et al. (2009). Adherence to antiretroviral medication regimens: A test of a psychosocial model. *AIDS and Behavior, 13,* 10–22.

Durvasula, R. S., Myers, H. F., Mason, K., & Hinkin, C. (2006). Relationship between alcohol use/abuse, HIV infection and neuropsychological performance in African

American men. *Journal of Clinical and Experimental Neuropsychology, 28*, 383–404.

Durvasula, R. S., Myers, H. F., Satz, P., Miller, E. N., Morgenstern, H., Richardson, M. A., et al. (2000). HIV-1, cocaine, and neuropsychological performance in African American men. *Journal of the International Neuropsychological Society, 6*, 322–335.

Elliott, A. (1998). Anxiety and HIV infection. *STEP Perspective, 98*, 11–14.

Ellis, R. J., Deutsch, R., Heaton, R. K., Marcotte, T. D., McCutchan, J. A., Nelson, J. A., et al. (1997a). Neurocognitive impairment is an independent risk factor for death in HIV infection. *Archives of Neurology, 54*, 416–424.

Ellis, R. J., Hsia, K., Spector, S. A., Nelson, J. A., Heaton, R. K., Wallace, M. R., et al. (1997b). Cerebrospinal fluid human immunodeficiency virus-type 1 RNA levels are elevated in neurocognitively impaired individuals with acquired immunodeficiency syndrome. *Annals of Neurology, 42*, 679–688.

Ellis, R., Langford, D., & Masliah, E. (2007). HIV and antiretroviral therapy in the brain: Neuronal injury and repair. *Nature Reviews. Neuroscience, 8*, 33–44.

Ellis, R. J., Moore, D. J., Childers, M. E., Letendre, S., McCutchan, J. A., Wolfson, T., et al. (2002). Progression to neuropsychological impairment in human immunodeficiency virus infection predicted by elevated cerebrospinal fluid levels of human immunodeficiency virus RNA. *Archives of Neurology, 59*, 923–928.

Ernst, T., Chang, L., Leonido-Yee, M., & Speck, O. (2000). Evidence for long-term neurotoxicity associated with methamphetamine abuse: A 1H MRS study. *Neurology, 54*, 1344–1349.

Ferrando, S., van Gorp, W., McElhiney, M., Goggin, K., Sewell, M., & Rabkin, J. (1998). Highly active antiretroviral treatment in HIV infection: Benefits for neuropsychological function. *AIDS, 12*, F65–70.

Forton, D. M., Allsop, J. M., Cox, I. J., Hamilton, G., Wesnes, K., Thomas, H. C., et al. (2005). A review of cognitive impairment and cerebral metabolite abnormalities in patients with hepatitis C infection. *AIDS, 19*(Suppl. 3), S53–63.

Galvan, F. H., Bing, E. G., Fleishman, J. A., London, A. S., Caetano, R., Burnam, M. A., et al. (2002). The prevalence of alcohol consumption and heavy drinking among people with HIV in the United States: Results from the HIV cost and services utilization study. *Journal of Studies on Alcohol, 63*, 179–186.

Goethe, K. E., Mitchell, J. E., Marshall, D. W., Brey, R. L., Cahill, W. T., Leger, G. D., et al. (1989). Neuropsychological and neurological function of human immunodeficiency virus seropositive asymptomatic individuals. *Archives of Neurology, 46*, 129–133.

Gongvatana, A., Woods, S. P., Taylor, M. J., Vigil, O., Grant, I., & The HNRC Group. (2007). Semantic clustering inefficiency in HIV-associated dementia. *Journal of Neuropsychiatry and Clinical Neurosciences, 19*, 36–42.

Gonzalez, R., Vassileva, J., Bechara, A., Grbesic, S., Sworowski, L., Novak, R.M., et al. (2005). The influence of executive functions, sensation seeking, and HIV serostatus on the risky sexual practices of substance-dependent individuals. *Journal of the International Neuropsychological Society, 11*, 121–131.

Gonzalez-Scarano, F., & Martin-Garcia, J. (2005). The neuropathogenesis of AIDS. *Nature Reviews. Immunology, 5*, 69–81.

Grant, I., & Atkinson, J. H. (1995). Psychiatric aspects of acquired immune deficiency syndrome. In H. I. Kaplan & B. J. Sadock (Eds.), *Comprehensive textbook of psychiatry* (Vol. 2, pp. 1644–1669). Baltimore: Williams and Wilkins.

Grant, I., Atkinson, J. H., Hesselink, J. R., Kennedy, C. J., Richman, D. D., Spector, S. A., et al. (1987). Evidence for early central nervous system involvement in the acquired immunodeficiency syndrome (AIDS) and other human immunodeficiency virus (HIV) infections. Studies with neuropsychologic testing and magnetic resonance imaging. *Annals of Internal Medicine, 107*, 828–836.

Grant, I., Sacktor, N., & McArthur, J. C. (2005). HIV neurocognitive disorders. In H. E. Gendelman, I. Grant, I. Everall, S. A. Lipton, & S. Swindells (Eds.), *The neurology of AIDS* (2nd ed., pp. 359–373). New York: Oxford University Press.

Greco, J. B., Westmoreland, S. V., Ratai, E. M., Lentz, M. R., Sakaie, K., He, J., et al. (2004). In vivo 1H MRS of brain injury and repair during acute SIV infection in the macaque model of neuroAIDS. *Magnetic Resonance in Medicine, 51*, 1108–1114.

Green, J. E., Saveanu, R. V., & Bornstein, R. A. (2004). The effect of previous alcohol abuse on cognitive function in HIV infection. *American Journal of Psychiatry, 161*, 249–254.

Haase, A. T. (1986). Pathogenesis of lentivirus infections. *Nature, 322*, 130–136.

Hammer, S. M., Eron, J. J., Jr., Reiss, P., Schooley, R. T., Thompson, M. A., Walmsley, S., et al. (2008). Antiretroviral treatment of adult HIV infection: 2008 recommendations of the International AIDS Society—USA panel. *Journal of the American Medical Association, 300*, 555–570.

Hardy, D. J., Hinkin, C. H., Levine, A. J., Castellon, S. A., & Lam, M. N. (2006). Risky decision making assessed with the gambling task in adults with HIV. *Neuropsychology, 20*, 355–360.

Harrigan, P. R., Hogg, R. S., Dong, W. W., Yup, B., Wynhoven, B., Woodward, J., et al. (2005). Predictors of HIV drug-resistance mutations in a large antiretroviral-naïve cohort initiating triple antiretroviral therapy. *Journal of Infectious Diseases, 191*, 339–347.

Heaton, R. K., Franklin, D. R., Clifford, D., Woods, S. P., Rivera-Mindt, M., Vigil, O., et al. (2009, February). *HIV-associated neurocognitive impairment (NCI) remains prevalent in the era of combination antiretroviral therapy (CART): The CHARTER study*. Paper presented at the 16th Conference on Retroviruses and Opportunistic Infections, Montreal, Quebec, Canada.

Heaton, R. K., Grant, I., Butters, N., White, D. A., Kirson, D., Atkinson, J. H., et al. (1995). The HNRC 500—Neuropsychology of HIV infection at different disease stages. *Journal of the International Neuropsychological Society, 1*, 231–251.

Heaton, R. K., Marcotte, T. D., Mindt, M. R., Sadek, J., Moore, D. J., Bentley, H., et al. (2004). The impact of HIV-associated neuropsychological impairment on everyday functioning. *Journal of the International Neuropsychological Society, 10*, 317–331.

Hinkin, C. H., Castellon, S. A., Durvasula, R. S., Hardy, D. J., Lam, M. N., Mason, K. I., et al. (2002). Medication adherence among HIV+ adults: Effects of cognitive dysfunction and regimen complexity. *Neurology, 59*, 1944–1950.

Hinkin, C. H., Castellon, S. A., & Hardy, D. J. (2000). Dual task performance in HIV-1 infection. *Journal of Clinical and Experimental Neuropsychology, 22*, 16–24.

Hinkin, C. H., Castellon, S. A., Levine, A. J., Barclay, T. R., & Singer, E. J. (2008). Neurocognition in individuals coinfected with HIV and hepatitis C. *Journal of Addictive Diseases, 27*, 11–17.

Hinkin, C. H., Hardy, D. J., Mason, K. I., Castellon, S. A., Durvasula, R. S., Lam, M. N., et al. (2004). Medication adherence in HIV-infected adults: Effect of patient age, cognitive status, and substance abuse. *AIDS, 18*(Suppl. 1), S19–25.

Hiscock, M., & Hiscock, C. K. (1989). Refining the forced-choice method for the detection of malingering. *Journal of Clinical and Experimental Neuropsychology, 11,* 967–974.

Iudicello, J. E., Woods, S. P., Parsons, T. D., Moran, L. M., Carey, C. L., & Grant, I. (2007). Verbal fluency in HIV infection: A meta-analytic review. *Journal of the International Neuropsychological Society, 13,* 183–189.

Iudicello, J. E., Woods, S. P., Weber, E., Dawson, M. S., Scott, J. C., Carey, C. L., et al. (2008). Cognitive mechanisms of switching in HIV-associated category fluency deficits. *Journal of Clinical and Experimental Neuropsychology, 30,* 797–804.

Jernigan, T. L., Gamst, A. C., Archibald, S. L., Fennema-Notestine, C., Mindt, M. R., Marcotte, T. D., et al. (2005). Effects of methamphetamine dependence and HIV infection on cerebral morphology. *American Journal of Psychiatry, 162,* 1461–1472.

Jia, H., Uphold, C. R., Wu, S., Reid, K., Findley, K., & Duncan, P. W. (2004). Health-related quality of life among men with HIV infection: Effects of social support, coping, and depression. *AIDS Patient Care STDS, 18,* 594–603.

Klusman, L. E., Moulton, J. M., Hornbostel, L. K., Picano, J. J., & Beattie, M. T. (1991). Neuropsychological abnormalities in asymptomatic HIV seropositive military personnel. *Journal of Neuropsychiatry and Clinical Neurosciences, 3,* 422–428.

Langford, D., Hurford, R., Hashimoto, M., Digicaylioglu, M., & Masliah, E. (2005). Signalling crosstalk in FGF2-mediated protection of endothelial cells from HIV-gp120. *BMC Neuroscience, 6,* 8.

Lawrence, A. D., Watkins, L. H. A., Sahakian, B. J., Hodges, J. R., & Robbins, T. W. (2000). Visual object and visuospatial cognition in Huntington's disease: Implications for information processing in corticostriatal circuits. *Brain, 123,* 1349–1364.

Letendre, S. L., Cherner, M., Ellis, R. J., Marquie-Beck, J., Gragg, B., Marcotte, T., et al. (2005). The effects of hepatitis C, HIV, and methamphetamine dependence on neuropsychological performance: Biological correlates of disease. *AIDS, 19*(Suppl. 3), S72–78.

Letendre, S., Marquie-Beck, J., Capparelli, E., Best, B., Clifford, D., Collier, A. C., et al. (2008). Validation of the CNS Penetration–Effectiveness rank for quantifying antiretroviral penetration into the central nervous system. *Archives of Neurology, 65,* 65–70.

Letendre, S. L., McCutchan, J. A., Childers, M. E., Woods, S. P., Lazzaretto, D., Heaton, R. K., et al. (2004). Enhancing antiretroviral therapy for human immunodeficiency virus cognitive disorders. *Annals of Neurology, 56,* 416–423.

Letendre, S., Paulino, A. D., Rockenstein, E., Adame, A., Crews, L., Cherner, M., et al. (2007). Pathogenesis of hepatitis C virus coinfection in the brains of patients infected with HIV. *Journal of Infectious Diseases, 196,* 361–370.

Letendre, S. L., Woods, S. P., Ellis, R. J., Atkinson, J. H., Masliah, E., van den Brande, G., et al. (2006). Lithium improves HIV-associated neurocognitive impairment. *AIDS, 20,* 1885–1888.

Levine, A. J., Hardy, D. J., Barclay, T. R., Reinhard, M. J., Cole, M. M., & Hinkin, C. H. (2008). Elements of attention in HIV-infected adults: Evaluation of an existing model. *Journal of Clinical and Experimental Neuropsychology, 30,* 53–62.

Levine, A. J., Hardy, D. J., Miller, E., Castellon, S. A., Longshore, D., & Hinkin, C. H. (2006). The effect of recent stimulant use on sustained attention in HIV-infected adults. *Journal of Clinical and Experimental Neuropsychology, 28,* 29–42.

Mapou, R. L., Law, W. A., Martin, A., Kampen, D., Salazar, A. M., & Rundell, J. R. (1993). Neuropsychological performance, mood, and complaints of cognitive and motor difficulties in individuals infected with the human immunodeficiency virus. *The Journal of Neuropsychiatry and Clinical Neurosciences, 5,* 86–93.

Marcotte, T. D., Deutsch, R., McCutchan, J. A., Moore, D. J., Letendre, S., Ellis, R. J., et al. (2003). Prediction of incident neurocognitive impairment by plasma HIV RNA and CD4 levels early after HIV seroconversion. *Archives of Neurology, 60,* 1406–1412.

Marcotte, T. D., Heaton, R. K., Wolfson, T., Taylor, M. J., Alhassoon, O., Arfaa, K., et al. (1999). The impact of HIV-related neuropsychological dysfunction on driving behavior. *Journal of the International Neuropsychological Society, 5,* 579–592.

Marcotte, T. D., Lazzaretto, D., Scott, J. C., Roberts, E., Woods, S. P., & Letendre, S. (2006). Visual attention deficits are associated with driving accidents in cognitively-impaired HIV-infected individuals. *Journal of Clinical and Experimental Neuropsychology, 28,* 13–28.

Marcotte, T. D., Wolfson, T., Rosenthal, T. J., Heaton, R. K., Gonzalez, R., Ellis, R. J., et al. (2004). A multimodal assessment of driving performance in HIV infection. *Neurology, 63,* 1417–1422.

Martin, A. (1994). HIV, cognition, and the basal ganglia. In I. Grant & A. Martin (Eds.), *Neuropsychology of HIV infection* (pp. 234–259). New York: Oxford University Press.

Martin, E. M., Novak, R. M., Fendrich, M., Vassileva, J., Gonzalez, R., Grbesic, S., et al. (2004a). Stroop performance in drug users classified by HIV and hepatitis C virus serostatus. *Journal of the International Neuropsychological Society, 10,* 298–300.

Martin, E. M., Pitrak, D. L., Robertson, L. C., Novak, R. M., Mullane, K. M., & Pursell, K. J. (1995). Global-local analysis in HIV-1 infection. *Neuropsychology, 9,* 102–109.

Martin, E. M., Pitrak, D. L., Weddington, W., Rains, N. A., Nunnally, G., Nixon, H., et al. (2004b). Cognitive impulsivity and HIV serostatus in substance-dependent males. *Journal of the International Neuropsychological Society, 10,* 931–938.

Martin, E. M., Sullivan, T. S., Reed, R. A., Fletcher, T. A., Pitrak, D. L., Weddington, W., et al. (2001). Auditory working memory in HIV-1 infection. *Journal of the International Neuropsychological Society, 7,* 20–26.

Mathias, J. L., Beall, J. A., & Bigler, E. D. (2004). Neuropsychological and information processing deficits following mild traumatic brain injury. *Journal of the International Neuropsychological Society, 10,* 286–297.

Mayeux, R., Stern, Y., Tang, M. X., Todak, G., Marder, K., Sano, M., et al. (1993). Mortality risks in gay men with human immunodeficiency virus infection and cognitive impairment. *Neurology, 43,* 176–182.

McCutchan, J. A., Wu, J. W., Robertson, K., Koletar, S. L., Ellis, R. J., Cohn, S., et al. (2007). HIV suppression by HAART preserves cognitive function in advanced, immune-reconstituted AIDS patients. *AIDS, 21,* 1109–1117.

Melrose, R. J., Tinaz, S., Castelo, J. M., Courtney, M. G., & Stern, C. E. (2008). Compromised fronto-striatal functioning in HIV: An fMRI investigation of semantic event sequencing. *Behavioural Brain Research, 188,* 337–347.

Meyerhoff, D. J. (2001). Effects of alcohol and HIV infection on the central nervous system. *Alcohol Research and Health, 25,* 288–298.

Miguez, M. J., Shor-Posner, G., Morales, G., Rodriguez, A., & Burbano, X. (2003). HIV treatment in drug abusers: Impact of alcohol use. *Addiction Biology, 8*, 33–37.

Mitchell, M., & Miller, L. S. (2008). Prediction of functional status in older adults: The ecological validity of four Delis-Kaplan Executive Function System tests. *Journal of Clinical and Experimental Neuropsychology, 30*, 683–690.

Mittenberg, W., Azrin, R., Millsaps, C., & Heilbronner, R. (1993). Identification of malingered head injury on the Wechsler Memory Scale–Revised. *Psychological Assessment, 5*, 34–40.

Mohsen, A. H., Murad, S., & Easterbrook, P. J. (2005). Prevalence of hepatitis C in an ethnically diverse HIV-1-infected cohort in south London. *HIV Medicine, 6*, 206–215.

Moore, D. J., Masliah, E., Rippeth, J. D., Gonzalez, R., Carey, C. L., Cherner, M., et al. (2006). Cortical and subcortical neurodegeneration is associated with HIV neurocognitive impairment. *AIDS, 20*, 879–887.

Morgan, E. E., & Heaton, R. K. (2009). The neuropsychological approach to predicting everyday functioning. In I. Grant & K. Adams (Eds.), *Neuropsychological assessment of neuropsychiatric disorders* (3rd ed., pp. 632–651). New York: Oxford University Press.

Morgan, E. E., Woods, S. P., Childers, M., Marquie-Beck, J., Ellis, R. J., Grant, I., et al. (2008). Predictive validity of demographically-adjusted normative standards for the HIV dementia scale. *Journal of Clinical and Experimental Neuropsychology, 30*, 83–90.

Munoz-Moreno, J. A., Rodriguez, C., Prats, A., Ferrer, M., Negredo, E., Garolera, M., et al. (2007, February). *Recommended earlier initiation of ART based on nadir CD4 cell count as a risk factor for HIV-related neurocognitive impairment* (abstract 383). Paper presented at the 14th Conference on Retroviruses and Opportunistic Infections, Los Angeles, CA.

Naval Aerospace Medical Institute. (2008). *Aeromedical Reference and Waiver Guide.* Retrieved February 16, 2009, from http://www.med.navy.mil/sites/navmedmpte/nomi/nami/arwg/Pages/AeromedicalReferenceandWaiverGuide.aspx

Neundorfer, M. M., Camp, C. J., Lee, M. M., Skrajner, M. J., Malone, M. L., & Carr, J. R. (2004). Compensating for cognitive deficits in persons aged 50 and over with HIV/AIDS: A pilot study of a cognitive intervention. *Journal of HIV/AIDS & Social Services, 3*, 79–97.

Newman, S. P., Lunn, S., & Harrison, M. J. (1995). Do asymptomatic HIV-seropositive individuals show cognitive deficit? *AIDS, 9*, 1211–1220.

Olesen, P. J., Schendan, H. E., Amick, M. M., & Cronin-Golomb, A. (2007). HIV infection affects parietal-dependent spatial cognition: Evidence from mental rotation and hierarchical pattern perception. *Behavioral Neuroscience, 121*(6), 1163–1173.

Panel on Antiretroviral Guidelines for Adults and Adolescents. (2008). *Guidelines for the use of antiretroviral agents in HIV-1-infected adults and adolescents.* Department of Health and Human Services. Retrieved February 1, 2009, from http://www.aidsinfo.nih.gov/ContentFiles/AdultandAdolescentGL.pdf

Paul, R. H., Ernst, T., Brickman, A. M., Yiannoutsos, C. T., Tate, D. F., Cohen, R. A., et al. (2008). Relative sensitivity of magnetic resonance spectroscopy and quantitative magnetic resonance imaging to cognitive function among nondemented individuals infected with HIV. *Journal of the International Neuropsychological Society, 14*, 725–733.

Pence, B. W., Miller, W. C., Whetten, K., Eron, J. J., & Gaynes, B. N. (2006). Prevalence of DSM-IV-defined mood, anxiety, and substance use disorders in an HIV clinic in the Southeastern United States. *Journal of the Acquired Immune Deficiency Syndrome, 42*, 298–306.

Pfefferbaum, A., Rosenbloom, M. J., Adalsteinsson, E., & Sullivan, E. V. (2007). Diffusion tensor imaging with quantitative fibre tracking in HIV infection and alcoholism comorbidity: Synergistic white matter damage. *Brain, 130*, 48–64.

Piatt, A. L., Fields, J. A., Paolo, A. M., & Tröster, A. I. (1999). Action (verb naming) fluency as an executive function measure: Convergent and divergent evidence of validity. *Neuropsychologia, 37*, 1499–1503.

Pomara, N., Crandall, D. T., Choi, S. J., Johnson, G., & Lim, K. O. (2001). White matter abnormalities in HIV-1 infection: A diffusion tensor imaging study. *Psychiatry Research, 106*, 15–24.

Powderly, W. G. (2002). Sorting through confusing messages: The art of HAART. *Journal of Acquired Immune Deficiency Syndromes, 31*(Suppl. 1), S3–9.

Power, C., Selnes, O. A., Grim, J. A., & McArthur, J. C. (1995). HIV dementia scale: A rapid screening test. *Journal of Acquired Immune Deficiency Syndromes and Human Retrovirology, 8*, 273–278.

Rabin, L. A., Barr, W. B., & Burton, L. A. (2005). Assessment practices of clinical neuropsychologists in the United States and Canada: A survey of INS, NAN, and APA Division 40 members. *Archives of Clinical Neuropsychology, 20*, 33–65.

Radkowski, M., Wilkinson, J., Nowicki, M., Adair, D., Vargas, H., Ingui, C., et al. (2002). Search for hepatitis C virus negative-strand RNA sequences and analysis of viral sequences in the central nervous system: Evidence of replication. *Journal of Virology, 76*, 600–608.

Reger, M., Welsh, R., Razani, J., Martin, D. J., & Boone, K. B. (2002). A meta-analysis of the neuropsychological sequelae of HIV infection. *Journal of the International Neuropsychological Society, 8*, 410–424.

Rippeth, J. D., Heaton, R. K., Carey, C. L., Marcotte, T. D., Moore, D. J., Gonzalez, R., et al. (2004). Methamphetamine dependence increases risk of neuropsychological impairment in HIV infected persons. *Journal of the International Neuropsychological Society, 10*, 1–14.

Robertson, K. R., Parsons, T. D., Sidtis, J. J., Hanlon Inman, T., Robertson, W. T., Hall, C. D., et al. (2006). Timed gait test: Normative data for the assessment of the AIDS dementia complex. *Journal of Clinical and Experimental Neuropsychology, 28*, 1053–1064.

Robertson, K. R., Smurzynski, M., Parsons, T. D., Wu, K., Bosch, R. J., Wu, J., et al. (2007). The prevalence and incidence of neurocognitive impairment in the HAART era. *AIDS, 21*, 1915–1921.

Rosenbloom, M. J., Sullivan, E. V., Sassoon, S. A., O'Reilly, A., Fama, R., Kemper, C. A. et al. (2007). Alcoholism, HIV infection, and their comorbidity: Factors affecting self-rated health-related quality of life. *Journal of the Study of Alcohol and Drugs, 68*, 115–125.

Rourke, S. B., Halman, M. H., & Bassel, C. (1999). Neurocognitive complaints in HIV-infection and their relationship to depressive symptoms and neuropsychological functioning. *Journal of Clinical and Experimental Neuropsychology, 21*, 737–756.

Ryan, E. L., Morgello, S., Isaacs, K., Naseer, M., & Gerits, P. (2004). Neuropsychiatric impact of hepatitis C on advanced HIV. *Neurology, 62*, 957–962.

Sacktor, N., Lyles, R. H., Skolasky, R., Kleeberger, C., Selnes, O. A., Miller, E. N., et al. (2001). HIV-associated neurologic disease incidence changes: Multicenter AIDS cohort study, 1990–1998. *Neurology, 56,* 257–260.

Sacktor, N., Nakasujja, N., Skolasky, R., Robertson, K., Wong, M., Musisi, S., et al. (2006). Antiretroviral therapy improves cognitive impairment in HIV+ individuals in subSaharan Africa. *Neurology, 67,* 311–314.

Sacktor, N., Schifitto, G., McDermott, M. P., Marder, K., McArthur, J. C., & Kieburtz, K. (2000). Transdermal selegiline in HIV-associated cognitive impairment: Pilot, placebo-controlled study. *Neurology, 54,* 233–235.

Sadek, J. R., Vigil, O., Grant, I., Heaton, R. K., & The HNRC Group. (2007). The impact of neuropsychological functioning and depressed mood on functional complaints in HIV-1 infection and methamphetamine dependence. *Journal of Clinical and Experimental Neuropsychology, 29,* 266–276.

Samuelson, K. W., Neylan, T. C., Metzler, T. J., Lenoci, M., Rothlind, J., Henn-Haase, C., et al. (2006). Neuropsychological functioning in posttraumatic stress disorder and alcohol abuse. *Neuropsychology, 20,* 716–726.

Schifitto, G., Sacktor, N., Zhang, J., Evans, S., Simpson, D., Millar, L., et al. (2006, February). *A phase II, placebo-controlled, double-blind study of the selegiline transdermal system in the treatment of HIV-associated cognitive impairment* (abstract 364). Paper presented at the 13th Conference on Retroviruses and Opportunistic Infections, Denver, CO.

Schulte, T., Mueller-Oehring, E. M., Rosenbloom, M. J., Pfefferbaum, A., & Sullivan, E. V. (2005). Differential effect of HIV infection and alcoholism on conflict processing, attentional allocation, and perceptual load: Evidence from a Stroop match-to-sample task. *Biological Psychiatry, 57,* 67–75.

Schweinsburg, B. C., Alhassoon, O. M., Taylor, M. J., Gonzalez, R., Videen, J. S., Brown, G. G., et al. (2003). Effects of alcoholism and gender on brain metabolism. *American Journal of Psychiatry, 160,* 1180–1183.

Scott, J. C., Woods, S. P., Matt, G. E., Meyer, R. A., Heaton, R. K., Atkinson, J. H., et al. (2007). Neurocognitive effects of methamphetamine: A critical review and meta-analysis. *Neuropsychology Review, 17,* 275–297.

Selnes, O. A., Galai, N., McArthur, J. C., Cohn, S., Royal, W., Esposito, D., et al. (1997). HIV infection and cognition in intravenous drug users: Long-term follow-up. *Neurology, 48,* 223–230.

Sevigny, J. J., Albert, S. M., McDermott, M. P., McArthur, J. C., Sacktor, N., Conant, K., et al. (2004). Evaluation of HIV RNA and markers of immune activation as predictors of HIV-associated dementia. *Neurology, 63,* 2084–2090.

Slick, D. J., Hinkin, C. H., van Gorp, W. G., & Satz, P. (2001). Base rate of a WMS-R malingering index in a sample of noncompensation-seeking men infected with HIV-1. *Applied Neuropsychology, 8,* 185–189.

Starace, F., Ammassari, A., Trotta, M. P., Murri, R., De Longis, P., Izzo, C., et al. (2002). Depression is a risk factor for suboptimal adherence to highly active antiretroviral therapy. *Journal of the Acquired Immune Deficiency Syndrome, 31*(Suppl. 3), S136–139.

Stout, J. C., Ellis, R. J., Jernigan, T. L., Archibald, S. L., Abramson, I., Wolfson, T., et al. (1998). Progressive cerebral volume loss in human immunodeficiency virus infection: A longitudinal volumetric magnetic resonance imaging study. *Archives of Neurology, 55,* 161–168.

Taylor, M. J., Schweinsburg, B. C., Alhassoon, O. M., Gongvatana, A., Brown, G. G., Young-Casey, C., et al. (2007). Effects of human immunodeficiency virus and methamphetamine on cerebral metabolites measured with magnetic resonance spectroscopy. *Journal of Neurovirology, 13*, 150–159.

Thompson, P. M., Dutton, R. A., Hayashi, K. M., Toga, A. W., Lopez, O. L., Aizenstein, H. J., et al. (2005). Thinning of the cerebral cortex visualized in HIV/AIDS reflects CD4+ T lymphocyte decline. *Proceedings of the National Academy of Sciences of the United States of America, 102*, 15647–15652.

Trepanier, L. L., Rourke, S. B., Bayoumi, A. M., Halman, M. H., Krzyzanowski, S., & Power, C. (2005). The impact of neuropsychological impairment and depression on health-related quality of life in HIV-infection. *Journal of Clinical and Experimental Neuropsychology, 27*, 1–15.

Tse, W., Cersosimo, M. G., Gracies, J. M., Morgello, S., Olanow, C. W., & Koller, W. (2004). Movement disorders and AIDS: A review. *Parkinsonism and Related Disorders, 10*, 323–334.

Tucker, J. S., Burnam, M. A., Sherbourne, C. D., Kung, F. Y., & Gifford, A. L. (2003). Substance use and mental health correlates of nonadherence to antiretroviral medications in a sample of patients with human immunodeficiency virus infection. *The American Journal of Medicine, 114*, 573–580.

Valcour, V., Yee, P., Williams, A. E., Shiramizu, B., Watters, M., Selnes, O., et al. (2006). Lowest ever CD4 lymphocyte count (CD4 nadir) as a predictor of current cognitive and neurological status in human immunodeficiency virus-type 1 infection—the Hawaii aging with HIV cohort. *Journal of Neurovirology, 12*, 387–391.

van Gorp, W. G., Baerwald, J. P., Ferrando, S. J., McElhiney, M. C., & Rabkin, J. G. (1999). The relationship between employment and neuropsychological impairment in HIV infection. *Journal of the International Neuropsychological Society, 5*, 534–539.

van Gorp, W. G., Rabkin, J. G., Ferrando, S. J., Mintz, J., Ryan, E., Borkowski, T., et al. (2007). Neuropsychiatric predictors of return to work in HIV/AIDS. *Journal of the International Neuropsychological Society, 13*, 80–89.

Vigil, O., Posada, C., Woods, S. P., Atkinson, J. H., Heaton, R. K., Perry, W., et al. (2008). Impairments in fine-motor coordination and speed of information processing predict dependence in everyday functioning in Hepatitis C infection. *Journal of Clinical and Experimental Neuropsychology, 30*, 805–815.

von Giesen, H. J., Heintges, T., Abbasi-Boroudjeni, N., Kucukkoylu, S., Koller, H., Haslinger, B. A., et al. (2004). Psychomotor slowing in hepatitis C and HIV infection. *Journal of Acquired Immune Deficiency Syndromes, 35*, 131–137.

Wang, X., Douglas, S. D., Metzger, D. S., Guo, C. J., Li, Y., O'Brien, C. P., et al. (2002). Alcohol potentiates HIV-1 infection of human blood mononuclear phagocytes. *Alcoholism: Clinical and Experimental Research, 26*, 1880–1886.

Weiland-Fiedler, P., Erickson, K., Waldeck, T., Luckenbaugh, D. A., Pike, D., Bonne, O., et al. (2004). Evidence for continuing neuropsychological impairments in depression. *Journal of Affective Disorders, 82*, 253–258.

White, D. A., Taylor, M. J., Butters, N., Mack, C., Salmon, D. P., Peavy, G., et al. (1997). Memory for verbal information in individuals with HIV-associated dementia complex. *Journal of Clinical and Experimental Neuropsychology, 19*, 357–366.

White, J. L., Darko, D. F., Brown, S. J., Miller, J. C., Hayduk, R., Kelly, T., et al. (1995). Early central nervous system response to HIV infection: Sleep distortion and cognitive-motor decrements. *AIDS, 9*, 1043–1050.

Woods, S. P., Carey, C. L., Tröster, A. I., & Grant, I. (2005). Action (verb) generation in HIV-1 infection. *Neuropsychologia, 43*, 1144–1151.

Woods, S. P., Conover, E., Rippeth, J. D., Carey, C. L., Gonzalez, R., Marcotte, T. D., et al. (2004a). Qualitative aspects of verbal fluency in HIV-associated dementia: A deficit in rule-guided lexical-semantic search processes? *Neuropsychologia, 42*, 801–809.

Woods, S. P., Conover, E., Weinborn, M., Rippeth, J. D., Brill, R. M., Heaton, R. K., et al. (2003). Base rate of Hiscock Digit Memory Test Failure in HIV-associated neurocognitive disorders. *The Clinical Neuropsychologist, 17*, 383–389.

Woods, S. P., Dawson, M. S., Weber, E., Gibson, S., Grant, I., Atkinson, J. H., & the HNRC Group. (2009). Timing is everything: Antiretroviral nonadherence is associated with impairment in time-based prospective memory. *Journal of the International Neuropsychological Society, 15*, 42–52.

Woods, S. P., Iudicello, J. E., Moran, L. M., Carey, C. L., Dawson, M. S., Grant, I., et al. (2008a). HIV-associated prospective memory impairment increases risk of dependence in everyday functioning. *Neuropsychology, 22*, 110–117.

Woods, S. P., Moran, L. M., Carey, C. L., Dawson, M. S., Iudicello, J. E., Gibson, S., et al. (2008b). Prospective memory in HIV infection: Is "remembering to remember" a unique predictor of self-reported medication management? *Archives of Clinical Neuropsychology, 23*, 257–270.

Woods, S. P., Morgan, E. E., Dawson, M., Scott, J. C., Grant, I., & The HNRC Group. (2006). Action (verb) fluency predicts dependence in instrumental activities of daily living in persons infected with HIV-1. *Journal of Clinical and Experimental Neuropsychology, 28*, 1030–1042.

Woods, S. P., Rippeth, J. D., Frol, A. B., Levy, J. K., Ryan, E., Soukup, V. M., et al. (2004b). Interrater reliability of clinical ratings and neurocognitive diagnoses in HIV. *Journal of Clinical and Experimental Neuropsychology, 26*, 759–778.

Woody, G. E., Donnell, D., Seage, G. R., Metzger, D., Marmor, M., Koblin, B. A., et al. (1999). Noninjection substance use correlates with risky sex among men having sex with men: Data from HIVNET. *Drug and Alcohol Dependence, 53*, 197–205.

The Neuropsychological Functioning of Prisoners of War Following Repatriation

10

JEFFREY L. MOORE

The stress of war tries men as no other test that they have encountered in civilized life. Like a crucial experiment it exposes the underlying physiological and psychological mechanisms of the human being. Cruel, destructive and wasteful though such an experiment may be, exceedingly valuable lessons can be learned from it regarding the methods by which men adapt themselves to all forms of stress, either in war or peace.

—Grinker & Spiegel, 1945, p. vii

INTRODUCTION

Both the Department of Veterans Affairs (VA) and the Department of Defense (DoD) provide long-term medical and psychological care of repatriated prisoners of war (repatriates, RPWs). In addition, RPWs are eligible for disability compensation for those diseases and disorders that were related to military service, combat, and internment as a prisoner of war. This DoD/VA program has records on 142,246 American military personnel who have been captured and interred during WWI, WWII, the Korean Conflict (KC), the Vietnam War (VN), Operation Desert Storm (ODS), and Operation Iraqi Freedom (OIF), as well as during the military actions in Somalia and Kosovo (Department of Veterans Affairs [DVA], 2008). Approximately 12% (17,009) of these prisoners of war (POWs) died during captivity. Of the 125,214 who were repatriated and returned to U.S. military control, 22,649 repatriates were alive as of January 1, 2008; however, nearly 6,500 repatriates died during 2007 (DVA, 2008). Although all 3,973 WWI repatriates have died, the current roster of repatriates eligible for care includes 20,327 from WWII, 1,739 from KC, 550 from VN, 21 from ODS, 8 from OIF, 1 from Somalia, and 3 from Kosovo.

To properly evaluate and treat RPWs, clinicians must appreciate those general captivity factors that appear to apply to nearly all POWs regardless of era, those captivity factors that are unique to each POW experience, factors that predate captivity (e.g., demographic, medical, and psychological) and postrepatriation factors (e.g., social support, continued military service, and availability of medical/psychological care). Clinical neuropsychologists in particular have provided crucial input in the integration of these factors. This multidisciplinary integration requires an understanding of psychiatric illness, known or suspected neurological illness or injury, psychological factors affecting medical illness and its treatment, and personality traits that may modify adjustment to captivity and repatriation. Clinicians with experience in providing comprehensive neuropsychological assessment routinely consider such issues in their selection of both tests to be administered and appropriate normative databases for test interpretation, as well as during their diagnostic formulations, prognostic predictions, and treatment recommendations.

The goal of this chapter is to provide neuropsychologists and other interested clinicians with a review of the scientific literature pertaining to the neuropsychological functioning of RPWs. This review will include a general description of the POW experience, unique era-specific aspects of the POW experience, medical and psychiatric morbidity with associated risk factors, and neuropsychological assessment as it relates to acquired cognitive deficits in general and, more specifically, posttraumatic stress disorder (PTSD). To protect their anonymity, no data will be presented on the 29 men and 4 women who were repatriated following captivity in ODS, OIF, Somalia, and Kosovo.

THE CAPTIVITY EXPERIENCE AND POW DEMOGRAPHICS

While serving their country as POWs, WWII, KC, and VN military personnel routinely experienced a variety of complex and chronic stressors. Among the typical physical stressors were exposure to temperature extremes (hot and cold), indigenous infections, environmental toxins, denial of medical care, dehydration, and nutritional deprivation. Isolation (both solitary confinement and controlled communications), uncertainty about captivity duration, unpredictability of captor behavior, lengthy interrogations, and the ever-present specter of death contributed to the development of hopelessness, helplessness, fear, anxiety, guilt, and shame.

In addition to physical stressors and isolation, torture was frequently used by the enemy. Torture is an experience that cuts across both the physical and psychological dimensions (Basoglu, Livanou, & Cronbaric, 2008; Molica & Caspi-Yavin, 1991). Torture may involve both passive (e.g., forced standing, forced kneeling, and sensory deprivation) and active (e.g., beatings, suffocations, mock executions, and various methods of joint dislocation) techniques. The specific torture techniques preferred by the enemy varied between the three wars and the specifics of the capture experience were also varied. However, for many POWs, the events surrounding capture and the subsequent transfer to their "permanent" detention camp or prison were among the most harrowing and stressful situations prior to repatriation.

The WWII POW experience comprised two distinct groups: those held by the Germans (European Theater [ET]) and those held by the Japanese (Pacific Theater [PT]). The majority of WWII POWs, with the exception of ET aviators, were high-school educated enlisted personnel, who were typically single and in their early twenties. In general, PT imprisonment was associated with more severe stressors and more pervasive long-term morbidity than ET captivity. More than 40% of PT POWs died in captivity, while the death rate associated with ET captivity was approximately 1% (DVA, 1980). Those PT POWs lucky enough to survive spent an average of 38 months under enemy control, whereas the average captivity duration for American servicemen in the German Stalags was approximately 11 months (DVA, 1980). Although at this late date mortality rates and rates of VA compensation for service-connected disability are equivalent (Creasy et al., 1999; Hunt et al., 2008; Skelton & Skelton, 1995), during the early years following repatriation both mortality rates and compensation rates were higher among POWs held by the Japanese (Beebe, 1975; Keehn, 1980; Nefzger, 1970). The Germans had two levels of camps: one for display to the International Red Cross inspectors that contained aviators and other prisoners held in high esteem, and the Stalags for the typical Army soldier. Treatment in these two camps varied greatly, with torture, attempts at political indoctrination, and deprivation being much more common in the Stalags (DVA, 1980). At times, black POWs, Jewish POWs, and other POWs considered undesirable by the Nazis were sent to one of the concentration camps. American POWs held by the Germans were subjected to bitter cold winters, chronic malnutrition (from a limited consumption of bread, sausage, and potato soup), frequent death threats, witnessing the deaths of fellow POWs, and forced marches between camps (DVA, 1980).

The most infamous forced march occurred during the spring of 1942 following the American surrender on the island of Bataan. During the so-called Bataan Death March nearly 17,000 men were either executed or died from a combination of dehydration, starvation, and tropical diseases (DVA, 1980). Additional POWs were captured on Corregidor, Wake Island, and various other remote locations. Since only a few aviators were shot down and captured while bombing Japan, as in Europe most PT POWs were young, high-school educated, single enlisted personnel. Unlike the United States and Germany, Japan had not participated in the Geneva Convention. Torture, beheadings, mock executions, punitive "medical care," and purposeful starvation were consequently common in Japanese POW camps and mainland prisons. Included in the Japanese torture repertoire (DVA, 1980) was a water torture technique that all too often resulted in death by drowning. Camp diet was typically limited to rice, augmented occasionally with meat and vegetables. As in Europe, transfers between camps were frequent and very hazardous to the American POW. Those POWs who made it to prisons in Manchuria or China faced extreme cold temperatures during the winter, unsanitary living conditions, and forced labor with exposure to occupational toxins (Robson, Welch, Beeching, & Gill, 2009). Unfortunately, a number of American POWs perished when the ships transporting them were sunk.

The death rate among KC POWs was approximately 38% (DVA, 2008; Ritchie, 2002) and those that survived spent an average of 26 months in captivity. As in WWII, the typical KC POW was enlisted, single, high-school educated, and in his early twenties. In contrast to WWII ET aviators, airmen captured by the Koreans were tortured severely with the goal of political confessions, interrogated regarding military intelligence, and charged with conducting germ warfare (DVA, 1980). All POWs were starved, dehydrated (average weight loss was between 40% and 50%), exposed to the elements, denied medical treatment, and forced to attend compulsory group indoctrination. The initial POWs were captured in July 1950. Within a few months of capture several of these soldiers had made propaganda tapes, and stories of "brainwashing" appeared in American newspapers (Ritchie, 2002). The Koreans and the Chinese had established interrogation techniques designed to indoctrinate the POWs into Communism and encourage collaboration (Biderman, 1957; Schein, Hill, Williams, & Lubin, 1957). Twenty-one KC POWs elected to remain in North Korea rather than be repatriated (DVA, 2008). When a portion of KC RPWs exhibited neurasthenia similar to the Konzentrationslagersyndrome (e.g., dysphoric mood, anergia, insomnia, irritability, loss of initiative, and failing memory), their psychological vulnerability was attributed to the effects of "brainwashing" (DVA, 1980) and initially labeled "give-it-upitis" (Ritchie, 2002). Although the issue of brainwashing was ultimately refuted, the stigma created by the topic has had a negative impact on many KC RPWs since their repatriation in 1953.

The first POWs held in Southeast Asia included those held by the Pathet Lao and those held by the Viet Cong. Although some of these men died in captivity, some escaped and some were released. An unfortunate few remained under enemy control (Rochester & Kiley, 1998). The longest held VN POW (Philpott, 2001) was kept in the jungles of South Vietnam until his repatriation during Operation Homecoming (O/H: Pettyjohn, 1998; Rayman, 1998) in the spring of 1973. His captivity lasted 9 days short of 9 years (approximately 108 months). The overall captivity-related death rate among VN POWs was approximately 15% (DVA, 2008), and the average VN POW spent 54 months in captivity. To better appreciate the captivity experience of the VN RPW, we must acknowledge two distinct factors: location of confinement and duration of captivity. The infamous "Hanoi Hilton," as well as other camps with names like Alcatraz, the Plantation, Hope (Son Tay), and the Zoo, confined the large group of Navy and Air Force aviators who were considered by the enemy to be "air pirates" and criminals outside purview of the Geneva Convention. These airmen were political prisoners of the North Vietnamese (NVN), and their torture was designed to obtain confessions, military intelligence, or denouncement of American policies (Rochester & Kiley, 1998). POWs created elaborate lies and fabrications to fool the enemy, but strict adherence to the Code of Conduct became so difficult that the senior ranking officers (SRO) created what was known as the "bounce back" policy. This policy acknowledged that individuals have different torture tolerance. The "bounce back" policy (Rochester & Kiley, 1998) encouraged the POW to renew his resistance, refuse to cooperate during the next interrogation, and force the captor to renew the torture. The SRO also issued an order that prohibited the NVN POWs from accepting an early release from captivity. According to this order, the terms of release were either all POWs simultaneously, those in need of expert medical assistance, or "first in, first out." Several aviators accepted early release against orders, and one enlisted sailor was ordered by his SRO to accept early release in August 1969 (Rochester & Kiley, 1998), bringing with him a memorized list of more than 250 known POWs that served as the first registry of POWs that had survived capture.

The typical NVN airman was a college-educated, married, career aviator officer who had completed survival training prior to captivity. The death rate in NVN was approximately 5%, average captivity duration was approximately 60 months, and two NVN POWs had also been POWs in WWII (ET). The longest held American aviator spent 102 months in NVN. Solitary confinement, starvation, restricted medical care, and torture were part of the daily routine for the "Old Guys"—those captured before the fall of 1969. As in previous wars, torture consisted of mock executions, forced standing or kneeling, placement in tight handcuffs, shackles or manacles, and beatings (Rochester & Kiley, 1998). One of the preferred torture methods in NVN was "the ropes," where the POWs arms were bound behind him and rotated upward until their shoulders dislocated (McGrath, 1975). The captivity experience changed for the better following the death of Ho Chi Minh in September 1969. The "New Guys," or "short-timers," consisted of those captured after that time and repatriated in 1973 as part of O/H. Although their captivity experience included torture, deprivation, and solitary confinement (Rochester & Kiley, 1998), these techniques were not routine, but rather applied as strategic punishments for violation of camp rules. Many of these aviators have written books (e.g., Alvarez & Pitch, 1989; Day, 1989; Denton, 1976; Johnson & Winebrenner, 1982; Risner, 1973; Stockdale & Stockdale, 1990) detailing their captivity experience in which they attribute their survival in NVN to their training, secret communications, maintenance of a military organization with a recognized command structure, humor and faith in each other, their family, their country, and their God (Gaither & Henry, 1973). The airmen held in NVN called themselves the "Fourth Allied POW Wing," and their adopted motto was "Return with Honor" (Day, 1989; Mock & Sanders, 1998).

The POWs held in the jungles of South Vietnam (SVN) were more similar demographically to POWs from other eras than they were to the NVN POWs in that they were typically young, high-school educated, single enlisted troops. The unique aspects of their experience related to being held in the jungle, at the end of enemy supply lines, by active combatant units (Rochester & Kiley, 1998). These active combatant units would frequently hold a small number of POWs. These SVN prisoners were chained or tied to trees, housed in bamboo huts called "tiger cages," or even kept in trenches or pits. Exposure, starvation, dehydration, denial of medical care, and beatings were common, although specific attempts to obtain either military intelligence or political conversion through torture were rare in comparison to the NVN experience (Brace, 1988; Purcell & Purcell, 2006). Tropical diseases, parasites, near constant relocations, and the continued risk of being injured or killed during fire fights between their Viet Cong captors and U.S. forces were part of routine captivity in SVN. The death rate in SVN was approximately 20%, and the average captivity duration was approximately 49 months. Unlike the NVN experience, where there were no successful escapes, several SVN POWs escaped and several others were returned to U.S. military control prior to O/H. Prior to repatriation, a number of the SVN POWs participated in a "forced march" to NVN (Rochester & Kiley, 1998), whereas the rest remained in SVN until O/H. Four SVN and four NVN POWs were awarded the Congressional Medal of Honor, four of which were posthumous awards (NamPows, n.d.).

MEDICAL CONSEQUENCES OF CAPTIVITY AFFECTING NEUROPSYCHOLOGICAL FUNCTIONING

The Veterans Administration presumes that the following medical conditions are directly related to the captivity experience: cold injury, stroke, heart disease, avitaminosis, chronic dysentery, helminthiasis, malnutrition (including associated optic atrophy), pellagra, any other nutritional deficiency, peptic ulcer disease, beriberi, cirrhosis of the liver (nonalcoholic), and peripheral neuropathy (DVA, n.d., 2005). Research has not only established a captivity-related increased risk for each of these conditions (e.g., Page & Brass, 2001) but has also established biologically plausible pathways between exposure and condition. Many of these presumptive conditions have predictable affects on neuropsychological functioning with which clinicians are already familiar. Brass and Page (1996) evaluated the effects of chronic stress associated with captivity in a cohort of 475 WWII RPWs approximately 40 years following repatriation. Among the RPWs there was a 9.3% incidence of stroke, whereas only 1.2% of the WWII veteran control group had suffered a stroke in this time period (relative risk [RR] = 7.5; 95% confidence interval [CI] = 1.05–53.7).

Within the RPWs there was a trend for those RPWs with PTSD to be at greater risk for stroke than those without PTSD (RR = 1.67; 95% CI = 0.95–2.93). A 50-year postrepatriation follow-up of nearly 9,500 (Page & Brass, 2001) found that the increased mortality risk for heart disease and stroke was greatest in RPWs aged 75 years and older (hazard ratio = 1.25; 95% CI = 1.01–1.56). Kang, Bullman, and Taylor (2006) found that RPWs with PTSD had an increased risk of cardiovascular disease, hypertension, and ischemic heart disease when compared to both RPWs without PTSD and non-RPW veterans from WWII.

In support of the presumptive compensation for neuropathies, research demonstrates that approximately 10% of PT repatriates had been shown to have long-term persistent neuropathies (Gill & Bell, 1982) and as many as 80% of VN repatriates exhibited evidence of upper extremity peripheral neuropathy nearly 30 years following repatriation (Holmboe, Wang, & Brass, 2002). These neuropathies can be associated with either torture or chronic nutritional deficiencies. Although attempts have been made to relate these same risk factors to what might be called premature aging, there is insufficient evidence to support compensation for specific neurological conditions such as Parkinson's disease (PD). Although early data suggested an increased risk of PD among British PT repatriates relative to controls (Gibberd & Simmonds, 1980), later British research (Gale, Braidwood, Winter, & Martin, 1999) found RPW status to be protective with regard to PD (standardized mortality rate [SMR] = 0.85; 85% CI = 0.83–0.87), and U.S. researchers failed to find any risk differences related to RPW status among WWII veterans (Page & Tanner, 2000).

In recognition of the differences in the captivity experiences of ET and PT repatriates, Klonoff, McDougall, Clark, Kramer, and Morgan (1976) administered the Wechsler Adult Intelligence Scale (WAIS; Wechsler, 1955) and the Halstead-Reitan Neuropsychological Battery (Reitan & Davidson, 1974) to 45 PT and 42 ET repatriates. In their sample, the captivity duration for the PT and ET repatriates were 3.7 and 2.1 years, respectively. The neuropsychological test results supported the authors' hypothesis that the higher levels of stress associated with PT captivity would result in poorer performance on these measures relative to the ET group. Significant differences were observed on WAIS Full Scale IQ (PT = 111, ET = 108), HRNB Category errors (PT = 72, ET = 57), Seashore Rhythm errors (PT = 4.89, ET = 2.95), Part B time on the HRNB Trail-Making Test (PT = 118 s, ET = 89 s), and the HRNB Impairment Index T-Score (PT = 46, ET = 59).

One hypothesized factor tying impaired neuropsychological dysfunction to captivity was weight loss associated with malnutrition. The first of three related articles (Sutker, Galina, & West, 1990) compared neuropsychological performance of two groups of WWII and KC repatriate subjects and a similar group of non-POW veterans (n = 50). Repatriates were assigned to groups based on their reported weight loss during captivity: greater than 35% (n = 60) and less than or equal to 35% (n = 113). Significant results supporting the research hypothesis of greater dysfunction associated with greater weight loss were found on the following measures: WAIS Performance IQ; WAIS subtests measuring Arithmetic, Similarities, and Picture Completion; Wechsler Memory Scale (WMS: Wechsler, 1974) Immediate Memory and WMS Delayed Memory.

In the second study (Sutker, Allain, Johnson, & Butters, 1992) an identical definition of weight loss was employed to define three groups of WWII and KC repatriates and matched veterans (all groups approximately 63 years old and high-school educated). After confirming a similar level of intelligence in the three groups (101–105), the authors evaluated the effect of weight loss on learning and memory as measured by the Revised WMS (Wechsler, 1987) and the Rey Auditory Verbal Learning Test (AVLT: Rey, 1964). Test results revealed significant group differences in support of the hypothesized detrimental effects of malnutrition on the AVLT Total Learning score (high weight loss = 33, low weight loss = 40, and combat veterans = 41). Within the Revised WMS, group differences were found on all measures except the Attention/Concentration Index.

In the third study, exploratory principal component analysis and multiple regression analysis were used to evaluate the relationship between neuropsychological performance, captivity-related weight loss, and measures of psychological distress (PTSD and depression) in a group of 108 WWII and KC repatriates (Sutker, Vasterling, Brailey, & Allain, 1995). As a group these repatriates averaged 17 months of captivity during which they lost an average of 48 pounds each (29%). Their average WAIS IQ was 105, and their average educational level was 12.6 years. Three domains of neuropsychological functioning were assessed: attention/tracking (Digit Span, Visual Span and Reitan Trail Making), learning and memory (Revised WMS Logical Memory and Visual Reproduction), and executive functions (Reitan Category Test and Wisconsin Card Sorting Test). The results of the principal component analysis with oblique rotation identified a three-factor solution that was identical to the three theoretical domains. These three component-based scores were subsequently entered into three separate multiple regression equations predicting weight loss, PTSD symptoms, and depressive symptoms. Weight loss was predicted by PTSD and learning and memory, whereas PTSD was predicted by weight loss, attention/tracking, and executive functions. Only attention/tracking performance was significant in predicting depressive symptoms. These three studies highlight the relationship between nutritional deprivation and neuropsychological dysfunction. They also provide a bridge to understanding the relationship between the physical and emotional stressors of captivity.

PSYCHIATRIC CONSEQUENCES OF CAPTIVITY AFFECTING NEUROPSYCHOLOGICAL FUNCTIONING

The Veterans Administration also presumes that the following psychiatric conditions are directly related to the captivity experience: psychosis, dysthymic disorder or depressive neurosis, PTSD, and all other anxiety disorders (DVA, n.d.). PSTD is a particular emphasis within the VA. Reports suggest that between fiscal years 1999 and 2004 the number of veterans, to include RPWs, receiving compensation for the disorder increased by 79.5%, while the benefits payments increased by 148.8% (Committee on Veterans Compensation for Posttraumatic Stress Disorder, 2007). The report also documented that within that time period, 8.7% of all claims were associated with PTSD and 20.5% of all compensation benefits were associated with PTSD. Although similar data are unavailable for WWII and KC repatriates, there are nevertheless a considerable number of these individuals who have been diagnosed with PTSD. The VA has been the focal point for the evaluation of combat-related PTSD, to include services for repatriates.

None of the WWII and KC repatriates were diagnosed with PTSD at the time of their release from enemy control. The diagnosis of PTSD was not included in the *Diagnostic and Statistical Manual of the American Psychiatric Association* until the third edition, published in 1980 (American Psychiatric Association), and studies describing the longitudinal trajectory of PTSD in this cohort are necessarily retrospective in nature. These retrospective assessments have been performed using structured interviews and a variety of symptom scales. Since 1980 the diagnostic criteria for PTSD have undergone various revisions. Regardless of the specific changes associated with symptoms of reexperiencing, avoidance/numbing, and arousal, the diagnosis has been considered one of the most controversial of all psychiatric diagnoses (Breslau, 2002; North, Suris, Davis, & Smith, 2009). This controversy relates to a lack of a biological marker for the illness, to a debate regarding categorical versus dimensional models, and to the etiological relevance of the traumatic event (Maier, 2006; Weathers & Keane, 2007). Traumatic events that may set the stage for PTSD include assault, injury, witnessed interpersonal violence, combat, and torture. In addition, the diagnostic criteria require that the patient react to the perceived threat with fear, horror, or helplessness. Regardless of the existing controversies and possible changes to the diagnostic criteria (Spitzer, First, & Wakefield, 2007), there can be little doubt that RPWs who may have been incarcerated and tortured daily by the enemy for years meet the entry criterion for the diagnosis of PTSD.

Given the lack of a biological marker, the subjective nature of most symptoms, and the potential for compensation, the search for objective signs of the disorder has been a prominent research focus. Of particular relevance to neuropsychologists is the issue of whether postdiagnostically observed neurocognitive deficits represent the aftermath of the condition or are risk factors for its development (McNally, 2006; Wolfe & Charney, 1991). A growing body of data based on twin studies of Vietnam-era combat veterans reveals that many of the intellectual, memory, and executive dysfunctions observed in combat veterans with PTSD (Crowell, Keffer, Siders, & Vanderploeg, 2002) are also observed in the noncombat twin (Gilbertson et al., 2006, 2007; Pittman et al., 2006). The work of Vasterling and colleagues, however, also present a convincing argument for the possibility that at least some neurocognitive deficits may be attributable to the effects of the illness (Uddo, Vasterling, Brailey, & Sutker, 1993; Vasterling, Brailey, Constans, & Sutker, 1998; Vasterling et al., 2002). The neuropsychological evaluation should place specific emphasis on verbal memory (Johnsen & Asbjornsen, 2008), various aspects of attention, emotional processing, and executive functions.

General estimates suggest that approximately 70% of adult Americans will experience a traumatic event during their lifetime of sufficient severity as to meet the entry criterion for the diagnosis of PTSD, yet the estimated prevalence of PTSD in the same population is in the 7–12% range. PTSD is a frequent and predictable consequence of captivity and torture, though epidemiological studies of PTSD among WWII and KC RPWs range 44–88% depending on the sample and specific RPW group being evaluated (Engdahl, Dikel, Eberly, & Blank, 1997; Kluznik, Speed, Van Vakenburg, & Magraw, 1986; Port, Engdahl, & Frazier, 2001; Sutker &

Allain, 1996; Zeiss & Dickman, 1989). It is important to note, however, that the prevalence of PTSD is not 100%, suggesting again that we must be as mindful of the type of person who had the experience as we are of the type of experience the person had. Estimates suggest that approximately one-third of PTSD in WWII and KC cases are uncomplicated by comorbid psychiatric illness. Based on retrospectively reported symptoms, there appears to be a pattern of acute symptoms that gradually decline in severity only to possibly increase again with advancing age. Weight loss, torture severity, injury, and disease during captivity have been positively correlated with symptom severity. Age, education, and military rank have been positively associated with resilience. Temporal symptom patterns seem to wax and wane for more than 40 years following repatriation, and without treatment PTSD is persistent. Up to 30% of WWII and KC RPWs may meet PTSD diagnostic criteria more than 40 years following release. In this group of chronically disabled patients there are also extremely high rates of comorbid generalized anxiety disorder (94%) and major depressive disorder (61%). Among repatriates, published data suggest that the severity of captivity trauma is more predictive of chronic PTSD than are either preexisting psychopathologies or familial risk factors.

The Minnesota Multiphasic Personality Inventory (MMPI; Hathaway & McKinley, 1951) has been employed as measure of the psychopathological profile of WWII and KC RPWs. In one of the earliest studies, Sutker, Allain, and Motsinger (1988) used Modal Profile Analysis to describe the MMPI profile of 60 RPWs. The average age of these men was 62 years (±5 years), and their educational level was 11 years (± 3 years). Two profile patterns emerged from this analysis. The mean profile elevation was somewhat higher in type I versus type II (70 vs. 63), and the interscale scatter was also greater within the type I group (16 vs. 12). The greatest difference between the two groups occurred on scales 2, 7, 8, 0, and A, with the type I profile group showing a higher mean score. The type I profile was also associated with significantly lower ego strength scores relative to the type II profile. Using a 16-item scale for "trauma index experiences," Sutker, Winstead, and Galina (1990) reported a higher incidence of capture-related injuries, beatings, physical torture, witnessing others being tortured, death threats, and forced marches among the RPWs in the type I group. This group also reported more marital problems, alcohol abuse, use of psychotropic medications, head injury, and postrepatriation adjustment problems than did the other group of repatriates in this study, with the implication that the type I profile was more indicative of PTSD than was the type II profile.

Subsequent research confirmed this prediction. In the first of these studies (Sutker & Allain, 1991), the MMPI profile was shown to successfully discriminate between groups of repatriates (n = 168) and combat survivors (n = 67). The mean profile for the combat survivor group was within normal limits, whereas the RPW group demonstrated clinically elevated scores on scales 1, 2, 3, 7, and 8. Through the use of stepwise discriminant function analysis, the authors demonstrated that the mean RPW profile was associated with "negative rumination, heightened anxiety, interpersonal anger, suspiciousness and low self-esteem." In a follow-up study that included 121 RPWs with PTSD and 40 non-PTSD RPWs (Sutker, Bugg, & Allain, 1991), the MMPI profile demonstrated a very high positive predictive power (0.93) in identifying the RPWs with PTSD using the following MMPI scales: F, Sc, and the Keane PTSD scale (Keane, Malloy, & Fairbank, 1984).

In summary, there is considerable evidence to document the higher prevalence of PTSD among WWII and KC repatriates. The results of personality testing demonstrate reliable differences between RPWs with and without PTSD in terms of captivity experiences, adjustment difficulties, and psychopathological symptoms. Repatriates from this era have also demonstrated that memory difficulties, attentional problems, and executive dysfunction are associated with the diagnosis of PTSD.

UNIQUE ASPECTS OF NEUROPSYCHOLOGICAL FUNCTIONING IN THE AVIATOR REPATRIATE

Unlike the WWII and KC RPWs, the modal Vietnam-era repatriate is a career aviator officer who was married and college educated at the time of capture and had met the psychiatric screening standards for military aviators (Fine & Hartman, 1968; Sours & Phillips, 1962). In addition, the VN POW was likely to complete at least a master's degree following repatriation and remain on flight status until their retirement. All VN RPWs have been eligible for neuropsychological, psychological, and psychiatric follow-up since repatriation, and most have elected to participate in this annual evaluation. Between 1973 and 1978, each service participated in a jointly designed, but separately controlled, program for their repatriates (Berg & Richlin, 1977a, 1977b, 1977c, 1977d). At the end of this planned 5-year program, the Navy program was continued under the leadership of Robert E. Mitchell, and a comparison group consisting of 138 combat-experienced naval aviators was incorporated into the program. Following the successful repatriation of the Desert Storm POWs, the Robert E. Mitchell Center for POW Studies, located in Pensacola, Florida, was able to incorporate the Air Force and Army VN RPWs into the program, and currently approximately 300 patrons participate each year. In addition, VN RPWs continue to receive care from the Veterans Administration and from mental health professionals in private practice. The following summary is provided as a framework for these neuropsychologists to use during their evaluations of these RPWs and other aviator veterans. Neuropsychologists should also remain aware of the probable existence of "baseline" and serial assessment data for their patients that may be obtained for comparison with current test results.

During the first few years following Operation Homecoming there were several articles addressing personality change, psychiatric illness, and resilience among Air Force repatriates. One of the earliest publications (Jones, 1980) reviewed the statements of 26 repatriates. Common themes focused on internal standards and means of coping with captivity. The most consistent themes were associated with faith and loyalty to self-image, family, fellow POWs, and country. Sledge, Boydstun, and Rabe (1980) compared 221 POWs separated into two groups based on captivity duration. The early group averaged 73 months of captivity, whereas the late group averaged 8 months of captivity. The long-term consequences of captivity were compared between groups, as were postrepatriation "benefits" of captivity. Similar data were also collected from 341 combat-experienced Air Force aviators who were not held as POWs. Reported physical and psychological suffering was greatest in the early group, as were the perceived benefits. This observed positive correlation between harsh treatment and enhanced self-concept was interpreted as "an attempt to make the most of an otherwise extraordinarily stressful situation" (Sledge, Boydstun, & Rabe, 1980, p. 443). This study did not directly address the risk for psychiatric illness among VN RPWs but rather raised the possibility that illness and growth could occur in the same individuals. In a related study (Ursano, 1981), information obtained from case studies, where the aviator had received comprehensive psychiatric evaluations before and after captivity, suggested that antecedent psychiatric disturbance was neither necessary nor sufficient for the development of posttraumatic psychiatric illness.

At the time of repatriation in 1973, approximately 23% of the 325 Air Force VN RPWs received psychiatric diagnoses, and the prevalence of these diagnoses did not vary as a function of captivity duration

(Ursano, Boydstun, & Wheatley, 1981). More specifically, there was only a slightly higher percent of the early group with diagnoses associated with neuroses or adjustment (stress) reactions (20% vs. 18% in the late group). Within the next 5 years, 253 of these RPWs participated in the voluntary follow-up program and the prevalence of diagnosed psychiatric illness remained unchanged (21%). At that time, members of the early group were more likely to obtain "pathological scale scores" (Ursano, Boydstun, & Wheatley, 1981, p. 312) on the MMPI than the late group (45% vs. 26%, respectively), with the largest group differences occurring on scales measuring physical complaints and suspiciousness. The authors noted that the relatively low prevalence of psychiatric illness may have been attributed to the psychiatric screening that these aviators underwent prior to combat, as well as to their motivation, maturity, and training. This study also noted a low and relatively constant prevalence of organic brain syndrome in this cohort (1–3%).

The relative cognitive status of U.S. Navy Vietnam-era POWs using data gathered at the Robert E. Mitchell Center has been evaluated to determine the effects of captivity on RPWs relative to CG subjects (Williams, Hilton, & Moore, 2002). Performance was compared between RPWs and controls on three cognitive batteries: the Halstead-Reitan Neuropsychological Battery (HRNB), WAIS, and the CogScreen-Aeromedical Edition (CogScreen-AE: Kay, 1999). Differences between groups and test sessions were assessed by multivariate analysis of variance. Although statistical issues, such as heterogeneous variance-covariance matrices, led to exclusion of 14 subtests of the HRNB, multivariate results using the remaining 9 subtests indicated significant differences between RPWs and controls, with controls having worse performance on six of the nine subtests.

Analysis of WAIS data (Williams, Hilton, & Moore, 2002) revealed a significant, but trivial, difference in average scores between RPWs (130) and controls (128). On the digit-span and picture completion subtests, RPWs out-performed the controls. Over time, there was significant improvement for arithmetic, vocabulary, picture completion, and block design subtests. The direction of the means suggested that the RPWs might have slightly better intellectual performance than their matched controls. Results of initial multivariate analysis of 64 CogScreen-AE subtests showed no significant between-group difference (Williams, Hilton, & Moore, 2002).

To examine the effect of aging and time since repatriation (Moore, 1994, 1998), the results of serial intellectual testing using the WAIS reveals minimal differences between the Navy VN RPW and comparison groups (Table 10.1). The mean IQ scores are in the superior to very

Table 10.1

U.S. NAVY AVIATOR RPW (*N* = 31) AND CG (*N* = 38) WAIS DATA, EACH EVALUATED THREE TIMES OVER A 17-YEAR PERIOD

VARIABLE		INITIAL WAIS		FOLLOW-UP WAIS #1		FOLLOW-UP WAIS #2	
		SCORE	COHEN'S *D*	SCORE	COHEN'S *D*	SCORE	COHEN'S *D*
Age	RPW	40.2	**0.36**	47.4	0.19	56.9	**0.21**
	CG	42.2		48.4		58.0	
FSIQ	RPW	130.1	0.14	130.2	0.00	134.1	0.18
	CG	129.1		130.2		133.0	
VIQ	RPW	128.2	0.16	126.9	0.11	130.5	0.14
	CG	127.0		127.7		129.6	
PIQ	RPW	128.7	0.05	130.1	0.02	134.5	0.13
	CG	128.2		130.3		133.5	
Inf	RPW	14.8	**0.24**	14.9	**0.47**	15.1	**0.29**
	CG	14.4		15.7		14.6	
Com	RPW	15.6	0.19	14.8	**0.39**	15.2	**0.20**
	CG	15.1		15.7		14.9	
Arith	RPW	15.0	0.15	14.9	**0.32**	14.4	0.15
	CG	14.7		14.3		14.7	
Sim	RPW	13.1	**0.52**	13.3	0.11	14.4	0.00
	CG	14.2		13.5		14.4	
DSp	RPW	14.2	**0.45**	13.3	0.00	13.4	**0.24**
	CG	12.9		13.3		12.8	
Voc	RPW	15.6	0.11	14.6	**0.24**	14.9	0.07
	CG	15.8		15.0		14.8	
DSy	RPW	12.5	0.05	12.4	0.14	12.3	0.00
	CG	12.4		12.7		12.3	
PC	RPW	14.8	**0.43**	13.6	**0.45**	13.4	**0.27**
	CG	13.8		12.6		12.8	
BD	RPW	14.6	0.11	14.3	0.00	13.5	0.11
	CG	14.4		14.3		13.7	
PA	RPW	12.1	0.00	12.4	**0.22**	12.6	0.27
	CG	12.1		11.9		12.2	
OA	RPW	12.8	**0.36**	13.7	0.17	13.2	**0.30**
	CG	13.6		13.2		14.1	

Numbers listed in bold reflect non-trivial effect sizes as follows: Small effect = 0.20; Medium effect = 0.50; and Large effect = 0.80.

Arith=arithmetic; BD=block design; CG=comparison group; Com=comprehension; DSp=digit span; DSy=digit symbol; FSIQ=full scale IQ; Inf=information; OA=object assembly; PA=picture arrangement; PC=picture completion; PIQ=performance IQ; Sim=similarities; VIQ=verbal IQ; Voc = vocabulary; WAIS=Wechsler Adult Intelligence Scale.

superior range, and group differences were trivial using Cohen's d as a measure of effect size (small = 0.2; medium = 0.5; large = 0.8). A review of the effect size of group differences at the subtest level reveals that RPWs sometimes score higher than the CG and that group differences on the digit symbol and block design subtests have been trivial.

The Navy VN RPWs have completed some or all of the HRNB several times over the years (Moore, 1994, 1998), and the serial HRNB results are presented in Table 10.2. The RPWs completed the HRNB shortly following repatriation and were reevaluated when the CG was added to the program. Although the superior performance by the RPW group at age 41 may have been partially attributable to practice, many of the effect sizes were similar 16 years later. At age 57, the mean impairment index scores of each group were within normal limits, as were each component scores of the Index.

A comparison of serial MMPI administrations (Moore, 1994, 1998) reveals that the effect size for group differences has most often been small. The Navy aviator VN RPWs have tended to obtain clinically normal profiles characterized by defensiveness and denial of psychiatric symptoms (Table 10.3). Although the RPWs and CG subjects rarely obtain profiles suggestive of psychopathology, on average the RPWs obtained twice as many scales above a typical cut score for clinical significance ($T > 70$). Between the ages of 44 and 57, there has been slight increase in endorsed physical complaints and depression among the RPWs. Mean RPW scores have been consistently higher than mean CG scores on most MMPI scales, but the groups have not differed on scales 5, 9, or Ego Strength.

The experienced clinician will recognize that military aviators often approach tests such as the MMPI with defensiveness, resulting in a risk of underdiagnosis of psychopathology. One way to address this issue is to obtain preliminary norms on various clinical instruments using aviators with known clinical status (Sipes, Moore, & Caldwell, 1991). Recently obtained data for symptoms of sleepiness (Porter, Moore, & Hain, 2005), divided attention (Moore, Ambrose, & Dolgin, 2002a, 2002b), depression, dissociation, and PTSD (Moore, Ellis, & Ambrose, 2001), as well as verbal memory performance and subjective memory self-rating are equivalent for RPW and CG subjects who are free of neurological (Fiedler, Hawkins, Moore, & Schroeder, 2002; Hawkins, Fiedler, & Moore, 2002; Moore, Hawkins, Fiedler, & Ambrose, 2001) and psychiatric illness.

For example, 323 older military aviators (average age = 62) completed the Geriatric Depression Scale (GDS; Yesavage et al., 1983). As

Table 10.2

U.S. NAVY AVIATOR RPW (N = 40) AND CG (N = 41) HRNB DATA, EACH EVALUATED 2–3 TIMES OVER A 19-YEAR PERIOD

VARIABLE		INITIAL RPW HRNB		RPW FOLLOW-UP HRNB #1 INITIAL CG HRNB		RPW FOLLOW-UP HRNB #2 CG FOLLOW-UP HRNB #1	
		SCORE	COHEN'S D	SCORE	COHEN'S D	SCORE	COHEN'S D
Age	RPW	38.3		40.5	0.11	56.8	0.08
	SD	5.6					
	CG			41.1		57.2	
Category	RPW	19.5		15.0	**0.78**	16.1	**0.52**
	SD	9.5					
	CG			24.1		20.8	
TPT D	RPW	4.3		4.5	**0.23**	4.0	0.08
	SD	1.7					
	CG			5.1		3.9	
TPT ND	RPW	3.1		3.7	0.04	3.1	**0.27**
	SD	1.5					
	CG			3.6		3.4	
TPT B	RPW	1.7		1.9	0.17	2.1	**0.44**
	SD	0.9					
	CG			2.1		2.5	
TPT T	RPW	9.1		10.0	0.14	9.1	**0.23**
	SD	3.3					
	CG			10.8		9.7	
TPT Mem	RPW	8.9		8.7	**0.20**	8.1	**0.27**
	SD	1.1					
	CG			8.5		7.8	
TPT Loc	RPW	6.6		6.8	**0.45**	4.8	**0.30**
	SD	2.4					
	CG			5.9		4.2	
Trails A	RPW	23.9		24.3	**0.47**	21.3	0.10
	SD	5.5					
	CG			27.7		20.8	
Trails B	RPW	52.7		50.2	**0.50**	49.6	0.11
	SD	13.8					
	CG			57.3		50.9	
Tap D	RPW			51.4	0.08	52.3	0.09
	CG			52.0		51.8	
Tap ND	RPW			46.5	0.16	47.6	0.06
	CG			47.5		47.9	
SRT	RPW					28.0	**0.40**
	CG					27.2	
SSPT	RPW					5.0	0.17
	CG					4.5	
Imp Index	RPW					0.14	0.15
	CG					0.16	

B=both hands; CG=comparison group; D=dominant hand; HRNB=Halstead-Reitan Neuropsychological Battery; Imp Index=Impairment Index; Loc=location; Mem=memory; ND=non-dominant hand; RPW=repatriated POWs; SRT=Seashore Rhythm Test; SSPT=Speech Sounds Perception Test; T=total time; Tap=Finger Tapping Test; TPT=Tactual Performance Test; Trails A=Trail Making Test Part A; Trails B=Trail Making Test Part B.

Table 10.3

U.S. NAVY AVIATOR RPW (*N* = 59) AND CG (*N* = 46) MMPI DATA, EACH EVALUATED THREE TIMES OVER A 14-YEAR PERIOD

VARIABLE		INITIAL MMPI SCORE	COHEN'S *D*	FOLLOW-UP MMPI #1 SCORE	COHEN'S *D*	FOLLOW-UP MMPI #2 SCORE	COHEN'S *D*
Age	RPW	44.4	0.09	47.6	0.11	57.8	0.19
	CG	44.0		47.1		56.9	
L	RPW	4.3	**0.36**	4.1	0.05	4.2	0.05
	CG	3.5		4.0		4.3	
F	RPW	3.9	**0.29**	4.1	**0.39**	4.6	**0.32**
	CG	3.1		3.2		3.7	
K	RPW	17.2	0.05	17.5	0.18	18.2	**0.28**
	CG	17.4		18.3		19.3	
Hs	RPW	4.5	**0.43**	5.7	**0.48**	6.1	**0.66**
	CG	2.9		3.8		3.6	
D	RPW	18.2	0.12	19.5	0.05	19.9	**0.55**
	CG	17.7		19.3		17.7	
Hy	RPW	21.6	**0.34**	23.2	**0.34**	23.0	**0.21**
	CG	20.0		21.8		22.1	
Pd	RPW	15.5	**0.27**	15.8	0.17	15.5	**0.22**
	CG	14.4		15.1		14.7	
Mf	RPW	25.1	0.02	24.6	0.00	25.0	0.10
	CG	25.0		24.6		25.4	
Pa	RPW	9.8	0.15	10.2	0.13	10.1	**0.35**
	CG	10.2		10.5		10.9	
Pt	RPW	7.0	0.16	7.6	**0.21**	6.4	0.14
	CG	6.2		6.5		5.7	
Sc	RPW	8.5	**0.26**	7.9	**0.28**	7.9	**0.36**
	CG	7.0		6.5		6.3	
Ma	RPW	16.2	0.03	15.6	0.12	15.5	0.16
		16.1		15.2		14.9	
Si	RPW	21.8	**0.33**	22.4	0.09	22.2	0.07
	CG	24.5		23.1		22.7	
# "Elevations"	RPW	0.7		0.9	0.33	0.9	**0.25**
	CG	0.5		0.5		0.6	
Es	RPW					50.3	0.04
	CG					50.5	
Mac	RPW					21.9	0.17
	CG					21.3	

CG = comparison group; D = depression; Es = ego strength; F = infrequency; Hs = hypochondriasis; Hy = hysteria; K = defensiveness; L = lie; Ma = mania; Mac = MacAndrew's Alcoholism Scale; Mf = masculinity/femininity; MMPI = Minnesota Multiphasic Personality Inventory; Pa = paranoia; Pd = psychopathic deviance; Pt = psychasthenia; RPW = repatriated POWs; Sc = schizophrenia; Si = social introversion; # "Elevations" = number of clinical scales with T-scores of 70 or greater.

the scores of repatriates and comparison group members did not differ, they were combined prior to analysis. In this study (Moore & Hain, 2004), 23 patients (7%) met *DSM-IV* criteria for major depressive disorders, while the remaining 300 aviators were without psychiatric diagnosis. The mean GDS score for psychiatrically healthy aviators (2.7) was significantly lower than that of depressed aviators (10.5). The GDS demonstrated adequate internal consistency ($r = 0.84$) and item-level comparisons revealed group differences on 20 of the 30 GDS symptoms. Only 48% of the depressed group scored above the published cut score.

A similarity between groups of neurologically and psychiatrically healthy RPW and CG subjects has also been observed on the Rey Auditory Verbal Learning Test (AVLT) and the Memory Assessment Clinics Self-Rating scale (MAC-S: Crook & Larrabee, 1990). One hundred and seventy-five retired military aviators completed the AVLT and the MAC-S as part of their medical follow-up at the Robert E. Mitchell Center (Moore, Ambrose, & Dolgin, 2002a, 2002b). The mean age was 61.4 years and mean years of education was 17 years. Subjects were grouped into three groups according to age: 55–59, 60–64, and 65–69. Aviator memory performance was superior to published age-corrected general norms. There were significant group differences on both objective and subjective memory measures. These differences were generally attributable to superior performance and higher MAC-S ratings in the youngest group, whereas the two older groups were generally equivalent. Age accounted for approximately 10% of AVLT total score variance in this healthy cohort. Older and younger aviators differed to a similar degree as the aviators differed from nonaviator norms.

Seven years later, 129 older military aviators who had remained neurologically healthy were reevaluated twice with the AVLT, the MAC-S, and the GDS (Moore & Porter, 2007). As before, there were no group differences as a function of RPW status and the data were combined for analysis. The initial and follow-up AVLT, MAC-S, and GDS scores were significantly correlated, but the effect sizes of these differences were typically trivial. Within each administration, MAC-S and GDS were significantly correlated, but neither correlated with AVLT. These results demonstrated that serial evaluation of neurologically healthy older aviators reveals that memory ability, subjective memory rating, and reported mood are remarkably stable across the decade of the 60s.

Despite these similarities between healthy older aviators, group differences have been observed as a function of diagnosed psychiatric illness. The relationship between depression, memory, memory complaints, concurrent PTSD symptoms, and peritraumatic dissociative symptoms has also been evaluated in this population (Moore, Larrabee, & Ambrose, 2000). Memory complaints are central components of PTSD, dissociative disorders, and major depression as currently described in the *DSM-IV* (American Psychiatric Association, 1994), and the predictive utility of peritraumatic dissociation for PTSD diagnosis is a topic of interest. Within the context of annual evaluation at the Robert E. Mitchell Center, 112 RPWs and 37 matched aviator comparison subjects (CG) completed the MAC-S, the AVLT, the GDS, the revised Impact of Events Scale (IES-R; Weis & Marmar, 1997) and the self-report version of the Peritraumatic Dissociative Experiences Questionnaire (PDEQ-SR; Marmar, Weiss, & Metzler, 1997). The POW experience was quantified using length of captivity (months), length of solitary confinement (weeks), and subjective torture severity. As before, the RPW and CG groups performed similarly on the AVLT, the GDS, and the MAC-S Ability ratings (Moore, Larrabee, & Ambrose, 2000). The two groups differed, however, on the IES-R, the PDEQ-SR, and the MAC-S Frequency ratings, with the suggested impairment being greater in the RPW group. The overall incidence of PTSD in the RPW group was 14%, and diagnosis was associated with lower memory ability, more depressive symptoms, higher peritraumatic dissociation, and more frequent memory complaints. Moore and colleagues (2000) reported that PTSD diagnosis did not affect MAC-S Ability ratings. RPW MAC-S Ability scores correlated significantly with AVLT, but not with IES-R or PDEQ-SR. RPW MAC-S Frequency scores correlated significantly with IES-R and PDEQ-SR, but not with AVLT. Stepwise linear regression revealed significant contributions of both GDS and age in predicting both MAC-S Ability and MAC-S Frequency; however, IES-R also contributed significantly to MAC-S Frequency. Memory ability was best predicted by a combination of age and IES-R.

SUMMARY

Many resources are available to assist the RPW with his or her medical and psychological needs. Proper treatment of these American heroes begins with an understanding of their captivity experience. Each war has had unique tortures and unique environmental exposures; however, the VA has identified a list of medical and psychiatric illnesses that are presumptively related to the captivity experience. Many of these conditions have known or suspected neuropsychological consequences.

As in any neuropsychological evaluation, care must be taken to select the appropriate normative database against which the patient's performance may be compared. The WWII and KC repatriates were similar to each other in terms of background demographics and different from the typical VN RPW who was a college-educated, career-designated, military aviator. This is not to say that there were no officer RPWs during WWII and the KC, or that there were no single, high-school educated enlisted RPWs during VN. Fortunately most normative databases allow for corrections due to gender, age, and educational level. Military aviators may be expected to perform in the superior range on most neuropsychological measures, and in some cases specifically designed instruments with unique aviator norms are available.

When evaluating a repatriate, neuropsychologists must also be aware of an increased risk for such conditions as cerebrovascular disease, severe malnutrition during captivity, torture-related injury, toxic exposure, and neuropathies. Although specific neuropsychological deficits may also be attributable to chronic PTSD, the neuropsychologist should not expect that all RPWs would suffer from this, or any other, psychiatric illness.

The availability of previous neuropsychological test data facilitates an understanding of illness trajectories, as well as neurocognitive strengths and weaknesses. Fortunately, many WWII and KC RPWs have been evaluated as part of research or clinical programs within the VA. All VN RPWs have completed such evaluations, and those results are available for release to neuropsychologists through the Robert E. Mitchell Center if appropriately authorized by the RPW.

Much remains to be learned from the men and women who have experienced the unique stressors associated with being a POW. Some of these stressors are physiological while others are psychological. Many POWs have not succumbed to even the most maximal stressor. Other POWs may have risk factors that precede captivity. Still others only cope with repatriation by reliance on extensive social support. Some repatriates have endured years of solitary confinement, isolation, and deprivation and yet have few problems. Other RPWs display chronic illnesses following brief periods of captivity. At this point it is impossible to predict which is more predictive of long-term illness: the type of experience the RPW had or the type of RPW who had the experience. As "cruel, destructive and wasteful" (Grinker & Spiegel, 1945, p. vii) as the POW experience may be, adaptation occurs. Nevertheless, no POW needs to be held as long as they were to learn everything they need to know about being a POW.

POW Medal: "For Honorable Service While A Prisoner of War".

REFERENCES

Alvarez, E., & Pitch, A. S. (1989). *Chained eagle.* New York: Donald I. Fine.

American Psychiatric Association. (1980). *Diagnostic and statistical manual of mental disorders* (3rd ed.). Washington, DC: Author.

American Psychiatric Association. (1994). *Diagnostic and statistical manual of mental disorders* (4th ed.). Washington, DC: Author.

Basoglu, M., Livanou, M., & Crnobaric, C. (2008). Torture vs other cruel, inhuman, and degrading treatment: Is the distinction real or apparent? *Archives of General Psychiatry, 64,* 277–285.

Beebe, G. W. (1975). Follow-up studies of World War II and Korean War prisoners: II. Morbidity, disability, and maladjustments. *American Journal of Epidemiology, 101,* 400–422.

Berg, W., & Richlin, M. (1977a). Injuries and illnesses of Vietnam War POWs: I. Navy POWs. *Military Medicine, 142,* 514–518.

Berg, W., & Richlin, M. (1977b). Injuries and illnesses of Vietnam War POWs: II. Army POWs. *Military Medicine, 142,* 598–602.

Berg, W., & Richlin, M. (1977c). Injuries and illnesses of Vietnam War POWs: III. Marine Corps POWs. *Military Medicine, 142,* 678–680.

Berg, W., & Richlin, M. (1977d). Injuries and illnesses of Vietnam War POWs: IV. Comparisons of captivity effects in North and South Vietnam. *Military Medicine, 142*, 757–761.

Biderman, A. D. (1957). Communist attempts to elicit false confessions from Air Force prisoners of war. *Bulletin of the New York Academy of Medicine, 33*, 616–625.

Brace, E. C. (1988). *A code to keep.* Central Point, OR: Hellgate Press.

Breslau, N. (2002). Epidemiologic studies of trauma, posttraumatic stress disorder, and other psychiatric disorders. *Canadian Journal of Psychiatry, 47*, 923–929.

Brass, L. M., & Page, W. F. (1996). Stroke in former prisoners of war. *Journal of Stroke and Cerebrovascular Diseases, 6*, 72–78.

Committee on Veterans Compensation for Posttraumatic Stress Disorder, Institute of Medicine, & National Research Council. (2007). *PTSD compensation and military service.* Washington, DC: National Academies Press.

Creasey, H., Sulway, M. R., Dent, O., Broe, G. A., Jorm, A., & Tennant, C. (1999). Is experience as a prisoner of war a risk factor for accelerated age-related illness and disability? *Journal of the American Geriatrics Society, 47*, 60–64.

Crook, T. H., & Larrabee, G. J. (1990). A self-rating scale for evaluating memory in everyday life. *Psychology and Aging, 5*, 48–57.

Crowell, T. A., Keiffer, K. M., Siders, C. A., & Vanderploeg, R. D. (2002). Neuropsychological findings in combat-related posttraumatic stress disorder. *The Clinical Neuropsychologist, 16*, 310–321.

Day, G. E. (1989). *Return with honor.* Mesa, AZ: Champlain Museum Press.

Denton, J. (1976). *When hell was in session.* New York: Reader's Digest Press.

Department of Veteran Affairs. (1980). *POW: Study of former prisoners of war.* Retrieved November 16, 2008, from http://www.vba.va.gov/bln/21/benefits/POW/POWBackground.htm

Department of Veterans Affairs. (2005). Presumptions of service connection for diseases associated with service involving detention or internment as a prisoner of war. *Federal Register, 70*(123), 37040–37042.

Department of Veterans Affairs. (2008). *American prisoners of war at end of 2007.* Retrieved November 16, 2008, from http://www.va.gov/opa/fact/pow.asp

Department of Veterans Affairs. (n.d.). *Former prisoners of war (POWs): What are the presumptive conditions for former POWs?* Retrieved November 16, 2008, from http://www.vba.va.gov/VBA/benefits/factsheets/serviceconnected/formerpows.doc

Engdahl, B., Dikel, T. N., Eberly, R., & Blank, A. (1997). Posttraumatic stress disorder in a community group of former prisoners of war: A normative response to severe trauma. *American Journal of Psychiatry, 154*, 1576–1581.

Fiedler, E. R., Hawkins, M. M., Moore, J. L., & Schroeder, D. (2002, June). *Use of the CogScreen to screen older aviators.* Poster session presented at the annual meeting of the International Congress for Applied Psychology, Singapore.

Fine, P. M., & Hartman, B. O. (1968). *Psychiatric strengths and weaknesses of typical Air Force pilots.* USAF School of Aerospace Medicine, TR-68–121, Brooks Air Force Base, Texas.

Gaither, R., & Henry, S. (1973). *With God in a POW camp.* Nashville, TN: Broadman Press.

Gale, C. R., Braidwood, E. A., Winter, P. D., & Martyn, C. N. (1999). Mortality from Parkinson's disease and other causes in men who were prisoners of war in the Far East. *Lancet, 354*(9196), 2116–2118.

Gibberd, F. B., & Simmonds, J. P. (1980). Neurological disease in ex-Far-East prisoners of war. *Lancet, 2*(8186), 135–137.

Gilbertson, M. W., Paulus, L. A., Willston, S. K., Gurvits, T. V., Lasko, N. B., & Pittman, R. K. (2006). Neurocognitive function in monozygotic twins discordant for combat exposure: Relationship to posttraumatic stress disorder. *Journal of Abnormal Psychology, 115,* 484–495.

Gilberston, M. W., Willston, S. K., Paulus, L. A., Lasko, N. B., Gurvits, T. V., Shenton, M. E., et al. (2007). Configurals cue performance in identical twins discordant for posttraumatic stress disorder: Theoretical implications for the role of hippocampal function. *Biological Psychiatry, 62,* 513–520.

Gill, C. V., & Bell, D. R. (1982). Persisting nutritional neuropathy amongst former war prisoners. *Journal of Neurology, Neurosurgery, and Psychiatry, 45,* 861–865.

Grinker, R. R., & Spiegel, J. P. (1945). *Men under stress.* Philadelphia: Blakiston.

Hathaway, S. R., & McKinley, J. C. (1951). *The Minnesota multiphasic personality inventory manual (revised).* New York: The Psychological Corporation.

Hawkins, M. M., Fiedler, E. R., & Moore, J. L. (2002, May). *WAIS correlates of CogScreen-AE performance for older aviators.* Poster session presented at the annual meeting of the Aerospace Medical Association. Montreal, Canada.

Holmboe, E. S., Wang, Y., & Brass, L. M. (2002). Long-term consequences of upper extremity peripheral neuropathy in former Vietnam prisoners of war. *Military Medicine, 167,* 736–741.

Hunt, R. C., Orsborn, M., Checkoway, H., Biggs, M. L., McFall, M., & Takaro, T. K. (2008). Later life disability status following incarceration as a prisoner of war. *Military Medicine, 173,* 613–618.

Johnson, G. E., & Asbjornsen, A. E. (2008). Consistent impaired verbal memory in PTSD: A meta-analysis. *Journal of Affective Disorders, 111,* 74–82.

Johnson, S., & Winebrenner, J. (1982). *Captive warriors.* College Station, TX: Texas A&M University Press.

Jones, D. R. (1980). What the repatriated prisoners of war wrote about themselves. *Aviation, Space, and Environmental Medicine, 51,* 615–617.

Kang, H. K., Bullman, T. A., & Taylor, J. W. (2006). Risk of selected cardiovascular diseases and posttraumatic stress disorder among former World War II prisoners of war. *Annals of Epidemiology, 16,* 381–386.

Kay, G. G. (1999). *CogScreen: Professional manual.* Washington, DC: CogScreen LLC.

Keane, T. M., Malloy, P. F., & Fairbank, J. A. (1984). Empirical development of an MMPI subscale for the assessment of combat-related posttraumatic stress disorder. *Journal of Consulting and Clinical Psychology, 52,* 888–891.

Keehn, R. J. (1980). Follow-up studies of World War II and Korean War prisoners: III. Mortality to January 1, 1976. *American Journal of Epidemiology, 111,* 194–211.

Klonoff, H., McDougall, G., Clark, C., Kramer, P., & Morgan, J. (1976). The neuropsychological, psychiatric, and physical effects of prolonged and severe stress: 30 years later. *Journal of Nervous and Mental Disorders, 163,* 246–252.

Kluznik, J. C., Speed, N., Van Valkenburg, C., & Magraw, R. (1986). Forty-year follow-up of United States prisoners of war. *American Journal of Psychiatry, 143,* 1443–1446.

Maier, T. (2006). Posttraumatic stress disorder revisited: Deconstructing the A-criterion. *Medical Hypotheses, 66,* 103–106.

Marmar, C. R., Weiss, D. S., & Metzler, T. J. (1997). The peritraumatic dissociative experiences questionnaire. In J. P. Wilson & T. M. Keane (Eds.), *Assessing psychological trauma and PTSD*. New York: Guilford.

McGrath, J. M. (1975). *Prisoner of war: Six years in Hanoi*. Annapolis, MD: Naval Institute Press.

McNally, R. J. (2006). Cognitive abnormalities in posttraumatic stress disorder. *Trends in Cognitive Sciences, 10*, 271–277.

Mock, F. L. (Director/Producer) & Sanders, T. (Director/Producer). (1998). *Return with honor* [Motion Picture]. Santa Monica, CA: American Film Foundation.

Molica, R. F., & Caspi-Yavin, Y. (1991). Measuring torture and torture-related symptoms. *Psychological Assessment, 3*, 581–587.

Moore, J. L. (1994, June). *The longitudinal neuropsychological evaluation of repatriated prisoners of war*. Paper presented at the Fourth Annual Navy Neuroscience Symposium, Portsmouth, VA.

Moore, J. L. (April, 1998). *Preliminary psychiatric and psychological findings in studies of Vietnam-era RPWs*. Paper presented at The Repatriated Prisoner of War Health Study: A Conference on the Long-term Effects of Captivity and Torture Among Vietnam-Era POWs. Washington, DC.

Moore, J. L., Ambrose, M. R., & Dolgin, D. L. (2002a, May). *Memory abilities among healthy older aviators*. Poster session presented at the Annual Meeting of the Aerospace Medical Association, Montreal, Canada.

Moore, J. L., Ambrose, M. R., & Dolgin, D. L. (2002b, October). *The evaluation of divided attention in older aviators using the CogScreen-AE*. Poster session presented at the Annual Meeting of the National Academy of Neuropsychology, Miami, FL.

Moore, J. L., Ellis, S. A., & Ambrose, M. R. (2001, December). *The relationship between peritraumatic dissociation and chronic PTSD symptoms among military aviators*. Poster session presented at the Annual Meeting of the International Society, for Traumatic Stress Studies, New Orleans, LA.

Moore, J. L., & Hain, R. E. (2004, May). *The evaluation of depression in older aviators*. Poster session presented at the Annual Meeting of the Aerospace Medical Association, Anchorage, AK.

Moore, J. L., Hawkins, M. M., Fiedler, E. R., & Ambrose, M. R. (2001, May). *The relationship between age and neurological status as predicted by the CogScreen-AE*. Poster session presented at the annual meeting of the Aerospace Medical Association, Reno, NV.

Moore, J. L., Larrabee, G. J., & Ambrose, M. R. (2000, November). *Peritraumatic dissociation, depression, memory ability and memory complaints among repatriated prisoners of war*. Poster session presented at the Annual Meeting of the National Academy of Neuropsychology, Orlando, FL.

Moore, J. L., & Porter, H. O. (2007, May). *A longitudinal evaluation of memory stability in neurologically healthy older aviators*. Poster session presented at the annual meeting of the Aerospace Medical Association, New Orleans, LA.

NamPows. (n.d.). *Three's in: The Vietnam POW home page*. http:/www.nampows.org.

Nefzger, M. D. (1970). Follow-up studies of World War II and Korean War prisoners: I. Study plan and mortality findings. *American Journal of Epidemiology, 91*, 123–138.

North, C. S., Suris, A. M., Davis, M., & Smith, R. P. (2009). Towar validation of the diagnosis of posttraumatic stress disorder. *American Journal of Psychiatry, 166*, 34–41.

Page, W. F., & Brass, L. M. (2001). Long-term disease and stroke mortality among former American prisoners of war of World War II and the Korean conflict: Results of a 50-year follow-up. *Military Medicine, 166,* 803–808.

Page, W. F., & Tanner, C. M. (2000). Parkinson's disease and motor-neuron disease in former prisoners-of-war. *Lancet, 355,* 843.

Pettyjohn, F. S. (1998). The return of Vietnam POWs—The aeromedical phase of Operation Homecoming 1973. *Aviation, Space, and Environmental Medicine, 69,* 1207–1210.

Philpott, T. (2001). *Glory denied: The saga of Jim Thompson, America's longest held prisoner of war.* New York: Norton.

Pitman, R. K., Gilbertson, M. W., Gurvitis, T. V., May, F. S., Lasko, N. B., Metzger, L. J., et al. (2006). Clarifying the origin of biological abnormalities in PTSD through the study of identical twins discordant for combat exposure. *Annals of the New York Academy of Sciences, 1071,* 242–254.

Port, C. L., Engdahl, B., & Frazier, P. (2001). A longitudinal and retrospective study of PTSD among older prisoners of war. *American Journal of Psychiatry, 158,* 1474–1479.

Porter, H. O., Moore, J. L., & Hain, R. E. (2005, May). *Symptoms of sleep disorders in older aviators.* Poster session presented at the annual meeting of the Aerospace Medical Association, Kansas City, MO.

Purcell, B., & Purcell, A. (2006). *Love & duty.* Clarksville, GA: Author.

Rayman, R. B. (1998). Operation Homecoming: 25 years later. *Aviation, Space, and Environmental Medicine, 69,* 1204–1206.

Reitan, R. M., & Davidson, L. A. (1974). *Clinical neuropsychology: Current status and applications.* New York: Winston/Wiley.

Rey, A. (1964). *L'examen clinique en psychologie.* Paris: Presses Universitaires de France.

Risner, R. (1973). *The pressing of the night: My seven years as a prisoner of the North Vietnamese.* New York: Random House.

Ritchie, E. C. (2002). Psychiatry in the Korean War: Perils, PIES, and the prisoners of war. *Military Medicine, 167,* 898–903.

Robson, D., Welch, E., Beeching, N. J., & Gill, G. V. (2009). Consequences of captivity: Health effects of Far East imprisonment during World War II. *Quarterly Journal of Medicine, 102,* 87–96.

Rochester, S. I., & Kiley, F. (1998). *Honor bound: American prisoners of war in Southeast Asia, 1961–1973.* Annapolis, MD: Naval Institute Press.

Schein, E. H., Hill, W. F., Williams, H. L., & Lubin, A. (1957). Distinguishing characteristics of collaborators and resisters among American prisoners of war. *Journal of Abnormal Psychology, 55,* 197–201.

Sipes, W., Moore, J. L., & Caldwell, L. (1991, October). *The Minnesota Multiphasic Personality Inventory (MMPI): Military pilot norms.* Paper presented at the 33rd Annual Conference of the Military Testing Association, San Antonio, TX.

Skelton, W. P., & Skelton, N. K. (1995). Environmental trauma in former prisoners of war. *Federal Practitioner, 12,* 42–47.

Sledge, W. H., Boydstun, J. A., & Rabe, A. J. (1980). Self-concept changes related to war captivity. *Archives of General Psychiatry, 37,* 430–443.

Sours, J. A., & Phillips, P. B. (1962). *Psychiatric aspects of aviation medicine.* Fifth European Conference for Psychosomatic Research, Madrid, Spain.

Spitzer, R. L., First, M. B., & Wakefield, J. C. (2007). Saving PTSD from itself in DSM-V. *Journal of Anxiety Disorders, 21*, 233–241.

Stockdale, J., & Stockdale, S. (1990). *In love and war.* Annapolis, MD: Naval Institute Press.

Sutker, P. B., & Allain, A. N. (1991). MMPI profiles of veterans of WWII and Korea: Comparisons of former POWs and combat survivors. *Psychological Reports, 68*, 279–284.

Sutker, P. B., & Allain, A. N. (1996). Assessment of PTSD and other mental disorders in World War II and Korean conflict POW survivors and combat veterans. *Psychological Assessment, 8*, 18–25.

Sutker, P. B., Allain, A. N., Johnson, J. L., & Butters, N. M. (1992). Memory and learning performance in POW survivors with a history of malnutrition and combat veteran controls. *Archives of Clinical Neuropsychology, 7*, 431–444.

Sutker, P. B., Allain, A. N., & Motsinger, P. A. (1988). Minnesota Multiphasic Personality Inventory (MMPI)–derived psychopathology subtypes among former prisoners of war (POWs): Replication and extension. *Journal of Psychopathology and Behavioral Assessment, 10*, 129–140.

Sutker, P. B., Bugg, F., & Allain, A. N. (1991). Psychometric prediction of PTSD among POW survivors. *Psychological Assessment, 3*, 105–110.

Sutker, P. B., Galina, Z. H., & West, J. A. (1990). Trauma-induced weight loss and cognitive deficits among former prisoners of war. *Journal of Consulting and Clinical Psychology, 58*, 323–328.

Sutker, P. B., Vasterling, J. J., Brailey, K., & Allain, A. N. (1995). Memory, attention, and executive deficits in POW survivors: Contributing biological and psychological factors. *Neuropsychology, 9*, 118–125.

Sutker, P. B., Winstead, D. K., & Galina, Z. H. (1990). Assessment of long-term psychosocial sequelae among POW survivors of the Korean conflict. *Journal of Personality Assessment, 54*, 170–180.

Uddo, M., Vasterling, J. J., Brailey, K., & Sutker, P. B. (1993). Memory and attention in combat-related posttraumatic stress disorder (PTSD). *Journal of Psychopathology and Behavioral Assessment, 15*, 43–52.

Ursano, R. J. (1981). The Viet Nam era prisoner of war: Precaptivity personality and the development of psychiatric illness. *American Journal of Psychiatry, 138*, 315–318.

Ursano, R. J., Boydstun, J. A., & Wheatley, R. D. (1981). Psychiatric illness in U.S. Air Force Viet Nam prisoners of war: A five-year follow-up. *American Journal of Psychiatry, 138*, 310–314.

Vasterling, J. J., Brailey, K., Constans, J. I., & Sutker, P. B. (1998). Attention and memory dysfunction in posttraumatic stress disorder. *Neuropsychology, 12*, 125–133.

Vasterling, J. J., Duke, L. M., Brailey, K., Constans, J. I., Allain, A. N., & Sutker, P. B. (2002). Attention, learning, and memory performance and intellectual resources in Vietnam veterans: PTSD and no disorder comparisons. *Neuropsychology, 16*, 5–14.

Weathers, F. W., & Keane, T. M. (2007). The criterian A problem revisited: Controversies and challenges in defining and measuring psychological trauma. *Journal of Traumatic Stress, 20*, 107–121.

Wechsler, D. (1955). *WAIS manual.* New York: The Psychological Corporation.

Wechsler, D. (1974). *Wechsler memory scale manual.* San Antonio, TX: The Psychological Corporation.

Wechsler, D. (1987). *Wechsler Memory scale—revised manual.* San Antonio, TX: The Psychological Corporation.

Weis, D. S., & Marmar, C. R. (1997). The impact of event scale—revised. In J. P. Wilson & T. M. Keane (Eds.), *Assessing psychological trauma and PTSD.* New York: Guilford.

Williams, D., Hilton, S. M., & Moore, J. L. (2002). Cognitive measures of Vietnam-era prisoners of war. *Journal of the American Medical Association, 288,* 574.

Wolfe, J., & Charney, D. S. (1991). Use of neuropsychological assessment in posttraumatic stress disorder. *Psychological Assessment, 3,* 573–580.

Yesavage, J. A., Brink, T. L., Rose, T. L., Lum, O., Huang, V., Adey, M. B., et al. (1983). Development and validation of a geriatric depression screening scale: A preliminary report. *Journal of Psychiatric Research, 17,* 37–49.

Zeiss, R. A., & Dickman, H. R. (1989). PTSD 40 years later: Incidence and person-situation correlates in former POWS. *Journal of Clinical Psychology, 45,* 80–87.

11

Cognitive Sequelae of Sustained Operations

NANCY J. WESENSTEN AND THOMAS J. BALKIN

Given the increase in deployments and operational requirements for service members, military psychologists must have a clear understanding of the effect of sleep loss on cognitive functioning. Sleep-deprived service members place themselves and others at risk for sleep-loss-induced errors and accidents. In addition, sleep-deprived members who present with symptoms of cognitive impairment may look severely impaired upon neuropsychological testing. Deployed military psychologists must be able to consult with commands regarding sleep issues and also be able to recognize decreased functioning as a result of sleep loss and differentiate it from other factors impacting operational readiness.

In this chapter, we describe the contribution of sleep to operational effectiveness. First, we review two case studies illustrating the devastating effects of sleep loss on mental operations; we then provide an overview of sleep loss effects on cognitive capacities relevant to current and foreseeable military operations. Last, we present an approach for managing sleep to sustain operational readiness.

Current operational realities involve round-the-clock, near-continuous operations with little or no opportunity for sleep. When sleep time is available, it may be out of phase with the usual sleep time (e.g., due to

This material has been reviewed by the Walter Reed Army Institute of Research, and there is no objection to its presentation and/or publication.

night operations, shift work), or the environmental conditions may not be conducive to sleep. Deployment to new time zones combines these factors: sleep lost as a result of travel and operations planning, poor sleep timing (due to time zone differences), and poor sleep environment (e.g., trying to sleep during troop transport). In short, lack of sleep is a reality for current and foreseeable military operations.

There is no question that falling asleep while on duty can lead to errors and accidents. Less well appreciated is that sleep loss degrades cognitive performance long before people become so sleepy that they fall asleep. Contrary to popular belief, high-optempo environments (the so-called adrenaline rush) do not insulate service members from the performance-impairing effects of sleep loss. Although results from laboratory studies indicate which aspects of cognitive processing (e.g., attention, vigilance) are impaired by sleep loss, it is from anecdotal evidence and case studies that the most deleterious effects of sleep loss in the operational environment become most apparent. These effects include impairments in cognitive executive functions (e.g., Hsieh, Cheng, & Tsai, 2007; Nilsson et al., 2005). These functions, originally described by Lezak (1983), include planning, anticipation, course-of-action determination, generation of novel strategies when current solutions fail or are ineffective, accurate assessment of threat (e.g., friend vs. foe), and appropriate risk taking. Below we describe two incidents in which it appears that sleep-loss-related decrements in one or more of these higher-order functions resulted in catastrophic outcomes.

CASE STUDIES: SLEEP LOSS EFFECTS ON COGNITIVE PERFORMANCE

Case Study 1: Attack on the 507th Maintenance Company

In the well-publicized March 23, 2003, attack on the 507th Maintenance Company (United States Army, 2003), the 507th had been traveling as part of a convoy heading northwest from its base camp to an objective in southeast Iraq in support of the 52nd Air Defense Artillery during Operation Desert Storm. This entailed movement along one route then switching to another route at a traffic control point (TCP) south of An Nasiriyah, then returning to the original route north of An Nasiriyah (Figure 11.1A). Figure 11.1B shows a timeline of events preceding the attack (shaded blocks indicate when the company reported obtaining sleep). The 507th arrived at the TCP at approximately 0100 hours on

March 23, where they were to switch to Route JACKSON to circumvent An Nasiriyah. At this point in time, they had been without adequate sleep for several days. What happened next was a series of missteps that ultimately led to the attack on the 507th.

In the first (and arguably most serious) misstep, the 507th continued along Route BLUE instead of switching over to Route JACKSON at the TCP (Figure 11.1C). In the next misstep, the 507th missed a left turn to stay on Route BLUE and continued north along Route 7/8 (Figure 11.1D, arrow 1). The company commander did not recognize this and continued north and on to Route 7/8. The convoy still had no reason to think they were off-route because armed Iraqi civilians along the route showed no hostile intent and actually waved at the convoy as it passed.

Finally, the commander realized that the convoy was off-route. He conferred with his first sergeant and decided that the best course of action was to route the convoy back along 7/8, through An Nasiriyah, to pick up Route BLUE again (Figure 11.1D, arrow 2).

After they had turned the convoy around and were heading back along route 16, they took some small-arms fire. In the next misstep, in the confusion of speeding up to get away from the small-arms fire, the commander (who was at the head of the convoy) missed the right turn at 7/8 to head back south (Figure 11.1D, arrow 3). The first sergeant radioed the commander to alert him that he had missed the right turn. In the process of turning around, the convoy disintegrated into small groups of independent vehicles, while still receiving fire (Figure 11.1D, arrow 4). En route back to Route BLUE various groups in the now fragmented convoy were ambushed (Figure 11.1D, arrow 5).

Of the 33 soldiers who entered An Nasiriyah in 18 vehicles on March 23, 2003, 11 Soldiers were killed, 7 Soldiers were captured, and 9 Soldiers were wounded. The executive summary of the event indicated that

> the 507th Maintenance Company was last in a march column of 600 vehicles. The company became isolated, as communications, already stretched to the limit, could not be extended to include them while they recovered heavy wheeled vehicles from soft sand and breakdowns along a cross-country route through the Iraqi desert. Over a period of 60–70 hours with little rest and limited communications, human error further contributed to the situation through a single navigation error that placed these troops in the presence of an adaptive enemy who used asymmetric tactics to exploit the Soldier's willingness to adhere to the Law of War.

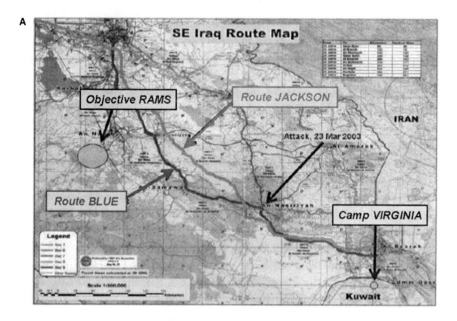

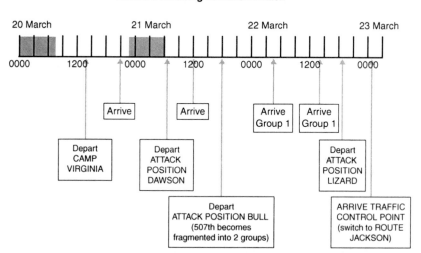

Figure 11.1 (A) 507th Maintenance Company convoy route from base camp to objective in southeast Iraq. Note planned switch from Route BLUE to Route JACKSON just south of An Nasiriyah. **(B)** Timeline of events preceding the attack; shaded blocks indicate when the company reported obtaining sleep. **(C)** Traffic control point at which the 507th was to switch from Route BLUE to Route JACKSON. **(D)** Series of incorrect routes (indicated by arrows 1–4) that ultimately resulted in the attack on the 507th occurring in the area marked by arrow 5.

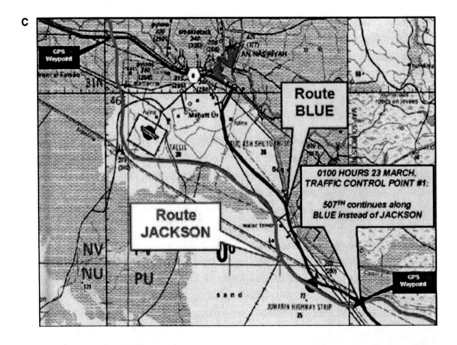

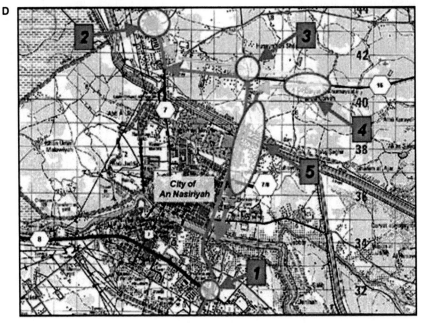

Figure 11.1 *Continued*

This example illustrates the deleterious effects of sleep loss on higher-order cognitive functions, in this case course-of-action determination and accurate assessment of threat.

Case Study 2: Crash of American International Airways Flight 808

The events leading to the crash of American International Airways (AIA) Flight 808 illustrate a case of sleep-loss-induced perseveration—in this case, the pilot's failure to realize his strategy was ineffective and consequent failure to change his course of action (National Transportation Safety Board, 1994). In the late afternoon of August 18, 1993, the crew of AIA Flight 808 were preparing to land at the U.S. Naval Air Station, Guantanamo Bay. Leeward Point Field could be approached two different ways: Runway 28 was a direct approach, whereas Runway 10 required a steep bank to avoid Cuban airspace. In the preceding 3 days, the crew had gotten little sleep due to their work schedules and had been continuously awake since the previous evening. For reasons that are unclear, the captain opted for the more difficult approach (implying impaired risk assessment), stating to the other crew members, "Otta make that one zero approach just for the heck of it to see how it is: why don't we do that…let's tell 'em we'll take [runway] one zero; if we miss we'll just come back around and land on two eight" (National Transportation Safety Board, 1994, p. 3) Approximately 10 minutes later (at 16:52:03), the air traffic controller transmitted, "Cuban airspace begins three quarters of a mile west of the runway" (referring to Runway 10). "You are required to remain…within the airspace designated by a strobe light." The first officer responded, "Roger, we'll look for the strobe light."

Table 11.1 is a transcript of the conversation among the crew as they approached the landing strip. The "strobe" to which the captain refers is the ground marker indicated by the air traffic controller, which marks where Cuban airspace starts. On that day, the strobe was not working. Even though the captain was clearly warned several times by the engineer that his airspeed was dangerously slow, he ignored the engineer and continued to look for the strobe rather than focus on keeping the aircraft aloft. The official report from the National Transportation Safety Board lists probable causes of the crash as

> the impaired judgment, decision-making, and flying abilities of the captain and flight crew due to the effects of fatigue; the captain's failure to properly assess the conditions for landing and maintaining vigilant situational awareness of the airplane while maneuvering onto final approach;

Table 11.1

COCKPIT VOICE RECORDER COMMUNICATIONS AMONG THE CAPTAIN, COPILOT, AND ENGINEER OF AIA FLIGHT 808 DURING THEIR APPROACH TO LEEWAY POINT FIELD, U.S. NAVAL AIR STATION, GUANTANAMO BAY

Engineer: Slow, airspeed.
Copilot: Check the turn.
Captain: Where's the strobe?
Copilot: Right over here.
Captain: Where?
Copilot: Right inside there, right inside there.
Engineer: You know, we're not gettin' our airspeed back there.
Captain: Where is the strobe?
Copilot: Right down there.
Captain: I still don't see it.
Engineer: #, we're never goin' to make this.
Captain: Where do you see a strobe light?
Copilot: Right over here.
Captain: Gear, gear down, spoilers armed.
Engineer: Gear down, three green spoilers, flaps, checklist.
???: There you go, right there, lookin' good.
Captain: Where's the strobe?
Copilot: Do you think you're gonna make this?
Captain: Yeah ... if I can catch the strobe light.
Copilot: 500, you're in good shape.
Engineer: Watch the, keep your airspeed up.
Copilot: 140. [sound of stall warning]
???: Don't—stall warning.
Captain: I got it.
Copilot: Stall warning.
Engineer: Stall warning
Captain: I got it, back off.
???: Max power!
???: There it goes, there it goes!
???: Oh no!

---

his failure to prevent the loss of airspeed and avoid a stall while in the steep bank turn; and his failure to execute immediate action to recover from a stall (National Transportation Safety Board, Executive Summary p. V).

SLEEP LOSS IMPAIRS EXECUTIVE FUNCTIONING

These two case studies are unfortunate examples of those aspects of cognitive functioning that are impaired by continuous operations (i.e., days or weeks with less than adequate amounts of sleep) or sustained operations (2–3 days of total sleep loss). In the case of AIA Flight 808, the impairment is easily identified from the cockpit data recorder conversation among the crew members: first, the captain's poor assessment of potential risk in choosing to attempt to land on Runway 10 rather than Runway 28; second, his subsequent perseveration in his failed attempts to locate the inoperable strobe and ignoring the engineer's warning that they were losing air speed.

In the case of the 507th, the cognitive impairment is not so readily identified, but it is exemplified in the commander's initial failure to ask the appropriate question (i.e., "Which way did the lead convoy go?" rather than "Is this Route BLUE?") coupled with the likely impaired condition of the TCP staff resulting from night shift work and their own "error of omission" in failing to point out to the Commander that the lead convoy had taken a different route.

Most of what we currently know about sleep loss effects comes from total sleep deprivation studies. Figure 11.2A illustrates the well-characterized decrement in response speed during a simple reaction time task (an effect that was initially described more than 100 years ago), particularly during the circadian nadir (approximately 0800–0900 hours in young, healthy adults who normally go to sleep at approximately midnight and awaken at approximately 0800). In addition, one's ability to maintain wakefulness under boring or nonstimulating conditions deteriorates (Figure 11.2B).

Over the past 20 years, interest has turned to the effects of sleep loss on executive functions. Those functions investigated to date and found to be impaired by as little as 24–36 hours of sleep loss include verbal fluency (Harrison & Horne, 1997), flexible or creative thinking (also referred to as "divergent" thinking; see Horne, 1988), the ability to update course-of-action determinations in light of new information or failed prior solutions (Harrison & Horne, 1999; Horne, 1998; Nelson, Dell'Angela, Jellish, Brown, & Skaredoff, 1995), planning (Horne, 1998; Wimmer, Hoffmann, Bonato, & Moffitt, 1992), prioritization, self-organization and self-monitoring (Nilsson et al., 2005), and the ability to detect errors and make corrections (Hsieh et al., 2007). Sleep loss also increases the time taken to make emotionally laden judgments (Killgore et al., 2007). Interestingly, although self-assessed risk-taking propensity decreases with sleep loss (Killgore et al., 2008), objectively measured risk taking (using gambling task paradigms) increases (e.g., Venkatraman, Chuah, Huettel, & Chee, 2007). A complete characterization of executive function deficits with

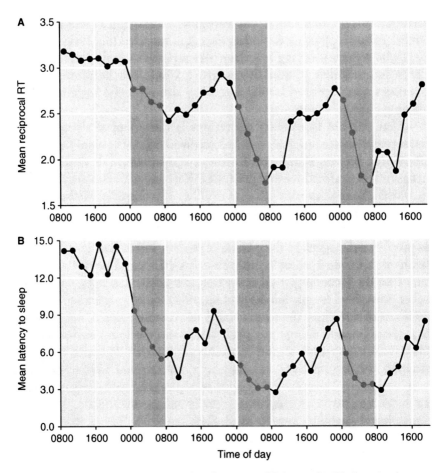

Figure 11.2 (A) Mean reciprocal reaction time across 87 hours of total sleep deprivation. Usual sleep periods are indicated by the darker-shaded bars. **(B)** From the same study, mean latency to sleep across the 87 hours without sleep. Shorter sleep latencies indicate a reduced ability to maintain wakefulness. (From Wesensten, Killgore, & Balkin [2005], with permission.)

sleep loss has been hampered in part by the fact that many tasks of executive functions are not repeatable, thus precluding establishment of non-sleep-deprived performance against which to compare effects of sleep loss across time awake. In addition, sleep-deprived individuals may not be aware of such deficits; however, complaints of difficulties concentrating or difficulties staying awake during meetings or other nonstimulating activities are symptoms of lack of adequate daily sleep. Consistent with these laboratory-based effects, results of the Army's fifth Mental

Health Advisory Team survey of warfighters serving in Operation Iraqi Freedom and Operation Enduring Freedom revealed that service members who reported having less sleep also reported a higher rate of accidents and mistakes (United States Army, 2008). Furthermore, service members who reported having less sleep also reported higher rates of abusing noncombatants.

Also relevant to military operations is the effect of sleep loss on team performance, an issue that has received little attention. One study (Banderet, Stokes, Francesconi, Kowal, & Naitoh, 1981, described in http://www.usafa.edu/isme/JSCOPE97/Belenky97/Belenky97.htm) involved a laboratory simulation of artillery fire direction center (FDC) team operations involving plotting target locations and deriving range, bearing, angle of gun elevation, and charge either for immediate fire or as preplanned targets. In the process of plotting target location, the FDC team must update its situation map and check the target on the map to be sure that the location plotted is not that of a hospital, school, church, or other proscribed target. Banderet et al. (1981) found that throughout the 36 hours of sleep loss, the team's ability to accurately derive range, bearing, elevation, and charge (relatively straightforward and well-practiced tasks) was unimpaired. However, after approximately 24 hours, the team stopped keeping up their situation map and stopped computing their preplanned targets immediately upon receipt. As a result, they no longer knew where they were relative to friendly and enemy units and thus no longer knew what they were firing at. Early in the simulation, when called upon for simulated fire on a hospital or other proscribed target, the team would check the situation map, appreciate the nature of the target, and refuse the request. After approximately 24 hours awake, without a current situation map, they would fire without hesitation regardless of the nature of the target. Early in the simulation, when called upon to engage in two concurrent fire missions and to fire on a preplanned target, the team would fire upon all three quickly and accurately, having already plotted and derived information for the preplanned target. Later in the simulation, when similarly called upon, the team—having neglected to plot and derive information for the preplanned target—would try to plot and derive information for three targets concurrently. In this effort they typically became disorganized and confused. The targets, if fired upon at all, were fired upon only after long delays. In a more recent study of team performance involving similar contingencies within a computer-based simulation of Naval shipboard surveillance and threat assessment (Baranski et al., 2007), it was reported that sleep loss impaired team decision-making accuracy and speed. However, these effects were less notable than the same decision-making metrics associated with individual performance, suggesting that being part of a team lessened the impact of sleep loss.

On average, 8 hours of sleep per 24 hours is required to sustain maximal operational readiness indefinitely. Humans can get by with less than 8 hours of sleep per 24 hours, but they will pay a performance penalty. Figure 11.3 shows results from a study we conducted to evaluate chronic sleep restriction effects (Belenky et al., 2003). Performance in a group that was allowed 9 hours time in bed (TIB) per night (obtaining approximately 8 hours of sleep) was sustained across the entire 7 days (Figure 11.3). However, decreasing TIB by only 2 hours, to 7 hours TIB per night, resulted in immediate performance decrements that became more pronounced across the 7 days. Likewise, the group allowed 5 hours TIB per night (who obtained approximately 4.5 hours of sleep) displayed immediate and substantial performance deficits that leveled off after approximately 4 days (but remained well below the performance of the 9-hour group). Finally, the group allowed only 3 hours TIB per night (obtaining approximately 3 hours of sleep) showed performance deficits

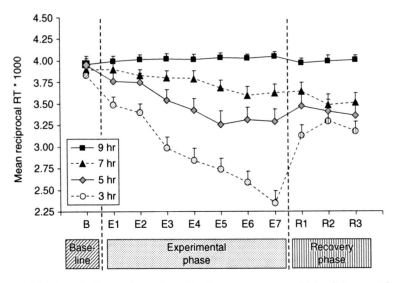

Figure 11.3 Mean daytime reciprocal reaction time across seven nights of sleep restricted to 3, 5, or 7 hours time in bed compared with 9 hours time in bed ("experimental phase"), followed by three nights of 8 hours time in bed ("recovery phase") for all groups. (Reprinted from Belenky et al., 2003, permission.)

that continued to mount across nights. In that group, performance was reduced by 70% of the levels maintained by the group allowed 9 hours TIB per night (Belenky et al., 2003). Furthermore, when the 3-, 5-, and 7-hour TIB groups were once again allowed 8 hours TIB (recovery phase), performance did not return to baseline levels even after three nights, indicating that chronic sleep restriction effects cannot be rapidly reversed.

Interestingly, Belenky et al. (2003) found that volunteers' self-rated sleepiness did not track objectively measured performance. In particular, for the 3-hour group, self-rated sleepiness did not continue to increase across days; rather, it peaked on the fifth day of sleep restriction but did not increase thereafter. Also, unlike performance, self-rated sleepiness returned to baseline levels after only one night of recovery sleep. These findings indicate that self-rated sleepiness is not a good substitute for objectively measured performance. The findings also suggest that sleep-restricted individuals are not good judges of their own performance capabilities.

In sum, sleep deprivation exerts two main effects. First, it increases time taken to respond, as well as susceptibility to falling asleep in a boring or nonstimulating environment (e.g., sentry duty). Second, even in a stimulating or high-optempo environment where the susceptibility to falling asleep is minimal, sleep loss directly impairs higher-order mental operations. Thus, sleep loss of any kind—whether acute total sleep loss or chronic partial sleep loss—impairs mental operations. However, whereas cognitive performance recovery from acute total sleep loss occurs after only one or two 8-hour recovery sleep periods, cognitive performance recovery from chronic restricted sleep appears to take days or even weeks (the exact recovery function is still unknown).

PHYSIOLOGIC BASIS OF SLEEP-LOSS-INDUCED COGNITIVE PERFORMANCE DEFICITS

The advent of neuroimaging techniques over the past 20 years has allowed for characterization of the neurophysiology underlying sleep-loss-induced cognitive performance deficits. Such techniques have revealed that sleep loss reduces brain metabolic activity, particularly in the prefrontal cortex, inferior parietal and superior temporal cortex, thalamus, and the anterior cingulate (Thomas et al., 2000), all of which are brain regions known to be involved in executive functioning (in fact, sleep loss can be thought of as causing a reversible functional lesion of prefrontal cortical areas; see Horne, 1988). Similarly, sleep (regardless of stage) restores waking metabolic activity to those regions deactivated by sleep loss (Braun et al., 1997).

The neurophysiologic basis of the delayed cognitive performance recovery process following chronic sleep restriction is unknown. However, one possibility outlined by the authors (Balkin, Rupp, Picchioni, & Wesensten, 2008) was suggested by recent animal work conducted by researchers at Harvard (McKenna et al., 2007). McKenna and colleagues showed that chronic sleep restriction (in the form of fragmented sleep) is associated with upregulation of AD_{A1} receptors (which in part may underlie reduced alertness during chronic sleep restriction). It may be that following reinstatement of adequate sleep amounts, return of AD_{A1} receptors to well-rested levels requires days or even weeks (Balkin et al., 2008). In contrast, acute total sleep deprivation does not result in upregulated AD_{A1} receptors, and thus its effects are rapidly reversed following a single recovery sleep period.

Furthermore, the known interindividual differences in vulnerability to sleep loss (which appear to be stable, trait-like characteristics; see Van Dongen, Baynard, Maislin, & Dinges, 2004) appear to have a genetic basis (Viola et al., 2007), which also is associated with preferred timing of sleep and morningness or eveningness preference (Archer, Viola, Kyriakopoulou, Von Schantz, & Dijk, 2008; Jones et al., 2007). In practical terms, a genetic (hard-wired) sleep need means that although some service members may be able to sustain cognitive readiness on less than optimal amounts of sleep, others by virtue of biology simply cannot. However, currently we cannot predict who is vulnerable and who is resilient to sleep loss. Therefore, a reasonable approach is to presume that (a) individuals need an average of 8 hours of sleep per day to sustain optimal operational readiness, and (b) those who obtain less than that are at increased risk of committing errors and causing accidents.

OPERATIONAL RELEVANCE OF SLEEP LOSS EFFECTS: NETWORK-CENTRIC WARFARE

The above case studies and laboratory results for sleep loss effects suggest that the individual service member, not technology, remains central to the success or failure of operational outcomes. On a broad scale, operational outcomes depend on speed of responding, that is, coming to the correct solution and acting before the enemy does (Col. John Boyd's notion of operating inside the enemy's decision loop; see http://www. d-n-i.net/dni/john-r-boyd/). In turn, rapidly coming to the correct solution depends on adaptability, foresight, anticipation, and course-of-action determination (i.e., executive functions).

Furthermore, the potential negative impact of sleep loss on operational readiness is likely to increase in the future rather than decrease as a direct function of the increasingly networked nature of military forces and the mental capabilities enabled (i.e., required) by this networking (Wesensten, Belenky, & Balkin, 2005). Stein (1998) outlined three capabilities enabled by a networked force:

1. Predictive planning and preemption: "ability to be proactive in the planning process...to be prepared to react and exploit opportunities...to shape expected actions to stay inside an enemy's decision cycle...to rehearse, evaluate, and adapt plans rapidly"
2. Integrated force management: "ability to achieve dynamic synchronization of missions and resources from components and coalitions; to synchronize distributed force operations"
3. Execution of time-critical missions: "ability to enable rapid target search and acquisition, battle coordination and target selection, handoff, and engagement of time-critical targets; acquire targets and execute timely response."

These capabilities are in essence executive functions, such as situational awareness, adaptability, mental agility, judgment, initiative, anticipation, and planning. One could speculate that networking will magnify the effects of stressors such as sleep loss on warfighter operational readiness, not minimize them as intended.

MANAGING SLEEP TO SUSTAIN OPERATIONAL READINESS

The idea of obtaining adequate sleep to sustain operational readiness is not new, and specific tactics for achieving this (e.g., appropriate sleep timing and sleep environment) have been described (Comperatore, Caldwell, & Caldwell, 1997). However, missing from previous sleep management guidelines is an overarching strategy. We (Belenky et al., 1996; Wesensten et al., 2005) proposed a strategy in which sleep is treated as an item of logistic resupply and measured and managed in the same way that food, fuel, and ammunition are managed. Three capabilities are critical to such a strategy: (a) the ability to measure sleep/wake under operational conditions, (b) a means to quantify (i.e., predict) the effects of the measured sleep/wake on operational outcomes, and (c) tools to improve the likelihood of successful operational outcomes. These capabilities are described next.

Measuring Sleep/Wake Under Operational Conditions

Treating sleep as an item of logistic resupply requires a means for quantifying it. The gold standard for recording and quantifying sleep amounts is polysomnography (PSG), which involves recording brain electrical activity, eye movements, and muscle tone using sensors applied to the skin and then visually scoring these recordings on the basis of accepted criteria. PSG-based quantification of sleep and wakefulness is neither logistically practicable nor cost effective in large numbers of individuals and over weeks or months.

Prior to PSG development, actigraphy was developed to measure and quantify sleep objectively on the basis of body movements (Szymansky, 1922). Interest in wrist-mounted actigraphy resurged in the 1970s and 1980s, fueled in part by technological advances that for the first time made it possible to measure and record actigraph signals over long periods (days, weeks, or even months). The primary issue then became the extent to which actigraph measures of sleep/wake correlated with PSG-based measurements. Results from validation studies using different actigraph scoring algorithms, subjects from various age ranges, varying sample sizes, and subjects with various sleep- and movement-related disorders indicate that wrist actigraphy is a valid and objective measure of sleep/wake state (Sadeh, Sharkey, & Carskadon, 1994). Although there are some differences among algorithms used to quantify sleep/wake from actigraphy, virtually all current actigraph scoring algorithms provide rates of agreement with standard PSG comparable to agreement rates between two experienced scorers visually scoring PSG on the basis of standard criteria (agreement rates ranging from approximately 85% to 93%). Figure 11.4 shows the basic schematic for actigraphy: The actigraph's accelerometer records wrist movements along three axes. Movement counts per time epoch (in this schematic, 1-min epochs) are calculated. Movement counts are then passed through an algorithm that assigns a score of "sleep" or "wake" to each epoch.

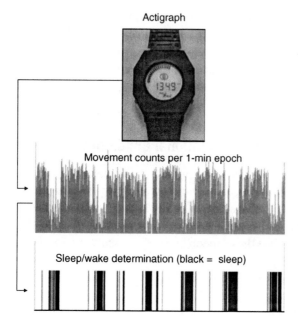

Actigraph

Movement counts per 1-min epoch

Sleep/wake determination (black = sleep)

Figure 11.4 Schematic showing an actigraph, movement counts per minute, and sleep/wake determinations. Note that in general, periods of higher movement activity are scored as wake whereas periods of low activity are scored as sleep.

Both our laboratory and others have demonstrated the feasibility of actigraphically recording sleep/wake amounts in the field under simulated as well as actual operational conditions. In one study, sleep was actigraphically assessed during the 58 days of U.S. Army Ranger School (Pleban, Valentine, Penetar, Redmond, & Belenky, 1990), involving simulated light infantry operations against a superior force. Ranger candidates averaged 3.2 hours of sleep each night over the 58 days of the school (Pleban et al., 1990). In a second study of two classes, Ranger candidates averaged 3.6 hours each night. Sleep was not accrued in a single sleep period but rather occurred as several naps over each 24 hours. Anecdotally (and consistent with executive function deficits noted earlier), mental performance in Ranger candidates is marginal, with frequent episodes of what the Rangers call "droning" (i.e., putting one foot in front of another and responding if challenged, but having difficulty grasping the situation or acting on one's own initiative).

Predicting Sleep/Wake Effects on Operational Outcomes

Most individuals inherently understand the value of sleep for sustaining operational readiness; we recognize that total sleep deprivation or brief, fragmented sleep exacts a substantial toll on operational readiness.

However, in order to manage sleep effectively, one must be able to predict or estimate objectively the impact of actual sleep obtained on cognitive performance and manage operational planning on the basis of these predictions—that is, a "miles per gallon" performance equivalent for sleep. Without this capability, estimating potential operational outcomes becomes a guessing game based on individual biases.

Whereas other groups have attempted to model sleep propensity, sleepiness, or other factors not directly related to operational outcomes, we developed a model that predicts cognitive performance quantified as speed of responding on a vigilance task (a measure shown to be sensitive to even small reductions in nightly sleep amounts; see Balkin et al., 2004). This model (the Walter Reed Army Institute of Research (WRAIR) Sleep Performance Model [SPM], most recently embodied as the Department of Defense Sleep, Activity, Fatigue and Task Effectiveness [SAFTE] model) predicts cognitive performance on the basis of those measurable factors known to account for the largest sources of variance in cognitive performance: (a) sleep/wake history and (b) time of day. Other factors may also contribute to variability in cognitive performance (e.g., environmental light, activity levels, environmental temperature; see Moore-Ede & Mitchell, 1995); however, such factors are not easily quantified, and the cost of quantifying them outweighs the gains in prediction accuracy. Figure 11.5 illustrates the separate contributions of sleep/wake history (Panel A) and time of day (Panel B) and their mathematically combined contributions (Panel C) to predicted cognitive performance. Predicted cognitive performance can be viewed as a reservoir. The sleep/wake function increases the cognitive performance reservoir during any time identified as sleep and depletes the cognitive performance reservoir during any time identified as wake. The time of day function modulates the sleep/wake prediction on circadian principles: It increases predicted cognitive performance from 0400 to 2000 hours and decreases predicted cognitive performance from 2000 to 0400 hours. The mathematical combination of these two processes results in the prediction seen in Figure 11.5C. A complete mathematical description of the sleep performance model can be found in Balkin et al. (2004) and related patents.

The performance prediction model can be used prospectively or retrospectively. Retrospectively, we used the model to estimate cognitive readiness in the 507th Maintenance Company on the basis of reports of sleep provided in the incident report. Our analyses revealed that when the convoy reached the TCP at 0100 hours, their estimated cognitive performance was only approximately 40% of well-rested levels. We also

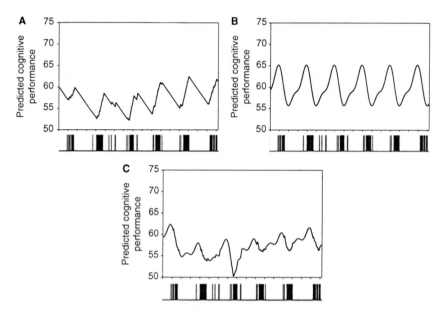

Figure 11.5 (A) Sleep performance model sleep/wake function. **(B)** Sleep performance model time of day or circadian function. **(C)** Mathematically combined sleep/wake and time of day functions resulting in predicted cognitive performance. Below all three panels is the actigraphically derived sleep/wake history (identical for all three panels) upon which the prediction is based.

used the model to estimate retrospectively cognitive readiness in the crew involved in the crash of AIA Flight 808. Those analyses revealed that at the time of the crash predicted cognitive readiness of the captain, copilot, and engineer was 71%, 70%, and 77%, respectively. In terms of simple response time, this means that if the captain could normally come to the correct decision within 300 msec, he would now take more than 400 msec to respond. In operational terms, 100+ msec could be the difference between firing first and being fired upon.

In terms of prospective applications, the Air National Guard Aviation Safety Division (National Guard Bureau/Safety Flight Division) has developed a user-friendly applet called Flyawake (www.flyawake.org) that overlays the SPM/SAFTE model. The Flyawake tool can be used to assess the risk of degraded cognitive performance (fatigue) associated with different flight schedules. Once points in the schedule associated with degraded cognitive performance have been identified, strategies (discussed below) can be applied to mitigate risk.

It is important to point out that like all other models, the WRAIR SPM/SAFTE model was developed to predict group averaged data rather than individual data. In fact, due to the large individual variability in response to sleep/wake amounts, none of the models accurately predicts individual cognitive readiness. As we learn more about the factors (including those noted above) that contribute to individual variability in cognitive readiness, we can adapt our models to take these factors into consideration. In the meantime, performance prediction models are a good first step in predicting, on average, how an individual will respond to a given sleep/wake history and thus serve as planning and risk management tools.

Tools to Improve the Likelihood of Successful Operational Outcomes

The third component of an effective sleep management strategy involves tools to improve the likelihood of successful operational outcomes. These generally fall into one of two categories: (a) tools for improving cognitive readiness when operators must go without sleep, and (b) tools for improving sleep under operational conditions.

Tools for Improving Cognitive Readiness During Sleep Loss

Both pharmacologic and nonpharmacologic tools for sustaining cognitive readiness during sleep loss have been examined. Nonpharmacologic strategies such as brief bouts of exercise or environmental stimuli (e.g., cold air, loud noise) are at best effective for only several minutes (Reyner & Horne, 1998). Furthermore, there is no evidence that dietary constituents (other than caffeine, discussed below) are effective.

In contrast, pharmacologic agents have been shown to sustain cognitive performance during short-term sleep loss (Bonnet et al., 2005). Lead pharmacologic agents include caffeine (which is available over the counter and in a variety of formulations such as beverages, food, and gum) and prescription-only agents such as dextroamphetamine and modafinil. These three compounds have been demonstrated to be safe and efficacious when used appropriately. However, none of these agents is a substitute for sleep; they merely allow the user to postpone sleep temporarily when necessary. Also, it is unlikely that prescription agents would gain widespread use among ground troops, and their use by aviators is governed by policy that requires the aviator to first use the compound under nonflight conditions ("ground trial") and is documented in the aviator's medical record (similar restrictions apply to the use of sleep-inducing agents or "no-go pills"). Under most circumstances, however, caffeine would be the stimulant of choice (and availability) for sustaining cognitive performance during sleep loss. Although it appears that at appropriate dosages all three compounds are equally efficacious for restoring simple response time and alertness (e.g., Wesensten, Killgore, Balkin, 2005), the goal of current and future work will be to determine the extent to which these (and other) stimulants differentially restore various aspects of executive functioning.

Tools for Improving Sleep Under Operational Conditions

A starting point for improving sleep under operational conditions involves the following commonsense (but often ignored) nonpharmacologic interventions: (a) protecting service members' sleep time by avoiding nonessential interruptions (e.g., the "hurry up and wait" phenomenon), scheduling meals and nonessential duties around the sleep period (Comperatore et al., 1997); (b) protecting service members' sleep environment by reducing noise and light (which includes providing separate sleeping quarters for operators working different shifts) and ensuring proper ambient temperature; and (c) proper sleep scheduling to include allowing sufficient sleep time (at least 8 hours per 24, even if this requires dividing available sleep time into two or more periods). However, such nonpharmacologic interventions may be insufficient for producing adequate-duration sleep (e.g., in night shift workers attempting to sleep during the daytime). Under these circumstances, prescription sleep-inducing agents can be used. It is critical that if prescription agents are used, sufficient downtime is allowed, because prescription sleep inducers impair learning and memory, often causing complete anterograde amnesia (Wesensten, Balkin, & Belenky, 1995; in contrast, retrograde memory remains intact). These amnestic effects last until the sleep inducer has cleared from the body. Thus, more downtime will be required after longer-acting agents (e.g., temazepam) than after shorter-acting agents (e.g., zaleplon).

CONCLUSIONS AND FUTURE DIRECTIONS

Warfighters of today and the future face increasing cognitive demands and decreased human redundancy on the battlefield. The effect of these realities is a magnification of sleep-loss-induced decrements in operational readiness, leading to increased risk of errors, accidents, and friendly fire incidents. Sleep is a commodity that must be effectively managed, similar to other items of resupply.

The objective (cognitive) and subjective effects of sleep loss overlap with effects associated with a broad range of other factors (including mental health disorders and brain injury). However, because the "cure" may differ depending on the cause, it is critical for clinicians to distinguish among causal factors. Querying service members about how much sleep they have obtained in the prior weeks or months takes little time but may provide the clinician with insight into the source of a particular symptom or complaint.

Current and future research needs include addressing the following: (a) the extent to which sleep sustains other, more subtle aspects of cognition (e.g., effective interpersonal interactions, moral decision making, ability to accurately detect and appropriately respond to others' emotions); (b) the extent to which sleep protects against combat-stress-related psychiatric disorders; (c) the extent to which pharmacologic countermeasures reverse sleep-loss-induced decrements in the various executive functions; (d) the identification of factors accounting for individual differences in vulnerability to sleep loss; and (e) characterizing the time course of recovery from chronic sleep restriction effects.

REFERENCES

Archer, S. N., Viola, A. U., Kyriakopoulou, V., Von Schantz, M., & Dijk, D. J. (2008). Inter-individual differences in habitual sleep timing and entrained phase of endogenous circadian rhythms of BMAL1, PER2 and PER3 mRNA in human leukocytes. *Sleep, 31*(5), 608–617.

Balkin, T. J., Belenky, G. L., Hall, S. W., Kamimori, G. H., Redmond, D. P., Sing, H. C., et al. (2004). *Method and system for predicting human cognitive performance. U.S. Patent No. 6,740,032.* Washington, DC: U.S. Patent and Trademark Office.

Balkin, T. J., Rupp, T., Picchioni, D., & Wesensten, N. J. (2008). Sleep loss and sleepiness: Current issues. *Chest, 134,* 653–660.

Banderet, L. E., Stokes, J. W., Francesconi, R., Kowal, D. M., & Naitoh, P. (1981). Artillery teams in simulated sustained combat: Performance and other measures. In L. C. Johnson, D. I. Tepas, W. P. Colquhon, & M. J. Colligan (Eds.), *The twenty-four hour workday: Proceedings of a symposium on variations in work-sleep schedules* (DHHS Publication No. 81-127, pp. 581-604). Washington, DC: U.S. Government Printing Office.

Baranski, J. V., Thompson, M. M., Lichacz, F. M. J., McCann, C., Gil, V., Pasto, L., et al. (2007). Effects of sleep loss on team decision making: Motivational loss or motivational gain? *Human Factors, 49*(4), 646–660.

Belenky, G., Balkin, T. J., Redmond, D. P., Sing, H. C., Thomas, M. L., Thorne, D. R., et al. (1996, June). *Sustaining performance during continuous operations: The U.S. Army's Sleep Management System. Proceedings of the 20th Army Science Conference,* Norfolk, VA.

Belenky, G., Wesensten, N. J., Thorne, D. R., Thomas, M. L., Sing, H. C., Redmond, D. P., et al. (2003). Patterns of performance degradation and restoration during sleep restriction and subsequent recovery: A sleep dose-response study. *Journal of Sleep Research, 12,* 1–12.

Bonnet, M. H., Balkin, T. J., Dinges, D. F., Roehrs, T., Rogers, N. L., & Wesensten, N. J. (2005). The use of stimulants to modify performance during sleep loss [A review by the Sleep Deprivation and Stimulant Task Force of the American Academy of Sleep Medicine]. *Sleep, 28,* 1163–1187.

Braun, A. R., Balkin, T. J., Wesensten, N. J., Carson, R. E., Varga, M., Baldwin, P., et al. (1997). Regional cerebral blood flow throughout the sleep-wake cycle. An H2(15)O PET study. *Brain, 120,* 1173–1197.

Comperatore, C., Caldwell, J. A., & Caldwell, J. L. (1997). *Leader's guide to crew endurance.* Fort Rucker, AL: United States Army Aeromedical Research Laboratory and the United States Army Safety Center.

Harrison, Y., & Horne, J. A. (1997). Sleep deprivation affects speech. *Sleep, 20*(10), 871–877.

Harrison, Y., & Horne, J. A. (1999). One night of sleep loss impairs innovative thinking and flexible decision making. *Organizational Behavior and Human Decision Processes, 78*(2), 128–145.

Horne, J. A. (1988). Sleep loss and "divergent" thinking ability. *Sleep, 11*(6), 528–536.

Hsieh, S., Cheng, I. C., & Tsai, L. L. (2007). Immediate error correction process following sleep deprivation. *Journal of Sleep Research, 16*(2), 137–147.

Jones, K. H. S., Ellis, J., Von Schantz, M., Skene, D. J., Dijk, D. J., & Archer, S. N. (2007). Age-related change in the association between a polymorphism in the PER3 gene and preferred timing of sleep and waking activities. *Journal of Sleep Research, 16,* 12–16.

Killgore, W. D., Grugle, N. L., Killgore, D. B., Leavitt, B. P., Watlington, G. I., McNair, S., et al. (2008). Restoration of risk-propensity during sleep deprivation: Caffeine, dextroamphetamine, and modafinil. *Aviation, Space, and Environmental Medicine, 79*(9), 867–874.

Killgore, W. D., Killgore, D. B., Day, L. M., Li, C., Kamimori, G. H., & Balkin, T. J. (2007). The effects of 53 hours of sleep deprivation on moral judgment. *Sleep, 30*(3), 345–352.

Lezak, M. D. (1983). *Neuropsychological assessment* (2nd ed.). New York: Oxford University Press.

McKenna, J. T., Tartar, J. L., Ward, C. P., Thakkar, M. M., Cordeira, J. W., McCarley, R. W., et al. (2007). Sleep fragmentation elevates behavioral, electrographic and neurochemical measures of sleepiness. *Neuroscience, 146,* 1462–1473.

Moore-Ede, M. C., & Mitchell, R. E. (1995). *Method for predicting alertness and bio-compatibility of work schedule of an individual. U.S. Patent No. 5,433,223.* Washington, DC: U.S. Patent and Trademark Office.

National Transportation Safety Board. (1994). Aircraft Accident Report: Uncontrolled Collision with Terrain, American International Airways Flight 808. Report Number AAR-94–04.

Nelson, C. S., Dell'Angela, K., Jellish, W. S., Brown, I. E., & Skaredoff, M. (1995). Residents' performance before and after night call as evaluated by an indicator of creative thought. *Journal of the American Osteopathic Association, 95*(10), 600–603.

Nilsson, J. P., Söderström, M., Karlsson, A. U., Lekander, M., Akerstedt, T., Lindroth, N. E., et al. (2005). Less effective executive functioning after one night's sleep deprivation. *Journal of Sleep Research, 14,* 1–6.

Pleban, R. J., Valentine, P. J., Penetar, D. M., Redmond, D. P., & Belenky, G. (1990). Characterization of sleep and body composition changes during ranger training. *Military Psychology, 2,* 145–156.

Reyner, L. A., & Horne, J. A. (1998). Evaluation of "in-car" countermeasures to driver sleepiness: Cold air and radio. *Sleep, 21*(1), 46–50.

Sadeh, A., Sharkey, K. M., & Carskadon, M. A. (1994). Activity-based sleep-wake identification: An empirical test of methodological issues. *Sleep, 17*(3), 201–207.

Stein, F. P. (1998). *Observations on the emergence of network centric warfare.* Retrieved from http://www.dodccrp.org/files/stein_observations/steinncw.htm

Szymansky, J. S. (1922). Aktivitaet und ruhe bei den menschen. *Zeitschrift fur angewandte Psychologie, 20,* 192–222.

Thomas, M., Sing, H., Belenky, G., Holcomb, H., Mayberg, H., Dannals, R., et al. (2000). Neural basis of alertness and cognitive performance impairments during sleepiness. I. Effects of 24 h of sleep deprivation on waking human regional brain activity. *Journal of Sleep Research, 9,* 335–352.

United States Army. (2003). *Attack on the 507th Maintenance Company, 23 March 2003, An Nasiriyah, Iraq.* Retrieved from http://www.army.mil/features/507thMaintCmpy/AttackOnThe507MaintCmpy.doc

United States Army. (2008). Mental Health Advisory Team V information. Retrieved from http://www.armymedicine.army.mil/reports/mhat/mhat_v/mhat-v.cfm

Van Dongen, H. P., Baynard, M. D., Maislin, G., & Dinges, D. F. (2004). Systematic interindividual differences in neurobehavioral impairment from sleep loss: Evidence of trait-like differential vulnerability. *Sleep, 27,* 423–433.

Venkatraman, V., Chuah, Y. M. L., Huettel, S. A., & Chee, M. W. L. (2007). Sleep deprivation elevates expectation of gains and attenuates response to losses following risky decisions. *Sleep, 30,* 603–609.

Viola, A. U., Archer, S. N., James, L. M., Groeger, J. A., Lo, J. C., Skene, D. J., et al. (2007). PER3 polymorphism predicts sleep structure and waking performance. *Current Biology, 17,* 613–618.

Wesensten, N. J., Balkin, T., & Belenky, G. (1995). Effects of daytime administration of zolpidem versus triazolam on memory. *European Journal of Clinical Pharmacology, 48,* 115–122.

Wesensten, N. J., Belenky, G., & Balkin, T. (2005). Cognitive readiness in network-centric operations. *Parameters, 35,* 94–105.

Wesensten, N. J., Killgore, W. D. S., & Balkin, T. J. (2005). Performance and alertness effects of caffeine, dextroamphetamine, and modafinil during sleep deprivation. *Journal of Sleep Research, 14,* 255–266.

Wimmer, F., Hoffmann, R. F., Bonato, R. A., & Moffitt, A. R. (1992). The effects of sleep deprivation on divergent thinking and attention processes. *Journal of Sleep Research, 1*(4), 223–230.

12 Neuropsychological Correlates of PTSD: A Military Perspective

JENNIFER J. VASTERLING, HELEN Z. MacDONALD,
ERIN W. ULLOA, AND NICOLE RODIER

Military duties often encompass exposure to life threat and other forms of extreme psychological stress. As such, posttraumatic stress disorder (PTSD) is of high relevance to military health care. The past two decades have brought significant advances in understanding PTSD from neurobiological and cognitive neuroscience perspectives. This chapter focuses on the neuropsychological correlates of PTSD. We begin by providing an overview of PTSD, including its epidemiology in military populations, its course, and its potential impact on day-to-day functioning. We next review the neuropsychological correlates of PTSD, including an overview of the neuroanatomical framework, a description of the neuropsychological findings, and a discussion of the clinical implications of neuropsychological evaluations involving military personnel with known or suspected PTSD. We conclude the chapter by summarizing evidence-based treatments for PTSD and their potential relevance to neuropsychology.

PTSD: AN OVERVIEW

Diagnostic Criteria

PTSD is unique among psychiatric disorders in that the diagnosis cannot be made without exposure to an environmental event (i.e., the trauma event). The text revision of the fourth edition of the *Diagnostic and Statistical Manual of Mental Disorders* (DSM-IV-TR; American Psychiatric Association, 2000) defines a traumatic event as one in which a person "experienced, witnessed, or was confronted with an event or events that involved actual or threatened death or serious injury, or a threat to the physical integrity of self or others" (criterion A1) and had a subjective response that involved "intense fear, helplessness, or horror" in adults or "disorganized or agitated behavior" in children (criterion A2). *DSM-IV-TR* groups symptoms into three criterion clusters: (a) reexperiencing of the traumatic event (e.g., intrusive thoughts, physiological and emotional responsivity to trauma reminders); (b) avoidance of external reminders or thoughts associated with the trauma and numbing of emotional responsiveness (e.g., inability to have loving feelings); and (c) hyperarousal (e.g., concentration impairment, hypervigilance to threat, irritability). Factor analytic studies, however, suggest that a 4-factor solution in which avoidance symptoms are separated from numbing and other symptoms may be more appropriate (King, Leskin, King, & Weathers, 1998; Simms, Watson, & Doebbeling, 2002). Finally, *DSM-IV-TR* requires that symptoms endure for at least 1 month and cause clinically significant distress or functional impairment.

Epidemiology

Epidemiological research indicates that over 50% of adults have experienced at least one psychologically traumatic event in the course of their lives (Kessler, Sonnega, Bromet, Hughes, & Nelson, 1995a). The minority of people who experience trauma, however, develop PTSD. The lifetime prevalence of PTSD in the general U.S. population is approximately 5% for men and 10% for women (Kessler et al., 1995a). Rates of PTSD are much higher in populations at increased risk for traumatization, including combat-exposed populations (e.g., Dohrenwend et al., 2006; Hoge & Castro, 2006; Hoge et al., 2004; Kulka et al., 1990). Population-based studies estimate that 14% of Operation Iraqi Freedom (OIF)/Operation Enduring Freedom (OEF) veterans currently experience PTSD (Tanielian & Jaycox, 2008), and almost 19% of Vietnam veterans have met criteria for PTSD during the course of their postwar lives (Dohrenwend et al., 2006).

Among deployment-related variables examined in military samples as potential mental health risk and protective factors, combat has figured prominently, showing a strong relationship to post-warzone PTSD and other mental health problems in military veterans (Fontana & Rosenheck, 1994; Foy, Siprelle, Rueger, & Carroll, 1984; Helzer, Robins, & McEvoy, 1987; Hoge, Auchterlonie, & Milliken, 2006; Kessler et al., 1995a; Kulka et al., 1990; Mellman, Randolph, Brawman-Mintzer, & Flores, 1992; Smith et al., 2008). Both the severity of trauma exposure and type of war-zone role are associated with PTSD in combat veterans (Hoge et al., 2004; Hotopf et al., 2006; Magruder et al., 2004; Sutker, Uddo, Brailey, Vasterling, & Errera, 1994), as is proximity to the enemy while deployed (Iversen et al., 2008). Other deployment-related risk factors include perceived threat to life in theater (Iversen et al., 2008; King, King, Foy, Keane, & Fairbank, 1999), a malevolent warzone environment (King, King, Gudanowski, & Vreven, 1995), poor preparation, low morale, perceived disinterest by supervisors, nonreceipt of a psychoeducational brief upon homecoming (Iversen et al., 2008), and physical injury (e.g., Grieger et al., 2006; Hoge et al., 2004; Koren, Norman, Cohen, Berman, & Klein, 2005). Of relevance to neuropsychological functioning, traumatic brain injury (TBI) may also exacerbate adverse mental health outcomes, including PTSD, following warzone exposure (e.g., Chemtob et al., 1998; Hoge et al., 2008; Vasterling, Constans, & Hanna-Pladdy, 2000b). Conversely, high levels of social support (Benotsch et al., 2000; Dikel, Engdahl, & Eberly, 2005; Green, Grace, Lindy, & Gleser, 1990a; Green & Berlin, 1987; King, King, Fairbank, Keane, & Adams, 1998; Neria, Solomon, & Dekel, 1998; Solomon, 1990; Solomon, Mikulincer, & Avitzur, 1988; Solomon, Waysman, Avitzur, & Enoch, 1991; Sutker, Vasterling, Brailey, & Allain, 1995) and unit cohesion (Brailey, Vasterling, Proctor, Constans, & Friedman, 2007; Eid & Johnsen, 2002; McTeague, McNally, & Litz, 2004), a multidimensional construct reflecting unit support and satisfaction with fellow soldiers and unit leaders, appear to buffer the adverse consequences of trauma exposure in military service members and veterans.

A more limited body of research has identified pretrauma vulnerability and protective factors impacting PTSD development. Premilitary factors associated with poorer PTSD outcomes in military samples include younger age (e.g., Magruder et al., 2004; Riddle et al., 2007; Turner, Turse, & Dohrenwend, 2007), previous trauma exposure (e.g., Riddle et al., 2007), childhood adversity (Cabrera, Hoge, Bliese, Castro, & Messer, 2007; Iversen et al., 2008), and lower rank (Ikin et al., 2007; Iversen et al., 2008). Of relevance to neuropsychological functioning, higher premilitary intellectual functioning and greater educational attainment appear to confer modest protective effects against PTSD in military samples (Iversen et al., 2008; Macklin et al., 1998; Riddle et al., 2007), especially at lower levels of combat exposure (Thompson & Gottesman, 2008).

The observed relationships of gender and ethnic minority status to PTSD are likely indirect. Although female gender has been associated with increased risk of PTSD in some studies using military samples (e.g., Riddle et al., 2007; Turner et al., 2007), there is also evidence that the effects of deployment on psychological symptoms do not differ among men and women (Rona, Fear, Hull, & Wessely, 2007). Military sexual trauma, however, estimated as occurring in 23–33% of servicewomen (Sadler, Booth, Neilson, & Doebbeling, 2000; Skinner et al., 2000; Suris, Lind, Kashner, Borman, & Petty, 2004), is associated with greater PTSD symptom severity and risk of developing PTSD (Kang & Hyams, 2005; Surís et al., 2004; Wolfe et al., 1998). Military veterans identified as ethnic minorities also report more PTSD symptoms than nonminority veterans (Green et al., 1990a; Koenen, Moffitt, Caspi, Taylor, & Purcell, 2003; Koenen, Stellman, Stellman, & Sommer, 2003; Kulka et al., 1990; Laufer, Gallops, & Frey-Wouters, 1984; Penk, Robinowitz, Black, & Dolan, 1989). The causes of these differences are not fully understood, though some research suggests that other factors, including ethnic minorities' greater trauma exposure, may be partially responsible (Dohrenwend, Turner, Turse, Lewis-Fernandez, & Yager, 2008; Green, Grace, Lindy, & Leonard, 1990b).

Course

Most commonly, PTSD symptoms develop immediately following trauma exposure (Flouri, 2005; Shalev, 2001). Whereas some individuals' PTSD symptoms remit within a few months of trauma exposure (Breslau, 2001), other people suffer a chronic course of PTSD lasting their entire lives (Yule, 2001). Orcutt, Erickson, and Wolfe (2004) found that Gulf War veterans demonstrated two distinct trajectories; (a) lower levels of PTSD symptoms over time with little change in symptom severity or (b) higher levels of PTSD symptoms initially with an increase in symptoms over time. More recently, in a population-wide screening of OIF-deployed soldiers, Milliken, Auchterlonie, and Hoge (2007) found that soldiers as a group reported higher levels of PTSD at the 6-month follow-up assessment compared with the initial assessment, but that 49–59% of those soldiers who reported PTSD symptoms at the initial assessment demonstrated reduced symptom severity at the follow-up assessment. For some individuals, symptoms may be cyclical, ebbing, and flowing depending on the time of year, other life circumstances, and subsequent trauma exposures. It is common, for example, for patients to report increased symptoms surrounding the anniversary of a particular war zone trauma (Morgan, Hill, Fox, Kingham, & Southwick, 1999; Morgan, Kingham, Nicolaou, & Southwick, 1998).

More often than not, PTSD occurs with other emotional and behavioral symptoms (e.g., see Brady, Killeen, Brewerton, & Lucerini, 2000, for a review), as well as decreased quality of life. The National Comorbidity Survey reported that 88% of men and 79% of women with a lifetime diagnosis of PTSD met criteria for at least one other psychiatric diagnosis (Kessler, Sonnega, Bromet, Hughes, & Nelson, 1995b). The most common disorders co-occurring with PTSD are substance use disorders, depression, and non-PTSD anxiety disorders (Brady et al., 2000). PTSD has likewise been shown to have a deleterious effect on military service members' and veterans' social, occupational, and physical health functioning (Beckham, Crawford, & Feldman, 1998; Boscarino, 1997; Buckley, Mozley, Bedard, Dewulf, & Greif, 2004; Engel, Liu, McCarthy, Miller, & Ursano, 2000; Hoge, Terhakopian, Castro, Messer, & Engel, 2007; Hoge et al., 2005; Kessler, 2000; Magruder et al., 2004; Schnurr, Spiro, & Paris, 2000; Vasterling et al., 2008; Zatzick et al., 1997). For example, Zatzick et al. (1997) found that PTSD among Vietnam veterans was associated with a wide range of functional impairments, including decreased well-being, poorer physical health, increased physical limitations, and increased perpetration of violence. More recently, Hoge et al. (2007) found that OIF veterans with PTSD reported lower ratings of general health, more sick call visits, more missed workdays, more physical symptoms, and high somatic symptom severity. Finally, there is extensive literature demonstrating associations between PTSD symptoms and multiple physical health problems, including respiratory and nervous system disorders (e.g., Boscarino, 1997), arterial, gastrointestinal, dermatologic, musculoskeletal disorders (e.g., Schnurr et al., 2000), and myocardial infarction and coronary heart disease (e.g., Kubzansky, Koenen, Spiro, Vokonas, & Sparrow, 2007).

NEUROPSYCHOLOGICAL CORRELATES OF PTSD

In this section, we begin with a brief overview of contemporary neuroanatomical conceptualizations of PTSD and follow with a discussion of the research findings of clinical neuropsychological test performance in individuals with PTSD. Although a comprehensive review is beyond the scope of this chapter, a robust body of literature has documented associations between PTSD and abnormalities in processing emotionally meaningful information. In sum, individuals with PTSD demonstrate attentional and interpretive "biases" toward threat-relevant stimuli (for a review of the literature, see Constans, 2005), likely at the expense of attention to emotionally neutral information. Likewise, we refer the reader to more comprehensive discussions of PTSD and autobiographical memory, including trauma memory (Verfaellie & Vasterling, 2009) and electrophysiological indices of PTSD-related information-processing abnormalities (Karl, Malta, & Maercker, 2006a; Metzger, Gilbertson, & Orr, 2005).

Neural Underpinnings of PTSD

When confronted with life threat, such as that encountered in military combat, the body responds with a state of physiological arousal, including acute increases in stress-related neurotransmitters and neuropeptides, such as corticotrophin releasing factor, norepinephrine, serotonin, dopamine, endogenous benzodiazepines, and endogenous opiates (Bremner, Southwick, & Charney, 1999b). These responses serve an immediate adaptive function by facilitating actions that promote survival (i.e., "flight or fight" responses). However, once perpetuated, the responses become maladaptive, playing an important role in the pathogenesis and maintenance of PTSD (Charney, Deutch, Krystal, Southwick, & Davis, 1993; Yehuda & McFarlane, 1995). The impact of chronic neurobiological dysregulation may be particularly relevant to current military deployment practices, in which service members deploy repeatedly, sometimes with relatively short periods of time between deployments, allowing biological systems little time to return to baseline.

Even when true threats are not repeated, as in the context of multiple deployments, cognitive processes may serve to perpetuate neurobiological stress responses. Specifically, anxiety is thought to influence the appraisal of environmental cues as threatening, resulting in exaggerated neurobiological and psychological responsiveness to cues that are often now harmless (Keane & Barlow, 2002). Thus, whether via repeated exposure to life threat or via cognitive appraisals of neutral cues as threatening, the central nervous system can become increasingly overresponsive and hence associated with increased neural dysregulation (i.e., "stress sensitization"; Southwick et al., 2007; Yehuda & McFarlane, 1995). In turn, this sensitization can lead to overresponsiveness to subsequent stress and fear cues. Over time, the cumulative biological strain produced by repeated stress responses, known as "allostatic load" (McEwen, 2000), can accelerate pathophysiology, including neuroimmune suppression and possibly neuronal damage. The chronic dysregulation of the noradrenergic system, hypothalamic-pituitary-adrenal (HPA) axis, and serotonergic system, in particular, are thought to result in dampened prefrontal and hippocampal functioning and reduced medial prefrontal inhibition of the amygdala, a limbic structure central to fear-based emotion (Southwick, Rasmusson, Barron, & Arnsten, 2005), and are therefore of particular relevance to the neuropsychology of PTSD.

The neuroimaging literature provides evidence that brain structure and function are indeed somewhat atypical in PTSD. Structural imaging studies have indicated that, as compared to control groups, PTSD diagnosis is associated with smaller hippocampal volume (e.g., Bremner et al., 1997, 2003a; Gurvits et al., 1996; Karl et al., 2006b; Kitayama, Vaccarino, Kutner, Weiss, & Bremner, 2005; Stein, Koverola, Hanna, Torchia, & McClarty, 1997), smaller left amygdala and anterior cingulate volumes (Karl, Malta, & Maercker, 2006a), smaller volumes of the frontal cortex (Carrion et al., 2001; De Bellis et al., 2002; Fennema-Notestine, Stein, Kennedy, Archibald, & Jernigan, 2002), including medial prefrontal cortex structures (Kasai et al., 2008; Rauch et al., 2003; Woodward et al., 2006; Yamasue et al., 2003), and smaller cortical thickness in much of the frontal gyri (Geuze et al., 2008). However, smaller amygdala (Bonne et al., 2001; Bremner et al., 1997; Carrion et al., 2001; De Bellis et al., 1999a; Gurvits et al., 1996) and hippocampal volumes (c.f., Schuff et al., 2001) have not been uniformly revealed, especially when samples with more recent trauma exposure were examined (c.f., Bonne et al., 2001; Carrion et al., 2001; De Bellis et al., 1999b). Moreover, hippocampal volume in PTSD patients is not necessarily associated with neurocognitive performances (Lindauer, Olff, van Meijel, Carlier, & Gersons, 2006). Finally, twin research has further suggested that reduced hippocampal volume may reflect vulnerability for, rather than a consequence of, PTSD (Gilbertson et al., 2002).

Functional neuroimaging studies of PTSD typically have demonstrated that individuals with PTSD, relative to comparison samples, show heightened amygdala responsivity and deactivation or decreased activation of the hippocampal, anterior cingulate, and orbital frontal cortex in response to symptom provocation (e.g., Bremner et al., 1999a, 1999c; Driessen et al., 2004; Lanius et al., 2001; Liberzon, Britton, & Phan,

2003; Liberzon et al., 1999; Rauch et al., 1996; Shin et al., 2004). A similar pattern has surfaced in studies using cognitive activation paradigms such as encoding and retrieval of threat-relevant stimuli (Bremner et al., 2003b; Dickie, Brunet, Akerib, & Armony, 2008; Rauch et al., 2000; Shin et al., 2001, 2005b), although activation of the anterior cingulate has also been observed under certain conditions in highly symptomatic patients (Pannu-Hays, LaBar, Petty, McCarthy, & Morey, 2009). In individuals with PTSD, relationships between activation in the amygdala and medial prefrontal cortex in response to threat-relevant stimuli further suggest a coordinated functional relationship between the amygdala and medial prefrontal cortex in PTSD (Gilboa et al., 2004; Shin et al., 2004, 2005b).

Multiple reviews of the vast neurobiological (e.g., Bonne, Grillon, Vythilingam, Neumeister, & Charney, 2004; Bremner et al., 1999b; Charney, Deutch, Southwick, & Krystal, 1995; Rasmusson, Vythilingam, & Morgan, 2003; Southwick et al., 2005; Yehuda, 2002) and neuroimaging (e.g., Francati, Vermetten, & Bremner, 2007; Grossman, Buchsbaum, & Yehuda, 2002; Karl et al., 2006a, 2006b; Rauch, Shin, & Phelps, 2006; Shin, Rauch, & Pitman, 2005a) literatures relevant to PTSD are available. Although beyond the scope of this chapter, there is also significant evidence of electrophysiological abnormalities in PTSD suggestive of neural processing abnormalities to both neutral and trauma-relevant stimuli (Metzger, Gilbertson, & Orr, 2005). In sum, therefore, multiple methodologies provide converging evidence of biological, physiological, and neuroanatomical abnormalities associated with PTSD that would be expected to be associated with neuropsychological impairment.

Description of Clinical Neuropsychological Findings

We organize our review by domains commonly assessed in clinical neuropsychological evaluations: intellectual functioning, attention, memory, language, visuospatial, and motor functioning. Much of the literature is based on military samples, but to allow full understanding of the nature of neuropsychological functioning in PTSD, we include also studies examining civilian samples. Other reviews are available (Danckwerts & Leathem, 2003; Horner & Hamner, 2002; MacDonald, Vasterling, & Rasmusson, in press; Vasterling & Brailey, 2005). Table 12.1 presents a summary of the most commonly used neuropsychological tasks in the empirical PTSD literature.

Intellectual Functioning

PTSD is associated with lower estimated and omnibus IQ scores when compared against trauma-exposed and nonexposed comparison groups

Table 12.1

COMMON CLINICAL NEUROPSYCHOLOGY MEASURES USED IN RESEARCH
STUDIES OF NEUROPSYCHOLOGICAL FUNCTIONING IN ADULT PTSD

Attention/executive function
Wisconsin card sorting test
Trail-making test (parts A and B)
Stroop color and word test
Paced auditory serial addition test
Continuous performance test
Digit span

Memory
Wechsler memory scales (partial or complete)
Rey-Osterrieth complex figure test

IQ
Wechsler intelligence scales (partial or complete)

without PTSD in civilian (Brandes et al., 2002; Gil, Calev, Greenberg, & Kugelmass, 1990; Gurvits et al., 2000) and military (Gilbertson, Gurvits, Lasko, Orr, & Pitman, 2001; Gurvits, Lasko, & Schachter, 1993; Hart et al., 2008; Macklin et al., 1998; Vasterling, Brailey, Constans, Borges, & Sutker, 1997; Vasterling et al., 2002) samples. Similarly, correlational studies indicate an inverse relationship between PTSD and intellectual performance (e.g., McNally & Shin, 1995). This pattern held in a study of Vietnam War veterans, even after controlling for the severity of combat exposure (Macklin et al., 1998). Studies of civilian (Gil et al., 1990) and military (Vasterling et al., 1997) samples that distinguished verbal and visual-spatial intellectual performances have additionally found that PTSD may be more strongly associated with relative weaknesses in verbal than in visual-spatial functioning.

Based on cross-sectional findings using tasks that estimate premorbid IQ, some researchers have hypothesized that higher intellectual functioning protects against the development of PTSD following trauma exposure (Hart et al., 2008; McNally, Lasko, Macklin, & Pitman, 1995; Vasterling et al., 2002). Gilbertson and colleagues (2006) used twin methodology to support this hypothesis and found that intellectual performance did not differ between warzone–exposed and nonexposed identical twin brothers. Instead, intellectual performance was less proficient among both brothers of twin pairs in which the exposed twin developed PTSD, as compared with twin pairs in which the exposed twin did not develop PTSD. This contention is also supported by studies using archival Army aptitude test scores obtained prior to warzone deployment (Gale et al., 2008; Macklin et al., 1998; Thompson & Gottesman, 2008).

The relationship between premorbid IQ and PTSD, however, may be complex. A study of Vietnam combat veterans using archival data revealed that pretrauma intellectual performance was protective against PTSD development only at lower levels of combat exposure. At higher levels of trauma exposure, precombat intellectual performance did not afford protection against PTSD (Thompson & Gottesman, 2008). Thus, cognitive resources may help military personnel exposed to lower levels of combat trauma adapt and recover from exposure to stress; however, when combat stress exceeds a certain threshold, cognitive resources alone are insufficient in buffering against the adverse emotional consequences of the exposure.

Attention and Executive Dysfunction

Executive functioning can be understood as the capacity to exert appropriate attentional control to participate in purposeful action and goal-directed behavior (c.f., Baddeley, 2002; Lezak, 1995). As such, attention and executive functioning may be of particular significance in military settings, in which decision making, planning, the ability to flexibly adjust to changing environmental demands, and vigilance may play a substantial role in saving lives. Because the two domains are integrally linked, they are reviewed together.

Despite the inclusion of concentration impairment as a diagnostic criterion, neuropsychological research suggests that PTSD is not associated with a general concentration deficit but, rather, with a specific pattern of attentional and executive deficits. In particular, PTSD has been linked to working memory decrements in both civilians (e.g., Brandes et al., 2002) and military veterans (e.g., Beckham et al., 1998; Gilbertson et al., 2001; Vasterling et al., 1997) and, to a lesser extent (c.f., Golier et al., 1997), to sustained attention abnormalities in both civilians (e.g., Jenkins, Langlais, Delis, & Cohen, 2000; McFarlane, Weber, & Clark, 1993; Veltmeyer et al., 2005) and military veterans (e.g., Vasterling, Brailey, Constans, & Sutker, 1998; Vasterling et al., 2002). Conversely, shift of attention and cognitive set (as measured by card sorting and visual selective attention tasks) and ability to focus attention (as measured by letter cancellation and the standard Stroop task) are rarely impaired in PTSD samples (e.g., Barrett, Green, Morris, Giles, & Croft, 1996; Gurvits et al., 1993; Jenkins et al., 2000; Leskin & White, 2007; Twamley, Hami, & Stein, 2004; Vasterling et al., 1998, 2002; Vasterling, Brailey, & Sutker, 2000a; Veltmeyer et al., 2005). It may be, however, that aging processes interact with PTSD, as demonstrated by PTSD-related deficits on card sorting tasks documented in elderly repatriated prisoners of war (Sutker et al., 1995).

From a neuroanatomical perspective, PTSD is understood to involve dysfunction of the prefrontal cortex, especially as relates to its inhibitory functions. Much of the literature documenting associations between PTSD and prefrontal disinhibition has been demonstrated in military veteran samples (Gilbertson et al., 2006; Kimble, Ruddy, Deldin, & Kaufman, 2004; Koso & Hansen, 2006; Samuelson, Neylan, & Metzler, 2006; Shucard, McCabe, & Szymanski, 2008; Vasterling et al., 1998). For example, Vasterling and colleagues (1998) reported a pattern of cognitive disinhibition and commission errors across attention and memory tasks in a sample of Persian Gulf War veterans. Similar findings have been revealed by studies using civilian and mixed military/civilian PTSD samples, which have documented cognitive disinhibition (Koenen et al., 2001; Leskin & White, 2007).

Two studies have also revealed findings consistent with prefrontal dysfunction in veterans using a sensory task in which participants were required to identify different odors on an olfactory discrimination task. Specifically, olfactory identification ability has been shown to be sensitive to orbitofrontal integrity (Savic, Bookheimer, Fried, & Engel, 1997). Both of these studies documented relative olfactory identification performance deficits in war veterans with PTSD when compared against combat-exposed and nonexposed veterans without PTSD (Dileo, Brewer, Hopwood, Anderson, & Creamer, 2008; Vasterling et al., 2000b), lending further support to neuroanatomical conceptualizations of PTSD that emphasize dysfunction within ventromedial structures.

Learning and Memory

Anterograde memory refers to new learning and consolidation of newly learned information into long-term memory. In the PTSD literature, anterograde memory has been the most frequently examined neuropsychological domain. Although some studies have failed to reveal a relationship between PTSD and anterograde memory functioning (e.g., Neylan et al., 2004; Pederson, Maurer, & Kaminski, 2004; Zalewski,

Thompson, & Gottesman, 1994), the majority of studies have found that individuals with PTSD demonstrate poorer performance on tasks of memory or learning when compared with those without PTSD. These findings span both civilian (e.g., Brandes et al., 2002; Bremner et al., 1995a; Bustamante, Mellman, David, & Fins, 2001; Gil et al., 1990; Golier et al., 2002; Jenkins, Langlais, Delis, & Cohen, 1998; Johnsen & Asbjornsen, 2008; Parslow & Jorm, 2007) and military veteran (e.g., Bremner et al., 1993; Burriss, Ayers, Ginsberg, & Powell, 2008; Gilbertson et al., 2001; Gurvits et al., 1993; Sachinvala et al., 2000; Samuelson et al., 2006; Vasterling et al., 1998, 2002; Yehuda et al., 1995) samples.

When conceptualized as a series of processes, anterograde memory can be broken down into several stages. In evaluating individual studies within the PTSD literature, the initial acquisition stage appears particularly vulnerable. In groups of military veterans with PTSD, there is also evidence of heightened sensitivity to proactive (i.e., previously learned information interferes with new learning) (Uddo, Vasterling, Brailey, & Sutker, 1993) and retroactive (i.e., new information interferes with recall of previously learned information) (Vasterling et al., 1998, 2002; Yehuda et al., 1995) interference. It is less clear, however, whether PTSD is associated with degraded retention of newly learned information over longer delay intervals. Whereas PTSD has been associated with less proficient memory retention in some studies (e.g., Bremner et al., 1995b), other studies, including several examining military veterans, have failed to reveal PTSD-related impairment of memory retention (e.g., Brandes et al., 2002; Gilbertson et al., 2001; Jelinek, Jacobsen, & Kellner, 2006; Stein, Hanna, Vaerum, & Koverola, 1999; Stein, Kennedy, & Twamley, 2002b; Vasterling et al., 1998, 2000a, 2002; Yehuda et al., 2005).

Two recent independent meta-analyses have attempted to address inconsistencies across studies examining the relationship between memory functioning and PTSD. One study focused on anterograde memory broadly, including verbal and visual memory, as well as immediate and delayed recall memory performance (Brewin, Kleiner, Vasterling, & Field, 2007), whereas the other study specifically examined the relation between immediate verbal memory and PTSD (Johnsen & Asbjornsen, 2008). Both studies found that PTSD was associated with less proficient memory performance. Brewin et al. (2007) found small to moderate magnitude memory decrements in individuals with PTSD across trauma type, with verbal memory, as compared with visual memory, more strongly associated with PTSD. These findings could not be attributed to head injury and did not differ significantly according to immediate versus delayed recall conditions. Johnsen and Asbjornsen (2008) similarly reported a moderate effect size for PTSD diagnostic status and immediate verbal memory but found that the effect was larger when specific memory instruments (Wechsler Memory Scale subtests and the Rey Auditory Verbal Learning Task, as compared with the California Verbal Learning Test) were used. In contrast to the study of Brewin et al., Johnsen and Asborjernsen also found a larger effect in military as compared with interpersonal trauma samples, such that the greatest verbal memory impairment was found in the war combat trauma groups (d = 0.82; large effect size). It could be speculated that larger effect sizes in military samples reflects the often repetitive, prolonged, and multi-faceted nature of combat trauma exposure. The diverse and repeated nature of the stressors to which many military personnel are exposed, in combination with often challenging environments, may result in more severe, chronic cases of PTSD and, relatedly, more serious memory impairments. Finally, recent longitudinal work has raised the question that at least some aspects of baseline memory abilities may predict PTSD outcomes subsequent to trauma exposure (Marx et. al., 2009).

Other Neuropsychological Functions

There is limited research examining basic language, visuospatial, and motor functioning in individuals with PTSD. Generally, the existing research in this area has failed to demonstrate PTSD-related deficits, except on those tasks with a dominant executive functioning component, such as complex figural copying (Barrett et al., 1996; Gurvits et al., 2000, 2002; Stein et al., 2002a), word list generation (e.g., Bustamante et al., 2001; Uddo et al., 1993), and motor sequencing (e.g., Gurvits et al., 1993, 2000). Experimental tasks have also revealed select visuospatial deficits associated with PTSD, including deficits processing distal contextual information (Gilbertson et al., 2007) and local, as opposed to global, stimulus attributes (Vasterling, Duke, Tomlin, Lowery, & Kaplan, 2004).

In a prospective study of Army soldiers, Vasterling and colleagues (2006) found that, in addition to decrements in attention and memory, OIF deployment was associated with enhanced reaction efficiency on a motoric reaction time task. Although the study did not specifically target PTSD, the authors speculated that faster, more efficient psychomotor responses might reflect an adaptation to a life-threatening context (i.e., warzone deployment) that comes at the expense of other cognitive resources. Although requiring replication, preliminary findings suggest that combat-related changes in response time are maintained over time but do not necessarily serve as a marker for PTSD (Marx et al., 2009).

Summary

Taken together, the existing body of literature indicates that individuals with PTSD demonstrate subtle, yet specific, cognitive deficits associated with tasks relying on attentional and executive functions (e.g., working memory and inhibition) as well as verbal memory functions. There is still much to be learned about the underlying relationship and directionality between neurocognitive dysfunction and PTSD.

Implications for Neuropsychological Evaluations

There are several applications for neuropsychological evaluations in active military and military veteran contexts involving PTSD as a component of the clinical presentation. These applications include, but are not limited to, ruling out alternative etiologies of neuropsychological impairment (e.g., TBI, neurotoxicant exposure), evaluating cognitive readiness to return to work or engage in vocational rehabilitation, and assisting in treatment planning. Clinical neuropsychologists are also occasionally referred cases in which the diagnosis of PTSD is still preliminary. In this section, we discuss issues salient to the neuropsychological evaluation of military patients with PTSD and highlight factors to be considered during clinical neuropsychological assessments.

Neurobehavioral Test Selection

The deficits associated with PTSD are generally subtle (Brewin et al., 2007; Johnsen & Asbjornsen, 2008), and thus decrements may be difficult to interpret at the individual level. However, documentation of the patient's strengths and weaknesses, whatever their magnitude, can help inform the development of treatment plans and the formulation of recommendations for the future, in addition to serving as a starting point from which to chart any subsequent changes in neuropsychological functioning. In this context, it is particularly important to select measures that are sufficiently sensitive and challenging.

In addition to selecting tasks that are appropriately challenging, the neuropsychological evaluation of military patients with suspected or confirmed PTSD diagnoses benefits from a broad assessment of multiple cognitive domains. Although deficits are typically circumscribed to attention, executive functioning, learning, and memory, the assessment of multiple neuropsychological domains can provide both confirmatory and disconfirmatory evidence of suspected etiologies. This approach is particularly useful in detecting alternative, non-PTSD–related etiologies requiring clinical attention.

Finally, a comprehensive neuropsychological evaluation typically benefits from assessment of effort to verify the validity of test findings and assess for suboptimal performance. There is no empirical foundation upon which to suggest that cognitive effort is more likely to be compromised in military populations. Nonetheless, given that mental health disorders may involve compensation claims and decisions regarding duty assignment, some patients may intentionally inflate PTSD or neurocognitive symptoms (chapter 4). For those military personnel with more severe emotional or psychological disturbances, mental health symptoms may also make it difficult to extend maximal effort on tests of cognitive functioning. Although cognitive effort tests may provide clinical information regarding the validity of the neuropsychological evaluation, there are two important caveats to consider in their interpretation. First, cognitive effort tests address the validity of neuropsychological measures, but, to date, there is no empirical basis that links performance on cognitive effort tests to the validity of PTSD symptom report. Second, these measures do not address why the patient's performance is suboptimal. There is a range of intentional (e.g., malingering) and nonintentional factors (e.g., severe sleep deprivation, transient somatic illnesses, acute distress) that could influence effort.

Differential Diagnosis: PTSD and TBI

An area of particular importance to the military population is the symptom overlap and comorbidity between PTSD and TBI (see Vasterling, Verfaellie, & Sullivan, 2009, for a review). Dubbed by some as the "signature injury" of OIF/OEF (Okie, 2005; Warden, 2006), TBI shares certain characteristics with PTSD in regard to neuropsychological deficits (Chen, Johnston, Petrides, & Ptito, 2008; Drake, Gray, Yoder, Pramuka, & Llewellyn, 2000; Kennedy et al., 2007; King, Hough, Vos, Walker, & Givens, 2006; Malojcic, Mubrin, Coric, Susnic, & Spilich, 2008; Milders, Fuchs, & Crawford, 2003; Moore, Terryberry-Spohr, & Hope, 2006; Raskin & Rearick, 1996; Ryan & Warden, 2003; Vanderploeg, Curtiss, Luis, & Salazar, 2007; Yang, Tu, Hua, & Huang, 2007), associated somatic symptoms (Fear et al., 2008; Hoge et al., 2008), and underlying neural abnormalities (Bigler, Young, Kane, & Nicholson, 2006; Wilde et al., 2007). The commonalities between some forms of PTSD and TBI can pose a unique challenge for clinicians in differentiating between the two disorders in terms of their relative contributions to particular neuropsychological deficits (Gaylord et al., 2008).

The relationship between TBI and PTSD is further complicated in that TBI may exacerbate PTSD and depression symptoms in trauma survivors (Chemtob et al., 1998; Mollica, Henderson, & Tor, 2002; Vanderploeg, Belanger, & Curtiss, 2009; Vasterling et al., 2000b). Military personnel with PTSD may also be more likely to engage in risk-taking behaviors that would put them at increased risk for sustaining a TBI. For example, upon returning home from deployments in support of OIF/OEF, some service members develop substance use disorders, which in turn increase the likelihood of driving while intoxicated or engaging in physical altercations, activities that increase the risk of head injury (Wolfe & Charney, 1991). In these cases, it is important to establish the temporal relationship between PTSD and TBI (i.e., understanding when the TBI[s] occurred in relation to the onset of PTSD), the relative severity of each disorder, as well as the degree to which there may be other complicating factors (e.g., headaches, comorbid substance abuse disorders) that influence current cognitive status and the course and prognosis of neuropsychological deficits.

Other Clinical Complications

As discussed in an earlier section, patients with PTSD often present with at least one other comorbid psychiatric or somatic condition. Complicating the primary diagnosis, overlap in symptom criteria (e.g., concentration difficulties) between PTSD and other psychiatric (e.g., depression) and somatic (e.g., postconcussion syndrome) disorders often creates diagnostic ambiguities. Comorbid conditions have the potential to impact the individual's neurocognitive functioning both directly and indirectly. For example, an individual with PTSD and comorbid depression may be more likely to attempt suicide or engage in serious self-harming behaviors (Oquendo et al., 2003), which could in turn result in long-standing neuropsychological deficits. In addition, psychopharmacological treatments for PTSD, depression, and other occurring disorders may impact neurocognitive functioning (Bremner & Yehuda, 2006; Constant et al., 2005; Davis, Frazier, Williford, & Newell, 2006; Siepmann, Grossmann, Muck-Weymann, & Kirch, 2003; Wadsworth, Moss, Simpson, & Smith, 2005). Finally, pre-existing neurodevelopmental disorders (e.g., learning disorders, residual attention deficit/hyperactivity disorder) and certain comorbid conditions, including drug and alcohol use disorders, mood disorders, TBI, and sleep disturbances, may influence neuropsychological performance directly (Austin et al., 1999; Himanen et al., 2006; Leroi, Sheppard, & Lyketsos, 2002; Meewisse et al., 2005; Ravnkilde et al., 2003).

In complicated clinical presentations, it can be challenging to distill the specific effects of PTSD on an individual's neurocognitive functioning. As a result, it is important that clinical neuropsychological evaluations of PTSD include the assessment of comorbid conditions (e.g., depression), health-risk behaviors (e.g., suicide attempts, excessive alcohol consumption), and contextual factors (e.g., concurrent pharmacological treatment, sleep deprivation) that potentially complicate interpretation of the assessment data. We recommend that the clinician examine the relative onset of PTSD and other comorbid disorders, behaviors, and contextual factors with relation to potential neurocognitive dysfunction. A thorough history of symptom course and presentation will assist in drawing conclusions and providing recommendations regarding etiology, treatment, and prognosis for PTSD and related neurocognitive impairment.

TREATMENT OF PTSD

Empirically supported interventions for treatment of PTSD fall into two primary categories: psychopharmacological approaches and psychotherapy. Both can be understood within neuropsychological frameworks. Below, we provide an overview of the most common PTSD treatments, integrating the neuropsychological implications of both. We conclude with a brief summary of early intervention and preventive strategies.

Psychopharmacological Approaches

As understanding of the specific psychobiological alterations associated with PTSD has grown, increased attention has been given to pharmacologic agents that may be effective in treatment of this disorder, including selective serotonin reuptake inhibitors (SSRIs), other antidepressants (e.g., tricyclics, monoamine oxidase inhibitors), antipsychotic medications, anticonvulsants, and alpha adrenergic blockers (Davis et al., 2006; Friedman, 2000; Thompson, Taylor, McFall, Barnes, & Raskind, 2008). Currently, however, the only pharmacological agents approved by the U.S. Food and Drug Administration for PTSD treatment are the SSRIs sertraline and paroxetine (Friedman & Davidson, 2007). Use of SSRIs has also been endorsed by the Departments of Veterans Affairs and

Defense (VA/DoD, 2004), the American Psychiatric Association (2006), and the International Society of Traumatic Stress Studies (Friedman, Davidson, Mellman, & Southwick, 2004); however, the Institute of Medicine cited inadequate evidence to support the efficacy of SSRIs or any other class of drugs in the treatment of PTSD (Committee on Treatment of Posttraumatic Stress Disorder, 2008).

Evidence for use of SSRIs for the treatment of PTSD is largely based on the role of serotonin in the human stress response and its direct effects on functioning of the adrenergic system and hypothalamic-pituitary-adrenal axis. Many fundamental brain mechanisms typically altered in PTSD, such as sleep regulation, aggression, cardiovascular activity, motor function, anxiety, and mood, have been linked to serotonin (Southwick et al., 1999). Of relevance to neuropsychology, in both human and animal research, SSRIs have successfully reversed stress-induced alteration of hippocampal morphology and deficits in hippocampal-based memory function (Duman, Nakagawa, & Malberg, 2001; Malberg, Eisch, Nestler, & Duman, 2000; Vermetten, Vythilingam, Southwick, Charney, & Bremner, 2003), suggesting that in addition to alleviating PTSD symptoms, they may also reduce neuropsychological dysfunction associated with PTSD.

Psychotherapy

It has been theorized that two separate processes, containment of re-experiencing symptoms (e.g., nightmares, flashbacks) and deliberate re-evaluation of the event, must be activated during effective treatment of PTSD (Brewin, 2003). These processes are well integrated into both exposure-based and cognitive-behavioral interventions, which have been identified as the most efficacious psychosocial treatments for PTSD (Friedman, 2000; Nemeroff et al., 2006; Resick, Monson, & Gutner, 2007). Although eye movement desensitization and reprocessing also incorporates an exposure component and has been demonstrated to be efficacious, its added benefit over other exposure-based interventions remains controversial (Bisson et al., 2007; Cahill, Carrigan, & Frueh, 1999; Lee & Drummond, 2008; Seidler & Wagner, 2006). Other treatment strategies, such as supportive counseling, psychodynamic therapy, and anxiety management, have also been used to treat PTSD; however, their evidence base remains incomplete (Committee on Treatment of PTSD, 2008; Nemeroff et al., 2006).

Exposure-based interventions provide a safe context for individuals to reconstruct the trauma in as much detail as possible with the aim of acclimating to the disturbing details, thus facilitating emotional processing, habituation of anxiety, integration of corrective information, and eventual mastery of the experience (Foa & Hearst-Ikeda, 1996). Cognitive-behavioral strategies focus on the identification and modification of distorted self-evaluations and interpretations of the traumatic experience. Clinically, elements of exposure and cognitive-behavioral interventions are often combined. However, the incremental benefit of combining exposure and cognitive elements has yet to be determined conclusively (Bryant et al., 2008c; Foa et al., 2005; Marks et al., 1998; Paunovic & Ost, 2001; Resick et al., 2008; Resick, Nishith, Weaver, Astin, & Feuer, 2002).

Cognitive processing therapy, for example, is an evidence-based treatment that incorporates both written exposure exercises and cognitive restructuring techniques (Resick & Schnicke, 1992, 1993). Whereas cognitive processing therapy has been found to result in greater reductions in PTSD symptomatology when compared with wait list control conditions (e.g., Chard, 2005; Monson et al., 2006), Resick et al. (2008) recently demonstrated in a dismantling study that cognitive restructuring alone, as compared with exposure alone or the standard combined treatment, was the most effective and most efficient means of symptom reduction. Conversely, some studies have suggested that the addition of cognitive restructuring to exposure is no more effective than exposure alone (e.g., Foa et al., 2005; Marks et al., 1998; Paunovic & Ost, 2001), whereas still others found that cognitive components enhanced exposure-based therapy (Bryant et al., 2003, 2008a, 2008b, 2008c).

The emphasis within exposure-based and cognitive-behavioral therapies on memory reconstruction and reinterpreting the experience suggests that executive (e.g., cognitive flexibility) and memory functions may be strongly related to response to these interventions. Sutherland and Bryant (2007), for example, found that reduction in re-experiencing symptoms following cognitive behavioral therapy (CBT) was associated with enhanced specificity of autobiographical recall. Several recent studies also suggest that neural integrity and cognitive functions may influence treatment response. Neuropsychological deficits encoding verbally acquired information (Wild & Gur, 2008), smaller volume of the rostral anterior cingulate cortex (Bryant et al., 2008b), and increased activation of the bilateral amygdala and ventral anterior cingulate (Bryant et al., 2008a) have been associated with poorer response to CBT.

Although preliminary, these studies emphasize the potential significance of neuropsychological parameters in relation to clinical outcomes and point to the potential utility of applying neuropsychological assessment to help tailor PTSD interventions to the individual characteristics of each patient. This may be a particularly important application in military populations in which TBI and other neurological insults acquired as part of military service can result in associated neuropsychological deficits that influence PTSD treatment response. Likewise, assessment of neuropsychological variables may provide an additional ecologically relevant index of treatment outcome.

Early and Preventive Interventions

Because exposure to stressful events cannot be prevented in many military contexts, prevention focuses on secondary prevention (preventing symptoms from developing following stressful exposures) and early intervention (preventing acute or postacute symptoms from becoming chronic). Secondary prevention efforts in military contexts have often relied on some form of Mitchell's (1983) critical incident stress debriefing (CISD), a semistructured intervention designed to promote open discussion, normalization, and unit cohesion among soldiers exposed to a potentially traumatic event (MacDonald, 2003). Despite its widespread use, empirical support for CISD remains incomplete. Some studies have found that CISD has led to poor outcomes (Bisson et al., 2007; Hobbs, Mayou, Harrison, & Worlock, 1996), mild improvements (Deahl, Srinivasan, Jones, Neblett, & Jolly, 2001; Shalev et al., 1998), or no change (Deahl, Gillham, Thomas, & Searle, 1994). In one of the most methodologically rigorous studies of CISD in a military context, Adler and colleagues (2008) found that CISD was no more effective in reducing symptoms of PTSD than no intervention; however, among soldiers exposed to the highest degree of mission stressors, CISD resulted in slight reductions in PTSD symptomatology as compared with a stress-management comparison group. Other secondary prevention efforts in military contexts have emphasized psychoeducational and supportive techniques aimed at normalizing experiences, enhancing coping options, and destigmatizing distress (Gould, Greenberg, & Hetherton, 2007; Grenier, Darte, Heber, & Richardson, 2007; Williams, Kos, Ajdukovic, Van der Veer, & Feldman, 2008). Although informed by evidence-based techniques, these interventions have not yet undergone evaluation sufficient to meet the criteria of evidence-based practice. To date, CBT (Ehlers et al., 2003; Kornor et al., 2008; Litz, Maguen, Friedman, Keane, & Resick, 2007; McNally, Bryant, & Ehlers, 2003) and exposure (Bryant et al., 2008c) are the only early interventions for PTSD with empirical support for their efficacious application.

CONCLUSIONS

With military service come duties that at times expose service men and women to life threat and other forms of extreme psychological stress. Such exposures are often accompanied by adaptive psychological and physiological responses that promote survival but, if perpetuated, can lead to PTSD and other psychological consequences. In addition to emotion-based symptoms, PTSD is associated with mild neuropsychological abnormalities. PTSD-related deficits found on clinical neuropsychology tasks include impairment of executive aspects of attention, sustained attention, learning, and memory. Performance on verbally mediated tasks, including IQ and anterograde memory tasks, is less likely to be proficient among trauma survivors who develop PTSD as compared to those who do not. However, recent work using experimental neuropsychology paradigms and error analysis suggests that select aspects of visuospatial functioning not necessarily detectable on standard clinical tasks are also impaired in PTSD. This pattern of neuropsychological strengths and weaknesses is consistent with neuroanatomical models of PTSD that emphasize the prefrontal cortex and limbic/paralimbic areas, including the amygdala and hippocampus, and raises the question of a relative functional cerebral asymmetry favoring the right hemisphere. Exciting new work suggests that neuropsychological principles may be applied to help predict treatment response and that neuropsychological functioning may be enhanced by treatment.

There remain, however, many questions about PTSD as a neuropsychological disorder. For example, the degree to which neurobiological and neuropsychological abnormalities represent predispositional factors versus sequelae of trauma exposure is uncertain. Likewise, the extent to which comorbidity (e.g., TBI) and treatment-related factors contribute to neuropsychological dysfunction in PTSD is not fully resolved. Methodological inconsistencies across studies have not permitted sufficient replication to create a highly delineated neuropsychological profile, although recent meta-analytic and longitudinal studies have begun to help address some of these issues. Finally, as it pertains to the military experience, the degree to which transient changes in neuropsychological functioning in the face of acute stress represents a desirable situational adaptation in which cognitive resources are redirected to survival versus a prognostic sign of poor long-term psychological and somatic outcomes is unclear.

REFERENCES

Adler, A. B., Litz, B. T., Castro, C. A., Suvak, M., Thomas, J. L., Burnell, L., et al. (2008). A group randomized trial of critical incident stress debriefing provided to U.S. peacekeepers. *Journal of Traumatic Stress, 21*(3), 253–263.

American Psychiatric Association. (2000). *Diagnostic and statistical manual of mental disorders* (4th ed., text revision). Washington, DC: Author.

American Psychiatric Association. (2006). Practice guidelines for the treatment of patients with acute stress disorder and posttraumatic stress disorder. In *American Psychiatric Association Practice Guidelines for the Treatment of Psychiatric Disorders: Compendium 2006* (pp. 1003–1071). Arlington, VA: Author.

Austin, M. P., Mitchell, P., Wilhelm, K., Parker, G., Hickie, I., Brodaty, H., et al. (1999). Cognitive function in depression: A distinct pattern of frontal impairment in melancholia? *Psychological Medicine, 29*(1), 73–85.

Baddeley, A. (2002). Fractionating the central executive. In D. T. Stuss & T. R. Knight (Eds.), *Principles of frontal lobe functioning* (pp. 246–260). New York: Oxford University Press.

Barrett, D. H., Green, M. L., Morris, R., Giles, W. H., & Croft, J. B. (1996). Cognitive functioning and posttraumatic stress disorder. *The American Journal of Psychiatry, 153*(11), 1492–1494.

Beckham, J. C., Crawford, A. L., & Feldman, M. E. (1998). Trail Making Test performance in Vietnam combat veterans with and without posttraumatic stress disorder. *Journal of Traumatic Stress, 11*(4), 811–819.

Benotsch, E. G., Brailey, K., Vasterling, J. J., Uddo, M., Constans, J. I., & Sutker, P. B. (2000). War Zone stress, personal and environmental resources, and PTSD symptoms in Gulf War Veterans: A longitudinal perspective. *Journal of Abnormal Psychology, 109*(2), 205–213.

Bigler, E. D., Young, G., Kane, A. W., & Nicholson, K. (2006). Mild traumatic brain injury: Causality considerations from a neuroimaging and neuropathology perspective. *Psychological knowledge in court: PTSD, pain, and TBI* (pp. 308–334). New York: Springer Science + Business Media.

Bisson, J. I., Ehlers, A., Matthews, R., Pilling, S., Richards, D., & Turner, S. (2007). Psychological treatments for chronic posttraumatic stress disorder: Systematic review and meta-analysis. *British Journal of Psychiatry, 190*(2), 97–104.

Bonne, O., Brandes, D., Gilboa, A., Gomori, J. M., Shenton, M. E., Pitman, R. K., et al. (2001). Longitudinal MRI study of hippocampal volume in trauma survivors with PTSD. *American Journal of Psychiatry, 158*, 1248–1251.

Bonne, O., Grillon, C., Vythilingam, M., Neumeister, A., & Charney, D. S. (2004). Adaptive and maladaptive psychobiological responses to severe psychological stress: Implications for the discovery of novel pharmacotherapy. *Neuroscience Biobehavioral Review, 28*(1), 65–94.

Boscarino, J. A. (1997). Diseases among men 20 years after exposure to severe stress: Implications for clinical research and medical care. *Psychosomatic Medicine, 59*(6), 605–614.

Brady, K. T., Killeen, T. K., Brewerton, T., & Lucerini, S. (2000). Comorbidity of psychiatric disorders and posttraumatic stress disorder. *Journal of Clinical Psychiatry, 61*(Suppl. 7), 22–32.

Brailey, K., Vasterling, J. J., Proctor, S. P., Constans, J. I., & Friedman, M. J. (2007). PTSD symptoms, life events, and unit cohesion in U.S. soldiers: Baseline findings from the neurocognition deployment health study. *Journal of Traumatic Stress, 20*(4), 495–503.

Brandes, D., Ben-Schachar, G., Gilboa, A., Bonne, O., Freedman, S., & Shalev, A. Y. (2002). PTSD symptoms and cognitive performance in recent trauma survivors. *Psychiatry Research, 110*(3), 231–238.

Bremner, J. D., Narayan, M., Staib, L. H., Southwick, S. M., McGlashan, T., & Charney, D. S. (1999a). Neural correlates of memories of childhood sexual abuse in women with and without posttraumatic stress disorder. *American Journal of Psychiatry, 156*(11), 1787–1795.

Bremner, J. D., Randall, P., Scott, T. M., Bronen, R. A., Seibyl, J. P., Southwick, S. M., et al. (1995a). MRI-based measurement of hippocampal volume in patients with combat-related posttraumatic stress disorder. *American Journal of Psychiatry, 152*(7), 973–981.

Bremner, J. D., Randall, P., Scott, T. W., Capelli, S., Delaney, R., McCarthy, G., et al. (1995b). Deficits in short-term memory in adult survivors of childhood abuse. *Psychiatry Research, 59*(1), 97–107.

Bremner, J. D., Randall, P., Vermetten, E., Staib, L. H., Bronen, R. A., Mazure, C., et al. (1997). Magnetic resonance imaging-based measurement of hippocampal volume in posttraumatic stress disorder related to childhood physical and sexual abuse—A preliminary report. *Biological Psychiatry, 41*, 23–32.

Bremner, J. D., Scott, T. M., Delaney, R. C., Southwick, S. M., Mason, J. W., Johnson, D. R., et al. (1993). Deficits in short-term memory in posttraumatic stress disorder. *American Journal of Psychiatry, 150*(7), 1015–1019.

Bremner, J. D., Southwick, S. M., & Charney, D. S. (1999b). The neurobiology of posttraumatic stress disorder: An integration of animal and human research. In P. A. Saigh & J. D. Bremner (Eds.), *Posttraumatic stress disorder: A comprehensive text* (pp. 103–143). Needham Heights, MA: Allyn & Bacon.

Bremner, J. D., Staib, L. H., Kaloupek, D., Southwick, S. M., Soufer, R., & Charney, D. S. (1999c). Neural correlates of exposure to traumatic pictures and sound in Vietnam combat veterans with and without posttraumatic stress disorder: A positron emission tomography study. *Society of Biological Psychiatry, 45*, 806–816.

Bremner, J. D., Vythilingam, M., Vermetten, E., Southwick, S. M., McGlashan, T., Nazeer, A., et al. (2003a). MRI and PET study of deficits in hippocampal structure and function in women with childhood sexual abuse and posttraumatic stress disorder. *American Journal of Psychiatry, 160*(5), 924–932.

Bremner, J. D., Vythilingam, M., Vermetten, E., Southwick, S. M., McGlashan, T., Staib, L. H., et al. (2003b). Neural correlates of declarative memory for emotionally valenced words in women with posttraumatic stress disorder related to early childhood sexual abuse. *Biological Psychiatry, 53*(10), 879–889.

Bremner, J. D., & Yehuda, R. (2006). The relationship between cognitive and brain changes in posttraumatic stress disorder. *Psychobiology of posttraumatic stress disorders: A decade of progress* (Vol. 1071, pp. 80–86). Malden, MA: Blackwell Publishing.

Breslau, N. (2001). Outcomes of posttraumatic stress disorder. *Journal of Clinical Psychiatry, 62*(Suppl. 17), 55–59.

Brewin, C. R. (2003). *Posttraumatic stress disorder: Malady or myth?* New Haven, CT: Yale University Press.

Brewin, C. R., Kleiner, J. S., Vasterling, J. J., & Field, A. P. (2007). Memory for emotionally neutral information in posttraumatic stress disorder: A meta-analytic investigation. *Journal of Abnormal Psychology, 116*(3), 448–463.

Bryant, R. A., Felmingham, K., Kemp, A., Das, P., Hughes, G., Peduto, A., et al. (2008a). Amygdala and ventral anterior cingulate activation predicts treatment response to cognitive behaviour therapy for posttraumatic stress disorder. *Psychological Medicine, 38*(4), 555–561.

Bryant, R. A., Felmingham, K., Whitford, T. J., Kemp, A., Hughes, G., Peduto, A., et al. (2008b). Rostral anterior cingulate volume predicts treatment response to cognitive-behavioural therapy for posttraumatic stress disorder. *Journal of Psychiatry Neuroscience, 33*(2), 142–146.

Bryant, R. A., Moulds, M. L., Guthrie, R. M., Dang, S. T., Mastrodomenico, J., Nixon, R. D. V., et al. (2008c). A randomized controlled trial of exposure therapy and cognitive restructuring for posttraumatic stress disorder. *Journal of Consulting and Clinical Psychology, 76*(4), 695–703.

Bryant, R. A., Moulds, M. L., Guthrie, R. M., Dang, S. T., & Nixon, R. D. (2003). Imaginal exposure alone and imaginal exposure with cognitive restructuring in treatment of posttraumatic stress disorder. *Journal of Consulting and Clinical Psychology, 71*, 706–712.

Buckley, T. C., Mozley, S. L., Bedard, M. A., Dewulf, A.-C., & Greif, J. (2004). Preventive health behaviors, health-risk behaviors, physical morbidity, and health-related role functioning impairment in veterans with posttraumatic stress disorder. *Military Medicine, 169*(7), 536–540.

Burriss, L., Ayers, E., Ginsberg, J., & Powell, D. A. (2008). Learning and memory impairment in PTSD: Relationship to depression. *Depression and Anxiety, 25*(2), 149–157.

Bustamante, V., Mellman, T. A., David, D., & Fins, A. I. (2001). Cognitive functioning and the early development of PTSD. *Journal of Traumatic Stress, 14*(4), 791–797.

Cabrera, O. A., Hoge, C. W., Bliese, P. D., Castro, C. A., & Messer, S. C. (2007). Childhood adversity and combat as predictors of depression and posttraumatic stress in deployed troops. *American Journal of Preventative Medicine, 33*(2), 77–82.

Cahill, S. P., Carrigan, M. H., & Frueh, B. C. (1999). Does EMDR work? and if so, why?: A critical review of controlled outcome and dismantling research. *Journal of Anxiety Disorders, 13*(1), 5–33.

Carrion, V. G., Weems, C. F., Eliez, S., Patwardhan, A., Brown, W., Ray, R. D., et al. (2001). Attenuation of frontal asymmetry in pediatric posttraumatic stress disorder. *Society of Biological Psychiatry, 50*, 943–951.

Chard, K. M. (2005). An evaluation of cognitive processing therapy for the treatment of posttraumatic stress disorder related to childhood sexual abuse. *Journal of Consulting and Clinical Psychology, 73*, 965–971.

Charney, D. S., Deutch, A. Y., Krystal, J. H., Southwick, S. M., & Davis, M. (1993). Psychobiologic mechanisms of posttraumatic stress disorder. *Archives of General Psychiatry, 50*(4), 295–305.

Charney, D. S., Deutch, A. Y., Southwick, S. M., & Krystal, J. H. (1995). Neural circuits and mechanisms of posttraumatic stress disorder. In M. J. Friedman, D. S. Charney, & A. Y. Deutch (Eds.), *Neurobiological and clinical consequences of stress: From normal adaptation to posttraumatic stress disorder* (pp. 271–287). Philadelphia: Lippincott-Raven.

Chemtob, C. M., Muraoka, M. Y., Wu-Holt, P., Fairbank, J. A., Hamada, R. S., & Keane, T. M. (1998). Head injury and combat-related posttraumatic stress disorder. *Journal of Nervous and Mental Disorders, 186*(11), 701–708.

Chen, J. K., Johnston, K. M., Petrides, M., & Ptito, A. (2008). Neural substrates of symptoms of depression following concussion in male athletes with persisting postconcussion symptoms. *Archives of General Psychiatry, 65*(1), 81–89.

Committee on Treatment of Posttraumatic Stress Disorder. (2008). *Treatment of posttraumatic stress disorder: An assessment of the evidence.* Washington, DC: The National Academies Press.

Constans, J. I. (2005). Information-processing biases in PTSD. In J. J. Vasterling & C. R. Brewin (Eds.), *Neuropsychology of PTSD: Biological, cognitive, and clinical perspectives* (pp. 105–130). New York: The Guilford Press.

Constant, E. L., Adam, S., Gillain, B., Seron, X., Bruyer, R., & Seghers, A. (2005). Effects of sertraline on depressive symptoms and attentional and executive functions in major depression. *Depression and Anxiety, 21*(2), 78–89.

Danckwerts, A., & Leathem, J. (2003). Questioning the link between PTSD and cognitive dysfunction. *Neuropsychology Review, 13*(4), 221–235.

Davis, L. L., Frazier, E. C., Williford, R. B., & Newell, J. M. (2006). Long-term pharmacotherapy for posttraumatic stress disorder. *CNS Drugs, 20*(6), 465–476.

De Bellis, M., Keshavan, M. S., Clark, D., Casey, B. J., Giedd, J. N., Boring, A. M., et al. (1999a). Developmental traumatology part II: Brain development. *Society of Biological Psychiatry, 45,* 1271–1284.

De Bellis, M. D., Keshavan, M. S., Clark, D. B., Casey, B. J., Giedd, J. N., Boring, A. M., et al. (1999b). Developmental traumatology: II. Brain development. *Biological Psychiatry, 45*(10), 1271–1284.

De Bellis, M. D., Keshavan, M. S., Shifflett, H., Iyengar, S., Beers, S. R., Hall, J., et al. (2002). Brain structures in pediatric maltreatment-related posttraumatic stress disorder: A sociodemographically matched study. *Biological Psychiatry, 52,* 1066–1078.

Deahl, M. P., Gillham, A. B., Thomas, J., & Searle, M. M. (1994). Psychological sequelae following the Gulf War: Factors associated with subsequent morbidity and the effectiveness of psychological debriefing. *British Journal of Psychiatry, 165*(1), 60–65.

Deahl, M. P., Srinivasan, M., Jones, N., Neblett, C., & Jolly, A. (2001). Commentary: Evaluating psychological debriefing: Are we measuring the right outcomes? *Journal of Traumatic Stress, 14*(3), 527–529.

Dickie, E. W., Brunet, A., Akerib, V., & Armony, J. L. (2008). An fMRI investigation of memory encoding in PTSD: Influence of symptom severity. *Neuropsychologia, 46*(5), 1522–1531.

Dikel, T. N., Engdahl, B., & Eberly, R. (2005). PTSD in former prisoners of war: Prewar, wartime, and postwar factors. *Journal of Traumatic Stress, 18*(1), 69–77.

Dileo, J. F., Brewer, W. J., Hopwood, M., Anderson, V., & Creamer, M. (2008). Olfactory identification dysfunction, aggression and impulsivity in war veterans with posttraumatic stress disorder. *Psychological Medicine, 38*(4), 523–531.

Dohrenwend, B. P., Turner, J. B., Turse, N. A., Adams, B. G., Koenen, K. C., & Marshall, R. (2006). The psychological risks of Vietnam for U.S. veterans: A revisit with new data and methods. *Science, 313*(5789), 979–982.

Dohrenwend, B. P., Turner, J. B., Turse, N. A., Lewis-Fernandez, R., & Yager, T. J. (2008). War-related posttraumatic stress disorder in Black, Hispanic, and Majority White Vietnam veterans: The roles of exposure and vulnerability. *Journal of Traumatic Stress, 21*(2), 133–141.

Drake, A. I., Gray, N., Yoder, S., Pramuka, M., & Llewellyn, M. (2000). Factors predicting return to work following mild traumatic brain injury: A discriminant analysis. *Journal of Head Trauma Rehabilitation, 15*(5), 1103–1112.

Driessen, M., Beblo, T., Mertens, M., Piefke, M., Rullkoetter, N., Silva-Saavedra, A., et al. (2004). Posttraumatic stress disorder and fMRI activation patterns of traumatic memory in patients with borderline personality disorder. *Biological Psychiatry, 55*(6), 603–611.

Duman, R. S., Nakagawa, S., & Malberg, J. (2001). Regulation of adult neurogenesis by antidepressant treatment. *Neuropsychopharmacology, 25*(6), 836–844.

Ehlers, A., Clark, D. M., Hackmann, A., McManus, F., Fennell, M., Herbert, C., et al. (2003). A randomized controlled trial of cognitive therapy, a self-help booklet, and repeated assessments as early interventions for posttraumatic stress disorder. *Archives of General Psychiatry, 60*(10), 1024–1032.

Eid, J., & Johnsen, B. H. (2002). Acute stress reactions after submarine accidents. *Military Medicine, 167*(5), 427–431.

Engel, C. C., Liu, X., McCarthy, B. D., Miller, R. F., & Ursano, R. J. (2000). Relationship of physical symptoms to posttraumatic stress disorder among veterans seeking care for Gulf War-related health concerns. *Psychosomatic Medicine, 62*(6), 739–745.

Fear, N. T., Jones, E., Groom, M., Greenberg, N., Hull, L., Hodgetts, T. J., et al. (2008). Symptoms of postconcussional syndrome are nonspecifically related to mild traumatic brain injury in UK Armed Forces personnel on return from deployment in Iraq: An analysis of self-reported data. *Psychological Medicine*, 1–9.

Fennema-Notestine, C., Stein, M. B., Kennedy, C. M., Archibald, S. L., & Jernigan, T. L. (2002). Brain morphometry in female victims of intimate partner violence with and without posttraumatic stress disorder. *Biological Psychiatry, 52*(11), 1089–1101.

Flouri, E. (2005). Posttraumatic stress disorder (PTSD): What we have learned and what we still have not found out. *Journal of Interpersonal Violence, 20*(4), 373–379.

Foa, E. B., & Hearst-Ikeda, D. (1996). Emotional dissociation in response to trauma: An information-processing approach. In L. K. Michelson & W. J. Ray (Eds.), *Handbook of dissociation: Theoretical, empirical, and clinical perspectives*. New York: Plenum Press.

Foa, E. B., Hembree, E. A., Cahill, S. P., Rauch, S. A. M., Riggs, D. S., Feeny, N. C., et al. (2005). Randomized trial of prolonged exposure for posttraumatic stress disorder with and without cognitive restructuring: Outcome at academic and community clinics. *Journal of Consulting and Clinical Psychology, 73*(5), 953–964.

Fontana, A., & Rosenheck, R. (1994). Posttraumatic stress disorder among Vietnam theater veterans: A causal model of etiology in a community sample. *Journal of Nervous and Mental Disease, 182*(12), 677–684.

Foy, D. W., Siprelle, R. C., Rueger, D. B., & Carroll, E. M. (1984). Etiology of posttraumatic stress disorder in Vietnam veterans: Analysis of premilitary, military, and combat exposure influences. *Journal of Consulting and Clinical Psychology, 52*, 79–87.

Francati, V., Vermetten, E., & Bremner, J. D. (2007). Functional neuroimaging studies in posttraumatic stress disorder: Review of current methods and findings. *Depression and Anxiety, 24*(3), 202–218.

Friedman, M. J. (2000). What might the psychobiology of posttraumatic stress disorder teach us about future approaches to pharmacotherapy? *Journal of Clinical Psychiatry, 61*(Suppl. 7), 44–51.

Friedman, M. J., & Davidson, J. R. T. (2007). Pharmacotherapy for PTSD. In M. J. Friedman, T. M. Keane, & P. A. Resick (Eds.), *Handbook of PTSD: Science and practice* (pp. 376–405). New York: Guilford Press.

Friedman, M. J., Davidson, J. R. T., Mellman, T. A., & Southwick, S. M. (2004). Psychotherapy. In E. B. Foa, T. M. Keane, M. J. Friedman, & J. A. Cohen (Eds.), *Effective treatments for PTSD: Practice guidelines from the International Society for Traumatic Stress Studies* (pp. 84–105). New York: Guilford Press.

Gale, C. R., Deary, I. J., Boyle, S. H., Barefoot, J., Mortensen, L. H., & Batty, D. B. (2008). Cognitive ability in early adulthood and risk of 5 specific psychiatric disorders in middle age. *Archives of General Psychiatry, 65*(12), 1410–1418.

Gaylord, K. M., Cooper, D. B., Mercado, J. M., Kennedy, J. E., Yoder, L. H., & Holcomb, J. B. (2008). Incidence of posttraumatic stress disorder and mild traumatic brain injury in burned service members: Preliminary report. *Journal of Trauma, 64*(2 Suppl.), S200–205; discussion S205–206.

Geuze, E., Westenberg, H. G., Heinecke, A., de Kloet, C. S., Goebel, R., & Vermetten, E. (2008). Thinner prefrontal cortex in veterans with posttraumatic stress disorder. *Neuroimage, 41*(3), 675–681.

Gil, T., Calev, A., Greenberg, D., & Kugelmass, S. (1990). Cognitive functioning in posttraumatic stress disorder. *Journal of Traumatic Stress, 3*(1), 29–45.

Gilbertson, M. W., Gurvits, T. V., Lasko, N. B., Orr, S. P., & Pitman, R. K. (2001). Multivariate assessment of explicit memory function in combat veterans with posttraumatic stress disorder. *Journal of Traumatic Stress, 14*(2), 413–431.

Gilbertson, M. W., Paulus, L. A., Williston, S. K., Gurvits, T. V., Lasko, N. B., Pitman, R. K., et al. (2006). Neurocognitive function in monozygotic twins discordant for combat exposure: Relationship to posttraumatic stress disorder. *Journal of Abnormal Psychology, 115*(3), 484–495.

Gilbertson, M. W., Shenton, M. E., Ciszewski, A., Kasai, K., Lasko, N. B., Orr, S. P., et al. (2002). Smaller hippocampal volume predicts pathologic vulnerability to psychological trauma. *Nature Neuroscience, 5*(11), 1242–1247.

Gilbertson, M. W., Williston, S. K., Paulus, L. A., Lasko, N. B., Gurvits, T. V., Shenton, M. E., et al. (2007). Configural cue performance in identical twins discordant for posttraumatic stress disorder: Theoretical implications for the role of hippocampal function. *Biological Psychiatry, 62*(5), 513–520.

Gilboa, A., Shalev, A. Y., Laor, L., Lester, H., Louzoun, Y., Chisin, R., et al. (2004). Functional connectivity of the prefrontal cortex and the amygdala in posttraumatic stress disorder. *Biological Psychiatry, 55*(3), 263–272.

Golier, J., Yehuda, R., Cornblatt, B., Harvey, P., Gerber, D., & Levengood, R. (1997). Sustained attention in combat-related posttraumatic stress disorder. *Integrated Physiological Behavioral Science, 32*(1), 52–61.

Golier, J. A., Yehuda, R., Lupien, S. J., Harvey, P. D., Grossman, R., & Elkin, A. (2002). Memory performance in Holocaust survivors with posttraumatic stress disorder. *American Journal of Psychiatry, 159*(10), 1682–1688.

Gould, M., Greenberg, N., & Hetherton, J. (2007). Stigma and the military: Evaluation of a PTSD psychoeducational program. *Journal of Traumatic Stress, 20*(4), 505–515.

Green, B. L., Grace, M. C., Lindy, J. D., & Gleser, G. C. (1990a). Risk factors for PTSD and other diagnoses in a general sample of Vietnam veterans. *American Journal of Psychiatry, 147*(6), 729–733.

Green, B. L., Grace, M. C., Lindy, J. D., & Leonard, A. C. (1990b). Race differences in response to combat stress. *Journal of Traumatic Stress, 3*(3), 379–393.

Green, M. A., & Berlin, M. A. (1987). Five psychosocial variables related to the existence of posttraumatic stress disorder symptoms. *Journal of Clinical Psychology, 43*(6), 643–649.

Grenier, S., Darte, K., Heber, A., & Richardson, D. (2007). The operational stress injury social support program: A peer support program in collaboration between the Canadian Forces and Veterans Affairs Canada. In C. R. Figley & W. P. Nash (Eds.), *Combat stress injury: Theory, research and management*. New York: Routledge.

Grieger, T. A., Cozza, S. J., Ursano, R. J., Hoge, C., Martinez, P. E., Engel, C. C., et al. (2006). Posttraumatic stress disorder and depression in battle-injured soldiers. *American Journal of Psychiatry, 163*(10), 1777–1783.

Grossman, R., Buchsbaum, M. S., & Yehuda, R. (2002). Neuroimaging studies in posttraumatic stress disorder. *Psychiatric Clinics of North America, 25*, 317–340.

Gurvits, T. V., Gilbertson, M. W., Lasko, N. B., Tarhan, A. S., Simeon, D., Macklin, M. L., et al. (2000). Neurologic soft signs in chronic posttraumatic stress disorder. *Archives of General Psychiatry, 57*(2), 181–186.

Gurvits, T. V., Lasko, N. B., Repak, A. L., Metzger, L. J., Orr, S. P., & Pitman, R. K. (2002). Performance on visuospatial copying tasks in individuals with chronic posttraumatic stress disorder. *Psychiatry Research, 112*(3), 263–268.

Gurvits, T. V., Lasko, N. B., & Schachter, S. C. (1993). Neurological status of Vietnam veterans with chronic posttraumatic stress disorder. *Journal of Neuropsychiatry & Clinical Neurosciences, 5*(2), 183–188.

Gurvits, T. V., Shenton, M. E., Hokama, H., Ohta, H., Lasko, N. B., Gilbertson, M. W., et al. (1996). Magnetic resonance imaging study of hippocampal volume in chronic, combat-related posttraumatic stress disorder. *Biological Psychiatry, 40*, 1091–1099.

Hart, J., Jr., Kimbrell, T., Fauver, P., Cherry, B. J., Pitcock, J., Booe, L. Q., et al. (2008). Cognitive dysfunctions associated with PTSD: Evidence from World War II prisoners of war. *Journal of Neuropsychiatry & Clinical Neurosciences, 20*(3), 309–316.

Helzer, J. E., Robins, L. N., & McEvoy, L. (1987). Posttraumatic stress disorder in the general population: Findings of the epidemiologic catchment area survey. *New England Journal of Medicine, 317*(26), 1630–1634.

Himanen, L., Portin, R., Isoniemi, H., Helenius, H., Kurki, T., & Tenovuo, O. (2006). Longitudinal cognitive changes in traumatic brain injury: A 30-year follow-up study. *Neurology, 66*(2), 187–192.

Hobbs, M., Mayou, R., Harrison, B., & Worlock, P. (1996). A randomized controlled trial of psychological debriefing for victims of road traffic accidents. *British Medical Journal, 313*(7070), 1438–1439.

Hoge, C. W., Auchterlonie, J. L., & Milliken, C. S. (2006). Mental health problems, use of mental health services, and attrition from military service after returning from deployment to Iraq or Afghanistan. *Journal of the American Medical Association, 295*(9), 1023–1032.

Hoge, C. W., & Castro, C. A. (2006). Posttraumatic stress disorder in UK and US forces deployed to Iraq. *Lancet, 368*(9538), 837.

Hoge, C. W., Castro, C. A., Messer, S. C., McGurk, D., Cotting, D. I., & Koffman, R. L. (2004). Combat duty in Iraq and Afghanistan, mental health problems, and barriers to care. *New England Journal of Medicine, 351*(1), 13–22.

Hoge, C. W., McGurk, D., Thomas, J. L., Cox, A. L., Engel, C. C., & Castro, C. A. (2008). Mild traumatic brain injury in U.S. Soldiers returning from Iraq. *New England Journal of Medicine, 358*(5), 453–463.

Hoge, C. W., Terhakopian, A., Castro, C. A., Messer, S. C., & Engel, C. C. (2007). Association of posttraumatic stress disorder with somatic symptoms, health care visits, and absenteeism among Iraq War veterans. *American Journal of Psychiatry, 164*(1), 150–153.

Hoge, C. W., Toboni, H. E., Messer, S. C., Bell, N., Amoroso, P., & Orman, D. T. (2005). The occupational burden of mental disorders in the US, Military: Psychiatric hospitalizations, involuntary separations, and disability. *American Journal of Psychiatry, 162*(3), 585–591.

Horner, M. D., & Hamner, M. B. (2002). Neurocognitive functioning in posttraumatic stress disorder. *Neuropsychology Review, 12*(1), 15–30.

Hotopf, M., Hull, L., Fear, N. T., Browne, T., Horn, O., Iversen, A., et al. (2006). The health of UK military personnel who deployed to the 2003 Iraq war: A cohort study. *Lancet, 367*(9524), 1731–1741.

Ikin, J. F., Sim, M. R., McKenzie, D. P., Horsley, K. W. A., Wilson, E. J., Moore, M. R., et al. (2007). Anxiety, posttraumatic stress disorder and depression in Korean War veterans 50 years after the war. *British Journal of Psychiatry, 190*, 475–483.

Iversen, A. C., Fear, N. T., Ehlers, A., Hughes, J. H., Hull, L., Earnshaw, M., et al. (2008). Risk factors for posttraumatic stress disorder among UK Armed Forces personnel. *Psychological Medicine, 38*(4), 511–522.

Jelinek, L., Jacobsen, D., & Kellner, M. (2006). Verbal and nonverbal memory functioning in posttraumatic stress disorder. *Journal of Clinical and Experimental Neuropsychology, 28*(6), 940–948.

Jenkins, M. A., Langlais, P. J., Delis, D., & Cohen, R. (1998). Learning and memory in rape victims with posttraumatic stress disorder. *American Journal of Psychiatry, 155*(2), 278–279.

Jenkins, M. A., Langlais, P. J., Delis, D. A., & Cohen, R. A. (2000). Attentional dysfunction associated with posttraumatic stress disorder among rape survivors. *Clinical Neuropsychology, 14*(1), 7–12.

Johnsen, G. E., & Asbjornsen, A. E. (2008). Consistent impaired verbal memory in PTSD: A meta-analysis. *Journal of Affective Disorders, 111*(1), 74–82.

Kang, H. K., & Hyams, K. C. (2005). Mental health care needs among recent war veterans. *New England Journal of Medicine, 352*(13), 1289.

Karl, A., Malta, L. S., & Maercker, A. (2006a). Meta-analytic review of event-related potential studies in posttraumatic stress disorder. *Biological Psychology, 71*(2), 123–147.

Karl, A., Schaefer, M., Malta, L. S., Dorfel, D., Rohleder, N., & Werner, A. (2006b). A meta-analysis of structural brain abnormalities in PTSD. *Neuroscience Biobehavioral Review, 30*(7), 1004–1031.

Kasai, K., Yamasue, H., Gilbertson, M. W., Shenton, M. E., Rauch, S. L., & Pitman, R. K. (2008). Evidence for acquired pregenual anterior cingulate gray matter loss from a twin study of combat-related posttraumatic stress disorder. *Biological Psychiatry*, 63(6), 550–556.

Keane, T. M., & Barlow, D. H. (2002). Posttraumatic stress disorder. In D. H. Barlow (Ed.), *Anxiety and its disorders: The nature and treatment of anxiety and panic* (2nd ed.). New York: Guilford Press.

Kennedy, J. E., Jaffee, M. S., Leskin, G. A., Stokes, J. W., Leal, F. O., & Fitzpatrick, P. J. (2007). Posttraumatic stress disorder and posttraumatic stress disorder-like symptoms and mild traumatic brain injury. *Journal of Rehabilitation Research and Development*, 44(7), 895–920.

Kessler, R. C. (2000). Posttraumatic stress disorder: The burden to the individual and to society. *Journal of Clinical Psychiatry*, 61(Suppl. 5), 4–14.

Kessler, R., Sonnega, A., Bromet, E., Hughes, M., & Nelson, C. (1995a). Posttraumatic stress disorder in the National Comorbidity Survey. *Archives of General Psychiatry*, 52(12), 1048–1060.

Kessler, R. C., Sonnega, A., Bromet, E., Hughes, M., & Nelson, C. B. (1995b). Posttraumatic stress disorder in the national comorbidity survey. *Archives of General Psychiatry*, 52(12), 1048–1060.

Kimble, M., Ruddy, K., Deldin, P., & Kaufman, M. (2004). A CNV-distraction paradigm in combat veterans with posttraumatic stress disorder. *Journal of Neuropsychiatry & Clinical Neurosciences*, 16(1), 102–108.

King, K. A., Hough, M. S., Vos, P., Walker, M. M., & Givens, G. (2006). Word retrieval following mild TBI: Implications for categorical deficits. *Aphasiology*, 20(2), 233–245.

King, L. A., King, D. W., Fairbank, J. A., Keane, T. M., & Adams, G. A. (1998). Resilience-recovery factors in posttraumatic stress disorder among female and male Vietnam veterans: Hardiness, postwar social support, and additional stressful life events. *Journal of Personality and Social Psychology*, 74(2), 420–434.

King, D. W., King, L. A., Foy, D. W., Keane, T. M., & Fairbank, J. A. (1999). Posttraumatic stress disorder in a national sample of female and male Vietnam veterans: Risk factors, war-zone stressors, and resilience-recovery variables. *Journal of Abnormal Psychology*, 108(1), 164–170.

King, D. W., King, L. A., Gudanowski, D. M., & Vreven, D. L. (1995). Alternative representations of war zone stressors: Relationships to posttraumatic stress disorder in male and female Vietnam veterans. *Journal of Abnormal Psychology*, 104(1), 184–196.

King, D. W., Leskin, G. A., King, L. A., & Weathers, F. W. (1998). Confirmatory factor analysis of the clinician-administered PTSD Scale: Evidence for the dimensionality of posttraumatic stress disorder. *Psychological Assessment*, 10(2), 90–96.

Kitayama, N., Vaccarino, V., Kutner, M., Weiss, P., & Bremner, J. D. (2005). Magnetic resonance imaging (MRI) measurement of hippocampal volume in posttraumatic stress disorder: A meta-analysis. *Journal of Affective Disorders*, 88(1), 79–86.

Koenen, K. C., Driver, K. L., Oscar-Berman, M., Wolfe, J., Folsom, S., Huang, M. T., et al. (2001). Measures of prefrontal system dysfunction in posttraumatic stress disorder. *Brain and Cognition*, 45, 64–78.

Koenen, K. C., Moffitt, T. E., Caspi, A., Taylor, A., & Purcell, S. (2003). Domestic violence is associated with environmental suppression of IQ in young children. *Development and Psychopathology*, 15, 297–311.

Koenen, K. C., Stellman, J. M., Stellman, S. D., & Sommer, J. F., Jr. (2003). Risk factors for course of posttraumatic stress disorder among Vietnam veterans: A 14-year follow-up of American legionnaires. *Journal of Consulting and Clinical Psychology, 71*(6), 980–986.

Koren, D., Norman, D., Cohen, A., Berman, J., & Klein, E. M. (2005). Increased PTSD risk with combat-related injury: A matched comparison study of injured and uninjured soldiers experiencing the same combat events. *American Journal of Psychiatry, 162*(2), 276–282.

Kornor, H., Winje, D., Ekeberg, O., Weisaeth, L., Kirkehei, I., Johansen, K., et al. (2008). Early trauma-focused cognitive-behavioural therapy to prevent chronic posttraumatic stress disorder and related symptoms: A systematic review and meta-analysis. *BMC Psychiatry, 8*, 1–8.

Koso, M., & Hansen, S. (2006). Executive function and memory in posttraumatic stress disorder: A study of Bosnian war veterans. *European Psychiatry, 21*(3), 167–173.

Kubzansky, L. D., Koenen, K. C., Spiro, A., III, Vokonas, P. S., & Sparrow, D. (2007). Perspective study of posttraumatic stress disorder symptoms and coronary heart disease in the normative aging study. *Archives of General Psychiatry, 64*(1), 109–116.

Kulka, R. A., Schlenger, W. E., Fairbank, J. A., Hough, R. L., Jordan, B. K., Marmar, C. R., et al. (1990). *Trauma and the Vietnam war generation: Report of findings from the National Vietnam Veterans Readjustment Study.* Philadelphia: Brunner/Mazel.

Lanius, R. A., Williamson, P. C., Densmore, M., Boksman, K., Gupta, M. A., Neufeld, R. W., et al. (2001). Neural correlates of traumatic memories in posttraumatic stress disorder: A functional MRI investigation. *American Journal of Psychiatry, 158*(11), 1920–1922.

Laufer, R. S., Gallops, M. S., & Frey-Wouters, E. (1984). War stress and trauma: The Vietnam veteran experience. *Journal of Health and Social Behavior, 25*(1), 65–85.

Lee, C. W., & Drummond, P. D. (2008). Effects of eye movement versus therapist instructions on the processing of distressing memories. *Journal of Anxiety Disorders, 22*(5), 801–808.

Leroi, I., Sheppard, J. M., & Lyketsos, C. G. (2002). Cognitive function after 11.5 years of alcohol use: Relation to alcohol use. *American Journal of Epidemiology, 156*(8), 747–752.

Leskin, L. P., & White, P. M. (2007). Attentional networks reveal executive function deficits in posttraumatic stress disorder. *Neuropsychology, 21*(3), 275–284.

Lezak, M. D. (1995). *Neuropsychological assessment* (3rd ed.). New York: Oxford University Press.

Liberzon, I., Britton, J. C., & Phan, K. L. (2003). Neural correlates of traumatic recall in posttraumatic stress disorder. *Stress, 6*(3), 151–156.

Liberzon, I., Taylor, S. F., Amdur, R., Jung, T. D., Chamberlain, K. R., Minoshima, S., et al. (1999). Brain activation in PTSD in response to trauma-related stimuli. *Society of Biological Psychiatry, 45*, 817–826.

Lindauer, R. J. L., Olff, M., van Meijel, E. P. M., Carlier, I. V. E., & Gersons, B. P. R. (2006). Cortisol, learning, memory, and attention in relation to smaller hippocampal volume in police officers with posttraumatic stress disorder. *Biological Psychiatry, 59*, 171–177.

Litz, B. T., Maguen, S., Friedman, M. J., Keane, T. M., & Resick, P. A. (2007). Early intervention for trauma. In M. J. Friedman, T. M. Keane, & P. A. Resick (Eds.), *Handbook of PTSD: Science and practice* (pp. 306–329). New York: Guilford Press.

MacDonald, C. M. (2003). Evaluation of stress debriefing interventions with military populations. *Military Medicine, 168*(12), 961–968.

MacDonald, H. Z., Vasterling, J. J., & Rasmusson, A. (in press). Neuropsychological underpinnings of PTSD in children and adolescents. In V. Ardino (Ed.), *Posttraumatic syndromes in children and adolescents*. Hoboken, NJ: Wiley-Blackwell.

Macklin, M. L., Metzger, L. J., Litz, B. T., McNally, R. J., Lasko, N. B., Orr, S. P., et al. (1998). Lower precombat intelligence is a risk factor for posttraumatic stress disorder. *Journal of Consulting and Clinical Psychology, 66*, 323–326.

Magruder, K. M., Frueh, B. C., Knapp, R. G., Johnson, M. R., Vaughan, J. A., III, Carson, T. C., et al. (2004). PTSD symptoms, demographic characteristics, and functional status among veterans treated in VA primary care clinics. *Journal of Traumatic Stress, 17*(4), 293–301.

Malberg, J. E., Eisch, A. J., Nestler, E. J., & Duman, R. S. (2000). Chronic antidepressant treatment increases neurogenesis in adult rat hippocampus. *Journal of Neuroscience, 20*(24), 9104–9110.

Malojcic, B., Mubrin, Z., Coric, B., Susnic, M., & Spilich, G. J. (2008). Consequences of mild traumatic brain injury on information processing assessed with attention and short-term memory tasks. *Journal of Neurotrauma, 25*(1), 30–37.

Marks, I., Lovell, K., Noshirvani, H., Livanou, M., & Thrasher, S. (1998). Treatment of posttraumatic stress disorder by exposure and/or cognitive restructuring: A controlled study. *Archives of General Psychiatry, 55*, 317–325.

Marx, B. P., Brailey, K., Proctor, S. P., MacDonald, H. Z., Graefe, A., Amoroso, P., et al. (2009). Association of time since deployment, combat intensity, and posttraumatic stress symptoms with neuropsychological outcomes following Iraq war deployment. *Archives of General Psychiatry, 66*, 996–1004.

Marx, B. P., Doron-Lamarca, S., Proctor, S. P., & Vasterling, J. J. (2009). The influence of pre-deployment neurocognitive functioning on post-deployment PTSD symptom outcomes among Iraq-deployed Army soldiers. *Journal of the International Neuropsychological Society, 15*, 840–852.

McEwen, B. S. (2000). Allostasis and allostatic load: Implications for neuropsychopharmacology. *Neuropsychopharmacology, 22*(2), 108–124.

McFarlane, A. C., Weber, D. L., & Clark, C. R. (1993). Abnormal stimulus processing in posttraumatic stress disorder. *Biological Psychiatry, 34*(5), 311–320.

McNally, R. J., Bryant, R. A., & Ehlers, A. (2003). Does early psychological intervention promote recovery from posttraumatic stress? *Psychological Science in the Public Interest, 4*(2), 45–79.

McNally, R. J., Lasko, N. B., Macklin, M. L., & Pitman, R. K. (1995). Autobiographical memory disturbance in combat-related posttraumatic stress disorder. *Behavioral Research and Therapy, 33*(6), 619–630.

McNally, R. J., & Shin, L. M. (1995). Association of intelligence with severity of posttraumatic stress disorder symptoms in Vietnam Combat veterans. *American Journal of Psychiatry, 152*(6), 936–938.

McTeague, L. M., McNally, R. J., & Litz, B. T. (2004). Prewar, war-zone, and postwar predictors of posttraumatic stress in female Vietnam Veteran health care providers. *Military Psychology, 16*(2), 99–114.

Meewisse, M. L., Nijdam, M. J., de Vries, G. J., Gersons, B. P., Kleber, R. J., van der Velden, P. G., et al. (2005). Disaster-related posttraumatic stress symptoms and sustained attention: Evaluation of depressive symptomatology and sleep disturbances as mediators. *Journal of Traumatic Stress, 18*(4), 299–302.

Mellman, T. A., Randolph, C. A., Brawman-Mintzer, O., & Flores, L. P. (1992). Phenomenology and course of psychiatric disorders associated with combat-related posttraumatic stress disorder. *American Journal of Psychiatry, 149*(11), 1568–1574.

Metzger, L. J., Gilbertson, M. W., & Orr, S. P. (2005). Electrophysiology of PTSD. In J. J. Vasterling & C. R. Brewin (Eds.), *Neuropsychology of PTSD: Biological, cognitive, and clinical perspectives* (pp. 83–102). New York: Guilford Press.

Milders, M., Fuchs, S., & Crawford, J. R. (2003). Neuropsychological impairments and changes in emotional and social behaviour following severe traumatic brain injury. *Journal of Clinical Experimental Neuropsychology, 25*(2), 157–172.

Milliken, C. S., Auchterlonie, J. L., & Hoge, C. W. (2007). Longitudinal assessment of mental health problems among active and reserve component soldiers returning from the Iraq war. *Journal of the American Medical Association, 298*(18), 2141–2148.

Mitchell, J. T. (1983). When disaster strikes...The critical incident stress debriefing process. *Journal of Emergency Medical Services, 8*(1), 33–39.

Mollica, R. F., Henderson, D. C., & Tor, S. (2002). Psychiatric effects of traumatic brain injury events in Cambodian survivors of mass violence. *British Journal of Psychiatry, 181*, 339–347.

Monson, C. M., Schnurr, P. P., Resick, P. A., Friedman, M. J., Young-Xu, Y., & Stevens, S. P. (2006). Cognitive processing therapy for veterans with military-related posttraumatic stress disorder. *Journal of Consulting and Clinical Psychology, 74*, 898–907.

Moore, E. L., Terryberry-Spohr, L., & Hope, D. A. (2006). Mild traumatic brain injury and anxiety sequelae: A review of the literature. *Brain Injury, 20*(2), 117–132.

Morgan, C. A., III, Hill, S., Fox, P., Kingham, P., & Southwick, S. M. (1999). Anniversary reactions in Gulf War veterans: A follow-up inquiry 6 years after the war. *American Journal of Psychiatry, 156*(7), 1075–1079.

Morgan, C. A., III, Kingham, P., Nicolaou, A., & Southwick, S. M. (1998). Anniversary reactions in Gulf War veterans: A naturalistic inquiry 2 years after the Gulf War. *Journal of Traumatic Stress, 11*(1), 165–171.

Nemeroff, C. B., Bremner, J. D., Foa, E. B., Mayberg, H. S., North, C. S., & Stein, M. B. (2006). Posttraumatic stress disorder: A state-of-the-science review. *Journal of Psychiatry Research, 40*(1), 1–21.

Neria, Y., Solomon, Z., & Dekel, R. (1998). An eighteen year follow-up study of Israeli prisoners of war and combat veterans. *Journal of Nervous and Mental Disease, 186*(3), 174–182.

Neylan, T. C., Lenoci, M., Rothlind, J., Metzler, T. J., Schuff, N., Du, A. T., et al. (2004). Attention, learning, and memory in posttraumatic stress disorder. *Journal of Traumatic Stress, 17*(1), 41–46.

Okie, S. (2005). Traumatic brain injury in the war zone. *New England Journal of Medicine, 352*(20), 2043–2047.

Oquendo, M. A., Friend, J. M., Halberstam, B., Brodsky, B. S., Burke, A. K., Grunebaum, M. F., et al. (2003). Association of comorbid posttraumatic stress disorder and major depression with greater risk for suicidal behavior. *American Journal of Psychiatry, 160*(3), 580–582.

Orcutt, H. K., Erickson, D. J., & Wolfe, J. (2004). The course of PTSD symptoms among Gulf War veterans: A growth mixture modeling approach. *Journal of Traumatic Stress, 17*(3), 195–202.

Pannu Hayes, J., LaBar, K. S., Petty, C. M., McCarthy, G., & Morey, R. A. (2009). Alterations in the neural circuitry for emotion and attention associated with posttraumatic stress symptomatology. *Psychiatry Research: Neuroimaging, 172,* 7–15.

Parslow, R. A., & Jorm, A. F. (2007). Pretrauma and posttrauma neurocognitive functioning and PTSD symptoms in a community sample of young adults. *American Journal of Psychiatry, 164*(3), 509–515.

Paunovic, N., & Ost, L. G. (2001). Cognitive-behavior therapy vs exposure therapy in the treatment of PTSD in refugees. *Behaviour Research and Therapy, 39,* 1183–1197.

Pederson, C. L., Maurer, S. H., & Kaminski, P. L. (2004). Hippocampal volume and memory performance in a community-based sample of women with posttraumatic stress disorder secondary to child abuse. *Journal of Traumatic Stress, 17*(1), 37–40.

Penk, W. E., Robinowitz, R., Black, J., & Dolan, M. P. (1989). Ethnicity: Posttraumatic stress disorder (PTSD) differences among Black, White, and Hispanic veterans who differ in degrees of exposure to combat in Vietnam. *Journal of Clinical Psychology, 45*(5), 729–735.

Raskin, S. A., & Rearick, E. (1996). Verbal fluency in individuals with mild traumatic brain injury. *Neuropsychology, 10*(3), 416–422.

Rasmusson, A. M., Vythilingam, M., & Morgan, C. A., 3rd. (2003). The neuroendocrinology of posttraumatic stress disorder: New directions. *CNS Spectrum, 8*(9), 651–656, 665–667.

Rauch, S. L., Shin, L. M., & Phelps, E. A. (2006). Neurocircuitry models of posttraumatic stress disorder and extinction: Human neuroimaging research—past, present, and future. *Biological Psychiatry, 60*(4), 376–382.

Rauch, S. L., Shin, L. M., Segal, E., Pitman, R. K., Carson, M. A., McMullin, K., et al. (2003). Selectively reduced regional cortical volumes in posttraumatic stress disorder. *Neuroreport, 14*(7), 913–916.

Rauch, S. L., van der Kolk, B. A., Fisler, R. E., Alpert, N. M., Orr, S. P., Savage, C. R., et al. (1996). A symptom provocation study of posttraumatic stress disorder using positron emission tomography and script-driven imagery. *Archives of General Psychiatry, 53*(5), 380–387.

Rauch, S. L., Whalen, P. J., Shin, L. M., McInerney, S. C., Macklin, M. L., Lasko, N. B., et al. (2000). Exaggerated amygdala response to masked facial stimuli in posttraumatic stress disorder: A functional MRI study. *Biological Psychiatry, 47*(9), 769–776.

Ravnkilde, B., Videbech, P., Clemmensen, K., Egander, A., Rasmussen, N. A., Gjedde, A., et al. (2003). The Danish PET/depression project: Cognitive function and regional cerebral blood flow. *Acta Psychiatrica Scandinavica, 108*(1), 32–40.

Resick, P. A., Galovski, T. E., O'Brien, U. M., Scher, C. D., Clum, G. A., Young-Xu, Y. (2008). A randomized clinical trial to dismantle components of cognitive processing therapy for posttraumatic stress disorder in female victims of interpersonal violence. *Journal of Consulting and Clinical Psychology, 76*(2), 243–258.

Resick, P. A., Monson, C. M., & Gutner, C. (2007). Psychosocial treatments for PTSD. In M. J. Friedman, T. M. Keane, & P. A. Resick (Eds.), *Handbook of PTSD: Science and practice* (pp. 330–358). New York: Guilford Press.

Resick, P. A., Nishith, P., Weaver, T. L., Astin, M.C., & Feuer, C. A. (2002). A comparison of cognitive-processing therapy with prolonged exposure and a waiting condition for the treatment of chronic posttraumatic stress disorder in female rape victims. *Journal of Consulting and Clinical Psychology, 70*, 867–879.

Resick, P. A., & Schnicke, M. K. (1992). Cognitive processing therapy for sexual assault victims. *Journal of Consulting and Clinical Psychology, 60*, 748–756.

Resick, P. A., & Schnicke, M. K. (1993). *Cognitive processing therapy for rape victims: A treatment manual.* Thousand Oaks, CA: Sage Publications.

Riddle, J. R., Smith, T. C., Corbeil, T. E., Engel, C. C., Wells, T. S., Hoge, C. W., et al. (2007). Millennium Cohort: The 2001–2003 baseline prevalence of mental disorders in the U.S. Military. *International Journal of Epidemiology, 60*, 192–201.

Rona, R. J., Fear, N. T., Hull, L., & Wessely, S. (2007). Women in novel occupational roles: Mental health trends in the UK Armed Forces. *International Journal of Epidemiology, 36*(2), 319–326.

Ryan, L. M., & Warden, D. L. (2003). Post concussion syndrome. *International Review of Psychiatry, 15*(4), 310–316.

Sachinvala, N., Von Scotti, H., McGuire, M., Fairbanks, L., Bakst, K., McGuire, M., et al. (2000). Memory, attention, function, and mood among patients with chronic posttraumatic stress disorder. *Journal of Nervous and Mental Disease, 188*(12), 818–823.

Sadler, A. G., Booth, B. M., Neilson, D., & Doebbeling, B. N. (2000). Health-related consequences of physical and sexual violence: Women in the military. *Obstetrics and Gynecology, 96*(3), 473–480.

Samuelson, K. W., Neylan, T. C., & Metzler, T. J. (2006). Neuropsychological functioning in posttraumatic stress disorder and alcohol abuse. *Neuropsychology, 20*(6), 716–726.

Savic, I., Bookheimer, S. Y., Fried, I., & Engel, J., Jr. (1997). Olfactory bedside test. A simple approach to identify temporo-orbitofrontal dysfunction. *Archives of Neurology, 54*(2), 162–168.

Schnurr, P. P., Spiro, A., III, & Paris, A. H. (2000). Physician-diagnosed medical disorders in relation to PTSD symptoms in older male military veterans. *Health Psychology, 19*(1), 91–97.

Schuff, N., Neylan, T. C., Lenoci, M. A., Du, A., Weiss, D. S., Marmar, C. R., et al. (2001). Decreased hippocampal N-acetylaspartate in the absence of atrophy in posttraumatic stress disorder. *Biological Psychiatry, 50*, 952–959.

Seidler, G. H., & Wagner, F. E. (2006). Comparing the efficacy of EMDR and trauma-focused cognitive-behavioral therapy in the treatment of PTSD: A meta-analytic study. *Psychological Medicine, 36*(11), 1515–1522.

Shalev, A. Y. (2001). What is posttraumatic stress disorder? *Journal of Clinical Psychiatry, 62*(Suppl. 17), 4–10.

Shalev, A. Y., Freedman, S., Peri, T., Brandes, D., Sahar, T., Orr, S. P., et al. (1998). Prospective study of posttraumatic stress disorder and depression following trauma. *American Journal of Psychiatry, 155*(5), 630–637.

Shin, L. M., Orr, S. P., Carson, M. A., Rauch, S. L., Macklin, M. L., Lasko, N. B., et al. (2004). Regional cerebral blood flow in the amygdala and medial prefrontal cortex during traumatic imagery in male and female Vietnam veterans with PTSD. *Archives of General Psychiatry, 61*(2), 168–176.

Shin, L. M., Rauch, S. L., & Pitman, R. K. (2005a). Structural and functional anatomy of PTSD: Findings from neuroimaging research. In J. J. Vasterling & C. R. Brewin (Eds.), *Neuropsychology of PTSD: Biological, cognitive, and clinical perspectives* (pp. 59–82). New York: Guilford Press.

Shin, L. M., Whalen, P. J., Pitman, R. K., Bush, G., Macklin, M. L., Lasko, N. B., et al. (2001). An fMRI study of anterior cingulate function in posttraumatic stress disorder. *Biological Psychiatry, 50*(12), 932–942.

Shin, L. M., Wright, C. I., Cannistraro, P. A., Wedig, M. M., McMullin, K., Martis, B., et al. (2005b). A functional magnetic resonance imaging study of amygdala and medial prefrontal cortex responses to overtly presented fearful faces in posttraumatic stress disorder. *Archives of General Psychiatry, 62*(3), 273–281.

Shucard, J. L., McCabe, D. C., & Szymanski, H. (2008). An event-related potential study of attention deficits in posttraumatic stress disorder during auditory and visual Go/Nogo continuous performance tasks. *Biological Psychology, 79*(2), 223–233.

Siepmann, M., Grossmann, J., Muck-Weymann, M., & Kirch, W. (2003). Effects of sertraline on autonomic and cognitive functions in healthy volunteers. *Psychopharmacology (Berl), 168*(3), 293–298.

Simms, L. J., Watson, D., & Doebbeling, B. N. (2002). Confirmatory factor analyses of posttraumatic stress symptoms in deployed and nondeployed veterans of the Gulf War. *Journal of Abnormal Psychology, 111*(4), 637–647.

Skinner, K. M., Kressin, N., Frayne, S., Tripp, T. J., Hankin, C. S., Miller, D. R., et al. (2000). The prevalence of military sexual assault among female Veterans' Administration outpatients. *Journal of Interpersonal Violence, 15*(3), 291–310.

Smith, T. C., Ryan, M. A., Wingard, D. L., Slymen, D. J., Sallis, J. F., & Kritz-Silverstein, D. (2008). New onset and persistent symptoms of posttraumatic stress disorder self reported after deployment and combat exposures: Prospective population based US military cohort study. *BMJ, 336*, 366–371.

Solomon, Z. (1990). Does the war end when the shooting stops? The psychological toll of war. *Journal of Applied Social Psychology, 20*(21), 1733–1745.

Solomon, Z., Mikulincer, M., & Avitzur, E. (1988). Coping, locus of control, social support, and combat-related posttraumatic stress disorder: A prospective study. *Journal of Personality and Social Psychology, 55*(2), 279–285.

Solomon, Z., Waysman, M., Avitzur, E., & Enoch, D. (1991). Psychiatric symptomatology among wives of soldiers following combat stress reaction: The role of the social network and marital relations. *Anxiety Research, 4*(3), 213–223.

Southwick, S. M., Davis, L. D., Aikins, D. E., Rasmusson, A., Barron, J., & Morgan, C. A. (2007). Neurobiological alterations associated with PTSD. In M. J. Friedman, T. M. Keane, & P. A. Resick (Eds.), *Handbook of PTSD: Science and practice* (pp. 166–189). New York: The Guilford Press.

Southwick, S., Paige, S. R., Morgan, C. A., Bremner, J. D., Krystal, J. H., & Charney, D. S. (1999). Neurotransmitter alterations in PTSD: Catecholamines and serotonin. *Seminars in Clinical Neuropsychiatry, 4*(4), 242–248.

Southwick, S. M., Rasmusson, A., Barron, J., & Arnsten, A. (2005). Neurobiological and neurocognitive alterations and PTSD: A focus on norepinephrine, serotonin, and the HPA axis. In J. J. Vasterling & C. R. Brewin (Eds.), *The neuropsychology of PTSD: Biological, cognitive, and clinical perspectives*. New York: Guilford Press.

Stein, M. B., Hanna, C., Vaerum, V., & Koverola, C. (1999). Memory functioning in adult women traumatized by childhood sexual abuse. *Journal of Traumatic Stress, 12*(3), 527–535.

Stein, B. D., Kataoka, S. H., Jaycox, L. H., Wong, M., Fink, A., Escudero, P., et al. (2002a). Theoretical basis and program design of a school-based mental health intervention for traumatized immigrant children: A collaborative research partnership. *The Journal of Behavioral Health Services and Research, 29*(3), 318–326.

Stein, M. B., Kennedy, C. M., & Twamley, E. W. (2002b). Neuropsychological function in female victims of intimate partner violence with and without posttraumatic stress disorder. *Biological Psychiatry, 52*(11), 1079–1088.

Stein, M. B., Koverola, C., Hanna, C., Torchia, M. G., & McClarty, B. (1997). Hippocampal volume in women victimized by childhood sexual abuse. *Psychological Medicine, 27*, 951–959.

Surís, A., Lind, L., Kashner, T. M., Borman, P. D., & Petty, F. (2004). Sexual assault in women veterans: An examination of PTSD risk, health care utilization, and cost of care. *Psychosomatic Medicine, 66*(5), 749–756.

Sutherland, K., & Bryant, R. A. (2007). Autobiographical memory in posttraumatic stress disorder before and after treatment. *Behavior Research and Therapy, 45*(12), 2915–2923.

Sutker, P. B., Uddo, M., Brailey, K., Vasterling, J. J., & Errera, P. (1994). Psychopathology in war-zone deployed and nondeployed Operation Desert Storm troops assigned graves registration duties. *Journal of Abnormal Psychology, 103*(2), 383–390.

Sutker, P. B., Vasterling, J. J., Brailey, K., & Allain, J. A. N. (1995). Memory, attention, and executive deficits in POW survivors: Contributing biological and psychological factors. *Neuropsychology, 9*(1), 118–125.

Tanielian, T., & Jaycox, L. H. (Eds.). (2008). *Invisible wounds of war: Psychological and cognitive injuries, their consequences, and services to assist recovery.* Santa Monica: RAND Corporation.

Thompson, C. E., Taylor, F. B., McFall, M., Barnes, R., & Raskind, M. (2008). Nonnightmare distressed awakenings in veterans with posttraumatic stress disorder: response to prazosin. *Journal of Traumatic Stress, 21*(4), 417–420.

Thompson, W. W., & Gottesman, II (2008). Challenging the conclusion that lower pre-induction cognitive ability increases risk for combat-related posttraumatic stress disorder in 2,375 combat-exposed, Vietnam War veterans. *Military Medicine, 173*(6), 576–582.

Turner, J. B., Turse, N. A., & Dohrenwend, B. P. (2007). Circumstances of service and gender differences in war-related PTSD: Findings from the National Vietnam Veteran Readjustment Study. *Journal of Traumatic Stress, 20*(4), 643–649.

Twamley, E. W., Hami, S., & Stein, M. B. (2004). Neuropsychological function in college students with and without posttraumatic stress disorder. *Psychiatry Research, 126*, 265–274.

Uddo, M., Vasterling, J. J., Brailey, K., & Sutker, P. B. (1993). Memory and attention in combat-related posttraumatic stress disorder (PTSD). *Journal of Psychopathology and Behavioral Assessment, 15*(1), 43–53.

Vanderploeg, R. D., Belanger, H. G., & Curtiss, G. (2009). Mild traumatic brain injury and posttraumatic stress disorder and their associations with health symptoms. *Archives of Physical and Medical Rehabilitation, 90*, 1084–1093.

Vanderploeg, R. D., Curtiss, G., Luis, C. A., & Salazar, A. M. (2007). Long-term morbidities following self-reported mild traumatic brain injury. *Journal of Clinical and Experimental Neuropsychology, 29*(6), 585–598.

Vasterling, J. J., & Brailey, K. (2005). Neuropsychological findings in adults with PTSD. In J. J. Vasterling & C. R. Brewin (Eds.), *Neuropsychology of PTSD: Biological, cognitive, and clinical perspectives* (pp. 178–207). New York: The Guilford Press.

Vasterling, J. J., Brailey, K., Constans, J. I., Borges, A., & Sutker, P. B. (1997). Assessment of intellectual resources in Gulf War veterans: Relationship to PTSD. *Assessment, 4*(1), 51–59.

Vasterling, J. J., Brailey, K., Constans, J. I., & Sutker, P. B. (1998). Attention and memory dysfunction in posttraumatic stress disorder. *Neuropsychology, 12*(1), 125–133.

Vasterling, J. J., Brailey, K., & Sutker, P. B. (2000a). Olfactory identification in combat-related posttraumatic stress disorder. *Journal of Traumatic Stress, 13*(2), 241–253.

Vasterling, J. J., Constans, J. I., & Hanna-Pladdy, B. (2000b). Head injury as a predictor of psychological outcome in combat veterans. *Journal of Traumatic Stress, 13*(3), 441–451.

Vasterling, J. J., Duke, L. M., Brailey, K., Constans, J. I., Allain, A. N., & Sutker, P. B. (2002). Attention, learning, and memory performances and intellectual resources in Vietnam veterans: PTSD and no disorder comparisons. *Neuropsychology, 16*(1), 5–14.

Vasterling, J. J., Duke, L. M., Tomlin, H., Lowery, N., & Kaplan, E. (2004). Global-local visual processing in posttraumatic stress disorder. *Journal of the International Neuropsychological Society, 10*, 709–718.

Vasterling, J. J., Proctor, S. P., Amoroso, P., Kane, R., Heeren, T., & White, R. F. (2006). Neuropsychological outcomes of army personnel following deployment to the Iraq war. *Journal of the American Medical Association, 296*(5), 519–529.

Vasterling, J. J., Schumm, J., Proctor, S. P., Gentry, E., King, D. W., & King, L. A. (2008). Posttraumatic stress disorder and health functioning in a nontreatment-seeking sample of Iraq war veterans: A prospective analysis. *Journal of Rehabilitation Research and Development, 45*(3), 347–358.

Vasterling, J. J., Verfaellie, M., & Sullivan, K. D. (2009). Mild traumatic brain injury and posttraumatic stress disorder in returning veterans: Perspectives from neuroscience. *Clinical Psychology Review, 29*, 674–684.

Veltmeyer, M. D., Clark, C. R., McFarlane, A. C., Felmingham, K. L., Bryant, R. A., & Gordon, E. (2005). Integrative assessment of brain and cognitive function in posttraumatic stress disorder. *Journal of Integrated Neuroscience, 4*(1), 145–159.

Verfaellie, M., & Vasterling, J. J. (2009). Memory in PTSD: A neurocognitive approach. In P. Shiromani, T. M. Keane, & J. LeDoux (Eds.), *Neurobiology of PTSD* (pp. 105–130). Totowa, NJ: Humana Press.

Vermetten, E., Vythilingam, M., Southwick, S. M., Charney, D. S., & Bremner, J. D. (2003). Long-term treatment with paroxetine increases verbal declarative memory and hippocampal volume in posttraumatic stress disorder. *Biological Psychiatry, 54*(7), 693–702.

Veterans Affairs/DOD. (2004). *VA/DoD clinical practice guideline for the management of posttraumatic stress. Version 1.0.* Washington, DC: Veterans Health Administration, DOD.

Wadsworth, E. J., Moss, S. C., Simpson, S. A., & Smith, A. P. (2005). SSRIs and cognitive performance in a working sample. *Human Psychopharmacology, 20*(8), 561–572.

Warden, D. (2006). Military TBI during the Iraq and Afghan wars. *Journal of Head Trauma Rehabilitation, 21*(5), 398–402.

Wild, J., & Gur, R. C. (2008). Verbal memory and treatment response in posttraumatic stress disorder. *British Journal of Psychiatry, 193*(3), 254–255.

Wilde, E. A., Bigler, E. D., Hunter, J. V., Fearing, M. A., Scheibel, R. S., Newsome, M. R., et al. (2007). Hippocampus, amygdala, and basal ganglia morphometrics in children after moderate-to-severe traumatic brain injury. *Developmental Medicine & Child Neurology, 49*(4), 294–299.

Williams, R., Kos, A. M., Ajdukovic, D., Van der Veer, G., & Feldman, M. (2008). Recommendations on evaluating community based psychosocial programmes. *Intervention, 6*(1), 12–21.

Wolfe, J., & Charney, D. S. (1991). Use of neuropsychological assessment in posttraumatic stress disorder. *Psychological Assessment: A Journal of Consulting and Clinical Psychology, 3*(4), 573–580.

Wolfe, J., Sharkansky, E. J., Read, J. P., Dawson, R., Martin, J. A., & Ouimette, P. C. (1998). Sexual harassment and assault as predictors of PTSD symptomatology among U.S. female Persian Gulf War military personnel. *Journal of Interpersonal Violence, 13*(1), 40–57.

Woodward, S. H., Kaloupek, D. G., Streeter, C. C., Martinez, C., Schaer, M., & Eliez, S. (2006). Decreased anterior cingulate volume in combat-related PTSD. *Biological Psychiatry, 59*(7), 582–587.

Yamasue, H., Kasai, K., Iwanami, A., Ohtani, T., Yamada, H., Abe, O., et al. (2003). Voxel-based analysis of MRI reveals anterior cingulate gray-matter volume reduction in posttraumatic stress disorder due to terrorism. *Proceedings of the National Academy of Science U S A, 100*(15), 9039–9043.

Yang, C. C., Tu, Y. K., Hua, M. S., & Huang, S. J. (2007). The association between the postconcussion symptoms and clinical outcomes for patients with mild traumatic brain injury. *Journal of Trauma, 62*(3), 657–663.

Yehuda, R. (2002). Posttraumatic stress disorder. *New England Journal of Medicine, 346*(2), 108–114.

Yehuda, R., Golier, J. A., Harvey, P. D., Stavitsky, K., Kaufman, S., Grossman, R. A., et al. (2005). Relationship between cortisol and age-related memory impairments in Holocaust survivors with PTSD. *Psychoneuroendocrinology, 30*(7), 678–687.

Yehuda, R., Keefe, R. S. E., Harvey, P., Levengood, R. A., Gerber, D. K., Geni, J., et al. (1995). Learning and memory in combat veterans with PTSD. *American Journal of Psychiatry, 152*, 137–139.

Yehuda, R., & McFarlane, A. C. (1995). Conflict between current knowledge about posttraumatic stress disorder and its original conceptual basis. *American Journal of Psychiatry, 152*(12), 1705–1713.

Yule, W. (2001). Posttraumatic stress disorder in the general population and in children. *Journal of Clinical Psychiatry, 62*(Suppl. 17), 23–28.

Zalewski, C., Thompson, W., & Gottesman, I. I. (1994). Comparison of neuropsychological test performance in PTSD, generalized anxiety disorder, and control Vietnam veterans. *Assessment, 1*(2), 133–142.

Zatzick, D. F., Marmar, C. R., Weiss, D. S., Browner, W. S., Metzler, T. J., Golding, J. M., et al. (1997). Posttraumatic stress disorder and functioning and quality of life outcomes in a nationally representative sample of male Vietnam veterans. *American Journal of Psychiatry, 154*(12), 1690–1695.

13 Cognition and Decision Making in Extreme Environments

JEFFREY A. McNEIL AND C. A. MORGAN III

War is the realm of uncertainty; three quarters of the factors on which action in war is based are wrapped in a fog of greater or lesser uncertainty.

Carl von Clausewitz, The Nature of War

In this chapter, we discuss what is currently known about how the stress associated with extreme situations and environments may negatively impact the ability of humans experiencing such stress to think clearly and to make decisions. The majority of what we know at present is derived from studies conducted in military populations. From a prevalence of exposure standpoint, military personnel are most at risk; what we learn from such studies may be used to develop ways of protecting military and other high-risk personnel from the negative cognitive and emotional impact of such stress and develop methods to enhance recovery from stress.

Military members are often called upon to make quick, life-dependent decisions in precarious and ambiguous environments (i.e., combat operations) where there is significant risk of serious injury or loss of life (Figure 13.1). In addition to traditional threats and stressors, military personnel also must learn to use new and emerging technologies designed to aid the warrior in combat. These new technologies place a premium on a warfighter's attentional capacity, ability to make decisions, and the ability

Figure 13.1 Iraqi Army Soldiers and U.S. troops from Company A, Third Battalion, 187th Infantry Regiment. ODRCD can impact service members' abilities to safely perform their missions. (Photo courtesy of U.S. Army.)

to engage motor control to apply these advantages (Janelle & Hatfield, 2008). Warfighters experience unique pressures and stress that have both acute and cumulative neurocognitive effects. In this chapter, we introduce the concept of operational demand–related cognitive decline (ODRCD), discuss the neurobiological and neurocognitive elements most likely to be impacted by significant operational stress, and address currently available and emerging performance enhancement techniques or methods designed to mitigate the harmful cognitive effects of acute stress.

THE CONCEPT OF OPERATIONAL DEMAND–RELATED COGNITIVE DECLINE

The idea of ODRCD traces its origins to the concept of *combat stress-induced cognitive decline*, explained by Lieberman et al. (2005). To better describe the *fog of war*, these researchers operationalized the condition and described it as pervasive decrements in both simple and complex cognitive abilities under combat conditions. While this definition has been useful for the development of specific measures and neurological models, the term has been insufficient for the purposes of investigating operational decision making in extreme situations.

In conceptualizing the cognitive decrement using the term "combat stress-induced," many operational situations are excluded, as much of what operational forces do is not conducted in a combat environment (e.g., pararescue, humanitarian operations). In addition, the term "combat stress" has taken on other connotations in current use, namely it has become synonymous with acute stress disorder and posttraumatic stress disorder (PTSD). ODRCD more accurately depicts the normal decrement of human cognition in extreme military and operational situations and negates the assumption that deficits observed in healthy service members are pathognomonic. Consequently, ODRCD is defined as *decrements in cognitive performance or decision making resulting from the manifold pressures or acute stressors characteristic of dangerous or extreme environments.* Given that this concept is a new one, much of the research used to develop the concept of ODRCD is based on clinical research and studies of PTSD. Fortunately, there is an emerging body of literature exploring performance in both normal and elite athletes and warfighters.

NEUROBIOLOGY OF STRESS

When discussing cognition in extreme environments and the concept of ODRCD, myriad physiological alterations that occur must be considered. Independent of whether such changes are caused by relatively benign stressors or by traumatic stressors (i.e., significant injury or threat to life, such as experienced in combat) they will involve the fight/flight systems of the human nervous system.

The current body of knowledge that informs us about human cognition under extreme stress is derived from research conducted in both military and civilian environments. The information provided from military studies has provided valuable clues about how human neurobiology is affected by acute and extended stress that is psychological and physical in nature. The bulk of this information comes from investigations of military members enrolled in military survival school training programs, combat diver qualification programs, or selection and assessment programs. The civilian studies of human cognition under extreme environmental conditions are largely derived from research on humans in high altitude chambers or in extreme temperature environments. In this chapter, we have drawn on findings from both military and civilian investigations and provide a brief review of the neurobiology of stress. Given that our current knowledge is likely to grow, the following description is not definitive, but rather a reflection of what is currently known. A brief review of the literature is provided for the neurobiological and neuroanatomical elements of acute stress.

Norepinephrine and Epinephrine

Norepinephrine (NE) and epinephrine (E) are critical hormones in the neurobiological response to stress. Acute stress-related increases in NE have been found in the amygdala, hippocampus, striatum, and prefrontal cortex (PFC). Rapid activation of the locus coeruleus/NE system facilitates the organisms' ability to respond effectively in dangerous situations (Southwick et al., 1999).

Specifically, exposure to stress will induce alterations in the hypothalamic pituitary adrenal axis. This refers to the mammalian system in which stress exposure increases sympathetic arousal in the brain, which then signals the release of adrenalin in the body. Adrenalin triggers, among many things, the release of glucose and noradrenalin in the brain (see Southwick et al., 1999, for an in-depth discussion). The point we would like the reader to focus on is this; the stress-induced increases in NE that occur in the human brain have significant consequences for how well the human will be able to respond to and deal with environmental events.

NE is involved in the organism's ability to selectively attend to meaningful stimuli. By selectively enhancing strong excitatory or inhibitory output, NE facilitates the processing of relevant stimuli (Southwick et al., 1999). However, under stressful conditions when NE release is increased above basal levels in the PFC, postsynaptic alpha receptors (alpha receptor sites on cell membranes are part of the G-protein-coupled receptor family and are intimately involved with regulating turnover of synaptive NE) become activated causing a decline in PFC functioning. It has been proposed that this inhibition of PFC functioning during stressful or dangerous situations has value for survival by allowing the organism to employ rapid habitual subcortical modes of responding (Arnsten, 1988; Birnbaum, Gobeske, Auerbach, Taylor, & Arnsten, 1999).

"Increased responsivity of noradrenergic systems is consistent with a sensitization model of some trauma related mental health problems (i.e., PTSD) where biochemical, physiological, and behavioral responses to subsequent stressors increase over time" (Southwick et al., 1999, p. 1200). There is compelling evidence for increased noradrenergic activity in those diagnosed with PTSD. (For a discussion of the neural underpinnings of PTSD, see chapter 12.)

With respect to cognition under high stress, both animal and human data indicate that increases in NE and E have been shown to enhance memory retrieval when administered at the time of memory testing. It has even been hypothesized that traumatic events stimulate the release of E and NE and that these neurotransmitters cause an overconsolidation of memory for the stressful event (McGaugh, 1989), which in turn propagate the re-experiencing subset of symptoms of PTSD. In addition, although numerous animal and human studies have provided evidence for the idea that increases in NE enhance memory, Morgan et al. (2004; Morgan, Doran, Steffian, Hazlett, & Southwick, 2006) found that human memory related to extremely high stress events is degraded and not enhanced by stress exposure.

Cortisol

Glucocorticoids, such as cortisol, are a class of steroid hormones that are released from the adrenal glands; they are essential for life and regulate a variety of important cardiovascular, metabolic immunologic and homeostatic functions. They play a critical role in human adaptation to stress. They mobilize energy, suppress nonessential anabolic activity, and increase cardiovascular tone. Mason (1968) detailed the psychoendocrine responses of monkeys exposed to uncontrollable stress and reported that cortisol significantly increases with animal distress and subjective awareness of distress.

Morgan et al. (2000a) found that the extreme stress of military survival training produced dramatic alterations in cortisol, percent free cortisol, testosterone, and thyroid indices, and provided further evidence that unavoidable stress exacerbates the physiological response to stress. In addition, if there is little psychological distress, such elevations of cortisol are not observed. The notion that subjective perception is intimately linked to neurobiological alterations has implications for the service member fighting on the modern battlefield. As service members become more uncomfortable or uncertain psychologically, the larger impact stress will have, in one sense because it is becoming "uncontrollable." The uncontrollable stress induced by a convoy mission in an improvised explosive device–infested area is one illustration of this principle. As service members traverse a route with a history of improvised explosive device strikes, there may be little (e.g., rudimentary security and countermeasures) that can be done to actively prevent a catastrophic event. In contrast, units for whom there are deliberate and carefully planned offensive raids may have at least the perception of "controllable" stress. In a deliberate assault, service members have control of timing, often have the element of surprise, a dedicated quick reaction force, and may have the availability of close air support. Therefore, the degree to which stress is uncontrollable is much lower and, as a result, would be expected to induce fewer cognitive and physiological alterations (i.e., lower ODRCD). While this is a simplistic example, it does illustrate some differences in the types of stress encountered in combat scenarios.

Prolonged exposure to uncontrollable stress (and associated elevations of cortisol) may cause physiological harm, specifically damaging the neurons in some specific areas of the brain. Foy, Stanton, Levine, and Thompson (1987, p. 138) reported that hippocampal slices prepared from adult rats that had experienced unpredictable and inescapable restraint-tailshock stress showed marked impairments of long-term potentiation (LTP). As LTP is related to information storage in the brain, uncontrollable stress can significantly impair memory processes.

Stress-induced levels of cortisol have been reported to correlate with cognitive deficits. For example, administration of stress levels of cortisol to normal human subjects has been found to selectively impair verbal declarative memory (Newcomer, Craft, Hershey, Askins, & Bardgett, 1994). Morgan et al. (2001a, 2001b) found that high levels of cortisol induced by uncontrollable stress were related to poorer cognitive performance (i.e., interrogation performance) in military survival training. The relationship between uncontrollable stress, elevated cortisol, and cognitive performance has significant implications for military decision making.

Neuropeptide-Y

Over the past decade, evidence from preclinical and clinical research studies have indicated that neuropeptide-Y (NPY) plays an integral role in the regulation of both central nervous system and peripheral nervous system functioning (Morgan et al., 2000b). Generally speaking, NPY serves to aid the organism in maintaining an ideal level of arousal in response to a stressor without being overwhelmed by it. Specifically, NPY, like corticotrophin-releasing factor (CRF), is released by populations of neurons critical to fear and threat responding (such as those in the amygdala; Morgan et al., 2000a, 2000b). While CRF increases anxiety and enhances fear, NPY exhibits anxiolytic functions and reduces alarm and arousal. NPY may play an integral role in human resilience and contribute to a physiological buffer from ODRCD.

Reductions in NPY have been discovered in combat veterans both with and without PTSD. Rasmussen et al. (2000) found that male Vietnam combat veterans with PTSD have low baseline and yohimbine-stimulated plasma NPY levels compared to healthy nontraumatized male subjects (Rasmusson et al., 1998). Within the PTSD group, baseline plasma NPY levels also correlated negatively with combat exposure scale scores, yohimbine-stimulated increases in plasma 3-methoxy-4-hydroxyphenylglycol MHPG (the major metabolite of NE), and baseline PTSD symptoms (Rasmusson et al., 2000).

These findings are consistent with numerous preclinical studies demonstrating the capacity of NPY to inhibit the release of NE from peripheral and central noradrenergic neurons and to diminish the firing of locus coeruleus neurons via presynaptic NPY Y2 receptor stimulation (Illes & Regenold, 1990; Colmers & Bleakman, 1994). This suggests that combat stress–induced decreases in *baseline* plasma NPY may mediate, in part, the noradrenergic system hyperreactivity observed in combat-related PTSD and the inappropriate expression of exaggerated alarm and anxiety reactions in veterans with PTSD long after war. However, it is also important to note that Rasmusson et al. (2000) measured plasma NPY in a group of Vietnam combat controls without PTSD who had been exposed to similar levels of combat as the PTSD subjects. This group demonstrated low baseline plasma NPY levels and peak MHPG responses to yohimbine comparable to those of the PTSD group, suggesting that the combat control group, like the PTSD group, may have adaptively acquired an enhanced capacity to rapidly trigger a fight or flight response. In contrast, the combat controls showed significantly higher peak NPY responses to yohimbine than the PTSD group. In addition, they showed no increase in anxiety and no PTSD symptoms in response to yohimbine, quite unlike the PTSD subjects. Thus, it seems possible that the combat control subjects were protected from elevated levels of anxiety by their robust NPY responses to yohimbine stimulation. This work suggests that a lowering of baseline plasma NPY levels may be a normal adaptive response to life-threatening stress exposure, but that a blunted NPY *response* to yohimbine stimulation may play a role in the generation of anxiety and distress (as demonstrated in the PTSD subjects). It has been shown, for instance, that a low intracerebroventricular dose of NPY increases anxiety in animals via activity at central Y2 receptors (Inui et al., 1998), whereas higher doses of NPY exert anxiolytic effects via central Y1 receptors (Inui et al., 1998). This suggests that a dose-dependent balance between activation of central Y1 and Y2 receptors may determine how much anxiety is experienced in response to increases in brain synaptic NPY levels. Therefore, it may be important that the yohimbine-stimulated NPY levels of the PTSD group were not significantly different from the placebo NPY levels of the healthy group. This suggests that recruitment of possible dose-dependent anxiolytic effects of NPY may not have occurred in the PTSD subjects. This possibility is supported by observations of Morgan et al. (2002) where plasma NPY levels achieved after simulated interrogation stress in military trainees correlated negatively with dissociative symptoms and symptoms of psychological distress and correlated positively with objective measures of good performance.

It should be noted, however, that at present it has not yet been confirmed whether yohimbine-induced changes in plasma NPY levels are paralleled in the brain or impact the central mediation of anxiety or fear. What is confirmed is that yohimbine crosses the blood-brain barrier and increases the central release of NE (Peskind, Veith, Dorsa, Bumbrecht, & Raskind, 1989), which suggests that NPY co-localized with NE in central noradrenergic neuronal terminals also may be released by the peripheral administration of yohimbine. In addition, peripherally circulating NPY may have direct access to brain areas that regulate visceral cardiac, respiratory, and gastrointestinal responses associated with anxiety and monitored in the study by Southwick et al. (1993); NPY-responsive Y4 receptors have been identified in the blood–brain barrier-free area postrema and subpostrema (Larsen & Kristensen, 1997). These nuclei interact with the immediately adjacent nuclei of the dorsal vagal complex and nucleus tractus solitarius, which, in turn, integrate afferent and efferent neural and humoral signals regulating the cardiovascular, respiratory, and gastrointestinal systems.

As mentioned, clinical studies in healthy military populations have provided evidence for the idea that NPY may buffer the negative impact of stress on human cognition. In two related studies (Morgan et al., 2000a, 2001b), plasma NPY concentration in humans exposed to military survival training were studied. Exposure to acute, uncontrollable stress affected levels of circulating plasma NPY in humans. NPY was significantly increased by the acute psychological stress of military interrogation and reduced in a subset of individuals 24 hours after the cessation of stress (Figure 13.2).

Special Forces (SF) soldiers had significantly higher NPY levels after exposure to acute stress and, after 24 hours, had returned to baseline pre-stress levels, whereas non-SF soldiers were significantly below baseline values. Relevant to the focus of this chapter, it is important to note that Soldiers who exhibited greater release of NPY in response to stress exhibited better performance—as rated by the military instructors—when performing an interactive task during stress exposure. In addition, Morgan et al. (2000a, 2000b) noted a negative relationship between NPY levels during stress and the degree to which Soldiers experienced altered cognitive processing known as symptoms of dissociation. Because such symptoms and interactive

Figure 13.2 Various aspects of captivity, particularly uncertainty and abusive interrogations, result in a variety of physiological consequences. Interrelationships between individual characteristics and environmental exposure impact a service member's ability to problem solve.

performance reflect central nervous system functioning, it is reasonable to hypothesize (and consistent with animal research data) that NPY may have preserved performance by sustaining function at the level of the PFC.

As noted above, neuronal structures integrally involved in the fear response (amygdala, locus coeruleus, hippocampus, and bed nucleus of the stria-terminalis) have dense networks of NPY fibers (Heilig et al., 1990), and it is likely these would be activated during exposure to extreme stress. Individuals with high NPY would be more capable of managing the stress-induced state of high arousal and maintain focus on the cognitive tasks at hand. Indeed, stress-induced NPY release was significantly greater in Soldiers who successfully completed extensive training and a rigorous selection process to obtain membership in U.S. Army Special Forces (Morgan et al., 2001a, 2001b). Induced NPY release was positively correlated with mental clarity and alertness, and this is consistent with findings that NPY demonstrates antianxiety properties, as well as enhancement of memory and alertness during stress (Herschbach, Henrich, & von Rad, 1999). While stress-induced E release did not differ between SF and Rangers/Marines, plasma NE was significantly higher in SF Soldiers under acute stress. Activation of CRF systems may lead to increases in central NE release along with NPY release. However, NPY and cortisol levels were related to interrogation performance, while NE and E were not significantly correlated with performance.

Dehydroepiandrosterone

Dehydroepiandrosterone (DHEA) is an endogenous hormone secreted by the adrenal cortex in response to adrenocorticotropin-releasing hormone. DHEA-S is the sulfated derivative of DHEA. A growing body of research has provided evidence that DHEA-S is involved in an organism's response to stress and that it may provide beneficial behavioral and neurotrophic effects (Morgan et al., 2004).

Morgan et al. (2004) investigated the relationship of plasma DHEA, cortisol levels, symptoms of dissociation, and military performance in military survival school students. The principal finding was that individuals with a higher DHEA-S–salivary cortisol ratio during stress experienced fewer symptoms of dissociation and exhibited superior military performance. Because indices of dissociation and military performance presumably measure central processes, the data provide support that in healthy humans, the ratio, or balance between circulating levels of DHEA-S to unbound cortisol may help buffer against centrally mediated, negative effects of stress (Morgan et al., 2004).

IMPLICATIONS FOR ASSESSMENT AND SELECTION

Sun Tzu states in his seminal work *The Art of War,* regarding a discussion of selecting scouts to conduct reconnaissance, "we should select the bravest officers and those who are most intelligent and keen..." (Sun & Giles, 1910, p. 105). It is not only intuitive that selecting the right individuals for jobs is imperative, but it has strong historical roots (for a discussion of this issue in the U.S. military, see chapter 1). Among other critical attributes, it is imperative for an assessment program to identify those with resistance to ODRCD.

While assessment and selection of military members is not the subject of this chapter, the studies cited in this chapter do provide confirmation of the importance of assessment and selection programs. Selecting individuals that can make good decisions in extreme environments has significant utility for a specialized unit or organization (Picano, Williams, & Roland, 2006). Inasmuch as a program has demonstrated validity and reliability, personnel selection based on cognitive, interpersonal, and emotional qualities provides potential advantages in both efficiency and effectiveness. It is most efficient to select warriors that learn quickly and adapt to ambiguous environments rapidly. Ostensibly, these select individuals should make better decisions and enhance mission effectiveness. For example, Morgan et al. (2001a, 2001b) reported significant differences in NPY release and superior interrogation performance for SF soldiers and non-SF Soldiers. Despite these neurobiological and cognitive differences between SF and non-SF Soldiers, it is difficult to ascertain if these are due primarily to endogenous factors, exogenous (i.e., training) factors, or a combination of both (i.e., self, military selection and subsequent training). However, for selection programs to work, a high percentage of candidates must be weeded out, and this lends itself to potential personnel shortfalls, especially in larger organizations. Ultimately, as we learn more about the neurobiology of cognitive performance, we may be able to investigate if by enhancing these factors (NPY, DHEA, etc.) we can get regular service members to function cognitively more like Army SF or other elite warriors.

NEUROCOGNITIVE FACTORS AND PERFORMANCE

This section includes an examination of select research on cognitive abilities and decision making. Investigating military training, athletic performance, and marksmanship training all have implications for studying military decision making in high-threat situations. While the survival school model includes more acute stress and has more fidelity with realistic high-stress combat scenarios, much of combat includes day-to-day decision making and engaging in "overlearned" activities or a habituation of perceiving threat over time due to success and perceived safety. This section illustrates the relevance of ODRCD across the spectrum of training that approximates the demands of combat. In addition, we cannot disregard the presence of complex and variable combat demands that may require cognitive abilities not tapped by neuropsychological tests. It is also important to mention that many fatal errors are made at times of low stress (i.e., negligent discharges, helicopter crashes). In some scenarios, duties become monotonous and a lack of novelty or stimulation can lead to a lackadaisical approach to otherwise perilous operations.

A majority of the research on the neuropsychology and cognitive factors of performance is based on sports research, including rifle marksmanship. While this research does not present a direct analogy of realistic life-threatening conditions, decision making, leadership, stress modulation, situational awareness, and preparation and training are critical to both sports and military environments (Janelle, Singer, & Williams, 1999).

Lieberman et al. (2005) studied both Army Rangers and Navy SEAL engaging in training scenarios designed with multiple stressors and intended to simulate combat conditions. One study was conducted during a Ranger training exercise intended to evaluate junior leaders. The Ranger subjects underwent nearly 72 hours of continuous wakefulness during an intense combat exercise. The Navy study was completed during U.S. Navy SEAL Hell Week, which includes extreme physical exertion, exposure to cold temperatures, and sleep deprivation. Performance decrements or ODRCD of the magnitude observed in the Rangers and the sea-air-land (SEAL) trainees could, in a combat situation, have led to failure to respond correctly to critical events (choice reaction time), failure to detect the enemy (impaired vigilance) and incorrect identification of friendly and enemy forces (attention and memory). Even an average of 9 years of experience in the Rangers' case did not prevent the onset of significant cognitive impairment (Lieberman et al., 2005).

Attention

Sustained attention, divided attention, and integration of visual and auditory cues are critical to military performance in extreme environments. Anxiety has considerable impact on attention and has received a great deal of coverage in previous research. For example, an interesting study with some analogous demands to tactical driving in an urban combat environment was conducted by Janelle et al. (1999). Janelle et al. (1999) measured visual search patterns (saccades induced by visual cues) and found in a car-racing simulation study that anxious drivers became increasingly distracted by the appearance of relevant and irrelevant peripheral cues, requiring foveation of the periphery, thereby detracting visual gaze from the race course. They postulated that anxiety caused constriction of the visual field and suggested that inefficient search strategies were more dominant when anxious (Janelle et al., 1999).

Working Memory

Working memory depends primarily on the PFC. In both rats and monkeys, high levels of dopamine and NE turnover in the PFC have been shown to induce cognitive deficits, including impairment in spatial working memory. Under conditions of high stress, NE release is increased above basal levels in the PFC and causes a decline in PFC functioning (Arnstein, 1998; Birnbaum et al., 1999).

Morgan and colleagues (2006) researched stress-induced deficits in working memory and visuoconstructive abilities in special operations Soldiers enrolled in SERE training (survive, evade, resist, escape). The Rey-Osterrieth Complex Figure (ROCF) drawing task is a standardized neuropsychological instrument that tests visual perception, visuospatial organization, motor functioning, and memory (Lezak et al., 2004). ROCF copy and recall results were within normal limits in the control group, whereas ROCF copy and recall were impaired in the stress group. The findings of this study suggest that exposure to realistic levels of acute stress results in significant decrements in visuoconstruction and visual working memory.

Shooting Performance

Emerging EEG and motor behavior research suggests that superior marksmanship performance is marked by mental economy, particularly of analytical associative processes, and that reduction of excessive cortico-cortical communication between such processes and motor regions underlies enhancement and consistency of shooting performance

(Hatfield & Hillman, 2001). Janelle et al. (2008) conducted a thorough review of studies investigating cortical activity and shooting performance (Bird, 1987; Hatfield et al., 1984 ; Hatfield, Landers, & Ray, 1987; Hatfield, Landers, Ray, & Daniels, 1982; Salazar et al., 1990). The subjects of the reviewed studies were members of the Army Marksmanship Unit from Fort Benning, Georgia, and successful intercollegiate performers. In general, the EEG electrodes were placed on the left and right occipital and temporal lobes to measure both verbal/analytic reasoning (left) and visuospatial reasoning (right). Based on this review, it appears that "expert marksmen economize brain activity that is essential and relax the neurocognitive processes unrelated to their current task demands" (Janelle & Hatfield, 2008). One hypothesis for this observation of economized brain activity is that expert marksmen had been selected due in part to their resilience or resistance to ODRCD. However, it is difficult to ascertain if training, innate abilities, or a combination of both contributed to the observed resilience.

Hauffler, Spalding, Santa Maria, and Hatfield (2000) conducted a study on EEG activity (recorded from the frontal, central, temporal, parietal, and occipital regions) with novice and expert marksmen including a target-shooting task as well as comparative verbal and spatial tasks. Their results from measures of frontal region activity suggest that expert marksmen are less reliant on effortful executive processing compared to their novice counterparts, and group differences in temporal activation during aiming suggest a reduction in the reliance of verbal analytic thinking with expertise. After an extensive review of extant research, Janelle and Hatfield (2008) reported that there is a robust and consistent picture of the cerebral cortical processes associated with superior shooting performance, which supports the notion of economy of cortical processes when the skilled marksman is free to concentrate and focus.

Neurofeedback and EEG

EEG biofeedback, or neurofeedback, is a sophisticated form of biofeedback based on specific aspects of cortical activity. It requires the individual to learn to modify some aspect of his/her cortical activity (Vernon, 2005). By identifying associations between particular patterns of cortical activity and specific states or aspects of behavior that are classified as optimal, one can attempt to train an individual to enhance performance by mirroring the pattern of cortical activity seen during such optimal states (Vernon, 2005). For example, Bird (1987) reported distinct cortical activity with expert riflemen as compared to amateur riflemen. Egner and Gruzelier (2004) studied 22 participants to investigate the influence of training low beta frequencies in healthy individuals, with the Test of Variable Attention as the dependent variable. Egner and Gruzelier (2004) concluded that the results represented a significant enhancement of attention scores in healthy volunteers through the use of neurofeedback. However, the current body of research on neurofeedback training and performance enhancement remains equivocal (Vernon, 2005).

A recent investigation by Kerick, Allendar, and Hatfield (2007) reported an increase in cortical activity (i.e., alpha suppression) in a study of U.S. Marines executing a target-shooting task under cognitive load (discrimination of enemy and friendly targets during shooting) relative to a nonstressed condition (i.e., shooting only enemy targets). The heightened activity under the condition of cognitive load was associated with declines in performance accuracy and decision making.

Saarela (1999) conducted an EEG performance study with marksmen and reported that the frontal asymmetry index was decreased when marksmen performed a target-shooting task under time pressure, relative to a nonstressed condition. This EEG measure provides an opportune target for neurofeedback training to enhance executive control over emotional responses and task engagement during response to challenge (Janelle & Hatfield, 2008).

Achieving control through psychological strategies to control attention, together with targeted neurofeedback training of the frontal region, may provide enhanced control over essential mental and physical processes that underlie quality performance while under stress (Janelle & Hatfield, 2008).

While there are apparent differences in brain activity between expert and novice marksmen, it is not clear at this point that neurofeedback training can effectively change performance on shooting or other sport-related tasks. However, one consistent finding is that highly skilled athletes' actions are characterized by effortlessness (Janelle & Hatfield, 2008). In addition, Deeny, Hillman, Janelle, and Hatfield (2003) studied EEG coherence and shooting performance and their results suggested that expert-level marksmen had more efficient cerebral cortex networking through a reduction of neuromotor "noise" and consequent interference with task-relevant motor functions.

ENHANCING COGNITIVE PERFORMANCE/ MITIGATING IMPAIRMENT

Pharmacological Prophylaxis: Implications of Early Intervention

Emerging research indicates that pharmacotherapeutic interventions may be a viable complement to existing programs for enhancing performance, preventing ODRCD, and preventing posttraumatic sequelae. A comprehensive review of pharmacological poststress interventions was conducted by Morgan, Southwick, and Krystal (2003), the results of which suggest that research in the area of glutamate and cognitive performance, as well as many initiatives investigating "resilience" in warfighters are likely to be productive in the development of new strategies for mitigating the negative effects of stress.

A brief exercise was designed to evaluate a nutritional intervention conducted with soldiers neither sleep deprived nor exposed to significant operational stress other than physical training and inadequate energy intake (Lieberman, Falco, & Slade, 2002). Each soldier was issued ambulatory vigilance and environmental monitors that were custom-designed and manufactured to wear on the nondominant wrist. The monitors were lightweight (68 g) devices somewhat larger than a large wristwatch. Provision of a carbohydrate beverage mitigated the decline of vigilance in Soldiers, whereas those not provided with the carbohydrate beverage exhibited a significant loss of vigilance on cognitive testing (Lieberman et al., 2005). In a similar study Morgan et al. (2009) used the same carbohydrate beverage used by Lieberman et al. (2005) to test how well poststress carbohydrate administration would restore stress-induced cognitive deficits in soldiers. Soldiers who received carbohydrate administration exhibited superior cognitive performance when compared to those who received placebo drinks. Importantly, the neuropsychological test that was improved was a type of test that is dependent upon intact PFC functioning. These data support the view that the PFC is impaired by high stress and that such impairment may be mitigated by interventions.

Research has shown that excessive arousal in the first several weeks following trauma exposure is related to the development of PTSD (Brewin, Andrews, Rose, & Kirk, 1999). Therefore, pharmacological agents that could mitigate excessive arousal and prevent the onset of PTSD may yield benefits for those exposed to combat trauma. Based on the current scientific literature, it seems reasonable that pharmacologic agents that modulate catecholamine release or block ca receptors in the PFC would be protective and/or maintain optimal PFC functioning during stressful situations. For example, the alpha-2 adrenergic agonist drugs clonidine and guanfacine (a long-acting agent) suppress the release of NE through actions at the presynaptic autoreceptor. These agents improve PFC functioning, reduce the impact of distracting sensory stimuli, provide inhibitory feedback to the amygdala, and help the organism concentrate on the contents of working memory (Arnsten, 1998).

In addition to alpha-2 receptor agents, it is also likely that pharmacologic agents affecting NE turnover via the Y receptors (i.e., that function like NPY) will be stress protective or restorative. Thus, a rational approach to mitigating cognitive impairment during stress may be administration of NPY posttrauma exposure. This may prevent sensitization of NE systems and related PTSD symptoms. At present NPY administration for the prevention of posttrauma distress has not been tested.

Opioids and Benzodiazepines

The early use of opiates posttrauma might diminish noradrenergic activity, block arousal-enhanced consolidation of memory, and decrease the likelihood of developing a sensitized NE system with potentially related hyperarousal and re-experiencing symptoms (Morgan et al., 2003). For example, Saxe et al. (2001) reported a negative association between amount of morphine administered and degree of PTSD symptomatology at 6-month follow-up for acute burn victims. In a study of trauma survivors with acute stress disorder (symptoms occurring 1–3 months posttrauma), the short-term use of benzodiazepines for sleep was associated with a significant reduction in PTSD symptoms (Mellman, Byers, & Augenstein, 1998). However, more prolonged use of benzodiazepines has been associated with higher rates of subsequent PTSD (Gelpin, Bonne, Peri, Brandes, & Shalev, 1996).

There are distinct challenges with treating service members posttrauma in combat with pharmacological agents. Each physician, physician's assistant, nurse practitioner, or medic/corpsman would have to be trained in the triage of psychological trauma. If the provider were organic to the service member's unit, they would ostensibly understand the soldier's baseline functioning and the unique operational demands characteristic of the particular unit's mission set. Stigmatization in the early stages may be a concern for those soldiers prescribed psychopharmacological agents either as prophylaxis or posttrauma. However, for service members that have deployed in support of GWOT, the prophylactic antimalarial drugs were routinely administered and serve as a model for successful pharmacological prophylaxis.

At this time, deployed mental health practitioners and other providers are evaluating or treating service members within hours posttrauma. While there may not be a strict algorithm for treatment of these soldiers, understanding and exploring additional treatment options are vital. Historically, the Critical Incident Stress Debriefing model (Mitchell) was seen as the primary tool for units involved in particularly traumatic events, but the preponderance of evidence indicates that these debriefings may be more damaging, especially to those with higher levels of arousal/activation and when not used as intended (Borders & Kennedy, 2006). There is need for a flexible standard of care for posttrauma interventions that is based on empirical research with warfighters in training scenarios and combat.

Cognitive Performance Enhancement and Training

The service members risking their lives conducting combat operations have a big stake in learning how they can do things better. While this is where the sports analogy can begin to break down, it does demonstrate that life or death can be an incredible impetus for seeking and applying performance enhancement.

A critical component in the management of fear is the executive control over limbic function and subcortical emotional circuits; such control would involve brain regions that are housed anatomically in the frontal regions of the forebrain (Janelle & Hatfield, 2008). Therefore, it is reasonable to hypothesize that cognitive interventions designed specifically to facilitate cortical modulation of arousal (i.e., interventions such as cognitive restructuring, stress inoculation training, mnemonics) are also likely to result in improved cognitive performance during stress. An example of this concept is an interesting study on American Olympic wrestlers that was conducted by Gould in 1993. He found that the most successful wrestlers reported an automaticity of the following coping strategies: (a) thought-control strategies (blocking distracters, perspective taking, positive thinking, prayer, etc.), (b) task-focused strategies (narrow, more immediate focus on goals), (c) behavior-based strategies (changing environment, routines), and (d) emotional or arousal control. These primarily cognitive coping strategies anecdotally improved performance through economizing mental activity and were inextricably linked with controlling physiological arousal.

At this point, however, interventions designed to sustain or improve cognitive functioning of warfighters are in their infancy. We believe that research on linking neurobiology with cognitive coping strategies across the spectrum of military-related athletic performance would be fruitful and lead to improved models for sustaining performance. Such a focus in neurobiological research would serve to integrate the burgeoning field of Sports Psychology with military performance research and related disciplines. The West Point Center for Enhanced Performance is one example of the integration of academic research with applied performance enhancement for U.S. Military Academy cadets (see Zinsser, Perkins, Gervais, & Burbelo, 2004).

CONCLUSION

Recent and contemporary military operations conducted by the U.S. military include complex counterinsurgencies and technologically advanced conventional warfare. For the warfighter, the future of warfare portends increased cognitive demands. Research on cognition in extreme environments for the military is critical for initiatives to strengthen resiliency to ODRCD, select personnel for high-risk missions, enhance training programs, and prevent posttraumatic sequelae. The confluence of neurobiology, neuropsychology, and sports psychology is imperative as we seek to identify critical factors, develop training programs, and ultimately improve the performance of our warfighters in extreme operational environments.

REFERENCES

Arnsten, A. F. T. (1998). Catecholamine regulation of pre-frontal cortex. *Journal of Psychopharmacology, 11*, 151–162.

Bird, E. I. (1987). Psychophysiological processes during rifle shooting. *International Journal of Sport Psychology, 18*, 9–18.

Birnbaum, S., Gobeske, K. T., Auerbach, J., Taylor, J. R., & Arnsten, A. F. T. (1999). A role for norepinephrine in stress-induced cognitive deficits: A-1 Adrenoceptor mediation in the prefrontal cortex. *Biological Psychiatry, 46*, 1266–1274.

Borders, M. A., & Kennedy, C. H. (2006). Psychological interventions following disaster or trauma. In C. H. Kennedy & E. A. Zillmer (Eds.), *Military psychology: Clinical and operational applications* (pp. 331–352). New York: Guilford Publishing.

Brewin, C. R., Andrews, B., Rose, S., & Kirk, M. (1999). Acute stress disorder and post-traumatic stress disorder in victims of violent crime. *American Journal of Psychiatry, 156*, 360–365.

Clausewitz, C. v. (1993). *On war*. New York: Alfred A. Knopf.

Colmers, W. F., & Bleakman, D. (1994). Effects of neuropeptide Y on the electrical properties of neurons. *Trends in Neurosciences, 17*, 373–379.

Deeny, S. P., Hillman, C. H., Janelle, C. M., & Hatfield, B. D. (2003). Cortico-cortical communication and superior performance in skilled marksmen: An EEG coherence analysis. *Journal of Sport and Exercise Psychology, 25*(2), 188–204.

Egner, T., & Gruzelier, J. H. (2004). EEG biofeedback of low beta band components: Frequency-specific effects on variables of attention and event-related brain potentials. *Clinical Neurophysiology, 115*, 131–139.

Foy, M. R., Stanton, M. E., Levine, S., & Thompson, R. F. (1987). Behavioral stress impairs long-term potentiation in rodent hippocampus. *Behavioral Neural Biology, 48*(1), 138–149.

Gelpin, E., Bonne, O., Peri, T., Brandes, D., & Shalev, A. (1996). Treatment of recent trauma survivors with benzodiazepines: A prospective study. *Journal of Clinical Psychiatry, 57*, 390–394.

Gould, D. (1993). Goal setting for peak performance. In J. Williams (Ed.), *Applied sport psychology: Personal growth to peak performance* (2nd ed., pp. 158–169). Palo Alto, CA: Mayfield.

Hatfield, B. D., & Hillman, C. H., (2001). The psychophysiology of sport: A mechanistic understanding of the psychology of superior performance. In R. N. Singer, C. H. Hausenblas, & C. M. Janelle (Eds.), *Handbook of sport psychology* (2nd ed., pp. 362–386). New York: John Wiley & Sons.

Hatfield, B. D., Landers, D. M., & Ray, W. J. (1984). Cognitive processes during self-paced motor performance: An electroencephalographic profile of skilled marksmen. *Journal of Sport Psychology, 6*, 42–59.

Hatfield, B. D., Landers, D. M., & Ray, W. J. (1987). Cardiovascular-CNS interactions during a self-paced, intentional attentive state: Elite marksmanship performance. *Psychophysiology, 24*, 542–549.

Hatfield, B. D., Landers, D. M., Ray, W. J., & Daniels, F. S. (1982). An electroencephalographic study of elite rifle shooters. *The American Marksman, 7*, 6–8.

Haufler, A. J., Spalding, T. W., Santa Maria, D. L., & Hatfield, B. D. (2000). Neurocognitive activity during a self-paced visuospatial task: Comparative EEG profiles in marksmen and novice shooters. *Biological Psychology, 53*, 131–160.

Heilig, M., & Widerlov, E. (1990). Neuropeptide Y: An overview of central distribution, functional aspects, and possible involvement in neuropsychiatric illnesses. *Acta Psychiatrica Scandinavica, 82*, 95–114.

Herschbach, P., Henrich, G., & von Rad, M. (1999). Psychological factors in functional gastrointestinal disorders: Characteristics of the disorder or of the illness behavior? *Psychosomatic Medicine, 61*, 148–153.

Illes, P., & Regenold, J. (1990). Interaction between neuropeptide Y and noradrenaline on central catecholamine neurons. *Nature, 334*, 362–363.

Inui, A., Okita, M., Nakajima, M., Momose, K., Ueno, N., Teranishi, A., et al. (1998). Anxiety-like behavior in transgenic mice with brain expression of neuropeptide Y. *Proceedings of the Association of American Physicians, 110*(3), 171–182.

Janelle, C. M., & Hatfield, B. D. (2008). Visual attention and brain processes that underlie expert performance: Implications for sport and military psychology. *Military Psychology, 20*(1), 39–69.

Janelle, C. M., Singer, R. N., & Williams, A. M. (1999). External distraction and attentional narrowing: Visual search evidence. *Journal of Sport and Exercise Psychology, 21*, 70–91.

Kerick, S. E., Hatfield, B. D., & Allendar, L. E. (2007). Event-related cortical dynamics of soldiers during shooting as a function of varied task demand. *Aviation, Space, and Environmental Medicine, 78*, B153–B164.

Larsen, P. J., & Kristensen, P. (1997). The neuropeptide Y (Y4) receptor is highly expressed in neurons of the rat dorsal vagal complex. *Molecular Brain Research, 48*, 1–6.

Lezak, M. D. (2004). *Neuropsychological assessment* (4th ed.). New York: Oxford University Press.

Lieberman, H. R., Bathalon, G. P., Falco, C. M., Morgan, C. A., Niro, P. J., & Tharion, W. J. (2005). The fog of war: Decrements in cognitive performance and mood associated with combat-like stress. *Aviation, Space, and Environmental Medicine, 76*(7), C7–C14.

Lieberman, H. R., Falco, C. M., & Slade, S. S. (2002). Carbohydrate administration during a day of sustained aerobic activity improves vigilance, as assessed by a novel ambulatory monitoring device, and mood. *American Journal of Clinical Nutrition, 76*, 120–127.

Mason, J. W. (1968). Organization of psychoendocrine mechanisms. *Psychosomatic Medicine, 30*(Pt.2), 565–575.

McGaugh, J. L. (1989). Involvement of hormonal and neuromodulatory systems in the regulation of memory storage. *Annual Review of Neuroscience, 2*, 255–287.

Mellman, T. A., Byers, P. M., & Augenstein, J. S. (1998). Pilot evaluation of hypnotic medication during acute traumatic stress response. *Journal of Traumatic Stress, 11*, 563–569.

Morgan, C. A., Doran, A., Steffian, G., Hazlett, G., & Southwick, S. M. (2006). Stress-induced deficits in working memory and visuo-constructive abilities in special operations soldiers. *Biological Psychiatry, 60*, 722–729.

Morgan, C. A., Hazlett, G., Southwick, S. M., Rasmusson, A., & Lieberman, H. R. (2009). Effect of carbohydrate administration on recovery from stress-induced deficits in cognitive function: A double blind, placebo-controlled study of soldiers exposed to survival school stress. *Military Medicine, 174*, 3.

Morgan, C. A., Hazlett, G., Wang, S., Richardson, E. G., Schnurr, P., & Southwick, S. M. (2001a). Symptoms of dissociation in humans experiencing acute, uncontrollable stress: A prospective investigation. *American Journal of Psychiatry, 158*(8), 1239–1247.

Morgan, C. A., III, Rasmusson, A. M., Wang, S., Hoyt, G., Hauger, R., & Hazlett, G. (2002). Neuropeptide Y and subjective distress in humans exposed to acute stress: replication and extension of previous report. *Biological Psychiatry, 52*, 136–142.

Morgan, C. A., III, Southwick, S., Hazlett, G., Rasmusson, A., Hoyt, G., Zimolo, Z., et al. (2004). Relationships among plasma dehydroepiandrosterone sulfate and cortisol levels, symptoms of dissociation, and objective performance in humans exposed to acute stress. *Archives of General Psychiatry, 61*, 819–825.

Morgan, C. A., Southwick, S. M., & Krystal, J. H. (2003). Toward a pharmacology of acute stress disorders. *Biological Psychiatry, 53*, 834–843.

Morgan, C. A., Wang, S., Mason, J., Southwick, S. M., Fox, P., Hazlett, G., et al. (2000a). Hormone profiles in humans experiencing military survival training. *Biological Psychiatry, 47*, 891–901.

Morgan, C. A., Wang, S. W., Rasmusson, A., Hazlett, G., Anderson, G., & Charney, D. S. (2001b). Relationship among plasma cortisol, catecholamines, neuropeptide-Y, and human performance during exposure to uncontrollable stress. *Psychosomatic Medicine, 63*, 412–422.

Morgan, C. A., Wang, S., Southwick, S. M., Rasmusson, A., Hazlett, G., Hauger, R. L., et al. (2000b). Plasma neuropeptide-Y concentrations in humans exposed to military survival training. *Biological Psychiatry, 47*, 902–909.

Newcomer, J. W., Craft, S., Hershey, T., Askins, K., & Bardgett, M. E. (1994). Glucocorticoid-induced impairment in declarative memory performance in adult humans. *Journal of Neuroscience, 14*, 2047–2053.

Peskind, E. R., Veith, R. C., Dorsa, D. M., Bumbrecht, G., & Raskind, M. A. (1989). Yohimbine increases cerebrospinal fluid and plasma norepinephrine but not arginine vasopressin in humans. *Neuroendocrinology, 50*, 286–291.

Picano, J. J., Williams, T. J., & Roland, R. R. (2006). Assessment and selection of high risk operational personnel. In C. H. Kennedy & E. A. Zillmer (Eds.), *Military psychology: Clinical and operational applications* (pp. 353–370). New York: Guilford.

Rasmusson, A. M., Hauger, R. L., Morgan, C. A., Bremner, J. D., Charney, D. S., & Southwick, S. M. (2000). Low baseline and yohimbine-stimulated plasma neuropeptide-Y (NPY) levels in combat-related PTSD. *Biological Psychiatry, 47*, 526–539.

Rasmusson, A. M., Southwick, S. M., Hauger, R. L., & Charney, D. S. (1998). Plasma neuropeptide Y (NPY) increases in humans in response to the a-2 antagonist yohimbine. *Neuropsychopharmacology, 19*, 95–98.

Saarela, P. I. (1999). *The effects of mental stress on cerebral hemispheric asymmetry and psychomotor performance in skilled marksmen.* Unpublished doctoral dissertation, University of Maryland.

Salazar, W., Landers, D. M., Petruzzello, S. J., Han, M. W., Crews, D. J., & Kubitz, K. A. (1990). Hemispheric asymmetry, cardiac response, and performance in elite archers. *Research Quarterly for Exercise and Sport, 61*, 351–359.

Saxe, G., Stoddard, F., Courtney, D., Cunningham, K., Chawla, N., Sheridan, R., et al. (2001). Relationship between acute morphine and the course of PTSD in children with burns. *Journal of the American Academy of Child and Adolescent Psychiatry, 40*, 915–921.

Southwick, S. M., Bremner, J. D., Rasmusson, A., Morgan, C. A., Arnsten, A., & Charney, D. S. (1999). Role of norepinephrine in the pathophysiology and treatment of posttraumatic stress disorder. *Biological Psychiatry, 46*, 1192–1204.

Southwick, S. M., Krystal, J. H., Morgan, C. A., Johnson, D. R., Nagy, L. M., & Nicolaou, A. (1993). Abnormal noradrenergic function in posttraumatic stress disorder. *Archives of General Psychiatry, 50*, 266–274.

Sun, B., & Giles, L. (1910). *Sun Tzu on the art of war: The oldest military treatise in the world.* Champagne, IL: Project Gutenberg.

Vernon, D. J. (2005). Can neurofeedback training enhance performance? An evaluation of the evidence with implications for future research. *Applied Psychophysiology and Biofeedback, 30*(4), 347–364.

Zinsser, N., Perkins, L., Gervais, P., & Burbelo, G. A. (2004, September–October). Military application of performance enhancement psychology. *Military Review*, 62–65.

14

The Future of Military Neuropsychology

ROBERT A. SEEGMILLER AND ROBERT L. KANE

New frontiers of the mind are before us, and if they are pioneered with the same vision, boldness, and drive with which we have waged this war we can create a fuller and more fruitful employment and a fuller and more fruitful life.

Franklin D. Roosevelt, November 17, 1944

As psychology matured professionally and developed bodies of knowledge in various areas, it emulated evolutions in medicine and increasingly developed subspecialties. The development of subspecialty areas is inevitable as a health-care profession expands its expertise along with the knowledge base that supports that expertise. Subspecialization has become increasingly evident in training with internships offering specialty tracks, in the expansion of postdoctoral training, with board certification, and with the clinical privileging process.

Despite the growing and necessary trend toward specialization, military psychologists are forced to function in diverse roles that reflect the overall needs of the services and service members at any given point in time. In peacetime psychologists may help service members deal with everyday stresses as well as with a range of mental health problems and family-related issues. The military psychologist may deal with a broad age range of patients and problems ranging from adult depression to learning problems with children. Behavioral health specialty clinics are a luxury of larger treatment facilities; they are not remote sites where a single psychologist may have to deal with a range of behavioral health issues.

During wartime, psychologists encounter additional issues dictated by the nature of the conflict. For example, posttraumatic stress disorder (PTSD) is a common problem occurring in all wars (Campise, Geller, & Campise, 2006; chapter 12). However, other issues involving psychological assessment and/or intervention emerge driven by the environment in which the service member is fighting or the tactics of the enemy. Weapons of war have always been destructive to the human central nervous system. However, concerns about chemical warfare, biological agents, radiation exposure, and concussion/traumatic brain injury related to impact or blast (chapter 5) have resulted in an increased focus on cognitive assessment with respect to both tools and training (chapter 6). These issues have also raised questions regarding scope of practice, including what training psychologists need to respond to neuropsychological questions, and how telehealth technology can be used to provide consultation to psychologists who lack specialist training.

The subspecialty of neuropsychology has expanded and matured at a remarkable pace during the past half century. Increased understanding of neurophysiology, neuropathology, and brain-behavior relationships has been accompanied by the corresponding burgeoning of neuropsychology as a profession (chapter 1). In many cases, recognition of a need for specific services has spurred the concurrent development of new assessment techniques, enhanced understanding of cognitive and behavioral disorders, and targeted interventions. The unique expertise and contributions of clinical neuropsychologists are now appreciated in a wide variety of settings, ranging from the classroom to the courtroom and even the locker room. Perhaps no other profession has so much to offer in terms of evaluating, understanding, and assisting persons with brain disorders.

The expansion of clinical neuropsychology services in schools, hospitals, rehabilitation centers, correctional facilities, and a myriad of other occupational settings has created opportunities to advance both the science and profession of neuropsychology. The same could also be said of military neuropsychology, particularly during the past decade. Social and political circumstances frequently stimulate scientific discovery and technological development. In an ironic twist, calamitous military conflicts have historically spurred important advancements in a variety of technical fields, including medicine. Terrorist attacks on the United States on September 11, 2001 set off a chain reaction of events resulting in the expansion of military neuropsychology as a profession, as well as a growing understanding of certain types of neuropathology, particularly traumatic brain injuries (TBIs). The widespread use of improvised explosive devices (IEDs) in Iraq and Afghanistan has resulted in thousands of TBIs. Determining the actual number of brain injuries sustained by military personnel deployed to the Middle East and Southwest Asia since 2001 is difficult. The RAND Corporation survey–based estimate is 320,000 (Tanielian & Jaycox, 2008). As of November 30, 2008, the Defense and Veterans Brain Injury Center (DVBIC) reported treating 9,100 service members with TBI diagnosis. As of this writing, the DVBIC number based on patient interview is being revised but is expected to remain below that obtained using survey methods. While estimates vary, the prevalence and seriousness of this problem has led politicians, veterans' groups, and the popular press to refer to TBIs as the "signature injury" of the war (Riccitiello, 2006).

The need to properly evaluate and assist service members who have sustained TBIs has already had a significant impact on military neuropsychology. In addition to the increased demand for qualified providers who can render clinical services, the spike in combat-related brain injuries will likely influence future directions in military neuropsychology. Just as other combat injuries have stimulated advances in medical knowledge in the past, military neuropsychologists have an opportunity and obligation to advance the scientific understanding of blast-related concussions and other neurological disorders resulting from military service. Other future challenges include obtaining baseline neuropsychological data for all military personnel and determining how such information should be used; developing effective tools and protocols for assessing suspected mild TBI (mTBI) or concussion in combat environments and making critical return-to-duty decisions; and refining assessment techniques to properly evaluate, diagnose, and treat injured military members who are often struggling with a complex combination of physical and psychological problems. Looking beyond the current conflicts, military neuropsychologists are faced with the challenge of maintaining their visibility and remaining relevant in times of peace, perhaps by offering their services to a broader patient population, becoming more involved in brain injury rehabilitation, and adopting expanded consultation roles.

IMPROVING BATTLEFIELD COGNITIVE ASSESSMENT

American involvement in military conflicts since 2001 has significantly expanded the demand for neuropsychological services. Increased enemy use of IEDs between the outbreak of hostilities in Iraq in March 2003 and the summer of 2007 resulted in a proportionate increase in the number of TBIs sustained by military personnel. The establishment of state-of-the-art medical treatment facilities in combat zones has saved thousands of lives, as injured personnel have been able to receive prompt, expert medical care in theater. Those with less serious injuries can return to duty, while those with more serious injuries are stabilized before being evacuated to medical centers in Europe and the United States for further treatment and rehabilitation.

While decisions regarding the medical evacuation of injured service members have always been at the discretion of their treating physicians, the surge in patients with head injuries has presented new diagnostic and dispositional challenges. The decision to medically evacuate personnel with moderate to severe brain injuries as evidenced by abnormal computed tomography (CT) findings and/or neurological impairment is simple. The decision-making process becomes much more complicated for those who have sustained concussion/mTBI. Neuropsychological assessment is an important part of the process for making return-to-duty decisions for these individuals.

The challenge, as with all illnesses and injuries that occur in combat zones, has been to accurately identify those who require medical evacuation versus those who can be retained in theater. Unnecessary evacuations are to be avoided as they waste resources, degrade mission capabilities, and are often not in the best interest of the individual. For those retained in theater, additional decisions must be made as to when those who have sustained mild concussions are ready to return to duty. An analogy can be made to the management of sports concussions, only the implications are far more serious in a combat zone. Injured troops are often eager to return to their friends and their units, and combat units are usually equally interested in the quick return of their troops. Premature return-to-duty decisions can, however, have dire consequences. Soldiers with ongoing attention problems, memory impairment, or reduced information processing speed may be killed or inadvertently endanger those with whom they serve. While there has generally been consensus in the military medical community that accurate evaluation of known or suspected brain injuries is critical, it has been much less clear how and by whom such evaluations should be conducted. Neuropsychologists have played a prominent role in addressing these questions.

The need for a valid, standardized neuropsychological screening instrument that requires minimal equipment, can be employed in remote locations, and can also be administered by persons without extensive neuropsychological training was recognized by the DVBIC, which spearheaded development of the Military Acute Concussion Evaluation (MACE) in 2006. The purpose of the MACE is to evaluate a person in whom a concussion is suspected, confirm the diagnosis, and assess his/her current clinical status. The MACE is an individually administered assessment tool that includes a brief history section with questions regarding how the service member was injured, whether there was a loss of consciousness or amnesia from the incident, and current symptoms. A brief cognitive and neurological examination follows, including assessment of orientation, memory, concentration, vision, speech, and motor functioning. The examination section of the MACE was derived from the Standardized Assessment of Concussion (SAC), a validated, widely used tool in sports medicine (McCrea et al., 1998). About the same time use of the MACE was implemented, the *Joint Theater Trauma System Clinical Practice Guidelines for In-Theatre Management of Mild Traumatic Brain Injury (Concussion)* was updated and disseminated. In November, 2008 the *Joint Theater Trauma System Clinical Practice Guideline—Management of Mild Traumatic Brain Injury (mTBI)/Concussion in the Deployed Setting* was revised to provide updated guidance for diagnosis, evaluation, treatment, follow-up, and return to duty of mild traumatic brain injury patients.

While the MACE proved to be a useful screening instrument, it is a fairly simple test and provides limited information. Its usefulness for assessing combat-related concussions is not clear. Anecdotally, word spread that some deployed service members were studying and memorizing the pocket and wallet card versions of the MACE that were readily available in theater so they would "know the answers" and be able to pass the test if they were ever injured, so as not to be found unfit for duty (Zoroya, 2007). Subsequently, alternate MACE items were developed. Experience on the ground in Iraq and Afghanistan highlighted the need for more sensitive instruments for assessing the mental status of injured military personnel and making critical return-to-duty decisions. One of the challenges was to select a reliable and effective test that could be quickly administered and interpreted by non-neuropsychologists.

A promising approach to neuropsychological screening in combat theaters of operation is the use of computerized assessment. Some of the potential advantages of computer-based testing include the ease and standardization of administration, the ability to measure reaction times and cognitive processing speed with great precision and accuracy, the ability to obtain instant and reliable results, the potential to assess multiple people at once when adequate hardware is available, and the intrinsic appeal of a challenging, well-designed computer administered test for assessing a population primarily composed of young adults. The use of computer-based assessment also makes immediate, individualized comparisons of pre- and post- injury functioning possible. While computerized neuropsychological tests are not intended to replace clinical judgment, they have the potential to greatly facilitate decision making that was often based on little more than subjective impressions in the past. Examples of computerized batteries that have already been used in Iraq include the Automated Neuropsychological Assessment Metrics (ANAM; Reeves, Winter, Kane, Elsmore, & Bleiberg, 2001) and the HeadMinder Cognitive Stability Index (CSI; Erlanger & Feldman, 1999). Both the ANAM and Cognitive Stability Index require approximately 30 minutes to administer and provide detailed information regarding cognitive domains such as response time, information-processing speed, attention, and short-term memory.

While the potential utility of computer-based neuropsychological assessment for military personnel appears to be great, a number of important issues have yet to be resolved. Ongoing research is aimed at determining which of the available instruments is best for evaluating the types of brain injuries typically sustained in combat environments. The validity and usability of computer-based assessment instruments are both important considerations. Policy must also be developed to specify who is qualified to administer and interpret the results of computer-based neuropsychological tests and how collected patient data will be used and stored. Another important consideration regarding the use of both computer-based and traditional pen and paper tests relates to the development of military-specific normative data for both types of tests. Efforts are currently under way to compare results obtained with different computerized batteries postconcussion, and the baseline process has produced a large body of military norms. Other military populations continue to gather their own normative data on traditional tests, such as the military aviation community.

While useful, population-based norms have potential limitations for assessing the cognitive functioning of injured military personnel. Normal individual differences might be misinterpreted as evidence of impairment in persons with below-average premorbid functioning, and higher functioning individuals may appear "normal" after being injured, even if they have suffered a decline from their baseline abilities. An additional method for assessing the extent of cognitive dysfunction following injury would be to compare a service member's cognitive functioning after an injury to his/her own pretrauma baseline, as is currently practiced by many sports neuropsychologists. Much like sports neuropsychologists now use individual pre- and postinjury data to make return-to-play decisions, military psychologists may in the future be able to use pre- and postinjury data to make critical return-to-duty decisions.

COGNITIVE BASELINE TESTING AND DEVELOPMENT OF A NEUROCOGNITIVE ASSESSMENT TOOL

Within the Department of Defense (DoD), the focus on factors affecting cognition in warriors is driven more by the research than the clinical community and has led to the development of computerized test batteries within various service branches (Kane & Kay, 1992) . The initial focus of the research was on environmental stressors including fatigue, temperature, medication effects, and altitude. Subsequent studies focused on the effects of atmospheric pressure, radiation, and toxic exposure (Lowe et al., 2007). Prior to the first Gulf War, efforts were made to study the effects of medications that would be used as countermeasures to toxic chemical exposures. General issues surrounding the 1991 Persian Gulf War drove research pertaining to service member monitoring and protection, cognition, as well as the adopting of pre- and postdeployment health assessments (Friedl et al., 2007). While the current focus on cognition within the DoD resulted from the need to assess service members and make return-to-duty decisions following concussion/mTBI, the notion that cognitive assessment is an important part of force health protection has deep roots.

In an effort to respond to clinical and operational needs and congressional mandate, DoD has embarked on a program to obtain baseline cognitive assessment on deploying service members. Recently the Defense Health Information Management System (DHIMS) began efforts to move the results of these baseline assessments into service members' electronic health records and make them available to clinicians in theater. The program is referred to as the Neurocognitive Assessment Tool (NCAT). The ANAM (Reeves, Winter, Bleiberg, & Kane, 2007; Figure 14.1) was designated to be the initial NCAT while systematic comparisons among available computerized test batteries continue. ANAM development was funded through the Army but was based on early work noted above done

Figure 14.1 An Air Force member takes the Automated Neuropsychological Assessment Metrics for her predeployment cognitive assessment.

by the Army, Navy, and Air Force to develop automated cognitive and performance assessment.

The NCAT effort within the DoD was driven by concerns pertaining to concussion/mTBI. However, it is applicable to a range of issues facing service members at war. One potential use of the neurocognitive baseline is to obtain information that might be useful in assessing service members related to various problems that may occur as a result of deployment and combat. However, a more specific application, and one with immediate implications for the psychologist, is the assessment of cognition following concussion/mTBI to facilitate triage, management, and return-to-duty decisions. A description of the predeployment testing program follows to discuss the potential implications of the program for military neuropsychology.

As the name implies, the initial objective of the program is to obtain baseline neurocognitive test results on service members prior to their being deployed. The directive from the Assistant Secretary of Defense for Health Affairs (May 28, 2008: Baseline Pre-deployment Neurocognitive Functional Assessment—Interim Guidance) indicated that the baseline should be obtained within 12 months of deployment. Because the DoD-wide program began well into the wars in Iraq and Afghanistan, the practical implementation required that many service members be tested just prior to deployment. In some cases, "baselines" are being obtained on individuals who were previously deployed on one or more occasions. Operationally, baseline is thus defined as the service member's functional level prior to a given deployment. From the standpoint of concussion/mTBI management, having the most recent baseline is useful. For broader questions related to deployment health, a more traditional baseline is preferable (i.e., prior to any deployments). Should DoD integrate neurocognitive assessment into a broader health-monitoring program, then the likelihood is initial baseline testing will be accomplished earlier in a service member's career with repeat testing at defined intervals based on normal changes with age or the individual service member's risk history.

The predeployment neurocognitive assessment program is ambitious from various standpoints. There are general issues related to testing a very large number of individuals, as well as specific issues related to the different methods of deployment used by the different services. There are also interface issues with the medical record. If the goal is to compare baseline test results with those obtained postinjury, then the preinjury baseline needs to be available in theater or wherever a service member is stationed. Medical informatics issues are beyond the focus of this chapter. However, the current approach being implemented by DHIMS is worth noting with respect to its impact on psychological practice.

An important aspect of the DHIMS implementation of the baseline testing program is "role-based" access. Psychologists have always had concerns about protecting test data from possible misinterpretation, and concerns remain regarding the appropriate use and interpretation of test information obtained from traditional psychological and neuropsychological tests. With neuropsychological tests there is the additional issue that the tests by themselves do not provide a specific diagnosis and have to be integrated with other medical and historical data by a trained provider. This integration is of clear importance on the battlefield where concussion/mTBI is a clinical diagnosis based on history and where multiple factors may impact neurocognitive test performance. An equally real and potentially conflicting concern is the portability of test information. Service members may be stationed at various locations both during war and peacetime and may incur an injury thousands of miles away from the site of their baseline examination. For predeployment assessments to be of practical value, they have to be accessible wherever a service member is stationed. Role-based access was designed to address the needs for appropriate data use, accessibility, and portability. The contract awarded by DHIMS calls for a solution to be implemented that allows for easy electronic upload of data into the military electronic health record system with worldwide access. Data will be stored in a manner so as not to be viewable without the appropriate test report software and only individuals assigned with the appropriate privileges will have access to the data and data report. Individual services will decide which of their health providers will be granted access.

One additional point prior to discussing implications of role-based access to the psychological community is the nature of the report generated by the current NCAT test system. The current NCAT has been used in previous military projects that yielded an initial normative base of over 2,300 soldiers from Ft. Bragg (Reeves et al., 2006). The expanded data set was based on over 5,000 soldiers from Ft. Bragg (Vincent et al., 2008) with additional norms being generated from baseline tests accomplished at other bases. As of this writing, over 200,000 service members have been tested from different branches of the armed services, although not all of these assessments constitute true "baseline" evaluations because many tests were completed on service members who had already deployed one or more times and may have previously been injured. Nevertheless, this number continues to grow. Hence, there is the potential to assemble an extensive military normative base that can afford the clinician multiple comparisons. These comparisons could be broken down in various ways including by service, rank, or military occupational specialty as well as by traditional factors such as age, education, and gender. The current database is composed primarily of young males, but future data collection should provide larger normative samples of females and persons in older age groups. The ANAM report program is designed to be flexible and display data based on clinician selected normative sets as well as comparing an individual service member's performance to his or her own baseline testing. The report is computer based and dynamic. It is produced on demand and allows the clinician to select various comparisons of interest.

Role-based access addresses the dual goals of appropriate data access and data portability. With respect to administration, the Army and Marines typically deploy large units at any one time point. To date, it has been possible to make use of mobile teams using trained administrators who travel to deployment sites. This method of testing is transitioning to having stable sites with trained testers at each site responsible for test administration. Air Force and Navy deploy in smaller groups and from diverse locations. Currently, this requires multiple test sites with individuals appropriately trained to administer testing. Obtaining baselines requires the establishing of training standards for test administrators.

The process of having a set of neurocognitive data permitting both normative and baseline comparisons requires the psychology community to define who should have access to the neurocognitive test performance data. Specifically, they will need to make decisions regarding whether this should be in the purview of neuropsychologists only, all psychologists, or all psychologists with additional training and consultative support. Each service will also have to address the question of whether any other health-care providers should have access to the test data. While these decisions will be the purview of each service, the decision may require some coordination since health care both in and out of theater is increasingly provided across services.

In the case of the NCAT, the initial impetus for implementing this long-contemplated strategy of baseline cognitive assessment was the problem of concussion/mTBI and the weapon choices of enemies in Iraq and Afghanistan that have produced blast-related injuries. The issue for psychologists is not just that of learning a new test procedure but also of learning how to use neuropsychological test data in general to contribute to the management of service members' post concussion/mTBI. The NCAT project and the timing of its implementation have brought together issues of test familiarity, general neurocognitive assessment expertise, and special knowledge of issues surrounding concussion/mTBI in an environment with multiple stressors and exposures, all of which could potentially affect cognition. The challenge for military psychology is to train psychologists for the complex roles they may be called upon to play as health-care providers in demanding environments and challenging circumstances (Figure 14.2).

Programs such as NCAT should be thought of as integrating technology with clinical demands to give psychologists an additional tool for force health protection and monitoring. The training demands associated with NCAT are those associated with bringing neurocognitive assessment into the force health protection arena. Further, concerns about evaluating concussion/mTBI have provided an opportunity to bring together various technologies for implementing neurocognitive assessment into military treatment and decision making.

Figure 14.2 Training is provided to military psychologists and psychiatric technicians in battlefield concussion assessment and management at Naval Medical Center San Diego.

RESOLVING COMPLEX DIAGNOSTIC CHALLENGES

The TBIs sustained by military personnel serving in Iraq and Afghanistan pose a number of challenges for military neuropsychologists. The majority of head injuries sustained in recent conflicts have been caused by IEDs. Research is ongoing to determine whether brain injuries sustained as the result of explosive blasts are qualitatively different from those caused by more familiar mechanisms such as blunt force trauma, penetrating injuries, acceleration/deceleration impact, and rotational forces resulting in axonal shearing. It appears that brain injuries may occur as the direct result of blast overpressure on soft tissues, or blast-induced neurotrauma (Cernak, Wang, Jiang, Bian, & Slavi, 2001; Elsayed, 1997; Leung et al., 2008). The mechanisms of blast-induced neurotrauma and the resulting impact on neuropsychological functioning are still not well understood. Further complicating the neuropsychological assessment of persons injured by blasts is the fact that many of these patients have also sustained ocular, otological, vestibular, and peripheral nervous system injuries. Substantial cognitive and sensorimotor deficits may occur in the absence of overt signs of trauma. It cannot simply be assumed that those injured by blasts will experience the same symptoms and outcomes as persons who have sustained concussions that are more traditional. (For a more detailed discussion of blast injuries, see chapter 5.)

The assessment of service members injured in combat poses a significant challenge for military neuropsychologists. Not only are the types of brain injuries being encountered perhaps unprecedented (see chapter 1), but numerous factors in addition to direct neurotrauma are affecting military members' cognitive functioning. Perhaps the most common complicating factor is the high comorbidity of acute stress or posttraumatic stress disorders (PTSD) among those with TBIs (chapter 12). Almost all military personnel injured in combat have also been exposed to "an extreme traumatic stressor involving direct personal experience of an event that involves actual or threatened death or serious injury, or other threat to one's physical integrity; or witnessing an event that involves death, injury, or a threat to the physical integrity of another person; or learning about unexpected or violent death, serious harm, or threat of death or injury experienced by a family member or other close associate" (American Psychiatric Association, 1994, p. 424). While not all returning service members experience significant emotional problems, the comorbidity of PTSD with combat-related mTBI appears to be quite high (Hoge et al., 2008). Distinguishing between PTSD and mTBI can be difficult because of the overlapping physical, emotional, and cognitive symptoms potentially associated with each condition. Further complicating differential diagnosis is the fact that the two conditions are not mutually exclusive.

In addition to assessing the impact of acute stress, PTSD, and other common mental health and substance disorders on cognitive functioning, neuropsychologists must also consider an array of other factors that often impact military members' cognitive functioning. Recently injured military personnel are often dealing with physical pain, sleep deprivation (chapter 11), and emotional distress including feelings of anxiety, fear, grief, anger, and depression. Neuropsychological evaluations of service members who have returned from deployment may also be complicated by readjustment issues, relationship problems, chronic pain and physical disabilities, preexisting learning disorders or attention-deficit/hyperactivity disorder (chapter 8), substance abuse (Kennedy, Jones, & Grayson, 2006) or attempts at "self-medication," and medication side effects from drugs that are often liberally prescribed for emotional problems, medical disorders, chronic pain, and insomnia. Motivational factors also significantly impact the clinical presentation and neuropsychological test performance of military personnel. Attempts at impression management can range from frank denial or minimization of symptoms to marked exaggeration or feigning of cognitive impairment. Personality testing and the use of symptom validity or effort measures are indispensable aspects of military neuropsychological evaluations (chapter 4). Conclusions and recommendations made by military neuropsychologists often influence medical board decisions including service members' level of impairment, degree of disability, and fitness for continued military service. Issues of level of impairment and disability rating are tied directly to financial compensation. Disentangling the complex interplay of physical, cognitive, emotional, social, occupational, and motivational factors will continue to be a major challenge for military neuropsychologists in the future.

MEETING THE DEMAND FOR SERVICES: CHALLENGES IN TRAINING AND UTILIZATION

Prior to the current wars in Iraq and Afghanistan, neuropsychology was a relatively small and sometimes overlooked subspecialty in the military medical community. There was an increased demand for neuropsychological evaluations following the first Persian Gulf War in the early 1990s, as neuropsychologists were called upon to evaluate military personnel who presented with symptoms of Gulf War syndrome, which included complaints of headaches, dizziness and loss of balance, and concentration and memory problems. Following this temporary spike in demand for services, military neuropsychologists generally settled into consultative roles in major military medical centers, evaluating military members and, as resources permitted, family members of military personnel and retirees with a wide range of brain-related disorders. The relatively young, predominantly male military population produced a steady stream of non-combat-related head injuries sustained in motor vehicle accidents, sports, and other high-risk activities. Military neuropsychologists also evaluated patients with academic problems, learning disorders, attention deficit disorders, and a wide range of neuropathological conditions (Ryan, Zazeckis, French, & Harvey, 2006). The demand for services was steady, but usually not overwhelming.

This all changed with the outbreak of new military conflicts beginning in 2001. The military medical community has subsequently scrambled to meet the increased demand for neuropsychological services. The current emphasis on providing services for combat-related casualties has unfortunately diminished access to care for other patient populations. The U.S. Army and Navy have responded by hiring civilian neuropsychologists to work in military hospitals. In fact, most of the neuropsychological services provided in military medical centers are delivered by nonmilitary providers, including civil service and contract employees.

Although many excellent civilian neuropsychologists now provide services to the military, this may not be an ideal solution for a few reasons. Civilian providers do not deploy with military personnel and may not fully comprehend or appreciate the nature of military duty, combat experiences, and even such things as military rank structure, discipline, and jargon (Reger, Etherage, Reger, & Gahm, 2008). Military patients may feel that civilian providers cannot relate to the physical and emotional trauma they may have experienced. Civilian neuropsychologists hired by the DoD must learn to operate in a unique environment where both the patient and the organization are "clients" and where strict regulations govern many aspects of clinical care (chapter 2). This is not to say that civilians cannot work with military members; however, to achieve cultural competency to work with the military population, systematic training geared to immerse the civilian into the military community is essential though, at this time, rarely provided.

While the DoD has responded to the need for additional neuropsychologists by hiring civilians, there has not been a corresponding push to either increase the number of active duty neuropsychologists or improve the utilization of active duty military neuropsychologists. Consequently, there is still a paucity of fellowship-trained neuropsychologists available to support unique military missions, including deployment to combat locations. While outstanding medical facilities have been set up at various locations in the Middle East and Southwest Asia in support of Operations Iraqi Freedom (OIF) and Enduring Freedom (OEF), a permanent neuropsychologist position has never been established at any of the frontline military medical centers where critical brain injury screening evaluations are conducted. Consequently, medical and mental health providers with little or no neuropsychological training have often been called upon to assess military members with TBIs and determine whether they are fit for duty or should be medically evacuated out of the combat theater. Military neuropsychologists who have deployed in support of the war effort have typically been assigned to generic mental health positions where their expertise in brain disorders and cognitive assessment was underutilized or not utilized at all.

Unfortunately, the underutilization of active duty military neuropsychologists is a perennial problem. Each year the Army and Air Force typically select one clinical psychologist for postdoctoral training in neuropsychology. The Navy usually selects one person for training every 2 years, though this has increased to one or two per year for at least the next 3 years. The Army trains their own personnel at accredited two-year postdoctoral fellowship programs at Walter Reed Army Medical Center in Washington, DC, and Tripler Army Medical Center in Honolulu, Hawaii. The Navy and Air Force do not have neuropsychology fellowship training programs but instead send their trainees to accredited civilian institutions. At the conclusion of their 2-year fellowships, military neuropsychologists may or may not be given the opportunity to practice their new skills. In many cases, military neuropsychologists split their time between clinical neuropsychology and other occupational demands, including general mental health practice, military specific duties, and leadership responsibilities. Newly trained Air Force neuropsychologists are typically sent to a major Air Force medical center where they may work full or part time as clinical neuropsychologists. New Navy neuropsychologists are usually given a single utilization tour, where they practice neuropsychology for an average of 3 years before being reassigned to positions that typically remove them from neuropsychological practice. Graduates from the Army postdoctoral neuropsychology fellowship programs may be given a utilization tour or sent to operational assignments with limited opportunities to practice neuropsychology and develop their new professional skills. Perhaps surprisingly, there are currently fewer than 10 designated clinical neuropsychology positions for active duty military officers within the entire DoD.

Military neuropsychologists, like all military personnel, ultimately serve in positions and perform duties deemed most critical by their superiors. In some cases, operational or expeditionary assignments are of paramount importance and may remove specialists from work within their area of expertise. Another reason why fellowship-trained military neuropsychologists often do not continue to practice neuropsychology is because full-time clinicians tend to be less competitive for promotion to the higher officer ranks. Promotion boards tend to value "career broadening" (i.e., diversification) and command (i.e., administrative) experience over clinical specialization and direct patient care. Military neuropsychologists interested in obtaining rank are often pressured to put aside their clinical practice in order to pursue command or other leadership experiences.

A future challenge for the military medical system will be to train an adequate number of neuropsychologists to meet the demand for services at forward operating locations as well as major medical centers in the United States and bases that have the highest numbers of deploying personnel, to properly utilize the expertise of trained providers, and to insure career progression opportunities for neuropsychologists who desire to continue serving as clinicians.

EXTENDING NEUROPSYCHOLOGICAL SERVICES THROUGH TELEMEDICINE

Telehealth

If war highlights the need for military psychologists to have grounding in threats to the central nervous system including concussion/mTBI and combat-related stress disorders, should the military be focused more on specialist rather than generalist training? The Department of Veterans Affairs has recently awarded new postdoctoral training programs. At least one of these combines parallel tracks where fellows specializing in PTSD get neuropsychology experience and those specializing in neuropsychology get additional background in the assessment and treatment of PTSD. Should this be a model for the military? The answer is probably yes, at least for a core group of military health providers. However, the addition of new demands will not lessen the need for psychologists to fulfill their traditional roles as health care providers. How then do military psychologists, whose training may have concentrated on a specific group of skills, transition among roles to meet the demands often placed on them by changing times and circumstances?

The most reasonable approach, in addition to the always present need for continued training and skill development, is telehealth and teleconsultation. The driving force behind telehealth efforts is to extend the range of providers with respect to geography and patients served. Telehealth brings specialized knowledge where needed, independent of the location of the provider. The use of telehealth negates the need for a specialty-trained neuropsychologist in every location where their services may be useful or required. However, to make maximum use of telehealth, psychologists at remote locations must have a general familiarity with procedures and issues, the use and interpretation of which can be expanded upon by the consulting specialist.

The use of telehealth dovetails well with the implementation of the NCAT project. As previously noted, serial testing results will be in the health record and available to be viewed by professionals with appropriate privileges independent of their locations. This capability facilitates easy access to test results providing both the consulting and treating psychologist the ability to look at test data, instantly compare current to previous results or to normative comparisons, review history and other relevant data, then decide on any follow-up testing procedures that are available to the treating psychologist. In essence, one has a melding of technologies that enhance the level of evaluation that can be provided to service members and extend the reach of the specialty-trained military psychologist.

Teleconsultation

As assessment of cognition takes on a greater role in theater, psychologists will be called on to administer neurocognitive measures and provide input into the overall assessment of the service member. Not all psychologists will be specialty trained, and it is unlikely any branch of the service will have a large number of neuropsychologists who can provide uninterrupted neuropsychological services to various theater-level medical facilities. As noted previously, a psychologist with more general training can be supported through teleconsultation. However, this system is more effective if the psychologist has skill in at least a limited number of tests that supplement the use of the NCAT and, most importantly, has some knowledge of the conditions they are most likely going to have to assess. In modern warfare, psychologists need backgrounds in brain injury, biological and toxic agents, and environmental stressors, in addition to acute and chronic stress reactions.

Training for the expanded role of the psychologist will require internships to tailor training experiences to provide additional background to their students in the assessment of cognition and in understanding how war-related injuries can affect cognitive performance. Training should include an understanding of the clinical practice guidelines associated with treating conditions such as concussion in and outside of theater and how neurocognitive assessment integrates with these protocols. Since it is unlikely that training during internship or fellowship will anticipate all contingencies, it will be important to pay attention to continued training needs and skill development. Meetings and workshops have long been part of continued education for the military psychologist. Increasingly, military psychology has made use of videoconferencing in training and skill development. There are additional techniques, however, that could assist the need for on-demand training independent of the location of the psychologist. These include distance learning and podcasts that could support the clinician in the field and facilitate psychologists in meeting changing and expanding demands.

Remaining Relevant

The dramatic rise in the number of military personnel sustaining brain injuries, particularly following the onset of OIF and OEF, has placed an unprecedented spotlight on the science and profession of neuropsychology. The increased demand for objective, empirical evaluation of post-traumatic cognitive functioning as well as compassionate, professional brain injury rehabilitation has elevated the prominence of neuropsychology in both the medical community and the general public. Even with increasing scientific understanding of the mechanisms of blast injuries and recent advances in neuroimaging, neuropsychologists are still the most qualified professionals to assess cognitive abilities and functional capacity. Even as hostilities decrease and fewer service members are injured, neuropsychologists will continue to play an important role in assisting and rehabilitating those who have sustained brain injuries and monitoring their recoveries over time (for more on brain injury rehabilitation in the military, see chapter 7).

While the needs of injured service members will not disappear overnight, military neuropsychologists may face the challenge of remaining visible and relevant in the future. As the number of persons sustaining combat-related brain injuries hopefully decreases over time, military neuropsychologists who now spend most of their time evaluating service members may be able to put more energy into treatment rather than assessment. Most service members who have sustained brain injuries during OIF/OEF have received rehabilitation services through Veterans Health Administration or Community-Based Health Care Organization programs. In early 2008, the Army, in collaboration with the DVBIC, began establishing multidisciplinary treatment programs at medical treatment facilities across the United States that provide care for service members with TBIs. Neuropsychologists are integral active members of such teams.

Military neuropsychologists also have an opportunity to build upon their new or strengthened alliances with other medical professionals to provide services to a broader patient population. While the recent emphasis has been on the evaluation and rehabilitation of combat-related TBIs, military neuropsychologists should seek to extend their services to a wider range of patients with brain-related disorders, such as learning disorders and ADHD, non-combat-related brain injuries, brain neoplasms, cerebrovascular disorders, epilepsy, autoimmune disorders, infectious encephalopathies, and neurodegenerative conditions.

To extend their services to such patients, military neuropsychologists should strive to strengthen their collaborative relationships with medical providers they have worked with closely during the war, including neurologists, rehabilitation therapists, psychiatrists, and family and general practitioners. As resources permit, military neuropsychologists should consider expanding their patient populations to include not only active duty service members, but also military dependents and retirees. With a growing population of elderly retirees, assessment of memory disorders and dementia screening may provide a valuable service to prior service members while enhancing the visibility and value of neuropsychologists to the military community.

Historically, military neuropsychologists have served primarily in evaluative and consultative roles. While direct patient care will continue to be a top priority, tremendous research opportunities also exist for neuropsychologists who work with military personnel. Extensive data derived from baseline testing, periodic reevaluations, and postinjury assessments could provide unprecedented information regarding both normal aging and cognitive changes associated with trauma and disease. Research opportunities also exist to study the neuropsychological sequelae of various vaccinations, prophylactic medications, and environmental hazards to which military personnel are exposed. Extensive neuropsychological data have already been collected on personnel in certain military occupational specialties such as aviators (Ryan et al., 2006), and valuable information might also be obtained regarding the cognitive functioning of those who serve in other unique military career fields, such as special forces, military intelligence, infantry, field artillery, divers, and ammunition and explosive ordnance disposal. Much has yet to be learned about the potential neuropsychological consequences of working in career fields with high inherent physical and psychological risks.

Fortunately, military neuropsychologists have been joined in their research efforts by scientists and practitioners at the DVBIC, Department of Veterans Affairs hospitals and rehabilitation centers, the Defense Advanced Research Projects Agency, universities across the United States, and other government and private agencies. In May 2008, Congress passed a supplemental appropriations act containing $300 million to support programs and activities relating to the treatment, care, rehabilitation, recovery, and support of the armed forces for TBI and psychological health issues. Four months later, the National Defense Authorization Bill for Fiscal Year 2009 was approved, with additional funding for medical treatment and research within the Defense Health Program, including $300 million for TBI and psychological health. Continuing research collaboration among the DoD, other governmental agencies, and civilian institutions is clearly needed to increase our understanding of brain injuries sustained by military members and provide appropriate treatment and rehabilitation. Neuropsychologists who work with military personnel should not only look for opportunities to participate in research, but must also stay informed of the latest developments in this rapidly evolving field to provide the highest quality services possible to ill or injured service members and veterans, both now and in the future.

REFERENCES

American Psychiatric Association. (1994). *Diagnostic and statistical manual of mental disorders: DSM IV* (4th ed.). Washington, DC: Author.

Campise, R. L., Geller, S. K., & Campise, M. E. (2006). Combat stress. In C. H. Kennedy & E. A. Zillmer (Eds.), *Military psychology: Clinical and operational applications* (pp. 215–240). New York: Guilford.

Cernak, I., Wang, Z., Jiang, J., Bian, X., & Slavic, J. (2001). Ultrastructural and functional characteristics of blast injury-induced neurotrauma. *The Journal of Trauma Injury, Infection, and Critical Care, 50*(4), 695–706.

Elsayed, N. M. (1997). Toxicology of blast overpressure. *Toxicology, 121*(1), 1–15.

Erlanger, D., & Feldman, D. (1999). *Cognitive stability index™*. New York: HeadMinder.

Friedl, K. E., Grate, S. J., Proctor, S. P., Ness, J. W., Lukey, B. J., & Kane, R. L. (2007). Army research needs for automated neuropsychological tests: Monitoring soldier health and performance status. *Archives of Clinical Neuropsychology, 22*(S1), s7–s14.

Hoge, C. W., McGurk, D., Thomas, J. L., Cox, A. L., Engel, C. C., & Castro, C. A. (2008). Mild traumatic brain injury in U.S. soldiers returning from Iraq. *The New England Journal of Medicine, 358*, 453–463.

Kane, R. L., & Kay. G. (1992). Computerized assessment in neuropsychology: A review of tests and test batteries. *Neuropsychology Review, 3*, 1–117.

Kennedy, C. H., Jones, D. E., & Grayson, R. (2006). Substance abuse and gambling treatment in the military. In C. H. Kennedy & E. A. Zillmer (Eds.), *Military psychology: Clinical and operational applications* (pp. 163–190). New York: Guilford.

Leung, L. Y., VandeVord, P. J., Dal Cengio, A. L., Bir, C., Yang, K. H., & King, A. I. (2008). Blast related neurotrauma: A review of cellular injury. *Molecular & Cellular Biomechanics, 5*(3), 155–168.

Lowe, M., Harris, W., Kane, R. L., Banderet, L., Levinson, D., & Reeves, D. L. (2007). Neuropsychological assessment in extreme environments. *Archives of Clinical Neuropsychology, 22*(S1), s89–s100.

McCrea, M., Kelly, J. P., Randolph, C., Kluge, J., Bartolic, E., Finn, G., et al. (1998). Standardized assessment of concussion (SAC): On site mental status evaluation of the athlete. *The Journal of Head Trauma Rehabilitation, 13*(2), 27–35.

Reeves, D. L., Bleiberg, J., Roebuck-Spencer, T., Cernich, A. N., Schwab, K., Ivins, B., et al. (2006). Reference values for performance on the automated neuropsychological assessment metrics V3.0 in an active-duty military sample. *Military Medicine, 171*, 982–984.

Reeves, D. L., Winter, K. P., Bleiberg, J., & Kane, R. L. (2007). ANAM® genogram: Historical perspectives, description, and current endeavors. *Archives of Clinical Neuropsychology, 22*(S1), s15–s38.

Reeves, D., Winter, K., Kane, R., Elsmore, T., & Bleiberg, J. (2001). *Automated neuropsychological assessment metrics user's manual: Clinical and research methods* (Special Rep. No. NCRF-SR-2002–01). The Army Medical Research and Material Command, National Cognitive Recovery Foundation.

Reger, M. A., Etherage, J. R., Reger, G. M., & Gahm, G. A. (2008). Civilian psychologists in an Army culture: The ethical challenge of cultural competence. *Military Psychology, 20*, 21–36.

Riccitiello, R. (2006). Iraq: A marine's experience of brain injury. *Newsweek.* Retrieved November 18, 2008, from http://www.newsweek.com/id/47236/output/print

Ryan, L. M., Zazeckis, T. M., French, L. M., & Harvey, S. (2006). Neuropsychological practice in the military. In C. H. Kennedy & E. A. Zillmer (Eds.), *Military psychology: Clinical and operational applications* (pp. 105–129). New York: Guilford.

Tanielian, T., & Jaycox, L. H. (Eds.). (2008). *Invisible wounds of war: Psychological and cognitive injuries, their consequences, and services to assist recovery.* Santa Monica, CA: RAND Corporation.

Vincent, A. S., Bleiberg, J., Yan, S., Ivins, B., Reeves, D. L., Schwab, K., et al. (2008). Reference data from the automated neuropsychological assessment metrics for use in traumatic brain injury in an active duty military sample. *Military Medicine, 173*(9), 836–853.

Zoroya, G. (2007, November 11). Troops cheat on brain-injury tests to stay with units. *USA Today.* Retrieved from http://www.usatoday.com

Index